THE GOOD CURRY GUIDE

PAT CHAPMAN was born in London's Blitz, with an addiction to curry inherited from his family's six-generation connection with India, the story of which is told in Pat's new book *Pat Chapman's Taste of the Raj* (*see* page 2). Virtually weaned on his grandmother's curries, he was taken to his first curry houses — Veeraswamy in Piccadilly, and Shafi's in Gerrard Street — at the age of six, at a time when there were only three such establishments in London, and six in the whole of the UK. Visits became a regular treat and confirmed in Pat a passion and a curiosity about the food of India. He was already a curryholic! Following education at Bedales and Cambridge, he did a short stint in the RAF, flying fast jets, then spent several years in industry.

He founded the now world-renowned Curry Club in 1982, at a time when the curry was just beginning to become nationally important, as the means to share information about recipes, restaurants and all things to do with spicy food. Soon a national network of curry restaurant reporters was established, whose voluntary contributions led to the publication of the first edition of this highly successful *Good Curry Guide* in 1984, and its prestigious awards to restaurants.

Assisted by his wife, Dominique, Pat frequently demonstrates at major food shows and appears on TV and radio, and they regularly stage cookery courses and events. His pioneering Gourmet Tours to India are now well-established holidays for *aficionados*.

With book sales exceeding 1 million, Pat is best known as a writer of easy-to-follow recipes. His succession of popular curry titles, some of which are listed on page 2, are published by Hodder & Stoughton, Piatkus, Sainsbury's and the BBC.

CURRY CLUB

THE 1999 GOOD CURRY GUIDE

EDITED BY
PAT CHAPMAN

In association with
Cobra Beer
&
The Taj Group of Hotels

CORONET BOOKS
Hodder & Stoughton

Assistant Editor: Dominique Chapman (D.B.A.C.)
Contributors: David Wolfe, Andy Munro, Andy Mitchell
Designer: Peter Ward
Fact verification: David Mackenzie
Statistics: Taylor Nelson, Sub Continent Publishing
Disk conversion: Tex Swan
Certification: James Le Boudec
Researchers: Karan, Arjay, Arjun, Samson and Bobbi
Edited and typeset: Grapevine Publishing Services, London

Good Curry Guide Reporters of the Year:
Hilary Chapchal of London
Malcolm Wilkins of Gravesend, Kent
plus many hundreds of others, without whom
this Guide would not exist

Hodder and Stoughton
A division of Hodder Headline PLC
338 Euston Road
London NW1 3BH

Author's Note

Sponsorship The continuing sponsorship of Cobra Beer as principal sponsor, and Taj Hotels as secondary sponsor, enables the author to finance the considerable costs of operating and producing this Guide which include: maintaining the restaurant database on computer; subscribing to a press-cutting service and other information suppliers; printing a detailed questionnaire and mailing it to all 7,550 restaurants on two occasions; mail-shotting the 1,200-plus restaurants that are selected to appear in this Guide; telephoning many for verification of information; producing, supplying and mailing the selected restaurants (free of charge) their wall certificates and window stickers; printing and mailing restaurant report forms for interested parties; collating and recording the information received (some 5,000 reports per annum) and operating the Awards Ceremony.

Accuracy The contents of this Guide are as up to date and accurate as possible, but we cannot be held responsible for any changes regarding quality, price, menu details, decor, ownership, health offences or even closure, following our processing of the reports.

Connections Pat Chapman, the publishers of this Guide and the proprietors of The Curry Club wish to make it quite clear that they have absolutely no financial or ownership connections with any restaurants, including those mentioned in this Guide.

False representation Restaurant reports are welcomed from any bona-fide source. We do not pay for reports – they are sent in spontaneously and voluntarily. Our own research and restaurant testing is normally done anonymously, the bill is paid, and often no disclosure is made as to our presence. On some occasions, such as openings, we accept invitations to visit restaurants as 'guests of the house'. Under no circumstances do we tout for free hospitality, and anyone doing so in the name of The Curry Club is an impostor. We have heard of cases where people claiming to be members of The Curry Club, or *Good Curry Guide* 'inspectors', request payment and/or free meals in return for entry into this Guide. In such cases, we would recommend that restaurants threaten to call the police. We would also like to be informed of any such incidents and we will not hesitate to take action against people acting illegally in the name of The Curry Club or *The Good Curry Guide*.

Discounts We invite all restaurants selected to appear in this Guide to participate in a discount scheme for members of The Curry Club. Those restaurants who agree to participate are indicated by the symbol © on their entry. The terms of this scheme are clearly spelled out to all parties. We cannot be held responsible if, at any time, the restaurant declines the offered discount. *See also* page 560.

Certificates and window stickers We send all restaurants appearing in this Guide a 1999 certificate, hand-signed by Pat Chapman, and a 1999 window sticker. As with the restaurant's entry, these items are supplied absolutely free of charge to all the restaurants in this Guide. Some choose not to display these items, others display them proudly and prominently. You may observe that our certificate is not displayed alone. There may well be a host of others, some bigger and flashier than ours including the Dome Grading certificates issued by Peter and Coleen Grove which are genuine, as are certificates issued by London's *Time Out*, Ronay, local council health departments and certain others. Unfortunately, some certificates are a pure sham. They are issued to any restaurant who cares to pay for them, in some cases, with a promise of entry into a Guide which does not even exist. The most recent scam is by *Good Food Guide*, yet again, but this is not <u>The</u> *Good Food Guide*. There is no Guide and this is the same outfit that were sued by the Consumers' Association some time ago having re-emerged at a different address. Masterchef is also back again after being exposed by BBC Food and Drink in June. Certificates are on offer for £67.50 with £10 for extra copies and £5 for window stickers. The Asian Food Guide was caught out on Radio 4. There are others on the bandwagon. Like Peter Groves, we would like to see this scam stopped. The problem is, selling a certificate is not illegal. And restaurateurs are anxious to impress their customers. The best thing to do is to tell your restaurant you are aware of the scam, and prefer awards which are given free on merit.

CONTENTS

THE DIRECTORY

County Index

See page 553 for Index of Towns

About this Guide

The Good Curry Guide broke new ground when it was first published in 1984, by being the first restaurant guide to specialise only in the British curry. This, its sixth edition, is the first time we have gone annual. Keen observers will note that there have been demotions and promotions since last time. We want continuity in each edition of the Guide, and because we do expect changes, we feel it important that each restaurant completes a questionnaire. For one thing, it means it actually wants to be in the Guide. It also verifies its current name, address, telephone number, and above all, prices. Despite our earnest endeavours, not all restaurants reply, even if they did so last time. So if we have not received a form back from a restaurant which was in the previous edition, after it has received a form three times from us, should it be delisted? I believe it should if it cannot be bothered, for what ever reason, to talk to us. But, this is a peculiar trade we are in, curry restaurants, communications are not easy, and normal rules do not apply. So I have decided that continuity of entry is also important.

The completed form from a restaurant does not itself guarantee entry to the Guide. We rely on a number of other sources of information. We ourselves can only visit a handful of restaurants each year, and we do not have a team of paid inspectors. Most important to us are the opinions of the customers, you, the diners. We do not pay for such reports, though from time to time The Curry Club gives prizes for your efforts. The report itself can be a simple short note, though we have a special form available for all who want one. (*See* page 559). One report may deal with just one restaurant. Some reporters write to us once in a lifetime. Others write repeatedly, and each report may include numerous restaurants. For this Guide, we received about 5,000 reports, which yielded information on up to 50,000 individual restaurant visits. We read and record every report, although it is becoming increasingly difficult to reply to all of them. I would like to take this opportunity, therefore, to thank all those who have been good enough to take the time to tell us where they have found the best, good, mediocre and even bad curries.

Of course reporting standards vary, and the The Wind of India in Puddlecome-on-the-Marsh may well be reported as the best in the world by its most ardent, youngest, novice, local fan (and I want such opinions), but it will probably not rate highly if compared with

London's best. Nevertheless, it will be a competent curry house in that area, serving standard formula curry. A good number of the entries in this Guide come into this category, and they are here because someone out there, maybe many more than one person, has taken the trouble to write in and praise the place, and to exclude it would be wrong. Quite simply, we want to know what you know.

Answering the question 'Name your favourite curry restaurant(s)' may not always be as easy as it sounds. It is worth quoting Sutton Coldfield's John Brockingham, a retired college lecturer: 'My favourite restaurants' he wrote 'range from opulent establishments, like Rajdoot, Birmingham, where I might take the family on special occasions, to cheap and cheerful places like Erdington's Balti Express, where a meal costs £11 a head. I have a favourite posh curry restaurant, when I can afford it, and a favourite posh Balti. But I have a favourite plonk version of both, and a favourite takeaway, and then there's a favourite lucky dip. Some of my favourites are good enough to tempt me in whenever I'm in the district, but could not be nominated for the highest accolade.'

Of course we do not receive reports on every single establishment. On occasion a restaurant we normally receive good reports on, gets damned. If this is the exception, we will probably still carry that restaurant. Some restaurants will have closed, and others should perhaps have been omitted. But not one restaurant gets into this Guide unless we have had at least one recent good report on it, preferably several. To get into the TOP 100 our rule is that we must have had several detailed excellent reports about the particular restaurant, including at least one by one of our elite sixty or so regular reporters. As editors we visit a TOP 100 restaurant anonymously when we are in the area whenever we can, but it's impossible to go to them all within one year. We do our best to filter out 'good' reports on bad restaurants, particularly those written by their hopeful owners. This time we requested restaurants selected for entry to get their customers to write to us, and many did, which has swelled our reporter base considerably. By doing this, we have almost weeded out those few restaurants who previously sent us phoney reports, purportedly from their adoring customers. However, even after fifteen years in the editor's chair, it is possible that I've been conned and a 'bad' restaurant has slipped into the Guide. Equally, I'll guarantee that, as usual, we've missed someone's favourite, and as usual there will be a few *faux pas* too. Please let us know about these. No doubt, we'll continue to get irate letters from people who won't have bothered to read this section, telling us that, because this or that restaurant was awful when they visited, 'it casts doubt on the credibility of the entire Guide'. In the last edition I singled out Malcolm Wilkins for doing this, and to keep the record straight, he not only promised to put things right, he has, during this year, become a prolific and interesting reporter, so much so that we have given him our Reporter of the Year award. Indeed there is more from Malcolm later.

We certainly do not enter restaurants just because they ask us to. After fifteen years of bona-fide operations, more than the great majority of the restaurants in this Guide, you would imagine that curry house owners would clamour to be in the Guide. And indeed some do. I have said in previous Guides, that more than one restaurant has made veiled references to the benefits that would be made available to the editors if that restaurant were declared the UK's number one. The idea that restaurateurs believe that they can buy their way into the Guide is abhorrent, and, of course, if one did accede to such bribery, word would soon get round risking the credibility of both author and publication. The book is paid for through book sales and sponsorship, not through bribes.

So what's new in this edition? Several readers have requested that we make it easier to find a particular restaurant or town. Regular readers will know that we go alphabetically in county order, then within that, alphabetically in town order, with the restaurants themselves in alphabetical order. We are continuing with this system, rather than, as many Guides do, listing alphabetically by town, since it is easier to see at a glance what alternative choices are nearby. We have also added a town index at the end of the book. At the start of each county's entry, we have also reintroduced our thumbnail county maps, which help pinpoint the location of that particular county, along with a new feature, which lists adjacent counties, and a few statistics. It should make this Guide more informative and finding your way around it easier.

And that, after all, is what this Guide is all about – finding good curries easily, and nothing else.

The Happenings of 1998

Before we get down to discussing the restaurants in detail, I must report on the happenings of the year since we last went to print. Firstly, your reactions to the 1998 Guide. Thank you for your wonderful letters, and for the useful ideas in some of them, hopefully implemented. Please do keep the correspondence flowing in. (The address is at the end of this Guide.)

Here are just a few extracts: 'We have become raving curry addicts. To my delight someone bought us your 1998 GCG, which has been invaluable, enabling us to try some more local and very good curry restaurants, and also to try things that perhaps we would not have done, thanks to your menu guide.' Jonathan Medling, Leigh, Lancs. 'We thought you'd like to know that the 1998 GCG is one of the most successful (Christmas) presents my husband got. His whole family have leafed through it and taken a note of various places.' Sally Writer, Hitchin. 'We bought your Guide to give as a Christmas present for someone, but we liked it so much, we kept it!' Simon Rollason and Lynda Gudgeon, Willenhall. 'I was very glad to receive a copy of your excellent Guide for Christmas and read it from cover to cover.' Simon Leng, Wakefield. 'I've read the Guide so many times, I can recite parts of it by heart!' Colin Snowball, Cheltenham. 'My 1998 edition is already somewhat dog-eared and well-thumbed and wife accused me of spending most of Christmas looking for its 'hot tips', rather than the family!!!' Malcolm Wilkins, Gravesend. 'I was given the 1998 GCG for Christmas by my 8-month-old nephew. He is going to be a man with great taste.' Phil Loudon, Sandy, Beds. 'We recently bought two copies of the GCG for Christmas. I bought one for my wife, and I unknowingly she bought one for me!!!' Gary and Katy Debono, High Wycombe. 'The 1998 Guide is bigger and better than ever and still fits in the jacket pocket!' Salma and Simon Ward, Croydon. 'It's most useful to read about restaurants we have already tried, and those we are now discovering.' Karen Harding Sutton Coldfield. 'Having just read the 1998 edition, I'm inspired to try out a few local hostelries which I've recommended. I'm guaranteed months of sampling the fruits of the Guide.' Brian George, Milton Keynes.

Regular readers will recall that last year's Brain-dead Award of the Year went to Ely's Surma, whose waiter denied all knowledge of both The Curry Club and the Guide to Brian George, our 1998 Reporter of the Year, despite our certificate being on his wall, our sticker on his window and references to both all over his menus. (The Surma Ely duly completed their 1999 form and have yet again offered to give a discount!) Regular readers will also remember Orpington's John Loosemoore, whose reports from all over Britain made him 1995 Reporter of the Year. Sadly we have heard nothing from him recently, but his absolute favourite restaurant was the Bengal Lancer in Chiselhurst. Interestingly in the 1992 Guide, we gave it a mixed report, but John was so passionate about it that he insisted we make it a TOP 100 restaurant. We did so in 1995. The legacy remained in 1998. And an eloquent report by Malcolm Wilkins shows how our 1992 judgement was, perhaps correct. Here is Malcolm's report: 'When I asked about the possibility of a Curry Club discount, the staff proclaimed no knowledge of the Curry Club. I pointed out their sticker in the window (dated 1992). I explained that someone had agreed with Pat Chapman to give a discount and showed him the Guide entry and the symbol indicating this. The manager (a Mr S. Choudhury) then said he *had* heard of the Curry Club, and of Pat Chapman, but was quite scathing about the Club, accusing Pat of "living off the backs of Indian restaurants' and 'taking money from Indian restaurants". He said they wanted nothing to do with it. He was uncomplimentary to say the least! I suggested that as entry to the guide cost nothing, if he cared to check he would find that no money had been paid by the restaurant to either Pat Chapman or the Curry Club. I said that the discount was purely voluntary, but if they didn't want to give one then he should write and say so. He said that he would. At this point the owner Mr A. Choudhury appeared and we went through the same discussion. He said he *had* heard of the Curry Club and knew Pat Chapman personally! Again I pointed out the sticker in the window, whereupon he said that as it was dated 1992, perhaps "someone" then had agreed to give a discount, but he knew nothing about it, and anything more recent was without his knowledge. The whole conversation was very polite and friendly and we ended up having a long and friendly conversation about restaurants in general and he urged me to try his other establishment, The Bengal Clipper in SE1 [which is also listed in the 1998 edition, but interestingly is not shown as giving a discount.] In the end he said he would write to you, although somehow I doubt it!' Malcolm concludes: 'All in all, a pleasant evening in comfortable surroundings, but not so good as to warrant the honour of a TOP 100 rating.'

Fortunately we do not get too much nonsense like this. We have not had any reports about this restaurant for 18 months, nor have they filled out their form. Curiously, though, someone has filled in and returned the form for the Bengal Clipper. It is unsigned, however, and the questions asking whether they will give discounts to CC members have been left studiously unanswered, leaving something of a black hole in the questionnaire. The flowing hand lists another restaurant as their branch, not the Bengal Lancer. Curiouser and curiouser! Exasperating though all this is, there is a funny side to it, and it does make amusing copy for this intro. Incidentally, can anyone tell me what exactly has happened to John Loosemoore?

Curryholic of the year award must go to Gareth Davis, 27. Ali Akbar, owner Barry Glam's Modern Balti, offered a bed-sit for rent above his restaurant. Gareth said he'd take it on condition he receives a 30% discount in the restaurant. Akbar said yes, and the deal was done. 'It's a dream come true,' says Davis. 'I love the smells coming through the floorboards. I've been a regular there since I was 12. Now I dine there daily.' Says Akbar: 'He's our best customer. It's a pleasure to have him in-house.'

Cyrus Todiwalla came to frequent notice this past year. The Café Spice Namasté concept is flourishing, and so is Cyrus. In a piece he wrote for *Tandoori Magazine*, in January, he wrote that only Indians could cook curry. It didn't go down too well with Bangladeshis, Pakistanis, Sri Lankans and Nepalese! It was this Guide that brought Cyrus to media and public attention by awarding him his first-ever award, Chef of the Year in 1992. Naturally, where this Guide goes, everyone else follows, and he was soon showered with awards by, well, everyone else. When we repeated the award in the next (1995) edition, we were not alone. But really Cyrus, on your 1999 questionnaire, to the question 'Has your restaurant been mentioned in any other Food Guides?' did you really need to write: 'Too many to mention.' This really must earn you the Bighead of the Year award. Still, I wish you well with your Café Spice Namasté cookbook, out this autumn.

I said last time that I was waiting for the first restaurant to call itself The Spice Girls. I'm still waiting, but Mokhtar Hussain's Leicester Monsoon has named five dishes after the fab five, now four! Baby Spice is a mild chicken curry, Posh Spice is a pricier meal made with regal king prawns, Sporty Spice is a curry made with runner beans, while Scary Spice is chicken or lamb cooked in a hot sauce! I have yet to hear whether Ginger Spice (contains lamb with ginger), has been taken off the menu since Ginger quit the group.

I hear nothing but reports about staff shortages at the Indian restaurant. Nearly everyone I talk to is down by a cook here or a waiter there. Some restaurants are down by three or four staff. This is very worrying. Indeed, pessimists are predicting closures for lack of personnel. There are several reasons for this phenomenon. Firstly, the curry restaurant sector has been expanding since 1950 when there were just six such restaurants in the whole of Great Britain. Now there are 7,500. But for the first time, growth has remained static for a year; new ventures are matched by closures. And a lot of the blame is put onto staff shortages. I believe there is still considerable potential for growth in the sector, providing the new generation of restaurants offers more than just formula curry. But in today's market, it is very hard to keep on finding skilled staff. There are no specific training schools for Asian cooks and waiters. A new course at Thames Valley University Catering Department is a step in the right direction. But it is a drop in the ocean. The schools at Tower Hamlets and Bradford failed for lack of funding, despite valiant attempts. So if an ever-increasing number of staff are required, where are they to be recruited from? Immigration and employment departments say such personnel must exist within the community. They point to the younger generation. One thing is clear – second-generation Asians, educated in Britain, do not, on the whole, wish to work in father's restaurant. It is well known that Asian children are high achievers, passing out of their colleges and universities with high scores. They prefer to pursue professional careers, and who can blame them?

There may not be schools specifically for the curry sector, but there are plenty of catering schools in Britain teaching mostly European cooking and management skills. They produce an annual flow of graduates into the market place, all of whom want work, but why do so few of these come into the Indian restaurant sector? One view is that they want better pay and conditions. The fact is the entire hotel and catering industry is booming, and new catering graduates can get work relatively effortlessly; perhaps it is felt by both sides, with less hassles and better career prospects outside the 'Asian' sector. A further important point concerns gender. I mentioned 'father' earlier. And I can't be accused of being sexist here, because it is a fact that there are 70,000 Bangladeshi waiters and cooks at work in our curry houses, and they are nearly all male. Why is this? Here we are in one of the most forward-looking countries in the world. There is no other employment sector in Britain where it's men only on the payroll. Behind every man, says the old phrase, there is a good woman. Somewhere then, there is a considerable number of Bangladeshi wives, whose culinary skills are not in dispute. Cultural resistance and language problems there may be, but these would soon be overcome, and the presence of waitresses in national costume would grace many a restaurant. I'd go so far as to say, it would increase trade. And they'd teach the cooks a thing or two.

However, it is one thing to say that there is a labour force potentially available. It is another thing to get it into employment in your venue, and keep it there. And so one turns to immigration. British immigration law is, quite rightly, very tough. To gain a three-year work permit, takes at least nine months from application, and requires certain criteria to be met. The most important of these is to prove that the job the person is being requested to do cannot be filled by someone already in the country. Secondly, the applicant must be able to prove he or she has the necessary skills. And this, according to the department, means paper qualifications. Certificates are impossible to come by in poor countries like Bangladesh. I have several times met a chef who works at the Mughal Sherton Hotel in Agra. He is a kebab specialist. He learnt his skill from his father, who learnt it from his father, and so on. Centuries ago, he says, his ancestors were kebab chefs for the Moghul emperors in Agra. This man can neither read nor write. He never went to school, but no one I know cooks a better kebab.

My conclusion is that, if the curry restaurant sector is to continue to boom, we must get hold of the best, most talented cooks and chefs in the subcontinent, whether they have paper qualifications or not. Both restaurateurs and customers must put pressure on the immigration and employment authorities to relax the rules regarding qualifications, and to speed up the permit-issuing process. In June I set up a petition, and sent a form to all 7,500 restaurants, asking each one to get 1,000 people to sign up. Forms are still flowing in, and the aim is to get over a million signatures. If you as a Guide reader wish to participate, then please get as many signatures (plus names and addresses) as you can and mail them to me. Well-known celebrities and your local councillors and MPs would be especially welcome. Keith Vaz MP was the first to sign up, and he is actively tabling motions in parliament. But we do need your voice — and 10 million people can't be wrong.

Much more of an issue was a piece by Iqbal Wahhab, published in the February edition of the Indian restaurant trade magazine, *Tandoori*, and repeated gleefully by most of the national press and media. Wahhab, himself a Bangladeshi, said, amongst other things, that all waiters at Indian restaurants were, and I quote 'miserable gits'. I'm sure you read about this, and I don't wish to dwell on his remarks, except to say that, hardly surprisingly, they infuriated many waiters, not to mention cooks and proprietors, who were certain that the restaurant trade would collapse overnight. They were wrong, of course, but matters were not helped by a spurious attempt by some to prolong the issue, and to ban *Tandoori* magazine, and anything related, from every curry house, including Cobra beer. Since I am Editorial Consultant, and a regular contributor to *Tandoori* magazine, and since Cobra beer is a sponsor of this Guide, I too was involved. One restaurant, and only one, returned our certificate because Cobra was mentioned on it, with an apologetic letter. Two weeks later, that same restaurant owner then filled in and returned his form for consideration for entry to this Guide. As it happens, he is entered in it, and I'll report back next time on whether he returns his 1999 certificate, and of course I'll name his restaurant if he does. True the hapless Wahhab overstepped the mark in his attempt to gain press attention. He could not have expected the amount of attention the incident got, and he has paid dearly. He was obliged to resign as Editor-in-chief of *Tandoori* magazine, issuing a much-publicised abject apology, and since even that was not enough to satisfy those out for his blood, he has not dared to show his face at the many gatherings, functions, new openings and celebrations at which his jovial manner had always previously lightened proceedings. There is not a single person in the community who does not know that Wahhab is an outspoken joker, who talks before he thinks, and no one who has met him can fail to enjoy his wit and humour. I am saddened by his expulsion, and wish him well in his new restaurant venture, The Cinnamon Club. A am delighted that the attempt to ban Cobra and Tandoori has been ineffective, but if a restaurant you patronise stopped selling Cobra Beer, now you know why. Perhaps your answer might be to take your custom elsewhere where they trade without bigotry. I am delighted to report that I continue to write for *Tandoori* magazine, and that Cobra Beer remain my sponsor. James Dudley and Ramjan Ali, owners of Bournemouth's Eye of the Tiger restaurant best sum up the sorry episode. 'Iqbal Wahhab's comments,' they say, 'are on a par with Edwina Curry's ill fated statement that salmonella existed in all eggs.'

The EC continue to ban things. During the year, they decided that Bengali and Thai King prawns were unhygienic, following the discovery of some bacteria in certain consignments. In typical EC fashion, every consignment was then banned. It's rather like saying if one car gets a puncture, all tyre sales must be banned. Not surprisingly, the price of king prawns doubled, and many restaurateurs either upped their prices or stopped selling them. Some even reprinted their menus. Within a few months the EC announced that the ban was lifted, and king prawns dropped to below their original prices. But despite all that, the ban on Bombay Duck, an eel-like fish native to Bombay, remains in place. It is processed by drying it in the sun, as it has been for thousands of years. And since this delicious dried fish is deep-fried before being served, any chance of a problem is simply cooked away. I miss my Bombay Duck at the moment and can't wait for this piece of madness to pass on by and for supplies to be resumed.

Finally, as ever, I hope this Guide will amuse and entertain you, as well as inform you and guide you to a good curry somewhere across the length and breadth of Great Britain. I hope reading its contents will make your mouth water as much as it did ours when we put it together, and that this will mean you'll just have to have a curry right now! If it's at a restaurant from the Guide, I hope you will enjoy the cuisine of the subcontinent of India at the highest standards. Or it might be a restaurant that's not in the Guide. Either way, and whatever you think of it, please let us know, so we can tell everyone next time.

If reading this book makes you want to rush off to the nearest curry house to have a fix, it will have served its purpose. Its title says it all – it is the *Good Curry Guide*.

Curry Statistics

Both Taylor Nelson and Mintel indicate that growth in the Indian restaurant sector is slowing down. We spent several weeks completely updating our database, and it reveals that there are somewhat fewer curry restaurants than we had previously believed, the difference largely being explained by name changes, duplication and rather more closures than we had been notified about. We said last time that the growth of new openings in the two years between mid-1995 and mid-1997, was 3%, or 300 restaurants. The number of new openings has continued during the last year at a slightly slower rate. We know of 125 openings nationwide, but we have heard of at least 300 closures. The net result, we believe, is 7,516 Indian restaurants operating in the UK in August 1998.

According to Mintel, the revenue at the Indian restaurant comes third at £1.66bn (excluding takeaway revenues) in 1997, after pub catering (£5.1bn), and non-ethnic restaurants (£6bn). But Mintel warn that over the period 1993 to 1997, revenue at the Indian has increased only by 13%, whereas several other sectors (including in-store restaurants, pizza and pasta, fish and chips, fried chicken, roadside food, and other fast food), currently with lower turnovers than the Indian sector, are showing average revenue growths of over 20% in the same period. Only the Chinese sector shows lower growth at 8% (£1.1bn in 1997). Thai food during the same period grew from £141m to £242m – a massive 38%.

But are restaurants making profits? Plimsoll Portfolio Analysts find 43% of restaurants increased their borrowings while 25% made a loss as a result of 'competitive pressures'. Half of these increased their levels of debt. Of those making profits, 39% increased their total asset value, though 75% of these borrowed to do so. The entire restaurant sector grew by 5.6% during 1997. 20% increased sales. Average industry margins were just 2.8%, though 20% made in excess of 10% pre-tax profit. Market Power's report on themed restaurants, tells us that according to government figures, there will be a 20% decrease in the number of 25 to 34 year-olds visiting these in the coming years. Themed restaurants have boomed from 250 in 1992 to double in 1997 and account for a £240m spend. Average spent there is £5-10 for lunch and £20-30 for dinner. Most are in the London area.

Indian meals are still very much the preserve of the younger consumer, remaining just about stable from last year – 24% are eaten by people aged between 16 to 24, 36% by those between 25 to 34, and 23% are eaten by 35 to 44 year-olds. An interesting comparison appears with the over-65s. Curry is still not a big thing in this age group. Only 6% consume it, although this figure has increased by 4% since 1995, whereas a total of 18% eat out at other (non-ethnic) restaurants. Of curry diners, 57% are male and 43% are female. On premises the split was 61%:39% respectively, while in takeaways and home deliveries it was 54%:46%. In the Curry Club, 65% of members are male, and of the restaurant reports we receive the percentage from males is around 75%, many of whom, it seems, are teachers, medics or policemen – all used to filling out paperwork! In socio-economic terms, AB consumers accounted for 21% of the total curry market, C1 31%, C2 28% and DE 18%. In the takeaway/delivery sector, it was 19%, 29%, 31% and 21% respectively. Despite media coverage saying the Indian restaurant is in decline, our figures remain virtually unchanged from last year. Over 2.5 million diners use the Indian restaurant each week. The average number of seats is 53. With an average bill of between £12-15, the total spend is now estimated at over £2bn. Old habits die hard, with 92% of curry house users preferring evenings. Saturday night accounts for 25% of all trade, Friday 18% and Thursday 12%. Sunday lunch only accounts for 2%. Indeed, with the curry house lunch trade amounting to only 9%, more restaurants have decided not to open at lunch times.

And what did these people order? Predictably, chicken remains the most popular ingredient, rising 1% to 66% in 1998 (from 52.5% in 1991 and 60% in 1995). Bad press or no, demand for meat at the curry house is constant at 22%, with lamb accounting for 10%, beef for 9% and venison and mutton nearly 4%. (Pork and veal rarely appear.) Fish and prawn has risen, despite high prices due to shortages, to 5% (up 1%) while vegetables account for just 7% (down 1%). According to Gallup (mid-1997), in that year there was a tiny gain of vegetarians to 5.4% of the population. Until then, the national figure for vegetarians had been around 5% for some years. Gallup point out that a further 14.3% of the population avoid red meat – the reasons given are taste 24%, BSE 22% and moral grounds 8%. Cost plays a factor, too. Called demi-vegetarians, many people still eat poultry and fish. This figure has hardly changed, either, over the years. At the curry house, Chicken Tikka Masala remains the number one ordered dish (16%), with Chicken Korma next (8%) and Jalfrezi, Masala, Roghan, Karahi and Tikka/Tandoori all close behind at around 6%.

Music (BBC watchdog – the Big Dinner) tested Schwartz spices (posh – expensive) spice and Rajah (cheap spice) on seven Balti restaurateurs. They asked which restaurateurs thought were best. Disagreement. They also found that classical music increases the spend by £11 per couple, whereas pop increases it by £7 and foyer music by under £1. They did not survey the effect that unpopular Indian music has, but there must be a lesson to be learned by the restaurateurs.

Main source: Taylor Nelson AGB. Subsidiary information: Mintel Gallup, Market Power, Plimsoll Portfolio Analysis, Tandoori Magazine Restaurateurs survey and Curry Club User Survey.

Those Price Checks

Throughout the Guide, when available, we publish the prices of certain commonly ordered items. We call it the Price Check and it always includes Papadams, Chicken Tikka Masala (CTM) and Pullao Rice. In selected cases we have included House Wine and Lager. It reveals an extraordinary divergence of prices from town to town. It's not as simple as London is dearest. Here are example highs and lows: let us know if you find higher or lower:

Papadams: Cheapest: Karahi Master, Hounslow, Middlesex – 10p Dearest: Woodlands, London w1 – £1.

CTM: Cheapest: Elmer Tandoori, Middleton-on-Sea, Sussex – £3.45 (YMCA w1 Lamb or Chicken curry – £2).
Dearest: Bombay Brasserie, sw7, £13.75

Pullao Rice: Cheapest: Elmer Tandoori, Middleton-on-Sea, Sussex 85p Dearest: Shezan, sw7, £4.50 + 10% service = £4.95

Pint Lager: Cheapest: Eastern Touch, Rusholme, Manchester – £1.50 Dearest: Rupee Room, ec2 – £4.95. Up high: Curry Mahal St Neots Cambs, £3.75 plus a 10% surcharge if you pay by credit card

House Wine, Bottle: Cheapest: Jewel in the Crown, Southsea, Hants – £3.95. Dearest: Tamarind, w1, £13.50; Tandoori of Chelsea, sw3, £2.50 glass + service 15% = £17.25 per bottle!

Cobra Indian Beer

You may be CC with
your Indian food,
but are you DC?

It's no secret, the British public's appreciation of Indian cuisine becomes ever more sophisticated. The great buzzword of the moment is 'authenticity', and lovers of Indian food are constantly striving to be CC (currinarily correct)! The great debate spills over into what is DC (drinkably correct) with such food, and as David Woolfe points out on page 31, if you wish to drink fine wine with curry, that's fine by him and many sophisticated Indians. But at many public curry, wine and beer tastings held by the likes of Safeway, there is equal response from the two camps. Wine lovers prefer wine with curry, beer drinkers, beer, and that's that. Or is it?

There is beer and there is beer. True, some wines may lose their subtlety when consumed with spicy food, but many beers have an even more negative effect. For example, real ale is too heavy to make it a satisfactory curry accompaniment, while typical European lagers are gassy. Both combine less well with spices than many wines, leaving an unpleasant bitter taste, and they tend to make you bloated. But to some, the thought of a long, cold glass of beer to go with an Indian meal is appealing.

Indian beer provides the solution and Cobra Indian Beer provides the best solution. Cobra was created in Bangalore in 1990 to go well with any Indian meal. After much research, a brew was formulated that is not just smooth, but extra smooth. A special double-filtration process helps create a beer that is much less gassy, while retaining a distinctive taste and the premium strength of 5% alcohol. Cobra is brewed using only top-quality barley malt, hops, maize, yeast and rice, giving it a clean, refreshing body and aroma. These attributes make it the ideal Indian food companion, because its hoppiness lends itself to spicy food, while its smoothness makes it dangerously easy to drink!

Cobra is now the biggest-selling Indian bottled beer in the UK, and has just recently also become available in selected restaurants on draught. Eye-catching, bright, rich new packaging, and an improved recipe, has enhanced Cobra's smoothness and introduces a more refreshing taste to the beer. It also gave curry-loving beer drinkers their first national icon. 'Dave the Curryholic' was introduced by Cobra, by advertising agency, Team Saatchi, to give a light-hearted look at the difficulties curry-lovers face in eating their curries with fizzy Euro-lagers. The campaign examines national eating habits and highlights for the first time, the popularity and importance of 'The Great British Curry'. As well as encouraging people to eat 'Indian', the campaign also establishes Cobra beer as an integral part of such meals – the smoother and less gassy texture making it 'the beer that lets you eat more curry.'

A recent survey showed that people are visiting their Indian restaurant earlier in the evening. These diners said they are seeking a more all-rounded Indian experience from their visit, and that, with Cobra, that experience is more complete. They said Cobra's larger bottle (66oml) is ideal for group dining because, just as with the food, one can share the bottles, thus adding to the communal experience of eating Indian. The regular 330ml bottle is increasingly becoming available outside Indian restaurants, most notably in Tesco's, Safeway's, Morrison's and Waitrose. Marks and Spencer's have just introduced their first ever Indian Lager brewed in association with Cobra Beer, specifically to be sold alongside their extensive Indian food range. Whether we are now eating Indian food at home or in the restaurant, Cobra makes the quest to bring us the real Indian experience that much easier, and that much more pleasurable.

*Cobra is brewed and bottled in the UK for Cobra Indian Beer Pvt. Ltd (India) and is distributed by Cobra Beer Ltd, 21 The Coda Centre, 189 Munster Road, Fulham, London, SW6 6AW. If you want more information about Cobra, call their head office on Freephone 0800 146 944. Tel: 0171 385 5300. Fax: 0171 385 2474.
E-mail: cobra-beer@cobrabeer.com Or visit their website: www.cobrabeer.com*

Our Top 100 Restaurants

Only one in every eight of the nation's curry restaurants achieves entry into this Guide, so they are all top restaurants and a cut above the norm. But, naturally, we are always asked to identify the best of the best, so to speak. And it is true that there is an élite number of really excellent restaurants including, by definition, those establishments about which we receive many consistently good reports. For over a decade we have listed them as our TOP 100 restaurants. This year there has been quite a lot of change. Twenty have been demoted from the list, only two as the result of closure. The others have lost their TOP 100 cachet because of a decline in performance. Six still exist, but sadly have been totally delisted from this Guide. Fortunately, from the many you have brought to our attention, we have promoted eighteen 'new' entrants (indicated *). Some are indeed new, although some are long-established (one, Anwar's, dating from 1962!). Three are previous TOP 100s returning after receiving many good reports this year. Once again we do not have an exact 100. This time the total is 112. However, this needs a little explanation because eleven of these are branches of just three restaurants (marked †). As ever, if there are yet others we feel we have missed, please report to us. For a restaurant to remain in our TOP 100 list, we also need your views.

There is a further, even more élite list, the cream of the cream, winners of our SPECIAL AWARDS (highlighted in bold type), all of whom attend the Guide's prestigious ceremony in London to receive their awards. For the record, previous winners of such an award are also indicated, since they all remain at the top of our TOP 100.

London

E1		Café Spice Namaste
N1		Sonargaon
N16	*	Rasa
NW1		**Diwana Bhel Poori** (BEST VEGETARIAN)
		Great Nepalese
NW4		Prince of Ceylon
NW5		Bengal Lancer
SE13	*	Spice of Life
SE23		Babur Brasserie

	Dewaniam
SE26	Jehangir (Previous Award Winner)
SW1	Saloos
SW3	Tandoori of Chelsea
SW5	Star of India
SW6	Blue Elephant (Previous Award Winner)
SW7	Bombay Brasserie (Previous Award Winner)
SW10	**Chutney Mary** (BEST IN UK FOR SECOND TIME)
SW12	**Tabaq** (BEST PAKISTANI FOR SECOND TIME)
SW13	Haweli (Previous Award Winner)
SW15	Ma Goa
SW17	Sree Krishna
SW18	* **Sharkhels** (BEST NEWCOMER)
SW19	* Zujuma's
W1	* Anwars
	Caravan Serai
	* Chor Bizarre
	La Porte des Indes (Previous Award Winner)
	Ragam South Indian
	Soho Spice
	Tamarind (BEST CHEF)
	Veeraswamy
W2	Khan's
	Old Delhi
W5	Monty's
W6	Tandoori Nights (Previous Award Winner)
W8	Malabar
W13	**Sigiri** (BEST SRI LANKAN, SECOND YEAR)
WC1	Malabar Junction (BEST SOUTH INDIAN)
	Mandeer (address change)
WC2	The India Club (Previous Award Winner)
	Punjab (BEST NORTH INDIAN)

Rest of England

BERKSHIRE
Theale   Café Blue Cobra (Previous Award Winner)
BRISTOL
Bristol   Rajdoot (Previous Award Winner)

BUCKINGHAMSHIRE
Milton Keynes   **Jaipur** (Best Outside London Restaurant)

CHESHIRE
Ellesmere Port   Agra Fort (Previous Award Winner)

DORSET
Poole   Rajasthan

ESSEX
Ilford   Curry Special
       Jalalabad

HAMPSHIRE
Fleet   Gurkha Square (Previous Award Winner)
Liss   Madhuban

HERTFORDSHIRE
Abbots Langley   Viceroy of India
St Albans   Mumtaj

KENT
Bromley   Tamasha (Previous Award Winner)
Folkestone   India
Welling   *   Tagore

LANCASHIRE
Adlington   Sharju

LEICESTERSHIRE
Leicester   Curry Fever
       Friends Tandoori

G MANCHESTER
Atherton   *   Savar
Manchester   Gaylord

MERSEYSIDE
Liverpool   **Gulshan** (Best in the North)

MIDDLESEX
Southall   Brilliant (Previous Award Winner)
       Madhu's Brilliant (Previous Award Winner)
       Omi's
       Sagoo and Thakhar
Wembley   Chetna's Bhel Puri
       Curry Craze

NORTHUMBERLAND
Corbridge   The Valley (Previous Award Winner)

NOTTINGHAMSHIRE
Nottingham   Chand

Saagar

OXFORDSHIRE

Oxford   Aziz

                Polash Tandoori

STAFFORDSHIRE

Kingsley Holt * Thornbury Hall Rasoi

Lichfield   Eastern Eye

SUFFOLK

Woodbridge   Royal Bengal

SURREY

Epsom   Le Raj (returns to the Top 100)

Oxted   * **Gurkha Kitchen** (BEST NEPALESE)

Tolworth   † Jaipur

Woking   † Jaipur

SUSSEX

Worthing   * Ma'hann

TYNE AND WEAR

Gateshead   Last Days of the Raj

Newcastle   Sachins

             * **Valley Junction 397** (MOST ORIGINAL)

                Vujon

WARWICKSHIRE

Leamington Spa Ashoka

WEST MIDLANDS

Birmingham   **Adil** (BEST BALTI HOUSE)(returns to the Top 100)

                Maharajah (BEST IN THE MIDLANDS, SECOND YEAR)

                Royal Naim (Previous Award Winner)

Coventry   King William IV (Previous Award Winner)

                Rupali

Warley   Rowley Village

N YORKSHIRE

Skipton   † **Aagrah** (BEST RESTAURANT CHAIN, SECOND YEAR)

Tadcaster   † **Aagrah** (BEST RESTAURANT CHAIN, SECOND YEAR)

S YORKSHIRE

Doncaster   † **Aagrah** (BEST RESTAURANT CHAIN, SECOND YEAR)

Sheffield   Nirmals (returns to the Top 100)

W YORKSHIRE

Bradford   † Nawaab

Garforth   † **Aagrah** (BEST RESTAURANT CHAIN, SECOND YEAR)

Huddersfield † Nawaab

Leeds		Darbar
Pudsey	†	**Aagrah** (BEST RESTAURANT CHAIN, SECOND YEAR)
Shipley	†	**Aagrah** (BEST RESTAURANT CHAIN, SECOND YEAR)
Wakefield†	*†	**Aagrah** (BEST RESTAURANT CHAIN, SECOND YEAR)

Scotland

FIFE

| St Andrews | | **New Balaka Bangladeshi** (BEST BANGLADESHI) |

LOTHIAN

Edinburgh	*	Far Pavillions
	*	**Gulnar's Passage to India** (BEST IN SCOTLAND)
		Lancers Brasserie
		Shamiana (Previous Award Winner)
		Verandah

STRATHCLYDE

| Glasgow | | The Ashoka (Previous Award Winner) |
| | * | Café India |

Wales

CLWYD

| Deeside | † | Bengal Dynasty (Previous Award Winner) |

GLAMORGAN

| Cardiff | * | **Jubraj 2** (BEST IN WALES) |
| Swansea | * | Moghul Brasserie |

GWYNEDD

| Llandudno | † | Bengal Dynasty (Previous Award Winner) |

A Taste of India

◈

THE TAJ GROUP *of* HOTELS

Taj Hotels ask: 'Why settle for a taste of India
when we can give you the whole banquet?'

No one can say they have seen India in all her entirety. No one can say
they know India completely. India is best described as an extraordinary
mosaic of languages, customs, traditions, religions, and, of course, cuisine, each indispensible, intricate piece contributing to make up that
comprehensive whole.

Other than taking up permanent residence in this magical land,
there is one other way to experience India in her magnificent diversity,
and that experience would lie exclusively behind the welcoming doors
of The Taj Group of Hotels. From its earliest days, taking up residence
with the Taj Group has been a grand occasion. For instance, when the
Taj Mahal Hotel, Mumbai, opened in 1903, the event was described the
The Times of London as 'a resplendent debut'. Consider that resplen-
dence multiplied by 50, spread over 30 destinations across the subcontinent, each an authentic representation of the culture of its surroundings, and what you have is The Taj Group of Hotels today.

Over the years, the Taj has garnered a reputation for its hospitality,
business accoutrements and, of course, its exquisite cuisines. Only the
renowned restaurants and the immaculately trained chefs of the Taj
Group can be trusted to bring the flavours, the spirit, the magic, the
pageantry and the riches of India through the ages to life in a feast
for all the senses. From the earliest days, cooks in India were given
an uncommonly high status. They were the maestros. And the heads
of different kingdoms would compete with each other to attract the
best cooks.

In fact, the Taj's commitment to recreating authentic ancient delicacies is evident in the Palace Hotels. The Taj has gone to great lengths
to hire chefs who are descendants of the cooks that served the Indian
royalty. Dining at 'Jharokha', the restaurant at the magical Lake Palace
proves the point. Your palate is treated to cuisine that the ancient rulers
of Mewar and their guests enjoyed. The menu offers secret

Rajashthani recipes passed down through generations by word of mouth.

You could well say that the food at the Taj takes you on a gastronomic journey of India. At any of the Taj hotels, it stops nothing short of magnificent. Take, for example, 'Haveli', the restaurant at the Taj Mahal, New Delhi. Here, you get to enjoy the finest North-West frontier cuisine – the *kebabs* and *kormas* so popular with the Mughrabi. At the Taj Lucknow – the city of refinement – is the 'Oudhyana', the restaurant which serves such delicacies as the fragrant *Dum pukht* biriyani. Redolent of cardamom and cloves. Studded with almonds and raisins. Another legendary creation is the *galouti* kebab – first created by the chef of a toothless *nawab* of Lucknow, to be so tender it melted in the mouth (the name *galouti* means 'melt-in-the-mouth'). Travel further south and, at the Taj Coromandel in Chennai, experience delicious Tamilian food. Fluffy *idlis*, cracklingly crisp *dosas*, fiery *rasams*. Or, even the authentic Mulligatawny which actually means 'pepper water' in Tamil.

Regardless of which Taj restaurant you eat at, you will always get the real taste of Indian food because the commitment of the chefs is legendary. After a rigorous training period of four years, most Taj chefs go out into the field and learn from the masters of Indian cuisine themselves. The chefs of the restaurant 'Southern Spice' at Madras' Taj Coromandel have spent an entire year staying with traditional Indian families, learning what no cookbook or catering school can teach. Such is the passion at the Taj to serve the most authentic recipes, that the chefs at 'Karavalli' (the coastal cuisine restaurant tucked away in a courtyard of the Gateway Hotel at Bangalore) travelled the entire western coast of India to understand the cuisine. Try the famous *Kori Gassi* and you'll know. It's spicy chicken in coconut gravy with expertly blended spices.

For those who want the taste of authentic Indian food, there is really no place like India. Here you can truly explore all the rich flavours of a land whose cuisine is as varied as her regions.

Taj Hotels is India's number one hotel group, with a portfolio of some fifty magnificent properties, ranging from tiny and large former palaces to brand new purpose-built extravaganzas. In addition, they have a further thirty equally splendid hotels worldwide. Taj has its own chef school at Aurangabad, where novices undergo a four-year apprenticeship then a year of work experience in a Taj Hotel. Only then are they qualified.

Wolfe on Wine

If you wish to drink fine wine with curry, that's fine by wine expert David Wolfe

Why drink wine with Indian food? A good question. But first consider an even more fundamental question – why drink wine at all? Not to get drunk. If we are silly enough to want no more than that, it is more easily achieved with spirits, or more cheaply with beer. So I am writing for the many sensible people who, while welcoming the pleasant feelings induced by a moderate amount of alcohol, drink wine for its flavour and as the best complement to food, not, I hasten to add, 'to wash it down'. That horrible expression implies horrible food.

Of course there are times when wine can be enjoyed on its own but it is usually better with a nibble, whether it be olives, cheese, sev or elaborate canapés in a luxury restaurant. Most wines seem to have this natural affinity with food. It is as true of Indian food as of any other. After all, much of what we now call Indian food began life in the north-west of the subcontinent bordering on Iran – and that grape-growing region is certainly one of the places where wine originated. 'One of the places' because the first wine must have been the result of an accident when a jar of grape-juice went past its sell-by date and started to ferment; it probably happened many times before someone invented the technology we now know as wine-making.

But restaurant guides going back to the earliest days of Indian restaurants in London, in the 1920s and 30s agree that Indian food ruins wine – or at least good wine. *Good Food Guides* of the 1960's are still full of warnings to avoid wine with Indian food, and even as I write, a wine journalist of a national newspaper has repeated this nonsense.

How did I find out about the happy marriage between wine and Indian food? That was another accident. I met a friend for lunch at the Bombay Palace, London W2, on a bitterly cold January day. We sat in the bar with only the window pane between us and the blizzard, and pondered what to drink. We didn't want spirits, certainly not cold beer and cocktails had not yet made their come-back. 'Let's have a glass of red wine,' I said, but there was none by the glass (it was 20 years ago). So I ordered a bottle of claret, a full-bodied St Emilion. We enjoyed a glass each, and drank the rest with our meal. It was a revelation. It was great with tandoori and fried starters – even with crab, which of all seafood, normally makes red wine taste awful. That is crab 'prepared in European style'. And it was sublime with the curries, both meat and fish. Was the flavour of the wine spoiled by the chilli, as is commonly said? Not at all. The wine clears the palate of chilli, and in its turn, but not before, the chilli clears the palate of wine.

The distinguishing feature of St Emilion clarets is the rounded softness characteristic of their main grape, the Merlot. But I cannot advise you to drink St Emilion in an Indian restaurant. Good ones are far too expensive for ordinary restaurants. Few places, perhaps a dozen in London, and fewer in the rest of the country, list them. In fact full-bodied French wines of quality are beyond the pockets of most of us, except for the few remaining Indian ex-Maharajas, and the rather more numerous Western showbiz and industrial Maharajas.

So is it back to the beer or lassi? Not at all. Forget father's, or grandfather's, advice about the superiority of French wines. For every-day drinking today look to Italy, Spain and above all the New World. Currently the best value is Chilean wine, and fortunately there are plenty of Chilean Merlots. And if there is no Merlot there may be a Cabernet Sauvignon. This is the great grape of the other side of Bordeaux, where the clarets of the Medoc and Graves come from. Its flavour is likened to that of blackcurrant. Again good ones are expensive. But Cabernet Sauvignon is also a leading variety in Australia, California, Chile and many other countries. Another of this 'claret family' of grapes is the Malbec, playing a minor part in Bordeaux, but Argentina's most important fine grape. And Argentine wines are improving so rapidly that they will soon be listed by most wine merchants.

The Syrah, known in Australia as Shiraz, is a major grape of the Rhone where it produces beefy reds; but while the Australians taste as if they will go beautifully with curry, they may unexpectedly lack the required depth of flavour. In Spain the Garnacha, which in France is the Grenache, is a major grape of Rioja, and of other Spanish wines from regions such as Navarra. They are often outstanding value. Italian wines are on the way up. One I dismissed in the past, even in previous editions of this Guide, is Valpolicella where recent fine vintages show great depth and body. Southern Italian wines often have plenty of flavour, together with a touch of homely roughness which is not unwelcome with Indian food.

The emphasis on fullness, depth of flavour, or in a word the 'amount' of flavour is the key to choosing wine for Indian food. But what about white wine I hear you asking? Isn't that the best thing to cool and refresh the palate? No it isn't. Because white wine is usually more, not less, alcoholic, than red from the same region, it is less cooling. It may actually make you thirstier because of the dehydrating effect of alcohol. But the main reason is that few whites have enough flavour to stand up to the strongest spices. I don't mean hot chillies, mustard and peppers but cloves, cinnamon, fenugreek, cardamom and many others.

If you really prefer white wine, again look for plenty of flavour. Don't bother with the great classic French names – Chablis for example, but consider sensibly priced French country wines, or basic Spanish whites, or Italian Orvieto (among many others) or New World Chardonnays. The Sauvignon has a place too, because of its fruit and crisp acidity which cuts the ghee or oil of fried starters such as samosas or bhajias. With tandoori grills, and kebabs, even tandoori prawns, I still prefer red. But if white is your choice don't shun the touch of sweetness, which can reveal extra flavour. Colombard and Chenin are grapes to look for, the latter especially in South Africa. And among white wines I must mention the great deception – the Alsace Gewürztraminer which for decades has traded on its name. Yes, the word 'Gewürz' does mean spicy. So those who make it and sell it, and many who write about it believe that it must go well with 'spicy' Oriental (not just Indian) cuisine. Matchings of wine and curry have confirmed my view that it just isn't so.

Finally a word about house wines. In many restaurants they are poor, thin, watery rubbish, unworthy of the name of wine. Always try a glass before ordering a bottle. And if it isn't good enough be prepared to pay not all that much more, for something infinitely better. Whether you are snacking on a samosa, devouring a dosa or feasting at an opulent banquet you may be pleasantly surprised at how much extra pleasure can be found.

David Wolfe, our regular wine expert, writes for wine magazines and gourmet Guides. He is also a specialist consultant to ethnic restaurants that need advice on their wine list selection and wine descriptions.

An Addict Confesses

Our wine man, David Wolfe, reveals all!

I lost my curry virginity to a Korma at the age of about thirteen. Soon I had worked my way through Rogan Josh, Dopiaza, Dhansak, Patia and so on, and tried Madras, Vindaloo and even a Phal — once each. But having experienced these delights I quickly returned to less volcanic dishes. This was because, even at that age, I thought of curries as a source of sensual pleasure, not as an Olympic sport with the gold medal going to whoever could eat the hottest.

From the 1940's I ate Indian from time to time but it was not until 1959 that I entered the Hell (and Heaven) of curry addiction. I was opening a restaurant, which would specialise in classic French cooking, and I should have been eating every meal in my future competitors' establishments. Instead I visited Indian restaurants nearly every day. On the rare occasions when I did not, I craved curry after 48 hours. A specialised taste was green curry, nothing like today's Thai green curry. Very few restaurants had even heard of it. So it had to be prepared at home. The basis was Bolst's green curry paste, one of the many excellent products of that brand at the time. The main ingredient was poppy seeds, and there were mustard seeds too. It was good with lamb or chicken, better with vegetables, best of all with potatoes. The only reference I can find to green curry now is in Camellia Panjabi's 50 Great Curries of India. It is Parsee style ras chawal, and includes only a tablespoon of poppy seeds for 10-12 oz of fish together with other green ingredients — cardamom, coriander leaves and stalks, and mint. It is pictured as dull yellow curry, flecked with green, nothing like the rich green produced by Bolst's paste.

To ginger up my memories I have consulted Good Food Guides going back to the 1955-6 edition. These list just seven Indian restaurants, of which only Veeraswamy's now exists. My recollection of it is somewhat negative. The first visit was less than successful because of a muddle about its name. The result was dinner, with little spice, and less pleasure, at Verrey's, also in Regent Street. So my attempt to impress a lady with my familiarity with London's oldest Indian failed. Perhaps it didn't matter because soon afterwards we were married. Then we continued to confuse restaurant names, and therefore failed to meet at the Light of the Himalayas, the Prince of Mahal or Taste of the Taj.

The 1963/4 Good Food Guide says there were rumoured to be over 300

Indian restaurants in London, and that many people regarded the Shah in Drummond Street as the best. The five listed in that edition included the Shah's off-shoot, the Star of India in Old Brompton Road. Interestingly there are two references to tandoori chicken. The Light of India was said to be one of the few restaurants where you could get it without ordering a day beforehand; the price, 17/6 (87½p.) curiously included rice. But Veeraswamy's offered it with only 20 minutes' notice. I suspect that tandoori chicken was then roasted in an ordinary oven, and nan was unknown here. But by 1973 one restaurant's 'impeccable nan' is recommended. And it was in the early 1970s that several restaurateurs boasted of using the first tandoori oven in this country. One was Anarkali in King Street, Hammersmith. That beautiful word 'Anarkali' literally means 'pomegranate bud' and is often the name of a specially beautiful woman in stage or film dramas. This Anarkali's chef was Mr Aziz who was not only a superlative classic cook, but also innovative – which in Indian terms, means that he was a revolutionary who had devised more than one new dish. A disadvantage of leading the pack of restaurants is that your ideas will be imitated. So it was that this border region between Hammersmith and Chiswick soon became a gastronomic province of India, with specialities unknown elsewhere; all were invented by Mr Aziz and copied by local competitors. Anarkali was also ahead of its time in decor, with great swathes of cotton or silk curving across walls painted cream from ceiling to floor. Mr Aziz is sadly no longer with us but his own restaurant Aziz still exists near by, although it was recently renamed the Ghandi.

A place of happy memories was Gerrard Street, Soho, long before it became the heart of Chinatown. Here was the Ganges, owned by Mr Ahmed and his wife, Heidi, who introduced Swiss efficiency and hygiene, and later became a fine Indian chef. Once I dined there at the same time as the Indian national hockey team, and I was privileged to share a 'home-style' mutton biriani prepared specially for them. This was my first encounter with a dish which can be so delicate when not made by combining meat curry with rice. The Ganges in Praed Street, Paddington is still in the family run by another Mr Khaled Ahmed, the founder's nephew. The mix of Indian and Far Eastern in Gerrard Street was spectacularly exploited by a man who ordered 24 papadams in the Ganges. They came piled on a single plate, only to be instantaneously demolished by the customer's ear-splitting 'hah' followed by a karate chop.

Twenty years ago I inspected Indian restaurants for the *Egon Ronay Guide*. Some were good, others not. Excuses for poor performance could sometimes be more interesting than the meal. At one place the only bread was stale papadams. There were no tandooris because 'the oven was not working'. Samosas? unavailable, no explanation. Spinach simply failed to arrive. Fried rice came instead of plain. Only when I insisted on changing it did the truth emerge. The chef had not come in that evening. The restaurant closed a few weeks later. Another time I remarked to a waiter that the standard of cooking and preparation suggested that the chef was taking a night off. 'No' he said, 'he is just very busy.' The 80-seat restaurant served five customers all evening.

Another famous Gerrard Street restaurant was the Shafi, founded in the 1930s. Its menu included a dish very rarely found today, akuri, charmingly described as curried 'scrabbled' egg. It was there that I did something I had never done before, nor since. The service, by a single wildly incompetent, thoroughly unspiritual, young man, had been awful. All the (mostly wrong) dishes were thrown on to the table, and beer was spilled. When, after a long delay, the bill arrived I crossed off the service charge. The manager appeared and politely pointed out the line on the menu – 'service 10%'. I equally politely replied that another line read 'cauliflower 60p'. This had not been charged because I had not had any. Nor had I had any service. 'Oh yes sir, that is very logical' said the manager. He paused. Then 'Please forgive him. This waiter does not know our ways. He has just arrived from the other side.'

The Cuisine of the Subcontinent

Afghan Afghanistan's location had always held the strategic key to India until this century, for it was through the solitary mountain passes that the invaders came and possessed India from as early as 3000 BC. Located between Iran (formerly Persia) and Pakistan (formerly N.W. India), it brought the cuisine of the Middle East to India – and that of India to the Middle East. Afghan food features Kebabs and Birianis, and skewered spiced lamb over charcoal. The only UK Afghan restaurants are Caravan Serai, London W1 and Afghan Kitchen, London N1.

Balti In the high mountains of north Pakistan, is the ancient state of Baltistan, sharing its border with China and India's Kashmir, and once on the Spice Route to China. These days, with Pakistan and India in a permanent state of war, the few roads connecting the two countries are permanently closed. Little may have been known about Balti food outside its indigenous area, had it not been for a small group of Pakistani Kashmiris, who settled in east Birmingham in the 1960s. There, they opened small cafés in the back streets, serving curries made aromatic with Kashmiri Garam Masala, and herbal, with plentiful coriander, in two-handled pots called the 'karahi' in India, but known here as the 'Balti pan'. Eating with no cutlery, using fingers and bread to scoop up the food, is the norm to the community, but a revelation to Birmingham's white population, who made Balti their own.

Bangladeshi/Bengali Most of the standard curry houses in the UK are owned by Bangladeshis and nearly all of those serve standard formula curries, ranging from mild to very hot. Bangladesh, formerly East Pakistan, is located at the mouth of the River Ganges. Before Partition, the area either side of the Ganges was Bengal. Today Bengal is the Indian state that shares its border with Bangladesh. In terms of food, Bangladesh is Muslim, so pork is forbidden. The area enjoys prolific fresh and sea-water fish – pomfret, boal, ruhi, hilsa and ayre, and enormous tiger prawns – and it specialises in vegetable dishes such as Shartkora and Niramish. Until recently, true Bangladeshi/Bengali cuisine was nigh on impossible to find in the UK. Hopefully we will find more and more of our Bangladeshi restaurants serving the delights of their own country.

Bombay   Bombay curries are mellow and light and, although a favourite restaurant dish, Bombay Potato (*see* glossary) is not found as such in Bombay but it is typical of Bombay tastes. Also in the glossary are Bombay Duck, presently banned from the UK, and Bombay Mix, re-invented under this name in Southall in the 1970s. Bhel Puri, also in the glossary, is Bombay's favourite kiosk food, most famously available at the city's Chowpatti beach. Years ago it found its way to the UK in the form of the Bhel Puri houses in Drummond Street, Wembley and other places around London. It is served cold and is delicious. Most of India's Parsees (q.v), with their distinctive food, live in Bombay.

Burmese   Burma, now renamed Myanmar, shares its boundaries with Bangladesh, India, China, Laos and Thailand. Its food is a combination of these styles. Rice is the staple and noodles are popular too. The curries are very hot and there are no religious objections to eating pork, beef or other meats. Duck and seafood are commonly eaten. The only UK Burmese restaurant is the Mandalay, London w2.

Goan   Goa is on the west coast of India, about 400 miles south of Bombay. It was established in 1492 by the Portuguese who occupied it until 1962. It is now a state of India where Christianity prevails and there are no objections to eating pork or beef. The food of Goa is unique. Their most famous dish is Vindaloo, but it is not the dish from the standard curry house. The real thing is derived from the Portuguese dish Vino d'Alhos, traditionally pork marinated (the longer the better) in wine vinegar and garlic, then simmered until tender. To this the Goans added hot red chillies, creating a rich red curry gravy. Goa also has delicious seafood and fish dishes. There is only one true Goan restaurant in the UK, Ma Goa in London sw15, although Goan dishes do appear at the better Indian restaurants.

Gujarati   Gujarat is a largely vegetarian coastal state, north of Bombay. The first British diplomat docked at the port of Surat in 1608, and the town was used as a British trading post, until Bombay was built in 1674. The soup-like dish, with gram flour dumplings, called Khadi, whose yellow gravy is made with turmeric, spices and yoghurt, may have been the very dish which gave curry its name. The food is India's least spicy. The Parsees, who lived in Gujarat for 500 years (*see* below), influenced the food, with subtleties of sour and sweet. Yoghurts and gram flour prevail. The famous Bhaji also originated here, as did the lesser known Dahi Vada, a gram flour dumpling in a tangy yoghurt sauce. Gujarati restaurants are prevalent in Leicester and Wembley, Middlesex, and they pop up elsewhere, too.

Moghul The curry from the standard curry house is based on rich, creamy dishes developed by the Moghul emperors. No one on earth was richer than the Moghuls, and it was during their time, four centuries ago, that Indian food was perfected. Authentically, this style of food should be subtly spiced. It can be found in an increasing number of 'haute cuisine' restaurants around the country, spelt variously Moghul, mogul, moglai, muglai mugal, mugul, etc.

Nawabi The Nawabs were the rich royals of the Lucknow area of India who lived over two centuries ago. Like the Moghuls before them, they perfected a style of cooking which was spicy and fragrant. Called Dum or Dum Pukt, it involves cooking the curry or Biriani in a round pot, whose lid is sealed into place with a ring of Chapatti dough. The resulting dish is opened in front of the diners, releasing all those captured fragrances, as found in some of the better UK curry restaurants.

Nepalese The beautiful mountain kingdom of Nepal, located North of India, in the Himalayas is home to the Gurkas, sherpas, the yeti, a virgin goddess princess and Everest. The Nepalese enjoy curry and rice, and wheat breads, many of which are familiar from the north Indian repertoire. Their own specialities are, perhaps, less well known. Momo, for example, are dumplings with a mince curry filling. Aloo Achar are potatoes in pickle sauce. Achari Murgh is chicken in a pickle and curry sauce. Pulses are important, and Bhat is fragrantly cooked rice. There is an increasing, although still small, number of restaurants with Nepalese specials on the menu, particularly in west London. More menu examples will be found in the entry for The Gurkha Kitchen, Oxted, Surrey and The Gurkha Square, Fleet, Hampshire.

Pakistani Until independence in 1947, Pakistan formed the northwestern group of Indian states. Located between Afghanistan and India, it contains the famous Khyber Pass. The people are predominantly meat-eaters, favouring lamb and chicken (being Muslim, they avoid pork). Charcoal cooking is the norm, and this area is the original home of the tandoor. Breads such as Chupatti, Nan and Paratha are the staple. Balti cooking originated in the northernmost part of

Pakistan (*see* earlier). In general, Pakistani food is robustly spiced and savoury. The area called the Punjab was split by the formation of Pakistan, and it is the Punjabi tastes that formed the basis of the British curry house menu (*see* Punjab, London wc2). Bradford, Glasgow and Southall have sizeable Pakistani populations.

Parsee/Persian It is quite common to see Persian dishes listed on the standard curry house menu. Dishes such as Biriani and Pullao did indeed originate in Persia (now called Iran). Bombay's Parsees came from there, having fled from Persia centuries ago. In India, they originated dishes of their own, such as Dhansak and Patia. The real thing is a subtle cooked-together combination of meat and vegetables and/or fruit. True Persian food is hard to find in the UK, although it is served at the Old Delhi, London w1. There is no Parsee restaurant in the UK but south-west London's Bombay Brasserie and Chutney Mary both have Parsee chefs who cook decent Parsee dishes.

South Indian Much of India's population is vegetarian, and the southern part of India is almost exclusively so. Until recently the extraordinary range of vegetarian specialities was virtually unknown in the UK. The introduction of more and more restaurants offering south Indian fare coincides with the increasing awareness of vegetarianism. Specialities include many types of vegetable curry including Avial, with exotic vegetables in a yoghurt base, and Sambar, a lentil-based curry. Other delights include huge, thin crisp rice- or lentil-flour pancakes called Dosas, with a curry filling (Masala) and Idlis – steamed rice- or lentil-flour dumplings. Restaurants serving this type of food are slowly springing up all around the UK.

Sri Lankan Sri Lanka is the small, pearl-shaped island, formerly Ceylon, at the southern tip of India. Its cuisine is distinctive and generally chilli hot. They eat similar fare to that eaten in south India, i.e. vegetarian dishes, but they also enjoy very pungent meat, squid, chicken and duck curries. Good Sri Lankan restaurants include Adjay, Southall, Middlesex, Prince of Ceylon, London nw4, Jehangir, London sw26, Sigiri, London w13.

The A to Z of the Curry Menu

To the first-timer, the Indian restaurant menu is a long and complex document. This glossary sets out to explain many of the standard, and some of the specialized, dishes and items that you will encounter at many a curry house. *See also* The Cuisine of the Subcontinent. Spellings of vowel sounds will vary vastly from restaurant to restaurant, reflecting the 15 languages and hundreds of dialects of the subcontinent. (*See* Masala, Moglai, Papadam and Rhogan Josh Gosht for some examples.) Our spelling here is as near as possible to the standard accepted way of spelling, when translating phonetically from Delhi Hindi, Lahori Urdu or Dhaka Bengali to Queen's English.

A

AAM or AM Mango.

ACHAR or ACHAAR Pickle, such as lime, mango, aubergine, etc. *Achar Gohst* is meat curry, curried in a pickle base, *Achar Murgh* is the chicken version.

AFGHANI CURRY Nuts and fruit are added for the standard curry house interpretation.

ALOO Potato.

B

BAIGAN or *BEGUN* see Brinjal.

BALTI Balti originated centuries ago in north Pakistan's Mirpur, Kashmir and Skardu (Baltistan). It found its way to east Birmingham in the 1970s, where any combination of ingredients was curried in a two-handled pot known as the *karahi* (q.v.) elsewhere, but the Balti there. Served to the table still cooking, the art is to eat the food – which should be spicy, herby and aromatic – Indian-style, with the bread as the scoop in the right hand. In the 1990s, Balti spread rapidly all over the UK and beyond. The Balti found at the standard Bangladeshi curry house, however, owes its flavours more to Patak's acidic Balti paste than to Mirpur, and unless it is cooked in its pan and served cutlery-free, it will (correctly) never convince the Brummy purist that it is anything other than hype.

BARFI or BURFI Indian fudge-like sweet made from reduced condensed milk (*koya* or *khoa*), in various flavours.

BASMATI The best long-grained rice.

BATERA Football-sized puri (q.v.) becoming increasingly popular.

BATTAR Quail.

BENGAL CURRY A chicken or meat curry with chilli, sugar, potato cubes and halves of tomato.

BHAJI or BHAJEE Dryish, pan-fried mild vegetable curry.

BHAJIA Deep-fried fritter, usually with sliced onion, mixed with spiced gram flour batter, then deep-fried. Bhajia is the correct term, meaning fried. Bhaji or Bhajee is the anglicisation (*see above* for the correct meaning). For the real thing, visit Maru's Bhajia House, Wembley, Middlesex. *See also* Pakora.

BHEL PURI This is the delicious street food snack from Bombay. It is a cold combination of those crunchy squiggles you find in Bombay Mix (q.v.), the smallest of which is called *Sev*. To this is added small-diced cooked potato, puffed rice (*mamra*), coriander leaf, onion and chilli. It is laced with brown sweet and sour tamarind (*imli*) sauce, yoghurt (*dahi*), coriander chutney (*dhania*) and chilli sauce, and topped with crispy puri biscuit chippings. The result is an exquisite combination of crisp, chewy and soft textures with sweet, hot, savoury and sour tastes. Variations include differing amounts of ingredients, under various similar names, such as *Sev Batata Puri, Dahi Batata Puri, Chat Aloo Papri* and *Batata Pava. Bhel* can be accompanied by Gol Goppas (q.v.). This delicious food is generally beyond the abilities of the average curry house, so is rarely found. Try it when you can (*see* London NW1's Drummond Street).

BHOONA or BHUNA Cooking process including slowly frying out all the water content to produce a dry, usually mild curry.

BINDI A pulpy, rather sappy vegetable also known as okra or ladies fingers. Correct cooking of this dish is a good test of a chef's ability.

BIRIANI Traditionally, rice baked between layers of meat or vegetable filling, enhanced with saffron and aromatic spices, traditionally served topped with edible silver leaf (*vark*). The restaurant interpretation is a cooked rice, artificially coloured, with filling stir-fried in. It is usually heavily garnished and served with a vegetable curry sauce (*see* Pullao).

BOMBAY DUCK A smallish fish native to the Bombay docks, known locally as *bommaloe macchi*. This was too hard for the British Raj to pronounce, so it became Bombay Duck. It is dried and appears on the table as a crispy deep-fried starter or accompaniment to a curry.

BOMBAY MIX An age-old traditional Indian snack nibble, called *muruku*, made from a savoury, gram-flour, spiced batter called *ompadi*, which is forced through a press straight into the deep-frier, to give different shapes and thicknesses of squiggly nibbles. Nuts, pulses, seeds and other ingredients are added. It should always be really crunchy and fresh. Re-invented by GK Noon, owner of Royal Sweets in Southall, under the catchy name Bombay Mix, it will to keep you going at the bar.

BOMBAY POTATO A popular invention of the curry house. Potatoes in curry sauce with onions and tomato.

BOTI KEBAB Marinated cubes of lamb cooked in a tandoor oven (*see* Tandoori).

BRINJAL Aubergine, also called *baigan* or *began*. In *Baigan Burtha*, aubergine is smoked, spiced and mashed, in *Baigan Bhaji* it is chopped and curried by pan-frying.

C

CTM Chicken Tikka Masala. Invented by a British curry house chef (identity unknown) *c.* 1980, as a way to exploit his already popular Chicken Tikka by adding it to a creamy, pink, mild sauce made tasty by skilful blending of curry sauce, tomato purée, tandoori paste, cream, coconut, mango chutney and ground almonds. It is now ordered by 65 percent of all diners. Not only that, it appears in supermarket sandwiches, flavours crisps, is a pizza topping and even flavours mayonnaise. If only that chef had copyrighted it, he'd be earning millions in royalties a year. *See* Makhani and Tikka.

CEYLON CURRY At the curry house, this is usually cooked with coconut, lemon and chilli.

CHANA A yellow lentil resembling, but not identical to, the split pea, used in Dhal (q.v.) and to make gram flour. *Kabli chana* is the chick-pea. Both can be curried or dried and deep fried as in Bombay Mix (q.v.). *See also* Paneer.

CHAT or CHAAT Literally means 'snack', though often a salad.

CHILLI Fleshy members of the capsicum family, ranging in heat from
    zero (the bell pepper) to incendiary. All chillies start green and, if
    left long enough, eventually become red, the one being no hotter
    than the other. The chilli normally used in Indian cooking is the
    narrow 7.5cm (3 in) cayenne. The hottest in the world are Mexican
    habaneros, Caribbean Scotch bonnets and Bangladeshi nagas.
    People build up a tolerance to chillies, coming to adore them, but
    they should never be inflicted upon the novice, not even in fun.

CHUPATTI A 15-cm (6-in) flat disc of unleavened bread, cooked dry on
    the tava (q.v.). It should always be served hot and pan-fresh. The
    spelling can vary – Chupati, Chapatti, etc.

CHUTNEY The common ones are onion chutney, mango chutney and
    tandoori chutney. There are dozens of others that rarely appear on
    the standard menu. *See* Sambals.

CURRY The only word in this glossary to have no direct translation
    into any of the subcontinent's 15 or so languages. The word was
    coined centuries ago by the British in India. Possible contenders for
    the origin of the word are: *Karahi* or *Karai* (Hindi) – the wok-like
    frying pan used all over India to prepare *masala* (spice mixtures);
    Karhi or *Khadi* – a soup-like dish made with spices, gram-flour
    dumplings and buttermilk; *Kari* – a spicy Tamil sauce; *Turkuri* – a
    seasoned sauce or stew; and *Kari Phulia* – Neem leaves, which are
    small and rather like bay leaves, used for flavouring. The Dutch,
    who were in India in the 17th century have their own derivation.
    They say it was used in Malaya of their Malay curries, and that it
    derived from the word *Lekker* meaning delicious, or in colloquial
    Dutch, *Lekkerie*.

CURRY HOUSE *See* Formula Curries.

D

DAHI or DOHI Yoghurt, used as a chutney (*see* Raita) and in the cook-
    ing of some curries. Most curry houses make their own, and it is
    delicious as an accompaniment to curry, being less sharp than the
    shop-bought equivalent. Incidentally, Dahi, not water, is the best
    antidote if you eat something that's too hot for you.

DAHI VADA South Indian savoury gram-flour doughnut, deep-fried,
    cooled and dunked into cold, spicy yoghurt (*see* Vada).

DAL or DHAL LENTILS There are over sixty types of lentil in the sub-

continent, all packed full of nutrients. The common restaurant
types are *massor* (red, which cooks yellow), *moong* (green), *chana* (also
used to make gram flour) and *urid* (black).

DEGCHI or DEKHCHI Brass or metal saucepan without handles.

DHANIA Coriander leaf or spice.

DHANSAK Traditional Parsee meat dish cooked in a purée of lentils,
aubergine, tomato and spinach. Restaurants use dal and methi, and
sometimes chilli and pineapple.

DOPIAZA Traditional meat dish. *Do* means two, *piaza* means onions.
Onions appear twice in the cooking, first fried and second raw. The
onions give the dish a sweetish taste.

DOSA South Indian pancake made from rice and *urid* (lentil) flour,
which, when made into a batter, soon ferments to give a superb
sour taste. *Masala Dosa* is a Dosa filled with mashed potato curry
spiced with onion, chilli, turmeric and mustard seed.

DUM Cooking by steaming in a sealed pot, invented by the Royal
Nawabs (*see* The Cuisine of the Subcontinent), e.g. *Aloo Dum*,
steamed potatoes. Also called Dum Pukt or Pukht (Pron as in
bucked).

E

ELAICHI Cardamom. Can major in curries — for example, *Elaichi Murgh*
is chicken curried with a predominance of green cardamom.

F

FOOGATH Lightly cooked vegetable dish found in the Malabar area of
South India. Any vegetable such as gourds or plantain can be used.

FORMULA CURRIES Many of our 'Indian' (q.v.) restaurants operate to a
formula which was pioneered in the late 1940s. In those days, a way
had to be found to deliver a variety of curries, without an un-
reasonable delay, from order to table. Since all authentic Indian
recipes require hours of cooking in individual pots, there was no
guarantee that they would even be ordered. So cubed meat, chicken
or potatoes, dal and some vegetables were lightly curried and
chilled, and a large pot of thick curry gravy, a kind of master stock,
was brewed to medium-heat strength. To this day, portion by por-

tion, on demand, these ingredients are reheated by pan-frying them with further spices and flavourings. At its simplest, a Medium Chicken Curry, that benchmark of middle ground, is still on many menus, though sometimes disguised as Masala, and requires no more than a reheat of some gravy with some chicken. For instance, take a typical mixed order for a couple at a table for two. She wants Chicken Korma (fry a little turmeric, coriander and cumin, add six pieces of chicken, add a ladleful of curry gravy, plenty of creamed coconut, almonds maybe and a little cream – result, a mild dish, creamy-golden in colour), and with it she'll have Vegetable Dhansak (fry some cumin seeds, dry methi leaves (q.v.), chopped onions, a little sugar, tomato, red and green capsicum with the gravy, add dhal and some cooked veg – result, colourful, and still medium-strength). He wants Meat Korma (as for the chicken, using meat), and he wants Prawn Vindaloo (fry spices and chilli powder, add the gravy which at once goes red and piquant, then cooked peeled prawns, fresh tomato and potato, simmer and serve). Maybe they'll also take a Sag Paneer (fry cummin, some thawed creamed spinach and pre-made crumbled paneer together, add fresh coriander – done). One cook can knock all these up, simultaneously, in five pans, within minutes. Rice is pre-cooked, breads and tandoori items made to order by a different specialist. And, hey presto, your order, sir and madam! Thus the menu can be very long, with a huge variety of dishes, sometimes numbered, sometimes heat-graded, mild, medium and hot, hotter, hottest, and any dish is available in meat, poultry, prawn, king prawn, and most vegetables, too. That's the formula of the standard curry house. Just because this is not authentic does not make it bad. It can be, and variously is, done well. This Guide is full of many such restaurants, about which we say 'a standard curry house, doing the formula well'.

G

GARAM MASALA Literally meaning hot (roasted) mixture (of pepper and aromatic spices), it originated in Kashmir and is added towards the end of cooking in certain north Indian curries. *See also* Masala.

GHEE Clarified butter or vegetable oil used in high-quality north Indian cooking.

GOBI Cauliflower.

GOL GOPPAS or PANI PURI are mouth-sized puffed-up crispy biscuits, served with *Jeera Pani* (water spiced predominantly with chilli, black salt and cumin water) and *Aloo Chaat* (potato curry) at Bhel Puri (q.v.) houses. To eat the correct way, gently puncture the top of the biscuit, pour in some *Jeera Pani*, and pop into the mouth in one. Chew and then add some *Aloo Chaat*.

GOSHT Meat, usually refering to lamb or mutton.

GULAB JAMAN An Indian dessert of cake-like texture. Balls of curd cheese paneer, or flour and milk-powder, are deep-fried to golden and served in light syrup.

GURDA Kidney. *Gurda Kebab* is marinated kidney, skewered and cooked in the tandoor.

HALVA Sweets made from syrup and vegetables or fruit. Served cold in small squares, it is translucent and comes in bright colours depending on the ingredients used. Orange – carrot; green – pistachio; red – mango, etc. Has a texture thicker than Turkish Delight. Sometimes garnished with edible silver leaf.

HANDI Cooking pot, sometimes earthenware, sometimes metal.

HASINA KEBAB Pieces of chicken breast, lamb or beef marinated in a yoghurt and spice (often tandoori) mixture, then skewered and barbecued/baked, interspersed with onions, capsicum and tomato. Turkish in origin. *See* Shaslik.

I

IDLI Rice- and lentil-flour steamed cake, about the size and shape of a hockey puck, served with a light but fiery curry sauce. South Indian in origin.

IMLI Tamarind. A very sour, date-like fruit used as in cooking or chutney which is of purée consistency, sweetened with sugar.

INDIAN In 1947, the subcontinent of India was partitioned. To cut a long story short, in Britain and the West we still generally erroneously refer to our curry restaurants as 'Indian'. In fact, over 85 percent are Bangladeshi, with only around 8 percent run by Indians and 8 percent run by Pakistani. There is a smattering of Nepalese and Sri Lankan restaurants, and only a single Afghan and a single Burmese restaurant in Britain. *See* Formula Curries.

J

JALEBI   An Indian dessert. Flour, milk-powder and yoghurt batter are squeezed through a narrow funnel into a deep-frier to produce golden, curly, crisp rings. Served in syrup.

JAL FREZI   Sautéed or stir-fried meat or chicken dish, often with lightly cooked onion, garlic, ginger, green pepper and chilli.

JEERA   Cumin or cummin seed or powder, hence *Jeera Chicken*, etc.

JINGRI or CHINGRI   Prawns of any size.

K

KALIA   Traditional Bengali/Bangladeshi meat, poultry or fish dish in which red coloured ingredients are mandatory, especially red chillies and tomatoes. *See* Rezala.

KARAHI   A two-handled Indian kitchen dish. Some restaurants reheat curries in small karahis and serve them straight to the table with the food sizzling inside. *See also* Curry and Balti.

KASHMIR CHICKEN   Whole chicken stuffed with minced meat. *See* Kurzi.

KASHMIR CURRY   Often a medium curry to which is added cream and coconut and/or lychees, pineapple or banana.

KEBAB   Kebab means 'cooked meat' in ancient Turkish, traditionally cooked over charcoal, in a process over 4,000 years old. It was imported to India by the Muslims centuries ago. Shish, incidentally, means 'skewer'. *See* Boti, Hasina, Nargis, Shami and Sheek Kebab.

KEEMA   Minced meat, e.g. as used in curry. *See also* Mattar.

KOFTA   Balls made from ground meat, poultry or fish/shellfish or vegetables, then deep-fried and simmered in a curry sauce.

KORMA   Probably derived from the Persian *Koresh*, a mild stew. The Moghuls made it very rich, using cream, yoghurt and ground almonds, fragranced with saffron and aromatic spices. But, traditionally, Kormas need not be mild. In Kashmir a popular dish is the *Mirchwangan Korma*, red in colour because it is full of Kashmiri chillies. To the curry house, Korma is terminology for the mildest curry, sometimes made sickly by the overuse of creamed coconut block, cream and nuts.

KULCHA   Small leavened bread. Can be plain or stuffed, e.g. *Onion Kulcha.*

KULFI   Indian ice cream. Traditionally it comes cone-shaped in vanilla, pistachio or mango flavours.

KURZI   Leg of lamb or whole chicken given a long marination, then a spicy stuffing, e.g. rice and/or Keema (q.v.), then slowly baked until tender. This is served with 'all the trimmings'. It is many a curry house's Special, requiring 24 hours' notice (because of the long preparation, and a deposit to make sure you turn up to eat it). Often for two or four, it is good value. Also called Khurzi, Kasi, Kozi, Kushi, etc. *See also* Murgh Masala.

L

LASSI   A refreshing drink made from yoghurt and crushed ice. The savoury version is *Lassi Namkeen* and the sweet version is *Lassi Meethi.*

M

MACCI or MACHLI   Fish. Today, fresh exotic fish from India and Bangladesh are readily available and, when a restaurant offers them, you have the chance of getting a truly authentic dish.

MADRAS   You will not find a Madras Curry in Madras, any more than you'll find a London Pie in London. Neither exists. But the people of the south eat hot curries, firing them up with as many as three different types of chilli – dry, powdered and fresh – added to the cooking at different stages. As the Brits got used to their early formula curries, they began to demand them hotter. With no time to add chillies in the traditional way, one of the pioneer curry house chefs simply added one teaspoon of extra-hot chilli powder to his standard sauce, along with tomato and ground almonds, and ingeniously called it 'Madras'. The name stuck. *See also* Chilli, Phal and Vindaloo.

MAKHANI   A traditional dish. Tandoori chicken is cooked in butter ghee and tomato sauce. Some say this was the derivation of CTM (q.v.).

MALAI Cream. So *Malai Sabzi Kofta*, for example, means vegetable balls
   in a creamy curry gravy. *See* Rasmalai.

MALAYA The curries of Malaya are traditionally cooked with plenty
   of coconut, chilli and ginger. In the Indian restaurant, however,
   they are usually based on the Korma (q.v.), to which is added
   pineapple and/or other fruit.

MASALA A mixture of spices which are cooked with a particular dish,
   e.g. *Garam Masala* (q.v.). It can be spelt a remarkable number of ways
   – Massala, Massalla, Masalam, Mosola, Moshola, Musala, etc.

MASALA DOSA *See* Dosa.

MATTAR Green peas. So *Mattar Paneer* is peas with Indian cheese, *Keema
   Mattar* is mince meat curry with peas, and so on.

MEDIUM CURRY *See* Formula Curries.

METHI Fenugreek, pronounced 'maytee'. Savoury spice. The seed is
   important in masalas. The leaves, fresh or dried, are used particularly in Punjabi dishes. At the curry house, the flavour of these
   leaves predominates in their *Dhansak*.

MOGLAI Cooking in the style of the Moghul emperors, whose chefs
   took Indian cookery to the heights of gourmet cuisine centuries
   ago. Few restaurateurs who offer Moglai dishes come anywhere
   near this excellence. Authentic Moglai dishes are expensive and
   time-consuming to prepare. Can also be variously spelt Muglai,
   Mhogulai, Moghlai, etc.

MULLIGATAWNY A Tamil vegetable consommée (*molegoo* pepper, *tunny*
   water), adapted by the Raj to create that well-known, thick, meat-
   based British soup.

MURGH Chicken.

MURGH MASALA or MURGH MASSALAM Whole chicken, marinated in
   yoghurt and spices for hours, then stuffed and roasted. See *Kurzi*.

N

NAN or NAAN Pronounced 'narn', it is flat, leavened bread, usually
   made from plain white flour (*maida*) dough, but sometimes from
   wholemeal flour (*atta*). After the dough rises, it is rolled out and
   baked in the tandoor (q.v.). It is teardrop-shaped and about 20-
   25cm (8-10 inches) long. It must be served fresh and hot. As well as
   Plain Nan, there are many variations involving the addition of other
   ingredient(s). *Keema Nan* is stuffed with a thin layer of minced,

spiced kebab meat. *Peshwari Nan* is stuffed with almonds and/or cashew nuts and/or raisins. Garlic, onion, pineapple, tomato, indeed anything, can be added. Double- or treble-sized *Karak*, Elephant or Family Nans are offered at Balti houses to share to scoop your food up with.

NARGIS KEBAB Indian scotch egg – spiced, minced meat around a hard-boiled egg.

NIRAMISH A Bangladeshi mixed vegetable, often cooked without garlic, and spiced only with *Panch Phoran* – Indian Five Spice mixture.

O

OOTHAPPAM *See* Uthappam.

P

PAAN Betel leaf folded, samosa-fashion, around a stuffing of aniseed, betel nut, sunflower seeds, lime paste, etc. and eaten in one mouthful, as a digestive after a meal. The leaf is bitter, the mouth-feel coarse and the taste acquired, but more acceptable (to Westerners) small spices and seeds (*supari*), sometimes sugar-coated in lurid colours, are often offered by the curry house after the meal.

PAKORA The true pakora is a whole piece of vegetable, lightly coated in gram-flour batter and deep-fried, although at the curry house it is to all intents and purposes the same as the Bhajia (q.v.).

PALAK *See* Sag

PANEER Cheese made from milk by separating the whey (liquid) from the curds (solids) which, when compressed, can be crumbled, chopped, fried, tandoori-baked and/or curried (*see* Mattar). In Bengali, Paneer is called *Chhana*, not to be confused with the lentil, Chana (q.v.).

PAPADAM or PAPAD Thin lentil-flour wafers. When cooked (deep-fried or baked) they expand to about 20cm (8 ins). They must be crackling crisp and warm when served. If not, send them back to the kitchen and deduct points from that restaurant. They come either plain or spiced, with lentils, pepper, garlic or chilli. There are many ways to spell papadam, using any combination of the vowels 'a', 'o'

and 'u', and double 'p' and double 'd'. But, despite many people call-
ing it so, it should never be referred to as a pampadom.

PARATHA Dough combined with ghee (q.v) thinly rolled out and folded over itself to create a layered disc, like puff pastry. It is pan-fried
to create a soft bread.

PASANDA Meat, usually lamb, which traditionally is thinly beaten, then
cooked in a creamy curry gravy to which some chefs add red wine.
The dish and wine were both true treats of Moghul emperor
Jehangir who, though Muslim, blessed the wine to make it 'holy
water' thus circumventing the rules of Islam. Then he and his court
proceeded to drink themselves legless while enjoying this dish.

PATIA Restaurant curry with a thick, dark, red sweet and sour sauce.
Based on a Parsee prawn or fish dish.

PATRA A Gujarati speciality, in which colcasia (patra) leaves are rolled
in gram-flour paste, like a Swiss roll, then steamed, sliced and finally deep-fried.

PESHAWARI NAN See Nan.

PHAL The hottest curry, also known as a Bangalore Phal, invented by
the British curry house restaurateurs.

PICKLE Pungent, hot, pickled vegetables essential to an Indian meal.
The most common are lime, mango, brinjal and chilli. Though
rarely seen at the restaurant, meat and game are made into traditional and very delicious Rajasthani pickles.

PODINA Mint. A fresh chutney, puréed from fresh mint, chilli and
onion. Can also be spelt Pudina.

PRAWN BUTTERFLY Usually a large or giant king prawn, cut so that it
opens out and flattens, butterfly-shaped, marinated in spices and
immersed in gram-flour batter, then deep-fried. A curry house
invention, whose name could also have derived from 'batter-fry'.

PRAWN PURI Prawns in a hot sauce served on a Puri (q.v.) bread.
Although sometimes described as Prawn Puree it is not a purée.

PULLAO Ancient Persia invented Pollou, with rice and meat and/or vegetables, cooked together in a pan until tender. Following Muslim
invasions it evolved into Turkey's Pilav, Greece's Pilafi, Spain's Paella
and, of course, India's Pullao. In many curry houses, the ingredients
are mixed after cooking, to save time. (See Biriani.) There are many
other ways to spell it: Pillau, Puloa, Pillar, Pilaw, Polaw, etc.

PULLAO RICE The restaurant name for rice fried with aromatic
spices, usually with rice grains coloured yellow and/or red and/or
green.

Puri Unleavened wholemeal bread: rolled out flat to about 10cm (4 ins) in diameter, it puffs up when deep-fried, and should be served at once.

Q

Quas Chawal or Kesar Chaval Rice fried in ghee (q.v.), flavoured and coloured with saffron (*kesar*).

R

Raita A cooling chutney of yoghurt on its own (*see also* Dhai) or vegetable, e.g. cucumber or mint (sometimes called Tandoori Sauce) to accompany papadoms, the starter or the main course.

Rasgulla Walnut-sized balls of paneer (q.v.), or semolina and cream cheese, cooked in syrup (literally meaning 'juicy balls'). They are white or pale gold in colour and served cold or warm. *See* Rasmalai.

Rashmi Kebab Kebab of minced meat inside an egg net or omelette.

Rasmalai Rasgullas cooked in cream, served cold. Very rich, very sweet.

Rezala Bengali/Bangladeshi speciality. Lamb cooked in evaporated milk, rich and subtly spiced, it would be milder than Korma except that green chillies are mandatory. Traditionally no red- or orange-coloured ingredients should be used. *See* Kalia.

Rhogan Josh Gosht Literally meaning 'lamb in red gravy'. Traditionally, in Kashmir, lamb is marinated in yoghurt, then cooked with ghee, aromatic spices and natural red colorants. It should be creamy but not hot. The curry house version omits the marinade and the aromatics, and uses tomato and red pepper to create a red appearance. There are many ways of spelling it – Rogon, Roghan, Rugon, Rugin, Rowgan, Ragan, etc., Just, Joosh, Juice, Jash, etc., Goosht, Goose, Gost, etc.

Roti Indian bread of any type, rolled out into thin flat discs.

S

Sabzi Vegetable.

SAG or SAAG   Spinach, also called *Shak* in Bengali, *Palak* in the Punjab and *Rai*, although these are mustard leaves. *Lalshak* is delicious red spinach.

SAMBAL   A Malayan term describing the chutneys accompanying a meal. Sometimes referred to on the Indian menu. Malays also refer to Sambal as a cooked dish of various ingredients cooked in a hot sauce, e.g. prawn sambal.

SAMBAR   A hot and spicy, runny, almost consommé-like south Indian vegetable curry made from lentils and exotic vegetables, such as the drumstick. In the Manchester/Merseyside area, the curry houses have a dish called *Samber*. It bears no resemblance to Sambar, except that lentils and a lot of chilli powder are added to meat, chicken or prawn curry.

SAMOSA   Celebrated triangular, deep-fried meat or vegetable patties, supreme as starters or snacks.

SHAMI KEBAB   Round minced meat rissoles.

SHASHLIK KEBAB   Shashlik in Armenia means 'to grill'. Cubes of skewered lamb or chicken are marinated (in an oil, garlic and chilli mixture) then grilled. *See* Hasina.

SHATKORA   A Bangladeshi citrus fruit, the size of a grapefruit but sharper in flavour, though softer than a lemon. Can be eaten fresh or used in cooking.

SHEEK KEBAB or SEEKH   Literally means (from Turkish *shish*) a skewer. Spiced minced meat, usually coloured lurid red at the curry house (from proprietary tandoori/kebab paste), is moulded onto the skewer, then baked in the tandoori and grilled.

STANDARD CURRY   *See* Formula Curries.

T

TANDOORI   An ancient style of cooking, which originated in the rugged north-west frontier of India (now Pakistan). It gets its name from the cylindrical clay oven, the tandoor, with its opening at the top, fired with charcoal in its base. Originally the ingredients were chicken and lamb, marinated for many hours in a spiced yoghurt-based sauce, traditionally slightly reddened with red chilli, then skewered and baked in the tandoor. Now the curry house product also includes fish, prawns, paneer (q.v.) and vegetables. But its lurid red or orange colour is created by the unnecessary use of tartrazine food colouring in proprietary ready-to-use pastes. *See* Boti Kebab, Tikka, Nan Bread and Raita.

TARKA DHAL   A tasty, spicy lentil dish, the Dhal being *massoor* (red) lentils, cooked to a purée, to which the Tarka (crispy, fried caramelized onion and/or garlic) is added as a garnish. This simple-sounding dish is a great test for the cook. It should taste very slightly burnt (from the Tarka), and be subtly, yet decisively, spiced, neither too thick nor too thin.

TAVA   A heavy steel, rimless, flattish frying pan, used to cook items such as Parathas.

THALI or TALI   A round tray (*thali*) with a low rim, averaging about 34cm (12 inches) in diameter. It is a food plate on which an entire meal is served for one person. Dry items, such as rice, bread and even dry curries, are placed directly on the thali. Wet portions, such as curries, dhals, soups and sweets, etc. are placed in matching serving bowls (*tapelis*) of different diameters, and they too reside on the thali. They were made of solid gold for the Moghul emperors, solid silver for the Maharajas, and stainless steel for the rest of us. To be found at certain restaurants serving 'special' meals.

TIKKA   Literally, a small piece. For example, *Chicken Tikka* is a filleted chunk of chicken, marinated (*see* Tandoori), skewered and baked in the tandoor. Traditionally, the marinade is identical to Tandoori marinade, and cooks a naturally russet brown colour. Proprietary Tikka paste, as used in the curry house, is lurid orange or yellow because of the tartrazine it contains.

TINDALOO   *see* Vindaloo

U

UPPUMA   South Indian dish. Lightly fried semolina with onion and spices.

UTHAPPAM   A spicy south Indian pizza, made from rice flour and topped with onions, tomatoes and chilli.

URID   A type of lentil, its husk is black, and it comes whole, split or polished. Available as a dhal dish in some restaurants, e.g. *Maharani Dhal*.

V

Vada or Vadai Lentil-flour spicy doughnut, enjoyed in Gujarat and south India. *See* Dahi Vada.

Vark Edible silver or gold leaf, made today in Hyderabad, but a Moghul speciality, said to be an aphrodisiac.

Vindaloo A fiery dish from Goa. (*See* The cuisines of the Sub-continent.) At the restaurant scene, it now means the second hottest dish (two spoonfuls of chilli powder), usually with a chunk of potato (Aloo). Also sometimes called *Bindaloo* or *Tindaloo* (even hotter). *See also* Chilli, Madras and Phal.

Y

Yakni Literally mutton, or a meat-based stock.

Z

Zaffron Saffron, also known as *Kesar* or *zafron*. The world's most expensive spice.

Zeera Alternatively called Jeera, which is cumin. *Zeera Gosht* is lamb cooked with cumin.

THE 1999
GOOD CURRY
GUIDE

THE DIRECTORY

CENTRAL LONDON

Area: British capital
Population: 5,694,000
Number of restaurants in central London: 1,431
Number of central London restaurants in Guide: 210

GREATER LONDON

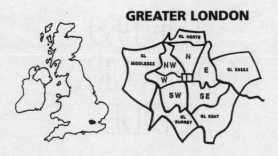

Greater London, established in 1965, absorbed Middlesex and parts of Essex, Hertfordshire, Kent and Surrey. For GL towns/boroughs in these areas, please see the relevant county (see list on page 8). For the purpose of this Guide we define London by its well-known 1870s postal districts. We run alphabetically as follows: E, EC, N, NW, SE, SW, W and WC.

Before we are accused of London bias, it is worth explaining that, of the 7,550 British curry restaurants on our nationwide database, nearly 20 percent of them are in London. Naturally, with such competition, many of the country's best are in the capital. Our coverage reflects this, with a strong London section. Furthermore, the choice of regional food is exhaustive, i.e., in addition to standard Bangladeshi curry houses, you'll find examples of every one of the regional cuisines, all of which are detailed on page 37.

©	Curry Club discount (see page 6)	☕	Unlicensed
√	Vegetarian		
BYO	Bring your own alcohol	▦	Delivery/takeaway

London E

Area: East London, postcodes E1 to E18
Population: 1,042,000
Number of restaurants in county: 220
Number of restaurants in Guide: 24

E1 – Brick Lane

Once predominantly Jewish, and bustling with tailors, cab drivers, and salt-of-the-earth street markets, the long and narrow Brick Lane, has, since 1971, become home to the country's largest Bangladeshi community. Running between Shoreditch and Aldgate East tube stations, plans are afoot to rename it *Banglatown*, indicating its proliferation of cheap and cheerful curry cafés, snack bars, restaurants and provisions shops, run by the thriving community. (To emphasise its roots you'll also find an all-night, fresh-baked bagel shop where cabbies queue for sustenance.) As for curry, some of the establishments have remained fairly spartan, and unlicensed (you can BYO). Here are your favourites:

EASTERN EYE BALTI HOUSE NAME CHANGE

63a Brick Lane, E1 © 0171 375 1696

Pakistani Baltis cooked by Bangladeshi chef-owner Babul, in the Brick Lane heartland. Whatever next, you may ask? But we hear they are good. Price check: Papadam 65p, BCTM £6.95 (incl. Nan or Roti), Bombay Potato £2.25, Pullao Rice £1.75, Pickles and Chutneys 65p per portion. You could buy a jar for that! Delivery: £12 minimum, 3-mile radius. Hours: 12pm-12am. Stocks Cobra.

BENGAL CUISINE

12 Brick Lane, E1 © 0171 377 8405

Traditionally decorated 60-seater, well-established in Brick Lane terms (1980). Taken over in 1993 by N. Choudhury. 'I was tired and cold and wanted somewhere to sit in comfort. At 4pm, I was their only customer. Food excellent.' BG. Price check: Methi Chicken £4.95, Sag Bhaji £2.45, Papadam 45p, CTM £6.95, Pullao Rice £2.15. £2.15, Peshwari Nan £2.15

Lager £2.45. Delivery: 3-mile radius. Hours: 12pm-12am non stop!
Branch: Taja, 199a, Whitechapel Road. E1. Stocks Cobra.

BHEL POORI BRASSERIE   √ BYO

63a Brick Lane, E1   © 0171 377 6412

Unusual for Brick Lane in that it serves Bhel Poori (*see* Glossary) and
south Indian dishes, all vegetarian. 'Extremely eye-catching decor –
black chairs complementing pink tablecloths and neatly laid-out tables.
Main course, Chef's Thali, was exceedingly good value. Eight small pots
of carefully prepared vegetable curries and side dishes surrounded a
larger central dish of Pullao Rice. BYO from the off-licence opposite.'
JT.

NAZRUL   BYO

130 Brick Lane, E1   © 0171 247 2505

I guess this Guide would be incomplete without the Nazrul, and it has
graced our pages since our first edition in 1983. Previously, DMW told us
of the loose toilet pedestal and leaky S-bends, but we never did hear
more on the subject! (Although I did get a review from a WC, which I
took to be a S-end up!) For the first-timer, the delights of the toilets in
such establishments are best avoided. Nazrul is an archetypal BYO,
really cheap, café-style venue, with a huge following of curryholics –
and fabulous food! It is for that you must go. New to the menu are Balti
dishes. 'Always appears to be busy – particularly popular with students.'
AS. 'Made the kids really welcome.' HC. Still has red banquettes and
flock, long may that last … somebody get it listed! Price check: Balti
Chicken £2.95, Chicken Curry £2.35. Set meal average £6. Branch:
Nazrul II, 49 Hanbury Street, E1.

SHAMPAN   ©

79 Brick Lane, E1   © 0171 375 0475

Unlike the rest of the lane, Shiraj Hoque's licensed, air-conditioned,
up-market (by Brick Lane standards) curry house Shampan makes a
point of serving the real Bangladeshi thing. So go for all your curry
favourites, if you must, but nowhere will you get a more authentic taste
of Bangladesh. Betki, Rup, Ayre and Rhui (Bengali fish) and the sour-
flavoured Shatkora (Sylheti citrus fruit) Gosht/Murgh, meat or chick-

en (£4.45), and seasonal veg such as Kakrol, Potol and Lalshak. 'Good portions, efficient service, overall good experience.' K&ST. Price check: Bangladeshi Thali £9.95, Papadam 35p, CTM £4.95, Pullao Rice £1.45. Branch: City Spice, 138 Brick Lane, E1. Stocks Cobra.

SWEET AND SPICY   BYO

40 Brick Lane, E1   © 0171 247 1081

Little changes at this friendly, formica-tabled Brick Lane veteran caff, founded in 1969 – its Bangladesh roots being emphasised by the Punjabi-Pakistani food 'being ladled out of containers onto plates as you wait. Excellent no-nonsense food and plenty of it at low prices. Karahi Gosht £3.50, spicy, plenty of meat and no fatty gristly bits. Aloo Gobi and Brinjal £2.20, large portion, excellent spice and flavour. Small plate of onion, Raita and red sauce free, water provided on each table. BYO policy for drink. They clearly have a similar policy for toilet paper, something to remember if likely to need to use the facilities!' MW. Will return for more!' PH. 'loved the grub, but would like a redec.' GR. (Rubbish – they'd put the prices up!) Closed during Ramadan.

Elsewhere in E1

CAFE INDIYA

30 Alie Street, E1   © 0171 481 8288

Some love the minimalist look of this 100-seater's polished wooden floors, charcoal-coloured tables and ladder-backed chairs, set off against cream walls. Others find the high decibels of the long-lunching city chatterers resounding off these reflective surfaces unpleasantly deafening. Michael Tarat (*see* Rupee Room, EC2) owns it, leaving its management to Ashik Al and the cooking to head chef Maq Sood for northern curries, and Taj-trained Antoinette D'Cruz, for Goan specialities. The limited but carefully chosen menu includes Chicken Mo Mo, a Nepalese dumpling starter £4.75, Tandoor-cooked Afghani Murghi Kebabish, chicken pieces marinated in vinegar, cashew paste, melon seeds and spices, Raan, sliced leg of lamb, from Rajasthan £9.75, Chicken Pista Korma from Hyderabad £7.95 and Chicken Pepper Fry from south India. Goan specialities are there, including a traditional Pork Vindaloo and Chicken Xacuti both £7.25, and some Goan fish dishes. Price check: Papadam 50p, CTM £5.95, Pullao Rice £1.75.

Hours: 12-4pm/6-11pm. Closed Sat. & Sun. Branch Rupee Room, EC2.
Stocks Cobra.

CAFE SPICE NAMASTE   TOP 100   ©

16 Prescot Street, E1   ℂ **0171 488 9242**

110-seater restaurant, opened in 1995 by Michael Gottlieb and Cyrus and
PervinTodiwalla, a Taj-trained husband and wife team, she managing
the front, he the cooking. This restaurant is the flagship of a proposed
value-for-money national chain, with a refreshing design concept in
modern vibrant colours. Located in the City, it does a really busy week-
day lunch trade. Evenings are generally quieter and are the best time to
go. The lengthy à la carte menu includes regional dishes from Gujarat,
Goa, Nepal, Kashmir and northern and southern India. Your eye is
caught by starters like Chilli Cheese Garlic Toast, for example, Shinanio
Balchao (mussels in a Goan sauce). Main dishes include Kerla Nandu
(crab curry), Galhina Xacutti (Goan chicken curry), Parsee Lamb Liver
and Kidney Curry or Rawa Kalwa (oysters marinated in Goan Piri Piri
Masala, dipped in dry semolina and crisply flash-fried, served with a
hot garlic dip). Curries are made from venison, goose, emu, bison, kan-
garoo, grouse and pheasant as well as the more conventional ingredients.
One of the most popular ingredients is Wensleydale Wild Boar – in
such guises as Jungli Maas Dhuanaar – where a haunch is marinated in
a masala, smoked over whole spices such as cinnamon, cardamom,
cloves, etc., then slowly oven-roasted. Curry-house all this is not! Our
advice is that you forgo your regular standard favourite and try things
new. That was the good news, however; I have to report a slowly declin-
ing level of satisfaction at the Café. Probably not amongst the city
lunchers who spend so much time yapping, and so much money on
their corporate credit cards, I wonder how they have time to masticate
let alone be discerning. Anyway, I've already made a few comments (on
page 14) about Cyrus. But on the day I am writing this very entry,
another huge piece this time in a national broadsheet arrived on my
desk. In it Giles MacDonogh extols the virtues of wine with curry,
quoting Cyrus at length. Cyrus, he says, is 'at the forefront of intro-
ducing wine to Indian restaurants. Cyrus,' the piece goes on, 'speaks
seven languages.' Really? Well one of these must be bullshit. Because,
long before Cyrus began wetting his ears as a cook's apprentice, Mr
Rajan of Tandoori of Chelsea, sw3 was quietly going about his business selling Château wines in 1965. And I wonder how the BB managed

it without you while you were working your way up through the Taj ranks in the 80s. Cyrus told MacDonogh that 'Parsees tend to be rich and exclusive, they employ cooks (as servants) and they don't sully their hands in the kitchen.' Enough Cyrus! The time has come for you to sully forth. Get back in there and focus on your job. And heed such remarks as: 'Disappointing starter despite this, the rest of the meal was excellent. Service very attentive, unusual surroundings – very Mediterranean feel. OK for a one-off, but be prepared to hurt the wallet!' – K&ST. Price check: Papadam 60p, CTM £8.95 (inc. Pullao Rice), Pullao Rice £2.35, Peshwari Nan £2.25. House wine £9.75. Delivery: £35 minimum, E1 area only. Hours: 12-3pm/6.15-10.30pm. Sat. 6.30-10pm. Bank Holiday Mon. & Sun. closed. Branch: Café Spice, 247, Lavender Hill, Battersea, SW11. Stocks Cobra.

LAHORE KEBAB HOUSE   BYO

2 Umberton Street, E1   © 0171 481 9737

For anyone who has not been to either Pakistan or to Sparkbrook, the LKH is what it's all about. Despite Brum's claim to be the inventor of the currinary world, this gaff has been doing Balti, under what some say is its true name, Karahi – or Karrai (*sic.*) – since it opened over twenty years ago – serving darned good food, geared to Asian tastes, without compromising it for Westerners. At least that's what it used to be. But its relatively new-found glory as a lunchtime dive for the money boys and girls from the City has permeated into the evenings, and it's had an effect on management. A redec has taken place. The tat beloved by LKH's *aficionados* and taken for granted by its Asian patrons, has been replaced by such inventory as arty line drawings. 'Is this the thin end of the wedge?' asks GR. I even hear they now allow discreet BYO, a big concession for strict Muslims. Cutlery is still for wimps (though you no longer have to ask for it). But when in Rome, eat the correct way, please, using a piece of Roti to scoop up your curry, in your right hand only – too bad if you're left-handed. And expect limitations if you're a veggie. Halal mutton, chicken and quail are it, in the karahi, from the tandoor as tikkas or kebabs, or as steam roast (Choosa), with robust lentils and fragrant rice. Real veterans show their spurs by enjoying the celebrated, and very filling and satisfying, Paya (lamb's trotters), laced with the Hot Chilli Raita, followed by their gorgeous Kheer rice pudding. Service is swift and accurate, but don't expect pampering, and don't expect to pay more than a tenner, including tip, in cash, please – nothing fancy like credit cards. It has a different atmosphere at different times of the day, different again at the weekend, depending on who's eating when. Despite one report telling of a decline in food quality and service, it remains very popular with local Asian families and well-heeled Indians and Pakistanis alike, indeed with all curry *cognoscenti*: 'My favourite restaurant.' RE. 'My number one restaurant.' RL. Hours: 12pm-12am. Branch: 19 Upton Road, E7.

NEW CLIFTON   NEW ENTRANT   © 10%

75-79 Wentworth Street, E1   **℡ 0171 377 9402**

The Clifton is dead (but watch this space!) and long live the New Clifton! So says proprietor, AR Haider, who opened his large, marble-walled 120-seater in 1997. Pakistani curries and Baltis by head chef Ali. His most popular dish is Mixed Grill £7.95. Price check: Papadam 50p, CTM £5.60, Pullao Rice £1.75, Peshwari Nan £1.75. Delivery: 3-mile radius. Hours: 12-3pm/6pm-12am. Sat. 6-11pm. Sunday Buffet £5.99, 11am-5pm. Stocks Cobra.

PRIDE OF ASIA   ©

207 Mile End Road, E1   **℡ 0171 780 9321**

A bog-standard, 65-seater serving all the favourites by chef Amir Uddin, owned and managed by Abdul Habiz. Price check: Papadam 45p, CTM £5.50, Pullao Rice £1.50. Delivery: £10 minimum, 3-mile radius. Hours: 12-2.30pm/6pm-12am. Stocks Cobra.

TAYYAB   🍴 BYO

89 Fieldgate Street, E1   **℡ 0171 247 9543**

A 36-seat truck-stop, according to one reporter. Well, an unlicensed (BYO tolerated, but discreetly please) caff, anyway, which now operates daytime. Owned by M. Tayyab since 1974, who is also the head chef serving Southall-style Pakistani/Punjabi kebabs and curries at ludicrously reasonable prices. 'One of my favourites.' RE. Its curious operating procedure would make any accountant faint at misused resources. Hours: 12-5pm. Then the same staff open up next door …

NEW TAYYAB   🍽 BYO

83 Fieldgate Street, E1   ✆ 0171 247 9543

... at this 65-seat venue, opened in 1995, where they curry on, in rather smarter premises. The food's the same, and it's OK with our regulars, especially the kebabs and the prices. And since the Tayyab family are the owners, accountants and cooks, it's OK with them too! Unlicensed and BYO with discretion please, i.e., don't flash it around and offend strict Muslims who are the real regulars. Price check: Papadam 50p, CTM £3.40, Pullao Rice £1.50. Both branches closed for Ramadan month.

TIFFIN   ©

165 Cannon Street Road, E1   ✆ 0171 702 3832

Abdul Kalam describes his 42-seat venue, just off the Commercial Road, as furnished with green and black marble-topped tables, high-backed iron chairs, café-style. We don't mind if the Kalam changes our previous description – 'A refreshing haven in London's East End' – to 'heaven'. Refreshing it is, with delights like Salmon Samosa £2.95, and Bathera, quails £8.50, or Lebu Murghi, special chicken, £9.95, but the Tiffin Royal Tandoori £13.95 would make Meena Patak blush the same red, so much of her paste is used on the ingredients. 'Good to busting, it is.' TH. 'We found Tiffin excellent.' D&LT. Price check: Papadam 50p, CTM £6.95, Pullao Rice £1.95. Set meal from £8.95. Hours: 12-3pm/6pm-12am, Sun. 6pm-12.30am. Stocks Cobra.

E2

AL-AMIN   ©

483 Cambridge Heath Road, E2   ✆ 0171 729 7415

Abdul Noor's two-room 39-seater remains a popular standard curry house with all the trimmings, including Balti. Price check: Papadam 50p, CTM £5.55, Pullao Rice £1.65. Delivery: £10 minimum, 2-mile radius. Hours: 12-2.30pm/6pm-12am. Stocks Cobra.

©	Curry Club discount (see page 6)	🍽	Unlicensed
√	Vegetarian		
BYO	Bring your own alcohol		Delivery/takeaway

E4 – Highams Park

PURBANI

34 The Avenue, E4   ✆ 0181 531 8804

'Takeaway for 1 teacher and 19 students: £140. Tarka Dal, Aloo Gobi, Mattar Paneer, Pullao Rice, Chapatti, salad and Papadoms. Portions so generous they served us for next day breakfast. The Indian students particularly liked the Tarka Dal and Aloo Gobi, the English students liked the Mattar Paneer, I liked it all!' BG. Proprietor is very friendly and keen to help. Price check: Papadam 40p, CTM £5.60, Pullao Rice £1.40.

E6 – East Ham

EASTERN EYE   ©

269 High Street, E6   ✆ 0181 470 8078

DMcC visits here 'many times', and she never has 'any complaints'. It's a good standard curry house run by Mabud Mussain, who also owns the Himalaya, 178 The Grove, Stratford, E15. Stocks Cobra.

MOBEEN   ☕

229 High Street North, E6   ✆ 0181 470 9365

The owners of this chain of Pakistani caffs are strict Muslims, so BYO is not permitted and it's unlicensed. Go for darned good, inexpensive, value-for-money, Punjabi, Kebabs, tandoori items and darned good curries of all sorts, selected from the counter, with specials varying from day to day. No credit cards. Hours: 11am-10pm. Branches: 222 Green Street, E7; 725 High Road, Leyton, E10; 80 Ilford Lane, Ilford, Essex.

E12 – Manor Park

THE EMPRESS INDIAN CUISINE   ©

729 Romford Road, E12   ✆ 0181 478 2500

The menu misses nothing. It's good formula curry house stuff, including Balti. Price check: Papadam 30p, CTM £5.20, King Prawn Korai Tandoori £6.90, Pullao Rice £1.40. Sunday buffet £6. Stocks Cobra.

E14 – Isle of Dogs

THE GAYLORD   NEW ENTRANT

141 Manchester Road, E14   ✆ 0171 538 0393

'The restaurant is tiny, only 34 seats around a central island. Service was friendly, and the food was delicious. All dishes were generously full of meat. My Sagh Gosht the most flavourful I've had.' JLN.

E17- Walthamstow

CHILLI HUT   NEW ENTRANT

195 High Street, E17   ✆ 0181 521 2425

'This is the Indian version of a pavement café (with the tables indoors). The staff are attentive and if you show enough interest you get to sample the dishes before you order. The pullao rice is a real treat, all the flavour and no food colouring in sight.' LC-S.

DHAKA TANDOORI

103 Hoe Street, E17   ✆ 0181 520 5151

'I used to live in E17 and my hall is littered with takeaway menus. But my winner, to whom I still return, is the Dhaka.' CJ. Stocks Cobra.

E18 – South Woodford

MEGHNA GRILL   ©

219 High Road, E18   ✆ 0181 504 0923

Long-established (1971), standard, competent Bangladeshi curry house stuff with no surprises from Siddiqur Rahman. Price check: Papadam 50p, CTM £6.50, Pullao Rice £1.70. Sunday buffet £6.95. Minimum charge per person £5. Takeaway-only branch down the road at no. 249.

ROSE OF INDIA   ©

65-67 High Road, E18   ✆ 0181 989 8862

The Rose has been operated for 22 years by Messrs Miah and Hoque, who offer all the favourite tandooris and curries at sensible prices.

London EC

Area: The City of London
Postcodes EC1 to EC4
Population: 140,000
Number of restaurants in county: 33
Number of restaurants in Guide: 3

EC1

BROKER'S INN   NEW ENTRANT

5 Clerkenwell Road, EC1   ✆ 0171 490 4468

It's bare and modern inside, with framed share certificates on the walls,
hence the un-Indian name. 'It was even more pleasing, better even, than
our first visit. The service is particularly good, friendly and efficient.'
HJC. 'We have been to this restaurant several times on our own, but this
was the first time we had guests, both of whom are frequent Indian
food eaters. They were most impressed. All the dishes were well above
average. A great asset to the Barbican area.' MR & MRS DRC. Stocks Cobra.

RAVI SHANKAR   √

442 St John Street, EC1   ✆ 0171 833 5849

DRC loves its south Indian vegetarian menu: 'choosing is always agonis-
ing. The Vegetarian Thali and a starter of yoghurt, spices, and what
appeared to be small pieces of idli, was delicious, spicy, sweet and sour
all at once. Our Paper Dosa, with usual relishes, was absolutely marvellous and served very eye-catchingly, vertically, curved around the back
of the stainless steel platter with the relishes in front, rather than the
more usual roll laid on the plate. How do they get it to stand upright?'

EC2

RUPEE ROOM

10 Copthall Avenue, EC2   ✆ 0171 628 1555

Michael Tarat's 1995 venture has an apt name. For rupee's the name,
rupee's the decor, and rupee's the game. Its City-suit brigade don't, it

seems, mind forking out mucho dinero while they fork up. Given a chance, chattering chef Abdur Rob happily boasts that his magnificent food leads to spends of over £75 a head! Tarat is more subdued, pushing Rob back where he belongs, behind stoves, but be prepared to spend half that. Hours: 11.30am-10pm weekdays, closed Sat., Sun. & Bank Holidays. Branch: Café Indiya, E1.

London N

Area: North London, postcodes N1 to N22
Population: 1,245,000
Number of restaurants in county: 197
Number of restaurants in Guide: 28

N1 – Islington

AFGHAN KITCHEN   NEW ENTRANT

35, Islington Green, N1   ✆ 0171 359 8019

'Not knowing anything about Afghan food, four of us were delighted to find a close resemblance to Indian with the Murgh Kofta, Gosht Qurma, the Suzhi (spinach) Gosht, each £4.50 with Nane Lavash bread as the staple, chilli pickle to liven up the delicate spicing, house wine to wash to all down.' GR. Small menu. No credit cards. Hours: 12pm-12am Tues.-Sat.

INDIAN VEG BHEL POORI HOUSE   √ ©

92-93 Chapel Market, N1   ✆ 0171 837 4607

'Although I have sung the praises of the excellent value eighteen buffet dishes e-a-m-a-y-l £2.95, I feel I must praise it again. I now lunch there once a week and the quality is always consistent. Occasionally there is a superb mashed potato and onion curry. Always a friendly welcome and my half lager is now brought automatically.' TN.

©	Curry Club discount (see page 6)	☕	Unlicensed
√	Vegetarian		
BYO	Bring your own alcohol	🔢	Delivery/takeaway

MILAN INDIAN PURE VEGETARIAN 　　　　🍵 √ ©

52 Caledonian Road, Kings Cross, N1　　© **0171 278 3812**

Mr and Mrs Verma (manager and chef) own this good-value vegetarian, unlicensed eatery. Hours: weekdays, 12-10pm, Sat. 12-2pm/6-10pm, closed Sun. Note the e-a-m-a-y-l buffet.

RAJMONI INDIAN CUISINE 　　　　　　　　©

279 Upper Street, Islington, N1　　© **0171 354 3821/1720**

Kalam and Jamal's Rajmoni's 70-seat restaurant is decorated simply in cream, with paintings on the walls and low lighting. Chef Ram Sing Pall's popular cooking includes all your favourite curries and side dishes. Price check: Papadam 50p, CTM £6.15, Pullao Rice £1.65, Peshwari Nan £1.70. Delivery. Hours: 12-3pm/6pm-12am. Branches: Rajgate, Ampthill, Beds; Villa Bombay, sw6.

SONARGAON　TOP 100 　　　　　　　　　©

46 Upper Street, Islington, N1　　© **0171 226 6499**

'On a training course in Islington a few of my colleagues from Manchester, knowing I am a curry addict, asked if I knew any good curry restaurants in the area. I opened my *Good Curry Guide* and to my great delight found that the Sonargaon was just around the corner from the training course. Off we went and had what proved to be one of the best meals any of us had ever had. The Manchester lads know their curries, as they are regular visitors to the Rusholme area, and to a man they declared that the Sonargaon well deserved its TOP 100 rating. We were met at the door by an extremely friendly waiter who invited us in. Service and atmosphere were good and we enjoyed a variety of excellent dishes. The Pall Masala turned out to be hot enough, even for me, and the taste was out of this world. One of my colleagues had Chicken Jalfrezi and voted it one of the best ever. The Chicken Tikka starter also received wide acclaim while the Nan bread, although not particularly large, was the tastiest I've had. The Lamb Roghan Josh, Chicken Tikka Masala and the Prawn Puri starters were all well appointed. It is rare to go to a restaurant with such a large group and find that to a man everyone reckoned it to be one of the best ever.' BG.

SURUCHI

82 Mildmay Park, N1   © 0171 241 5213

Khalil Miah's Suruchi serves more than the standard curry. Try their dosas for a change. It has a patio garden which, we hear is worth gold dust to its loyal clientele. Hours: 12-2.30pm/6-11.30pm. Branches: Babur, 32 Mill Lane, NW6; Ruchi, 92 Kingsgate Road, NW6.

N2 – East Finchley

MAJJOS FOODS   NEW ENTRANT   ©

1 Fortis Green, N2   © 0181 883 4357

Established in 1993 by Mrs Ashraf. Manager S. Mogul. A shop with a seating area for just 10 diners, so you can enjoy some spicy dishes while shopping for your Indian groceries. Kashmiri, Pakistani and Indian food. Meat curries £5.25 (large) £3.50 (small), Vegetable curries £3.50 (large) £2.30 (small). Price check: CTM £5.25, Pullao Rice £1.25. Hours: 10.30am-10.30pm (10pm on Sun.).

N3 – Finchley

RANI   √

3 Long Lane, N3   © 0181 349 2636

Jyoti Pattni's vegetarian menu, with its mainly Gujarati specials (cooked by his wife and his mother), makes this restaurant different. 'Food has always been superb here but I found that the relatively small menu became rather monotonous. Welcomed the new menu. It has some cold starters which are "to die for". Rashia Vall, great. Rice and breads as good as usual.' CT. Branch: Richmond, Surrey. Stocks Cobra.

N4 – Finsbury Park

JAI KRISHNA   ⬛ √ BYO

161 Stroud Green Road, N4   © 0171 272 1680

Mr and Mrs S. Choudhury's unpresumptuous café, seating 50 on rickety chairs; its gaudy Hindi decor and the smells from the food at the counter are so redolent of India. And, of course, it's the food which matters here. At that counter are superb pure vegetarian dishes, differing daily, depending on the availability of seasonal exotic vegetables. Make your choice. No credit cards accepted. Unlicensed: BYO, corkage 75p wine, 25p lager. In 1996, they committed a health offence, (for grease on the walls and floor). Price check: Papadam 35p, Masala Dosa £2.50, Sambar £2.50, Coconut Rice £1.90. Set Lunch: £5.75. Hours: 12-2pm/5.30-11pm, closed Sun.

SUNDERBAN   ©

50 Blackstock Road, N4   ℭ 0171 359 9243

'This is a basic, standard – but clean – curry house. Decor – flock. Service is very good if you mention Curry Club. We have been here on numerous occasions, the food is always excellent.' AS.

N6 – Highgate

KIPLINGS   ©

2 North Hill, N6   ℭ 0181 340 1719

From the Stanley Krett stable (*see* Bengal Lancer, NW5), it has established a good reputation with everything 'as it should be.' JE. Stocks Cobra.

N8 – Hornsey

JALALIAH   ©

163 Priory Road, N8   ℭ 0181 348 4756

Moen Uddin's well established (1974) 40-seater. Curry formula remains 'inexpensive and very good'. Price check: Papadam 40p, CTM £3.70, Pullao Rice £1.10, Peshwari Nan £1.30. Delivery: £10 minimum, 2-mile radius. Hours: 12-2.30pm/6pm-12am. Stocks Cobra.

JASHAN

19 Turnpike Lane, N8   ℭ 0181 340 9880

Messrs Rohit and Rashmikant Khagram's restaurant is decorated with plants, abstract painting and a water fountain, it seats 52 diners in one dining room. Northern Indian food on the menu, specials include: Elachi Raan, whole butt-half of lamb cooked (pot roasted), served with rice and vegetables, Bhape Chingre, delicately steamed prawns, with mustard. Jashan's food is at Selfridges and Harrods food halls. Price check: Papadam 50p, CTM £5.95, Pullao Rice £2.95, Peshwari Nan £2.70. Hours: 6-11.30pm, closed Mon. Stocks Cobra.

MEGHNA ©

55 Topsfield Parade, Tottenham Lane, Crouch End, N8   © 0181 348 3493

Omar Farook Khan's 52-seat wedge-shaped room lends itself to spacious, typical Indian-arch decor with relaxing alcoves for privacy. Chef Moynul Haque's standard items are supplemented by quality specials such as Bangladeshi fish dishes and FS's favourite Lemon Chana Chicken. 'Quantities large, quality good, comfort fine.' GP. Price check: Papadam 50p, CTM £5.25, Pullao Rice £1.45, Peshwari Nan £1.40. Delivery. Hours: 12-2.30pm/6pm-12am. Sun. 12pm-12am, serving e-a-m-a-y-l buffet all day. Branch: Meghna, 2 Abbey Parade, Hanger Lane, Ealing, W5. Stocks Cobra.

N9

JAYS   NEW ENTRANT   √

547, Kingsbury Road, N9   © 0181 204 1553

'Another good vegetarian unlicensed Indian café, with a menu that is fairly similar to Sakoni's (*see* Wembley, Middlesex). The open-plan kitchen enables you to see how the food is cooked. Also serves Indian-Chinese.' RM. At the burgeoning Chinese restaurants in India, Chinese food is cooked with an Indian twist, adding a new spicy perspective, which you either like or you don't. RM does. He says: 'particularly liked the Shanghai Potato. Overall, a bit expensive given the location and decor.' Another like it or not option is available – Hindi music. Spend over £10 on food, and you will receive five tapes free! Price check: Mogo Crisps: £1.75, Bhel Poori £2.50, Masala Dosa £3.75. Delivery: £15 minimum, 2-mile radius. Hours: 12.30-11pm.

©	Curry Club discount (see page 6)		Unlicensed
√	Vegetarian		
BYO	Bring your own alcohol		Delivery/takeaway

N10 – Muswell Hill

DEENA TAKEAWAY   NEW ENTRANT

97 Colney Hatch Lane, N10   ✆ **0181 444 5025**

Managed by Miss Shaharun Miah. A spacious takeaway-only establishment with good lighting. Standards cooked by Mr Miah, Chicken
Madras is his most popular dish. Price check: Papadam 40p, CTM
£5.95, Pullao Rice £1.65, Peshwari Nan £1.55. No credit cards. Delivery:
£10 minimum, 4-mile radius. Hours: 5.30-12pm.

TASTE OF NAWAB   NEW ENTRANT   ©

93 Colney Hatch Lane, N10   ✆ **0181 444 6146/883 6429**

Taken over in 1996 by Mujibur Rahman, the comfortable air-
conditioned Nawab has 'all the old favorites plus exciting dishes. The
Chicken Kori is a must – really delicious, spicy and full of flavour. All
dishes are large, reasonably priced and tasty. Service great!' SM. Price
check: Papadam 50p, CTM £5.95, Pullao Rice £1.75, Peshwari Nan
£1.75. Lager £2.10 pint, £6.95 house wine. Delivery: £10 minimum.
Hours: 12-2.30pm/6pm-12am. Sunday buffet 12-5.30pm.

N11 – New Southgate

BEJOY   ©

72 Bounds Green Road, N11   ✆ **0181 888 1268/1262**

Established 1995, Abdul Sukur's restaurant seats 54, party room 16.
Bangladeshi standards and side dishes cooked by chef M. Rahman.
Price check: Papadam 50p, CTM £6.30, Pullao Rice £1.60, Peshwari
Nan £1.75. Delivery: £8 minimum, 2-mile radius. Hours: 12-2.30pm
(Sat.-Thurs.)/6pm-12am. Sunday buffet £5.95 per person, 12-11pm.
Branch: Sunderban, N4. Stocks Cobra.

NEW ARJUN   ©

35-37, Friern Barnet Road, N11   ✆ **0181 368 1504**

A. Rahman's 70-seat (party room 20) consistently good air-conditioned
restaurant, decorated in shades of blue, with mahogany chairs, trailing
plants and gilt framed pictures and mirrors, has been around since 1978.

Head chef Mr Choudhury cooks northern Indian and Kashmiri style curries. Price check: Papadam 50p, CTM £5.95, Pullao Rice £1.70, Peshwari Nan £1.95. Hours: 12.30-2.30pm/6pm-12am (1am on Fri. & Sat.). Stocks Cobra.

N12 – North Finchley

FINCHLEY PAN CENTRE   🍺 BYO

15 Woodhouse Road, N12   ✆ 0181 446 5497

A tiny, unlicensed Indian snack bar, frequented by Indians. Kebabs, samosas, veg. rissoles, etc., very inexpensive. Friendly service. Cash please. Hours: 12-10pm (Fri., 3.30-10pm). Closed Tues.

N14 – Southgate

ROMNA GATE TANDOORI

14 The Broadway, N14   ✆ 0181 882 6700

Everyone remarks on the decor – 'impressive', 'outstanding'. The room is made spectacular and intimate by the skilful use of elegant coloured glass, mini waterfalls and wrought-iron work. The little service bell on each table is a good idea. 'The glass screens each side of the table cut out cigarette smoke from other diners.' DCG. We do hear about it getting very busy, particularly at peak times, which is always taxing for the best-run restaurants, and occasionally leads to a less than perfect occasion. However, most reporters remain happy with all aspects of the Romna, though CF tells of the same red sauce appearing on several dishes and watery dal, etc. Reports, please.

N15

GUPTA BHEL PURI   🍺 √ ©

460 West Green Road, N15   ✆ 0181 881 8031

If you like Bhel Puri, you'll love Gupta's. It's vegetarian, unlicensed, expensive, satisfying and very more-ish. Hours: 11am-11pm.

N16 – Stoke Newington

ANGLO ASIAN TANDOORI

60-62 Stoke Newington Church Street, N16 ✆ 0171 254 3633

New to the 1998 Guide, following good reports. CT finds it 'very fine with service friendly and extremely attentive. Chicken Patia outstanding, CTM very good, though far too red, Chicken Bhuna, Bindi Bhajee, and Tarka Dal, simply superb.'

MASALA HUT   NAME CHANGE

18 Stoke Newington Church Street, N16   ✆ 0171 254 4429

The name change here seems not to have diminished its regular following, from whom we hear of a menu full of old favourites, with a good vegetable selection as well, at reasonable prices. Stocks Cobra.

RASA   NEW TO THE TOP 100   √

55 Stoke Newington Church Street, N16   ✆ 0171 249 0344

Since Atique Choudhury's Spices went Thai and became the excellent Yum Yum, Shiva Das Sreedharan – Das to you and me – his former manager went solo on the same street, with his wife Alison, with the Rasa. Decor is very relaxing, with about fifteen tables. They specialise in southern Indian vegetarian cooking, mostly from Kerala, India's most southerly state. Cooking uses coconut, mustard, curry leaves, curds, chillies, lentils and rice. Exotic vegetables include plantains, gourds, sour mangos. 'On my one visit so far, I had Thayir Vadal as a starter. This is fried urid bean doughnut marinated in freshly spiced yoghurt. For my main course I had Moru Kachiathu, a Travancore speciality of yoghurt curry prepared with green banana and sweet mangoes, served lukewarm (as it should be, apparently) on Lemon Rice. Both dishes were new to me and were delicious!' DS. The 'very good' from DR CF and his tribe of highly critical medics is praise indeed! We would be remiss not to include this restaurant in our TOP 100, though in truth it doesn't need this accolade. It's always full, so book. Branch: Dering St, W1.

LE TAJ NAME CHANGE ©

56 Stoke Newington Church Street, N16   ℂ 0171 249 0799

Formerly the Spice of Asia, Mrs F. Khanom's 46-seater, now Le Taj, serves le curry and les side dishes. Notable specials include: Achar Goshti, pickled meat, Muglai Murgh, creamy chicken, Hash Masala, duck curry and Fish Jalfrezi, fish dry stir-fried. Price check: Papadam 55p, CTM £5.95, Pullao Rice £1.60. Delivery: £10.50 minimum, 3-mile radius. Hours: 6-11.45pm, closed Tues. Stocks Cobra.

N19

RAJ VOGUE ©

34 Highgate Hill, N19   ℂ 0171 272 9091

Established in 1985 Abed Choudhury's restaurant seats 44 with a 30-seat party room. Chef Mr Suhail cooks up Bangladeshi, Pakistani and northern Indian curries. 'All my fussy-eater colleagues and I were happy and full. Food, a variety of dishes, well cooked, well spiced and promptly served. Rice just right. One innovation, a dish made with lots of marrow-bone, meat attached, which got everybody trying to get the marrow out. Very tasty. Highly recommended!' DR CF. That's funny Conal, I thought it was you who was the fussy-eater! And are Red Ken (who's he?) and Spurs football stars (and who are they?) still visiting regularly? Price check: Papadam 40p, CTM £5.70, Pullao Rice £1.70, Peshwari Nan £1.70. Lager £2.20 pint, house wine £8. Hours: 12-2.30pm

N21

RAJ OF INDIA

10 Station Road, Winchmore Hill, N21   ℂ 0181 360 9543

js advises us not to be 'fooled by the tatty exterior of this restaurant. Inside is a traditional (red flock wallpaper), largish – 20 tables – Indian eatery. The food wheeled in on a wooden trolley is superbly cooked and nicely presented. There is nothing lavish or exotic about the food or surroundings but don't let that detract from a very pleasant meal. The dishes are not very spicy, so if you like the food hot you can go for the Vindaloo without ordering a gallon of water. The waiters were helpful and pleasant.

London NW

Area: North West London, postcodes
 NW1 to NW11
Population: 675,000
Number of restaurants in county: 170
Number of restaurants in Guide: 32

NW1 – Drummond Street

*I am often asked where the best restaurants are. It's the reason for producing this Guide.
Drummond Street is one such area. West of Euston Station, it will not win any beauty awards, and it lacks the ethnic glamour of Southall and Wembley, or the intensity of
purpose of Brick Lane. Its assets are a concentrated selection of extremely good, mainly
inexpensive Indian food vendors. There are greengrocers, a Halal butcher and ingredient
stores, such as Viranis, where Pataks began trading in the 60s. It is open all hours for
all things Indian including Cobra (useful for the nearby BYOs), a dozen or so takeaways and restaurants. Here in alphabetical order is our Drummond Street selection:*

AMBALA SWEET CENTRE

112 Drummond Street, NW1   © 0171 387 3521

Ambala started trading in 1965. It specialises in takeaway-only savoury
snacks (Pakoras and Samosa, etc.), Indian sweets (Halva, Jalebi, Gulab
Jamun, Barfi, etc.) and a few vegetarian curries such as chickpea.
Established initially for Asians, it now has branches in Birmingham,
Bradford, Derby, East Ham, Finchley, Glasgow, Leicester, Leyton,
Luton, Manchester, Slough, Southall, Tooting and Wembley.
Drummond Street is the flagship. All branches serve identical items at
identical prices. The quality is first-class and the prices are always rea-
sonable. Be prepared to queue, and pay cash. Open daily, 10am-11pm

---

©	Curry Club discount (see page 6)		Unlicensed
√	Vegetarian		
BYO	Bring your own alcohol		Delivery/takeaway

CHUTNEYS √

134 Drummond Street, Euston, NW1 ℄ 0171 388 0604

Serves only vegetarian food, including Bhel Puri. True it's all cheaper down the street, but our scribes are not as dismissive as one of the less accurate London food guides. 'Set buffet lunch, at £4.95, is still one of central London's best feed-ups.' CJ. 'Great, imaginative, cheap menu, possibly my favourite restaurant on this street.' RJL. Set dinner £8.95. Service 10%. Hours: 11am-2.30pm/6-11.30pm. 12-10.30pm Sun. Branches: Haandi and Ravi Shanka. Stocks Cobra.

DIWANA BHEL POORI TOP 100 √ BYO

121 Drummond Street, Euston, NW1 ℄ 0171 380 0730

Established in 1971 by Kris Patel, who manages, assisted by Eddie Labak, and describes his gem as serving 'authentic Gujarati, Bombay and south Indian food'. It's functional, more or less café-style, unlicensed, open all day, still very cheap, highly successful 100-seat restaurant, divided into two ground-floor sections plus a further floor. The food is all vegetarian, with much vegan, and above all, it's all fabulous, and it's most certainly all authentic. And Diwana is an original. As is often the way, the originator of a concept (in this country at any rate) usually remains the best. Diwana pioneered Bombay pavement kiosk snack food in the UK and is now much copied. And it is undoubtedly still the best of its kind. It is one of DBAC's 'favourites, not to be visited for the decor, nor for a long and relaxing meal – sitting on the floor would be more comfortable than sitting on the bolted-down benches, so opt for chairs if you can. I have the same thing every time I visit, Papadam with Coconut Chutney, Rasam, a soup, whose chillies without fail give me attention-drawing hiccups, then a Dosa £3.00 to £4.60 depending on type, with more Coconut Chutney, with its mustard seed and chilli and Sambar. If Pat and I share, I try to get all the drumsticks before him. And of course I never miss out on one of their adorable Bhel Puris, their masthead and their most ordered dish.' Bhel Puri, or Poori, is defined on page 42. Diwana offers several types -Batata Puri, Dahi Batata Puri, Chat Aloo Papri and Batata Pava, all £2.10. Bhel can be accompanied by Gol Goppas (*see* page 47). A super alternative starter is Dahi Vada (*see* page 44). By now you've spent £5 or £6, and you're probably full. But try to leave a little space for the Diwana's desserts. Their legendary Kulfi, perhaps, or 'the highlight of our meal, the

Falooda – an Indian knickerbocker glory – probably the best in London. The quality of the food outweighs the numbness in your backside!' DB. 'The back of the bill has a questionnaire. I was pleased to tick excellent for everything.' HC. Booking is hit and miss, so expect a queue (especially at peak hours). Probably the best value in London and don't forget to BYO (no corkage charge). Off-licence with chilled Cobra available at Viranis up the street. Buffet lunch £3.95. Hard to exceed £12 for a good veggie blow-out! It remains high in our TOP 100. Dosa from £3.00 to £4.60. Thali from £4.00 to £6.00. Hours: 12pm-11pm Daily buffet: £3.95 till 2.30pm.

GUPTA CONFECTIONERS   🏢 ☕ √

100 Drummond Street, Euston, NW1   © 0171 380 1590

Overshadowed,perhaps by the nearby Ambala, Gupta is nonetheless a very good, long-established, less flashy vegetarian snack and sweet take-away. Samosas and Pakoras, plus their unique, delightful, and often still-hot Pea Kebab, a Gujarati speciality, being freshly cooked in the kitchens behind. Their sweets achieve a lightness of touch, and seem to avoid the taste of tinned evaporated milk that sometimes spoils those made by others. Cash or cheque. Branch: Watford Way, Hendon, NW4.

HAANDI

161 Drummond Street, Euston, NW1   © 0171 383 4557

In decor terms this licensed venue is the smartest of the Chutneys, Haandi, Ravi Shankar trio. It has all the south Indian favourites but this is the only one of the three to offer meat dishes. 'Upon ordering the waiter asked if we would like a complimentary glass of white wine or onion bhajia starter.' JT. Branches: Chutneys, Ravi Shankar, NW1.

RAAVI KEBAB HALAL

125 Drummond Street, Euston, NW1   © 0171 388 1780

Kebab tells you it's very much a meat place, Halal that there's no pandering to Western tastes, as one can tell by its local mostly Muslim patronage (so no alcohol allowed). 'Had three Roti which were freshly made, very good and moist. Main course – Haleem, the rarely encountered Hyderabadi/Pakistani dish, cooked with meat, wheat, lentils and spices – very nice and spicy. The rest of the menu wasn't extensive with

five grills, four specials, four meat, three curry, four vegetable dishes.' GH.
'One of my favourites. Cheap and cheerful. Food superb. Sheek Kebabs
amongst the best anywhere.' RE. Cash only. Hours: 12.30-11pm.

RAVI SHANKAR

133 Drummond Street, Euston, NW1   ℂ 0171 388 6458

The least pretentious of the Chutneys, Haandi group (and the first), it
is slightly (but only just) more up-market than, but otherwise similar in
most respects to the Diwana which it followed into Drummond Street.
It is licensed, but prices are still very reasonable and it is usually busy at
peak hours. Recommended are the two Thali set dishes, the Mysore and
the Shankar, and the Shrikand dessert. Hours: 12pm-11pm. Branches:
Chutneys, and Haandi, NW1. and Ravi Shankar, EC1.

Elsewhere in NW1

GREAT NEPALESE TOP 100   ©

48 Eversholt Street, Euston, NW1   ℂ 0171 388 6737

A regular TOP 100, and justly so. Established in 1982 this small 48-
seater is the best of London's few Nepalese restaurants because, unlike
many of these, the Great actually has a Nepalese chef (Masuk) and
owner (Gopal P. Manandhar) and, more particularly, it has a decent
number of Nepalese specialities on the menu. Masco Bara, black lentil
pancakes with curry sauce £3.25, Mamocha or Momo – steam-cooked
meat-filled pastries, £3.30 – and Kalezo Ra Chyow (chicken liver) are
three such starters. Main courses include Dumba (mutton), Pork
Bhutwa (the Nepalese have no proscriptions of either pork or alcohol)
and Hach Ko (duck) curries. There is also a range of eleven Nepalese
vegetable dishes. Add those to sixteen 'standard' curry house vegetable
dishes and the vegetarian will be spoilt for choice. In addition, the Great
does all the standard curries and tandooris, from Phal, 'very very hot',
to Shahi Korma, 'very very mild', though why you'd go there for these
is beyond me. Go for Nepalese food, and if virgin to it, check out the
Nepalese set meal (£12). For consistency, reliability and for a range of
choice, plus quality that is way above average, we are pleased to keep the
Great in our TOP 100. 'The Great is is my regular eating place, when
on business. Consistently good food and service. Prices are reasonable
for London. Always book especially in the summer.' PAW. Price check:

Papadam 55p, CTM £4.95, Pullao Rice £1.50, Peshwari Nan £2.25. Service 10%. Minimum charge £5.50. Hours: 12-2.30pm/6-11.30pm. Stocks Cobra.

MUMTAZ

4 Park Road, NW1   © 0171 706 2855

'"Very" is perhaps the keyword to describe Mumtaz. The restaurant is very smart, very clean – the food was very excellent and very expensive. I think it's worth the very extra cost. Chicken Tikka Masala was very!' DW. A sense of humour, Lord Latif-style (*see* Rupali, Newcastle, Tyne & Wear) has crept into the menu, with a 'very' hot dish challenge: Hot Pot Chicken Chilli Masala, £8.50, is cooked with five types of chilli, including the Bangladeshi Naga incendiary – 'Finish the entire dish, and you get a free beer'. and you'll need it! Price check: CTM (Mumtaz Masala) £7.75, Buttery King Prawns £12.50, Pullao Rice £3, Thali £12-18. Fill-your-face Sunday buffet good value at £14.

TANDOORI NIGHTS   ©

108 Parkway, Regents Park, NW1   © 0171 482 1902

It is unusual to see a woman working in a Bangladeshi restaurant, but this does not deter the eloquent and elegant owner Mrs Yasmeen Rashid, who is regularly to be seen here. Manager Raj is equally smooth and, being from Goa, he might point you at a Goan dish or two (Goan Fish is £7.95). Price check: Papadam 50p, CTM £6.95, Pullao Rice £2.30. Service 10%. Branches: Cockfosters, Herts; Covent Garden, WC2.

NW2

FINCHLEY PAN CENTRE NEW ENTRANT

15 Woodhouse Road, North Finchley, NW2 © 0181 446 5497

Takeaway only, owned and managed by S. Sayed. Kenyan Asian curries and accompaniments, Biryani being the most popular dish. Pan on offer. No credit cards. Price check: Vegetable Samosa (2) 90p, Meat Samosa (2) 90p, Chicken Biryani £4.25, Mutton Masala £3.60. Hours: 12-10pm, 3.30-10pm Fri., closed Tues.

SHAMA   BYO ©

66 Cricklewood Broadway, NW2   © 0181 450 9052

The Shama is one of those places that local communities thrive on. It's small (50 seats) and comfortable, but not plush. Owned by Messrs Rawat (manager) and Ahmed (chef) since they started it in 1980. The food is competent and inexpensive. You can BYO (despite it being licensed). Price check: Papadam 25p, CTM £4.30, Karahi Chicken/Lamb £3.60, Pullao Rice £1.20.

NW3

CURRY MANJILL

34 England's Lane, NW3   © 0171 722 4053

A typical, long-standing (1970) family-run curry house with a typical menu boosted by some nice specials – Pomphret Mosalla (*sic*) and Koliza Bhuna (chicken liver in a creamy sauce). There are some Balti dishes here, too, all at reasonable prices. Stocks Cobra.

CURRY PARADISE

49 South End Green, NW3   © 0171 794 6314

'Served us well for over ten years. Unfortunately, recent indoor redecoration has lessened seating power, increasing likelihood of sitting next to smokers. A pity. Otherwise, superb Phals – fire-eaters' dream! An excellent and extremely reliable curry house, reasonably priced.' DMcC.

FLEET TANDOORI   ©10%

104 Fleet Road, NW3   © 0171 485 6402

'A good restaurant for those seeking a dependable, quiet and inexpensive meal. The Sunday buffet is a must for those who wish a cheap alternative to meat and two veg. An additional attraction is the Special on the menu – Pomfret Fish, which comes either tandoori or, for those with a rich palate, bathed in a curry sauce flavoured with a multitude of spices. Good prices enhanced by a 10% discount to Curry Club members at any time!' AD. Stocks Cobra.

PAPADAM

58 Belsize Lane, NW3	© 0171 794 0717

'It is a lovely, small and attractive restaurant, with charming staff. Generous quantities of food served in square, classy china dishes. Danny had huge success with the Garlic Duck, I stuck to CTM, we shared Garlic Mushrooms, Veg Dhansak, Nan, Papadoms, relishes and bhajis. Not a grand place like the BB (Bombay Brasserie), but one of the best. The bill, with drinks and coffee, about £49.' Stocks Cobra.

NW4

PRINCE OF CEYLON TOP 100   ©

39 Watford Way, NW4	© 0181 202 5967/203 8002

Owned by Abdul Satter for the last twenty years. A large restaurant seating 120 diners in four rooms, so you don't feel you are eating in an aircraft hangar. Linen yellow-ochre and brown, olive green leather bar stools, a lot of natural dark wood – tables given privacy by carved wood screens. It has a colonial feel. There is a party room for 30 diners. The Prince's standard menu of tandooris, kebabs, curries and all the business, all perfectly competently cooked, are not what you go there for. It is the Sri Lankan specials. And if these items are unfamiliar, ask the waiter's advice, but be patient if explanations are unclear at first. It is a rice (Buth) cuisine. Jaffna Thossai, soft pancake made of soaked and ground urid dal, served with coconut chutney £2.25. Devilled Squid curry £4.50. Fried Cabbage with onion £2.75. Coconut Chutney £1.50. Hoppers or Appas are rice and coconut-flour pancakes; String Hoppers, like string made of wheat or rice flour dough, but resembling vermicelli nests (10 for £3); or Pittu – ditto dumpling. These or straight rice are accompanied by pungent watery curries, in which coconut, turmeric, tamarind, curry leaves and chillies feature. But they can be mild, too. Look out for aromatic black curries and fragrant white ones. Fish dishes, such as Ambul Thial (a Sri Lankan national dish – a sour, spicy fish dish) and the Ceylon Squid (Dhallo) curry are popular. And there are substantial curries such as Lumpri (chicken, meat and egg). Sambols, or relishes, include dried fish and chilli (Seeni Sambol is a cooked version). I mentioned last time that Fay Maschler did not agree with my review of the Jehangir, SE26. She wrote to me that she rated the Prince better for Sri Lankan food. It shows the slight difficulty we have in relying on reports because the reports we receive on the Prince are by different people from those who write about the Jehangir. They are, after all, poles apart, literally – at the extreme north and south of London. At the time, we revisited both, anonymously, and agreed with Ms M. enough to upgrade the Prince and give it our TOP 100 rating. Why though, do we get good reports, interspersed with poor ones? 'The starters were excellent and couldn't be faulted, but the curries were not good at all. Fish, squid and chicken all tasted the same, as did the vegetables. Sorry Pat, we cannot agree it should be in the TOP 100, and by the number of diners last night, I don't think we are alone.' sj. Others, like Fay, love the Prince. Hours: 12-3pm/6pm-12am. Sat. & Sun. 12pm-12am. Sunday buffet £8.00. More reports please. Serves Cobra.

NW5

BENGAL LANCER TOP 100 ©

253 Kentish Town Road, NW5 ✆ 0171 485 6688

Stanley Krett and Akram Ali's brainchild brasserie, now ten years on, pioneered a wave of Raj reminiscence-theme restaurants, including one of their own (*see* below). The Lancer soldiers on, attracting good reports a-plenty. 'This is a restaurant whose standard has remained consistently high. Always a pleasure to visit. The service is efficient, but not obtrusive, and the quality of food very high, thus guaranteeing that we will be visiting again shortly.' DM. 'A monthly outing of the Jubilee Line Extension Project curry clan. Good food presented with some style even when faced with nine very hungry people. Service good, portions reasonable. Highlights from the menu included Potato Chat and Jeera Chicken. The Peshwari and Keema Nan were also extremely good.' P.C. 'A genuine classy restaurant with an excellent menu range. Liver Hazra, liver cooked and tossed in spices, rich and almost a meal in itself. Unusual, good and great taste. Tiger Wings are chicken drumsticks tandoori-style. Service first-class, attentive and despite a packed peak-time Saturday night they kept checking up to see if we required anything else. Food up among the best for quality, portions more than adequate and at value-for-money prices. Deserves its rating in the TOP 100.' AS. Some criticism, though, about the service, the cover charge and 'lighting too intense for an intimate dinner.' DW. It remains in our TOP 100. The discount for Curry Club members will go some way to offset these minor criticisms. Branch: Kiplings, N6.

INDIAN LANCER   ©

56 Chetwynd Road, NW5   © 0171 482 2803

Established in 1990 by MY Hashmi, it seats 42 diners and serves Pakistani-Punjabi food. House specials include: Karahi Ghost, Punjabi Tinda, Shalgam (Turnip) and Paneer Tikka. Cover charge 40p. Price check: Papadam 40p, CTM £5.50, Pullao Rice £1.60, Peshwari Nan £2. Delivery: £10 minimum, 2-mile radius. Hours: 6pm-12am, Sat. 12pm-12am. Stocks Cobra.

SHAHANA TANDOORI   ©

343 Kentish Town Road,
Kentish Town, NW5   © 0171 485 5566

Owner ME Muslim is on hand in this popular local curry house, again offering formula curry house food at reasonable prices.

NW6

GEETA SOUTH INDIAN

57 Willesden Lane, NW6   © 0171 624 1713

It's vegetarian food at which Geeta excels, and has done for two decades, with never a decline in standard. Dosas, Idlis, Upamas Karela (bitter gourds), drumsticks (long pithy marrow which you suck to extract the tender flesh), Rasams, Sambars and more. It's all fine stuff, served in less than glamorous, but typically Indian surroundings, to a thoroughly devoted following. Actually, they do have meat and tandoori items on their menu but, good though these are, the *aficionados* prefer the authentic vegetarian. All at reasonable prices – even with the ridiculous 10% service, you'll spend less than a tenner, with drink. Serves Cobra.

PANSHI   ©

31 Malvern Road, Maida Vale, NW6   © 0171 328 1226

Panshi, meaning a Bangladeshi royal barge of yore, is a 48-seater run by Messrs Abdul Salam and Bahar, between Maida Vale and Kilburn. Chef Adbul Hakim offers true Bangladeshi curries, such as Gosht Kalia, highly spiced lamb, onions, ginger, garlic and fresh chilli, £5.50, Rezala, a kind of korma with coconut and chilli, and Gowa, even hotter – Naga chillies, £4.95. Full marks for that. Price check: Papadam 40p, CTM £5.50, Pullao Rice £1.75, Peshwari Nan £1.50. Delivery: £10 minimum, 3-mile radius. Hours: 12-2.30pm/6pm-12am. Sun. 3pm-12am. Stocks Cobra.

SURYA ✓ ©

59-61 Fortune Green Road, NW6 ✆ 0171 435 7486

Mr (front of house) and Mrs Tiwari (chef) really pack 'em in at this tiny, 34-seat vegetarian, licensed restaurant – there's no room to move, almost literally – it's always full. The dish of the day (it changes daily) excites several of our regulars. We hear well of Gujarati dishes such as Patra and Kaddu Kari and inexpensive prices. Hours: 6-10.30pm, and Sunday lunch. Branch: Shree Ganesha, 4 The Promenade, Edgwarebury Lane, Edgware, Middlesex.

VIJAY

49 Willesden Lane, NW6 ✆ 0171 328 1087

Correct me if I'm wrong, but Vijay, founded in 1966, predated nearby Geeta (*see* above) by several years, so it can take the crown for being the earliest to provide south Indian food for NW6, and its menu contains all the vegetarian items listed in Geeta's entry, at much the same prices. Vijay has its own clan of loyal regulars who know they'll get 'very nice tasty food.' B&WW.

NW7

BRENT TANDOORI ©

24 High Road, Willesden Green, NW7 ✆ 0181 459 0649

This takeaway-only is reported as being clean, generous, prompt and efficient. The food is evidently well-liked and the prices reasonable. Owner Monojir Ali welcomes Curry Club members to whom he will give a discount on his already reasonable prices, at his quieter times.

©	Curry Club discount (see page 6)		Unlicensed
✓	Vegetarian		
BYO	Bring your own alcohol		Delivery/takeaway

DAYS OF THE RAJ ©

123 The Broadway, Mill Hill, NW7   **© 0181 906 3363**

Established in 1989 by S. Miah, who tells us that he changes the wallpaper every six months to 'maintain standards'. M. Miah manages the
100-seater, whose extensive menu appears to be formula stuff from
Kurma (*sic.*) to Phal, etc. But a closer look provides a number of
'unique' dishes. What are Noorane, Sherajee, Kushboo, Dilkush and
Bakhara curries, for example? Each available in chicken, lamb, beef,
prawn, king prawn and vegetables (the menu explains their attributes),
they are clearly house inventions. So is the dish Days of the Raj, gently
cooked with pineapple, lychees and sultanas in a thick creamy sauce
sprinkled with nuts. It sounds like a fruit salad but is, we're assured,
'really quite delicious, the chicken quite succulent, and mild enough for
my boss who is a curry novice.' GC. It is more than a 'safe-bet' curry
house. It is very smart indeed and is a place to go for an enjoyable meal
out. Price check: Papadam 45p, CTM £7.25, Duck Bakhara £7.90,
Pullao Rice £1.90, Peshwari Nan £2.10. House wine £8.25. Service 10%.
E-a-m-a-y-l lunch buffet daily £6.90. Delivery: £12 minimum, 3-mile
radius. Hours: 12-2pm/5-11.30pm. Stocks Cobra.

NW9

KABANA NEW ENTRANT

43 Blackbird Hill, NW9   **© 0181 200 7094**

'Are you coco not entering the Kabana?' asks GR. He and others adore
that distinctive Kenyan Asian Punjabi taste. 'When formula curries pall
a bit, drool while they cook in the open kitchen over a drink (they're
licensed), and recharge your taste batteries when the food is served.' As
do many local Asians, who come for honest-to-goodness inexpensive
gosht and murgh karahis and kebabs, punctuated with African-influ-
enced banana chips and Mogo (Casava).

©	Curry Club discount (see page 6)	☕	Unlicensed
√	Vegetarian		
BYO	Bring your own alcohol	⊞	Delivery/takeaway

NW10

ANN MARIE AT THE TASTE OF THE TAJ   ©

4 Norbreck Parade, off Hanger Lane,
Ealing, NW10   ℂ 0181 991 5366

Ann Marie won't mind if I repeat myself about location, location, location. Her Taste, which has been going since 1989, *is* in Ealing. It's also
in NW10, which Ealing isn't (but it used to be W5). The North Circular
Gyratory rebuild caused mayhem with Ann Marie's access, if you follow me, not to mention with her postcode. She says herself it's 'essential to phone and ask for directions, because the access to the front is
now closed from the NCR'. As in Birmingham, you can see it, but you
cannot touch it. But find this 64-seater you should. Relax to the warm
and cosy red decor, admire the many tiger pictures on the walls, then
avail yourself of a personalised service and advice that some of Ann
Marie's regulars have known and delighted in for over 30 years, in another Ealing venue. Enjoy the memsahib's personal touches that turn this
very ordinary-looking menu into a welcoming taste experience. Chef
Nazrul converts it all into stimulating cuisine. We hear of a 'fabulous
fresh Chicken Dapeaza (*sic.*) floating in fresh glistening onions' from CR;
'cooked original-style with crispy fried onion, a "mean" Dhansak and
very succulent Tandoori dishes, served with fluffy Nans – basically curries with attitude!' and 'a rather unexpected delicacy of touch in the
Courgette Bhaji' from RG. Lager £2.30 pint, house wine £8.50. BYO on
champagne only, but please ask. Price check: Papadam 40p, CTM
£4.95, Pullao Rice £1.60, Peshwari Nan £1.60. Delivery: £12 minimum.
Hours: Lunch weekdays only and 6pm-12am daily.

BALTI HUT BRENT TANDOORI   NEW ENTRANT

24 High Road, Willesden Green, NW10   ℂ 0181 459 0649

'Had a terrific Egg Madras, which took a while because the eggs were
freshly boiled. Good value.' RDL. Halal. Price check: Papadam 40p (plain
or spicy), CTM £4.50, Bombay Potato £1.95, Pullao Rice £1.45,
Chutney and Pickle 50p each portion. Delivery: £10 minimum, 3-mile
radius. Hours: 12-2.30pm/5.30-12pm, (12.30am Fri. & Sat.).

KADIRI KITCHEN   ©

26 High Road, Willesden, NW10   © 0181 451 5525

It's a small place (36 seats) that has been around for a long time (since 1974). Sayed Kadiri's 150-item menu surely has something for everyone, 'including fish curries (Wednesdays only) and a great selection of Paneer dishes, e.g., Paneer Chilli Masala.' GB. Good food, good value.

SABRAS   √

263 High Road, Willesden, NW10   © 0181 459 0340

Hemant and Nalinee Desai are great survivors, and their tiny 25-year old Sabras proves it. Regulars keep returning (and telling us so), ignoring the tacky shopfront for the 'great home-style vegetarian Gujarati and south Indian food. Vadas, Dosa, Bhel Puri, samosas, home-made chutneys, and heavenly curries redolent with curry leaves and fluffy rice.' DN. The prices are still really attractive, and help is at hand if you are unfamiliar with the food. Even with the silly 10% service charge, expect to pay between £12 and £15 for a worthy meal. Hours: 6-10.30pm, Tues.-Sun. Stocks Cobra.

NW11

GURKHA BRASSERIE   ©

756 Finchley Road, NW11   © 0181 458 6163

One of the best places to go for Nepalese food. Owner-chef Hari K.C. is often on hand to explain what's what amongst the Gurkha's Nepalese specials. The regular curries are 'pretty darned good too.' SW. Branch: Gurkha Brasserie, W1.

©	Curry Club discount (see page 6)		Unlicensed
√	Vegetarian		
BYO	Bring your own alcohol	⊞	Delivery/takeaway

London SE

Area: South East London, postcodes SE1
to SE28
Population: 901,000
Number of restaurants in county: 185
Number of restaurants in Guide: 24

SE1

BENGAL CLIPPER

**11-12 Cardamom Building, 31 Shad Thames,
Butlers Wharf, SE1** ✆ 0171 357 9001

Finding it is the problem. It's a fair walk from the tube! Taxis will find
it (it's behind Conran's). If you're driving, and you've squeezed through
the narrow one-way streets, you'll then have to find a parking space
(min. £4). Once inside, you'll find Kenneth Lynn's sophisticated and
expensive interior. The grand piano is still in evidence but was silent on
our last visit, thank heavens, so we could hear each other talk. Service
has become slicker and there is no doubt that everyone cares about
image. Chef Azam Khan's relatively short menu takes a good gastronomic tour of India. The results are less slick, owing more to the house
one-pot gravy, than to regional Indian or Bangladeshi cuisine. Expect to
pay more than average here. Price check: Papadam 75p, CTM £9.25,
Dahi Dover Sole £13.95, Tiger Prawns £15.50, Pullao (Pilaw – *sic.*) Rice
£2.25. Cover charge £1.50, incl. Papadoms. Stocks Cobra.

CASTLE TANDOORI

**200-201 Elephant and Castle
Shopping Centre, SE1** ✆ 0171 703 9130

Mr Uddin's Castle is a spirited place, and a regular entrant in our
Guide. He tells us, and you, if you care to be entertained by him, that
he's outlived twenty-two Hoovers, two recessions, and several prime
ministers, and served enough nan bread to stretch from Waterloo to
Paris. The menu is pretty much formula (135 items) but includes duck,
lamb chops and trout in various guises. Reports tell of the value for
money. We know of no longer hours in London. (Tell me if you know

better.) So, if you're an insomniac curryholic, or just a late-night revel-
ler, note this place well. Hours: Lunch Mon.-Fri., and from 6pm-1am
daily (extended to 2.30am on Fri. & Sat.). Stocks Cobra.

IMPERIAL TANDOORI   NEW ENTRANT   ©

48 Kennington Road, SE1   ℂ 0171 928 4153

'MPs love it.' winks Mohibad Rahman, though, despite attempts,
he doesn't elaborate. Price check: Papadam 40p, CTM £6.45,
Tandoori Shashlik £5.95, Pullao Rice £1.75. Minimum charge £7.95.
Stocks Cobra.

THAMES TANDOORI

79 Waterloo Road, SE1   ℂ 0171 928 3856

Established in 1985, Kalkur Rahman's 52-seater is doing it under the railway bridge, and, yes, its neighbour, the Fishcotheque, is still doing it
too. And no name-change to Tikkateque! HC still loves it – 'Brinjal Bhaji
so good, we ordered a second.' Price check: Papadam 50p, CTM £6.75,
Pullao Rice £2.30, Peshwari Nan £1.95. House wine £7.75. Delivery: £20
minimum, 2-mile radius. Hours: 12-2.30pm/5.30-11.30pm. Branch:
Strand Tandoori, WC2. Stocks Cobra.

TOWER TANDOORI

74 Tower Bridge Road, SE1   ℂ 0171 237 2247

Well-established (1978 and in our first Guide) by H.M. Shab Uddin,
seats 80 (plus party room for 40). Chef Hafizur Rahman cooks formula curries and side dishes. Price check: Papadam 55p, CTM £6.70,
Pullao Rice £1.60. House wine £6.95. Minimum charge £10. Delivery:
£15 minimum, 2-mile radius. Hours: 12-2.30pm, 6pm-12am (12.30am on
Sat.), Sun. 12pm-12am – buffet £6.95.

SE2

ABBEY WOOD TANDOORI   NEW ENTRANT

13 Wickham Lane, Abbey Wood, SE2   ℂ 0181 310 3534

DP and his girlfriend have eaten in over 100 curry restaurants, but the
one nearest their home is their favourite. She says there's nothing he has

not eaten on the menu over the past three years! They deliver, too. Price check: Papadam 40p, CTM £4.95, Balti Lamb £5.25, Pullao Rice £1.45.

SE3

SOPNA

39 Tranquil Vale, Blackheath Village, SE3   ℂ **0181 852 7872**

A return to the Guide after two absences, because we hear good things about S. Miah's food. Appetisers include Fish Amritsari, strips of fish fried with a spicy coating £2.95. Bater Asmeri, marinated quails cooked in a garlic and lemon sauce £2.95. Main dishes include sharp and hot Chicken Green Masala, cooked in a variety of fresh green herbs, spices, crushed garlic, ginger and green chillies, lemon juice £5.95. Saffron Gosht, tender spring lamb cooked in a creamy sauce flavoured with coconut, poppy seed and cashew nuts and garnished with saffron £5.95.

SE5 – Camberwell

CAMBERWELL TANDOORI   ©

22 Church Street, Camberwell, SE5   ℂ **0171 252 4800**

Sam Huda owns and manages this 42-seater. Plenty of fomula plus interesting specials, e.g.: Kebab-E-Coxbazza (*sic.*), a fish dish from that region of Bangladesh (Cox's Bazaar!) and Murug-E-Makoney (*sic.*), a type of CTM £6.50 And there's Balti on the menu – Balthee (*sic.*) chicken. Price check: Papadam 50p, Pullao Rice £1.50. Peshwari Nan £1.65. Lager £2.50 pint, house wine £7.95, Minimum charge £6.95. Delivery £10 minimum, 3-mile radius. Hours: 12-2.30pm (Fri. & Sat.) and 6pm-12am. Sun. 12pm-12am.

NOGAR   ©

59 Denmark Hill, SE5   ℂ **0171 252 4846**

Owned and managed by K. Hussain, with A. Islam as chef. 'We liked the idea of Chicken Flaming – whole breast mediumly (*sic.*) cooked, sizzling with a flame of Sambuca. And we liked it when it came.' bk. And we liked the move towards Bengal fish specials (there are four); we also note a Balti dish here. Stocks Cobra.

SE9 – Eltham

RUCHITA TAKEAWAY   ⊞ ©

31 Avery Hill Road, SE9   © 0181 850 1202

Unusually for a takeaway-only, Miss Salma Yousuf's and Chef A.
Mukid's Ruchita is licensed. It's been going since 1975, so they know
what they're doing. Price check: Papadam 40p, CTM £5.50, Pullao Rice
£1.50. Peshwari Nan £1.70. Set meal £12.90. Delivery: £18.00 mimimum,
3-mile radius. Hours: 5pm-12am. Stocks Cobra.

WELL HALL TANDOORI   ©

373 Well Hall Road, SE9   © 0181 856 2334

A competent curry house owned and managed by Tuahid (front) and
Abdul (chef) Ali and Muhan Miah. Stocks Cobra.

SE13

BENGAL BRASSERIE   ©

79 Springbank Road, Hither Green, SE13   © 0181 244 2442

This 60-seater restaurant, prettily decorated in pale shades of pink, is
owned and managed by Syed Ahmed. CT describes chef M. Chowdhury's efforts as 'a nice little menu, now containing a few originals'. 'The
spinach in Lobster Saghee (£6.95) makes this a fine dish' E.S. And others enjoy the Sea Thali (£8.50) – clever name. Most popular dish Sali
Ana Roshi, chicken or meat with pineapple and honey, lightly spiced
£4.75. Price check: Papadam 40p, CTM £5.50, Pullao Rice £1.30.
Peshwari Nan £1.50. House wine £6.50. Minimum charge £15. Parties:
of 20 diners, eat and drink as much as you like for £25 per diner! Service
10%. Cover charge £1. Delivery 3-mile radius. Hours: 5.30-11.30pm,
(12am on Sat.). Stocks Cobra.

SPICE OF LIFE   NEW TO TOP 100   ©

260 Lee High Road, Lewisham, SE13   © 0181 244 4770

Owned by Syed Ahmed since 1989, his restaurant seats 58 diners. 'One
of the best I've eaten in. Service by either Moody or Harris is unfail-
ingly polite and prompt, even when they are full. Food is always deli-

cious, beautifully presented and hot (temperature). Favourite dishes include Murghi Masala and the Prawn Pathia is to die for!' CS&PB. Specials include: Shatkora Bhuna, lamb chop, highly spiced with Bangladeshi citrus fruit. £4.75. 'As usual welcomed warmly into the friendly atmosphere of the restaurant and had a well served, beautifully presented, flavoursome and tasty meal.' GM. 'Particular favourites Chicken Shatkora and Tiger Fish. Extended range of vegetable dishes, exciting experience for vegetarians.' MB. The daily blackboard specials are very popular, and are so rare in the curry business. But it's such a simple way of varying the menu, and everyone loves that. It's one of my bones of contention, and we should go on nagging at the other curry restaurants until they all do it. Meanwhile, my apologies to The Spice for certain confusion last time, sorted by returning your questionnaire this time (I am chastened by those who told me off!) and congratulations for your promotion to the TOP 100. Gilian, you have your wish (along with many others). I hope it doesn't change The Life of Spice. Price check: CTM £5.50, Pullao Rice £1.30, Peshwari Nan £1.50. Delivery: £8 minimum, 3-mile radius. Hours: 5.30-11.30pm, (12am on Sat.). Stocks Cobra.

SE15

TWO SISTERS INDIAN TAKEAWAY   NEW ENTRANT ©

4 Gibbon Road, Nunhead, SE15   ✆ 0171 277 7635

Taken over by Miss Salima Rahman in 1994. Chef Shafique Rahman prepares curries and Baltis. Price check: Papadam 40p, CTM £6.30 (incl. Rice), Pullao Rice £1.40. Delivery: £15 minimum, 3-mile radius. Hours: 5.30-12pm, Sun. 6-11.30pm.

SE16

SURREY QUAYS TANDOORI   ©

30-32 Albion Street, SE16   ✆ 0171 237 1876

Forty-seater, est. 1989 by S.U. Ahmed, who is also the manager. Bengal Fish Tikka Masala £6.95 a house special and very popular. Price check: Papadam 50p, CTM £5.65, Pullao Rice £1.50. Delivery: £12.50 minimum. Hours: 12am-2.30am/6-11.30pm(except Sat.), Sun. 12pm-12am. Stocks Cobra.

SE18

MEGHNA TANDOORI   NEW ENTRANT

297 Plumstead High Street, SE18 ℰ 0181 312 2091

'A takeaway only, yet I can say without doubt the food is the best I've ever had. My verdict: Pat, go there. You will not be disappointed.' DP.

SE19

PASSAGE TO INDIA

232 Gipsy Road, SE19   ℰ 0181 670 7602

'I have been eating here for years. It is still excellent. I ate there last week and had a wonderful meal.' GG. Reports please. Stocks Cobra.

SE22 – East Dulwich

MIRASH

94 Grove Vale, East Dulwich, SE22   ℰ 0181 693 1640

'A crisp and smart interior.' says VG. Formula curries include all the favourites. Value-for-money Sunday set lunch. Stocks Cobra.

SURMA   ©

42 Lordship Lane, East Dulwich, SE22   ℰ 0181 693 1779

Muzahid Ali opened the popular 46-seat Surma in 1976. Mr Islam's now the chef. 'Food in our opinion is second to none, service is first class.' PR. Price check: Papadam 35p, CTM £4.75, Taba Gosht £5.50, Pullao Rice £1.40, Peshwari Nan £1.50. House wine £5.95, Set meal £25 for two. Delivery: £10 minimum, 2-mile radius. Hours: 12-2.30pm/6pm-12am. Sunday Buffet £5.95, 12pm-12am. Stocks Cobra. Branch: Joy Bangla Curry House, 39 Denmark Hill, SE5.

©	Curry Club discount (see page 6)		Unlicensed
√	Vegetarian		
BYO	Bring your own alcohol		Delivery/takeaway

SE23 – Forest Hill

BABUR BRASSERIE TOP 100   ©

119 Brockley Rise, Forest Hill, SE23   © 0181 291 2400

Babur established the Moghul Empire in 1483 through his courage and
daring in capturing Delhi. This restaurant captured Forest Hill in 1985,
though its ownership by the dynamic Rahmans did not occur until
1992. Quite simply, it's in our TOP 100 because everything the
Rahmans do, they do well. If you are a regular, you'll get frequent mail-
shots telling you what is happening here, from festivals to their new al
fresco dining outside the restaurant. Talking about outside, the front is
really attractive, with white Mogul arches, each one enhanced by hanging baskets and floor tubs. The white decor continues inside, offset by
56 air-force blue chairs. Dining is intimate in a screened area or in the
conservatory. While perusing the menu, you may be tempted by a range
of cocktails, including Monsoon Hurricane, £4.25, making you 'hot,
heavy and ready to go'. But, we presume, not too heavy to order! The
menu is a careful compilation of well-known favourites, with an above-
average selection of unusuals. Fish, crab, mussels and the rarely-seen
Patra, steamed, then deep-fried, Gujarati savoury Swiss roll of Besan
and patra leaf, £2.60. Aloo Choff, £2.75 is a rissole of mashed potato
and vegetable, rolled in chopped cashew and pan-fried. Main courses
include the gorgeous traditional Parsee dish, Sali Jardaloo, £6.50, lamb
slowly cooked with spices, enhanced with the sweet and sour tastes of
dried apricots (jardaloo) and honey, garnished with straw potatoes
(sali). Goa is well represented with Chicken Cafriel, £6.95, Badak Xec
Xec, pronounced 'shek-shek', fragrant duck, and hot tangy Tuna
Bulchao, both £7.50, and the even hotter Lobster Peri Peri, £13.95. From
the Raj is Ginger Roast Lamb, £6.95. Among a satisfactory choice of
vegetables, you'll find Dum Tori, £3.25, courgettes tossed with sour
mango powder, and Shorvedar Makhani, £3.50, involving beetroot. All
co-owner chef Enam Rahman's cooking is bright and fresh. Front of
house is equally so, under the careful supervision of co-owner manager
Emdad Rahman. Keep an eye out for their regular cuisine festivals and
special offers. There is plenty of attention to detail, good food, service
and ambience which keeps this restaurant in our TOP 100. For the
record, here's our standard price check: Papadam 50p, CTM £6.25,
Pullao Rice £1.95. Peshwari Nan £15. Minimum charge £7.95. House
wine £7.95. Hours: 12-2.30pm (Sat.-Thurs.)/6-11.30pm. Branch: every-

thing is available for takeaway, or delivery, evenings only, closed Tues., from Babur Takeaway, 443 Brockley Road, Crofton Park, SE4. Stocks Cobra.

DEWANIAM TOP 100

133-5 Stanstead Road, Forest Hill, SE23   ✆ 0181 291 4778

Forest Hill has a further TOP 100 restaurant, the Dewaniam, meaning a Moghul Hall of Public Audience. Owned by Rashid Ali and chef Fozlu Miah. Unlike its near neighbour, the Dewaniam sticks hard and fast to the Bangladeshi curry house formula. But there are surprises throughout. There is the usual complement of tandooris and kebabs, ranging from £2.50 for Chicken Tikka to £7.95 for Tandoori King Prawn. The surprise in this section is Tandoori Sri Lanka, £7.50, augmented with hot spices! Curries range from Kurma (sic.) – very mild – to Phall – extra hot – through eighteen others, including the surprise, with bamboo shoots, and all with meat. Chicken, prawn, all around £3.20, or King Prawn, £5.20. Add the sundries and veg side dishes, and that's the formula. You can, of course, have a thoroughly good meal there, choosing nothing but these favourites. But there are some truly outstanding alternative choices. Specialist ingredients include game birds, pheasant, quail, duck, lobster, trout, venison and hare. Don't panic about Heron Tikka, however – it's not that elusive, well-loved river bird, it's 'marinated deer meat barbecued in the tandoor'. (The Hindi/Urdu word for venison is Heeran!) Chef Fozlu is an innovator. His skilful use of alcohol, unusual in Indian cooking, matches anything you'd find in the French repertoire. Mugli Batak, for example, is duck cooked with mince, egg, cream, green herbs and red wine. But it's not just red wine that appears in a number of dishes – white wine enhances the Tandoori Trout marinade, brandy is used as a flambé (for tandoori pheasant or quail), Tia Maria as a marinade in Chicken Indropuri. There's one Bangladeshi fish dish, Fish Masallah (sic.), and a no-compromise vegetable dish, Sabzi Satrang, of okra, bitter gourd, sour tinda and aubergine. While you peruse the menu, you can indulge in an 'Elephant Trunk' cocktail. Price check: Papadam 55p, CTM £5.50, Pullao Rice £1.70. Hours: 12-2.30pm/6pm-12am. Sunday lunch e-a-m-a-y-l buffet, 12-5.30pm, £6.95, kids £3, under-5s free. Branches: Dewaniam Takeaway, 3 Westdale Road, SE23 evenings only, minimum charge £7.50. Muglai, 61a Dartmouth Road, SE23.

RAJ BALTI HOUSE NEW ENTRANT

16-18 Sunderland Road, Forest Hill, SE23   © 0181 291 0870

'Have now been there countless times, and every time it has been excellent. I hope to see it included in your next book.' NO. Price check: Chicken Tikka Biryani £5.95, Pullao rice £1.40, Vegetable Thali £6.95.

SE25 – South Norwood

JOMUNA BRASSERIE   ©

165 Portland Road, South Norwood, SE25   © 0181 654 9385

E. Ali's 44-seat 'nicely decorated long narrow layout has pleasant background jazz and a good full menu. Aromatic fish dishes shown as a speciality, e.g.: Machi Koiful – Bangladeshi fish with Sylheti vegetables, £4.60. Settled for a pleasant Chicken Dupiaza £3.70, Chicken Tikka £4.25, a good Chana Masala with fresh onion £1.90, and the nicest ever Bombay Aloo £1.95. Good friendly service. Hot lemon towels.' TN. Price check: Papadam 45p, CTM £5.30, Pullao Rice £1.45. Minimum charge £7.50. Hours: lunch and dinner, daily, Sun.: 1-6pm e-a-m-a-y-l, £5.95, kids £3.95. Stocks Cobra.

SE26 – Sydenham

JEHANGIR TOP 100   ©

67 Sydenham Road, Sydenham, SE26   © 0181 244 4244

It is, perhaps, irrelevant to compare one particular Sri Lankan with another, (*see* Prince of Ceylon, NW4). We could equally bring Jaffna SW17, Thamouline, Hayes, Middx and Sirgiri, W13 into the frame. And for Sri Lankan food that's about it in the UK. It is my firm belief that such rarities should be treated like protected species. They are like tigers in a mass of indifference. And if we are to see the true authentic regional food of the subcontinent ascend from the one pot formula of food colouring, and coconut cream block, we must nurture such ventures. The Jehangir's dining room is light and airy and gorgeously decorated, with vaulted archways, marble floors, hand-painted ceiling, complete with huge colonial fan, mahogany carvers and Wedgwood crockery. But it's the food that counts. The Jehangir's menu is astonishing. It runs to 10 pages and contains a massive 143 numbered items. The takeaway version comes as a little booklet, and even that has 87 items! Get one. It gives really good descriptions of each item. In fact, the Jehangir gives a combination of north and south Indian and Sri Lankan food, with a touch of the Maldive Islands thrown in. There are 23 starters. Hot Tempered Prawns are indeed hot, and the Gothamba Roti, a thin bread, is indeed silky. There are eight types of Dosai (urid and rice-flour pancakes), idlis and three hoppers. Main courses include thirteen chicken, twelve lamb and ten seafood dishes, many of which use imported Sri Lankan fish. Breads, rice and biriyanis (*sic.*) are followed by one of the most remarkable vegetarian selections we've seen – over 23 dishes. And the service? Good on our visit, and we hear they are extremely good with customer care. On the special occasions, cards, flowers, cake or champagne is given by the management. Recent reports received are contented. 'Everything you say about this is correct. It is superb and I have used this restaurant many times since discovering it.' GG. MR TN liked the view into the kitchen, 'en-route to the mediocre loos. It was quite full of couples on a Sunday evening, but we were the only couple to have the Sunday buffet, which proffered a starter of papadoms, salad and two hot chutneys, followed by five curries and rice, with rice white buns (idlis), which cost £21, incl. Cokes and service.' MRS TN, though, found the dishes too hot. This is a problem with the food of this region, so ask manager S. Nathan for advice about mild curries, if that's your bag. Chefs Mrs Mano and Mrs Kughan will oblige so, with that proviso, our advice here, as ever, is to go at quieter times for the best food and service, and to order Sri Lankan/south Indian items, rather than north Indian. We're happy to keep the Jehangir in its TOP 100 slot. For the record, here's our standard price check: Papadam 55p, CTM £5.25, Pullao Rice £1.95. Minimum charge £10, set meal from £6.95, plus 12½% service, all relieved by the Curry Club discount!

©	Curry Club discount (see page 6)		Unlicensed
√	Vegetarian		
BYO	Bring your own alcohol		Delivery/takeaway

London SW

Area: South West London,
  postcodes sw1 to sw20
Population: 703,000
Number of restaurants in county: 260
Number of restaurants in Guide: 52

SW1

GREAT INDIA

79 Lower Sloane Street, SW1   ✆ 0171 730 2207

'Situated in a parade of shops and several restaurants. Decor is completely plain cream, modern and could be any cuisine – no Indian artifacts or pictures at all. At 10.15pm the restaurant was almost full and had the most wonderful atmosphere. The menu is very large but standard with extremely reasonable prices for Chelsea. Average Papadam with relishes. Onion Bhajia, very good, flat disc style with a wonderful flavour. Excellent Prawn and Bean curry, Butter Chicken Tikka Masala, an unusual combination which turned out to be spectacularly good, a sort of Chicken Tikka Masala with a butter chicken sauce, rich with coriander and coconut, over the top. Good Brinjal Bhajia, large chunks. Pullao Rice good and generous. Altogether a very enjoyable meal with good service.' HC.

KUNDAN NEW ENTRANT

3 Horseferry Road, SW1   ✆ 0171 834 3434

There are 117 seats at the Kundan (and 200 or so at the House of Lords and 632 at the Commons). And like as not you'll spot many a political face in here, all enjoying right-wing-raitas with Commons seeds and red-Vindaloos or Matar Peers, perhaps. Our Honourable and Right Honourable members enjoy curry so much that they've even formed a branch of The Curry Club at their House, and are frequently seen practising at the Kundan. We've not heard of Blair Biriani, or Major Madras, Prescott Patia, or Kinnock Kebab, but I wouldn't put it past owner Nayab Abbasi, who just loves all this, of course. Given half a chance, if he's not at his San Francisco branch, he'll explain that they, and many other politirati, have been seen tucking in here, as often as not. Ask him to explain about the loud bell that rings here from time to time. And since so many of you have asked me to explain, I will: it's not the fire alarm, so don't make a move! It's an extension of the division bell. In times of tight majorities, it means a mad exodus of smart, dark Armani suits (unless it's Ken Clarke, of course), leaving half-eaten plates of curry. Standard food, with some nice specials from Chef Mohamed Aziz Khan. Not cheap, but such delights wouldn't be, and it *is* Westminster! Hours: Lunch, dinner from 7pm Closed Sun. & Bank Holidays. Stocks Cobra.

SALOOS TOP 100

62-64 Kinnerton Street, Knightsbridge, SW1   © 0171 235 4444/6845

I continue to get more praise about Saloos from my Indian friends than about any other restaurant, and I do mean Indian. Saloos is very much Pakistani, owned by M. Salahuddin. As I say, it is immensely popular with London's well-educated wealthy Indians, who ignore politics when it comes to good food. As in 1995, we took our seat at a table near the back stairs, the route to the kitchen. We decided to order the same meal. The large, genial head waiter was there. The ordering system is unchanged – to throw a copy of the chit down the stairs with a screech. It is collected by an unseen minion, and later is transferred into food, carried aloft up the stairs by a seen minion, complete with long white Marigold gloves, who silently waits until the maître d' takes his offerings and ceremoniously delivers to the appropriate table. Also watching these proceedings, as before, was a well-dressed gentleman who spent his time preparing bills, raising his eyes to the heavens and from time to time muttering in our direction. I took him to be Mr Salahuddin himself. And what about the food? Meat, meat and more meat ('A vegetarian-free heaven' says RA who, unlike Bernard Shaw, despises vegetables) predominates. There is a comprehensive tandoori section providing succulent, natural-coloured, divinely flavoured offerings. Chicken Shashlik superb. Lamb chop and Shami Kebab were both lean and melt-in-the-mouth. Hard-to-find, acquired taste Haleem, pounded meat cooked with wheat, supplied complete with a DIY spice kit of chillies, ginger, garam masala and onion tarka, which you add yourself, was well spiced this time. The Chicken Jalfrezi was fresh and poignant. The Pullao Rice was, again, superb and definitive. Aloo Paratha was fantastic. 'I was impressed with Salloos and I didn't think it was over expensive, although I did have the set lunch. Food and service were both very good. Waiter kindly informed me the Seekh Kebab was a spicy dish, he needn't have bothered!' RC. It is essential to book. The elegant Farizeh Salahuddin (daughter of the house – she can be heard out of hours on the answer machine) handles bookings with considerable aplomb. Our bill for two with an aperitif, wine, starter, main course and coffee came to £120 (up £20) which still makes it probably the most expensive Pakistani, Indian or Bangladeshi restaurant in the UK, if not the world. The place is an institution and is worth at least one visit. Set Lunch £16, dinner £25. Cover charge £1.50. Service 12½%. Hours: Mon.-Sat., 12pm-2.30pm/7-11.45pm. Remains in our TOP 100.

WOODLANDS   √ ©

37 Panton Street, SW1   © 0171 930 8200/ 839 7258

Long-established (1985) licensed, vegetarian, south Indian 55-seat restaurant, just off Haymarket, is managed by Mr Valaiya, head chef Mr Bhatt. It is the tiniest of three Woodlands and sponge-effect green walls with Indian wall-hangings are old hat along with the 'rocky tables, and nasty music, forgivable for Woodlands' orgasmic food, and nearly forgivable for its 12½% service charge.' RC. 'I particularly like southern Indian food, and find the menu so appealing, it makes choice difficult. We chose one exceptionally good-value set Thali, £6.50, which was quite generous, with good variety, and the Paper Dosa, £3.95. Upma, £2.95, Lhassi, £1.25) and Channa, £3.75 are as good as ever. Also glad to have a choice of Indian desserts. Good value.' HC. Price check: Papadam £1.00, Pullao Rice £2.75. House wine £8. Hours: 12-2.45pm/ 5.30-11pm. Branches: London, W1, Wembley, Middlesex. Stocks Cobra.

LANCER OF BENGAL   ©

220 Brixton Hill, Brixton, SW2   © 0181 674 4736/671 7372

40-seater, established in 1989 by Sarfraz Ali. Good formula. Specials include: Dall and Kodhu Bhaji (lentils with marrow – 'super' GR). Price check: Papadam 40p, CTM £5.20, Pullao Rice £1.60, Peshwari Nan £1.50. House wine £6.95. Delivery: £10 minimum, 3-mile radius. Hours: 12-2.30pm/6pm-12am. Stocks Cobra.

SW3

SHAHEEN OF KNIGHTSBRIDGE   ©

225 Brompton Road, SW3   © 0171 581 5329

AK Trehan's 38-seater is just a chupatti throw from Harrods. Good standard stuff from chef Mustafa Kamal, with one or two 'unusuals'. The
Maahn Dal is a Gujarati special with black lentils, ginger, tomato and
chillies, and Mango Lassi is a favourite with some. Being patronised by
tourists, it's more expensive than average (£35 per head, with drink, service and cover charges), but it is competent and friendly. Delivery.
Hours: 12-3pm/6-11.30pm. Sat. & Sun. 12-11.30pm. Stocks Cobra.

TANDOORI OF CHELSEA TOP 100

153 Fulham Road, Chelsea, SW3   © 0171 589 7617

This elegant 70-seat basement restaurant quietly goes about its business
without fanfare or hype. It is, and always has been since it opened in
1965, a leader in style, from its carefully selected small number of dishes
to its decor and wine list. It is, of course, Indian, not Bangladeshi, and
owned by A. Rajan, whose timeless quote cannot be omitted: One
should certainly not drink lager with his food – 'Spice and gas don't
mix!' he explodes. 'Good wine does go with well-cooked Indian food. It
is not overpowered by subtle spicing. That is why we have Château
Latour on the menu.' 'How much?' say I. '£100 a bottle!' 'Who the heck
can afford that?' 'Arabs,' he winks knowingly. The wine list is exemplary,
and a leader in its field. 'An indisputably smart place, where dressing up
is part of the fun.' says EB. The food is indeed subtly spiced, but the
chefs will step up both spice levels and chilli heat if requested. Here is
what one of our ace reporters (MRS HC) says: 'I've walked by this restaurant dozens of times and always admired the Indian-dressed doorman
and imagined the basement restaurant would be attractive. Every dish
we had was marvellous, service was good, prices fair for the quality and
area. We were very impressed.' 'Very upmarket, one of the finest I have
been to. Dining with my father, requested not to have a romantic table
for two. On arrival, given the choice of two tables. Glad we both wore
suits – it's not the place to wear jeans and T-shirt. Tandoori Lamb
Chops being a house special, and Tandoori King Prawns in spicy sauce,
served in a Karahi – outstanding. Food, service and ambience faultless.
Deserves its long-standing place in the TOP 100.' PJ. Price check:

Papadam 40p, CTM £6.90, Pullao Rice £2.50. House wine £2.50 glass.
Service 15%. Hours: 12.30-3pm/6.30-12pm. Sun. 6.30-11.30pm. Stocks
Cobra.

SW4 – Clapham

GOLDEN CURRY TANDOORI

131 High Street, SW4   © 0171 720 9558

Clapham's second oldest (1971), owned by Abdur Rhaman Choudhury.
His restaurant seats 72 diners and head chef Shiraze Ahamed serves
well-liked curries and side dishes and has some Indo-French specials up
his sleeve, £6.25-£8.95. Price check: Papadam 55p, CTM £5.50, Pullao
Rice £1.75, Peshwari Nan £1.75. House wine £7.50. Delivery: £10 minimum. Hours: 12-2.30pm/6pm-12am. Sun. 12pm-12am; buffet £5.75 –
12-4.30pm. Stocks Cobra.

MAHARANI

117 High Street, SW4   © 0171 622 2530

The 30-minute TV programme, on the growth of the Indian restaurant
in Britain, I mentioned last time was screened nationally on BBC2. The
producer wanted me to tell the story of a very long-established subur-
ban curry house. The 104-seat Maharani immediately came to mind. It
was established in 1958, at which time there were under 200 curry houses in the whole of the UK. It was not only Clapham's first curry house,
opened long before Cla'am became trendy ma'am, it was one of the first
to open in a London suburb. It has always earned its keep by providing
good, bog-standard, formula curries; indeed, owner S.U. Khan was one
of the pioneers of the formula. Under the same ownership for all these
years, Khan has kept up with the trends, though, and everything is as it
should be. Branches: Maharani, NW4; Sonargaon, SW9; Taste of India,
334 Kennington Road, SE11. Price check: Papadam 50p, CTM £5.25,
Pullao Rice £1.80, Peshwari Nan £1.50. House wine £6.95. Hours: 12-
2.30pm/6pm-12am. Sun. 12pm-12am.

©	Curry Club discount (see page 6)	🍵	Unlicensed
√	Vegetarian		
BYO	Bring your own alcohol	▦	Delivery/takeaway

ROYAL INDIA NEW ENTRANT   ©

31 Clapham Park Road, SW4   © 0171 622 3332

From the old to the new! Enamul Kabir, A. and S. Alam's 40-seater was
established in 1997. It serves Bangladeshi style curries and side dishes.
Specials include: Chicken Tikka Dhakewari £7.15. Price check: Papadam
45p, CTM £4.75, Pullao Rice £1.50, Peshwari Nan £1.50. House wine
£6.50. Have agreed to give CC members a complimentary drink as their
CC discount. Delivery: 2-mile radius. Hours: 6pm-12am (1pm on Sat.).
Stocks Cobra.

SW5

NIZAM   ©

152 Old Brompton Road, SW5   © 0171 373 0024

M. Mian's Nizam (Nizam was the former ruler of Hyderabad, once the
richest man in the world) is indeed a small (65 seats in two rooms) but
smart place, 1989 vintage, with colour washed walls and large gilt
framed mirrors. Miss Sumaira Lateef-Mian's service is said to be exemplary, with smartly waistcoated waiters, exuding expertise. North West
Frontier and Moghul cuisine is carefully executed by chef M. Riaz.
Price check: Papadam 50p, CTM £7.95, Hyderabadi Lamb £7.95, Pullao
Rice £2.50. Peshwari Nan £2.25. House wine £8.95. Cover charge £1.
Delivery: £12 minimum. Hours: 12-2.30pm/6-11.45pm. Stocks Cobra.

STAR OF INDIA TOP 100

154 Old Brompton Road, SW5   © 0171 373 2901

The redec, now some years old, still has everyone talking, and we continue to get comments about the murals, the stars, the lighting, the flora
and the prices – above all, the prices. No one talks louder or more pro-
fusely than Reza himself, and since I'm not one to let a good quote die,
here it is again: 'Such luxury doesn't come cheap.' he says. 'What do you
expect for the Sistine Chapel directed by Zeffirelli?' Ah me! He's such a
showman. But who's to argue – his 94-seater is always packed with
tourists and regular fans (booking essential), who presumably adore
Reza's rhetoric. And good for him. We loudly applaud such theatre.
Dining out is supposed to be fun and escapist. The recent departure of
chef Vineet Bahtia to pastures new took place after all our reports were

received. He's a hard act to follow and we hope his successors will maintain the specials such as their bench-mark Patrani Maachli (pomfret
with coriander wrapped in banana leaf), the red mullet, red chilli variant, and the smoky-tasting Baigan-e-Bahar (aubergine stuffed with
paneer and spiced with curry leaf, mustard and sesame). Incidentally, I
have heard nothing from Reza about his scornful dismissal of all things
Balti on BBC-TV's *Good Food* programme last year. Brum's Balti boys are
still waiting for their right to reply, when Reza shows up in Sparkbrook!
Maybe, they should pay a visit to sw6! Retained in our TOP 100 pen-
ding reports please. Prices around £30 including drink and £1 cover
charge. Hours: 12-2.45pm/6-11.45pm (7-11.15pm Sun.). Stocks Cobra.

SW6

THE BLUE ELEPHANT TOP 100

4-6 Fulham Broadway, SW6   ℭ **0171 386 6595**

The best Thai restaurant in the UK qualifies, as ever, for entry to this
Guide because of its Thai curries. Its blue neon frontage stands out in
the Broadway, throbbing with life of all ages when we were last there on
a Saturday night. Inside, you get a warm welcome from the staff in
national costume. There's a bar and a cloakroom, and some tables.
Nothing out of the ordinary here but, when you book, insist on being
seated further in. There are 250 seats, and you soon realize this is no
ordinary place. Ahead of you is the jungle: literally hundreds of strate-
gically-placed plants. Bamboo on the walls and ceiling, and pagodas
transport you at once from Fulham to Phuket. And just when you think
you've seen it all, there's more. The restaurant goes on and on. Small
bridges traverse ponds, inhabited by huge golden carp and lilies.
Waterfalls tinkle gently down. So does your small change if you want a
lucky wish. The perfumes from exotic flowers fill the air. Little Thai
houses surround the walls, and different dining areas have different
characteristics. Some are secluded, some communal. Yet one is simply
not aware of its size and it somehow manages to retain a feeling of intimacy. The blue elephant motif appears again and again – on the carpets, on the tablecloths, on the crockery, in the display cabinet among
items for sale and on the menu.

What of the menu? Well, there are two, actually (three, if you count
the wine list). One is the main menu, the other is the vegetarian menu.
The main menu contains seventeen starters, five soups and thirty-four

meat, chicken, duck and seafood dishes. Chilli heat is indicated by elephant symbols (three for hottest) on the menu, and there are a number
of Thai curry dishes. For those who like to try a wide range of dishes,
the Banquet for £27 without soup, £30 with, provides a massive selection of dishes although you need a large party to take advantage of this.
Smaller groups, even singles, can sample a selection of starters and
main-course dishes by ordering Pearls and Royal Platter. The Blue
Elephant flies in fresh produce every week. Ingredients such as lemon
grass, aubergines, green peppers, chillies, holy basil and banana leaves
(they make disposable doilies from them), orchids and galingale combine to produce those memorable Thai fragrances. And flying in their
own food ensures a freshness unmatched in rival Thai restaurants.
Portions are more than ample. Service is gracious, smiling and accurate.
Don't forget to book – it is always full. Parking is nigh on impossible
so go by taxi. (It's opposite the Tube, but if you can't afford a taxi you
might as well forget the Blue Elephant.) It's a top-price restaurant (for
Indo-Thai that is, but still much less than Roux/Little/Hilton-type
places). Expect to pay between £30 and £50 per head depending on how
lavish your extras are, and that may not include the 15% service charge
and £1.50 cover charge. If you want to carp about that, do it to the carp
at the restaurant, not me! The food at the Blue Elephant is spot on, and
since even three elephants is nowhere near as hot as you'd get in
Bangkok, you only have to ask! The place has become an institution. For
two or three hours you can escape from the world in here. It is fun and
it is theatre. What more can one ask? Remains very high in our TOP
100. Indian branch: La Porte des Indes, w1.

THE EAST INDIAN RESTAURANT   ©

448 Fulham Road, SW6   ✆ **0171 381 2588.**

Anyone trading since 1962 in one venue knows what they are doing.
Habibur Rahman at Fulham's first curry restaurant, certainly does. He's
an old hand at the game. Everything smacks of it. The right formula
things are here on the menu, even the spelling is 100% (so often a give-
away with the new boys). Chef Islam's cooking is 100% too, so go there
and enjoy curry house cooking as it should be. Price check: Papadam
50p, CTM £6.25, Bhaja Mas (trout) £6.95, Pullao Rice £1.95. Minimum
charge £9. Branch: Modern Tandoori, Stanley Road, Teddington. Stocks
Cobra.

MAMTA √

692 Fulham Road, SW6   © 0171 736 5914

A Gujarati vegetarian restaurant is a rarity in Fulham. Gujarati food is
based on yoghurt and gram flour, and is sweetish and quite bland and,
frankly, not to everyone's taste. And I don't just mean Brits who adore
the Bangladeshi formula. One of my Punjabi friends gets withdrawal
symptoms if expected to eat it, and not just because he's an inveterate
meat-eater – he simply finds it too bland. So if it's new to you, try it all
from the starters onwards, and enjoy the results, served on a Thali. Ask
for advice from the helpful staff and, above all, tell them to spice it up,
if that's how you like it – they're not mind-readers!

NAYAB ©

309 New Kings Road, SW6   © 0171 731 6993

Owner Praveen Rai's up-market menu is full of 'some dishes you won't
recognise and some that you will.' The latter are Indian and Pakistani
specials cooked by head chef Akeel Ghani. These include: Nihari Kohe
Avadh, pot roast shank of lamb, £7.95. Most popular dish ordered is
Goan Galinha Xacutti (Sha-Coo-Tee), browned onion, fresh coconut,
£6.95. Meat Dhaba Wala Lamb cooked in bone marrow stock and
mince (ask Rai to tell you about this). This is all dedicated stuff, and
well spoken of by the regulars. For the if-you-must-brigade, Mr Rai
offers 'old curry house favourites' which includes everything except
Phal. (he'll explain how it came to be 'invented by chefs as a revenge
against the lager lout – and he'd never serve it or them!') So if you are
chilli-addicted, as Praveen himself is, then choose the hotter specials.
Price check: Papadam 50p, CTM £5.95, Pullao Rice £2.75, Peshwari
Nan £2.25. House wine £8.95. Set menus for two at £13 and £16 pp.
Delivery: Fulham area only. Hours: 12-2.30pm/6-11.45pm (11.30pm on
Sun.). Stocks Cobra,

©	Curry Club discount (see page 6)		Unlicensed
√	Vegetarian		
BYO	Bring your own alcohol		Delivery/takeaway

SW7 – Kensington

BOMBAY BRASSERIE TOP 100

Courtfield Close, Courtfield Road, SW7   © 0171 370 4040

The Bombay Brasserie, managed by Adi Modi and Harun, is still, amazingly, the Taj Hotel Group's only UK Indian restaurant. Opening in 1982, as an experiment, it was the brainchild of Taj director Camelia Panjabi, who explains: 'I wanted to launch regional Indian cuisine in England – home-style Bombay dishes such as Patrani Macchli, fish embalmed in green chutney, baked in a banana leaf, and Bhel Puri streetside food for starters, and regional main-course dishes, such as Parsee Jardaloo Sali Boti, lamb cooked with apricot, and garnished with potato straws.' But such a venture in 1982 was by no means a safe bet. Such food was new to Britain. By coincidence, it was the year in which I founded the Curry Club, so I know with certainty that there were then 3,500 'Indian' restaurants, and though the market was beginning to grow, there were some who felt London was already saturated. The BB in its out-of-the-way location, they felt, would not succeed. In those days I was too low on the Indian food chain to receive an invite to that glittering, star-studded opening-night, but I soon went there and found it to be as good as the best Taj hotels in India. True to the vision, BB cooking was, and still is, shared by specialist chefs from Goa, and elsewhere, doing their own regional thing. Camelia's story can be read in her book *50 Great Curries*. The dishes mentioned above, and many other similar authentic dishes, have remained on the menu all these years and are always in demand. It is the regional specialities that you should go for when you visit. Of course, the BB does some well-known Punjabi dishes too. Tikka, kebabs and tandoori come luscious and succulent and devoid of artificial food colouring. Familiar main courses include Rogan Josh, Chicken Tikka Makhani and Biriani. There are plenty of vegetarian choices and several set-meal Thalis.

Two things have happened at the BB this last year. One was unplanned (the departure of exec. chef Udit Sharkel to found his own empire – see Sahrkels, SW19), leaving Vikram Sundera to take over, and for a while things wavered about while he found his feet with the brigade. The new conservatory has finally opened. It has been so cleverly done that you would hardly notice its doubling in size to accommodate a further 80 covers, making the entire capacity some 250 seats. This too had to be coped with by the kitchens, and again there was a detectable learning curve. 'Fantastic service, the best I've ever encountered, good food (Goan fish curry) though hideously expensive.' RC. 'Wonderful food, great ambience – you've heard it all before. The thing I most like is the basket of different breads including a type of Paratha I have not found elsewhere they call Lacha Paratha. It's dry and crispy with a reddish tinge. The area they could improve on is their Sunday Buffet. This comment is in fact aimed at most Indian style restaurants. They seem to be aiming their Sunday lunchtime produce at customers who they think want a cheap meal. *"All you can eat for £15.95"* screams the advert. When I dropped in, it was easy to get a table, choice of three meat dishes, two vegetables, rice and breads. Good value for £15.95 but not what I was looking for. I wish that there was a decent Indian restaurant that decided to let me try dishes that I've never tried!' AF. 'Visited in the evening for a special opening party of the new conservatory, it really is lovely. Ate from a buffet of Bombay snack foods, e.g. Sev Batata (Bhel) Puri and Gol Goppas, which the chef prepared in front of us, to order. All absolutely delicious, as you would expect from this Top Indian restaurant.' It reminds us of when we visit the Taj Intercontinental Hotel in Bombay. Lunch is always a dash up the stairs opposite the swimming pool, to the Sea Lounge for a plate full of these delicacies, accompanied with a Nimboo soda.' DBAC. The Bombay Brasserie, despite being an even larger machine than last year, operates very smoothly with a very experienced team. It has the benefit of an even bigger operation and team in the form of its owners, the Taj Hotel Group. Who elso could have survived a chef change and a major rebuild and still be full every night? The food is again as good as it gets, if you want to sample Indian regional cooking that's as near to authentic as you can get outside of the Indian home. It will probably not satisfy if it's formula one-pot curry-stuff that you're looking for. Despite its enlargement, booking well ahead is still essential, unless you're lucky. If you prefer the conservatory, ask for it when booking. As ever, the Bombay Brasserie is the yardstick at the top of our TOP 100. House wine £11.95. Price check: Papadam 50p, CTM £13.75, Pullao Rice £3.50, Nan £2.75. Set lunch buffet £15.95. Hours: 12.30-3pm / 7.30pm-12am.

©	Curry Club discount (see page 6)		Unlicensed
√	Vegetarian		
BYO	Bring your own alcohol		Delivery/takeaway

CAFE LAZEEZ

23-29 Old Brompton Road, SW7   ℂ 0171 581 9933

Lazeez, meaning 'delicate and aromatic', describes itself as a 'new type of Indian restaurant'. It operates in true café mode, with nonstop opening hours. It has a striking frontage, with 26 outside good-weather seats. Inside are 130 seats, on two floors. Downstairs in stark, minimalist surroundings, is a short-menu café (which changes to full menu after 7pm). Upstairs is decorated with an illuminated, white, tented roof, and a full menu. Its owners are Pakistani, in the persons of the elegant Ms Sabiha Kasim and her brother Zahid. If they suffer criticism, it's because its dishes try to be two things, authentic and evolved. Nothing wrong with either aspiration, but somehow the result just isn't quite right. We have mixed reports, though one totally reliable reporter, HC. glows: 'Spicing different, and not necessarily Indian. A good place to take people who say they don't like Indian food. Succulent prawns, sizzling lamb chops, well-spiced vegetables, rich and creamy Korma, the Lamb Sag, not enough lamb, but good flavour, Saffron Rice fantastic, firm, fresh and spicy mushrooms, star dish, aubergine – superb – and the Nan, small, round, lightest and crispest I've had. Expensive, but first class. Overall, a wonderful meal.' That Korma is a good example. It's authentic as done in the Pakistani heartlands, where the meat is marinated in yoghurt to tenderise it, resulting in a mild, aromatic dish with subtle, spicing, including a hint of garam masala, *ergo* Lazeez! It's a lively place. Average snack price £6, meal price £30, incl. service and cover charge. Hours: 11am-11pm. (10.30pm on Sun.). Stocks Cobra.

DELHI BRASSERIE

134 Cromwell Road, SW7   ℂ 0171 370 7617

Owner Mr A. Jabber says 'shop out and pop in ' (it's near Sainsbury's). A bright comfortable spacious 60-seater. Chef Ram Singh's food and service excellent. Hours: 12-11.30pm. Stocks Cobra.

KHAN'S OF KENSINGTON

3 Harrington Road, SW7   ℂ 0171 584 4114

60-seater, est. 1991 by Mr Khan (no relation to Khan's, w2). 'Indian in a modern way. We were made very welcome, and all the food was above average and prices very reasonable for central London,' DRC. Plenty for veggies, though the rarely-found south Indian meat dish, Narial Gosht (lamb in coconut), and Machli Gowala (pomfret), are highlighted. Price check: Papadam 55p, CTM £6.95, Pullao Rice £1.90. Delivery: £20 minimum. Hours: 12-2.30pm; 6-11.30pm. Sat. 12pm-12am. Sun. 12.30-11pm. Stocks Cobra.

KWALITY   ©

38 Thurloe Place, SW7   ✆ 0171 589 3666

Sultan Khan says his Kwality, established in 1984, 'seats 48 in a modern Indian style'. It serves formula curries and side dishes. Price check: Papadam 45p, CTM £5.95, Pullao Rice £1.80. Service 10%. Hours: 12-2.30pm; 6-11.30pm (11pm on Sun.).

MEMORIES OF INDIA

18 Gloucester Road, SW7   ✆ 0171 589 6450/581 3734

Managed by N. Islam, seating 70, with a 30-seat party room. Curries and side dishes cooked by head chef M. Uddin. Price check: Papadam 50p, CTM £6.95, Pullao Rice £1.95. Hours: 12-11.30pm. Stocks Cobra.

MOTI MAHAL

3 Glendower Place, SW7   ✆ 0171 584 8428

An old hand (1956) 50-seater in two rooms. B Rahman's specials include: Chicken Malabar, King Prawn Jalfrezi and Murge Akbari. 'Above average, very comfortable. Service swift, very polite and with a smile, despite the late hour we arrived. The Memsahib fancied the Mixed Grill for two, so that's what we had (I'm a coward!) with a bottle of Beaujolais. Beautifully presented on silver plates, Papadams, Samosas, Onion Bhajia, Mixed Grill, Veg Curry (lovely), Special Fried Rice and Coffee, £40. Thoroughly enjoyable. London prices of course but nothing over the top.' MS. Price check: Papadam: 60p, CTM £6.90, Pullao Rice £2.30, Peshwari Nan £2.40. House wine £8.75. 12% discount on collected takeaways. Delivery: £20 minimum, 3-mile radius. Hours: 12-2.45pm; 6-11.30pm. Sat. and Sun.

SHEZAN   ©

16-22 Cheval Place, Knightsbridge, SW7   ℂ 0171 584 9316

This 1966 120-seat Pakistani restaurant, is in the street opposite the
world's number one store. The downstairs dining room, past the bar, is
elegantly simple, with its downlighters, pewter plates and candlelight.
Chef Khan's food is as sophisticated as the service to match the prices,
which *are* Knightsbridge. Are you sitting comfortably? Price check:
Papadam free, CTM (sorry, Makhni) £11.75, Karahi Kebab £12.75,
Pullao Rice £4.50. Set lunch £12.95. Minimum charge dinner £25.
Service 10%. Cover charge £1.50. Stocks Cobra.

SW10 – Chelsea

CHUTNEY MARY   TOP 100   BEST IN UK

535 Kings Road, SW10   ℂ 0171 351 3113

Established in 1990 by Ranjit Mathrani and Namita Panjabi, this 150-
seater is easy enough to find, near Lots Road, though it's not near a
Tube, so it's taxi, bike or shanks. Parking is iffy, but worth a try. You
can tell they are getting busier. The ground floor bar has more tables
than ever and is now the overflow, though its scheduled redec will, we're
told, make this arrangement feel as though it is intended. Admire the
raj-style decor and count the brass cobra lamp stands – a grand apiece
from up-the-street Christopher Wray. Downstairs is gorgeous with its
murals, Indian props and conservatory. Chutney Mary would be dull
without its conservatory (though not everyone opts for it – some tell us
they prefer the interior!). But the conservatory nearly wasn't there. The
offices which overlook it obtained an injunction to prevent its being its
built, despite the correct permissions being in place. Mathrani and
Panjabi had to pay five figures to get the injunction overturned. Now
even those same office residents, couldn't imagine the place without it.
Ah me! Such is life – one has to fight for all the best things. But this is
typical of this husband and wife team. They will not accept second
best. They are true professionals, and do everything by the book, punc-
tiliously, down to the last detail, like those lamp stands. There is a large
highly-trained house team headed by G.M. Eddie Khoo, and assisted by
Neeraj Mitra delivering impeccable service. The menu is a brief document. Nothing on it resembles formula curry house, of course, but I
believe most diners are aware of that. Namita despises the formula with

its one-pot (of curried onion purée gravy). 'If you go down that road,' she says, 'everything ends up tasting the same. Every dish we make has its own unique spice mixture. All the curries are freshly cooked from scratch in their own pan. Wet masalas are ground on our own motorised stone grinder, imported from India.' Chef Hardev Singh Bhatty and his brigade of five chefs are each from a different region of India. Between them they can accurately cook dishes from Kashmir, the Punjab, Lucknow, Goa, Bombay, Mangalore, and Kerala. Each has his own work station and his own ingredients. 'We supply them whatever they need,' continues Namita. 'It means flying-in certain ingredients unobtainable in Britain, such as Kashmiri chillies, Goan coconut and palm sugar, to mention just three items. It's very hard work for chefs used to having plentiful kitchen help back home, but the economics of the west preclude a large kitchen and oodles of helpers. It becomes a nightmare when their work permits run out after three years and they must return to India. We have to find and train replacements. The brigade has learnt to cover for each other for holidays and days off – no mean feat with such specialist dishes. If we get accused of being expensive, compare our tag to say Le Gavroche or Nico's – we're less than half of theirs for at least equal costs and effort! I sometimes wonder whether it's all worth it.' She doesn't mean that, of course. But why is it that people are prepared to pay £100 and over per head for what they perceive to be '*haute cuisine*'? Yet they baulk at paying for 'haute Indian'! But such attention to detail is only possible with constant owner supervision. There can be no stricter quality control than Namita's kitchen taste, face-to-face with the chefs, whenever she feels like it. 'Anyway, it's my local, so I expect it to be good,' she told me. 'Why own a restaurant if you don't dine in it?' And dine she does, in the company of her co-owner husband Ranjit and friends. Chutney Mary must be doing something right. It's packed full of *aficionado*s, mostly regulars, who delight in its real Indian food.

On the menu is still a trio of Anglo-Indian dishes – Kedgeree, Country Captain and Masala Roast lamb shank, but it is the Indian regional specialities to go for. Acceptance by the Indian community proves that the food is as close to Indian home cooking as you could get in any restaurant. Go for the set meals for good value, or for the food festivals that Namita stages from time to time. 'Always quite an experience but we can't afford to go there too often.' sw. 'I have always had an exceptionally authentic meal with the best puddings ever!' DC. 'I was slightly disappointed, the food was pretty nice, different. In retrospect, I'd been to the cup final, Man U had lost to Everton so I wasn't in the mood.' RC. 'About as good as that style can be. I'd travel to London just for the Okra dishes, any of them.' PT. 'Tried one of their many food festivals recently. First class food, service and company.' DBAC. They have a superb wine list, and for the you-can't drink-wine-with-curry brigade, what do you think Namita and Ranjit delight in? Good red wine, of course! Oh, and just in case your visit to the toilet mystifies you, a Pickle John was the derogatory, arrogant term bestowed by both snooty Brits and Indians upon young Indian men who dared to wear western clothes and adopt western attitudes in the 1920s and 1930s Raj. The equivalent female was called a Chutney Mary! For the reasons given above, Chutney Mary is a one-off. Its cooking standards should never be lowered. No way could it ever be a contender for branches. Now that their rescue of Veeraswamy (W1) is done, I suspect that, as if all this isn't enough, this ambitious couple are planning something additional to keep them occupied. And if it is to take the one-pot formula to new heights, so much the better for the industry. It's time Chutney Mary regained its BEST IN BRITAIN category. Price check: Set lunch £12.50 for two courses, £14.50 for three courses. House wine £10.95. Cover charge £1.50 – includes ample spicy Papadams with home made chutney and pickle. Average spend £38. Hours: 12.30-2.30pm; 7-11.30pm. Sun. 12.30-3pm/7-10.30pm. Stocks Cobra

---

EXOTIKKA OF INDIA   ©

35 Stadium Street, SW10   ℂ **0171 376 7542/ 351 7274**

Someone had to think of the name! And it may as well be owners Hye and Hussain. Competent curries from chef A. Kalam at this 40-seater. Price check: Papadam 40p, CTM £5.95, Pullao Rice £1.75. Set lunch £6.95. Hours: 6-11.30pm, to 12 on Sat. Stocks Cobra.

VAMA – THE INDIAN ROOM   ©

438 Kings Road, London SW10   ℂ **0171 351 4118**

Established in 1997 by Andy and Arjun Varma, and Ritu Dakmia. Their sophisticated, stylishly decorated restaurant (though DW thinks it looks like an expensive Chelsea clip joint – that's a bordello to DBAC) seats 110 and serves North West Frontier cuisine. Tandoori Jhinga, Tiger prawns marinaded in cream, yoghurt, mustard oil, garlic, ginger and Kashmiri chilli, roasted on charcoal, £10, being the most popular dish ordered.

'Expensive, 3 scallops £7.75. £88 for two including one bottle of wine. Poor service, missing on 3 scallops £7.75. £88 for two including one bottle of wine. Poor service, missing one meat and bread.' DW. Price check: Papadam 75, CTM £8.75, Pullao Rice 2.50. House wine £8.75. Service 12½%, cover charge £1. Hours: 12.30-3pm; 6.30-11.30pm. Stocks Cobra.

SW11 – Battersea

BATTERSEA TANDOORI

515 Park Road, Battersea, SW11   © 0171 585 0487

'Fairly standard menu but the food is good.' A. Miah's 40-seater serves chef Tara Miah's standards, well cooked, always arrives at the table hot. Quantities are very generous and prices reasonable,' DRG. Price check: Papadam 40p, CTM £5.25, Pullao Rice £1.50, Peshwari Nan £1.40. House wine £5.95. Hours: 12-2.30pm; 6pm-12am.

CAFE SPICE NAMASTE   NEW ENTRANT   ©

247 Lavender Hill, SW11   © 0171 738 1717

Opened in 1997 by Cyrus Todiwala and Michael Gottlieb. Hours: 12-3pm; 6.15-10.30pm. Sat. 6.30-10pm, closed Sun. Branch E1 (see entry for menu details). Stocks Cobra.

SW12

BOMBAY BICYCLE CLUB

95 Nightingale Lane, SW12   © 0181 673 6217

Known to some an the BBC! 'Something wonderfully luxurious, elegant decor, massive vase of flowers dominates the room, charming staff, starched white tablecloths and napkins. In the winter, it's cosy and snug, in the summer the windows and doors are thrown open, the colonial ceiling fans whirr and it all looks extremely pretty and atmospheric. The food is absolutely delicious, with plenty of crunchy green pepper in the main-course dishes and beautifully presented vegetable dishes. Although the Nan was a great disappointment, very dense. Masala Papadams arrive at the table at the same time as your bottom hits the chair. However, the waiting staff feel duty bound to chivvy you along.

In some restaurants you wonder what you have to do to get served. At the BBC you wonder what you have to do to get them to leave you alone. The staff are in over-drive, the message very strong and most persistent: eat up–pay up–and get up. The staff asked us for a wine order, when we were holding full pint glasses of beer. At one point they tried to remove dishes that we were eating from! It leaves you feeling miffed, when you've shelling out nearly £50 for dinner!' JM. 'When you telephone to book, it is an answer phone, which informs you to leave your details. Promptly shown one of too many tables (insufficient room between chairs – staff tried in vain to squeeze through). Given the menu. Papadams served but no chutneys. Trying to rush us through. You could not fault the starter – absolutely beautiful. Tellicherry Squid, in a non greasy batter, very delicate spicing, excellent. No plate warmers. Portions small compared to cost. Waitress cleared table, when one in our party hadn't finished, height of bad manners. Disappointing ice creams and luke-warm coffee. Expensive.' MW. Hours: 7-12pm, Mon.-Sat. Stocks Cobra.

TABAQ TOP 100 BEST PAKISTANI   ©

47 Balham Hill, Balham, SW12   © 0181 673 7820

Run by the brothers Ahmed. Mushtaq is front-of-house manager. His domain consists of pale walls giving a spacious feel, enhanced by richly embroidered tapestries of rural Lahore, and tables with pink cloths, around which are just 50 seats, so booking is necessary, and good old fashioned silver service. The other Ahmed brother, Manoor, is head chef, and the culinary magic emanates from him and his brigade. But don't expect quick food from him. He cooks everything freshly, and a 30-minute wait is not uncommon. The menu is pure Lahori cuisine. Lahore, now in Pakistan, was once one of four major palace cities, resided in by rotation by the great Moghul emperors, rather in the way that QEii rotates round Buck Pal, Windsor, Sandringham and Balmoral. Agra, Delhi and Srianagar, Kashmir were the others, all linked by still extant tree-lined trunk roads. Lahore is famous for its cuisine. Grills and tandoori, meat and chicken predominate, and there are fish, prawn and vegetable dishes too. At Tabaq, they do it all well. Specials include Lahori Steam Roast Chicken, Masala Machli Lahori, robustly spiced white fish, Quail Masala, Baby Chicken Tabaq. The daring will go for liver (but can no longer try that great Pakistani speciality, goat brain, because it's still banned). Their Pullao Rice Masaledaar gets thumbs up. 'I think it gives fair value for money and fine quality. They really care about their cooking. My favourite is Gosht Ka Lazeez Masala.' RB. 'They made us welcome.' CHC. 'In my Top Four. Superb lunchtime special, great value. Included best ever Peshwari Nan.' RL. Tabaq means large serving dish. And if you want to stage something really spectacular for a party, order (at least 24 hours in advance, of course) a whole baby lamb, cooked Raan-style, or even a leg or two. Deservedly promoted to our TOP 100. Price check: Papadam 60p, CTM £6.50, Pullao Rice £2.75. Set lunch £6.95. Peshwari Nan £2.75. House wine £8.50. Hours: 12-2.45pm; 6-11.45pm. Closed Sun. Stocks Cobra.

SW13 – Barnes

HAWELI TOP 100   ©

7 White Hart Lane, SW13   © 0181 876 4441

Manju Choudhury is an energetic Bangladeshi entrepreneur, whose Haweli chain (*see* below) has been an inspiration and an example to all in the trade. From just one restaurant, he expanded it, with the help of his extended family, to nine, and all do really excellent food with good service. Keeping it in the family helps, but so does the fact that Manju likes nothing better than hands-on cooking. In fact, the place where you are most likely to find him isn't here, the current flagship, but at his St Margarets, Twickenham, takeaway-only branch. 'It's much harder to do takeaway,' he says. 'It's faster, and it keeps you on the go for hours, non-stop.' I make no secret of the fact that I was commissioned by Manju to consult as a chef, cooking with Manju in the kitchens of this very branch. It was not the first time I have cheffed at Indian and Bangladeshi restaurants, but this was an exciting brief. Manju wanted unusual dishes. He had seen some in my cookbooks and he wanted, among other things, Balti. So together we worked out a new and exciting menu, then I trained the other chefs to use ingredients new to them. For example, Mirchwangi Korma is from Kashmir. There, a special root is used to achieve a dark red colour. Here, we use beetroot (not otherwise used in curry restaurants), with red chilli, capsicum and tomato, and it dispels the myth that all Kormas are mild! And the Harlyala Murgh is chicken, marinated with a coriander, spinach and mint purée, then baked. The Balti dishes available are herbal and aromatically spiced, and were not only the first in London but are correctly made, with specially roasted and ground spices, rather than that acidic horror paste, straight from a well-known manufacturer's bottle, as offered by most Bangladeshi restaurants. You tell us you like the Hawelis very much so, with my declaration of interest made, how could we not continue to give this restaurant a TOP 100 award? Haweli (meaning 'palace') gets very busy at the weekends so booking is advisable. Manager Nazrul (Nigel) Choudhury will give a discount to Curry Club members. Hours: 12.30-3pm; 6-11.30pm. Haweli branches: Belmont; Epsom; New Malden; St Margarets, Middlesex (takeaway only); Surbiton; Sutton; Wallington; West Byfleet. Guru Express, 146 Fulham Road, sw6. Stocks Cobra.

SW15 – Putney

GANGES

205 Lower Richmond Road, SW15   © 0181 789 0357

Bodruzzamam Ahmed's cosy 35-seater's menu has all the usual favourites. Price check: Papadam 45p, CTM £5.95, Pullao Rice £1.80. Delivery: £12 minimum, 2-mile radius. Hours: 6pm-12am.

MA GOA TOP 100

244 Upper Richmond Road, SW15   © 0181 780 1767

Goa is one of India's 24 states, not a country in its own right, as some think. It is on the western coast of India and because it was Portuguese for nearly 500 years, it inherited different characteristics from the rest of India, including a small pork-eating, Christian population. Goan cooks were prized in the Raj (because they would handle beef and pork and could cook well). My family had one for years. Until a few decades ago, Goan cooks were frequently to be found in merchant ships. In the sixties Goa was 'discovered' by hippies, and in the last decade, it has been 'discovered' by holiday companies offering the cheap package at formerly beautiful, exclusive, caring hotels. I first witnessed this at the Ramada Renaissance hotel in 1993. £700 bought a winter fortnight, and still does. On that occasion the type of clients this attracted were British (and German) lager louts who spent all their time at the pool, tanning, drinking, belching, and swearing. At meal times they gorged on the 'international buffet' wanting steaks, burgers, pizzas, chips and the like, and avoiding all things Indian like poison. They never left the hotel, and it was irrelevant to them that they were in India, let alone Goa. All they wanted was to go home to show off their status-symbol of a winter sun tan. Imagine the shock to the local staff and Indian guests, who, till then genuinely believed that all Europeans still exuded the gentlemanly manners of the Raj. I felt saddened and embarrassed. It's bad enough to have to tolerate the lager lout as a home product, taking the curry industry downmarket, and worse losing our once highly-regarded reputation for decent behaviour, at international football matches and the dreaded Costa fortnight, but exporting them to India leaves Cosmos and their ilk with a lot to answer for in the name of their god – profits! Having got that off my chest, let's talk about Goan food. Firstly it is rarely found in Britain. Indeed only two resturants do it exclusively: Palms of Goa, w1 and Ma Goa. The Bombay Brasserie sw17 and Chutney Mary sw10 have excellent Goan cooks. Often they are female, and are always called 'auntie'. Even the BB has one. So has Ma Goa. Sushma Kapoor is the co-owner along with Deepak Kapoor, in fact she's his mum, not his auntie, so easy on the Ma Goa gags! And what of her food? As a regular visitor to Goa, I can vouch that it's as good and as near to home-cooking as it gets. Goan food is unique, having that Portuguese influence – any meat goes and pork is the favourite, as is the chilli. *Aficionados* must try the Vindaloo. But this isn't the formula interpretation of standard curry gravy, with two spoons of chilli powder and a chunk of potato (aloo). This is the real thing, based on the Portuguese dish, *Vinho d'alhos*, or wine vinegar and garlic. In the Goan version, pork is marinated with the above and plenty of chillies. It is then slow-cooked, and that's that, with nary a potato in sight! Ma Goa serve it in traditional earthenware Handis. Try Chorizo, Goan chilli pork sausage. There are many other Goan delights, too numerous to list here. Specials are on the blackboard. Advice is forthcoming. If you ask for Goan heat, you'll get it hot! Meat, chicken, fish and veg are all authentic. There are even Goan puds. But a word of caution. Please be patient. This is not your wham-bam-and-thank-you-ma'am, multi-dish, rapid-fire curry house. Relax with their chilled Portuguese Vinho Verde, and nibble something while you wait for your order to be cooked. Think *manyana*, as they do in Goa, and plan your next holiday there. Before you can say 'goan, goan, gone', a super meal will be with you. 'Groan, groan, groan, Pat,' says fact-verifier DMCK. 'and tomorrow is *tolice* in Portuguese.' 'A quick BIG rave about a restaurant which I think it's just "ab-fab". Real authentic stuff with great service'

SM. Even with the new extension its seating is a modest 50, so booking essential. Hours: Lunch: Weds.-Sun., and 6.30-11pm Mon.-Sat. A rarity, deserving our TOP 100 cachet. Sells Indian artifacts. Stocks Cobra.

MUNAL TANDOORI NEW ENTRANT   ©

393 Upper Richmond Road, SW15   ℂ 0181 876 3083

You'll find all the standards at this 65-seater, but try some Nepalese items, such as Chicken Bhutuwa, £4.95. Ask owner-manager Khem Ranamagar for explanations, and enjoy chef Bijaya Thapa's good food. Price check: Papadam 40p, CTM £5.30, Pullao Rice £1.80. Set meal £7.95. Minimum charge £8. Delivery: £10 minimum, 3-mile radius. Hours: 12-2.30pm; 6-11.30pm (12am Sat & Sun). Stocks Cobra.

SW16

MEMORIES OF INDIA   ©

109 Mitcham Lane, SW16   ℂ 0181 677 8756

M. Iqbal's restaurant seats just 30. Specials include: Chicken Langwaki, diced chicken with herbs, fresh tomato, cucumber and French beans. Papadam 35p, CTM £5.25, Pullao Rice £1.50. Delivery: £10 minimum, 2-mile radius. Hours: 6-11.30pm, Sunday Buffet £5.95 – 6-11pm.

MIRCH MASALA NEW ENTRANT   BYO

1416 London Road, SW16   ℂ 0181 679 1828

Mirch Masala, 'pepper mixture', is a good example of a London Balti house under another name, such as have dominated Southall and Wembley for years. It's an offspring of the ever-popular Karahi King, where meat is king, cutlery is out, and BYO is in, no corkage charge. This unlicensed cafe is pleasant, light and bright, air-conditioned and seats 70. Open kitchen, with unusual Kenyan-Asian specials by owner Raza Ali's brigade. Cassava chips (mogo) can substitute for papadoms, before you plough into a wide selection of dechi (saucepan) or karahi dishes, kebabs and all the trimmings. Most popular dish Karahi Methi Chicken. Good veggie stuff, too. Price check: Papadams 30p, CTM £6, Pullao Rice £1.50. Hours: 12pm-12am, Tues.-Sun. Newly-opened Branch: Lavender Hill SW11

SHAHEE BHEL POORIA   √ ©

1547 London Road, Norbury, SW16   © 0181 679 6275

Lebas Miah's 75-seater, opposite Norbury Station, serves Gujarati vegetarian/vegan food. Thalis and Dosas are the most popular dishes served. Specials include Chappati Chana (hot), chick peas marinated in a balanced blend of spices and sauce, served with green coriander, £1.70. Bhelpoori (cold), delicious mixture of Indian savouries blended with spices and exotic sauces which make this dish unique, £1.70. Dahi Vada (Bhalle) (cold), spicy black-pea-flour fritters, with yoghurt and sweet and sour sauce, £1.70. Rava Onion Dosa, a crispy onion vegetable pancake stuffed with delicately spiced potatoes, served with coconut chutney and Sambar, £4.10. House wine £5.50. Hours: 12-2.30.pm; 6-11pm. Sunday buffet. Stocks Cobra.

SPICE COTTAGE

78 High Road, Streatham, SW16   © 0181 677 1719

Praful Shah's restaurant, decorated in white with walnut fixtures and fittings, seats 40 (alcoves) with a party room for 30. Chef Abdul Rahim cooks formula curries and side dishes. Price check: Papadam 50p, CTM £5.80, King Prawn £9.90, Pullao Rice £1.60. Delivery: £15 minimum. Hours: 12-2pm (Mon.-Fri.) and 6-12. Stocks Cobra.

SW17 – Tooting

Watch out Southall! Upper Tooting Road (UTR) just gets better and better. For years, the area has reflected the varied roots of its Asian population. Its one kilometre, between Tooting Bec and Tooting Broadway tube stations, is home to two of London's best south Indian restaurants – Sree Krishna 192 UTR and Kolam 58, a Sri Lankan – Jaffna at the Broadway, three Gujarati vegetarians havens – Milan 158 and Kastoori 188 and Gossip 180. Veggy Indian sweet and snack takeaways include Ambala 48 and Alaudin 98, with Royal beyond UTR (north of Tooting Bec) while at Masaladar 121, you get Bhel Poori and meat curries alike. Handis 164 and Lahore Karahi at the Broadway represent Pakistan and fill the carnivore gap, Southall-style. As if that were not enough there are two formula Bangladeshi curry houses, the Peacock 242 and Nazim's which has niftily added Balti house. to its name. The shops are getting better and more varied too, with more openings, and longer hours. Sakoni 204-208 UTR is still the best Asian veg shop in London and there is no better Indian grocer than next-door Dadus, 210. There are several Sri Lankan grocers too. Utensils shops, sari boutiques and halal butch-

ers have sprung up too. Unlike Southall and Wembley, parking has not yet reached Sunday traffic-warden proportions but I fear it will soon. Meanwhile, UTR, with the tube so convenient, is an all-day curryholic's theme park. Here's more detail:

HANDIS

164 Upper Tooting Road, SW17   © 0181 672 6037

A 60-seater Pakistani restaurant owned by Mrs S. Sheikh. Managed by Mr J. Sheikh. Cooking down one entire side. The Handi is a clay cooking pot, and dishes are served either in this or in the karahi. 'Usual very high standard. Onion Bhajia particularly superb. Chicken Jalfrezi also great, plenty of chicken breast with onion, green pepper and lots of fresh chilli, garnished with a generous amount of ginger strips, great! Superb Chappati. Clean, unremarkable decor.' CT. Price check: Papadam 30p, CTM £5, Pullao Rice £2.25. House wine £6. Hours: 11am-11pm. Stocks Cobra.

JAFFNA HOUSE

90 High Street, Tooting Broadway, SW17   © 0181 672 7786

We don't mind the new license. But we do worry that K. Sivalogarajah's and M. Sivanandan's Jaffna, which built its name on its authentic, no compromise, chilli hot (as-it-should-be) Sri Lankan dishes (and south Indian) with its particularly popular different Friday, Saturday and Sunday specials, will turn over completely to its recently added range of tandoori items and north Indian curries cooked by Aziz and Kannan, They tell us Biryani is now their most popular dish. If the formula takes over, I suppose we only have the customers to blame. But why endanger this rarity? Why can't they go elsewhere for such things? There's enough choice nearby. Very cheap, huge choice of good food. Cash preferred, cheques minimum £5. Some credit cards accepted, minimum £15. Price check: Papadam 25p, CTM £4.25, Mutton Kotthu £2.50, Masala Dosai £1.50, Pullao Rice £1.25. Minimum charge £5. Delivery £15 minimum. Hours: 12-12, last sit-down orders 11pm. Stocks Cobra.

©	Curry Club discount (see page 6)	🍵	Unlicensed
√	Vegetarian		
BYO	Bring your own alcohol	⊞	Delivery/takeaway

KASTOORI

188 Upper Tooting Road, SW17   © 0181 767 7027

This African-Asian family specialize in both Gujarati and Kenyan vegetarian dishes. The former include Dahi Vadas and Kadhi, yoghurt and
besan sauce, with dumplings, and Katia Wahd, a tomato-based curry.
Karela Bharah is stuffed bitter gourd. The latter gives Cassava Chips,
Kasodi, sweetcorn in a peanut and yoghurt-based sauce, and Matoki,
plantain curry. Their Bhel Poori is a crunch snip at £2.10, and this is one
of the few places where you can experience Bhatura, giant puri bread,
£1, which puffs up to balloon-size when deep-fried. It's all the rage in
New York's curry houses at the moment, and about the only curry thing
NY does passably. Incidentally I wonder what are the 32 spices they
claim go into their garam masala? I can get to about twelve. Which
reminds me again of the US. Following a recent demo in Albuquerque,
in which I showed how to blend and roast my nine spice garam masala,
I was dogmatically told by a large, don't-mess-with-me blue-rinse, that
curry was a single spice which grows in Texas, not a complex Indian
blend! Average meal £12. Hours: 1230-2pm, Wed.-Sun. and 6-10.30pm
daily.

KOLAM   BYO ©

58-60 Upper Tooting Road, SW17   © 0181 767 2514

Established in 1982 by S Rajakumar. Seats 52 in one long thin dining
room which is decorated quite simply: pale pink wall paper, beechwood
chairs and red carpet. The food served is authentic South Indian, as they
have it in Tamil Nadu, plus standard north Indian items. It was two
years since we last ate here, but they remembered Dom, Erik and me,
plus Helena taking a break from the kids, and they welcomed us like
long lost friends. And friendly they are, albeit at freeze-frame slowness.
Manyana is far too fast, which again reminded us greatly of India. As
ever, patience will reward you with a good inexpensive meal, and as ever
go for the South Indian delights, which is what they know best. Masala
Dosa £3, Sambar £2.50 and Coconut Chutney, still as good as ever.
BYO is allowed: £1 corkage. Price check: Papadam 50p, CTM £4.25,
Pullao Rice £1.75. Hours: 12-2.30pm, Tues.-Sun./6-11pm (12pm on Sat.).
Stocks Cobra.

LAHORE KARAHI   BYO

1 High Street, Tooting Broadway, SW17   ℂ 0181 767 2477

A Karahi-house in Tooting! It's been open since late 1995 and was long-awaited, now much-patronised by Asians, and is being copied around and about the area. It's Southall in style and Southall in name, though, as far as we know, the owners are new to the game, having copied, not without hiccups, an established formula. For example, they originally offered a choice of dishes unlikely to be eaten by most of Tooting's Asians, such as Haleem – ground meat and wheat grains – and Raan. The former a central Indian Muslim speciality from Hyderabad and Pakistan, the latter a Kashmiri Mogul dish. Both are complex to cook. Not even Southall offers them. So out they've gone, and sticking to kebabs, tandoori and Punjabi food is a safer bet for them for now. And it's all good stuff. Maybe a dish-of-the-day concept, at a future date, can bring back these unusual items. Cash preferred. Waiter service, with the cooking on view. Unlicensed and BYO welcomed. 'Exceptional flavours,' CHC. Average meal around £10. Hours: 12pm-12am.

MASALEDAR   NEW ENTRANT   NO ALCOHOL

121 Upper Tooting Road, SW17   ℂ 0181 767 7676

A smart frontage is not the norm on the Tooting street scene, not yet anyway. But it draws attention to itself and, no doubt, it won't be long before others copy. But what lies behind the smokey plate glass? Terracotta tiles on split-level floor and table. Plants in pots and trailing. Smart up-lighters behind large halved karahis. You can sit outside watching all this through that window, at the five pavement tables. But the food is good. Starters include Bhel Poori, and Mandazi, samosa-shaped deep-fried bread with an African-Asian name, both £1.50. Our advice is to stay with vegetable main course dishes, but if you must have meat/chicken there's ample choice. Don't expect a wine list – strict Muslim rules apply and BYO is not permitted. Price check: Papadam 40p, Chilli Chicken £3.95, Veg Thali £3.50. Hours: 12pm-12am.

©	Curry Club discount (see page 6)		Unlicensed
√	Vegetarian		
BYO	Bring your own alcohol	⊞	Delivery/takeaway

MILAN   √ ©

158 Upper Tooting Road, SW17   ℰ 0181 767 4347

If it's robust meat you want, you're in the wrong joint. Taj Mehta's, this vegetarian café is just the sort of place we like to recommend. It's unpretentious, and unexpectedly licensed and a/c. But for the vegetarian, what more could you ask for? If I were you, I'd start with papadams and their adorable fresh home-made relishes. Next I'd ask for their fabulous Bhel Poori. I'd avoid the Masala Dosa (they do it better at Sree Krishna), and I'd go for its subtly-spiced Gujarati curries, made largely from besan flour and yoghurt, spiced with turmeric and curry leaves. If it's new to you, ask for help, or for a Thali, from £4.50. The dish of the day is always a good option. And do try the fresh Rotla (millet bread). Leave some room for the terrific Indian sweets on display. And buy some fresh 'Bombay mix' items. 'Another good one' SM. Minimum charge still a ridiculous £2. Average meal under £10. Takes no credit cards so cash preferred. Price check: Papadam 35P, Masala Dosa £3, Nan £1. Sunday lunch £5.75. Hours: 10am-9.30pm, (10pm on Sat. & Sun.). Stocks Cobra.

PEACOCK TANDOORI   ©

242 Upper Tooting Road, SW17   ℰ 0181 672 8770

Yogi Anand's 52-seater is tasteful, warm and cosy with Tooting Tudor-beam ceiling. Chef Baboo does all the favourite, and his specials include: Batair-e-Khas (quail) £7.65, and Rajma, kidney bean curry. Price check: Papadam 50p, CTM £5.60, Batair-e-Khas, Pullao Rice £1.90. Peshwari Nan £1.95. House wine £7.95, Delivery. Hours: 6pm-12am.

SREE KRISHNA   TOP 100   ©

192-194 Tooting High Street, SW17   ℰ 0181 672 4250

Sree Krishna is a revered, playful Hindi god. His picture is in this corner restaurant, which has been in our Guide since we started. Taken over in 1988 by T. Haridas, J. Dharaseelan and Mrs Pillai. This unpretentious 120-seat south Indian restaurant, shows exactly how Keralan cuisine should be done at totally affordable prices. The slightly tacky decor transports one straight back to Kerala, and the food transports you to heaven. It's a no-frills place. Paper tablecloths, methodical but sure service, bizarre toilet location, and plenty of regulars, Indian and white. Cobra, Kingfisher and Kaliani Indian beers are all here, and they never seem to muddle the labelled glasses. Its specialities are south Indian vegetarian food. We always start with a Papadam 35p and the hot red coconut chutney, and/or the hotter green one, then we go for the best Masala Dosa in town, £1.95 − a thin, crispy pancake made from fermented rice/urid-flour batter (wherin lies the secret of success), wrapped around a tasty mashed potato curry. Nobody does it as well, not even the India Club, wc2. It explains why it is this restaurant's most popular dish. Take it accompanied with Rasam (pepper soup), and Sambar (thin lentil curry) £3.45. Other south Indian house specials include Rava Dosa, a light and crispy pancake made of semolina, rice flour, cummin and spices, served with coconut chutney and Sambar £4.15. Uthappam: a South Indian version of pizza made of rice and lentil flour with a topping of chopped onions, green chillies, tomatoes, curry leaves and ginger, served with a special chutney and Sambar. Poori Masala: a fried South Indian puffed bread made of wheat flour, served with lightly spiced potato masala £2.45. Vadai, doughnut made of black grams, ginger, onion, curry leaves, green chillies, soft centre with crunchy exterior, served with chutney £1.35. Our bill for two never exceeds £20, with Cobra and service, but could obviously be twice that if we pigged out! House wine £7.50. Minimum charge £5. 10% service charge, Credit cards accepted. Remains high in our TOP 100. Hours: 12-3pm; 6-11pm Sun.-Thurs. (12am on Fri. & Sat). Branch: Ragam, Cleveland St, w1. Stocks Cobra.

SW18

NAZMIN BALTI HOUSE   ©

398 Garratt Lane, Earlsfield, SW18   ℭ 0181 946 2219

An oldie (1966) taken over in 1994 by Shajan Miah, who is also the head chef. He cooks Bangladeshi styled curries and accompaniments for his 40-seater restaurant, which is very cosy, decorated with flowers and foliage. Price check: Papadam 45p, CTM £5.50, Baltis from £6.95, Pullao Rice £1.60. Peshwari Nan £1.50. House wine £6.95. Minimum charge £8. Delivery: £12 minimum. Hours: 12-2.30pm; 6pm-12am. Stocks Cobra.

SARKHELS   NEW TO OUR TOP 100   BEST NEWCOMER

199 Replingham Road, Southfields, SW18   © 0181 870 1483

'When we first heard that Udit Sharkel, was leaving the Bombay
Brasserie (sw7), we thought it was a posting back to Bombay. Déjà-vu!
When we heard that he and his delightful Chinese wife, Veronica were
about to open their own venture in Wimbledon we were really excited.
Veronica once managed the Bombay Taj Mahal Intercontinetal's flagship restaurant, the Tanjore in Bombay. The site could be better. It's on
the yellow-lined, outside curve of a bend on a busy road. Evening parking is feasible. The place looks unlikely. The shop front of the
restaurant isn't the most attractive in the world, but don't be put off;
inside is smart and simple, tiny with stylish white walls, terracotta-tiled
floor, 35 small wooden chairs at white-linened intimate tables of 2 and
4. It is uncluttered giving a cool and relaxing feel. We hadn't booked and
it was empty at 8pm on a Tuesday. We were lucky – by 9pm it was
packed. There is a good menu with all our Indian favourites, and a daily
specials board. Plain and spicy Papadams with three home-made chutneys, thick Mint Raita, chunky Mango Pickle and Mango Chutney,
were promptly delivered. Service is very professional. We ordered a
bottle of French red wine. While this was being served, Pat and I argued
over who was having the Sev Puri, crisp round flour crackers with cubed
potato, onion, chillies, sprouted moong beans, a mix of sauces topped
with gram flour vermicelli £2.95. Reluctantly, he decided I could share.
Ragara Pattice, tempered mashed potato cakes served with spiced chick
peas and chutneys (one was clearly chilli enhanced tomato ketchup),
£2.95. We had a third starter, from the specials, Prawn stuffed
Mushroom, baby prawns, spicy mashed potato and fried onion, covered
in sev and deep-fried. Everything was delicious and quickly disap-
peared. For our main courses we ordered from the menu and specials
board, chef's pièce de résistance Hyderabadi Lamb Biriani, garnished
with an onion tarka served in a beaten copper Handi with matching lid
dum-sealed, traditionally by dough. When the waiter released the lid,
saffron fragranced rice steamed into the air. Oven-roasted Shank of
Lamb, smothered in a creamy sauce – the meat literally fell off the
bone, it was so tender. Chicken Makhani £5.95, this is CTM, except it
is cooked the traditional way and is truly delicious, smokey, spicy with
chilli, tomatoey, smooth with cream and butter but not sickly and not
one sultana in sight! – even Pat liked it. Two vegetable dishes, both
served in copper Handis with lids, Baigan Bhurta, char-grilled, mashed

and spiced aubergines £4.95, not quite char-grilled enough for us – we like a really smokey flavour and Sarson, mustard leaf, a stronger flavour than spinach, with slivers of fresh garlic. Accompanied with a tandoor-cooked Laccha Paratha, a much neglected bread, light and buttery. BB food at Southfield's prices.' DBAC. 'Wonderful service. Very good food.' DW. Deservedly goes straight into our prestigious TOP 100. Hours: 6-10.30pm (11pm on Fri. & Sat.). Sun. only: 12-2.30pm. Stocks Cobra.

SW19 – Wimbledon

POPADOME   NEW ENTRANT

186, The Broadway, Wimbledon, SW19

'Small, seats 28. Service was unhurried. Kitchen entirely on view. Stuffed pepper £1.75 to start comes whole, complete with lid, stuffed with Pullao Rice, sweetcorn, red peppers, green beans and peas. Gently spiced, very fresh flavour, delicious. Balti Mixed Vegetables £4.95, Vegetable Madras £2.75, not much difference between them, Green Dal £2.50, whole green lentils, gentle garlic taste, lovely. Garlic Nan and Coriander Nan both £1.55, very definite flavours. The waitress rushed off to do a delivery – forget a moped ridden by someone with a death wish – she drove off in the family Mercedes – that's Wimbledon for you!' JM. Price check: Papadam 35p, CTM £4.95, Pullao Rice £1.50. Delivery. Hours: 5.30-11pm, closed Mon.

ZUJUMA'S   NEW TO OUR TOP 100

58a Wimbledon Hill Road, SW19   ✆ 0181 879 0916

Hyderabadi cookery writer Zuju Shareef's evolved food and brewer Whitbread did not mix. Her perfectionism and their aspirations for a nation-wide mass market chain misfired. Somehow she extricated herself from the arrangement, closed for a rethink and a redec, and reopened in 1998, with a change of menu. Though modern in the bright spice colours currently in vogue, the food is closer to authenic. The menu features Mushqaabs, a main course served with a selection of accompaniments. Baghare Baigan, a classic Hyderbadi preparation of aubergine in a dark tangy sauce with coconut and sesame seeds. Narangi Dopiaza, succulent lamb lifted by the zest of citrus fruit. Fez-un-Jun, an Iranian dish of chicken in walnut and pomegranate sauce. 'Delicious and HUGE.' DBAC. 'Infinitely better, but lacks variety, though homely.' DW. 'Sampled each of the home made puddings: Qoobani £3.50, stewed Hunza apricots, Jaam Ka Mitha £3.75, poached guavas, Andon Ki Peosi £3.75 a golden spongy egg and saffron dessert, sweet but not sickly – fabulous!' DBAC. Hours: 6.30-11pm. Stocks Cobra.

London W

Area: West End postcode W1
  and West London W2 to W14
Population: 624,000
Number of restaurants in county: 313
Number in Guide: 39

W1

ANWARS NEW TO OUR TOP 100	BYO
64 Grafton Way, W1	© **0171 387 6664**

Old hands will remember the Grafton Way's Bombay Emporium, when London had just a couple of spice stores. In 1962, Anwars opened down the street, and buying spices had a new excitement. It was taken over in 1985 by Muhammad Afzal Zahid. His 52-seater serves gutsy, spicy Pakistani food and is redolent of Southall. Basic, clean café-style. Make your choice from the serving counter, from the dishes of the day (no menu as such), then carry your tray to a formica table, jugs of water in place, and enjoy it. It has good local Asian patronage. 'Another little gem. Wide selection on display, take a tray and choose. Food authentic and first class, plenty of underlying flavour.' MW. 'Our favourite. We go every 2 to 3 weeks for cheap and cheerful wonderful food. Needs to be in the TOP 100'. SR. (You're quite right – don't know why I didn't give my erstwhile water hole this accolade before!- Ed) – Price check: Papadam 30p, Biryani £3.30, Karahi Chicken £4 and Haleem £3. Hours: 12-11pm.

©	Curry Club discount (see page 6)	🍵	Unlicensed
√	Vegetarian		
BYO	Bring your own alcohol	🔳	Delivery/takeaway

CARAVAN SERAI TOP 100   BYO ALLOWED

50 Paddington Street, Marylebone, W1   ℭ 0171 935 1208

Mr Nayed's 50-seat Afghani restaurant est. 1975 starts with a very nice
touch – free hot Pakoras with chutney, given at the beginning while you
examine the menu. Try the Logery – leg of lamb, flavoured with spices
and saffron – or the Sekonia (skewered lamb, cooked in the tandoor).
Ashaks are pastries, filled with a spicy leek and mince filling, with
yoghurt. Kohi is roast lamb, spiced with Char Masala and blackcurrant.
Yoghurt and garlic, root vegetables and pulses are also popular. End
with Carrot Kulfi or Coconut Halva. 'Comfortable restaurant with
attractive decor. Interesting menu, Starters delicious. Spiced Roast
Lamb on the bone was so tender it fell off the bone. First class vegetables, aubergine particularly tasty. First rate meal.' MW. House wine £9.95,
mineral water £3.50. BYO allowed: £2 corkage. 20% discount on takeaway. Hours: 12-3pm; 6-11.30pm.

CHOR BIZARRE NEW TO OUR TOP 100

16 Albemarle Street, W1   ℭ 0171 629 9802

In Delhi the Chor Bazaar (literally 'thieves' markets') is a kind of permanent car-boot-sale, where you can buy anything at knock-down
prices. Canny entrepreneurs Rohit Khattar and M.Kaul bought the furniture from there for their hugely succesful Delhi restaurant. No two
items were the same. Judging by our mail bag, it works, the more so in
London because the 85-seat dining room is so totally unexpected.
Hence the linguistic twist from 'Bazaar' to 'Bizarre'. 'Antiquities' abound
and one table, for example, is encased in an '18th-century four-poster
bed' from Calcutta. While it is worth visiting for the interior alone, the
cuisine on offer gives a rare opportunity to savour chef Deepinder
Sondhi's Kashmiri house specials which include: Goshtaba, a Kashmiri
speciality of minced lamb balls cooked in a yoghurt gravy £12; Kerala
Prawn Curry, prawns cooked in coconut milk and black pepper gravy
£13.50; Nadroo Yakhani, lotus stem in spiced yoghurt gravy £7. 'The
much-publicised decor is certainly is quite amazing. Made very welcome. Menu is marvellous. Prices are high, but many of the dishes are
large, and intended for sharing. Overall, a very good restaurant, definitely a "would-go-back" venue.' HJC. Better speak to the bank manager
for an overdraft before you try this place, or perhaps increase your
mortgage, prices certainly aren't bizarre but bi-gantic. Price check:

Papadam complimentary, CTM £10, Pullao Rice £3.95, house wine
£11.95. Service 12½%. Hours: 12-3pm; 6-11.30pm, Sun. 6-10.30pm. Stocks
Cobra.

DHAKA BRASSERIE   NEW ENTRANT   ©

36-38, Charlotte Street. W1

'From the ashes of the Neel Akash (ex Hanway Street – its home demolished), rises Sheikh Ashik Miah's 110-seater. The new site is a lot
nicer with additional seating downstairs.' RL. Hours: 12-3pm; 6pm-12am.

GURKHA BRASSERIE   ©

23 Warren Street, W1   ✆ 0171 383 4985

'Genuine Nepalese restaurant. Superb decor with Gurkha photos on
the walls (including owner Hari K.C.'s father with the Queen at a regi-
mental do). The thatched hut decor transports you straight to Nepal,
as does the food. Nepalese food is very different and must be sampled.
Momos (spicy dumplings) are highly recommended as are all the
dishes.' GH. 'Try the Choala – cold lamb with garlic ... hmmm!' DL.
Branch: 756 Finchley Road, NW11.

INDIAN YMCA CANTEEN

41 Fitzroy Square, W1   ✆ 0171 387 0411

Nothing changes at this favourite eating hole. It's the downstairs can-
teen for the YMCA residents, many of whom are Asian students. It's
basic, unsophisticated but authentic Indian school-dinner style food.
No bookings, no licence, no BYO and no nonsense! Outsiders welcome, but only now at lunchtimes. Take a plastic tray, join the
always-busy queue. Point to your choice which is unceremoniously dol-
loped onto your plate. Top up with chupatties, tea or coffee, and pay at
the till, cash only. It's absurdly cheap – hard to exceed £4. Then jostle
for space at a shared formica table. The food may not be brilliant, but
the company can be, when you share your table with talkative, friendly
students. 'Marvellous.' MW. Price check: Lamb or Chicken Curry £2,
various Vegetable Curries £1 to £1.20. Hours: 12.30-1.30pm daily,
prompt!

MAHARANI

77 Berwick Street, W1   © 0171 437 8568

Est. 1971 by S. Khan, F.R. Choudhury and A. Kalam (who manages).
Chef Abu Fazal cooks good curry house stuff. 'Heinz was the only customer, and the one "aged" staff member took the order, cooked it with
much banging and clattering, produced a meal only loosely related to
the order, which was, I am assured, extremely good, then entertained
him with the philosophy of life throughout.' MWS. Price check:
Papadam 60p, CTM £7.25, Pullao Rice £2.25, Peshwari Nan £2.10.
Hours: 12pm-12am (1am on Sat.). Stocks Cobra.

PALMS OF GOA   NEW ENTRANT

12 Charlotte Street, W1   © 0171 636 1668

Established in 1994 by Eugene Dias, who also manages. His restaurant
seats 40 and serves Goan and regular curries and side dishes. House
specials include: Lamb Xacutti, prepared with coconuts, vinegar and
hot spices £5.95, Goan Green Fish Masala, spicy sauce with fresh
coriander and chillies £5.95 and Pumpkin Curry, a speciality of
Mangalore £2.95. Price check: Papadam 35p, CTM £6.50, Pullao Rice
£1.95. Delivery. Hours: 12-3.30pm/6-11.30pm. Closed Sun. and '2 weeks
for Christmas'. Stocks Cobra.

LA PORTE DES INDES   TOP 100   ©

32 Bryanston Street, W1   © 0171 224 0055

It cost £2.5 million for designer Yves Burton to convert the enormous
former Mayfairia ballroom into the country's most extraordinary
Indian restaurant. Its entrance is unremarkable, tucked away one block
behind the Marble Arch Odeon. Parking can be hell, though there's an
NCP down the street. The reception area is deceptive, too. It's attractive enough, with its dark, polished wood floor, but it gives you no hint
of what is to come. But prowl around and you begin to see where the
money went. Go down the nearest stairs into the bar. It is made of cane,
with bamboo furniture and palms in beaten copper pots, and it's OK
but still not breathtaking. There's a sandstone arch and a 40-foot water-
fall, too, but take a good look at the sweeping staircase and make a
point of going up and down it. It is made of white marble with pink
sandstone balustrades, imported especially from India's pink city,

Jaipur. Airy, domed skylights enhance La Porte's daytime atmosphere, making it a different place in darkness. There is a forest of jungle plants, a wealth of Indian artefacts, and antiques. Ask to see the adorable antique bronze coconut scraper, and the range of eating rooms, including the tiny private dining rooms, seating 12 and 24 respectively, to areas of 60-plus.

La Porte purports to present cuisine from 'French India'. True the French did belatedly arrive there, in 1664, staying until 1954. But despite a few skirmishes, their minor presence had little effect on either India or the British. According to Indians who live in the main ex-French area, Pondicherry there is no such thing as Pondicherry cuisine! Be that as it may, the opening section of the main menu, a massive missive, gives French names to Indian dishes, described in English. I suppose 'beignet' sounds better than 'doughnut', and 'Cassoulet de Fruits de Mer', £11 more impressive than 'sea food stew'. Kari des Boulettes, £9.80 undoubtedly sound more enticing than meat ball curry! Demoiselles, £7.50 are defined as unmarried females in my dictionary, and it's not for me to say whether referral to 'juicy scallops' is appropriate. Poulet Rouge, £12.80 – chicken in red, creamy sauce – sounds suspiciously like CTM to me! One or two recipes have Creole features: Rasoul, £4.90 is a samosa with a Creole sauce. Couside, £5 is a Creole broth. Main courses include Magret de Canard Pulivaar – Mme Lourde Swamy's Duck, £12.50 – and Policha Meen is Mme Blanc's Mullet, £11.75. If all this sounds a bit pretentious, all I can say is that dining out is meant to be theatre on occasions. And I guess that La Porte des Indes sounds more impressive than India Gate! The second section of the menu is no less costly but it drops the French and offers many other classic dishes from all over India. For those who wish 'to try a bit of everything', the last page's 'menu maison' sounds better than 'set meals', at £31 per person without soup, or £33 with minimum two people, and there is a seasonal menu changed monthly at £18. The lunch presentation of food on raised copper salvers is opulent and attractive, and you can eat your fill for £15. On Sundays it's called brunch, at the same price, with a live jazz band. And even if some of the prices have come down since last year, and though there is no service charge, be warned: à La Porte Les Prix du Menu Français sont Très Chers, but at least they're half those of Le Gavroche – but there they *are* French!! As you have gathered I am not impressed by the use, outside France, of perfectly ordinary French food words on British menus, no matter how grand. (Imagine if the French described their food in English to bump up the prices!) As for this Marble Arch Frindain, I suspect it evolved from the Brussels branch. It is a pity that with all this French influence, the wine list (sorry carte des vins), though large, is really weak on the new world.

But please don't get me wrong. I am impressed by La Porte – the ambience, the decor, the service and the food is all as good as it gets. I gave it our Best in UK award last time, and though I've now moved that award on, it does not detract from Mernosh's fabulous food. Indeed, many Indians have now 'found' La Porte. One restaurateur couple, whose own top-100 venture has graced these pages since we began, have now switched their weekly 'Cinema and Chinese' Tuesday night off to an intimate night out at La Porte. They tell us they love it, and others do too. We have many contented reports from regulars and one-offs alike. Malcolm Gluck was less complimentary, finding the food too un-curry-house to recommend wines for it. 'When are they going to put some spices in?' he asked. And this is an occasional cause of complaint from those unused to authentic Indian food, as far removed from the formula as it can be. The French connection may be tenuous, but Mernosh Mody's cooking keeps it high in our TOP 100. Hours: 12-2.30pm (Sun.-Fri.) and 7-12pm (Mon.-Sat.). Sun. 6-10.30pm. Branches: Blue Elephant Thai, sw6, and others in Europe. Stocks Cobra.

RAGAM SOUTH INDIAN TOP 100   ©

57 Cleveland Street, W1   © 0171 636 9098

Established in 1984 by J. Dharmaseelan, Haridas and S. Pillai. This restaurant seats 34 upstairs, 20 downstairs. Chef Nair cooks standard curries and, good though they are, our advice is to concentrate only on the authentic south Indian food. Uthappam, a pizza-style pancake made of rice and lentil flour with a topping of onions, green chillies, tomatoes and herbs, served with Sambar and Coconut chutney £4.20. Kaalan, made with yoghurt, coconut and sweet mango, goes well with rice £2.80. Service 10%. House wine £9. Price check: Papadam 40p, Pullao Rice £2.60. It remains safely in our TOP 100. Delivery: mini-mum £10, city area only. Hours: 12-3pm; 6-11.30pm. Sat. 12-3pm. Sun. 6-11pm. Branch: Sree Krishna, Tooting, sw17. Stocks Cobra.

©	Curry Club discount (see page 6)		Unlicensed
√	Vegetarian		
BYO	Bring your own alcohol		Delivery/takeaway

RAJ TANDOORI   ©

72 Berwick Street, W1   ✆ 0171 439 0035

Abdul Haque and chef Rouf's 40-seater, does an 'honest-to-goodness standard menu, well done' GR. Price check: Papadam 50p, CTM £6.50, , Pullao Rice £1.85, Chutney & Pickle 50p. Sunday lunch £5.95. Hours: 12-3pm; 5.30-12pm. Fri. & Sat. 12pm-12am. Stocks Cobra.

RASA NEW ENTRANT   √

6 Dering Street, W1   ✆ 0171 629 1346

It seems Das Sreedharan's vegetarian Rasa does two full sessions every night, plus a full week-day lunch trade. It shows. With no room to move, the atmosphere was hurried, the service patronising. A good start was made with Rasa's unique pre-starters, £4 and the home-made chutneys, £2.50. The fried starters £4.25 each, were weak and samey, and would benefit from being daintier. Despite a vain attempt to make our own choice of main course, nanny-knew-best, and we were bossed into accepting four set meals, £22.50 each, with, it transpired, enough food to serve eight, and insufficient table space to set down all the dishes. Maybe that would have been OK, but when we finished, the plentiful remaining food was whipped away without nanny even asking if we'd like a doggie bag. Some of these dishes were true Keralan, and were superb in appearance, texture, colour and taste. All that was lacking, curiously, was a lentil dish. We only had room for one pudding between us – nothing more nor less than a fancifully named, average-tasting banana fritter. The place is so tiny that there's hardly room to breath. The tables with four seats may be OK for the couples prevailing that night, but not for four, and the chairs were too short in the squab to be comfortable. But there's no chance of comfort. Das's pack-em-in policy leads to muddled service, with no one asking if we were OK, things either arriving twice or not at all, and stress clearly showing all round. The awkward-looking party waiting for our 9pm shift-change could have had our table 20 minutes earlier had I not had to ask repeatedly for the bill. Who said there's a recession on? True it included two bottles of wine, but £150.75 for four, hugely boosted by a 12½% service charge, already on the bill, described as 'optional', makes this one of the most expensive Indian restaurants in London, especially when you consider that vegetables are so very much cheaper than meat, and easier to cook! Good food, some of it excellent, most of it Keralan, let down as described. Get that right and it could be in our TOP 100. Branch: Rasa 55 Church St, N16.

SOHO SPICE TOP 100

124-126 Wardour Street, W1   © 0171 434 0808

Amin Ali's 180-seat is on two floors. Striking and spirited decor. Shiny wood floor, aqua blues and mint greens on the ground floor, and reds and saffron downstairs. As expected, the breakfast experiment failed, just as Stanley Krett's Greek Street attempt did a decade before. Soho Spice now doesn't open until later, so at least the staff get a lie in! Kuldeep Singh's short but intriguing menu all-day offerings include such starters as vermicelli-coated, golden-fried Spiced Prawns, £4.50, Chicken Wings or Bhajis £3.50, Papri, mini poories with sweet and sour yoghurt dressing £3.50. Main courses come with pullao rice, dal, nan and vegetables: Sula Salmon, classical Rajasthani Tandoori gravy, £8.95. Chilli Aubergines, cooked in yoghurt, peanut and coconut sauce, £7.95. Jungli Maas is still there, with the rather less alluring name 'Hot Lamb Curry', £8.95. Originally meat was caught and cooked with ghee and dry red chillies, for hunting parties in the Rajasthan jungle. It's from the concrete jungle that the parties prevail at Soho Spice. It's the haunt not hunt of the Soho suits, spearing the bill with the prestigious corporate credit card. 'Deserves its TOP 100 placing. It may be the future of curry houses, but you will never replace the tiny, dark, empty venue with dodgy music in the background. Food, service, and Mango Lassi all exactly what you want.' RDL. Service: 12½%. House wine £10.95, mineral water £2.75. Hours: 11.30am-12am. Sat. 12pm-12.30am. Sun. 12-10pm. Branch: Red Fort W1

TAMARIND TOP 100 BEST CHEF AWARD

20 Queen Street, Mayfair, W1   © 0171 629 3561

If you come by car they'll valet it for you (evenings only). The welcome is as good as ever, and the staircase down to the action is no obstacle. The dining room is spacious and the 100 seats do not feel cramped. The decor, in tones of blonde, gold, copper, brass and pine, is Mayfair not Madras, Todhunter not Tandoori, and subdued not sub-continent. The main feature is two long glass wall panels, displaying six metre pink silk saris. I still dislike their pallid look, but I'm still smitten with the

wrought iron chairs. Still, love or hate either, you can't eat 'em. I told
last time how Oberoi-trained chef Atul Kochhar found himself with no
chef help when the restaurant opened in 1995. Chefs from Delhi, planning to arrive in our summer, were delayed by months of work permit
nonsense caused by the obduration of British immigration (they say
Indian bureaucracy, originally learned from us, has evolved into an art-
form of rubber-stamping and immobility, but those wallahs can still
teach the subcontinent a thing or two!). The chefs arrived in December
just as the first (and only) snow fell that winter. Finding themselves
without dozens of minions (kitchen help comes cheap in Delhi) and
taking an instant, pathological dislike to the English climate, they last-
ed about seven days before high-tailing it back to Delhi! Kochhar
continued slogging it out on his own, refusing to compromise his time-
consuming touches, such as long preps for individual dishes, and
home-made chutneys, which have always made this restaurant stand out.
Atul's courage paid off and he now has a well-coached team which has
matured into Bhalla Papri Chaat, dumplings of lentil with cummin,
yoghurt and mint sauce £4.80. Chicken Liver Masala, £5.80. is a spicy
melt-in-the-mouth appetizer, as is Atul's Shami Kebab, £4.80. There is
a choice of kebabs and tandooris, the making of which is on view,
behind glass, culminating in the platter selection, £28 for two. The small
selection of eight curries from £13.50-17, is perhaps as minimalist as the
decor, with just two prawn, one fish, three chicken (e.g. Murgh
Khurchan, strips of chicken with spring onion, ginger, pepper and
tomatoes £13.50) and two meat dishes, but this allows the kitchen to create each dish as its own entity and not from a central stock-pot. The
result is a delicacy of touch found in the best Indian homes. There is a
satisfactory range of vegetable dishes, including some classics, all £4.80.
There are two good birianis and a selection of breads, and if you have
not seen a Romali Roti – handkerchief bread, £2.50 – being 'thrown',
ask to see it. It is a skill that takes years to learn, so is rarely found in
UK restaurants. A lump of dough is spun rotating into the air (pizza-
style) repeatedly until it is like a huge round handkerchief. It is then
cooked until it goes as pink as those pallid saris and just as silky.
Service, headed by Patrice Mossadek, is equally silky and proficient. Of
course, all of this does not come cheap. Remember where we are!
Mayfair does not come cheap! Tamarind is at the top end of Indian
restaurant pricing. The average dinner will cost at least £40, assisted by
a 12½% service charge. The daily lunch (closed Sat.) is £16.50, though be
prepared for a relatively small plateful that might leave trenchermen

wanting. Price check: Papadam 50p, Murgh Makhani £13.50, Pullao Rice £4., Nan £2.50. House wine £13.50, mineral water £4. Delivery: Mayfair area. Hours: 12-3pm (Mon.-Fri.)/6-11.30pm (10.30pm Sun.).

TASTE OF MUGHAL   ©

29 Great Windmill Street, W1   ℂ 0171 439 8044

M.S. Khan and Abdul Khalam's good, formula curry. Price check: Papadam 40p, CTM £5.95, Pullao Rice £1.95. Set meal £6.95. Service 10%. Hours: 12-11.45pm. Stocks Cobra.

VEERASWAMY   TOP 100

99-101 Regent Street, W1   ℂ 0171 734 1401

When Namita Panjabi and Ranjit Mathrani of Chutney Mary (SW10) fame bought Britain's oldest Indian restaurant (founded 1926) its reputation had been at rock-bottom for a decade. They knew they would soon restore it to better things, concerning management and food, but what to do with the decor? Replace the nondescript hotel-foyer look, yes, but should they do a Raj recreation? 'My dears,' said some of their friends, 'you must bring back the good old days!' (whatever they are). So what would you do with an institution blessed with the best site in Britain, which has been patronised for decades by teams of opinionated Raj colonels, Indian foodies, and old fogeys, coupled with undiscerning tourists and suits on corprate business? You give the place a re-launch which will take it fighting into the next century, and give it the best chance it's had since the sixties, to last another 70 years. If it means sweeping out the Raj, so what. It's only a sentimental memory now, anyway. More important was to sweep out the lazy chefs, the complacent management, and for that matter, if they don't appreciate it, the former fusty-crusty customers too. This is brave stuff, and not without criticism. How was it done? The street entrance is still on the aptly-named Swallow Street. Go up the stairs one floor, or take the lift. Once there, the geography never felt right in its previous incarnation. Now it does. The first masterstroke was moving the entrance position to amidships, (where it once was apparently) so that dining areas are to your left and your right, making the 130 seats feel more intimate. The floors are polished expensive hardwood, the lighting is modern, the view to Regent Street dominant. The small reception table is discreet, and the wine glass display is a work of art. The walls are painted in vibrant glowing earth colours: aubergine, saffron, garam masala, coriander leaf. Discreet artefacts and etched glass take it far, far away from its early days. The old upstairs room has been connected with a new staircase and is planned to be added later as a further dining area. But you do not let your customers forget Veeraswany's USP. A few carefully select-ed pictures of yore are displayed on a small wall area to remind us of its heritage. 'Wonderful, talented and stunningly modern transform-ation. Some might not like it, but they are in the minority – it is truly amazing. It is vibrant and energetic, forward thinking and for the young at heart.' DBAC. The management is in the hands of Preman Mohan with his deputy, Andreas Kirshnev, and is skilled and smooth. Cooking is headed by Gowtam Kumar. Start with popadam or the more unusual rice vadam with home-made chutneys. Choose from a dozen or so starters, which include oysters and mussels. Main course dishes come with rice or nan and vegetable curries. Roghan Josh, from Lucknow, lamb shanks slow-cooked in an intense broth for 5 to 6 hours till the meat is falling off the bone, served with rice and vegetables, £11, is the most popular dish. Malabar Prawn Curry with fresh turmeric and raw mango served with rice and vegetable £11.50. 'Started Vada with lentil dumpling in yoghurt, £3.50 and delicious main course of Chicken Tikka, rice, chickpeas and salad. Superb food.' RL 'Chutney and Vadams, Pani Puri (Bhel), very small, surprised that they were cold and far too much runny tamarind dip. Fishcakes, much better, tasty, nicely served. Roghan Josh, flavoursome. Did not like the austere basic decor and thought it overpriced.' GCM. (Perhaps the menu should state when a dish is intended to be cold.) 'Pani Puri is served as it should be, quite cold, and is quite delicious.' NBD. House wine £9.95. Price check: Papadam 50p, CTM £10.50, Pullao Rice £1.50, Nan £1.50. Hours: 12-2.30pm and with pre-theatre from 5.30-11.30pm (Sun. 10.30pm). Stocks Cobra.

WOODLANDS   √ ©

77 Marylebone Lane, W1   © 0181 835 1799

A branch of Mr Sood's well-liked, small chain of southern Indian veg-etarian restaurants. Managed by My Ullur, it seats 75, is decorated in sponge painted blue walls and Indian artifacts. The bar is made of black granite.Chef Rao's house specials include Cashewnut Pakoda (*sic.*), cashew nuts coated in batter with aromatic spices and deep-fried, £2.75. Kancheepuram Idli, soft rice puffs with chilli, spices and cashewnuts, £3.25. Eight varieties of Dosa, £3.50 to £4.95. Service 12½%. Price check:

Papadam £1, Pullao Rice £3.50. House wine £9, Hours: 12-2.45pm; 6-10.45pm. Branches: SW1 and Wembley, Middlesex. Stocks Cobra.

W2

BOMBAY PALACE

**50 Connaught Street,
Hyde Park Square, W2**   ✆ **0171 723 8855**

'Although in general it was okay, we were not thrilled to bits. Food was pricey, starters too expensive. Vegetarian Thali at £16 was acceptable and you would not go home on an empty stomach. My wife's Chef's Special Tandoori Vegetables, very un-Indian. Food delivery fairly quick, but took over half an hour to clear.' RM. Stocks Cobra.

EVEREST

41 Craven Road, Lancaster Gate, W2   ✆ **0171 262 3853**

This 'old' venue (1961), owned by Mohammed Ali and managed by M. Ahmed, has light decor, cane furniture and interesting framed photographs of old India. 'Papadoms and pickles, Meat Samosas (lean mince) and crisp salad were followed by Chicken Tikka Bhuna (one of the best I have had) and Paratha (very light) washed down by large bottles of Cobra. The bill was £14 for a small meal but the quality was good. Many of the diners were local residents who commented on their high regard for the Everest,' AE. Price check: Papadam 35p, CTM £5.95, Pullao Rice £1.60. Set meal £12.95. Stocks Cobra.

GANGES   ©

101 Praed Street, Paddington, W2   ✆ **0171 723 4096**

Closed for 'works' at our final verification (August 98). Reports please.

©	Curry Club discount (see page 6)	☕	Unlicensed
√	Vegetarian		
BYO	Bring your own alcohol	⊞	Delivery/takeaway

GOLDEN SHALIMAR   ©

6 Spring Street, W2   © 0171 262 3763

This concise report comes from regular AE: 'Decor traditionally ethnic, dim, small and cosy. Seats 56. Busy, good service, fast. There are 10 curry houses in Paddington, this is the best. Onion Bhajia (£1.50), crispy. Tikka Bhuna (£5.65) was good. Big bottles of iced Cobra.'

INDIAN CONNOISSEURS   ©

8 Norfolk Place, W2   © 0171 402 3299

A bright and airy, 46-seat cosy interior (booking advisable). The menu has all the favourites, and much more. Interesting appetisers include Bombay Roll, ground steak coated in potato paste and deep-fried, £2.95. and Ayre Cutlet, Bangladeshi fish lightly spiced and pan fried with onion £2.95. Main course dishes include Hass Baas, spicy duck cooked with bamboo shoots, £7.95. Potato Tilli, lamb kidney cooked with potato £5.50. Khashi Gazar, goat meat cooked with baby carrots £6.95. Parrot Fish, pan fried in a thick spicy sauce, £7.50. Shorisha Ayre, £5.75 is 'magnificent' DR. 'Or Venison, pheasant, grouse and quail Bhoona. Congratulations to chef Kabir Miah for adding authenticity to the formula. Paddington sleuth AE found a warm haven on a cold night and was 'swiftly served with free papadom and excellent pickles. The Meat Thali £9.50 was excellent value, good quality, nicely presented and very filling.' Regional cuisine: Price check: CTM £5.95, Pullao Rice £1.60, Peshwari Nan £1.70. Hours: 12-2.30pm; 6pm-12am. Branch: Golden Orient, 639 High Road, E11.

MANDALAY NEW ENTRANT

444 Edgware Road, W2   © 0171 258 3696

Since the British left Burma (renamed Myanmar) 50 years ago, this beautiful country has descended into unnecessary poverty, caused by a brutal totalitarian regime, whose 'year of the tourist', just gone, was not in itself sufficient incentive to cause the free world to want to visit. Nor should they, until free speech and democracy return, especially when there are the delights of Thailand and India next door, whose tourist incomes are fast-expanding. Sadly, this needlessly deprives us of a taste for Burmese food, lamentably demonstrated by the success of Thai and Indian UK restaurants, and the paucity of Burmese. Indeed since this restaurant's no relation Greenwich name-sake closed a few years ago, the nation has been without even one. If Burmese food is strange to you, (imagine a marriage of Indian and Thai foods – *see* page 38), the Ally brothers' Mandalay is the only place where you can satiate your curiosity. The decor's not up to much being somewhat café-style, but the waiters will give good heedable menu guidance. Starters include Hanatsone, a spicy chilli laden salad £3.90, spicy potato egg Samosa, £1.70. and the national fishy soup Mohinga. Main course curries include the fishy Nga hin, £5.50 and Seit-tha-thay- nat, £4.90 lamb in tamarind/chilli sauce. Rice and noodles are the staples, and if you have room for pud – the Indian-style creamy Falooda, £2.50 is an example. Average meal £12 Set lunch from £3.50. Hours: 3pm; 6pm-1am. Closed Sun.

OLD DELHI   TOP 100

48 Kendal Street, W2   ℂ 0171 724 9580

You'll often find so-called 'Persian' dishes on the standard curry house menu. There is a centuries-long link between Persia (now Iran) and India. Dishes such as Biriani, Patia, Pullao and Dhansak had their origins in Persia. But to most curry houses these dishes are merely a modification to formula curries. Not so at the Old Delhi, whose owner is Iranian, and whose son Jay is manager. You can certainly get superbly cooked curries in its superb setting, but venture further and try at least some of the rather less spicy but authentically cooked Iranian specials. Faisenjan (chicken marinated, then cooked in a purée of pomegranate, spices and nuts) goes divinely with Saffron Rice and Doog (minty lhassi). A must for serious spicy food *aficionados*. In our TOP 100.

Westbourne Grove – W2 and W11

This short street, whose postcode changes midway, is well-known for its many curry houses. These are worthy of mention:

KHAN'S   TOP 100

13-15 Westbourne Grove, W2   ℂ 0171 727 5420

For those who don't know Khan's, nothing changes at this 22 year old venue, and it never will, so here's the usual caveat: it's a love it or hate it place. You'll love the decor. The main room's high, cloud-painted ceiling is supported by a forest of gilt palm trees. There is a huge Hindi-arched mahogany bar and countless tables with pink cloths and black bentwood chairs. It is huge (180 seats upstairs, plus 100 in the basement) and is as full at lunchtime as dinner. Apparently it is not unusual for them to do 1000 covers a day. And therein lies the problem. This sheer volume results in a New York-style 'have- a-nice-day/take-it-or-leave-it/don't mess with me' attitude. You'll either love that for a kind of perverse entertainment value, or you'll hate it. Even Americans are shocked: 'Reasonably friendly service this time, which wore off when the place got busier – we had to ask five times for our pudding!' DB. 'I'm a regular here and if they don't make a mistake on my order and blame me for it, I'd think I was somewhere else!' PD. As first impressions count, we would not recommend it for a curry first-timer, nor to demure foreign tourist groups. But, for seasoned curryholics, it is an institution and decidedly not to be missed. Indeed, Khan's has built up a very large customer base of frequent (some three-times-a-week, say owners Mrs QN and Salman Khan) regulars from far and wide, who certainly love Khan's, and especially its north Indian food. 'Given the opportunity, I'd eat here every day. Their food is so fresh and full of flavour. On a purely food basis, it is the best.' RW. 'Had a wonderful visit to Khan's, food superb, decor and ambience very interesting.' CM. As ever it remains in our TOP 100. Price check: Papadam 50p, CTM £3.80, Pullao Rice £1.65, Peshwari Nan £1.60. Service 10%. House wine £6.75. BYO is not encouraged, except 'on rare occasions' (you'll have to work out for yourself when that is). £3 per bottle corkage is charged. Hours: 12-3pm; 6pm-12am. Stocks Cobra.

KHYBER ©

56 Westbourne Grove, W2   ✆ **0171 727 4385**

Mr Lamba's formula curries. Branch: Laguna, W13. Stocks Cobra.

©	Curry Club discount (see page 6)		Unlicensed
√	Vegetarian		
BYO	Bring your own alcohol		Delivery/takeaway

STANDARD

23 Westbourne Grove, W2   ✆ 0171 727 4818

Apt name for the street's oldest curry house. Stocks Cobra.

SULTAN TANDOORI BUFFET   ©

57 Westbourne Grove, W2   ✆ 0171 792 2565

Messrs Khan and Majid continue to fill this 150-seater with the fill your face e-a-m-a-y-l 20-dish (menu changed weekly) self-serve buffet for £6.99. Included are table-served Papadoms and starters. The bonhomie from all this tummy-bursting spreads to the 'always pleasant' ED, waiters. Talking of the tummy, as if all this isn't enough, on Tuesdays there's an added attraction – Cathy the International Belly Dancer. Hours: 12-2.30pm; 5-11.30pm. 12am-12pm Sat. & Sun. Branch: Kebabish, Wembley; Manor Park, E12. Stocks Cobra.

W5 – Ealing

CLAY OVEN

13 The Mall, Ealing, W5   ✆ 0181 840 0313

Go for Bhadur Chelleri's cooking. Branch: Ealing Cottage, 76 Uxbridge Road, W13.

MONTY'S TOP 100

1 The Mall, The Broadway, Ealing, W5   ✆ 0181 567 8122

Mahanta (Monty) Shrestha's 68-seater venue, managed by Donald, remains Ealing's most popular. with standard curries, done exceedingly well, plus some Nepalese specials e.g: Chicken Choala, Chicken Ledo. 'Worthy of TOP 100.' RL. Price check: Papadam 50p (p & s), CTM £6.95, Bombay Potato £3.40, Pullao Rice £1.95, Pickle Tray 40p. Hours: 12-3pm; 6pm-12am. Stocks Cobra.

SAMRAT

52 Pitshanger Lane, Ealing, W5   ✆ 0181 997 8923

Horuf Miah's formula 36-seater. Specials include: Peshwari dishes £5.95, made with diced onions, green peppers, in a thick masala. Price check:

Papadam 40p, CTM £5.95, Pullao Rice £1.75, Peshwari Nan £1.95. Lager £2.30 pint, house wine £7.95. Hours: 12- 2.30pm/6pm-12am.

W6 – Hammersmith

ANARKALI

303-305 King Street, Hammersmith, W6   © 0181 748 1760

'Party of 13 had excellent meal of vegetarian dishes.' HS. Price check: Papadam 50p (plain or spicy), CTM £7.50, Bombay Potato £3.25, Pullao Rice £2.10, Pickle Tray 50p. Hours: 12-2.30pm/6pm-12am.

INDIAN SUMMER NEW ENTRANT

291 King Street, Hammersmith, W6   © 0181 748 7345

Rafique Miah's menu describes itself as Indian neo-classical, with the likes of kebabs, paneer, tikka and korma with a few dishes from SE Asia e.g. Namprig Kai, £9.50 – a Thai chicken curry and Crab Crumble, steamed crab and chicken, deep-fried with chilli sauce, £4.50. Price check: CTM £8.50 inc rice & 2 veg, Saffron Rice £2.75. Average spend £20. Hours: 12-3pm weekdays, 6-11.30pm. Sun. 11.30am-5pm. 6.30-10.30pm.

TANDOORI NIGHTS TOP 100   ©

319 King Street, Hammersmith, W6   © 0181 741 4328

Mr Modi Udin's Tandoori Nights still gets the best-in-the-area vote from our reporters. One local couple write again to remind us of their regular King Street curry crawl, lucky them, from time to time – a kind of bindi-bender, I suppose, taking in them all, but they always find Tandoori Nights their favourite. 'The bright white facade is as inviting as the manager, AB Choudhury, and his staff. The pink decor is relaxing, and the food from chef Mabul Miah is curry house at its best,' J.W. Excellent food- rapidly served as requested.' HS. 'Worthy of TOP 100.' RL. Price check: Papadam 55p, CTM £7.95, Meat Thali £11.95, Pullao Rice £2.25. Service 10%. Set meal average for two £24.90. Hours: 12-3pm/6pm-12am. Stocks Cobra.

W8 – Notting Hill

MALABAR TOP 100

27 Uxbridge Street, W8   ✆ **0171 727 8800**

The simple decor and the eclectic menu haven't changed at Jo and Tony Chalmers' and Anil Bis's three floor 56-seat Malabar since it opened in 1983. After all, why change a good thing? Starters include Devilled Kaleja, charcoal grilled chicken livers, marinated in yoghurt and spices £4, Prawn Philouries, shelled prawns deep-fried in potato flour, £3.80, Hiran, tamarind-marinated venison, £6, and my late gran's favourite Bhutta sweetcorn with chillies, £3.10. Main courses include Long Chicken – medium-hot with cloves and ginger, £5.10 and Kayla Foogarth, sliced banana cooked with ginger and spices £3.10. 'This is a real find, thanks to your Guide. After so many recent formula curries, it's a treat to see different offerings on the menu and all superbly cooked. The Murgh Makhani and Keema Nan are among the best I have tasted, and the "menu for two, £31.50" delivers a substantial and economical feast.' JPL. Jo Chalmers has now been joined front of house by her daughter Sophie, and we hear constant praise for their customer care. Remains secure in our TOP 100. Prices are reasonable, but the Sunday lunch buffet at £6.95 is a real bargain. Price check: Papadam 55p, Murgh Makhni £6, Pullao Rice £1.95, Peshwari Nan £1.90. Hours: 12-3pm/6-11.30pm. Closed one week in August. Stocks Cobra.

W12

NEPALESE TANDOORI   ©

121 Uxbridge Road, Shepherds Bush, W12   0181 740 7551

Prabin Pradhan's cosy 38-seater's specials include: Chicken Nepal, boneless chicken with fresh fruits and cream £4.75, Nepalese Murgh Masala, chicken off the bone with sauce and boiled egg £5.75, Vegetable Nepal, seasonal vegetables with fresh fruits and cream £3.75. £2.20 pint of lager, house wine £6.95, stocks a Nepalese brand called Iceberg. Price check: Papadam 50p, CTM £5.25, Pullao Rice £1.70, Peshwari Nan £1.70. Delivery: £12 minimum, 3-mile radius. Hours: 12-2.30pm/6am-12pm.

W13 – West Ealing

LAGUNA   ©

127-129 Uxbridge Road, Ealing, W13   ✆ 0181 579 9992

Established in 1984 by Sunil Lamba. Huge frontage, decorated with
individually planted conifers in square wooden tubs. Northern Indian
food is served in his 120-seater restaurant. Stylishly decorated in pastel
shades, with arches and ceiling fans. Laguna Special Butter Chicken
£5.25 is the most popular dish. Service 10%. House wine £7.55. Price
check: Papadam 35p, CTM £5.25, Pullao Rice £1.95, Peshwari Nan £1.95.
Hours: 12-3pm/6pm-12am. Sun. 12pm-12am. Branch: Laguna Banquet
Hall, N Acton Road, NW10 and Khyber, W2. Stocks Cobra.

SIGIRI TOP 100 BEST SRI LANKAN

161 Northfields Avenue, W13   ✆ 0181 579 8000

The Sigiri is a true gem in the unlikely setting of Northfields, serving
delightful, authentic Sri Lankan food, and there are precious few such
restaurants in the whole UK. Find the corner site with its smoked glass
windows, inset in red bricks. Enter to understated elegant decor of slate
floor and green walls, and its 50 seats. Enjoy the sensible service and its
good atmosphere. The food's good, too. Try Banana Chips, £2.60 with
Pol Sambol, with Maldives fish, £1.25 followed by squid or pork (devilled they say, but if you like things hot and spicy, tell 'em – the devil is
quite a mild chappie at the Sigiri). The rice-based items, Hoppers
(Apa), Dosa and Uppaamas – with their glorious Coconut Chutney –
are almost old hat. Regulars tell of peppery meat and cashew chilli
chicken, around £5-6. Leave room (Sri Lankan food is deceptively filling) for Wattalappam, a very sweet, jaggery-based Sigiri signature
pudding. All good Sri Lankan Sinhalese stuff, and all at good prices
(average £15), especially the nine-dish Sunday lunch and dinner buffet
at £5.50. 'The starters and puddings were excellent, especially the egg
hoppers and the Wattalappam – as good as you get in Sri Lanka, but
the main courses were not truly Sri Lankan. We would go again' SJ. Safe
in our TOP 100. Hours: 6.30-11pm daily.

London WC

Area: West End postcodes WC1, WC2
Population: 164,000
Number of restaurants in county: 53
Number of restaurants in Guide: 8

WC1 – Holborn

MALABAR JUNCTION TOP 100 BEST SOUTH INDIAN

107 Great Russell Street, WC1 ℂ **0171 580 5230**

The conservatory, bamboo chairs, glass-domed roof with its planters, fountain, colonnades, gilt pictures and pastel walls give a relaxing welcome. So do the Keralan staff. The menu specialises in Keralan cuisine, with dishes from the cities of Cochin, Malabar and Travancore. Hot is the norm in Kerala but they cool it for 'western tastes'! So if you want to up the chilli strength, tell them and the kitchen will be more than happy to oblige. Contrary to popular belief, meat, chicken and fish dishes are the norm there. Try Lamb Cutlets: patties made of minced lamb and spices with bread crumbs and fried, served with tomato sauce and salad. £4.50. Malabar Chicken, £7.50 is cooked with coconut, curry leaves, garlic and mustard. Fish Mollee, £7.50 is a classic dish, so mild and gentle in its coconut base that even the Raj allowed it at table. Cochin Prawn, £7.90 with the ubiquitous coconut, this time with tomato, is another. Chemeen Poriyal – King Prawn Fry: king prawns marinated in ginger, garlic, spices and sliced coconut, fried in seasoned oil, £7.90. All the now familiar vegetarian south Indian rice-based offerings are here, such as Masala Dosa (crispy, potato curry-stuffed pancake), Uthappam (an intriguing rice-flour, crisp disc, baked with a spicy topping), Paripu, Sambar (lentil dishes) and Rasam, peppery soup and wonderful coconut chutneys. Other less familiar vegetarian offerings include Vellappam: a Keralan crumpet made of flavoured rice and served with vegetable stew, £6. Spinach Vadai: fried crunchy doughnut of channa dal, green chillies, onion, ginger, curry leaves and fresh spinach served with a variety of chutneys, £3 and for pud Banana Leaf Cake: made of rice with a sweet filling of grated coconut, banana and jaggery wrapped in banana leaf and steam cooked. £4. 'My second favourite restaurant.' RL. Hours: Restaurant: 12-3pm/6pm-12am, Café and Bar: 11am-11pm.

MANDEER TOP 100

8 Bloomsbury Way, WC1   © 0171 323 0660

Mr and Mrs Ramesh Patel's ever-popular Mandeer went the same way
as the Minara and the Neel Akash (see Dhaka Brasserie, later) in the
name of property development. Their new premises have now opened,
and although we've not yet been to try it out, we assume that the standard of this vegetarian restaurant continues to be as high as that of
their previous establishment and are, therefore, leaving it in our TOP
100 this time. Reports please.

RED PEPPER   ©

65 Red Lion Street, WC1   © 0171 405 8072

Manager Mujeeb Sayeed's cutely-named first floor 40-seater has a good
pedigree (Chutney's, Ravi Shankar and Handi are in the same ownership). Some good, unusual dishes on offer: Pattice (spicy potato
rissoles) and Shakoothi (*sic.*) Goan chicken, with plenty of red chilli
pepper, Karahi Chicken £5.20, Mirch Masala £5.95 and Vegetable Bhujia
£3.95. Price check: Papadam 50p, CTM £5.25, Pullao Rice £1.95,
Peshwari Nan £1.75. House wine £7.20, mineral water £2.95. Service
10%. Hours: 12-3pm/6-11.30pm

WC2

BHATTI   ©

37 Great Queen Street, WC2   © 0171 831 0817

Taken over in 1990 by N. Ruparel. The restaurant seats 95 in two rooms
and serves northern Indian food. It is situated in a 17th century listed
building. 'Concerned when we sat down to hear another customer pas-
sionately complaining about the service. He had been waiting a whole
20 minutes! We waited 20 minutes too, but it was worth it! Murgh Chat
– quite a plateful and delicious. Chicken Jalfrezi, interesting with shards
of lemon peel. Good value for central London.' ST. Price check:
Papadam 50p, CTM £6.75, Bombay Potato £3.25, Pullao Rice £2.05.
House wine £8.10. Delivery: £25 minimum, 4-mile radius. Hours: 12-
2.45pm (2pm on Sun.)/5.30-11.45pm (10.30pm on Sun.). Stocks Cobra.

DACCA   ©

46 Bedford Street, WC2   ℰ 0171 379 7623

Established in 1981 by Thahirul Islam; an air-conditioned 66-seater.
'Happy Hour discount of 20% for meals ordered between 5.30pm and
7.30pm, obviously a great draw as within minutes the restaurant went
from empty to full. This did put a strain on the service and that left
something to be desired.' HC. Service 10%. Price check: Papadam 45p,
CTM £5.85, Pullao Rice £1.95, Peshwari Nan £1.95. House wine £9.95.
Hours: 12-3pm/5.30pm-12am (11.30pm on Sun.) Sat. 12pm-12am.

THE INDIA CLUB   TOP 100   BYO

143 The Strand, WC2   ℰ 0171 836 0650

The India Club has been here since 1950, and it's a landmark, though
several correspondents have asked for more specific directions as to
where exactly it is. To find it turn right (west) at Waterloo Bridge/
Strand junction and it's a short distance along on your right. Find the
door-width entrance – there's a new sign, gold on black, saying 'India
Restaurant and Hotel'. Or use a taxi but be prepared for an opinion. As
I mentioned before, London black cab drivers know everything about
everything. Even their driving test is called the 'knowledge', so when a
cabbie tells our ace reporter about the India Club – 'this is the place *afi-
cionados* go to exchange recipes' – you know the India Club's arrived!
Now so must you. Climb the narrow stairs. (In typical Indian style, the
owners do not see the need to redecorate – it's clean enough, though.)
At the first floor is the hotel reception. I believe it is called the Strand
Continental Hotel. With singles £29, and doubles £39 it's cheaper than
Delhi. We've never dared to stay here, so reports from the brave please!
Old hands know it's unlicensed and you can BYO – no corkage, and
they stock up with Cobra at the first floor so-called hotel residents' bar.
One year we asked a waiter about this and were told some incompre-
hensible nonsense about joining their drink club (cost £1.10) to permit
you to do this. We duly paid up, to the unquenchable amusement of the
elderly bar waitress who, in between cackles, advised us that the waiters
'know nothing'. From the bar return to reception then proceed up
another floor. In front of you is the door to the L-shaped restaurant.
It's a cheap café style, with laidback, friendly waiters. Please don't expect
modern decor, or indeed any decor. I swear nothing has changed since
the India Club opened, including, I do believe, the barmaid! As in India,

minimalist here means flaking plaster, no tablecloths, flies a-buzzing, bare chairs, and pictures askew. It's all part of the charm, and the regulars don't want change. 'Someone has been round straightening the pictures, including Gandhi's! Let us hope that this is just a prank, not official policy.' GR. And, shortly after: 'Gandhi is askew again – thank heavens!' GR. Who am I to argue with a London cabbie? But don't expect the place to be full of recipe exchangers. In all the 38 years I've been going there, I've never once seen recipes exchanging hands, nor have I been asked to participate. Pity, really! What does change hands, and has done for nearly 50 years, is fabulous, uncompromisingly Indian food, served in unpretentious surroundings. The part printed part hand-written menu, still with its 01 (not even 071 let alone 0171) phone number, is a testament to economy. No need for a reprint (and very wise too, with BT planning another 'it-will-never-happen-again' number change in London next year!) Don't expect formula curries. Head chef Puroshothaman is from south India, and it's that food at which they excel. True there are meat and chicken curries, from £4.50, but to us they always lack sparkle, though the Keema Peas is excellent. (If it's korma-CTM-balti that you crave, go to the nearby Sitar Balti.) We greatly prefer the south Indian Rasam (served in a tea cup with saucer – hot as hell), Sambar, Masala Dosa and Coconut Chutney. Chilli bhajias are wonderful. Don't over-order – portions are generous. Despite my caveats even more clearly spelled out this time, RW was: 'Disappointed, food obviously freshly prepared but lacking in taste.' Here's one quote from the dozens of devotees: 'Whatever you have heard hardly prepares you. The decor is truly awful, but it matters not – food was excellent. Egg curry, boiled rice and Nan were superb. Waiters are unique too. I turned round to order a Papadam and caught the head waiter swigging a can of super-strong cider!' RDL. Despite its quirks (which give it a 'charm of its own,' says CD.) it decidedly remains firmly in our TOP 100. There is a bar downstairs (part of the hotel). Price check: Papadam 30p, Chicken Curry £4.60, Pullao Rice £2.20. Hours: 12-2.30pm/6-11pm. Closed Sun. The last words, as always go to PD: 'Long may the Club remain open.' Stocks Cobra.

©	Curry Club discount (see page 6)		Unlicensed
√	Vegetarian		
BYO	Bring your own alcohol		Delivery/takeaway

PUNJAB TOP 100 BEST NORTH INDIAN   ©

80-92 Neal Street, Covent Garden, WC2   ℭ 0171 240 9979

The Punjab is even older than the India Club. It was London's third
Indian restaurant (after Veeraswamy W1, *see* entry, and Shafi, now long
closed), opening in 1947 in Aldgate. Even with its move to its present
site in 1951, it is still the oldest Punjabi restaurant in the UK. And for
all its life, it has been in the capable hands of just two men, the late
founder and now his son, Mr S. Maan. Of course, by definition, the
Punjab was one of the original pioneers of the curry formula. Only
here it is done as it has always been done, and as it should be. The result
is unlike the newer Bangladeshi clones, and is probably what old curry
hands think they remember when they say 'curry isn't like it used to be
in the old days'. The food is meat-orientated, spicy, savoury and very
tasty. 'The menu is very good with a number of more unusual dishes.
Pumpkin is featured in about half a dozen different dishes. The chef's
special fish curry was excellent. I was more than satisfied'. HJC. One of
its former regulars used it twice a day, five days a week, for forty years,
before retiring (GL). This astounding claim (no one has bettered it) got
Geoff onto a BBC-TV Noel Edmonds programme. Such is their loyalty to the place that regulars have their own club, the 'Punjabbers'.
Remains high in our TOP 100.

TANDOORI NIGHTS   ©

35 Great Queen Street, WC2   ℭ 0171 831 2558

Owner Mrs Yasmeen Rashid opened her first Tandoori Nights in
Cockfosters, Herts, in 1988, and her second in NW1 (*see* entries), months
later. In 1993 she opened this branch with Manager Salil, and chef Waris
Miah. Price check: Papadam 50p, CTM £6.75, Mixed Grill £12.95,
Pullao Rice £2.15. Lunch buffet £8.95. Service 12½%. Reports, please.
Stocks Cobra.

THALI INDIAN VEGETARIAN NEW ENTRANT   √ ©

3-7 Endell Street, WC2   ℭ 0171 379 6493

A useful new addition in London's heartland, a 12-11.30pm vegetarian-
only, licensed place, from N. Hussain of Royals, WC2 (*see* entry). South
Indian Dosai and Idlis, north Indian Mutar Panir (*sic.*), Samosas and
Ragara Patice, a Bombay-style potato cake. The Gujarati Thali, £6.95, is

a three-course meal, and Bhel Puri addicts will find it in the £8.95 set meal. Selection of Indian puddings. 'Went for lunchtime buffet, excellent. Fair selection of dishes, but rice pudding bit past its best. Major quibble, pint of lager £3.' RDL. Price check: Papadam 55p, Pullao Rice £2.25. All-day e-a-m-a-y-l 12-dish buffet £4.95. Service 10% (not on buffets). Stocks Cobra.

ENGLAND

The method in this Guide is to record our entries in alphabetical order: first the county then, within that, the town, then the restaurant. With the demise of Avon, we now start with Bedfordshire, the first town we record is Arlesey, and its first restaurant is Raj Villa, and so on. Our last English county is Yorkshire West, and Wetherby is the last recorded town.

©	Curry Club discount (see page 6)	🍵	Unlicensed
√	Vegetarian		
BYO	Bring your own alcohol	🎲	Delivery/takeaway

BEDFORDSHIRE

Area: Central
Population: 536,000
Number of restaurants in county: 73
Number of restaurants in Guide: 8

Arlesey

RAJ VILLA   ©

27 High Street, Arlesey   ℰ 01462 835145

Akthar Ali has owned and managed this 70-seater since 1996. Price
check: Papadam 40p, CTM £5.75, Pullao Rice £1.60, Peshwari Nan
£1.50. Lager £1.95 pint. Delivery. Hours: 12-2.30pm/6pm-12am.
Branches: Raj Gat, 8 Bedford Street, Ampthill. Raj Moni, 279 Upper
Street, London, N12.

Bedford

ALAMIN   ©

51-51a Tavistock Street, Bedford   ℰ 01234 327142

Owner Gulzar Miah plans a conservatory at this 40-seater. Chef Altab
Hussain cooks formula curries and Balti dishes. Price check: Papadam
40p, CTM £5.15, Pullao Rice £1.40, Peshwari Nan £1.40. Sunday
Buffet £5.95. Delivery: £10 minimum, 5-mile radius. Hours: 12-
2.30pm/6pm-12am. Stocks Cobra.

AMRAN TANDOORI   ©

53b Harpur Street, Bedford   ℰ 01234 352359

We've not heard from the erstwhile Amran (established 1958, changing
hands to Shabbir Raja back in 1966). It has consistently served competent and good curries ever since. We hope it still has its red flock
wallpaper and Taj Mahal pictures. Precious few Indian restaurants now
have that once-celebrated trademark, though we're delighted to see that
the Amran keeps up with the trends and serves Baltis, done well by
Inayat Khan Raja in the Pakistani way, including Balti Chicken Quetta

Earthquake (£7.30). It uses chillies, chillies and more chillies. I wonder where Shabbir got that wicked idea from. Open daily 6pm-12am.

GULSHAN ©

69 Tavistock Street, Bedford   © 01234 355544

JS Nijjer and his wife BK are the owner/managers. 150 seats. Painted marble-effect walls and wooden lattice partitions. Chef Shanu Miah cooks Pakistani and North Indian curries and Baltis. Specials include Lamb Sharab, lamb tikka cooked in cream and almond liqueur, served with Pullao Rice (£6.95). Price check: Papadam 60p, CTM £6.95, Pullao Rice £1.45, Peshwari Nan £1.75. Delivery £10 minimum, 15-mile radius. Hours: 12-2pm/6pm-1am. Stocks Cobra.

MAGNA TANDOORI

50 Tavistock Street, Bedford   © 01234 356960

Taken over in 1995 by Mrs Rufia Rahman. Mohammed Rahman manages the restaurant with chef Monsur Ali specialising in Bangladeshi and Balti curries. It is a large restaurant seating 140 diners on two floors, in three rooms. There is a car park at the rear of the restaurant for 10 cars. Price check: Papadam 40p, CTM £6.95, Pullao Rice £1.40, Peshwari Nan £1.85. Delivery: £10 minimum, 5-mile radius. Hours: 12-2.30pm/6pm-12am. Branch: Magna, 199, Bedford Road, Kempston, Beds. Stocks Cobra.

Leighton Buzzard

INDIAN OCEAN ©

13 Wing Road, Linslade, Leighton Buzzard © 01525 383251

M. Ali owns and manages this cosy 35-seater, where Chef H. Ullah cooks Bangladeshi-style curries. Price check: Papadam 40p, CTM £5.10, Pullao Rice £1.45, Peshwari Nan £1.40. Delivery: 3-mile radius. Hours: 5pm-12am. Stocks Cobra.

©	Curry Club discount (see page 6)		Unlicensed
√	Vegetarian		
BYO	Bring your own alcohol		Delivery/takeaway

Luton

ALANKAR ©

276 Dunstable Road, Luton   ✆ **01582 455189**

Deva Odedra (Dilip)'s beamed mock-Tudor house, complete with
tower (don't expect Hampton Court, though – it's strictly 1930s) seats
75 in two rooms. Chef Whahid cooks regular curries with some
Gujarati specials. Price check: Papadam 40p, CTM £4.90, Pullao Rice
£1.40. Delivery: £10 minimum, 3-mile radius. Hours: 12-2.30pm/6pm-
12am. Sunday 12-2.30pm – eat all day, five course meal with all the
trimmings for only £5.95. Stocks Cobra.

MEAH TANDOORI ©

102 Park Street, Luton   ✆ **01582 454504**

Seats 52 diners. 'Quick meal prior to a football match. Very impressed,
particularly with the honesty of the proprietor, K Ahmed. Paid a bill
of £32.60. He chased down the street – our bill was only £25.20. How
refreshing!' AW. Price check: Papadam 50p, CTM £5.30, Pullao Rice
£1.75, Hours: 12-2.30pm/6pm-12am. Stocks Cobra.

BERKSHIRE

Area: Home Counties (west of London)
Population: 756,000
Number of restaurants in county: 85
Number of restaurants in Guide: 11

Bracknell

PASSAGE TO INDIA

3 Market Place, Bracknell   ✆ **01344 485499**

Owner Mr Hussain. Seats 80. Price check: Papadam £1.60 (portion of
four), CTM £5.95, Pullao Rice £1.95, Peshwari Nan £1.95. Delivery.
Hours: 12-2pm/6-11.30pm. Stocks Cobra.

Maidenhead

NABHA TAKEAWAY   NEW ENTRANT

39 King Street, Maidenhead.   ✆ 01628 770193

Taken over by Zahire Khan in 1998. A Balti takeaway. Price check: Papadam 40p, CTM £5, Pullao Rice £1.50, Peshwari Nan £1.75. Delivery: £8 minimum, 3-mile radius. Hours: 5.30pm-12.30am.

Reading

BINA

21 Prospect Street, Caversham, Reading   ✆ 0118 946 2116

We reported last time that we had received a disappointing report (published in the *Sunday Times*, no less) amongst many good reports. I am sorry to say that we have now had several such disappointing reports. We still believe this to be a good restaurant, but we do wonder whether owner Abdul Miah has taken his eye off the ball, his core business, in pursuit of other matters. He certainly has not bothered to return his questionnaire, which should remove the Bina from the Guide. (It will next time!) Here are some of the comments: 'A reasonable restaurant with some interesting dishes, Crab Bhuna, Tandoori Quail!. Service a bit on the slow side.' AF. 'Can feel cramped.' N&GT.

EVEREST TANDOORI

9 Meadway Precinct, Honey End Lane,
Tilehurst, Reading   ✆ 0118 958 3429

Says MW: 'Although the decor and service are nothing special, the cuisine is extremely good. The portions are enormous. Be careful not to over-order – you need a few friends to help you.' 'Promoted as a Nepalese restaurant, it has plenty of seating.' SP. 'We like this one, they certainly do the hottest Phals.' N&GT.

INDIA PALACE   ©

83-85 Wokingham Road, Earley, Reading   ✆ 0118 962 2711

The Palace is jointly owned by Mrs L.C. Payne and chef Bhadracen, and managed by A. Ahad. 'Impressed by the cleanliness, crisp linen, light ambience of lighting and decor and background music. Chicken Chat £2.50 was delicious. Palace Spring Chicken £6.40, Haandi Saag Chicken £6.50, Pullao Rice, Tarka Dal and Bombay Aloo with Kulcha Nan, all really excellent. With three Cobras and a G&T £31.25.' RT.

Slough

ANAM TANDOORI AND BALTI HOUSE   ©

1a Baylis Parade, Oatland Drive, Slough   © 01753 572967

A typical competent curry house owned by Javeed Ali, open evenings only. 'Baltis are a speciality here and very tasty too.' RE.

BARN TANDOORI

Salt Hill Park, Bath Road, Slough   © 01753 523183

We know of restaurants in old schools, fire stations, churches, garages, even Portakabins, but the Barn takes the papadom! It's in a rather grand, ex-cricket pavilion in the middle of nowhere – well, a park, actually, and next to the tennis courts. Taken over in 1996 by Messrs Mehbub, Rahman, Alam and Kandakar. Serves formula curries. 'I have revisited this excellent Indian restaurant in the park twice with large business parties at very short notice. The staff copes admirably, delivering many different orders at the same time, maintaining high-quality cuisine with superb service.' TE. Price check: Papadam 50p, CTM £5.75, Bombay Potato £2.60, Pullao Rice £1.85, Pickles 25p. Lager £2.10 pint. Sunday lunch buffet £5.95, children under 12, £3. Delivery: £20 orders qualify for a free bottle of wine, 5-mile radius. Hours: 12-2.30pm/6-11.30pm.

Sunningdale

TIGER'S PAD   NEW ENTRANT

3 Station Parade, London Road, Sunningdale.   © 01344 621215

'Expensive, minimalist, open plan decor. Oak tables. Perfect papadams. Onion Bhajias £2.95 like tennis balls, really good. Scallops Chilli Fry £6.95 and Seekh Kebab £3.95, both very good. Lamb Vindaloo £6.95, excellent tender very tasty. Subz Hyderabadi £7.95, vegetables roasted in the tandoor and glazed with cheese. OK but not enough cheese and too much onion. Everything was served in solid brass pots with large heavy matching spoons. Nan £1.95, one of the best I've ever had. Packed full by 8pm. One complaint, wine list is outrageously expensive – £16.95 for an ordinary bottle of Australian Chardonnay. Unusual (for an Indian restaurant) 4 out of 7 staff were female.' AF. Price check: Papadam 50p, CTM £7.50, Bombay Potato £3.25, Pullao Rice £2.25, Chutney and Pickles 50p. Sunday Buffet £9.95 from 12-5pm.

Theale

CAFE BLUE COBRA TOP 100

20 High Street, Theale   © 0118 930 4040

Here's a new (mid-1996) place with a real difference, in an unlikely location – a tiny, pretty village just off the M4's J12. It is owned by the enterprising Abssar Waess, whose curry connections extend to his celebrated uncle, Wali Udin, curry restaurateur and Bangladeshi Consul in Scotland. With such a pedigree, it was not surprising that Waess would want to open his own restaurant, but he decided to do something ambitious and unique. The clue is in the name. The venue opens at noon and operates, café-style, until midnight. The first-timer is struck by the coolness and fresh cleanliness of the decor. The bar area, with its marble and cane furnishings, seats 30. It leads on to the main dining area, whose 60 ormolu seats are designed to evoke airy oriental verandas. The light walls are a regularly changing 'gallery', home to the works of local professional artists. The Cobra Express Platter lunch can be advance-ordered by phone and served on arrival – useful for the busy exec. Those with less demanding timescales can choose à la carte until 2.30pm, or simply linger in the bar over the snacks menu until 6pm, with cappuccino, or sample some of the 16 worldwide beers, including Cobra, which are on offer. From 6pm the full menu comes into play, and an interesting document it is. Naturally there is a wide range of Bangladeshi and Bengali dishes, some of which will be familiar to the curry *aficionado*. Delights include Tikka (£ 3.95), Methi Saag Gosht (£6.45) and Birianis (£8.85). But there are so many other dishes and ingredients that 'it takes several visits, and we're still just learning.' MN. There is duckling, crab, venison, veal, pomfret, ayre, surma river fish and much more.

Indeed, so far I've only touched on half the menu. The other half is Thai food. Two different master chefs have their own stations in the kitchens. The Thai operation includes some classics, such as, for starters, steamed mussels (£5.50), Chicken Sateh (£3.95) or a mixed platter (£9.95). Tom Yam soups start at £2.95, and the main courses range from Thai Green Chicken Curry (£7.50) to Ped Pad Prik – Hot Duck (£13.90) with Pad Thai noodles (£5.95). Egg-fried rice is £2.75. Expect to spend around £35 per head for a three-courser with drink and coffee. There are themed set meals from £17.90, but Waess reports that many diners happily mix and match the two cuisines. And why not? Eating has no rules other than enjoyment. Traditionalists who insist that nothing can be changed are bores. Café Blue Cobra is far from boring. Remains in our TOP 100. Stocks Cobra.

Windsor

VICEROY NEW ENTRANT

27 St Leonard's Road, Windsor   © 01753 858005

'Very big and beautifully refurbished. Seems to have attracted the best waiters from other restaurants in the area – they recognised me! Service slow on the two times I've been there but was well worth the wait. Meat Thali excellent. Wonderful Tandoori Chicken and Sheek Kebab with Chicken Bhuna. Hot Jalfrezi. Very fresh Papadams and Chutneys.' AF.

Wokingham

ROYAL INDIAN TANDOORI   ©

72 Peach Street, Wokingham   © 0118 978 0129

A 70-seater established in 1978 by T Ali, serving excellent Bangladeshi and Kashmiri-styled curries by chef M Miah. Banquets on Sundays. Price check: Papadam 70p, CTM £6.50, Pullao Rice £1.95, Peshwari Nan £1.95. Takeaway menu 15% cheaper than restaurant menu. Hours: 12-3pm/6pm-12am. Stocks Cobra.

©	Curry Club discount (see page 6)	☕	Unlicensed
√	Vegetarian		
BYO	Bring your own alcohol	⊞	Delivery/takeaway

BRISTOL

Area: West Country
Population: 400,000
Number of restaurants in county: 76
Number of restaurants in Guide: 7

BRITISH RAJ   NEW ENTRANT

**1-3 Passage Road, Westbury on Trym,
Bristol**   ✆ 0117 950 0493

Our scribes say this classical, upmarket restaurant, open since 1973, is
one of the most highly respected in the south-west. 'Not cheap, £40
for two with drinks. Excellent service, food quality was outstanding,
fresh, hot and tangy.' NO. Price check: Papadam 45p, CTM £6.25,
Bombay Potato £2.15, Pullao Rice £1.45, Chutney 25p, per portion.
Hours: 12-2pm/6-11.30pm.

LAL JOMI PAVILION

2 Harcourt Road, Redland, Bristol   ✆ 0117 924 4648/1640

Mocklis Miah and Abdul Noor's popular 90-seater serves formula curries. 'I've been here many times, comfortable, usual decor but nice
booths to hide in.' AW. Price check: Papadam 40p, CTM £6.30, Pullao
Rice £1.40, Hours: 12-2pm/6pm-12am.

MEENAR   ©

143 Church Road, Redfield, Bristol   ✆ 0117 939 5534

Open plan, 36 seats café-style, owned by Shaukat (Shaun) Alime and
his chef wife, Bushra, who cooks Pakistani food on view with Abdul
Nasir, and it's really good value. Off-street parking. Balti and Pakistani
curries on the menu. Price check: Papadam 25p, CTM £4.90, Pullao
Rice £1.20, Peshwari Nan £1.40. Pickle and Chutney 40p. No credit
cards accepted. Delivery: £10 minimum, 4-mile radius. Hours: 5pm-
12am, (2am on Fri. and Sat.). Stocks Cobra.

THE NEW TAJ TANDOORI

404 Gloucester Road, Horfield, Bristol   © 0117 942 1992

Takeaway only, evenings only. Says AJWP: 'I have been eating Indian food for 35 years, and in the last 10 years or so I thought my palate had become jaded since all the normal Indian restaurant food tended to taste the same and was indifferent in flavour, not like it used to be in the 50s and 60s. However, the New Taj has restored my faith. It is first class.' Owned and run by Parvin Rayman, a Bangladeshi Muslim woman described by all our reporters as helpful and friendly. Her takeaway is spotless, decorated with flowers and serving fresh, tasty food.

PUSHPANJLI   √

217a Gloucester Road, Bristol   © 0117 924 0493

'A wonderfully informal yet smart Gujarati vegetarian restaurant fitted with formica tables and plastic chairs, with all food displayed under a glass counter. All food is home-cooked. Huge variety of starters, Dal Bhajia, Samosa, Kachori, Bateta Wada, Mogo Chips, all superb. Large assorted pickle tray offering wide choice and lovely Papads. Masala Dhosas enormous with Sambar and coconut chutney. Many lovely vegetable curries, rice and breads. I visit this restaurant several times a month and it is truly brilliant.' DR. 'My no 1. Can't fault the food. Bhel Puri great, portions good, sweets are very indulgent. They hold buffet evenings – help yourself for £10-12ish – eat until you drop!' JM.

RAJDOOT TOP 100   ©

83 Park Street, Bristol   © 0117 926 8033

Established in 1970 by Indian architect Des Sarda. The attractive decorations are very Indian with beaten copper tables in the bar area and bronze statues. Manager Sukhi Sharma. We get contradictory reports about all the Rajdoots, despite the caveat, which I'll repeat: as most restaurants are Bangladeshi-run, Rajdoot's food may come as a surprise to some. It is much truer to the authentic food you'll find in homes in northern India. It is this very fact that leads to the disappointment which is expressed to us by some of Rajdoot's first-and-only-time diners, who simply do not find the food matching their expectations. The complaints, and I stress again that they are few but persistent, are that the food is bland and the prices high. It's the same at all three Rajdoot branches (*see* Birmingham; Dublin; Manchester). I personally continue to dine here (and at the others), and I have to say that I find it excellent on all counts. Actually, we have had fewer such reports this time. But here are examples: 'Saw the entry in the Guide. Decided to try the Rajdoot to see who is right. I went on a quiet night, service was very fast. Only six customers in. Decor very comfortable and clean. FOOD WAS OUT OF THIS WORLD. Concerns about portion size and spiciness are wrong thankfully. Shish Kebab was passable on the palate but had a pleasant spicy "after burn". Lamb Jalfrezi was heaven. Large portion, succulent cuts of lamb, wonderful lingering spice taste which was not chilli hot but lastingly pungent. Chana Bhuna a wonderful complementing side dish. Refreshing Kulfi to cool things down. A truly memorable meal – well worth a TOP 100 slot. Final nice touch a jug of water was requested and delivered without any charge or hassle to buy bottled water.' PAW. Then we get: 'Had high hopes for this restaurant, but these were ill founded. On entering, the manager didn't look like he'd quite forgiven the British by the expression on his face. Even a mention of the Curry Club didn't throw misery guts into fits of ecstasy. Anyhow, big bowls of nibbles were nice while you waited. Restaurant atmosphere was very pleasant and restful, I liked the fact that the food wasn't dyed to radioactive levels or dripping in grease, but we wouldn't return. TSM was watery and tasted of cloves. Chicken Tikka Biriani was no better and at £9.20, totally unjustified. Keema Nans were stodgy and small.' HS. 'My colleague and I had an excellent meal, both in quality and quantity. Lamb Tikka £3.30, Fish Kashmiri £6.90, Fish Shajah £6.60. He was particularly impressed by the Peshwari Nan £2.20. Even though the restaurant was crowded, the service was pleasant and efficient. Comfort and decor good with a comfortable lounge area. I revisited two evenings later and was warmly welcomed by the manager. Again, a first class meal, I felt very much at home.' DR WOL. Price check: CTM £7.20, Bombay Potato £3.90, Pullao Rice £1.80. Lager £2.50 pint. Hours: 12-2.30pm (closed on Sunday) and 6.30-11.30pm.

SPICE OF NEPAL TAKEAWAY   NEW ENTRANT   ©

245 Lodge Causeway, Fishponds   © 0117 956 0664

A Nepalese takeaway opened in 1997 by Pradeep Karki, head chef. Dilip Karki manages front of house. Momo, dumplings filled with mince, steamed, served with Nepalese Tomato Pickle. Kastamandapa, a mild dish, flavoured with ground nuts, cream, with a hint of garlic, highly recommended. Price check: Papadam 25p, CTM £3.95, Pullao Rice £1.25, Peshwari Nan £1.40. Delivery £10 minimum, 3-mile radius. Hours: 6-11.30pm, closed on Sun.

BUCKINGHAMSHIRE

Area: Home Counties (west of London)
Population: 642,000
Number of restaurants in county: 74
Number of restaurants in Guide: 20

Aylesbury

GOLDEN BENGAL   ©

1-2 Villiers Building, Buckingham Street, Aylesbury   *©* **01296 384001**

Established in 1971, taken over in 1996 by Sayad Miah and Harunur Rashid. Restaurant decorated in cream, red and gold, seats 40. Price check: Papadam 35p, CTM £7.40 incl. Pullao Rice, Pullao Rice £1.50, Peshwari Nan £1.25. Lager £1.90 pint. Delivery: £10 minimum, 3-mile radius. Hours: 12-2.30pm/6pm-12am.

TAJ MAHAL NEW ENTRANT   ©

73 Buckingham Street, Aylesbury   *©* **01296 399617**

Opened in November 1993 by Abdul Khaliq. Formula curries served competently in this 50-seater curry house, CTM, Jalfrezi and Korma being the most popular dishes ordered. Price check: Papadam 50p, CTM £6.35, Pullao Rice £1.60, Peshwari Nan £1.65. Delivery: £10 minimum, 3-mile radius. Hours: 12-2.30pm/5.30pm-12am. Stocks Cobra.

©	Curry Club discount (see page 6)		Unlicensed
√	Vegetarian		
BYO	Bring your own alcohol		Delivery/takeaway

Beaconsfield

BUCKS TANDOORI

7 The Broadway, Penn Road,
Beaconsfield   ✆ 01494 674580

'I am a regular, and I mean most Friday nights. The food is Nepalese-style and is freshly prepared, so don't expect to get out in record time. Service is comfortably good with friendly, polite waiters. Sunday buffet e-a-m-a-y-l for £7.50 per person. Everything that has been tried is excellent, and well worth a visit. Watch for special events.' MS.

Bourne End

LAST VICEROY

74 The Parade, Bourne End   ✆ 01628 531383

Back in the Guide after two editions of absence because we're getting good reports again. 'Really great restaurant. Wonderful food, sauces out of this world. Friendly service, you can take your time over your meal. I always enjoy a Madras. My husband raves about their Masala dishes. We have never been disappointed.' BP. 'Food was quite simply superb! Bollywood Rolls – spiced lamb, chicken, king prawn and vege-tables, all neatly wrapped up in pastry. Mussels cooked in herbs and spices, carefully preserving the delicate flavour of the seafood. Botikka Lamb – tender and spicy.' CF. 'Great welcome, table good, drinks quickly delivered. Large, warm Popadoms with exceptional Lime pickle. Plate warmers, superb food, excellent quantities. Hot towels. Lovely evening.' BR. Price check: Papadam 35p (plain) 40p (spicy), Aloo Jeera £2.20, Pullao Rice £1.60, Chutney and Pickles (per person) 50p. Hours: 12-2.30pm/6pm-12am.

Buckingham

DIPALEE   ©

18 Castle Street, Buckingham   ✆ 01280 813151

A regular Guide entrant because it is a well-established (1980) 90 seater curry house under the watchful ownership of Salique Ahmed. Head Chef Ashik Miah cooks competent formula curries. Price check:

Papadam 50p, CTM £5.95, Peshwari Nan £1.75. Hours: 12-2.30pm/6-11.30pm. Stocks Cobra.

Burnham

AKASH TANDOORI   ©

21 High Street, Burnham   © 01628 603507

Foysol Ahmed's Akash is a regular entrant in these pages. Indeed, our regular correspondent of many years, who still wishes to remain anonymous, now claims to be eating his way round the menu for the sixteenth time – every dish at least once.

Chesham

CHESHAM TANDOORI   NEW ENTRANT

48 Broad Street, Chesham   © 01494 782669

Faizul and Mojibul Hoque's air-conditioned 62-seater serves competent formula curries and Balti. Price check: Papadam 45p, CTM £6.25, Pullao Rice £1.85, Peshwari Nan £1.75. 10% discount on takeaways. Hours: 12-2.30pm/6pm-12am. Stocks Cobra.

High Wycombe

CURRY CENTRE   ©

83 Easton Street, High Wycombe   © 01494 535529

Whenever the owners are personally looking after front of house (A. Musowir) and kitchen (MA Mali) respectively, you can be sure of getting their best (or at least you know who to tell if not). They also own the Indian Delight Takeaway, 189 Farnham Road, Slough. 'Food and service of a consistently high standard.' GD.

ELACHI

188 Cressex Road, High Wycombe   © 01494 510810

Elachi, as all good cooks know, means cardamom. Same ownership as Reading's Bina. Opened February 1995. An extremely pretty restaurant with hand-painted figures on the walls reminiscent of Michelangelo. Food including unusual dishes generally commended.

Little Chalfont

PUKKAH SAHIB

13 Nightingale Corner, Cokes Lane,
Little Chalfont   ✆ 01494 763144

Opened early 1997, we said last time 'It's one to watch.' Sadly, no one did evidently, as we lack any reports, not even from the restaurant. We said last time: 'Menu reminiscent of the Bombay Brasserie and Chutney Mary, with classic Raj and Indian dishes, e.g.: Calamari Chilli, Salmon Samosa, Goan Green Chicken Curry and Lamb and Saffron Biriani, cooked, layered in the pot, complete with chupatti lid (called Dum). Prices above average. Traditional items are all here if you want them.' Reports please, restaurant please note, or we delist you.

Milton Keynes

AKBAR TANDOORI   ©

10-12 Wolverton Road, Stony Stratford,
Milton Keynes   ✆ 01908 562487

Taken over by M. Sattar. Air-conditioned. 64 seats. Adequate car-parking space. Price check: Papadam 35p, CTM £5.95, Pullao Rice £1.50. Delivery: £15 minimum. Hours: 12-2.30pm/6pm-12am. Sunday buffet 12-11.30pm. Stocks Cobra.

EASTERN PARADISE   NEW ENTRANT

8 Church Street, Wolverton,
Milton Keynes   ✆ 01908 312969/225765

'I'm slightly surprised this has never been listed before – it's been here a long time and seems to do well! It announces itself as the "first Balti House in Milton Keynes" and has recently been "decorated" with masses of artificial plants covering the walls and dangling from the ceiling – tasteful or naff? Service friendly, full of regulars.' BG.

©	Curry Club discount (see page 6)	☕	Unlicensed
√	Vegetarian		
BYO	Bring your own alcohol	⊞	Delivery/takeaway

GOLDEN CURRY   ©

4 Duncombe Street, Bletchley,
Milton Keynes   ✆ 01908 377857

MK's oldest (1971) now owned by Ismail Ali. Seats 58. Serves formula
curries. Price check: Papadam 40p, CTM with Pullao Rice, £6.20.
Pullao Rice £1.60, Peshwari Nan £4.95, Pickles and Chutneys 50p each.
Lager £2 pint. Hours: 12-2pm/5.30-11.30pm.

JAIPUR   BEST OUTSIDE LONDON TOP 100   ©

502 Elder Gate, Central Milton Keynes   ✆ 01908 669796

Firstly, let's tell the world what owner Abdul Ahad has been delight-
edly telling all his regulars this last year. The Jaipur will be moving
within MK into a £2m detached, sumptuous, purpose-built, opulent,
Maharajah-style, domed palace in its own gardens. Until then it continues operating, beside the station. Watch out for the cycle-rickshaw
(you can have your photo taken in it with the ebullient Mr Ahad).
Despite the imminent move, a brand new carpet has been installed, and
it has been redecorated, in its familiar shades of pink, reflecting its
namesake city, Jaipur in Rajasthan (the city where all the buildings are
made from the local pink-coloured sandstone). Walls, chairs, tablecloths, ceiling (the centrepiece of which is a chandelier) are gorgeous.
Life at the Jaipur never stands still. Additions to the menu, special
functions. Oberoi-trained Indian chef Vijendra Singh has settled in
well with the excellent resident chef Sufian Miah. We continue to get
many reports singing the Jaipur's praises. Those readers who like happy
endings will be thrilled to hear that Dr Ho Yen and his medic friends
have patched it all up and have been back and back again. So have many
others, literally too numerous to mention. Here's the tip of the iceberg:
'What can I say? Excellent! Gold premium award. I had the Chicken
Jalfrezi, my partner had non-vegetarian Thali, Popadoms, Pickles,
Peshwari Nan, Prawn Puree. Really enjoyed my meal. No wonder it is
in the top ten.' MM. 'My friend has the Gosht Garlic Masala with Nan
£7.95, one of the best she'd ever had. Absolutely delightful.' BG. 'Drove
up to MK to visit Ahad and experience the 1st Monday of the month
Banquet. Restaurant absolutely packed. Set menu, but large, large portions of a different dishes. Fabulous. Started with Chicken Samosa,
Aubergine Stuffed Tomato with a delightful coriander chutney, yum
yum. Twice marinated trout, I'm not a fish eater, but I did try it, and I

would try it again. Main Course – two curries, traditionally cooked on the bone, one lamb with Shatkora (Indian lime) sour but great, the other one chicken. Vegetables – Mushrooms and Spinach, good as was the Cumin Cauliflower. Fluffy hot Nanbread and a good portion of rice. Forced down delicious fresh Indian sweets, Carrot Halva being my favourite and a Saffron Barfi. Staggered home.' DBAD. 'Sunday evening Vegetarian Buffet at £7.50, remarkable value with too many dishes to remember! Brinjal was fabulous, including frittered slices and the Spinach and Peas was sensational. A wonderful Dal, a chana cooked with red and green capsicum, a Vegetable Dhansak, Aloo Ghobi, a beautiful Raita and on and on it goes.' BG. Price check: Papadam 50p, CTM £6.95, Pullao Rice £1.75. Service charge 10%. Hours: 12-3pm/6-11.30pm. Branch: Dipalee, 18 Castle Street, Buckingham. I am happy to repeat that you will not find a restaurateur who cares more about his restaurant and his customers than Mr Ahad. Everything from the decor to presentation is first-class.

JALORI   NEW ENTRANT   ©

23 High Street, Woburn Sands,
Milton Keynes   ✆ **01908 281239**

Abdul Hai and Ahad's 70-seater is bigger than it looks. Managed by Abdul Kadir, chef Abdul Hanaan prepares food that is 'First class.' BG. Most popular dish is Chicken Cashew Pasanda. Price check: Papadam 45p, CTM £6.50, Pullao Rice £1.70, Peshwari Nan £1.70. Delivery £12 minimum, 6-mile radius. Hours: 12-2pm/6-11.30pm.

MOGHUL PALACE   ©

7 St Paul's Court, High Street, Stony Stratford,
Milton Keynes   ✆ **01908 566577**

'It's an old monastery school where monks once beat knowledge into the sons of local gentry.' LT. Now the local curryholic gentry beat a path through its Gothic arch, complete with wrought-iron gate, beyond which stands the imposing clerestoric building. Owners Monowar Hussain and Anfor Ali greet you, and given a chance, will tell you how much they spent in 1994 converting this Victorian former cigar-factory-cum-orphanage-cum-school into their 100-seat Palace. And impressed you will be, with the spacious reception area with its armchairs and comfortable sofas where you wait to be seated, and the scale, height, tiled floor, stonework and wood panels of the dining room. Be nice to the gargoyles, there to ward off bad vibes! And wonder what the monks would think of the menu offering all the familiar curry items. 'Service and food quality were both excellent although portions were on the small side. I had my usual favourite, Chicken Zalfraji (£5.75). It was very tasty as were the Chicken Madras (£4.95), Thali Special (£9.95) – delicious – and Chicken Biryiani.' BG. Price check: Papadam 45p, CTM £6.45, Pullao Rice £1.80. Several set meals from £12.95. Hours: 12-2.30pm/6-11.30pm.

MYSORE

**101 High Street, Newport Pagnell,
Milton Keynes**   © **01908 216426**

Another MK high-standard goodie from the Ahad stable, this one operated by brother M. Abdul Odud. The dining room, cleverly housed within two cottages, seats 98, yet provides a number of secluded areas, which 'give a good feeling of privacy.' HG. North Indian curries and Balti on the menu. Join the Mysore VIP Club to qualify for discounts. 10% discount for takeaways. Hours: 12-2.30pm/6-11.30pm. Stocks Cobra.

THE NIGHT OF INDIA   ©

**Agora Centre, Church Street, Wolverton,
Milton Keynes**   © **01908 222228/322232**

Night of India sums up this takeaway – it stays open until 1.30a.m. to please the MK night owls and, not surprisingly, it doesn't do a lunch trade. Home delivery seems to do better than in-house, despite a 20% discount on takeaway orders collected (over £10). Food is good, the House Special Biriani includes lamb, chicken and prawns with salad dressing. The Dal a delight.' BG.

Wendover

THE RAJ

23 Aylesbury Road, Wendover   © **01296 622567**

In a 300-year-old listed building in a beautiful old street, in a picture-postcard town. Inside are 'exposed beams, with walled partitions, dividing the 60 seats into almost separate rooms, creating an agreeable ambience and comfort. We enjoyed our second visit more. Starters, Machli Biran – fish parcels and Chicken Shaee, in mint cooked over charcoal and both terrific. Main course – Lamb Jeera and Garlic Chilli Masala, plenty of meat, beautifully spiced.' MS . Price check: Papadam 50p, CTM £6.95, Bombay Potato £2.50, Pullao Rice £1.80.

Winslow

MAHABHARAT   NEW ENTRANT   ©
---
25 Market Square, Winslow   © 01296 713611

Mr Islam's ground-floor restaurant seats 44 diners plus private room for 26. Price check: Papadam 40p, CTM £5.75, Pullao Rice £1.60, Peshwari Nan £1.70, Chutneys 25p per person. Lager £1.90 pint. Hours: 6-12pm. Takeaway 15% discount.

CAMBRIDGESHIRE

Area: East
Population: 665,000
Number of restaurants in county: 60
Number of restaurants in Guide: 7

Cambridge

GOLDEN CURRY   ©
---
111 Mill Road, Cambridge   © 01223 329432

Shaista Miah's pleasant, air-conditioned, large 98-seater, is divided into booths. Chef Abdul Tahid creates 'Wonderful tastes. Everything piping hot including the plate' JB. Price check: Papadam 40p, CTM £6.25, Pullao Rice £1.70, Peshwari Nan £1.95. Minimum charge £10. Hours: 12-2.30pm/6pm-12am. Branch: Gulshan, Regent Street, Cambridge. Stocks Cobra

TAJ TANDOORI   ©

64 Cherry Hinton Road, Cambridge   © 01223 248063

Taken over by SA Haque in 1992. Restaurant seats 72. 'Food is very good. Puri with a large helping of Prawn Bhuna on top set the scene. Excellent Chicken Tikka Jalfrezi.' RW. Price check: Papadam 45p, CTM £6, Pullao Rice £1.55, Peshwari Nan £1.60. Hours: 12-2pm/6pm-12am. Stocks Cobra.

Ely

SURMA TANDOORI   ©

78 Broad Street, Ely   © 01353 662281

Established in 1979 by M.A. Ossi and S.A. Choudhury. Seats 64 in 2 dining rooms. 'This is the best curryhouse for miles. We regularly eat here once or twice a week.' GS. 'We have always had good meals here – the quantities and quality are always good.' JS. 'Had a very enjoyable curry.' DW. Price check: Papadam 40p, CTM £6.95 incl. Pullao Rice, Pullao Rice £1.50, Peshwari Nan £1.50. Lager £2 pint, house wine £4.95! Hours: 12-2pm/6pm-12am.

Peterborough

BOMBAY BRASSERIE   ©

52 Broadway, Peterborough   © 01733 565606

Owned by Rony Choudhury (front manager) and Mahbub Khan (chef). An attractive red-brick 70-seat interior with a brass-work bar as a feature serving generous curries. Price check: Papadam 40p, CTM £5.90, Pullao Rice £1.50, Peshwari Nan £1.50. Minimum charge £10. Branch: Planet Papadam, 10a Park Road, Peterborough.

INDIA GATE   ©

9 Fitzwilliam Street, Peterborough   © 01733 346160/346485

Taken over in 1996 by Mohammed Farooq. This elegant 44-seater is full of Eastern trinkets and atmosphere. The menu consists of a full house of curry favourites, competently cooked by Chef Kamal Uddin. Air-conditioned. Price check: Papadam 45p, CTM £6.10, Pullao Rice

£1.65, Peshwari Nan £1.60. Sunday lunch buffet £6.50. Delivery: £13.50 minimum. Hours: 12-2pm/6pm-12am (1am on Sat.). Stocks Cobra.

TAJ MAHAL ©

37-39 Lincoln Road, Peterborough ✆ 01733 348840

Taken over in 1995 by Haq Nawaz, who is also the manager. Seats 100. Serving Pakistani and Kashmiri-style curries. Air-conditioned. Price check: Papadam 50p, CTM £6.50, Pullao Rice £1.70, Peshwari Nan £1.65. Lager £2.50 pint, House wine £9.50 Delivery: £10 minimum, 5-mile radius. Hours: 12-2.30pm/6pm-12am. Sat. 6-1am.

St Neots

CURRY MAHAL

1-2 Longsands Parade, Longsands Road, St Neots ✆ 01480 407099

Established in 1993 in a former modern pub by Z. Rahman. Decor good if spartan. Price check: Papadam 50p, CTM £5.80, Pullao Rice £1.80, Peshwari Nan £1.80. Lager £3.75 pint! House wine slightly redeeming £6.95. If you pay by credit card you will be charged 10% extra! So beware this dubious practice. Hours: 12-2pm (3pm on Sun.) and 6-11pm, (12am on Fri. & Sat.).

CHESHIRE

Area: North West
Population: 959,000
Number of restaurants in county: 61
Number of restaurants in Guide: 6

Chester

THE ASIA ©

104 Foregate Street, Chester ✆ 01244 322595

Opened originally in 1962. Under the ownership of Nurun Nahar Chowdhury since 1997. Serves formula curries. Price check: Papadam

40p, CTM £5.75, Pullao Rice £1.45. Hours: 5.30pm-12am (2am on Fri. & Sat.), Sun. 4-10pm.

GATE OF INDIA

25 City Road, Chester   **℃ 01244 327131**

Chester's second oldest (1961), and in Moinuddin Ahmed's hands since 1992. Two floors seating 64. Chef Sundar Ali serves formula curries. Private party room seating 20. Price check: Papadam 60p, CTM £6.25, Pullao Rice £1.55, Peshwari Nan £1.90. House wine £7.90. Hours: 6pm-2.30am, to 1am on Sundays. Useful for Chester night owls and curry-insomniacs. Stocks Cobra.

Ellesmere Port

THE AGRA FORT TOP 100

1-7 Cambridge Road, Ellesmere Port   **℃ 0151 355 1516**

Owned by Shams Uddin Ahmed. A rather damning report from one of our respected critics rocks the boat, since all the rest are happy: 'The restaurant itself is spacious, clean and we felt very welcomed on our arrival. Had Chicken Chat and Prawn Puri (excellent, the helping larger than we get at other restaurants) as starters. Mutton Jalfrezi and CTM as main dishes. Deserves its accolade.' H&MS. 'Impressed with the vegetable curry sauce served with the chicken shaslicks, an interesting variation. Prices very reasonable.' S&KT. 'Large, warm amiable restaurant. Will go again.' DB. 'Sunday Buffet is especially good value at £6.95 each. Monthly gourmet evenings.' RC. Price check: Papadam 45p, CTM £6.25, Pullao Rice £1.60, Peshwari Nan £1.75. House wine £1.75 glass. Hours: 12-2pm/6-11.30pm (12.30am on Sat.). Sunday buffet 1-11.30pm. We'll keep it in our TOP 100, but more reports please. Stocks Cobra.

©	Curry Club discount (see page 6)	☕	Unlicensed
√	Vegetarian		
BYO	Bring your own alcohol	▦	Delivery/takeaway

Lymm

THE SAHIB

4-6 The Cross, Lymm   © 01925 757576

Situated upstairs in an old cottage. 'Excellent Onion Bhajis crisp and
delicately spiced, Shami comes with "rashmi" egg wrap, is moist and
delicately coriandered. Main courses good quality. Traditional village
setting.' IEF-E. 'Tandoori Chicken Masala makes love to your tastebuds!
King Akban Cham Cham seduces your tongue and then proceeds to
nail it to the table – one for those who like a spicy kick.' JC.

Sandbach

THE TASTE OF THE RAJ   ©

11 High Street, Sandbach   © 01270 753752

Opposite the old cobbled square which contains the Sandbach Cross,
Anam Islam's small 38-seater 'gets very busy when the pubs close. Very
neat and tidy. Panner Pakora and Fish Pakora, tasty. Chicken Lajawab
with green chillies, good and spicy. Superb Brinjal.' RK. Price check:
Papadam 40p, CTM £6.50, Pullao Rice £1.40. Minimum charge £10.50.
Five-course set lunch £5. Service charge 10%. Sunday buffet £8.95.
Lunch and dinner, daily, except Sat.s 3pm- 12.30am.

Warrington

BALTI EMPORIUM NEW ENTRANT   BYO

111 High Street, Golborne, Warrington   © 01942 511010

Mr Khan's 36-seater curry house serves formula curries and Baltis.
Price check: Papadam 55p, CTM £5.85, Pullao Rice £1.45, Peshwari
Nan £1.75. Lager £1.80 pint, but you can BYO. Delivery £10 minimum.
Hours: 6pm-12am, Fri. & Sat. from 5pm.

CORNWALL

Area: West Country
Population: 468,000
Number of restaurants in county: 22
Number of restaurants in Guide: 7

Bude

TASTE OF INDIA   NEW ENTRANT   ©

11 Queens Street, Bude   ✆ **01288 356591**

Established in 1995 by A.M. Choudhuri. 'Onion Bhajia, high onion
content, ill-formed, inside undercooked – a bit like my efforts really!!
[but are you charging £1.95 Malcolm?]. CTM and Dhansak sauces reasonable flavours. Average Balti Vegetable Bhajee. Service very quick.'
MW. Price check: Papadam 40p, CTM £6.95, Pullao Rice £2, Pickles
50p per person. Takeaway menu 20% cheaper. Delivery: £10 minimum,
3-mile radius. Hours: 12-2pm /5.30pm-12am. Stocks Cobra.

Launceston

SAGOR   NEW ENTRANT

4 Western Road, Launceston   ✆ **01566 777088**

'Excellent restaurant a real find in the depths of Cornwall. Spotless
toilets, floral displays. Good quality food, served hot.' JG. Chicken Tuk
Tuk, marinated in butter sauce and deep-fried £3.20. Price check:
Papadam: 50p, CTM £7.10, Pullao Rice £1.75. 10% off on collected
takeaways over £10. Hours: 12-2pm/6-11.30pm.

Newquay

THE NEW MAHARAJAH

39 Cliff Road, Newquay   ✆ **01637 877377**

Vasant Maru's restaurant has the unusual distinction of having one
chef from south India, the other from Nepal, resulting in 'fresh and
tasty, unusual food, such as Patra (rolled leaves in batter).' CP.

Penzance

GANGES BALTI NEW ENTRANT

18 Chapel Street, Penzance   ✆ **01736 333002**

'A large restaurant. Superb quality Chicken Kahlin, huge chunks of chicken, the largest I've ever seen. Many different flavours in the meal, top quality stuff.' GGP. 'Chicken Karahi £6.25, cooked with black pepper, attractive sour taste. Egg Bhuna £2.95. Quality very good but slightly greasy. Very prompt, efficient service. Restaurant too dark to see my meal.' MP. Price check: Papadam 35p, Pullao Rice £1.65.

St Austell

EASTERN PARADISE

26 Beach Road, Carlyon Bay, St Austell   ✆ **01726 813141**

'Comfortable 50-seat surroundings. Booking organisation is chaotic, unreliable. Had to wait for a booked table and then manager N. Uddin overruled the waitress who had our booking, and gave our table to a party who were waiting with us but had not booked. Overall the food was good and starters plentiful. Onion Bhajia and Prawn Puri good and an excellent sharp and spicy Chicken Chat. Vegetable Samosa a little on the small side. Fiery Madras, Dhansak even hotter. Tikka Masala very tasty and Special Biriani enormous.' MW. Price check: Papadam 40p (plain), 45p (spicy), CTM £5.95, Bombay Potato £1.95, Pullao Rice £1.50, Chutneys and Pickles, per person 40p. House wine £6.80. Hours: 12-2pm/5pm-12am, to 12.30am weekends.

TAJ MAHAL NEW ENTRANT

57 Victoria Road, Mount Charles, St Austell   ✆ **01726 73716**

'Just 7 single-table alcoves. Faded decor, with old-style atmosphere. Menu standard, recent addition of obligatory Balti section. Onion Bhajias spicy with plenty of onion. Tasty Tikkas and Dhansak, hot and full of flavour. Excess oil should have been drained off. Service left room for improvement. Waiter unsmiling throughout, bordering on surly.' MW. Price check: Papadam 40p, CTM £6.95, Bombay potato £2.10, Pullao Rice £1.60, Pickles, Chutneys and Mint Sauce (each) 40p. Hours: 12-2pm/6pm-12am.

Saltash

SHALIMAR

37 Lower Fore Street, Saltash   © 01752 840404

We received a lovely letter from proprietor Syed Munawar Ali. Not normally sufficient to get a Guide entry, but if he cares that much to write, we reckon he'll care about you. 'Chicken Badshahi is highly recommended. Chickpeas in the Chana Masala very well cooked, which makes a change from the bullets a lot of places present you with.' DB. Price check: Papadam 40p, CTM £5.20, Pullao Rice £1.60.

CUMBRIA

Area: Lake District
Population: 492,000
Number of restaurants in county: 26
Number of restaurants in Guide: 10

Barrow-in-Furness

GOLDEN VILLAGE   ©

36 Dalton Road, Barrow-in-Furness © 01229 430133/430033

Owned and managed by Janet Cheserwith, head chef Aba Fateh Choudhury. The restaurant in two rooms seats 58. Price check: Papadam 45p, CTM £6.50, Pullao Rice £1.40, Peshwari Nan £1.70. Delivery: £10 minimum, Barrow area. Hours: 6pm-12am, closed Mon. Stocks Cobra.

MITHALI NAME CHANGE   ©

252-254 Dalton Road,
Barrow-in-Furness   © 01229 432166/431947

Evan Ahmed's 42-seater has changed name from the Monihar. Thumbs up for Chef Abida Choudhury. 'Excellent Thali dishes. Good selection of Biriani dishes – eight different. Curry Club members 10% discount and free bottle wine with the Kurzi Lamb (for four).' AY. Price check:

Papadam 40p, CTM £5.50, Pullao Rice £1.45, Peshwari Nan £1.70. Delivery: £6.50 minimum, 10-mile radius. Hours: 12-2pm/5pm-12am (12.30am Fri. & Sat.). Stocks Cobra.

Bowness on Windermere

EMPEROR OF INDIA NEW ENTRANT

The Arcade, Crag Brow,
Bowness on Windermere   © 015394 43991

Some interesting dishes include Banana Raitha £1.10 and Palak Nan £2.10. 'We ordered a prawn puree to start. Fresh – an even balance of spices so as not to spoil the taste of the prawns. The main course was equally well prepared and presented. Overall an excellent meal £36 for 2 including a reasonably priced St Emilion.' DH. Price check: Papadam 60p (plain), 65p (spicy), CTM £8.95, Bombay Potato £2.95, Pullao Rice £1.90, Pickles/Chutney 50p each. Hours: 12-2pm/5.30-10.45pm (11.30pm on Fri. & Sat.).

Carlisle

DHAKA TANDOORI   ©

London Road, Carleton, Carlisle   © 01228 523855

You'll find A. Harid's 100-seater 'marbled-effect restaurant with chandeliers on the edge of town approaching junction 42 of the M6. Consistently good, smart up-market restaurant. Try Chef M. Ali's Kebab Kyberi, diced chicken in mild spices with fresh tomatoes, onions, served sizzling in iron karahi.' AY. House wine a very reasonable £5.95. Delivery: £12 minimum. Hours: 12-2pm/6pm-12am, Sun. 12pm-12am. Stocks Cobra.

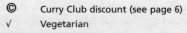

©	Curry Club discount (see page 6)		Unlicensed
√	Vegetarian		
BYO	Bring your own alcohol		Delivery/takeaway

THE VICEROY

Rigg Street, Shaddongate, Carlisle   ✆ 01228 590909

It's near the castle, just out of the city centre and not easy to find. The
outside resembles a garage workshop, but owner Sukar Ali's hospitality is renowned and there is a transformation when you step inside. You
start in a conservatory, where you can browse over a drink, Bombay
mix, and the huge menu. There you'll find most Indian favourites, plus
Balti, Thalis and Jalfrezi. Very good Tandoori. Sultana Lamb Pasanda,
pieces of sliced lamb cooked in fresh cream, cultured yoghurt with
almonds and cashews. Do NOT have a starter if you order the Thali,
you won't be able to eat it all. Best Pickle tray, five varieties.' AY. Hours:
12-2.30pm/6pm-12am. The opening of Ali's Takeaway, opposite, has rid
the Viceroy of its endless queues.

Cockermouth

TASTE OF INDIA   ©

4-5 Hereford Court, Main Street,   ✆ 01900 822880
Cockermouth

F. Rahman's 60-seater is divided into two rooms with a 44-seat private
room. It's 'nicely decorated, and Chef NI Khan offers good choices.'
AY. Price check: Papadam 45p, CTM £6.95, Pullao Rice £1.70,
Peshwari Nan £1.90. Hours: 12-2.30pm/ 5.30pm-12am. Branches: Red
Fort, 5 St Street, Keswick, and Emperor of India, Crag Brow, Bowness,
Cumbria. Stocks Cobra.

Kendal

FLAVOURS OF INDIA

20 Blackhall Road, Kendal   ✆ 01539 722711

Yaor Miah's 95-seater 'used to be a carpet warehouse. A huge water
fountain in the centre of the restaurant refreshes the senses. Choice of
dishes is bewildering. Every dish is good but many are outstanding.
particularily Shahi Korma. Excellent Methi dishes. Thithir Frezi, quail
marinated in herbs and spices and finished off in the clay oven, then
cooked with minced meat, egg, tomatoes, onions, and capsicum, served
in a hot sizzler.' AY. Price check: Papadam 35p, CTM £5.80, Pullao Rice

£1.50. Hours: Lunch: Mon.-Fri., and daily: 5.30pm-12am (1am on Sat.).
Stocks Cobra.

Keswick

MAHARAJAH

6a Herries Thwaite, off Main Street,
Keswick   © 017687 74799

Write off the pencil museum and lap up the lake, then curry on to
Zahangir Ali's 56-seater, for Chef Mofiz Ali's formula delights. CTM
is the most ordered dish. Price check: Papadam 40p, CTM £7.50,
Pullao Rice £1.55, Lager £1.90 pint. Set meal £11.95. Kurzi Special for
two £40, paid in advance. Takeaway menu 15% cheaper than restaurant
menu. Hours: 12-2pm/5.30pm-12am.

Penrith

CAGNEYS TANDOORI   ©

17 King Street, Penrith   © 01768 867721

Established in 1987 by Messrs Imdabul (chef) and Fazul Haque (call
me Hawk!). OK! Hawk manages the restaurant, so well patronised by
local regulars that plans are under way to increase from 50 to 90 seats.
'Table immaculate, seating comfortable and staff courteous throughout.' MR. 'Lamb Masala came up trumps, encompassing a depth and
range of flavours. Aloo Sag was mild and fragrant' MR. 'Unusual decor,
gold leaf wallpaper. Best Pathia.' AY. Price check: Papadam 50p, CTM
£6.95, Pullao Rice £1.55. Takeaway 10% discount. Hours: 12-2.30pm/
6pm-12am. Stocks Cobra.

Whitehaven

AKASH NEW ENTRANT   ©

3 Tangier Street, Whitehaven   © 01946 691171

Nurul Hoque's cooking attracts a loyal following. Owners Abdul
Karim and M.K. Rayman operate a customer loyalty scheme – 5% off
the bill when dining in, and 10% off party bookings of 10 or more.
Price check: Papadam 45p, CTM £6.25, Pullao Rice £1.65, Peshwari

Nan £1.45. Takeaway 20% discount. Delivery. Hours: 12-2.30pm/6pm-12am. Stocks Cobra.

DERBYSHIRE

Area: North Midlands
Population: 933,000
Number of restaurants in county: 49
Number of restaurants in Guide: 8

Ashbourne

RAJAH

1-5 Digg Street, Ashbourne　　　　　　　℡ **01335 342537**

Motin Miah's well established (1978) restaurant seats 56. Chef Harun Miah's specials include Chicken Bengal bhuna-style curry, cooked with onions, tomatoes, green beans, fried egg, £6.40. Price check: Papadam 35p, CTM £6.50, Pullao Rice £1.60, Peshwari Nan £1.90. Delivery: £15 minimum, 5-mile radius. Hours: 6pm-12am (1am on Fri. & Sat.). Stocks Cobra.

Buxton

TAJ MAHAL　NEW ENTRANT

35 High Street, Buxton.　　　　　　　　℡ **01298 78388**

'We use it virtually once a week, since moving to Buxton. Favourites include Madras, Moglai and Jalfrezi, which are pretty hot! Two of us recently had the vegetarian set meal and after completely stuffing ourselves there was still sufficient left over for a light lunch the next day. Staff are young and friendly.' MR&SM. Price check: Papadam 40p , CTM £5.45, Bombay Potato £1.80, Pullao Rice £1.40, Chutney 30p, Pickle 40p. Takeaway 10% discount. Hours: 5-11.30pm.

Castle Donington

PAKEEZA NAME CHANGE   ©

43-45 Borough Street, Castle Donington   ✆ 01332 814455

Formerly Tandoori Nights. Taken over in 1997 by Mohammed Abdul Basit. Seats 55 in two simply decorated dining rooms. Pakistani curries on the menu. Specials include: Balti Sp Cocktail £8.75. Price check: Papadam 50p, CTM £8.50, Pullao Rice £1.75, Peshwari Nan £1.95. Lager £1.95 pint. Delivery: £10 minimum, 5-mile radius. Hours: 6pm-12am.

Chesterfield

GULAB NEW ENTRANT   ©

**207 Chatsworth Road, Brampton,
Chesterfield   ✆ 01246 204612**

R. Miah and A. Rahman's Gulab. seats 40 and serves formula curries. Price check: Papadam 40p, CTM £5.95, Pullao Rice £1.60, Peshwari Nan £1.75. Lager £1.90 pint. Minimum charge £6 Hours: 6-11.45pm (12.45am on Fri. & Sat.).

Derby

ABID TANDOORI   BYO ©

7 Curzon Street, Derby   ✆ 01332 293712/344786

Mohammed Ilyas' 90-seater serves Pakistani and Kashmiri curries. 'This particular evening the food was delicious. It always is, but tonight the dishes were really on form. The dishes are always very generous and the service is always quick and the waiters are helpful. It's comfortable but by no means up-class, just right.' NH, 'but you can BYO, £2.50 a cork.' Price check: Papadam 40p, CTM £7.50, Pullao Rice £1.50, Peshwari Nan £1.80. Delivery: £15 minimum, 6-mile radius. Hours: 5.30pm-3am. Branches: Abid, Dale Road, Matlock. Abid Balti, Causley Road, Alfreton. Stocks Cobra.

Ilkeston

SHAH JAHAN   ©

1 Awsworth Road, Ilkeston   © 0115 932 3036

Taken over by Mr Aziz in 1994, who is also the head chef, cooking curries and Baltis at his red decorated 36-seater. Price check: Papadam 30p,
CTM £7.50, Pullao Rice £1.50, Peshwari Nan £1.40. Delivery: £15 minimum. Hours: 6-12.30am. Stocks Cobra.

Matlock Bath

ABID TANDOORI   ©

129 Dale Road, Matlock Bath   © 01629 57400

Mohammed Bashir's 70-seater is in this delightful Peak District spa
town, nestling on the River Derwent, with its many pleasant walks and
even a cable car to take you to the top of the cliffs. Just the thing to
work up an appetite for Chef Maroof's Pakistani and Kashmiri cooking. 'The Lamb Bhuna was huge and excellent. The rice was a little *al
dente* and the Sag Aloo was a disappointment. Massive menu.' AGR. Price
check: Papadam 40p, CTM £6.50, Pullao Rice £1.50, Peshwari Nan
£1.70. Delivery: £20 minimum, 5-mile radius. Hours: 6pm-12am (1am
on Fri. & Sat.). Branches: Abid, Curzon Street, Derby. Abid Balti,
Causley Lane, Alfreton. Stocks Cobra.

Ripley

SHEEZAN II   ©

11 Church Street, Ripley   © 01773 747472

Opened in 1983, by N. Hussain (head chef) and M. Sharif (manager).
Pakistani and North Indian-styled curries. Air-conditioned, 42-seater
restaurant. Price check: Papadam 40p, CTM £5.85, Pullao Rice £1.45,
Peshwari £1.70. Hours: 6pm-12am (1am weekends).

©	Curry Club discount (see page 6)		Unlicensed
√	Vegetarian		
BYO	Bring your own alcohol		Delivery/takeaway

DEVON

Area: West Country
Population: 1,031,000
Number of restaurants in county: 62
Number of restaurants in Guide: 8

Exeter

GANDHI

7 New North Road, Exeter   ✆ 01392 272119

'Remains reliable. Good sized tables, pleasant atmosphere and friendly staff. Lamb Tikka Karahi a firm favourite. Chicken Patia in a dark, hot, sweet and sour sauce.' PJ.

Ilfracombe

RAJAH   ©

5 Portland Street, Ilfracombe   ✆ 01271 863499

Ralph Wild is the owner-chef here, assisted by his son James. The menu is short but comprehensive. A small restaurant, seating 30, decorated in red, with Indian ornaments. 'The dishes taste like I wish my home-cooked curry dishes would taste. All are made from scratch with fresh, basic ingredients, according to the manageress. Also (and I use this as a yardstick to determine how well made a curry is) in all the dishes we had, there was no residue of oil on top of the dish when it was served or left over in the dish once the contents had been eaten.' MC. 'We found a warm welcome and excellent food. We particularly enjoyed the Jeera Mushrooms, the Allu Bunda and the nut rice.' PL. Price check: Papadam 40p, CTM £6.50 incl. rice and Nan, Pullao Rice £1.85. House wine £6.50. Delivery: £13.50 minimum. Hours: 6-10.30pm, holiday season only. Stocks Cobra.

Newton Abbot

PASSAGE TO INDIA NEW ENTRANT

137 Queen Street, Newton Abbot

'A good restaurant and fairly crowded for early Sunday evening. Despite this the service was good and food excellent. Tandoori Chicken Shorati £6.10, Pullao Rice £1.85, Chutney and Pickles 35p, Nan £1.30. Still had that awful Carlsberg on draught, but had a pint of Tetley Bitter £2.30. Should be in the Guide.' BP-D. 25% discount for collected takeaways. Price check: Papadam 35p, CTM £6.10, Bombay Potato £2.10, Pullao Rice £1.85. Hours: 12-2pm/5.30-11.30pm, (12am on Fri. & Sat., 11pm on Sun.).

Plymouth

BABA INDIAN   NEW ENTRANT

134 Vauxhall Street, Plymouth   © 01752 250677

Established by and named after E.H. 'Baba' Laskar, founder of Devon's Ganges chain, the 84-seat restaurant is decorated with oak panelling, Indian silk cloth paintings and brass ornaments. 'Comfortable, smart, with consistently excellent food.' SH. Menu contains all the old favourites, plus a host of unusuals. Shahi Akbari Chicken and Chicken Kahlia (both about £5) are particular favourites, presented in copper pots. There is a 9-course monthly banquet £9.95, pre-booked only. 'Good, but not ambitious enough for the discerning palate.' SH. Price check: Papadam 45p, CTM £6.95, Pullao Rice £1.85, Peshwari Nan £1.95. Delivery: £10 minimum, 4-mile radius. Hours: 5.30pm-12am. Sunday 12pm-12am, family buffet available 12-5.30pm. Stocks Cobra.

JAIPUR PALACE   NEW ENTRANT   ©

146 Vauxhall Street, The Barbican,
Plymouth   © 01752 668711

Established in 1984 by Syed Abdul Wahid. The two-roomed restaurant seats 70. Chef Rumel Ahmad's cooking is 'recommended to anyone who enjoys quality food in a comfortable atmosphere. My wife says that no one cooks a lamb passanda like the Jaipur.' LC. 'I can think of no better restaurant to put in your guide for the best curry I have had the pleasure to taste.' JK. 'The menu was a good mix of all curries. The quality of food, service and comfort were all above excellent.' J&K. Price check: Papadam 35p, CTM £6.75, Pullao Rice £1.85, Peshwari Nan £1.80. Set lunch: £5.95. Delivery: £10 minimum, 4-mile radius. Hours: 12-2pm/5.30pm-12am, Sunday 5.30pm-12am. Stocks Cobra.

TAJ INDIAN   ©

49 Mayflower Street, Plymouth   *C* 01752 669485

Syed Lutfus Rahman's 80-seat Taj is one of the 'old hands' of Plymouth, being here since 1971. Such experience always tells. GMO talks of 'a lovely meal with really helpful waiters'. Price check: Papadam 40p, CTM £5.95, Pullao Rice £1.70, Peshwari Nan £1.80. Delivery: £12 minimum, 5-mile radius. Hours: 12-2.30pm/5.30pm-12am. Sat. and Sunday open all day. Stocks Cobra.

VEGGIE PERRINS   √

97 Mayflower Street, Plymouth   *C* 01752 252888

Despite the silliest name, you'll like it. 'Plain decor and lacking ambience, but go for the food. Buffet night – £5.50. Plain Papadams and chutneys. Bateda Vada and Mixed Bhajia. Vegetable Tikka, Courgette Bhajee, Madras, Aloo Palak, Chana Dal, Basmati rice and Parathas and salad. All very good. Service a little slow but very friendly.' TI. Hours: 12-2.30pm (Sat. 3.30pm)/5-11pm, closed Sundays.

Tavistock

GANGES

9 West Street, Tavistock   *C* 01822 616731

The popular Ganges was taken over in 1996 by N. Miah. Seats 56 in two rooms, decorated with Indian mirror paintings. Reports please. Price check: Papadam 40p, CTM £6.05, Pullao Rice £1.80. Peshwari Nan £1.75. House wine £6.50 Takeaway prices 20% off. Hours: 5.30-11.30pm. Stocks Cobra.

DORSET

Area: South West
Population: 658,000
Number of restaurants in county: 59
Number of restaurants in Guide: 10

Bournemouth

BOURNEMOUTH TANDOORI NEW ENTRANT ©

**8 Holdenhurst Road, Lansdowne,
Bournemouth** ℰ **01202 296204**

Shuab Ahmed's 50-seat restaurant, is 'tastefully decorated in apricot
and green. Papadam and pickles arrived without asking within minutes. Started with a Madouri Kebab (£3.95), new to me, diced lamb,
tomato, cucumber, etc, succulent and tasty, with mint sauce in a jug to
pour on, how sensible! Followed by one of my favourites, Chicken
Jalfrezi and rice (£6.95), bread and Mushroom Bhaji (£2.15). I rate this
ten out of ten. Service pleasant and swift. One of the best in Bournemouth.' MS. Specials include: Delight, cooked with Grand Marnier
liqueur, fresh cream, almonds, £8.95. Price check: Papadam 50p, CTM
£6.95, Pullao Rice £1.50, Peshwari Nan £1.95. Lager £2.90 pint. Hours:
12-2.30pm/6pm-12am.

THE EYE OF THE TIGER ©

**207 Old Christchurch Road,
Bournemouth** ℰ **01202 780900**

'Opened in 1992 by James Dudley and Ramjan Ali. Managed by Anum
Miah with Showkat Ali in the kitchen. Seats 80. 'We were a bit concerned that it was empty at 7pm on a Saturday night, but we dived in
to find a pleasant restaurant with helpful waiters. It was the best curry
we'd had for many a long month. I was amused to see a machine in the
men's toilet selling curry-flavoured condoms! The meal (without this
particular item) cost us £25 including four drinks, and by the time we
left, it was packed.' CS. JS says her 'mind boggles. Imagine a Phal-
flavoured version!' Really, Jane, behave yourself – this is a respectable

publication! Price check: Papadam 45p, CTM £8.35, Pullao Rice £1.75,
Peshwari Nan £1.70. Hours: 12-2pm/6pm-12am.

TOUCH OF SPICE   ©

**3-4 Granville Place, off Yelverton Road,
behind Barclays Bank, Bournemouth   ✆ 01202 789438**

Established in 1996 by Jakir Hussain. Managed by Alishar Noor with
Abdur Noor in the kitchen. Business lunch, Monday to Friday 2 courses £4.95. Price check: Papadam 50p, CTM £7.05, Pullao Rice £1.65,
Peshwari Nan £1.60. Delivery: £10 minimum, 2-mile radius. Hours: 12-
2pm/6-11.30pm. Stocks Cobra.

Christchurch

STARLIGHT   ©

54 Bargates, Christchurch   ✆ 01202 484111

Ian Clasper's and Abdul Hai's eye-catching, popular Starlight is decorated with hand-painted murals Price check: Papadam 60p, CTM
£8.30 incl. Pullao Rice, Pullao Rice £1.95, Peshwari Nan £2.25. £7.20
house wine. Hours: 12-2pm/6pm-12am. Stocks Cobra.

Poole

THE GATE OF INDIA   ©

**54-56 Commercial Road,
Lower Parkstone, Poole   ✆ 01202 717061**

Messrs Choudhurys' Gate seats 70 in two rooms. 'Friends unexpectedly called on New Year's Eve. They were booked to capacity, but said if
we could be out by 8.30, they'd fit us in. Arrangement worked like a
dream. Splendid meal in delightful ambience, thoroughly charmed and
spoiled. Chicken Moglai, cream, egg, sultanas and almonds. Mozadar
Lamb, tomatoes and coriander. Chicken Dhansak, heavenly, Karahi
Chicken, diced marinated chicken, fried capsicum, brought to table
sizzling hot in superb, characterful sauce. Nothing short of miracu-
lous, four of us stuffed to the gills for £55 inc wines.' RG. 'Reputation
grows apace. Colleague so enamoured of the Mustard Chicken, he
needs it on a regular basis. Assures me that after a few days he begins

to shake and hallucinations follow within a week. Value for money – outstanding. Chicken Rezala my wife told me was the kiss of heaven and Patia Chicken (to die for). They're geniuses.' JC. Price check: Papadam 45p, CTM £6.85, Pullao Rice £1.40, Peshwari Nan £1.60. Monday Balti Night £7.95, Sunday Buffet Lunch £5.95. Lager £3.40 pint, House wine £6.75. Hours: 12-2.30pm/6pm-12am.

MOONLIGHT ©

9 Moor Road, Broadstone, Poole   ℭ 01202 605234

A. Malik's restaurant seats 80, with a 30-seat function room. 'Strongly recommend a visit. No Balti but excellent food, including very interesting specials.' JL. 'Good staff, food excellent.' CC. Mr Malik tells us of a group of customers who visit five times a week. Who are these curry-holics? Declare yourselves and write in! Price check: Papadam 45p, CTM £7.95, Pullao Rice £1.75, Peshwari Nan £1.85. Lager £1.20 pint, house wine £6.95. Hours: 12-2pm/6pm-12am.

RAJASTHAN TOP 100

127 Pennhill Avenue, Poole   ℭ 01202 718966

'Tasteful and very spacious, napkins are of top quality, damask. There is a spacious, well-stocked bar. Tandoori meals are all very good. Shashlik and Tava Murg are blissful. Sabji Korai, green chillies and ginger, splendid experience. Chilli Chicken I had here will rank as one of the finest curry meals I have ever eaten, full, rich, spicy with a kick like a howitzer. They cook authentic Rajasthan dishes here, as well as standard high-street favourites. 'We enjoyed a memorable evening. My wife's Rajasthani Tava Murg – a dry curry, stir-fried marinated chicken garnished with cheese (£7.50) – was exotic, fragrant and delicious. My nephew had a splendid rich Lamb Madras Curry and my Chicken Biryani was out of this world – not the usual faked-up dish with cooked rice and a few bits of chicken, but the genuine slow-cooked classic regal dish of India. All the vegetables, including the Bindhi (£2.20), are fresh. The waiters are charming, helpful, amiable and obliging without being obsequious. Value for money. Extremely impressive.' 'General tone is highly sophisticated. I would especially praise Rajasthan Dakana – chicken drumsticks, marinated in yoghurt, spices and garnished with fried onion. Brilliant Tandoori Mixed Grill. Sabzi Pathia, hot and sour vegetables, laced with chillies and lemon lingers in my memory. Range of different rices, coconut, lemon, mushroom, pullao and beautiful breads.' JL. The Rajasthan is where good curries go when they die.' RG. Glad to keep it in our TOP 100.

TANDOORI NIGHTS   ©

50 High Street, Poole   ✆ 01202 684383

Adul Hannan Choudhury's Nights is a popular restaurant seating 105 Managed by Russell Choudhury. Chef Suza Miah cooking the formula. Price check: Papadam 50p, CTM £7.50, Pullao Rice £1.60, Peshwari Nan £1.80. Hours: 12-2.30pm/6pm-12am.

Sherborne

RAJPOOT   ©

The House of the Steps, Half Moon Street,
Sherborne   ✆ 01935 812455

Owned by Mizanur Rahman, managed by Fajul Hoque with Abdul Kussus in the kitchen, the spacious restaurant has lots of traditional tapestry and upholstery seats for 58 in two rooms. Specials include Rui, Pomfret and Ayre Jalfrezi (£6.95). Bangladeshi fish, 'all very good and generous. Shatkora, a tangy Bengali citrus fruit is used, when available, in chicken, meat or prawn. Service very slow. Onion Bhaji awful, stodgy and lukewarm. Replacement the same but hot. Brinjal Bhaji absolutely wonderful, ingredients chopped very fine, no sauce, no tomatoes, superb flavour, nearly had a second helping. Butter Chicken marvellous and generous. Garlic Nan very good.' HC. Price check: Papadam 50p, CTM £6.20, Pullao Rice £1.80, Peshwari Nan £1.80. Lager £2.10. Hours: 12-2.30pm/6-11.30pm. Branch: Akash Takeaway, 147, Wareham Road, Corfu Mullen, Wimbourne.

WEYMOUTH BALTI HOUSE

24 Commercial Road, Weymouth.   ✆ 01305 783515

Owned and managed by Shalim Abdul. Chef Abdul Shahid. Seats 100. Bangladeshi style curries and Balti dishes on the menu. 'The mangoes were great.' R&CP. 'Over several years, we have been impressed by consistently high standard of service and cuisine.' M&JH. 'Lively spicy food, perfectly cooked, sensitive service.' J&JS. Price check: Papadam 50p, CTM £6.90, Pullao Rice £1.90, Peshwari Nan £2.20. Lager £2.30 pint. Hours: 12-2pm/5.30-11pm.

COUNTY DURHAM

Area: North East
Population: 599,000
Number of restaurants in county: 40
Number of restaurants in Guide: 6

Bishop Auckland

THE KING'S BALTI NEW ENTRANT   ©

187 Newgate Street,
Bishop Auckland   **📞 01388 604222/605222**

Owned by Mohammed Boshir Ali Hussan. Baltis and Bangladeshi curries on the menu. Chutneys and Pickles 50p a portion but if you buy a jar from an assortment they are £1.90 a jar – brilliant idea! Price check: Papadam 40p, CTM £4.80, Pullao Rice £1.45, Peshwari Nan £1.25. Hours: 5pm-12am (11.30pm on Sun.).

Darlington

SHAPLA   ©

192 Northgate, Darlington   **📞 01325 468920**

S.A. Khan's green and beige 80-seat restaurant has two large trees and engraved glass divisions, with a private room seating 60. 'Brilliant.' PJ. 'Excellent' DMC. Price check: Papadam 40p, CTM £5.60, Pullao Rice £1.60, Peshwari Nan £160. £7.50 house wine. Hours: 12-2pm/6-11.30pm. Closed Fri. lunch. Stocks Cobra.

Durham

SHAHEEN'S

The Old Post Office, 48 North Bailey,
Durham   © 0191 386 0960

'Established in 1989 by Mrs S. Khan. The restaurant seats 40 in two
rooms. Kashmiri curries are on the menu. Price check: Papadam 50p,
CTM £8.90, Pullao Rice £1.50, Peshwari Nan £1.60. Hours: 6-11pm.
Closed Mon. Stocks Cobra.

TANDOORI CENTRE   ▦

28 Front Street, Framwellgate Moor,
Durham   © 0191 384 6493

'I enjoyed the Moong dishes – in my ignorance, I expected the beans
to have sprouted. I recommend those waiting for takeaways to drink in
the adjacent Tap and Spile. This is the only real-ale pub I know with a
no-smoking bar; T-shirts and beer-bellies are optional.' DMc.

Stanley

MONJU TANDOORI   ©

33 Park Road, South Moor, Stanley   © 01207 283259

Established in 1987 by Ala Miah, who is also the manager. Cooking by
Moyz Uddin. A small restaurant seating 30 diners in two rooms. Price
check: Papadam 45p, CTM £4.25, Pullao Rice £1.40, Peshwari Nan
£1.25. Delivery: £10 minimum, 8-mile radius. Hours: 12-2pm/6pm-
12am. Stocks Cobra.

Stockton-on-Tees

THE ROYAL BENGAL   ©

Prince Regent Street, Stockton-on-Tees   © 01642 674331

'Formula curry house, marginally better than the rest.' PT.

ESSEX

Area: Home Counties (east of London)
Population: 1,566,000
Number of restaurants in county: 285
Number in Guide: 40

Part of Essex was absorbed by Greater London in 1965. We note affected towns with the letters GL.

Benfleet

AKASH ©

219 High Road, Benfleet © 01268 566238

Mr L. Ali's restaurant is friendly and popular. 'I have a restrictive diet, and need my curries to be as oil-free as possible. Mokis Khan, chef, is very happy to do this for me.' LA. Price check: Papadam 50p, CTM £6.50 incl. rice, Akash Special £5.95, Pullao Rice £1.40. Stocks Cobra.

MAHARAJA NEW ENTRANT

358 London Road, Thundersley © 01268 792141

Est. 1995 by Muhammed Siraj Ali, it seats an impressive 184, plus a party room for 30. Akmal Ali's specialities are popular: Nawab Ka Kana, lamb cooked with ground almonds, cashew nuts, cream, mango pulp, honey and cream, garnished with pistachio nuts, £5.95. Price check: Papadam 50p, CTM £6.95, Pullao Rice £1.85, Peshwari Nan £1.95. House wine £7.95. Hours: 12-2.30pm/5.30-11.30pm.

SPICE 'N' NICE NEW ENTRANT ©

261 High Road, South Benfleet. 01268 759848

Taken over in April 1998 by A.A. Karin (manager) and M.J. Ahmed (head chef), who plan to refurbish their a/c, 40-seater before the end of the year. Specials include Darul Kebab, minced chicken with a spicy sauce £5.95. Price check: Papadam 50p, CTM £5.95, Pullao Rice £1.60. Hours: 12-2.30pm/6-11.30pm. Stocks Cobra.

TANDOORI PARLOUR

63 Hart Road, Thundersley, Benfleet   © 01268 793786

'Another good evening out enjoyed here with entertainment and music quiz. The service, however, although good and helpful can be slow at peak times. Plentiful food, prices a little higher.' PEH. 'What makes it so special is the food, decor and service and entertainment. Holds about 200 people. Decor is modern and very appealing, with a polished wooden dance floor area, and a stage that holds a white grand piano. A curry house with a difference, this one not only tantalizes your tastebuds with gastronomic delights but also entertains you in the process at no extra cost! Every Friday and Saturday night, resident DJ runs a Karaoke and music quiz evening, with music to listen to whilst eating, and prizes to be won. These evenings are lively, and therefore perhaps not for those wishing to spend a quiet, intimate evening. Shar, the owner, and his team of waiters are excellent, and certainly know their job. Food is fabulous and you get loads of it, Tandoori Seafood being their speciality. A very satisfied customer.' BO. 'Dinner dance at the weekend. Magician entertains at our table.' RL.

Braintree

BRAINTREE CURRY PALACE   ©

28 Fairfield Road, Braintree   © 01376 320083

Established in 1975 by A. Noor. His restaurant seats 38 diners in a smart, clean, attractive and friendly atmosphere. House specials include: Butter Chicken and the very popular Kushbue. Price check: Papadam 50p, CTM £5.90 (incl. rice), Pullao Rice £1.60, Peshwari Nan £1.80. House wine £8.20. Hours: 6-11pm. Fri. & Sat. 5.30-11pm, closed on Mon.

Burnham-on-Crouch

POLASH

169 Station Road, Burnham   © 01621 782233

A/c 67-seater well managed by S.A. Motin. Most popular dish: Chicken Makhani, chicken tikka in a medium thick sauce with crushed green pepper and tomatoes, £6.95. Price check: Papadam 40p, CTM

£6.60, Pullao Rice £1.80, Peshwari Nan £1.80. Lager £2.30 pint, house wine £7.50, mineral water £2.10 bottle. Hours: 12-2.30pm/6-12am. Branch: Polash, Shoeburyness.

Chadwell Heath, GL

BHANGRA BEAT BALTI

108 High Road, Chadwell Heath   © 0181 590 2503

58-seater, managed by Babul Hussain. 'Very good. We were stuffed and walked the 3 miles back to Romford.' TL&MR. Price check: Papadam 40p, CTM £5.95, Pullao Rice £1.65. Delivery: £12 minimum, 2-mile radius. Hours: 12-2.30pm/6-12.30am. Stocks Cobra.

Chelmsford

SHAFIQUE

30 The Green, Writtle, Chelmsford   © 01245 422228

M.A. Shafique's baby, it's a mile or three out of town and is in 'beautiful surroundings.' JT. 'Elegant, well decorated, large restaurant. Sun. buffet, good selection of food with fair pricing.' PEH.

Clacton-on-Sea

EAST INDIA TAKEAWAY

182 Old Road, Clacton-on-Sea   © 01255 436445

M.A. Salam's 'takeaway portions are generous. Lamb Tikka Vindaloo £4.25, hot and tasty. Only disappointment was the Nan, slightly overdone.' LG. Price check: Papadam 40p, CTM £4.85, Pullao Rice £1.40 Peshwari Nan £1.50. Delivery: £10.50 minimum, 6-mile radius. Hours: 5-11.30pm (12am on Fri., Sat. & Sun.).

©	Curry Club discount (see page 6)	🍵	Unlicensed
√	Vegetarian		
BYO	Bring your own alcohol	▦	Delivery/takeaway

Colchester

ALISHAN

19 Osbourne Street, Colchester   ✆ 01206 574486

'Very clean and well presented, air-conditioned. Menu, usual offerings.
Service prompt and polite. Good quantities, outstanding quality.
Chicken Tikka brilliant. My best in Colchester.' NF. Price check:
Papadam 50p, CTM £5.50, Pullao Rice £1.60. Set lunch £3.95.

CURRY INDIA

119-121 Crouch Street, Colchester   ✆ 01206 762747

Owned and managed by M. Farid and H. Rahman, since 1968, with
cooking by Abdul Kalam. 'No background music, but a lovely "hub-
bub" from the diners. Plentiful atmosphere and justifiably popular.
The mature waiters in black waistcoats, and the two younger waitress-
es in Indian dress worked flat out all the time. Very competent.' HJC.
Price check: Papadam 40p, CTM £8.50, Pullao Rice £1.90, Peshwari
Nan £1.95. Delivery: 4-mile radius. Hours: 12-2.30pm/6-11.30pm (Fri.
& Sat. to 12am). Stocks Cobra.

INDUS MAHAL BALTI HOUSE

59 East Street, Colchester   ✆ 01206 860156

A.M. Khan's restaurant seats 50, with a party room for 20. Chef Batin
cooks Bangladeshi curries and side dishes. Price check: Papadam 45p,
CTM £6.10, Pullao Rice £1.80. Delivery: £10 minimum, 4-mile radius.
Hours: 12-2.30pm/6-12. Sun. 12pm-12am.

PALASH   ©

40 St Botolphs Street, Colchester   ✆ 01206 578791

'The drab outside could put you off, but we know the food is the best
available in town. The interior is old-fashioned flock wallpaper, curry
house standard, and a little dreary, although kept very neat and tidy.
Chutneys and dips are delivered to your table within moments of
being seated, and drinks orders are promptly attended to. All portion
sizes are very generous, especially the Nan breads – almost a meal in
themselves. All was superb – really proves the old adage of not judg-

ing a book by its cover. The bill for three persons, including one round of drinks, came to £30.10 including service.' HN. Owner N.I. Khan tells us he's happy to give Curry Club members, either a free starter, drink or a percentage off the bill; please ring him to discover which one he is giving tonight! Price check: Papadam 50p, CTM £6.95, Pullao Rice £1.50, Peshwari Nan £1.60. House wine £6.50. Delivery: 5-mile radius. Hours: 12-2.30pm/6-11.30pm. Stocks Cobra.

Dagenham, GL

CURRY MAHAL

27 Gorsebrook Road, Dagenham   © 0181 592 6277

Fakrul Islam's 50-seater does standards cooked by L Miah. Price check: Papadam 50p, CTM £5.60, Pullao Rice £1.50, Peshwari Nan £1.75. Hours: 12-2.30pm/6pm-12am.

Epping

RAJ   NEW ENTRANT

75 High Street, Epping.   © 01992 572193

Mumin Ali's a/c 40-seater is, he tells us, 'beautifully decorated with artificial plants with cosiness and elegance'. Chef, Abdul Ali cooks formula curries. Price check: Papadam 45p, CTM £6.95, Pullao Rice £1.75, Peshwari Nan £1.75. Delivery: £10 minimum, 5-mile radius. Hours: 12-2.30pm/6pm-12am. Sunday lunch buffet £6.95. Branches: Raj Lodge & Garden of India, Harlow, and Rajah, Waltham Abbey, Essex.

Halstead

SIZZLERS

1 High Street, Halstead.   © 01787 478674

'Mr Khan is a wonderful host' JA. He's also adept at getting his customers to tell us so – all on our own copied report forms too! And why not? We encourage restaurants to get their regulars to tell us things such AS: 'I have no hesitation in recommending Sizzlers to others.' DAW. So thanks to AR, AS, AG, DLM, MS, SS, TAB, TAW, AR, SD, SJ to mention but a few. Last words, which we assure Mr Khan are praise indeed from A&DK. 'As my husband says, it is the "dog's bollocks"!'.

Hornchurch, GL

TASTE OF BENGAL ©

194 High Street, Hornchurch © 01708 477850

'Decor very swish and food surpassed expectations. The staff were really helpful and didn't mind us taking nearly three hours over our meal on a busy evening.' PW. Owner Jamal Uddin will give a discount to Curry Club members, here and at his branch: Passage to India, 99 Upminster Road, Hornchurch. Stocks Cobra.

Ilford, GL

CURRY SPECIAL TOP 100 ©

2 Greengate Parade, Horns Road,
Newbury Park, Ilford © 0181 518 3005

Family-run by G.L. and Paul Luther, Punjabi Kenyan Asians as are their relations, the Southall Anands (*see* Madhu's Brilliant, Middlesex), resulting in a different menu from that at the formula curry house. This is the real taste of the Punjab – savoury, powerful, delicious and satisfying, and as near to Punjabi home food as you'll get in Britain. Such items as Palak Lamb, £5, 'lamb so tender with spinach so savoury – it just blends.' DR. 'I adore the Chicken Keema, £6.50, really tasty spicing, with Aloo Cholai, £3, potatoes and chickpeas, Tinda Masala, £3, and a delicious Vegetable Biriani. The food was quite unlike any we'd experienced before.' GT. The family signature dishes are Karai Mexican Mixed Vegetables, and the renowned Butter Chicken, Jeera Chicken and Chilli Chicken. A full portion for four is £12-13. Half-portion £6.50-7. These are starters, and are huge. And the fun is to go in large parties and share each of these. That's the way the local Asians enjoy it, leaving lots of room and lots of choice for the main course. Clues to the Luthers' Kenyan background is also in the menu. Mogo Chips are fried cassava, £3 and Tilapa Masala is an African fish curry, starter £3, main £6.50. Try the Kenyan Tusker lager. For the record here's our standard price check: Papadam 40p, CTM £6.50, Pullao Rice £1.50. Remains in our TOP 100. Hours: 12-2.30pm Tues.-Fri./6pm-12am daily, except Mon., closed.

HAWA BENGAL NEW ENTRANT   ©

530 High Road, Seven Kings, Ilford   © 0181 599 9778

Mr Bashir Ullah is the owner-chef here, while Mr Hudda Kabir runs
front of house. 'We visit regularly and find the staff very helpful,
pleasant and knowledgeable and have sampled many of their dishes.
We have also been guinea-pigs on occasions and had the opportunity
to try new and tasty dishes not yet on the menu. Our favourites are Sag
Chicken, CTM, Balti Chicken, Chicken and Mushroom Biriani and
especially the Dilkush Special.' AN. Price check: Papadam 50p, CTM
£5.80, Pullao Rice £1.50. Minimum charge £8. Hours: evenings only.

JALALABAD TOP 100

247 Ilford Lane, Ilford   © 0181 478 1285

55-seater established in 1977 by Nazrul Islam (head chef) and Badrul
Islam (manager). It serves 'good-as-they-get' formula curries. No new
comments about this TOP 100, I don't know why, so reports please.
Here's a précis from last time, plus up to date info from the restaurant
'Have yet to find anywhere remotely up to the Jalalabad's standard.' IB.
'Outstanding dishes of the highest quality – gorgeous.' MF. 'Starters
plentiful and delicious. Waiters very attentive without being overload-
ing. Our main course curries were all top-class. CTM the best I've
tasted. When the Peshwari Nan arrived it was the best I've had. I asked
the waiter if the bread had been cooked in a tandoor, at which I was
invited into the kitchen to see the tandoor. Immaculate with everything
laid out ready.' TL. Hopefully, restaurants as well-established as this one
do not change, so we'll keep it in our TOP 100. Price check: Papadam
50p, CTM £6.90 (incl. rice), Pullao Rice £1.60, Peshwari Nan £1.60.
House wine £8.50. Delivery: £15 minimum, 3-mile radius. Hours: 12-
2.30pm/6pm-12am (1am on Fri. & Sat.).

Loughton

BENGAL SPICE

12 Forest Road, Loughton.   © 0181 508 7185

'Well let us tell you, the Bengal Spice is mighty damn hot (no pun
intended). Both Lucy and myself feel this is our best haunt yet.
Reasons for this are numerous: great decor, superb cuisine, very friend-

ly and efficient staff, posh loos ... I could go on. When you're there, do a wee samba on your table, and Lucy and I will say hello. It goes without saying that we'll be there.' LD&SK.

Leigh-on-Sea

TAJ MAHAL

77 Leigh Road, Leigh-on-Sea	✆ 01702 711006

Owned by Shams and Noor Uddin, manager and chef respectively, it's hugely popular. 'In my role as a Licensing Magistrate, I can recommend the Taj Mahal.' [no I don't understand the connection either -Ed] 'Relaxing atmosphere, decor spotless and service friendly and attentive. My wife and son particularly enjoy the wide range of curries, whilst I prefer the Tandoori dishes.' AGH. 'Been a regular for more than 15 years, on average about twice a week. Good surroundings, well prepared, generous dishes. Fair prices.' GSH. 'The food is always well prepared and delicious. The Chicken Tikka Massala is the best I've tasted in Southend. Loved Patrani Machli – whole trout coated in coriander, cooked in a banana leaf – delicious! Portions generous. All in all, my family and friends agree it deserves continuation in your guide.' PFT. Price check: Papadam 45p, CTM £5.85, Pullao Rice £1.75, Peshwari Nan £2.10. Hours: 12-2.30pm/6pm-12am. Stocks Cobra.

Maldon

HEYBRIDGE TANDOORI NEW ENTRANT   ©

5 Bentall's Shopping Centre, Heybridge, Maldon	✆ 01621 858566

Abdul Rofik, Abdul Hannan and Nazrul Islam's 70-seater, decorated in bright colours with blue table cloths, pink napkins, has a non-smoking room. The centre has ample 24hr-security-guarded car parking facilities. Fish specials include Chandpuri Hilsha, Boal, Ayre and large Chingri (prawns). Price check: Papadam 50p, CTM £5.95, Tandoori King Prawn Special £7.95, Pullao Rice £1.60. Minimum charge £7.95. Set meal £7.95. Delivery: £10 minimum, 3-mile radius. Hours: 12-2.30pm/6-11.30pm. Sat.-12. Stocks Cobra.

Rayleigh

RAYLEIGH SPICY TAKEAWAY NEW ENTRANT ▦ ©

159 High Street, Rayleigh.   © 01268 770768

'You must include this t/a' DR. Est. 1997 by Shelim Uddin and chef Moynur Miah. Specials include: Mancherian, mango and peach pulp, herbs, sweet and mild £5.10. Price check: Papadam 50p, CTM £4.95, Pullao Rice £1.50, Peshwari Nan £1.50. Delivery: £10 minimum, 4-mile radius. Hours: 5.30-11.30pm (12am on Sat., 11pm on Sun.).

Rochford

ROCHFORD TANDOORI   ©

45 North Street, Rochford   © 01702 543273˙

Aktar Hussain's 67-seater, delivering the formula. Price check: Papadam 50p, CTM £6, Pullao Rice £1.65. Delivery: £10 minimum, 5-mile radius. Hours: 12-2pm/6-11.30pm. Stocks Cobra.

Romford, GL

INDIA GARDEN   ©

62 Victoria Road, Romford   © 01708 762623

Originally opened in 1970 and under the present management (Yeabor Ali) since 1975. A medium-sized restaurant seating 54 diners. Branch: Rupali, South Woodham Ferrers, Essex. Stocks Cobra.

Saffron Walden

ROSE TAKEAWAY

11 Market Row, Saffron Walden   © 01799 520987

'Chicken Vindaloo £3.70 and Pasanda £6.30, extremely flavoursome, quite delightful.' JP. 10% discount on collected orders. Price check: Papadam 50p, CTM £6.30, Bombay Potato £2, Pullao Rice £1.70, Chuckney (sic.) and Pickles 40p. Delivery: 4-mile radius.

Shoeburyness

POLASH   ©

84-86 West Road, Shoeburyness   © 01702 293989

The Polash and its slightly younger branch have been in our Guide
since we began, which makes them old friends to these pages. Manager
S.A. Motin tells us his decor is 'wonderful, air conditioned, with water
fountain'. But there's a third Polash in the same ownership. Not in
Essex, nor even Britain. It's in Sylhet, Bangladesh, the town where so
many of our curry-house workers come from. Polash is the best hotel
in town, and their restaurant, the Shapnil, has an item on its 200-dish
menu that amazed us when we visited. Item 95 is no less than CTM!
It is the only place in the whole of Bangladesh where it is to be found.
And, says owner Sheik Faruque Ahmed, 'it sells really well!!!' His UK
partner, M. Khalique, agrees. Price check: Papadam 40p, CTM £6.60,
Pullao Rice £1.80. Peshwari Nan £1.80. Set meal, 'Kipling's Favourites'
– for two £26.95. Minimum charge £9.50. Hours: 12-2.30pm/6pm-
12am. Sun. 12am-12pm. Branch: Polash, Burnham on Crouch. Stocks
Cobra.

Southend-on-Sea

ANAND

363 Victoria Avenue, Southend-on-Sea   © 01702 333949

'Our favourite, frequented for years without mishap!' PM.

SOUTHEND TANDOORI

36 York Road, Southend-on-Sea   © 01702 463182

'Apart from no flock wall paper it is as traditional as possible, small,
Indian music, pictures of Indian scenes, standard menu. Staff very
friendly, helpful. Food good in every way without being exceptional.
Low prices. Papadam and relishes very good. Chicken Tikka Pasanda,
made more spicy on request, including Pullao Rice £7.50. Sag and
Brinjal Bhajee both £1.90.' HC. No credit cards accepted.

Southminster

VILLAGE TANDOORI

High Street, Southminster   © 01621 772172

'Consistently excellent. Standard menu, generous portions, friendly service.' MP. 'We've tried most things on the menu, and have never been disappointed. The Kurzi Lamb's a dream. Customers are treated like friends to the extent that, when one night there was no taxi available, Mr Kadir gave my son and his girlfriend a lift home.' SJ.

South Woodham Ferrers

RUCHITA

Unit 1b, Guildway, Town Square,
South Woodham Ferrers   © 01245 323855

66-seater, est. 1981 by Nazrul Islam (Izzy), cooking by S. Miah. Party room 20. Price check: Papadam 40p, CTM £5.50, Pullao Rice £1.50. Delivery: £10 minimum, town area only. Hours: 12-2pm/6pm-12am.

NAWAB   NEW ENTRANT

1 Chipping Row, Reeves Way,
South Woodham Ferrers   © 01245 321006

'One of my favourites is "King Prawn delight with Eggs Net". Sometimes a cocktail umbrella appears on it! No quiet evening here, but do expect always excellent food served by very friendly staff.' SJ.

RUPALI   NEW ENTRANT

10 Guild Way, Inchbonnie Road,
South Woodham Ferrers   © 01245 322926

'King Prawn Bhuna Puree absolutely special. Tandoori King Prawn just as good. Chicken Tikka Chillies – tikka pieces in curry sauce with as many chillies as you can stand, always excellent. The best Mushroom Bhajee I can remember – Vindaloo hot.' LG. Price check: Papadam 50p, CTM £5.80, Pullao Rice £1.50. Delivery: £10 minimum, town area only, 6-11pm. Hours: 12-2.30pm/6-11.30pm (12am on Fri. & Sat.).

Tilbury

MINAR BALTI HOUSE TAKEAWAY NEW ENTRANT ©

166 Dock Road, Tilbury   © 01375 855181

A takeaway establishment only. Price check: Papadam 35p, CTM £5.50, Pullao Rice £1.40. Hours: 5-11.30pm.

Waltham Abbey

SHUHAG   ©

16 Highbridge Street, Waltham Abbey   © 01992 711436

19 years is how long M.H. Rashid has been going at his Shuhag. Everything from Roagan Goast (*sic.*) to Butter Chicken (£5.75) is on the menu and, as you'd expect, it's all done with an experienced hand. Price check: Papadam 45p, CTM £5.95, Pullao Rice £1.70. Minimum charge £8. Four-course lunch £6.95, kids half-price. Stocks Cobra.

Wanstead

PURBANI

153, High Street, Wanstead   © 0181 989 4174

'Gives the impression of being in a shed adjoining The George, a vast pub. Friendly welcome. Stand at the bar with drinks till a table comes free. Service fast and reliable, customers packed in but happy. Instant papadoms, with good pickle tray. Chicken Phal well up to litmus, or should it be blue touch-paper test. (no, red – Ed!). Good Moghlai, creamy Masala.' cj. Price check: Papadam 40p, CTM £6.30, Bombay Potato £2.10, Pullao Rice £1.50. Stocks Cobra.

Westcliff-on-Sea

MOTI MAHAL   ©

186 Station Road, Westcliff-on-Sea   © 01702 332167

'Thank heavens for Shahi Khan's Moti. It gets my money any day.' gc.

PURBANI

387 London Road, Westcliff-on-Sea   ✆ 01702 391947

'Excellent food has got us thoroughly addicted. Service is good and the waiters are friendly and helpful.' PEH.

Wickford

MARCO POLO

9-11 Lower Southend Road, Wickford   ✆ 01268 764002

'A large, spacious, well decorated restaurant, now very popular so booking advisable . . . Goan cooking is a feature, and unusually there are around half a dozen fish curries. One of our party ordered a prawn dish which arrived served in a king coconut.' SJ.

GLOUCESTERSHIRE

Area: South West
Population: 550,000
Number of restaurants in county: 54
Number of restaurants in Guide: 20

Cheltenham

INDIAN BRASSERIE   ©

146 Bath Road, Cheltenham   ✆ 01242 231350

A pretty 56-seater in pastel shades with cane furniture, managed by A. Rakib. CS still thinks it's the best in town. 'Waiters are always very cheerful and friendly, there's a nice atmosphere.' Branch: Dilraj Tandoori, Dursley.

INDUS TANDOORI

266 Bath Road, Cheltenham   ✆ 01242 516676

Noorl Allam's Indus was recently extended to seat 120, with a party room for 60. Specials include: Chilli Chicken, a very popular stir-fry with fresh coriander, served on a sizzler £9.95. Sun. 12-course buffet meal £10.95 (£6.95 for children), bookings only. Price check: Papadam 50p, CTM £6.95, Pullao Rice £1.95, Peshwari Nan £2.10, Pickle Tray (per person) 50p. Hours: 12-2.30pm/6-11.30pm.

SHEZAN   ©

4 Montpelier Street, Cheltenham   ℂ 01242 525429

Owned by C. White, managed by N. Chaudhry, and still a favourite among Cheltenham's 17 curry houses. Price check: Papadam 55p, CTM £5.95, Pullao Rice £1.95. Average meal £15. Stocks Cobra.

Cinderford

AKASH

92 High Street, Cinderford   ℂ 01594 827770

'Decor is to a high standard and spotlessly clean. Tasty Shami Kebabs if a little small followed by a quite excellent Meat Madras with lashings of fresh coriander.' MB. Stocks Cobra.

Cirencester

ALISHAN

1 Farrell Close, 39 Castle Street, Cirencester ℂ 01285 658987

Good food and service continues to be recorded. Stocks Cobra.

RAJDOOT   ©

35 Castle Street, Cirencester   ℂ 01285 652651

Equally good reports recorded at Fozlur and Ataur Rahman's place.

Dursley

DILRAJ

37 Long Street, Dursley   ℂ 01453 543472

DH continues to 'visit once a week and have never had anything less than an excellent Tandoori Machli followed by Chicken Madras or

Dhansak with Madras Dal Sambar being an exciting and different side dish. Rashid and Rakib play cricket with the local club.' 'Our favourite restaurant. The food, and we have tried most of the dishes, is always well prepared.' FG. Branch: Indian Brasserie, Cheltenham.

Gloucester

BALTI KING   NEW ENTRANT   BYO ©

32 Bristol Road, Gloucester   © 01452 330990

Established in 1995 by N., L. and F. Miah. Their restaurant, decorated in green, seats an intimate 22. Shah Lepaz's cooking includes Jaipuri Special, juicy chunks of chicken tikka cooked in a special ginger, coriander sauce £5.95. Unlicensed so BYO, no corkage. Price check: Papadam 45p, CTM £5.50, Pullao Rice £1.45, Peshwari Nan £1.60. Delivery: £7.50 minimum. Hours: 12-2pm/5.30pm-12am. Branch: Maharajah, 140, Barton Street, Gloucester.

BENGAL LANCER

24-26 London Road, Gloucester   © 01452 501731

'Seats 80 in a light, airy room with windows the length of two walls, affording a panoramic view of the somewhat tatty buildings – well, you can't have everything! It has its own car park at the back and full air-conditioning. Tables are polished black. There is a large reception area/bar where you can relax over whatever while choosing from the menu. Lamb Pasanda was light and creamy, Murgh Jalfrezi, aromatic and delicious loaded with the required green chillies. The Pilau Rice was also very fragrant. Had a good night.' MS. 'Cooking is truly excellent, especially the Birianis. Comfortable and spacious.' PN.

HILLTOP

19 Worcester Street, Gloucester   © 01452 308377

DGT goes frequently: 'The menu is familiar, but the tastes are different. They serve Nepalese and south Indian food. Bhajis are particularly good, so is the Aloo Masala Dosa, and the Nepalese Murgh Masala is very good. Our food for two £22 plus drink.' Stocks Cobra.

Lechlade

BRITISH RAJ

Burford Street, Lechlade   © 01367 252952

'Comfortable intimate atmosphere. Friendly and efficient, no delays but sufficient time given between courses.' C&SR. Stocks Cobra.

Lydney

MADHUMATI TANDOORI

3 Cavendish Building, Hill Street, Lydney   © 01594 842283

'Smart and clean, olde-cottage style complete with coach lamps on the walls. I think the chef got a little carried away with my Madras, it was a real fork-melter. Portions plentiful and Nan fresh and light.' MB.

Moreton-in-Marsh

MORETON TANDOORI

High Street, Moreton-in-Marsh   © 01608 650798

'Excellent meal, pleasant surroundings. Service quick and efficient. Balti Vegetable Bhoona especially good. Decent-sized starters.' JM.

Nailsworth

PASSAGE TO INDIA

Old Market, Nailsworth   © 01453 834063

'On entering I was met with a wonderful aroma of spices. Lamb Phal and Pilau Rice well-cooked, well-balanced but so huge, I couldn't eat it all.' AEJ. 'A very tastefully decorated restaurant with friendly and courteous staff. Food is freshly cooked and mouthwatering. I will return.' ST. 'A bit expensive, but worth it, food very good.' PJ.

©	Curry Club discount (see page 6)		Unlicensed
√	Vegetarian		
BYO	Bring your own alcohol		Delivery/takeaway

Staple Hill

TANDOORI NIGHTS

36 Broad Street, Staple Hill,
South Gloucestrshire   © 0117 970 1353

Opened in 1989 but taken over in 1993 by Masuk Miah (manager),
Angur Alam (head chef) and Faruk Miah. Seats 42 diners in two
rooms. Bangladeshi, Kashmiri and Northern Indian curries. We told
last time that AEJ proposed to his girlfriend here. We haven't heard
more but hope he still 'can't get enough!' (of the place!!!). Price check:
Papadam 80p, CTM £6.40, Pullao Rice £1.90, Peshwari Nan £2.10.
Lager £2.40 pint. Hours: 12-2pm/6-11.30pm.

Stroud

RAJDOOT   NEW ENTRANT

16 Gloucester Street, Stroud   © 01453 765430

Owned by Mr Hussain, who is also in charge of the kitchen. Price
check: Papadam 40p, CTM £6.26, Pullao Rice £1.60. Hours: 12-
2.30pm/6-11.30pm (12am on Fri. & Sat.).

Tewkesbury

MUNIRA   ©

69 Church Street, Tewkesbury   © 01684 294353

Remains popular and well spoken of. Branch: Munira, 60 Upper High
Street, The Strand, Cheltenham. Stocks Cobra.

Thornbury

MOGHUL'S BRASSERIE

High Street, Thornbury   © 01454 416187

AE-J tells us he was Moghul's first customer a few years back when it
opened. He tells us in his reports how much he likes it. Stocks Cobra.

MUMTAZ INDIAN   ©

7 St Mary's Centre, Thornbury   ✆ 01454 411764

The Mumtaz is on two levels. The downstairs seating area and small bar are for takeaway customers and perusal of the menu. The restaurant is upstairs. 'Menu not too extensive, but food extremely good and large portions. Clean European-style decor and music! Very helpful staff and friendly. Would go back.' ww. KB was less enthusiastic about the decor and other reports talk of standard curries of generous proportions. AE.-J found the Phal too hot on one occasion and too mild on another, although his fiancée 'loves the Kormas'. Evenings only.

Wotton-under-Edge

INDIA PALACE

13 Church Street, Wotton-under-Edge   ✆ 01453 843628

A 'welcome holiday discovery in the beautiful Cotswolds'. Average food and service reported. MD. Stocks Cobra.

HAMPSHIRE

Area: South
Population: 1,600,000
Number of restaurants in county: 209
Number of restaurants in Guide: 31

Aldershot

JOHNNIE GURKHA'S   ©

186 Victoria Road, Aldershot   ✆ 01252 328773

'Glad to see the restaurant is still as seedy as ever, although it's not quite so easy to accept since the prices are now as much as anywhere else. Mint sauce is excellent. Famous Dil Kusa Nan – an enormous bread topped with cherries and coconut.' PD. 'Food is very plentiful, beautifully cooked and spiced and nothing was left!' JW. Stocks Cobra.

Alresford

SHAPLA NEW ENTRANT

60, West Street, Alresford   © 01962 732134

'Up there with the best of them, 60 seats, half downstairs, where it's best to be, with the atmosphere. Food is excellent and portions better than norm. My wife can't see past the Murgh Rossa £6.95 and I recommend the Chilli Masala or Garlic Chilli Chicken, £6.95 for those who like it on the hot side. Service is friendly. Smoking and non-smoking areas. Book at weekends.' TB. Price check: Papadam 50p, CTM £6.25, Pullao Rice £1.90. Branch: Gandi, Winchester.

Alton

ALTON TANDOORI   ©

---

7 Normandy Street, Alton   © 01420 82154

48-seater, owned and managed by M. Shahid. Forhad Miah's 'food is very good and in plentiful quantities.' JM. 'Chicken Bharta was delicious.' JW. Price check: Papadam 50p, CTM £8.50 (incl. Special Rice), Pullao Rice £1.80, Peshwari Nan £1.90. Hours: 6-11.15pm.

Andover

MUGHAL TANDOORI NEW ENTRANT   ©

---

33 Andover Road, Ludgershall, Andover   © 01264 790463

Owned by Towidar Rahman, managed by S. Miah. 'Tucked away at the end of a modest row of shops is this trip to memory lane. Food like I used to eat as a student in the '50s. All the old favourites, slightly tarted up with chopped fresh coriander. Madras and Vindaloo are really hot and very rich, done to Colonel Blimp's wholehearted approval. By Gad sir! You may enter as a Rookie in the growing ranks of the Curry Army, but you'll be an Old Sweat when you leave. The service is genial, well worth looking out for.' RG. Price check: Papadam 45p, CTM £5.95, Mughlai Kopta (fish) Dupiaza £6.10, Pullao Rice £1.50. Stocks Cobra.

Ashurst

EURO ASIA INDIAN CUISINE   ©

179 Lyndhurst Road, Ashurst   ✆ 01703 292885

Azad Miah runs the front while Mr Rahman cooks the food, which
we continue to hear is fine. Price check: Papadam 55p, CTM £5.80,
Kurzi Lamb for four £42.25, Pullao Rice £1.70. Hours: 6pm-12am.
Branches: Prince of Bengal, Hythe, Dynasty, Brockenhurst, Lal Quilla,
Lymington, all Hampshire. Stocks Cobra.

Basingstoke

AGRA BALTI HOUSE   NEW ENTRANT

34 Winchester Street, Basingstoke   ✆ 01256 475566

'Rough and ready decor. Very good and friendly service. Papadam very
crisp, superb chutneys. Excellent Meat Thali, £9.40. Chicken Tikka,
£2.30 a bit too sweet. Great Nan. Great tasting Chicken Madras £3.75,
right heat level. Will return.' JP. Price check: Papadam 40p, CTM £5.65,
Bombay Potato £1.95, Pullao Rice £1.75. Delivery: £10 minimum,
3-mile radius, orders over £20, free bottle of wine.

BENGAL BRASSERIE   ©

4 Winchester Street, Basingstoke   ✆ 01256 473795

This 'old hand' originally opened in 1978 and has been under Shelim
Ahmed's careful ownership since 1985. Hours: 12-2.30pm/6pm-12am.

Eastleigh

GREAT MOGHUL   NEW ENTRANT

1 High Street, Eastleigh   ✆ 01703 612018

'Service immediate and attentive. I enjoyed fresh Papadams, the most
delicious Lamb Samosas, followed by giant pieces of superbly spiced
Chicken Tikka Bhuna with a Paratha. Definitely worth a visit.' TE.

Fareham

FAREHAM TANDOORI

174a West Street, Fareham   ✆ 01329 286646

36-seater owned by Mr Begum, managed by Jakir Hussain, a haunt of
MS. Here's his latest: 'Menu's OK, grub's fine. Things went swimming-
ly until two English girls came on duty at 8pm. They gave very good
impersonations of wax dummys except when chatting to each other or
(presumably) boyfriends on the restaurant phone. I feel sorry for the
owner getting lumbered with these two "superior" workshy girls.' Price
check: Papadam 45p, CTM £5.45, Pullao Rice £1.70. Delivery: £1.50
Fareham area. Hours: 12-2.30pm/6pm-12am. Stocks Cobra.

Farnborough

GURKHA VILLAGE   NEW ENTRANT

Lynchford Road, Farnborough   ✆ 01252 541419

'Opened by an ex-Gurkha serviceman. Easy parking. Pictures of Nepal
adorn the walls. Service very friendly and impeccable. Set menu banquet for £8.50 a head, Mon. to Thurs., excellent value. Food well
cooked. Sizzlers much in evidence. Especially remarkable: 2 bhajis the
size of tennis balls! Quite busy for a wet Thursday evening.' SM.

POPADOMS   ©

33 Medway Drive, Cove, Farnborough   ✆ 01252 376869

Owner Sean Usher claims to be the UK's only English owner (you're
not Sean – read this Guide!). The 36-seater is painted cream and earthy
red, the woodwork indigo blue, the furniture is simple wood giving an
airy feeling. Swathes of cream, red and blue hang from the ceiling.
Nepalese. Bikash Devkota is manager. Sanjiv Singh's specials include:
Chicken Monsourri – slices of chicken tikka in a Madras-style sauce
that also features sliced green chillies and soy sauce. Price check:
Papadam 50p, CTM £5.90, Pullao Rice £1.90, Peshwari Nan £1.90.
Delivery: £8 minimum. Hours: 6-10.30pm. Stocks Cobra.

SHAMPAN NEW ENTRANT

54 Cove Road, Cove, Farnborough   © 01252 370226

'Off the beaten track, worth discovering. Chutneys fresh, service very friendly, chatty waiters advise on selections (unusual round here!). Does a very good Chicken Rezala and Prawn Purée. Only gripe – the prices. £80 for four.' SM. 'Having just moved, I found my new local near my front door, what luck! Even better, it's really good. Decor of highest quality, back-lit glass etchings. Aloo Chat exceptional, not your average bit of boiled spud in the leftover Bhuna from yesterday, nicely presented, just to get the tastebuds in the feel of things. Chicken Vindaloo, an excellent choice, a little runnier than usual but had a good kick to it. Paratha, really good, flaky bread. Prices reasonable.' RV.

Fleet

THE GURKHA SQUARE TOP 100   ©

327 Fleet Road, Fleet   © 01252 810286

Nearby is Church Crookham, the Gurkha base, and you'll find a few good Nepalese restaurants in the area, actually patronised by Nepalese. This 67-seater, owned by A.B. Gurung, managed by Om Gurung, is as good as you'll find. 'Thought Wednesday night should be quiet, no need to book – but we were wrong. Absolutely packed out. Second sittings. Polite, smart waiters. Food delicious. Sel Roti, traditional Nepali roti made from rice flour, yoghurt, sugar, fennel and cardamom, served golden brown in colour with aloo achar £3. Momo, steamed dumplings, delicately spiced and served with tomato pickle £2.90. We also tried Aloo Tamam Bodi for the first time, typical fermented bamboo shoots, black eye beans and potatoes, £2.90. OK if you like the sourness of bamboo. One lonely little chap from the Gurkha regiment was having a solo meal. I did notice that he had learnt how to drink lager (Nepalese Tiger lager £2.90 pint) in fairly large quantities, probably from his British squaddy mates.' DBAC. Main courses include a variety of chicken (Kukhara), lamb (Kashi) or prawn (Jhingay) dishes. Swadilo is mild, Khorsani hot. Bhat is rice. We chose Kukhara Bhutawa, fried chicken, £5.75 and the Kashi Ledo Bedo, £4.20 – lamb in a Nepalese gravy, with Yogi Bhat £5.20. It all transported us back to Nepal.' MB. 'Absolutely delicious. Belgian chocolate with the bill.' JWG. 'Food was excellent but no service added, because it was much too slow.' RV. (not slow when the editors visited anonymously). Delivery: 3-mile radius. Hours: 12-2.30pm/6-11.30pm.

Gosport

DIL TAKEAWAY   ©

73 Forton Road, Gosport   © 01705 521997

Abdul Rob took over in 1998. Price check: Papadam 40p, CTM £5, Pullao Rice £1.40, Peshwari Nan £1.70. Hours: 6pm (5pm on Sat.)-12am. Branch: Bombay Aloo, 293, Commercial Road, Portsmouth. Delivery: £10 minimum.

TASTE OF INDIA   ©

5 Bemisters Lane, Gosport   © 01705 601161

Taken over in 1997 by Abdul Ahad, his restaurant seats an intimate 36 diners. 'The quality of food and service was excellent. Rarely have I seen so much sweat over a meal as from my companion, who said his Jalfrezi was the hottest curry he had ever had.' SF. House specials include: Shatt dishes – a shatt is a Himalayan lemon with a sour taste – he tells us that they are proving very popular. Price check: Papadam 40p, CTM £6.45, Pullao Rice £1.60, Peshwari Nan £1.60. Delivery: £8 minimum. Hours: 12-2.30pm (Tues. & Sat. only)/5pm-12am (1am on Fri. & Sat.). Stocks Cobra.

Hook

HOOK TANDOORI   ©

1 Fairholme Parade, Station Road, Hook   © 01256 764979

Syed Ahmed's 67-seater is: 'Highest quality, full of flavours. Particularly the King Prawn, Chicken Vindaloo – especially good. Staff well presented and friendly.' MJBK. Price check: Papadam 50p, CTM £8.95, Pullao Rice £1.95, Peshwari Nan £1.85. Hours: 12-2.30pm/6-11.30pm. Branch: Mogul, 13 London Road, Bagshot, Wiltshire.

Horndean

INDIAN COTTAGE NEW ENTRANT   ©

4 The Square, Horndean   ✆ **01705 591408**

Taken over in 1997 by Abbas Karim (manager) and Anor Miah (head chef), his most popular dish is Chicken Jalfrezi. Has a cottage effect with leaded lights, cosy and comfortable. Price check: Papadam 50p, CTM £5.50, Pullao Rice £1.65. Sun. buffet £6.95. House wine £6.95, Hours: 12-2.30pm/6pm-12am. Stocks Cobra.

Liss

MADHUBAN TOP 100

94 Station Road, Liss   ✆ **01730 893363**

I told last time how this is my best nearby local. Lodue (pronounced Ludo) Miah, is one of the most caring perfectionists I know. And I do know, because he still uses me as his consultant. This year I took on the design of his menu. I thought it would take 3 days – it took 10! But I was determined, like he was, that this would be the menu of menus and I was delighted to see the end of his nasty, lurid plastic-laminated offering. You know the species well, complete with 23 spelling mistakes. This is typical at the curry house. I blame the printers 150%. Is it a prerequisite to employ dyslexic illiterates, who are often colour blind as printers? There is no excuse for 'meat balls spicy cokked with chick peas' or 'grilled ona charcoal flame', 'avarcado … in a vinigrete', 'savory meat' or 'corriander' six times. I don't think it's funny, and it's all too prevalent. You can't blame the restaurateur – English is the world's hardest language to spell. He trusts his printer. (How would such a worm manage if he had to print his c/v in Bengali?) What, incidentally happens to the computer spell-check? Such a menu becomes the butt of all humour – the whole industry slides further down market. But what can be done? Originating a menu is expensive, and corrections can only be done at proof stage. I urge all restaurateurs to ask their trusted customers or the bank manager to read the proofs, and *vice-versa* customers to offer to do it.

Anyway, Lodue's new menu is error-free, guaranteed. That will get everyone looking. And it should because it's not just a pretty menu which makes a restaurant. It is service, decor, ambience and food. Oh and one more thing – the toilets. One correspondent wrote saying that we should carry a toilet-grading on all our entries. Great idea, madam, but it's hard enough to get their new prices out of them!

Well, at the Maduban, it's full marks for all of these – though DBAC says: 'A pretty blue restaurant with glittering chandeliers and a pedestal fountain, containing a resident duck. They obviously like river birds … if you order a brandy, they serve it to you supported by a brass swan with flame!' But she adds 'the decor is getting a bit used. It's time for a complete re-dec'. What's all this about a duck asks a Scottish scribe? It lives, with three ducklings in the fountain (which Lodue plans to rebuild to monumental proportions). They're all just plastic – and just a little gag! Fernhurst's I.A. Brown has not dared to reappear having dismissed the regulars as 'ignorant yuppies'. The regulars would still like to interview Mr Brown on this topic. They still come from far and wide. The Kent regular augmented her weekly visits this year with a special wedding reception held at the Madhuban for 35 guests (all from Kent) all day one Sat. Lodue is usually out front, with his brothers Bedar and Dodu in their smart waistcoat uniforms. He does supervise the cooking, though day-to-day it's in the hands of an uncle and cousins. Finally, what of the food?

The new eight-page menu fully describes all the dishes. 22 starters, 7 items from the tandoor, plus 5 nans. There is an ample choice of old favourites, and they are all done well. Unusual items include Hyderabadi Shorba, £1.60, a soup with chicken and potato, flavoured with coconut and lemon; and Hussaini Kebab, £2.50, meat stuffed with raisins; Dhaba Meat, £5.50 a 'roadside dish of lamb'; while Elaichi Gosht, £5.50 is meat flavoured with cardamom and coriander. In addition there is a supplementary menu sheet, with some specials such as Murgh Deluxe, £7.50, keema-stuffed boned chicken leg in a CTM creamy sauce, Jingha Pineapple – prawns in a scooped-out pineapple £10.95, and sliced Raan, £7.50. Price check: Papadam 50p, CTM £5.95, Pullao Rice £2.20. Remains in our TOP 100. Stocks Cobra.

Portsmouth

NEW TAJ MAHAL   ©

54 Kingston Road, Buckland, Portsmouth   ℮ 01705 661021

Nothing 'new' about this 1965 curry house. Now owned by Lilu Miah and Abdul Matin. It's a safe bet on curry alley!

SHANTI NAME CHANGE

124 Kingston Road, North End,
Portsmouth   ✆ 01705 664045

Ownership change to Shakut Ali, and inexplicable name change at the former Palash and no diner reports take it out of our top listing.

STAR OF ASIA ©

6 Market Way, City Centre, Portsmouth   ✆ 01705 837906

Established in 1992 by Abdul Mothen, who also manages his 40-seater restaurant. Chef Gian Uddin cooks the curries. Hours: 12-2.30pm/ 6pm-12am. Sat. & Sun. 12pm-1am.

Ringwood

CURRY GARDEN ©

10 High Street, Ringwood   ✆ 01425 475075

Between them, Feroze Khan and chef Runu Miah continue to satisfy the needs of their diners.

Romsey

SHAHEB NEW ENTRANT

5 Church Street, Romsey   01794 517431

'Well cooked food. The lady in the booth next to me left her sleeping five-year-old behind (apparently he likes Chicken Vindaloo but it knocks him out) and the owner ran after her with him!' MS. Price check: Papadam: 40p, CTM £5.20, Bombay Potato £1.90, Pullao Rice £1.60. Delivery: minimum £10. Hours: 5.30pm-12am.

Southampton

LAST VICEROY NEW ENTRANT ©

4-7 High Street, Southampton   01703 452285

Owned by Mrs Begum Bahar since 1989, her restaurant seats 60 diners. Northern Indian cuisine is supervised by head chef M. Abdul Hassan;

his most popular dish is Roghan Josh. House wine £8.95, mineral water £3.50 bottle. Price check: Papadam 50p, CTM £6.75, Pullao Rice £1.90, Peshwari Nan £1.80. Hours: 12-2pm/6pm-12am. Stocks Cobra.

Southsea

GOLDEN CURRY TOP 100   ©

16 Albert Road, Southsea   ℭ 01705 820262

Owner Salim Hussein (manager) and Razak Ali (head chef) since 1979 tell us they're about to redecorate their a/c, 52-seater. That's fine, but please don't change the food quality. I was recently interviewed by a local TV station there, and I sampled many dishes from the korma to the phal. They were spot on. Colours, aromas, tastes, textures, service and price – all done right by experienced 'old hands'. 'Excellent food and service. Our regular curry restaurant.' D&KM. 'For some 24 years, the Golden Curry is the only location that my family and I have used locally. My brother genuinely impressed. My wife's cousin more than pleased. Classing them as "professional eaters", I relish their observations.' RB. House special include: Bengal Star, chicken, king prawn, mushroom, cooked together with tomato, onion and green pepper, garnished with tomato and cucumber, medium spiced, served with Pullao Rice £8.15; Trout Biran, a dry dish, fresh, whole trout, fried with spices, served with lightly spiced spinach, sliced lemon, served with boiled rice £8.25. Price check: Papadam 45p, CTM £7.05, Pullao Rice £1.80, Peshwari Nan £1.70. Hours: 12-2pm/5.30pm-12.30am. Sun. 12pm-12am. Stocks Cobra.

INDIAN COTTAGE

257 Albert Road, Southsea   ℭ 01705 826010

'Lovely decorations, apricot, green, blue, high-quality furnishings, including wood screens. Heavy silver cutlery, white crisp cotton table-cloths on dark wood polished tops. Papadoms arrived as I sat down, my Lamb Tikka starter arrived five minutes later with the chutneys! Followed with Chicken Shashlik Kebabs – two huge skewers more like swords on a bed of shredded lettuce and white cabbage. Great lumps of chicken, onion, green pepper all burnt on the edges – yummy! Excellent food, cheerful and speedy service and good ambience.' MS. Price check: Papadam 40p, CTM £5.95, Pullao Rice £1.95. Hours: 12-2.30pm/6pm-12am. Stocks Cobra.

JEWEL IN THE CROWN

60 Osborne Road, Southsea   ✆ 01705 827787

Chef Sikandar Ali recommends Murgh Makani, 'nice and very mild' £5.95. Price check: Papadam 40p, CTM £5.40, Pullao Rice £1.80. Delivery: £12 minimum. Hours: 12-2.30pm/6pm-12am. Stocks Cobra.

Waterlooville

INDIAN COTTAGE   ©

51 London Road, Cowplain,
Waterlooville   ✆ 01705 269351

D&BR and L&AC have been coming as a foursome for many years to Sheik Shab Uddin's tiny 30-seater (exposed oak beams, blue walls and tablecloths, red velvet chairs) because chef AH Khan's 'food is excellent and the staff always attentive'. Price check: Papadam 50p, CTM £5.50, Tandoori Trout £6.50, Pullao Rice £1.95. Minimum charge £5.55. Hours: 12-2.30pm/5.30pm-12am. Branches: Indian Cottage, Port Solent Marina, near Portsmouth, and at The Square, Horndean. Stocks Cobra.

SHALIMAR NEW ENTRANT   ©

9 Hambledon Parade, Hambledon Road,
Waterlooville   ✆ 01705 251565

A/c 56-seater, with smoking and non-smoking sections, is managed by Mujib. 'Does the simple things well. Chicken Korma one of the best. Lamb Jalfrezi, hotter than usual. Young friendly staff – polite and efficient.' GS. Price check: Papadams 40p, CTM £5.50, Pullao Rice £1.60, Peshwari Nan £1.60. Hours: 12-2.30pm/5.30-11.30pm.

Winchester

GANDHI

163 High Street, Winchester   ✆ 01962 863940

'Agree with BPD in the last GCG …' (to remind us, he said: 'superb ambience. Most of the tables (50-60 covers) arranged for four in cabins, which can be partitioned by curtains – very unusual, but very nice

for a young couple in need of a quick cuddle before a curry! BPD).
'…ambience is very welcoming and good use is made in what is actually not a very big restaurant. Food was very good indeed. Freshly
cooked Onion Bhajia, very generous portion, four pieces. Very good
Lamb Tikka. Stuffed Fried Eggs, two eggs cooked and halved with the
yolk replaced with some sort of whipped mixture and whole prawns,
then deep-fried in batter – great!! Only table there at 6pm, waiters were
prompt, attentive and polite.' CT. Stocks Cobra.

SUHEL'S BALTI HOUSE

8 St Georges Street, Winchester   © 01962 862838

Established in 1993 by Suhel Ahmed, with, he says a ceiling painted as
an Indian equivalent of the Cistene (*sic.*) Chapel, seats 50 diners. House
wine £6.95, mineral water £2.50 bottle. Price check: Papadam 40p,
CTM £6.25, Pullao Rice £1.95, Peshwari Nan £1.65. Private parking
behind the restaurant for 10 cars. Delivery: £10 minimum, 3-mile
radius. Hours: 12am-2pm/6pm-12am. Stocks Cobra.

HEREFORDSHIRE

Area: Welsh Border
Population: 215,000
Number of restaurants in county: 18
Number of restaurants in Guide: 4

Bromyard

BOMBAY PALACE   ©

22 High Street, Bromyard   © 01885 488668

Mr Sofik Miah's 60-seater is 'the friendliest in town. Food a pleasure
to look forward to,' RW 'and service excellent.' CT. Hours: 5.30pm-12am.

Hereford

TASTE OF RAJ NEW ENTRANT

67 St Owens Street, Hereford   © **01432 351075**

Goyas Miah and Azmol Hussain's restaurant seats 44 diners. House specials include: Mughlai Duck Mosallah (*sic.*), duck marinated in tandoori sauce, barbecued in the clay oven, then further cooked in ground nuts and cream £9.95. Price check: Papadam: 35p, CTM £6.20, Pullao Rice £1.65, Peshwari Nan £1.70. Sunday buffet lunch, £7.50, kids £3.75, bookings recommended. Hours: 6-11.30pm. Stocks Cobra.

Leominster

JALALABAD

33 Etnam Street, Leominster   © **01568 615656**

Well promoted by the ebullient owner-manager Kamal Uddin. (though, curiously not to us). Owner-chef Abdul Mukith's food menu attracts regular praise from Leominster locals. Stocks Cobra.

Ross-on-Wye

OBILASH

19a Gloucester Road, Ross-on-Wye   © **01989 567860**

A smallish restaurant seating 40. Some unusual Bangladeshi authentic dishes on the menu include Shathkora Curry and Ada Lembu Curry.

©	Curry Club discount (see page 6)		Unlicensed
√	Vegetarian		
BYO	Bring your own alcohol		Delivery/takeaway

HERTFORDSHIRE

Area: Home Counties (north of London)
Population: 996,000
Number of restaurants in county: 143
Number of restaurants in Guide: 32

Part of Hertfordshire was absorbed by Greater London in 1965. We note affected boroughs with the letters GL.

Abbots Langley

VICEROY OF INDIA   TOP 100   ©

20 High Street, Abbots Langley   ✆ **01923 262163**

Established in 1989 by Ronney Rahman. His 80-seater restaurant, he tells us, has been redecorated this year. House specials include: Makhoni Hash (mild) tandoori grilled duck, tossed in butter, cultured yoghurt, fresh cream and mild spices £5.75 and Karahi Jhinga (hot), jumbo prawns cooked with a medium dry gravy, herbs, tomatoes, onions and green pepper, served from a iron karahi £6.95. Price check: Papadam 45p, CTM £5.75, Pullao Rice £1.70, Sunday buffet £6.95. Reports please. Hours: 12-2.30pm/6-11pm. Stocks Cobra.

Barnet, GL

KING TANDOORI   ©

92 East Barnet Road, New Barnet   ✆ **0181 441 9272**

M.D. Salim opened his 46-seater in 1995 and we hear well of it, especially of the Happy Hour Half Price Meal. 'It makes me happy at that price.' NL. Price check: Papadam 40p, CTM £5.30, Pullao Rice £1.50. Evenings only, except Sun. e-a-m-y-l buffet £5.95, lunch and dinner.

SHAPLA TANDOORI ©

37 High Street, Barnet © 0181 449 0046

S.I. Ahmed's smart restaurant seats 50 and is popular. 'My local, always very reliable. Standard menu. Excellent Dhansak, generous Shashlik and very good side dishes. A clean, cosy restaurant.' CT. Price check: Papadam 40p, CTM £4.95, Pullao Rice £1.45. Minimum charge £7.50. Parking in Fitzjohn Avenue. Hours: 12-2.30pm/6pm-12am. Stocks Cobra.

BARNET TANDOORI   NEW ENTRANT

86 High Street, Barnet © 0181 364 9804

Established in 1980 by Nazir Ahmed (manager) and Foyzul Islam (head chef). Their 48-seater restaurant is (they tell us) nice and cosy, like a train carriage. Price check: Papadam 45p, CTM £5.75, Pullao Rice £1.65, Peshwari Nan £1.60. Delivery: £10 minimum, 3-mile radius. Hours: 12-2pm/6-11.30pm. Stocks Cobra.

Berkhamsted

AKASH ©

307 High Street, Berkhamsted © 01442 862287

'We particularly like owner Foysol Ahmed's service – greeted at the door, coats taken, napkins placed in your lap, staff are attentive without hovering' LB. Hours: 12-2.30pm/6pm-12am.

CURRY GARDEN ©

29 High Street, Berkhamsted © 01442 877867

'An old converted pub, lovely low beams and cosy booths. Very impressed. Will most definitely be back.' SW. Stocks Cobra.

©	Curry Club discount (see page 6)		Unlicensed
√	Vegetarian		
BYO	Bring your own alcohol		Delivery/takeaway

Bushey

INDIA GARDEN NEW ENTRANT

88 High Street, Bushey   © **0181 950 2061**

At Abdul Koyes Choudhury's 52-seater, we hear of the good value:
Sunday 12-course buffet lunch, £6.95. Price check: Papadam 50p, CTM
£5.95, Pullao Rice £1.60, Peshwari Nan £1.40. Hours: 12-2.30pm/6-
11.30pm. Branch: Taste of India, High Street, Kings Langley.

Cheshunt

RAJ VOGUE NEW ENTRANT   ©

48 High Street, Cheshunt   © **01992 641297**

Established in 1991 by Khalek Quazi, who also manages the 82-seater
restaurant. GR likes the Nawab Nargis, cooked with spicy minced
chicken and fresh mint. Price check: Papadam 45p, CTM £6.55, Pullao
Rice £1.95, Sunday lunch buffet £6.95. Delivery: £15 minimum, 3-mile
radius. Hours: 12-2.30pm/6-11.30pm.

Cockfosters, GL

TANDOORI NIGHTS   ©

27 Station Parade, Cockfosters Road,
Cockfosters   © **0181 441 2131**

At the end of the Piccadilly Line is Mrs Yasmeen Rashid's good, reliable 60-seater managed by H. Karim and we regularly get satisfactory
reports about it. Price check: Papadam 40p, CTM £6.95, Roast Quail
and Kurzi Lamb dinner for four, ordered in advance, £110, Pullao Rice
£2.30. Sunday buffet £6.95. Service 10%. Branches: Parkway, London
NW1; Great Queen Street, London WC2. Stocks Cobra.

©	Curry Club discount (see page 6)		Unlicensed
√	Vegetarian		
BYO	Bring your own alcohol		Delivery/takeaway

Harpenden

DHAKA COTTAGE

1a Harding Parade, Station Road,
Harpenden   ✆ 01582 769317

A 40-seat smart establishment with a large modern frontage, which is
home to several exotic palm and rubber plants. 'Amongst my very enjoyable meal was a green vegetable dish in cashew sauce. I can't remember
its name (my wife says slime!) but it was composed of fresh broccoli,
sprouts, chilli and an Indian leaf [Patra? Ed]. The sauce was sublime —
crunchy and sweetish.' PFM. Stocks Cobra.

Hatfield

PRINCE OF INDIA   NEW ENTRANT   ©

10, Market Place, Hatfield.   ✆ 01707 265977

Established in 1993, managed by SF Ali. The restaurant seats 48 diners,
and is newly decorated, we are told, in a romantic and pleasant atmosphere. Price check: Papadam 40p, CTM £6.05, Pullao Rice £1.45,
Peshwari Nan £1.50. Delivery: £8.95 minimum. Hours: 5.30-11.30pm.

TASTE OF INDIA   NEW ENTRANT   ©

33-34 Salisbury Square, Old Hatfield   ✆ 01707 276666

Owned by Mrs A. Khatun and managed by Golam Yahna, the Taste has
become a popular local haunt. Price check: Papadam 40p, CTM £6.95,
Duck Korai £6.95, Balty (sic.) Tropical £6.50, Pullao Rice £1.40.
Mondays, four-course banquet £9.95. Stocks Cobra.

Chelmsford

GURU TANDOORI   ©

5 Bridge Street, Hemel Hempstead   ✆ 01442 254725

Owner S.M. Rahman. Chef S. Uddin. 36 seats. MBS says he eats here
twice a week for twenty years, and that he always recommends it to his
friends, who in turn have become satisfied customers. Price check:
Papadam 50p, CTM £6.90, Pullao Rice £1.50, Peshwari Nan £1.70.

Delivery: £15 minimum, 5-mile radius. Hours: 12-2.30pm/6-12. Branch: Guru, 630, Uxbridge Road, Hayes, Middx. Stocks Cobra.

PARADISE TANDOORI   ©

**79-81 Waterhouse Street,
Hemel Hempstead**   ℭ **01442 243595**

M. Ruez opened his 60-seater in 1988. 'The Pasanda, cooked with wine, was just divine.' MS. Hours: 12-2pm/5.30-12. Branch: Raja, below. Stocks Cobra.

RAJA   ©

**84 London Road, Apsley,
Hemel Hempstead**   ℭ **01442 252322**

'Both spacious and intimate. Portions generous, brought sizzling.' JP. Delivery: 'service was fast. Large and very tasty portions arrived piping hot within 30 minutes.' JH. Branch: Paradise, above. Stocks Cobra.

Hertford

GURU

6 Parliament Square, Hertford   ℭ **01992 551060**

'Always ample, always served promptly, always v g quality. Ask to inspect the kitchen at any time.' KR. Free delivery or collected takeaway 20% discount. Hours: 12-2.45pm/6pm-12am. Sun. 12pm-12am (buffet until 6pm).

Hitchin

INDIA BRASSERIE   ©

36 Bancroft Road, Hitchin   ℭ **01462 433001**

M Chowdhury's restaurant seats 32. Chicken Makhani Tikka £5.95, Rezala Chicken £4.50 and Fish Bhuna £5.25. 'The best in Hitchin.' SW. Hours: 12-2.30pm Tues.-Thurs./5.30pm-12am. Sun. 1-11pm, buffet £7.95. Stocks Cobra.

Letchworth

CURRY GARDEN   ©

71 Station Road, Letchworth   ✆ 01462 682820

Afiz Ullah is the head chef and owner of this 72-seater, which has a
'huge friendly menu.' MT. Hours: 12-2.30pm/6pm-12am. Sun. 12pm-
12am, buffet 12-5.30pm. Branches (all named Curry Garden) at:
Berkhamsted; Rickmansworth; Dunstable, Beds; Hornchurch, Essex.

SAGAR   ©

48 The Broadway, Letchworth   ✆ 01462 684952

Motiur Rahman's 'Trout Masala, £8.50 is one of the best.' LV. Price
check: Papadam 50p, CTM £6.95, Pullao Rice £1.65. Service 10%.
Lunch buffet, weekdays £5.50, Sun. £5.95. Branches: Aashiana,
Broadway, Beds; Ahkbar Takeaway, Abbot's Walk, Biggleswade, Beds.

Radlett

RADLETT INDIA CUISINE

70e Watling Street, Radlett   ✆ 01923 856300

'Chicken Chockro Vorty, marinated strips, grilled, served with salad,
exceptional starter. Jeera Kata Garlic Chicken brilliantly tasty, no cloy-
ing curry gravies. Nan, chewy and delicious.' CJ. Stocks Cobra.

Rickmansworth

EASTERN SPICE   ©

9 Penn Place, Northway, Rickmansworth   ✆ 01923 711101

Ekbal Hussain's 40-seater remains popular with its local following.
Price check: Papadam 45p, CTM £5.45, Pullao Rice £1.60. Hours 12-
2.30pm/6-11.30pm. Branch: Gadebridge Balti, Hemel Hempstead.

©	Curry Club discount (see page 6)		Unlicensed
√	Vegetarian		
BYO	Bring your own alcohol	⊞	Delivery/takeaway

Royston

BRITISH RAJ   ©

55 High Street, Royston   © 01763 241471

Established in 1976 by Nazir Uddin Choudhury, whose restaurant is
decorated with embossed ivory wallpaper and pictures of the Raj, seats
44 diners in an L-shaped dining room. House specials include: a real
Bengali cod fish curry with tomatoes, chillies in a sauce £6.55. After
your meal you can finish the night off by ordering the fifth course –
Hukkah (Hubble Bubble) £2.55. 'The person behind the counter
belched loudly with no apology or an excuse me. Conclusion: Average.
We get better food at home. Worthy of the guide, but NOT TOP
100.' sw. Sorry Mr Choudhury, but this is not the only such report.
We have to agree. Time to update the image, *n'est ce pas?* Price check:
Papadam 50p, CTM £6.75, Pullao Rice £1.65, Peshwari Nan £1.85.
Hours: 12-3pm/6pm-12am. Stocks Cobra.

St Albans

MUMTAJ TOP 100

115 London Road, St Albans   © 01727 858399

We promoted Muklasur Rahman Mojumder's 44-seater to our TOP
100 last time and reports agree with that decision. It was influenced
by PFM, who said then: 'I am lucky enough to travel widely on business,
and never without your Guide. Having visited many, many curry houses in the UK, as well as Brussels (ugh), Amsterdam (great), Stockholm
(ugh), Riyadh (ummm), and the US (hmmm) [I meant to ask last time
where you eat in the US, Peter? If it's only 'hmmm', it ain't where we
eat. Where we go is food is generally worse than 'ugh' especially curry,
and we've been all over the country six times in the last 3 years. Why
do people still rave on about the US being so far ahead of Britain? In
what, pray tell me? Have they even been there? NY – that once awe-
some, faster-than-light city typifies today's land-of-opportunities. It's
now smelly, ill-maintained, unkempt, dirty, honking, grid-locked, rude,
aggressive, sweltering or freezing. It's like the 3rd world with money!
Mind you we always go back for more, but, like Peter, could never live
there. Awaiting the flack in the correspondence. -Ed]. PFM went on: "I
am always pleased to get home and eat at the Mumtaj. Its location and

interior are grand but its food is sublime. Too many curry houses serve their food coated in the same general brown gravy. But in the Mumtaj each flavour stands out on its own. The owner's son Chad Rahman now runs the kitchen. He worked for some time in curry houses in Houston, Texas. [Whoops! But been there — curry ugh! Space centre fab though-Ed]. Our favourite dish is Karachi Kebab — sizzling Chicken Tikka in a spicy sauce, with peppers and tomatoes. This is a very commonly found dish (CTM), but none has brought it to the height that The Mumtaj has.' Incidentally, the name dates from their first menu when the English printer mistook the name 'karahi' and they have kept it ever since. Price check: Papadam 50p, CTM £7.50, Pullao Rice £1.65, Peshwari Nan £1.80. House wine £7.50, mineral water £3.50. Delivery: £11 minimum, town area only. Hours: 12-2.30pm/6pm-12am. Stocks Cobra.

Sawbridgeworth

STAR OF INDIA   ©

51 London Road, Sawbridgeworth   ℂ 01279 726512

Est. 1982 by Dilwar and Jamal Ahmed, it seats 70 in two rooms. Specials include: Hundi (*sic.*) dishes £7.50. We hear again smooth service and good food, notably about superb onion bhajias, 'the size of melons at my all-time-favourite.' DW. Price check: Papadam 50p, CTM £6.20, Pullao Rice £1.75. Delivery: £10 minimum, 5-mile radius. Hours: 12-2pm/5.30-11.30pm (12am Fri. & Sat.). Stocks Cobra.

TANDOORI NIGHT   NEW ENTRANT

Knight Street, Sawbridgeworth.   ℂ 01279 722341

'Chicken Tikka, excellent huge pieces, very tasty. Onion Bhajias size of tennis balls. [must be the thing round here -Ed]. Very hot and tasty Madras, plenty of Vegetable Biriani. Friendly staff.' JP. Price check: Papadam 50p, CTM £5.95, Bombay Potato £2.10, Pullao Rice £1.60, Hours: 12-2.30pm/6-11.30pm (12am on Fri. & Sat.).

©	Curry Club discount (see page 6)	🍷	Unlicensed
√	Vegetarian		
BYO	Bring your own alcohol	⊞	Delivery/takeaway

Stevenage

NEW GATE OF INDIA NEW ENTRANT   ©

20 The Glebe Chells Way, Chells, Stevenage ✆ 01438 317619

Abdul Salam's 57 seats are divided between 4 rooms. Chef Arosh Ali cooks all the favourites. Price check: Papadam 50p, CTM £6.15, Pullao Rice £1.60, Peshwari Nan £1.70. Delivery: £10 minimum, 4-mile radius. Hours: 12-2.30pm/6pm-12am. Stocks Cobra

STEVENAGE TAKEAWAY NEW ENTRANT

22 Wedgewood Gate, Stevenage   ✆ 01438 749203

Owner Dilwar Ali and Chef Yabor Ali recommend: Chicken Silsila, marinated chicken tikka cooked in a sauce with cream, £5.95. Price check: Papadam 40p, CTM £4.45, Pullao Rice £1.50, Peshwari Nan £1.50. Hours: 5pm-12am. Private parking in front of the premises. Delivery: £6 minimum, town area, £10 minimum, Walkern area.

Tring

JUBRAJ   ©

53a High Street, Tring   ✆ 01442 825368

Special dinners for two at Monnan Miah's 90-seater, adjacent to the town car park. Hours: 12-2.30pm/6-11.45pm.

Ware

NEELAKASH

1-3 Amwell End, Ware   ✆ 01920 487038

'Everything good.' PC. 'Sunday buffet, enjoyable.' AS. Stocks Cobra.

Watford

JAIPUR   ©

37 Market Street, Watford   ✆ 01923 249374

Owner-manager Mohammed Abullaes has completely refurbished his

70-seater. Chef Isakali Motahir recommends his Peshwari Chicken or Lamb Bhoona Tikka Mossola (*sic.*) £5.95. Price check: Papadam 45p, CTM £5.50, Pullao Rice £1.50. Minimum charge £10. Service 10%. Delivery: £10, 3-miles. Hours: 12-2pm/6-12 (1am Sat.). Stocks Cobra.

Welwyn Garden City

RAJ OF INDIA

16 Hall Grove, Welwyn Garden City   ✆ 01707 373825

Abdul Noor tells us his 58-seater is 'luxuriously decorated with a hanging garden from the ceiling'. 'When in an unknown area we always use the guide and we weren't disappointed. Every dish, without exception, was well cooked and well presented, all tasting freshly cooked. Will certainly visit again if in the area.' SJ. Price check: Papadam 35p, CTM £6.60, Pullao Rice £1.55. Hours: 12-2.30pm/6-11.30pm.

KENT

Area: South East
Population: 1,560,000
Number of restaurants in county: 312
Number of restaurants in Guide: 42

Part of Kent was absorbed by Greater London in 1965. We note affected areas with the letters GL.

Ashford

CURRY GARDEN   ©

31 Bank Street, Ashford   ✆ 01233 620511

'Bajloor Rashid 80-seater's house specials include: Chicken Khandary, mince meat, chicken, onion, capsicum, herbs and spices £6.25. Vegetable Thali, containing six items £8.50. Sunday buffet lunch £6.95, kids £3.50. Price check: Papadam 45p, CTM £6.95, Pullao Rice £1.70. Hours: 12-2.30pm/6-11.30pm Stocks Cobra.

Barnehurst, GL

JHAS TANDOORI   ©

158c Mayplace Road East, Barnehurst   © 01322 555036

Est. 1989 by Kuldip Jhas, who is also head chef; Robinder Jhas is the
manager – a family business. Punjabi style Chicken and Lamb Balti is
a house special and most popular with customers. 10% discount on
takeaways. Price check: Papadam 40p, CTM £5.15, Pullao Rice £1.55,
Peshwari Nan £1.95. Lager £2.70 pint, house wine £8.35. Hours: 6-
11.30pm, Sat.-12, closed Sun.

Beckenham, GL

ROSE OF INDIA

406 Upper Elmers End Road, Eden Park,
Beckenham   © 0181 650 0919

Formerly Rose Tandoori. Taken over in 1997 by Abdul Quadir. His
simply decorated restaurant seats 40. Chicken Green Masala is the
most popular dish. Price check: Papadam 40p, CTM £5.95, Pullao
Rice £1.75, Peshwari Nan £1.65. Set Dinner: £7.95. Delivery: 4-mile
radius. Hours: 12-2.30pm/6-11.30pm. Sat. 6-12. Stocks Cobra.

Bexley, GL

CURRY HUT TAKEAWAY   NEW ENTRANT   ©

166 Mayplace Road East, Bexleyheath.   © 01322 550077

Est. 1995 by Muhammed Jahangir Alam. He tells us it's very modern,
with an open kitchen. Set dinner £12.95 vegetarian, £14.95 non-vegetarian. Price check: Papadam 35p, CTM £5.45, Pullao Rice £1.65.
Delivery: £10 minimum, 3-mile radius. Hours: 5-11.30pm.

SAGGOR   ©

145 Blendon Road, Bexley   © 0181 303 7549

Ali Uddin's Sugati Mussala (£6.50) – chicken with coconut, the Mase-
e-Masala (£5.50) – fish cooked with wine, and the Subze Tandoori
(£2.80) – vegetables, marinated then tandoor-cooked, are popular.

Price check: Papadam 50p, CTM £6.10, Pullao Rice £1.55. Delivery: £10 minimum. Hours: 12-2.30pm/6-11.30pm. Sun. 6-11pm.

Biggin Hill, GL

RAJ NEW ENTRANT ©

187 Main Road, Biggin Hill ✆ **01959 572459**

70-seater, managed by AM Crorie, decorated in an 'olde worlde' style. Price check: Papadam 70p, CTM £5.85, Pullao Rice £1.90, Peshwari Nan £1.90. Delivery: £10 minimum, 3-mile radius. Hours: 12-2.30pm (3.30pm on Sun.)/6-11.30pm (12am on Sat.). Stocks Cobra.

Bromley, GL

SURUCHI ©

466 Bromley Road, Downham, Bromley ✆ **0181 698 8626**

Modern, simply decorated, 60-seater. North Indian curries. Recommended Kaliya Galda, tiger prawns prepared with fresh coconut, ground mustard and ghee £9.95. Sunday buffet £5.95, kids £3.95, babies free. Owner Mr Dey promises CC members a free drink as their discount. Price check: Papadam 50p, CTM £5.70, Pullao Rice £1.70, Peshwari Nan £1.80. Service 10%. Delivery: £12 minimum, 2-mile radius. Hours: 12-2.30pm/6-12. Stocks Cobra.

TAMASHA TOP 100 ©

131 Widmore Road, Bromley ✆ **0181 460 3240**

Owner is Shekor Tarat and manager Pramod Dey's 85-seater is attached to a small hotel, so if you need a decent curry, followed by a bed for the night, now you know. Tamasha means 'something worth seeing'. And it is! There is ample car parking, and you enter past a smartly saluting geezer, via an awning flanked by tub plants. Inside, there's a well-stocked bar with a fine selection of wines and beers including Cobra. The dining room, in two parts, is superbly decorated like a British Raj club, with polo sticks and hats, black and white photos of polo teams, Maharajas and sumptious banquets. Cane furniture with palms in copper planters. Have the Kama Sutra pictures in the ladies' been removed? Head chef Rajinder Kumar, cooks food from north and south India, Goa and Kashmir. One correspondent told us that the award-winning menu described in out last guide has changed – it has not; the same delicious food is still being served. But curry house formula, it certainly is not. Favourite starters include Bhajis (Pakoras), Kebabs and Tikka, and main courses Jalfrezi and Chicken Tikka Masala, both £6.95. Good they are, too. But a little exploring can yield some treasures: Chicken Nilgiri Tikka, boneless chicken marinated in spices, fresh coriander and mint, cooked in the tandoor £4.25. Sev Pappri, a type of Bel Puri, gram flour threads, with chick peas and potatoes with coriander leaves, mint and a tart tamarind sauce on a bed of crispy puri £3.95. Keema Khumb, £3.95, mince-stuffed mushrooms. Goan Fish Curry, £6.95, cooked in coconut with red chillies is to be commended, as is the Raan Jaipuri, £8.50, marinated, roasted leg of lamb, and Tandoori Pomfret, £7.95. Mixed Kebab Karara, £4.25 is pop-ular, and Abrakebabra! so is the table magician who entertains the kids during their Sunday lunch. There's live entertainment on Monday (jazz) and Tuesday (Latin) evenings. 'Overall exceptional, large por-tions that were well-presented and full of flavour. Service polite, precise and helpful.' MW. 'In my top three.' KT. 'Very busy, obviously popular, we visited as it was in your Top 100. The food I found expen-sive. 12½% service is automatically added on to the bill, a practice which I despise.' DP. Price check: Papadam 75p, CTM £6.95, Pullao Rice £2.25, Peshwari Nan £2.25. House wine £7.95. Set lunch £7.95. Service 12½%. Hours: 12-2.30pm/6-11.30pm. Remains high in our TOP 100. Stocks Cobra.

ZANZIBAR   ©

239 High Street, Bromley   ℂ 0181 460 7130

Ebullient owner Ken Modi opened his Carioca in 1971 but changed its name because 'I got fed up with Karaoke requests'. The main room seats 50, its walls and ceiling decorated with coconut matting, giving the feeling of being in a fisherman's hut. The party room, which includes a mock Pullman railway carriage, seats 70. The menu contains the regular favourite tandooris, baltis, curries and accompaniments. 'After a morning shopping on a Saturday, we headed to the Zanzibar for a lunchtime buffet. The food is on view from the outside, as it is displayed on a warming table in the window. This sounds awful but it's actually well done, the dishes, polished and spanking clean, the food,

fresh. We were politely served our starters first: a fresh, crisp salad with
flat Onion Bhajis and half a Nan with chutneys, raita and a Coconut
Chutney which was incredible, with a slight hint of heat from its mustard seed. The service became very friendly and helpful when we were
given huge warm bowls for the self-serve buffet. The dishes were
explained to us: Chicken Tikka Masala (smoky flavour – great),
Bhoona Gosht, Mild Chicken Curry, Meat Madras, Bombay Aloo
(excellent – new potatoes), Cauliflower Bhajee, Dal Makhani, Brinjal
Bhajee, Plain and Pullau Rice and Nan bread. After two visits to this
array of food, I was stuffed and delighted. Good food from a clean,
well-decorated restaurant.' MPW. Price check: Papadam 40p, CTM
£5.95, Pullao Rice £1.55. Set lunch £4.95, children £2.95, dinner £9.95.
children £4.95. Lunch buffet £4.95. 10% service. Dinner buffet – 20
dishes £7.95. Hours: 12-2pm and 6-11pm, Mon. to Fri. (11.30pm Sat.),
12.30-3pm Sun. Stocks Cobra.

Canterbury

GANDHI

36 North Gate, Canterbury   © 01227 765300

Opened in 1984 by Nurul Islam Khan. Head chef Fokrul Islam Khan,
good formula. Price check: Papadam 60p, CTM £6.25, Pullao Rice
£1.70, Peshwari Nan £1.80. House wine £6.25. Delivery: £15 minimum,
3-mile radius. Hours: 12-2.30pm/6pm-12am. Stocks Cobra.

Chatham

MONUMENT OF BANGLADESH   NEW ENTRANT

50 New Road, Chatham

Proprietor, F. Uddin. Specials include: Ayer Maachher Karahi, freshwater Bengal catfish, £6.30. Rooshon Palook Baji, Indian spinach leaf
fried with aniseed and garlic, £2. Price check: Papadam 50p, CTM
£6.10, Aloo Moreech Baji, small potatoes fried with chilli and curry
leaves £2, Pullao Rice £1.60, Pickles, Chutneys and Raita 40p. Hours:
12-2.30pm/6-11.30pm.

Chislehurst, GL

JAIPUR   ©

53 Chislehurst Road, Chislehurst   ℂ 0181 467 9390

Owner Abdul Mushahid and manager Abdul Hannan have put together 'an exciting, different menu.' PP. Starters include Lacy Cutless, £2.95,
an Anglo-Indian Keema-stuffed potato rissole, and Fish Roe, £2.95,
breadcrumbed and deep-fried. Main courses include a wealth of interesting items, such as Green Goan Chicken Curry and a Sylheti red
version, both £5.95. There is a creditable selection of Bangladeshi
dishes. Ayre and Roop, Bengali fish, and the super Baingan Torkari –
aubergine with tamarind cooked Sylheti-style in black terracótta. Price
check: Papadam 50p, CTM £6.25, Pullao Rice £1.75. Minimum charge
£10. Hours: 12-2pm/6-11.30pm.

Dartford

MAHATMA COTE   NEW ENTRANT   ©

77 Station Road, Longfield, Dartford   ℂ 01474 705735

Owned by David Wood. Managed by Paul Puvenanthiran. The restaurant opened in 1992 and seats 50 diners. It is decorated with a red
carpet, cream walls, black high-backed chairs, white table linen and
with plants hanging down from the ceiling and a central ceiling fan.
The blackboard gives details of special starters and main courses.
Incidentally, they've heard all the cloakroom hat and coat jokes.
Delivery: £20 minimum, 3-mile radius. Hours: 6-11pm daily. Sunday
lunch 12.30-3pm. Stocks Cobra.

Dover

LIGHT OF INDIA

Town Wall Street,Dover   ℂ 01304 241066

A pretty 100-plus-seater furnished with blue upholstery and gold curtains and tablecloths. 'Menu is standard but the food of high quality,
portions ample. Prawn Puri was full of prawns, excellent value.' JSK.

Folkestone

INDIA TOP 100   ©

1 The Old High Street, Folkestone   © 01303 259155

One regular reporter, a driver, has sent us just one report a year since
chef-proprietor Ali Ashraf opened his 46-seater India in 1985. 'Chance
routed me into Folkestone, rather than my usual Dover to cross the
channel. Now I always use Folkestone, the arrival of the Chunnel
adding spice to my choice of route, because I always spice up at the
India each trip on departure and on arrival.' PJ. Mr Ashraf is a French-
trained Indian chef and speaks French, too. He serves 'freshly cooked,
grease-free Indian food from all over the country, many of the recipes
are centuries old.' and, he tells us, French cuisine too! Parts of his menu
are in French, Fish – Poisson, Chicken – Poulet. Plats Français (French
dishes) include Ratatouille Provençale, Steak au Poivre and Poulet au
Citron. In some cases he combines the French use of cream, wine and
brandy with spices to provide an original interpretation of his Indian
dishes. The starters include Sabzi-ka-Soup, £2, a freshly-made spicy
vegetable soup, Sita's Dosha, £2.95, pancake stuffed with prawn, mushroom, crab and coriander, Crab Kochin, £3.50, crab with a southern
Indian spicing of ginger and fresh coriander. Main courses range far
and wide. The Beef Hyderabadi, £4.95 is spiced with mustard seeds,
and Lamb Roghan Gosht is delicately and correctly spiced with nutmeg
and mace and pistachio nuts. Old hands swear by the special dishes for
two, requiring 24 hours' notice and a deposit – Murog Masallam,
£20.95, whole chicken in cream, with poppy, cinnamon and bay, Vath,
£25.95, duck with cashews, raisins and cardamom, and Raan, £30.95, leg
of lamb, marinated then roasted and topped with saffron, nuts and
lemon. 'Just the place to take my father, since he doesn't like curry, cos
of all the garlic, but will happily eat French, who probably use more
garlic than the rest of the world put together. But sadly for him, I don't
(won't) take him anywhere, cos he's a miserable git who never pays the
bill!' DBAC. Specials include: Vath – duck, cashew nuts, raisins, cardamom and cinnamon £30.50 for two – sounds fabulous. Price check:
Papadam 50p, CTM £5.75, Pullao Rice £1.60. Peshwari Nan £1.95.
House wine £7.25. Hours: 12-2pm/6-10.30pm. Remains in our TOP
100. Stocks Cobra.

Gravesend

CURRY EXPRESS TAKEAWAY NEW ENTRANT

125 Rochester Road, Gravesend   © 01474 331303

Formerly Simla. 'Everything well up to local standards, Chicken Tikka Dhansak hot and tasty. Patia in a nice sweet and sour sauce. Tarka Dal well spiced. All portions plentiful.' MW. Price check: Papadam 40p (plain & spicy), CTM £4.95, Bombay Potato £1.9, Pullao Rice £1.40, Chutney and Pickles 45p. Delivery. Hours: 5pm-12am.

GANDHI BALTI HOUSE   ©

66 West Street, Gravesend   © 01474 536066

Restaurant decorated in light pinks and light green, seats 60. Owned by Abdul Basith Khan, serves Bangladeshi styled curries. 'Couldn't fault any dish, standard Popadoms with good vaiety of pickles [though at 50p each per person, we think expensive -Ed] of varying strengths. Aloo Chat, served on a puri, tangy and tasty. Chot Pote, chick peas and egg, spiced in hot and sour sauce, different and delicious. Jalfrazi as expected, excellently cooked with plenty of chillies. Chicken Sali, an East Bengal dish, spiced with garlic, onion, ginger with a crispy pota-to topping, full of flavours. Sell Cobra lager, 10 out of 10 for the water test. No problem in getting 10% discount for CC members. Rate high-ly.' MW. 'Chicken Chat up to standards, as was the Chicken Patia. Sheek Kebab extremely tasty and the accompanying salad, varied and large. Meat Madras satisfyingly hot in a dark rich sauce and the Mixed Vegetables excellent.' MW. Price check: Papadam 50p, CTM £5.90, Pullao Rice £1.80, Peshwari Nan £1.70. Sunday lunch buffet £6.50, children £5.50. Hours: 12-2.30pm/5.30-11pm (11.30pm on Sat.). Stocks Cobra.

©	Curry Club discount (see page 6)		Unlicensed
√	Vegetarian		
BYO	Bring your own alcohol		Delivery/takeaway

Meopham

INDIA PALACE,

Station Approach, Meopham, Gravesend   ℡ 01474 812088

'Comfortably furnished in two rooms. Onion Bhajia £2.20, starters
were very solid and stodgy with insufficient onion. However, all other
dishes were good, if a little oily. Dhansak £4.50 nicely spiced and
"lentilly." Friendly and efficient service.' WJW. Price check: Papadam:
45p, CTM £5.50, Pullao Rice £1.60. Khorzi Lamb £26.50 and Khorzi
Chicken £24. Delivery: £12 minimum, 8-mile radius. Hours: 12-
2.30pm/5.30-11.30pm.

MEOPHAM TANDOORI   ©

2 The Parade, Wrotham Road, Meopham,
Gravesend   ℡ 01474 812840

Jahir Ali's 60-seater is 'very attractive. Decor, comfort and toilet facilities all good. Comprehensive menu of all the favourites. Onion Bhajias
£2.25 solid, but surprisingly tasty. Chicken Chat Massala £2.70 a bit
disappointing, being oily, chicken of indifferent quality. Tandoori
Chicken £5.50 tasty and well marinated but with basic salad. Dhansak
£5.50 good, thick lentil sauce and nicely hot. Tasty Mixed Vegetable
Bhajee £2.10, plenty of fresh coriander. Good portions. The two waiters looked like students in a temporary job and while pleasant, lads
were inattentive and not cut out to be waiters.' MJW. Sunday lunch
£6.95. Lager £2.40 pint, house wine £6.95, £2 bottle mineral water.
Price check: Papadam: 45p, CTM £5.95, Pullao Rice £1.70, Peshwari
Nan £1.85. Hours: 12-2.30pm/5.30-11.30pm. Branch: India Palace Balti
House, Station Approach, Meopham, Kent. Mr Ali has promised a
10% discount for CC.

MILAAD TAKEAWAY

18 Milton Road, Gravesend   ℡ 01474 567768

'Extensive, imaginative menu. Badami – mild, creamy, peanut and pistachio sauce. Dhansak, Patia, Jalfrezi dishes are particularly to my taste
– hot, well spiced in good thick sauce. Quantities ample, although
prices may be marginally higher than other takeaways, are in line with
most Indian takeaways. Free home delivery: regardless of the size of

order. Consistently provided good quality takeaway service.' MJW. 'Portions always generous, now huge, containers packed to the brim. Jalfrezi well endowed with green chillies. Dal Sambar very hot – a mouth tingling meal!' MW. Price check: Papadam 30p (plain), 35p (spicy), CTM £5.50, Pullao Rice £1.40. Hours: 5.30pm-12am.

Maidstone

SHAMRAT BRASSERIE   ©

36 Upper Stone Street, Maidstone   ℰ 01622 764961

Est. 1989 by chef, Jamal Hussain; you say 'Chicken Jalfrezi, one of the best, appeals to me as a fire-eater!' BP-D. 'Always an excellent welcome. Good warm food on a cold night. Bottomless coffee, liqueurs, orange slices, Suchard Mints, hot towels and an excellent house white wine. How do they do it?' PS. 'The warmth of a real blazing fire and Bombay Mix helped thaw me out whilst I looked through the menu. Quality, tasty, large portions of food.' NG. Price check: Papadam 50p, CTM £6.50, Pullao Rice £1.75, Peshwari Nan £1.80. Sunday lunch buffet £6.95. Delivery: £12, 5-mile radius. Stocks Cobra.

Margate

ALI RAJ

65 Canterbury Road, Westbrook,
Margate   ℰ 01843 297151

'A small, 40-cover, impeccably clean, well-decorated, air-conditioned restaurant which has gained regular clientele with a good reputation. Staff charming and polite. A full menu at reasonable prices. Often go for complete set meals for two at £19.95 consisting of Papadams, chutneys, Chicken and Lamb Tikka, Chicken and Meat Dupiaza, Aloo Gobi, Mushroom Bhajee, Pilau Rice and Nan breads. Can only eat the large portions if we haven't had lunch.' TN.

©	Curry Club discount (see page 6)		Unlicensed
√	Vegetarian		
BYO	Bring your own alcohol		Delivery/takeaway

Orpington, GL

THE BOMBAY

76 High Street, Green Street Green,
Orpington   © 01689 862906

Owned by Hannan Miah and M. Ali since 1986. 'Deceptively large
restaurant, divided by partitions with further tables round a corner.
Seating about 90, but intimate. Pleasant atmosphere, friendly welcome.
Good decor and comfortable seating. Service – like eating your dinner
in a hurricane!! Popadoms, crisp and light, good pickle selection,
together with Raita, which was left throughout the meal. Chicken Chat
tasty but lacked sharpness. Onion Bhajia contained plenty of onions,
enjoyable. Patia was flavoursome and acceptably hot, without any dis-
cernible sweetness or sourness to it. Garlic Chicken Bahar was so
overwhelmed by garlic flavour that it masked any other. Overall enjoyable and portions sufficient. Restaurant scores highly on the trimmings
– Bombay Mix in waiting area, ice and lemon with water. Hot scent-
ed towels, endless coffee, mints with coffee and again with the bill;
seeds mixture and guest book to sign etc.' MW. Price check: Papadam
50p, CTM £5.50, Pullao Rice £1.60. Banquet Balti Night – every
Wednesday night, 5 courses £9.95. Service 10%.

CURRY HOUSE   ©

24 Station Square, Petts Wood,
Orpington   © 01689 820671

Opened 1971, since 1989 son Basth (Baz) Wahab has been running the
42-seater. 'Superb cuisine, professional service and hospitality of Basth
and his team – recommended.' RSC. 'Have been regulars for more than
seven years. Value for money.' PL&VR. Price check: Papadam 35p, CTM
£5.50, Pullao Rice £1.35. Hours: 12-3pm (not on Fri.) and 6pm-12am.
Closed Mon. Stocks Cobra.

RAJ OF INDIA   ©

4 Crescent Way, Orpington   © 01689 852170

Owner-manager Muzibur Rahman's 70-seater. Chef recommends:
Akbori Lamb, cooked with sultanas and almonds in a yoghurt sauce
£5.95. 'Smart restaurant. They do me an ultra-hot Phal, which some-

times is too hot to eat in one sitting, so I have the rest for breakfast! Aubergine Bhaji is worthy of a mention.' PW. Price check: Papadam 40p, CTM £6.15, Pullao Rice £1.80, Peshwari Nan £1.80. Hours: 12-2.30pm/6pm-12am. Branches: Raj of India Sheerness, Swanley and Sittingbourne; Raj Bari Sevenoaks; Maharajah Bexley; Juboraj Brentwood, Essex. Stocks Cobra.

Ramsgate

RAMSGATE TANDOORI ©

17 Harbour Street, Ramsgate   © 01843 589134

Owned by Rezaur Rahman, managed by Mrs Rahman. Bangladeshi and Pakistani curries on the menu, cooked by head chef Joyanti Mendas. Restaurant seats 70. Sunday buffet £3.95. Price check: Papadam 45p, CTM £5.95, Pullau Rice £1.70, Peshwari Nan £1.75. Delivery: £10 minimum. Hours: 12-2.30pm/6pm-12am.

Rochester

BENGAL BRASSERIE ©

356 High Street, Rochester   © 01634 841930

Ashahin Ali (manager), Abdul Roob (chef) and Ashamim Ali (chef) have plans to enlarge their busy 44-seater in 5 dining rooms. 'Most friendly, family-run restaurant. Food plentiful, hot and very fresh. Waiters very friendly and helpful.' JEG. Lobster £10.50 or Duck Sizzler £6.95 are recommended. 'Have been a regular customer for at least 4 years. Food and atmosphere is like home from home, every dish they serve is freshly cooked.' JEG. Price check: Papadam 55p, CTM £6.95, Pullao Rice £1.90, Peshwari Nan £1.95. Hours: 12-2.30pm/5.30pm-12am. Delivery: £12 minimum, 4-mile radius. Stocks Cobra.

SINGAPORA ©

51 High Street, Rochester   © 01634 842178

Dr and Mrs Shome's 150-seater spreads over three floors, with tables in odd alcoves. 'Food spans East Asia, Singapore, Malaysia, Indonesia, Thai and Japanese. Curries on offer are Singaporean/Malaysian style, not Indian. Friendly welcome and efficient staff. Variety of starters, meat and vegetable satay served with traditional spicy peanut sauce, nice but fairly standard. Gorent Wan Ton, small fried meat parcels and Butterfly Prawns, both with a sweet and sour dip, tasty. Curries, relatively mild with a coconut base while the hotter dishes are those cooked with fresh chillies, such as Kai Paed Prik. Portions not particularly large, except rice, but sufficient. Enjoyed.' MW. Hours: 11am-3pm/6-11pm, Sun. 11am-10.30pm. Branches: Singapore Garden, Maidstone; Gordon Hotel, Rochester.

Sandwich

INDIAN VILLAGE

The Old Fire Station, 11 The Butchery,
Sandwich   © 01304 611926

'It really did once house horse-drawn fire-engines, giving reason for its gently uplit long, low ceilings. It is a classy 50-seater, with the restaurant name woven into the carpet and onto the seat backs. Smart, efficient waiters offer just the right amount of attentiveness. We had all the business including pudding and wine for only £30.' TN.

Sidcup, GL

BLACKFEN TANDOORI   ©

33 Wellington Parade, Blackfen Road,
Sidcup   © 0181 303 0013

A friendly, pleasant, competent 48-seat curry house, owned by Muzammil Ali since 1983.

OVAL BRASSERIE   ©

49 The Oval, Sidcup   © 0181 308 0274

Ansar Miah has owned and managed the aptly-named Oval since 1988 (head chef Mohibur Rahman). Monday and Tuesday £7.95, starter, main course, side dish, rice or Nan – excellent value. Price check: Papadam 50p, CTM £5.10, Pullao Rice £1.60. Delivery: £10 minimum, 3-mile radius, free Papadam. Hours: 12-2.30pm/6-11.30pm. All day Sunday buffet £6.95, £4 for kids. 12-11.30pm. Stocks Cobra.

Staplehurst

MALONCHO   NEW ENTRANT

17 The Parade, Staplehurst   ℂ 01580 892769

Owners Ahasan, Barua, Sil and Misson tell us that their 52-seater is beautifully decorated. Price check: Papadam 40p, CTM £5.50, Pullao Rice £1.80, Peshwari Nan £1.60. Hours: 6-11. Sun. 7-10.30. Branch: Maloncho Takeaway, Peacehaven, Sussex. Stocks Cobra.

Strood

SHOZNA INDIAN CUISINE   NEW ENTRANT   ©

18 High Street, Strood   ℂ 01634 710701

J.U. Ahmed's cosy 34-seater, is decorated in green with white plaster cornices. Specials include: Bangladeshi Chicken or Lamb, tikka cooked in butter with a fresh garlic sauce £6.90 and Jinga Masala, cooked with mincemeat, egg and spiced king prawns £7.90. Chicken Chatt is the most popular dish ordered. Price check: Papadam 45p, CTM £5.30, Pullao Rice £1.40. Minimum £10.50 p.p. Hours: 12-1.30pm/5.30pm-12am.

Swanley

BENGAL LANCER   ©

3 Station Road, Swanley   ℂ 01322 662098

A popular curry house, seating 48, owned by chef Hiron Miah and Feruz Ali, out front. Hours: 12-2.30pm/6pm-12am.

GURKHA PALACE   ©

9 High Street, Swanley   ℂ 01322 663608

A Nepalese 80-seater owned by J. Gautam. Miss Mass is the most popular, cooked by chef Bhim Lal Gautam, whose 'Nepalese touch is subtle and different.' PP. Price check: Papadam 40p, CTM £5.10, Pullao Rice £1.75. Hours: 12-2.30pm/6pm-12am. Stocks Cobra.

Tonbridge

SIMLA CUISINE

2 Church Road, Paddock Wood,
Nr Tonbridge   © 01892 834515

Abdal Miah's 90-seater is air-conditioned and decorated in cream and black. Good formula curries on the menu. Price check: Papadam 40p, CTM £5.60, Pullao Rice £1.50, Peshwari Nan £1.60. Hours: 12-2.30pm/6-11pm (11.30pm on Fri. & Sat.).

Tunbridge Wells

BOMBAY MASALA   NEW ENTRANT   ©

90, London Road, Southborough,
Tunbridge Wells   © 01892 537551

Established in 1994 by Shamim Khandakar (manager). His 48-seater restaurant is air-conditioned and serves Bangladeshi styled curries and Balti dishes. Price check: Papadam 40p, CTM £5.50, Pullao Rice £1.50, Peshwari Nan £1.70. Lager £2 pint, house wine £6, mineral water £2 bottle. Hours: 12-2.30pm/6-11.30pm. Branches: Anglo India, Tunbridge Wells. Jubo Raj, Brentwood.

Welling, GL

FALCON   ©

16 Falconwood Parade, The Green,
Welling   © 0181 303 7219

A. Gofur's 54-seater is spacious, with plants all around. Chef Tamij Ali's ace is Chicken Indo Purie, a marination cooked with Tia Maria in creamy gravy, served with Special Fried Rice £8.80. 'Amazing!' LM. Price check: Papadam 50p, CTM £6.90, Pullao Rice £1.90. Hours: 12-2.30pm/6-11.30pm. (12am on Fri. & Sat.). Stocks Cobra.

©	Curry Club discount (see page 6)		Unlicensed
√	Vegetarian		
BYO	Bring your own alcohol		Delivery/takeaway

TAGORE   NEW TO OUR TOP 100   ©

3 High Street, Welling   ✆ 0181 304 0433

Nur Monie's 40-seater is decorated with swathes of silk on the ceiling
and pleated saris on the walls. Bombay-trained chef Rajendra Balmiki
cooks Northern Indian curries and specials from Pakhtoomn, assisted
by head waiter Tapesh Majumber. This refers to the Pathan tribal people of Afghanistan and the rugged Pakistani passes, whose name for
themselves is Phuktana or Pukhtun. Afghan food is pretty basic (*see*
page 37), especially at tribal level, involving kebab-skewer cooking and
slow-cooking in pots. This is translated at The Tagore into a select
menu. Kebab Ke Karishma, a selection of kebabs £16 for two, is popular). Main dishes are divided between six chicken dishes, five meat, six
from the tandoor and three fish dishes. At £6, Patrani Mahi, pomfret
coated in herbal chutney, leaf-wrapped and baked, is a rarity to be trea-
sured. Murgh Chennai, £5 is none other than Chicken Madras, and
Koh-e-Avadh, £5.50 is lamb knuckles simmered in the dum method.
Raan E. Buzkazi, leg of lamb from the NW Frontier £19.50. The fact
that it's not formula leads to adverse comment: 'Very poor meal.' DW
Others like it: 'On all occasions I have found their food to be a world
apart from the traditional curry houses with the dishes being expertly
cooked. Excellent value for money, service and explanation of the
dishes is of a very high quality.' PG. Price check: Papadam 50p, CTM
£7.50, Pullao Rice £2.25, Peshwari Nan £1.80. Average meal £20.
Takeaway prices 20% cheaper. Hours: 8pm to 11pm.

Westerham

TULSI

20 London Road, Westerham   ✆ 01959 563397

Tulsi, *Ocimum Sanctum*, is the sacred basil plant of India, where it is
grown as a symbol of good luck and good health. Owned by A.K. Deb,
it has a small waiting area with tables and chairs, and an extended,
slightly elevated, well-decorated eating area, with a polished wooden
floor. Walls covered by framed posters of Bollywood film stars.
Ambience is good with very friendly staff, well-dressed in national costume. Chef Anil K. Hazra's specials include: Goan fish curry, cooked
in coconut milk, red chillies and garnished with fresh coriander £6.95.
Tandoori Paneer Shashlik, pieces of cottage cheese, mushroom, capsi-

cum, tomatoes and onion, cooked on a skewer in the tandoor and served on a sizzler with grilled onion £6.50. 'Chicken Nilgri, so tender and excellent. Murgh Makhani, lovely and creamy. Manchoori had real bite from the chillies. Best of all was the Peshwari Nan – absolutely exquisite, light and brushed with hot ghee. Shared a melon sorbet. Hot towels and mints with coffee.' CD. Price check: Papadam 70p, CTM £6.25, Pullao Rice £1.95, Peshwari Nan £2.25. Hours: 12-2.30pm (closed Sunday lunch) and 6-11.30pm. Branch: Tamasha, Bromley. Stocks Cobra.

Whitstable

SHAPLA ©

36 Harbour Street, Whitstable © 01227 262454

Messrs Rashid, Khan, Rahman and Uddin's 42-seater continues to get the best-in-town nomination from our scribes. Price check: Papadam 40p, CTM £7.75 (incl. Pullao Rice and Nan), Pullao Rice £1.40, Peshwari Nan £1.75. Sunday lunch: £6.95. Hours: 12-2.30pm/6-11.30pm Branches: Curry Garden, Ashford, Kent. Khan, Herne Bay, Kent. Delivery: £15 minimum, 3-mile radius.

Wye

JOSHAN OF WYE

2-4 High Street, Wye © 01233 812231

'Quantities of food – while not piled high – are on the generous side of average. A very friendly welcome and service.' RCD. Reports, please.

LANCASHIRE

Area: North West
Population: 1,420,000
Number of restaurants in county: 153
Number of restaurants in Guide: 28

We have adhered strictly to the official county of Lancashire here. Please also refer to the entries for Greater Manchester (listed under Manchester, Greater) and Merseyside for other restaurants within the former (1965) Lancashire boundary.

Adlington

SHAPLA TAKEAWAY ©

178 Chorley Road, Adlington ✆ 01257 474630

Est. 1992 by Shiraz Ali (manager) and MD Rahmin Ullaj (chef). 'Addiction from an early age, satisfied on my doorstep.' AL. 'A wide range of excellent food.' AH. Price check: Papadam 30p, CTM £5.50 (incl. Pullao Rice), Pullao Rice 95p, Hours: Sun.-Thurs. 4pm-12am.

SHARJU TOP 100 ©

Church Street, Adlington ✆ 01257 481894

This is an old favourite of our Guide, and of its loyal following. 'Congregation' may be a more appropriate word because this was surely the first restaurant to occupy a former church. And, yes, they've heard all the gags: from Vestry Vindaloo, RC Roghan, Baptistry Biriani, C of E Tikka to 'will they be serving papadoms with communion wine?' Now owned by Mithu Dhar, the opportunity was taken in 1984 to convert this building to its now ideal use. In fact, it is not a large room, in clerical terms, but it has made for a large number of seats in restaurant terms. Reached by an imposing staircase, the plum seats are on the balcony, which extends around the remaining three sides of the room. From here one has a view of downstairs diners.

MKM says: 'It has bags of atmosphere, with its oak beams and strategically placed Indian artefacts. We go fairly regularly on the Thursday evenings for the £12.95 per person Candlelight Dinner.' Other reporters tell of the special 'royal' dishes. 'From time to time we treat ourselves to one or other of these.' KL. Two of these are chef Faruk Ali's signature dishes – Chicken Shagorika (£10.45) and Lashuni Chicken Flambé (£12.45), both with rice. The former is tikka pieces twice-cooked in a very spicy sauce with peas, the latter consists of a tandooried long fillet of chicken breast, which is flambéed in brandy, in a creamy garlicky sauce at your table. 'Huge portions of everything. There is only one word which covers the experience – magnificent.' DB. 'Madras is very hot but with bags of flavour right down to the last grain of excellent Pullau rice, all helped down with a Nan bread of the highest quality.' MB. It is managed by BB Choudhury. Price check: Papadam 50p, CTM £7.25, Pullao Rice £1.50. Set meal from £9.25. Eat-your-fill Sunday lunch, 12-4.30pm, £7.95, kids £3.50. Service 10%. Minimum charge £10. Branch: Shanti, 466 Bromley Road, Bromley, Kent. Remains in our TOP 100.

Blackburn

SHAJAN ©

Longsight Road, Clayton-le-Dale, Mellor,
Blackburn   ✆ 01254 813640

Mohammad Ali (Shaju) is at pains to tell you his 144-seater is easily found on the A59. Its resemblence to a residential bungalow ceases on entry. It is stylishly decorated with cream walls, ceiling and table linen, blue carpet, 144 wicker chairs, in two dining rooms. Wooden fretwork screens give tables privacy. Baltis are very popular. Price check: Papadam 30p, CTM £6.25, Pullao Rice £1.65, Peshwari Nan £1.95. Discounts for CC members, lunches only. Takeaway 15% off. Hours: 12-2pm/5.30-11.30pm (12am on Fri. & Sat.). Stocks Cobra.

Blackpool

ALIRAJ NEW ENTRANT

65 Topping Street, Blackpool   ✆ 01253 292225

'Surprisingly all the meat was beef, the only lamb was Tikka or Passanda. Very tasty Onion Bhajia. Meat Madras, good.' RE. 10% off takeaway. Minimum charge: £12. Price check: Papadam 40p, CTM £7.30, Pullao Rice £1.50. Hours: 12-2.30pm/6-12. Stocks Cobra.

BOMBAY   ©

227 Dickson Road, Blackpool   © 01253 296144

Askor Ali's dusky pink restaurant seats 30. 'The Chilli Masala is just
fabulous but, good though it is, I don't think anyone's Roghan Josh
originated in Rangoon!' RT. Price check: Papadam 50p, CTM £5.90,
Pullao Rice £1.80. Set meal £4.95. For delivery, you pay for the taxi!!!
Hours: 12-2pm/6pm-12am. Fri. & Sat. to 1am. Stocks Cobra.

SHABAB   NEW ENTRANT

129 Church Street, Blackpool   © 01253 292180

Owned by Waheed and Soni. Pakistani food on the menu cooked by
Farooqui. 'What a wonderful eatery. Green and gold decor, with fixtures and fittings imported from Pakistan. Good food. Smashing
starters of Vegetable Samosa and Aloo Tikki. Superb Chicken Karahi
with Pullao Rice.' RK. Price check: Papadam 50p, CTM £6.95, Pullao
Rice £1.50. Hours: 6pm-12am, Fri. & Sat. to 3am!

SUNAM

93 Redbank Road, Blackpool   © 01253 352572

Dudu Miah, A. Ali and chef A. Basar's pretty 70-seater. Red brick
building with arches, swags and tails, seats. Parking for 4 cars on the
forecourt. BIG secret – don't tell – Ian Botham eats here (proof in our
October CC magazine). Hours: 12-2.30pm/6pm-12am. Stocks Cobra.

Burnley

AGRA

Horse Hill Farm, Hapton, Nr Burnley   © 01282 770113

'A most impressive converted barn in the last place you'd expect to find
a restaurant, let alone an Indian. Someone has gone to long lengths to
create a rich and comfortable Indian atmosphere. Food was as good as
the interior. Chicken Tikka and Shammi Kebabs were perfect. Chicken
Tikka Makahan and Royal Bengal Special both excellent mopped up
with a large succulent Nan. Well recommended.' MB. Stocks Cobra.

SHALAMAR ©

56 Church Street, Burnley ℭ 01282 434403

'Service good – not pushy. Food presented well, portions ample, but not generous. Started with Vegetable Pakora £1.50. Chicken Bhuna £4.30 excellent with delicious side dishes of Tarka Dhal £1.90 and Aloo Palak £1.90. Karahi Lamb £5.60. Definitely revisit.' AC. Price check: Papadam: 40p, CTM £5.90, Pullao Rice £1.20. Stocks Cobra.

Carnforth

FAR PAVILION

25 Bye Pass Road, Bolton-le-Sands,
Carnforth ℭ 01524 823316

'Difficult to fault this 70-seater. Decor and welcome second to none. Service efficient and courteous.' FS. 'Sampled my usual benchmark meal of Shami Kebab, which was excellent, followed by Chicken Madras, which was standard curry house.' MB. Stocks Cobra.

Cleveleys

TASTE MI TA   NEW ENTRANT

17 Knowle Avenue, Cleveleys ℭ 01253 779949

Abdul Latif tells us he has recently spent £40,000 on refurbishment. Minimum charge: £5. Price check: Papadam 30p, Pullao Rice £1.20, Delivery: 3-mile radius. Hours: 5-11pm (11.30pm Sat.). Stocks Cobra.

Chorley

HYATT   NEW ENTRANT

1 Dole Lane, Chorley ℭ 01257 231975

'Very smart restaurant. "Nice" touches include a very extensive mobile wine rack and cloth napkins. Service is excellent. Extra rice can be requested at no additional price. Boti and Mushroom Kebab, a richly flavoured mini-curry in a thick sauce. Chicken Tikka Bhaji, a delicate mix of chicken, tomatoes, onion, coriander and spices, set on a puri bread. Main courses, Lamb Kashtoori, with bananas and fresh orange juice as well as chillies, coriander and a delicate mixture of herbs and spices. Chicken Karai Kabuli, Madras hot, bursting with flavour!' AE

VEENA   NEW ENTRANT

64 Brooke Street, Chorley   ✆ 01257 234235

'Smart restaurant, just outside Chorley centre. Very reasonable prices. Fish Hasina — succulent cod pieces in a rich, red, tangy masala sauce with crunchy vegetables. Also the Tikka Chicken Puri — with a rich spicy sauce, bursting with flavour. Bombay Machan, similar to Korai but laced with brandy, Chicken Kashmir a deliciously decadent mix of peaches, bananas and a rich array of herbs and spices. Indian food *à la haute cuisine!*' AE. Price check: CTM £6.45, Bombay Potato £1.95, Pullao Rice 90p, Papadam relish 70p. What are Bombay Fries? perhaps chips with a little spice — I do hope so!

Clitheroe

DIL RAJ   ©

7-9 Parsons Lane, Clitheroe   ✆ 01200 427224

Seats 48, owned by Mr Raj. Sunday buffet £6. Set dinner £12.50 each, four people share. Papadams, Tandoori Chicken, Lamb and Chicken Tikka, Sheek Kebab starters, Beef Roghan Josh, Karahi Gosht, Mogulai Chicken, CTM, vegetable Pullao, Raita, pickles and chutney, followed by desserts and coffee. 10% off takeaways. Price check: Papadam 60p, CTM £6.95, Pullao Rice £1, Peshwari Nan £1.40. Hours: 5-12.30pm, Sun. 12pm-12am. Stocks Cobra.

Darwen

ANAZ

110-112 Duckworth Street, Darwen   ✆ 01254 703357

'We chose from the very extensive menu, Chicken Sambar, which is tender juicy chicken cooked in a very spicy lentil sauce and absolutely delicious. Lightest of Nans. First-class.' MB. Stocks Cobra.

Haslingden

SUNAR GAW   ©

16 Regent Street, Haslingden   ℂ 01706 212137

Owner-manager NA Malik and owner-chef A. Quddus share owner-ship and roles at this popular 1987, evenings-only restaurant. RK says: 'The Kyber Murghi Maladari (£5.50) – chicken cooked with ginger, green chilli, onion, garlic and coriander – was out of this world. Brinjal Bhaji delicate. It's another gem.' Stocks Cobra.

Lancaster

BOMBAY   NEW ENTRANT   ©

Jubilee Hall, China Street, Lancaster   ℂ 01524 844550

Opened in 1997 by Askor Ali, his 70-seater, plainly decorated restaurant serves chef Babul Ahmed's curries. Price check: Papadam 50p, CTM £5.90, Pullao Rice £1.80, Chutney Tray £1.20. House wine £5.90, mineral water £2 bottle. 20% discount on takeaways. Hours: 12-2pm and 6pm-12am. Stocks Cobra.

NAWAAB

32 Parliament Street, Lancaster   ℂ 01524 847488

'Of exceptional quality, serving wonderful food.' DB.

Leyland

ROYAL SHAH   NAME CHANGE

Thornlees, Wigan Road, Leyland   ℂ 01772 622616

Former Mughal. 'Very tastefully decorated with no-smoking area. Will go again and again. Menu superb. Free Papadams with dishes of onion and spices. Food of a very high standard.' KP. Stocks Cobra.

©	Curry Club discount (see page 6)		Unlicensed
√	Vegetarian		
BYO	Bring your own alcohol	⊞	Delivery/takeaway

Longridge

POLASH

23-33 Berry Lane, Longridge   © 01772 785280

Owner/manager Runuk Ullah, known as Ronnie. His restaurant seats
80, and serves formula curries under the eye of head chef Shah i Noor.
He recommends Tangri Massala, drumsticks marinated in yoghurt,
herbs, spices and grilled in the tandoor then cooked with minced lamb
£9.50. Price check: Papadam 65p, CTM £8.95 (incl. Pullao Rice or
Nan), Pullao Rice £1.85, Chutney Tray £1.75, phew!! Delivery: £15 minimum, 5-mile radius. Hours: 5.30pm (Sun. from 5pm)-12am Mon.-Fri.
& Sat. 5pm-12.30am. Stocks Cobra.

Morecambe

MORECAMBE TANDOORI

47 Marine Road West, Morecambe   © 01524 832633

Opened in 1991 by M.A. Quadir, who is also the head chef. Butter
Chicken is the most popular dish ordered. Set Dinner £13.50. Price
check: Papadam 40p, CTM £6.25, Pullao Rice £1.45. Lager £1.95 pint,
house wine £5.75. Hours: 12-2pm and 6pm-12am.

Ormskirk

PASSAGE TO INDIA

Moor Street, Ormskirk   © 01695 578979

'Small, tastefully decorated, impeccably clean restaurant serves a decent
range of dishes cooked and presented with above-average care.' AGJ.
Stocks Cobra.

©	Curry Club discount (see page 6)	🍵	Unlicensed
√	Vegetarian		
BYO	Bring your own alcohol	🏠	Delivery/takeaway

Preston

DILSHAD

121-122 Friargate, Preston   © 01772 250828

Established in 1993 by Arshad Din, 'pleasant and homely.' 84-seater restaurant serving Kashmiri and Pakistani curries. Korma is the most popular curry ordered. Set lunch: £4.99. Price check: Papadam 30p, CTM £7.50, Pullao Rice £1.60. Hours: 12-2pm and 6pm-12am.

SAGAR PREMIER

Clayton Brook Road, Bamber Bridge,
Preston   © 01772 620200

'Disappointing exterior, rather like a community centre built onto the edge of a housing centre, but initial impression rapidly altered by the quality of the food. Very smart internally with partitioned seating. Fresh, light Popadoms with a wide range of chutneys, including a red sauce. Starters include hoppers, similar to rice pancakes, very nice and different. CTM of top class.' JL.

SANGAM   NEW ENTRANT

14-15 Hope Terrace, Lostock Hall, Preston   © 01772 628616

The new management has injected some fire here: 'Wings of Fire were – wow! The main course dish, Tava Chicken Lahori, was great, as was the Pullao Rice. We didn't know whether to eat it or climb it, so big was the portion! Luckily they supplied doggy bags!' RK. Stocks Cobra.

Rawtenstall

SAMRAT   ©

13 Bacup Road, Rawtenstall   © 01706 216183

Alkas Ali is owner-chef here, and he's proud of his cooking – so proud, in fact, that you can ring him on his mobile on 0973 328426 and he'll explain about his dishes. A unique service, we believe. Price check: Papadam 40p, CTM £7.65, Pullao Rice £1.95, Peshwari Nan £1.65. Minimum charge £8.50. Hours: 5pm-12am. Stocks Cobra.

St Annes

MOGHUL   ©

12 Orchard Road, St Annes   © 01253 712114

M. Liaquat Ali owns and presides over a very sunny, friendly 60-seat restaurant, decorated in pastels and pine, serving all the usual Dansak, Madras, Vindaloo, Baltis and Karahis. We hear well of the Moghul Jeera Chicken (£5.90), with cummin flavour predominating, and Keema Patila (£5.90), a tasty mince curry, which one couple enjoy for takeaway — and they also like the special box provided. Stocks Cobra.

Whalley

TRISHNA

25 King Street, Whalley   © 01254 822394

'Very nice restaurant, bigger inside than it first appears (seats 72 diners). Food absolutely gorgeous — could not fault it. Biggest Nan bread ever seen! Polite service. On leaving, ladies get a flower, men a lollipop.' SP. Stocks Cobra.

LEICESTERSHIRE

Area: East Midlands
Population: 898,000
Number of restaurants in county: 104
Number of restaurants in Guide: 16

Leicester

Leicester is home to a good number of Gujaratis from India. In addition, many of its Asian community settled there in the 1970s when they became exiled from Africa, specifically Kenya and Uganda, where they had lived for generations, having been taken there as clerks and semi-skilled plantation labour by the British. Most contemporary Leicester Asians have little concept of the Indian subcontinent, few having ever visited it, but you would not know this from the quality of the food, particularly in the cheap and cheerful cafés, snack bars and sweet shops all over town. The first curry house, the Taj Mahal, opened in 1961 and is still there! I dined there that year, and when I asked for chilli pickle the anxious owner appeared and spent half an hour counselling me against eating hot food! (To no avail, I might add!) Now there are over 80 'Indian' restaurants on our database which, with a city of around 300,000 population, is a ratio of one 'Indian' restaurant per 3,750 people, making Leicester our second most densely curry-housed city in the UK (see Bradford, West Yorkshire).

ASHOKA NEW ENTRANT

257 Melton Road, Leicester   © 0116 261 1331

Red brick exterior, smokey plate glass window and door. Nicely deco-rated, comfortable chairs, large chandelier. An air-conditioned Bangladeshi and Pakistani restaurant serving formula fare to 90 diners. Price check: Papadam 40p, CTM £5.10, Pullao Rice £1.80. House wine £8.50 wine, mineral water £3.75 bottle. Hours: 12-2.30pm/6pm-12am.

BOBBY'S GUJARATI VEGETARIAN   ⊞ ☕

154 Belgrave Road, Leicester   © 0116 266 2448

Ever-popular cafeteria-type atmosphere, you pay (cash please) at the till. Hours: All day.

CURRY CUISINE NEW ENTRANT   ©

1261 Melton Road, Syston, Leicester   © 0116 260 5535

Owned by Kumar since November 1997. The curry house seats 52 diners on two floors and is, at the time of writing this guide, under refurbishment. Popular orders include: Jeera and Chilli Chicken. Take-aways over £25 qualify for a free bottle of wine. Price check: Papadam 40p, CTM £5.50, Pullao Rice £1.60, Peshwari Nan £1.75. Lager £2.20 pint, house wine £5.95, mineral water 90p. Delivery: £12 minimum, 3-mile radius. Hours: 6pm (5.30pm Fri. & Sat.)-12am. Tues. closed.

©	Curry Club discount (see page 6)		Unlicensed
√	Vegetarian		
BYO	Bring your own alcohol	⊞	Delivery/takeaway

CURRY FEVER TOP 100   ©

139 Belgrave Road, Leicester   ℰ 0116 266 2941

Established in 1978 by Anil Anand (head chef) and Sunil Anand (manager). They are related to the Brilliant and Madhu's Brilliant of Southall and Curry Craze of Wembley. The Fever is pleasantly decorated, pink walls, green carpet and chandeliers. Northern Indian food is on the menu, Punjabi dishes as they eat them at home. House specialities, which show the restaurant's Kenyan background include: Jeera Chicken, Butter Chicken and Pili-Pili Chicken (most popular), all priced at full £12.60 and half £7.35, all are dry and on the bone. 10% discount on takeaways. Price check: Papadam 65p, CTM £7.17, Pullao Rice £2.30, Peshwari Nan £1.95. Lager £2.20 pint, house wine £8.50, mineral water £1.80. Hours: 12-2.30pm (Sun. closed) and 6-11.30pm, (12am on Fri. & Sat.). Mon. closed, except Bank Holidays. Stocks Cobra.

CURRY HOUSE

63 London Road, Leicester   ℰ 0116 255 0688

Red-bricked, double shop-front. Owner/head chef Hilsar Kolia. His Pakistani-style curries are served by manager, Iqbal Kolia to 70 diners. Decorated in cream walls, red carpet, padded velvet chairs, pale pink linen, ceiling fans, Indian pictures, copper vases and climbing plants. Price check: Papadam 35p, CTM £5.95, Pullao Rice £1.50, Peshwari Nan £1.85. House wine £7.25, mineral water £3.80. Hours: 6-11.45pm. Stocks Cobra.

FRIENDS TANDOORI TOP 100   ©

41-45 Belgrave Road, Leicester   ℰ 0116 266 8809

110-seater opened in 1982 by T.S. Pabla. The interior is attractive in peach and midnight blue, with its mahogany spiral staircase, enormous 'hookah' and works of art. Separate upstairs drinks lounge in which to peruse the menu or to relax over a coffee after your meal. As to that menu, first-timers will need time to peruse it. It's practically a book! It begins with starters, ordinary enough with Tikkas, Kebabs and Bhajis. Vegetarians are catered for with a decent selection of dishes. Odd moments of Pabla wit come to the fore in the menu. Here are some in descending order of wit: Gulab Jamun is 'the missing holes out of doughnuts'; Kulfi is 'a legend in its own lunchtime'; Bhindi Masala is 'fresh okra (Winfrey!)'; and it gets worse: Roti is 'Pavarotti – I mean 'ave a roti – Tandoori Roti.' Since I do the funnies in this Guide, I'd go for 'Pablarotti' – and you can 'ave that one on me, Mr Pabla!. I continue to get get glowing reports about the cooking now led by son Bobby Pabla and his brigade.

Getting back to the menu, the wine list is clearly a labour of love, apparently of other son Manjit Pabla, and is probably as good an exposition of wines which go well with spicy food as you'll find anywhere. Fourteen pages are given over to very professional explanations though these, too, are not immune from Pabla humour. What getting his hands on Brigitte Bardot (mentioned twice) has to do with wine, ask him, not me, but there are 109 very interesting wines, ranging in price from £6.95 (house red or white) to £39.95 (a delicious Deuxième Grand Cru Classe red from St Estephe). Excellent though this is, there is another list, unique, I believe, to the Indian restaurant trade, and rare in any restaurant. It is a 22-strong malt whisky list, which Pabla calls his 'collection'. Prices go from £2 for Glenfiddich to £5.25 for a rare Laphroaig 1968, although the 100%-proof Macallan, said to 'cure all ills', will certainly create some if you don't stagger home by taxi! Talking of staggering, whisky is the favourite tipple in India, in the form of a chota peg (two-finger measure), topped up with still water, and no ice. At all the parties, at all the best homes, this is what you drink for a couple of hours until the food comes. Nothing is drunk with the actual meal itself, and then you go (staggering) home! Friends is a caring restaurant that deserves to remain in our TOP 100. Price check: Papadam 40p, CTM £6.95, Pullao Rice £1.95, Peshwari Nan £2.10. Minimum charge £8.50. Takeaway 15% off above prices. Hours: 12-2pm (Sun. closed) and 6-11.30pm.

GRAND DURBAR

294 Melton Road, Leicester   © **0116 266 6099**

Owned and managed by Kibria Wahid since inception, 1988. He tells us that 'it is traditionally decorated but with a strong contemporary feel, in warm colours.' The Bangladeshi restaurant seats 76 diners and has about 20 car parking spaces in front. Lager £1.90 pint, house wine £6.75, mineral water £2.95. Minimum charge £7. Delivery: £12 minimum, 5-mile radius. Hours: 12-2pm/6pm-12am.

MANZIL BALTI   NEW ENTRANT

200 Narborough Road, Leicester   © 0116 223 0366

Owned by Minara Begum Choudhury since 1975. Assisting her she has
M.U. Raj, front of house and S.D. Khan as head chef. 60-seater, Balti
is very popular. Price check: Papadam 50p, CTM £6, Pullao Rice £1.70,
Peshwari Nan £1.50. House wine £6.50. Minimum charge: £8. Sunday
lunch buffet £6.95. Hours: 12-2pm/5.30pm-12am. Stocks Cobra.

MONSOON   ©

194 Evington Road, Leicester   © 0116 273 9444

Established in 1995 by Mokhtar Hussain and Monrul Huda. A pretty
restaurant, seating 40. Blue hand-printed curtains with white elephants
hang at the large plate glass windows, comfortable rounded wooden
chairs, square and round tables (I prefer round tables). Some unusual
items. Halim (*sic.*) soup (£2.30) is a meat- and lentil-based spicy broth,
Haash Masala (£8) is half a duck on the bone, marinated and deep-
fried, and Roup Chanda Bhaza (£7.50) is Bangladeshi fish, marinated
and pan-fried. With 24 hours' notice and a deposit, you can have
Shagorana (£35), a feast for two, with, amongst other things, mussels,
crab, lobster and Bangladeshi vegetables. Price check: Papadam 40p,
CTM £5.50, Pullao Rice £1.75. Delivery: £10 minimum, 3-mile radius.
Hours: 12-2pm/6-11.30pm. Closed Mon. Stocks Cobra.

NAMASTE   ©

65 Hinckley Road, Leicester   © 0116 254 1778

Proprietors Dwssendra Kumar Dey (manager) and Rakhal Paul (chef)
opened in April 1994, serving formula curries to a restaurant seating 52
diners. Balti Mixed is the most popular dish ordered. Minimum charge
£9.50. Sunday buffet lunch £5.95. Tuesday and Wednesday £6.50 e-a-m-
a-y-l dinner. Price check: Papadam 45p, CTM £7.55 (incl. Rice or
Nan), Pullao Rice £1.60. Hours: 12-2 and 5.30-11. Stocks Cobra.

SHARMILEE VEGETARIAN   √ ©

71-73 Belgrave Road, Leicester   © 0116 261 0503

Opened way back in 1973 by Gosai brothers (manager, LK Goswami),
this is a two-part venue. The sweet mart serves a rich assortments of

Indian sweets, and such delightful items as Vegetable Samosas, Pakoras and Dahi Vadia, from 9.30am-9pm, daily, except Mondays. The restaurant is upmarket and vegetarian, decorated with marble pillars in shades of brown and dusky blue marble-effect walls, high-backed black chairs, white table linen. Tasty starters of Pani Puri, crispy puris served with spicy sauce, chickpeas and onion £2.25. Chanabateta, chickpeas and potatoes in a tamarind sauce garnished with onions £2. South Indian specialities: Masala Dosa, thin crispy pancake filled with potato and onion £4.25, Idli Sambhar, flat pulse balls £2.50, both served with Sambhar and coconut chutney. Price check: Papadam 40p, Pullao Rice £1.50. Takeaway 10% discount. Mininum charge £4.95. Hours: 12-2.30pm/6pm-9.30pm (closed Sun.). Sat. 12-9pm. Closed on Mon., except Bank Holidays. 10% discount to CC Members. Stocks Cobra.

LE SPICE   NEW ENTRANT

1b Conduit Street, Leicester

S. Alam has been the current proprietor since 1997, but it opened originally in 1965, wow! Bangladeshi and Pakistani curries feature on the menu, cooked by A. Uddin. Price check: Papadam 40p, CTM £5.95, Bombay Potato £2.40, Pullao Rice £1.65. Hours: 6pm-1am.

SPICE OF INDIA

67 Blaby Road, South Wigston, Leicester   © 0116 278 6236

Owner/manager Sarfaraz Nasrulla since 1997. His restaurant seats 54 diners. Bangladeshi formula curries on the menu. Price check: Papadam 40p, CTM £5.50, Pullao Rice £1.40, Peshwari Nan £1.75. House wine £6.95, mineral water £2.30 bottle. Delivery: £10 minimum, 4-mile radius. Hours: 5.30pm-12am. Stocks Cobra.

Loughborough

AMBER TANDOORI

5a High Street, Loughborough   © 01509 215754

'Decor is pleasant and clean. Food and service always good and prompt.' MG. Open 12-2.30pm/5.30pm-12.30am (1.30am on Fri. & Sat.).

Market Harborough

SHAGORIKA

16 St Mary's Road, Market Harborough   © **01858 464644**

Ala and Ablas Uddin have been trading successfully here since 1980. Seats 70 diners. Party room seats 25 guests. Formula curries. Price check: Papadam 40p, CTM £6.25, Pullao Rice £1.80, Peshwari Nan £2.25. Hours: 12-2pm/6-11.30pm. Stocks Cobra.

Melton Mowbray

PARI TANDOORI   ©

38 Leicester Street, Melton Mowbray   © **01664 410554**

Home-delivery service available at Babul Ali's Pari. Menu offers all the usual curries, tandooris and Baltis. Hours: 6pm-12am.

LINCOLNSHIRE

Area: East
Population: 591,000
Number of restaurants in county: 42
Number of restaurants in Guide: 18

Barton-upon-Humber

GANDHI TANDOORI

28 High Street, Barton-upon-Humber   © **01652 634890**

'Tandoori dishes are excellent, with Chicken Tikka worth singling out. Curries are distinctive and aromatic.' BT.

©	Curry Club discount (see page 6)		Unlicensed
√	Vegetarian		
BYO	Bring your own alcohol		Delivery/takeaway

Boston

STAR OF INDIA

110-112 West Street, Boston   🕾 01205 360558

Owned by Tanvir Hussain. Air conditioning and completely redecorated in 1997, seating increased from 52 to 76 diners, serving Pakistani
formula curries with traditional accompaniments. 'Very pleasant decor,
typical Indian restaurant style enhanced by large numbers of cotton
flowers. Service attentive but not intrusive. Balti Chicken was quite
delicious. Keema Nan was piping hot and filled with ample quantity
of minced meat. Highly recommended.' MS-R. 'Best-ever Tandoori
Chicken starter followed by superb Dhansak.' AG. It continues to get
plentiful one-liners of satisfaction. This year fifteen people nominated
it among their top three in our 'list your favourite' slot on our report
forms. Minimum charge: £5. Takeaway 10% discount. Price check:
Papadam 35p, CTM £5.75, Pullao Rice £1.40, Peshwari Nan £1.50.
House wine £5.75, Perrier £2.25. Hours: 12-2.30pm/6pm-12am.
Branches (both takeaways): Chilli Master, 2 Red Lion Street,
Stamford; Chilli Master, 11 Winsover Road, Spalding. Stocks Cobra.

TASTE OF BOMBAY   NEW ENTRANT   ©

53 West Street, Boston   🕾 01205 359944

Established in 1994 by Mohammed Faruk. The restaurant is traditionally designed with arches and pillars. It seems that this restaurant has
its own regular fans who prefer it to the Star and vice-versa. More
reports please on both. Minimum charge: £5.50. Price check: Papadam
40p, CTM £6.25, Pullao Rice £1.45, Peshwari Nan £1.60. Lager £3 pint,
house wine £6.95 wine, mineral water £2.59. Hours: 12-2.30pm/
6-11.45pm, (12.30pm on Fri. & Sat.). Branch: Bombay Brasserie, 24,
Railway Road, Kings Lynn, Norfolk.

Bourne

PRINCE OF KASHMIR   ©

8 Abbey Road, Bourne   🕾 01778 393959

Co-owners Ali Ashker, Ali Akbar (chef), Ali Arshad and Ali Amjad,
told me last time that they have made a lot of new customer friends

since they appeared in the Guide, and they really welcome Curry Club members for their discount, so get booking and enjoy all your favourites. Hours 5.30pm-12am (12.30am on Fri. & Sat.).

Cleethorpes

AGRAH

7-9 Seaview Street, Cleethorpes   © **01472 698669**

Established in 1979 by Bashir Miah. Seats 60, serves formula curries. Specials include: Dabari Kash, tandoori chicken cooked in butter, tomato and cream, served with green salad and Pullao Rice £6.25. Takeaways 5% discount. Price check: Papadam 25p, CTM £5.50, Pullao Rice £1.25, Peshwari Nan £1.50. House wine £6.50. Hours: 12-2.30pm/6pm-12am. Branch: Shahi Mahal Takeaway, 6 Pinfold Lane, Cleethorpes. Stocks Cobra.

TASTE OF PUNJAB   ©

9-11 Market Street, Cleethorpes   © **01472 603720**

Established in 1989 by Mr and Mrs Sagoo. Their restaurant seats 38 diners and serves Pakistani formula food. Takeaway 10% discount. Sunday lunch: £3.50. Price check: Papadam 30p, CTM £5.90, Pullao Rice £1.10, Peshwari Nan £2. House wine £7, mineral water £1.20. Delivery: £10 minimum. Hours: 12-2.30pm/5.30pm-12am (2am on Sat., 12.30am on Sun.). Stocks Cobra.

Grantham

BOMBAY BRASSERIE   ©

11 London Road, Grantham   © **01476 576096**

Large, but well spaced tables, seats 104. Festoons of red silk and satin hang from the ceiling, blue and pink chintz curtains hang by an arch dividing the dining room. Pink and white table linen, air-conditioned. Price check: Papadam 40p, CTM £6.90, Pullao Rice £1.75, Peshwari Nan £1.50. House wine £7.90, mineral water £2.50. Hours: 5.30pm-12am (1am on Sat.). Stocks Cobra.

Grimsby

ABDUL'S TANDOORI

152 Victoria Street, Grimsby   ✆ 01472 356650

Owned by Abdul Salique since 1982. Seats 46 diners and serves
Pakistani style curries and side dishes. 'Modern Indian decor, reasonably comfortable. Wide and conventional menu but unadventurous.
Potato Pakora and Vegetable Cutlet both £1.95. Generous quantities.
Achari Chicken Balti £5.20. Service slow, late on Saturday night and
very busy.' GGP&MP. Sunday lunch £4.95. Price check: Papadam 40p,
CTM £5.75, Pullao Rice £1.20, Peshwari Nan £1.35. House wine £6.95,
mineral water £2.50. Delivery: £8 minimum, 3-mile radius. Hours: 12-
2.30pm/6pm-12am, (12.30am on Fri. & Sat.). Stocks Cobra.

Lincoln

SARGA TAKEAWAY NEW ENTRANT

133 Burton Road, Lincoln   01522 511777

'Went for my birthday. Plain and stuffed Paratha, hot and delicious.
Mushroom Rice nice, big pieces of mushroom, large slices of onion.
Mixed vegetable Korma, creamy, coconut sauce.' NT. The menu
includes a rather odd curry: 'Gandhi's Revenge' described as, extremely hot and volatile curry, with special red bullet chillies, this should
bring a grin to Gandhi's soul after you have eaten it! £6.25 – Sounds
great! If anyone orders it, tell us. Price check: Papadam 30p (plain),
40p (spicy), CTM £5.50, Bombay Potato £1.75, Pullao Rice £1.50,
Chutney 50p each. Delivery: £8.50 minimum. Hours: 5.30pm-12am.

RAJ DOUTH

7 Eastgate, Lincoln   ✆ 01522 548377

In a quaint building in the exclusive part of town. Restaurant com-
prises several rooms, linked together by the reception area. You get a
special offer for birthdays: one main course free upon proof of birth!

Louth

HELAL TANDOORI

1 Mercer Row, Louth   © 01507 607960

Bashir Miah's restaurant seats 80 divided between three dining rooms (party room seats 18) and serves   formula curries and side dishes. Specials include: Chicken Tikka Biriani £6.25. 'Service, by youngsters, was very casual. We had booked a table, but on arrival, this had not been noted. Waited for our wine until the main course was served, then we had to ask and they were not busy.' SL. Takeaways 10% off. Price check: Papadam 25p, CTM £5.75, Pullao Rice £1.50. Hours: 12-2.30pm/6pm-12am. Branch: Shahi Mahal Takeaway, 6 Pinfold Lane, Louth.

Scunthorpe

RAHMAN'S TANDOORI   ©

143 Frodingham Road, Scunthorpe   © 01724 841238

Bangladeshi curry house taken over in 1984 by A. Miah, who says it's 'very pinky at the moment' but not for much longer, 'plans for a new colour scheme and function room upstairs.' Price check: Papadam 40p, CTM £5.95, Pullao Rice £1.50, Peshwari Nan £1.70. Lager £1.80 pint, house wine £5.95, mineral water £2.50. Delivery: £10 minimum. Hours: 12-2pm/6-12pm.

THE TAJ TAKEAWAY   ▦ ©

159 Frodingham Road, Scunthorpe   © 01724 862220

Established in 1989 by chef Rehman Rahman, who says he 'provides excellent food and service', and also that his reception area is, 'as good as any top star hotel.' He has sent me a photo and I can confirm that it is extremely prettily decorated with chandeliers, palms and comfortable cane chairs with squashy chairs. Mr Rahman has promised a 5% discount for CC members collecting a takeaway during the week. Hours: 5.30-11.30pm, closed Tuesday.

Sleaford

SHAH JEHAN NEW ENTRANT   ©

19 Market Place, Sleaford   01529 415313

Air-conditioned restaurant seats 54 diners, serving Pakistani food.
Decorated in burgundy and cream. Balti dishes are most popular,
served with Nan. Chicken Balti £5.95. BYO allowed, no corkage. Price
check: Papadam 50p, CTM £5.95, Pullao Rice £1.60, Peshwari Nan
£1.75. Lager £1.95 pint, house wine £8.50, mineral water £2.50. Hours:
5.30-11.30pm (12am on Fri. & Sat.).

Spalding

CHILLI MASTER

11 Winsover Road, Spalding   © 01775 762221

Takeaway offering Pizza (make your own, toppings 45p and 55p each –
garlic and chilli free!), Curry, Balti, Tandoori, Doner Kebabs, Southern
Fried Chicken and Burgers. Fast and free delivery available locally.
Hours: 5pm-1am (3am on Fri. & Sat.). Branch: Chilli Master, 2 Red
Lion Street, Stamford.

INDUS NEW ENTRANT

9 Winsover Road, Spalding   © 01775 760088

'Situated right next door to our favourite takeaway Chilli Masters. Pale
blue 'rag-roll' walls. Interesting menu – venison and duck. Smiling
waiters. Impressed.' PA. Hours: 5.30pm-12am, Sun. 12pm-12am. Sun.
buffet 12-5.30pm, £8.90, children under twelve, £4.45.

Stamford

RAJ OF INDIA   ©

2 All Saints Street, Stamford   © 01780 753556

'On being asked by friends to find a good curry house near Peterborough, I opened my trusty bible to the Raj of India. Staff very
pleasant. Chatting to the head waiter, boasted of best in Lincolnshire.
Couldn't fault. Fifteen of us. Xal Fari (!) very hot but very tasty, good

sized portions, lovely surroundings. Another great, successful curry.'
DP. 'Given I didn't have much time — I telephoned ahead and found
crisp fresh Papadams waiting at my table for one. Large portion of
Pullao Rice, equally big CTM — quite spicy, required a Cloret or two
before my afternoon meeting, quite simply the best Mushroom Bhajee
I have had, lightly spiced, thinly sliced button mushrooms, garnished
with chopped fresh coriander — excellent. Clean and inviting restau-
rant.' AG. Raj Suite for private parties. 10% discount on takeaway.
Owner Rohom Ali has promised a 10% discount off the bill for CC
Members. Price check: Papadam 40p (plain), 50p (spicy), CTM £7.20,
Bombay Potato £2.20, Pullao Rice £1.90, Chutney or Pickles (per portion) 40p. Hours: 12-3pm (Sun. closed) and 6pm-12am. Stocks Cobra.

Woodhall Spa

INDIA VILLAGE

6 The Broadway, Woodhall Spa   © 01526 352223

Wasn't this the Dam Busters' HQ? Not the India Village, though the
chaps would have loved it — the actual village, I mean. I know that
Scampton, which is relatively near, was their base. Anyway, MS LN found
it 'a little slow, but the food OK'. Price check: Papadom 55p, Green
Herbal Chicken Kebab £5.80, CTM £5.95, Very Hot Pili Pili Chicken
£5.95, Pullao Rice £1.85.

GREATER MANCHESTER

Area: North-west
Population: 2,578,000
(Manchester postcodes, M1 to M46
  pop: 433,000)
Number of restaurants in county: 309
Number of restaurants in Guide: 60

*Although Greater Manchester was introduced as a county in 1965, it is still disregarded
by many of its residents who prefer to refer to the counties that Greater Manchester
gobbled up, e.g., parts of Lancashire and Cheshire. We have adhered strictly to the official current Greater Manchester territory for town locations in this Guide.*

Altrincham

MUGHAL   ©

86 Park Road, Timperley, Altrincham   © 0161 973 4513

M. Hoque's Mughal remains just as popular. Open 5pm-12am. Branch:
Tondori Royale, Manchester, M19.

SHERE KHAN

Old Market Place, Altrincham   © 0161 926 8777

Owned by Rafiq Awan and managed by Saleem Bakir. 'Located next to
the Orange Tree Pub (CAMRA award-winner) in an attractive old
town, its reputation has grown – it's busy every night. Two floors of
beautiful decor, bamboo, pine and gold. Waiters pounce from all corners, service is excellent. Papadam, perfect with complimentary side
salad and the usual pickles, including a coleslaw. Delicious Chicken
Tikka curries, slightly spicier than expected. Breads and Rice very
tasty.' TE. Price check: Papadam 60p (two), CTM £5.20, Bombay
Potato £3.50, Pullao Rice £1.10. Halal Food.

RAJ TAKEAWAY NEW ENTRANT   ▦ ©

175 Ashley Road, Hale, Altrincham   © 0161 929 6399

Owned by Anwar Ahmed Choudhury. Formula northern Indian and
Balti dishes on the menu. Price check: Papadam 35p, CTM £5.20,
Pullao Rice £1.50, Peshwari Nan £1.70. Hours: 4.30pm-12am.

RAJDAN TAKEAWAY NEW ENTRANT   ▦ ©

401 Stockport Road, Timperley, Altrincham   0161 903 9334

Also owned by Anwar Ahmed Choudhury. Popular orders include
Masala and Balti dishes. Set Lunch £8.50 for two. Price check:
Papadam 35p, CTM £5.20, Pullao Rice £1.50. Hours: 4.30pm-12am.

©	Curry Club discount (see page 6)		Unlicensed
√	Vegetarian		
BYO	Bring your own alcohol	▦	Delivery/takeaway

Ashton-under-Lyne

INDIAN OCEAN   ©

83 Stamford Street East, Ashton   ✆ 0161 343 3343

Pakistani curry house, seats 120. Owned by Nahim Aslam. House specials include: Lamb Jalfrezi, Chicken Chilli Masala, cooked with fresh green chillies and Chicken Chat Masala, chicken pieces with chick peas, garnished with roasted cashew nuts, all at £5.25. Minimum charge: £8. Buffet £8.95. Price check: Papadam 45p, CTM £7.25, Pullao Rice £1.70, Peshwari Nan £1.60. House wine £8, mineral water £1.10. Delivery: £7.95 minimum, 3-mile radius. Hours: 5 (Sun. 4)-11pm, (12am on Fri. & Sat.). Stocks Cobra.

Atherton

FAR PAVILION   NEW ENTRANT

138 Bolton Road, Atherton   ✆ 01942 875077

'The food is always out of this world. Prawn Patia, Seekh Kebab and Onion Bhajia are our favourite starters. All main courses are superb. The complimentary cream liqueur was a nice touch. This restaurant must appear in your 1999 guide as to us it is the best.' JM.

SAVAR   NEW TO OUR TOP 100   ©

39-41 Mealhouse Lane, Atherton   ✆ 01942 875544

Established in '94 by Haq (head chef), Uddin and Ali (manager). Restaurant seats 56 diners. Have recently refitted carpet and wallpaper. 'We simply cannot contain ourselves any longer, we must tell you about our favourite restaurant in the whole wide world. My hubby and myself have eaten in numerous restaurants throughout Europe – 50% at least were of the Indian variety and we cannot find a meal to equal – indeed, approach – the quality, flavour, texture and total experience of the Savar's Balti dishes. Good-quality meat and vegetables wallow in a variety of thick, rich, tangy sauces, delicately suffused with a multi-tude of fragrant spices and lavishly strewn with fresh coriander. The Nan breads are as light as clouds and as large as duvets, the portions reach well halfway up the side of the washing-up-bowl-sized Balti dishes – and you must try the special red sauce that arrives with the pickles and starters. The Savar is a pleasant, unassuming restaurant, situated in a converted chapel. The staff are lovely – especially Ranu, the chatty manager. The prices are extremely modest. All in all, this is an experience not to be missed.' IF-E. 'Has a Balti chef from Birmingham, so we expected authenticity – and we got it. Portion quantities were just about right, and the quality was superb thanks to the liberal use of fresh ingredients. King Prawn Puri quite delicious. Balti Lamb Jalfrezi was mind-blowing – love those chillies! I'm going to enjoy being a regular here.' MS. 'Papadams with fabulous Tamarind Chutney. Followed by Aloo Chat on Puri. Balti Chicken liberally covered in coriander with rice. Fabulous Tikka Chilli Masala, hot and spicy. Utterly delicious, delicately spiced Brinjal Bhajee.' RK. Thanks for the photos, showing a couple's wedding reception; we will print these in the magazine. Price check: Papadam 40p, CTM £6.10, Pullao Rice £1.40, Peshwari Nan £1.50. House wine £6.50, mineral water £2. Minimum charge £5.50. Hours: 5-11.30pm (12.30am on Fri. & Sat.). Sun. 4-11.30pm. New to our TOP 100. Stocks Cobra.

Bolton

AMIR NEW ENTRANT

2 Broad Gate, Ladybridge, Bolton ℭ **01204 660114**

Opened in '94 by Omar Dey. Serves Northern Indian curries. Price check: Papadam 45p, CTM £6.45, Pullao Rice £1.50. House Specials include Jali Bhuna, served with rice for £7.95. Hours: 5.30-10.45pm. Branch: Tandoori Ghar, Drake Street, Rochdale.

ANAZ TAKEAWAY

138 St Helens Road, Bolton ℭ **01204 660114**

Takeaway established in '94 by Yunus Ahmed. Specials include: Moglai, Masala, Aloo Gosht, Aloo Methi, Chilli Masala and Garlic Curries. 'Spotless, service first-class and I was offered a fresh cup of coffee whilst I waited.' MB. Price check: Papadam 30p, CTM £4.75, Pullao Rice £1, Peshwari Nan £1.50. Delivery: £7.50 minimum, 2-mile radius. Hours: 5pm-12am, (1am on Fri. & Sat.), closed Monday.

HILAL TANDOORI   NEW ENTRANT   ©

296 Chorley Old Road, Bolton   © 01204 842315

This one was opened in 1975 by Surat Ali, and he's still here with Anor Liiah as manager. Chef Abdul Monaf cooks the curries. A nice touch is the free liqueur at the end of the meal. Takeaways qualify for a free can of lager and Papadam. Price check: Papadam 40p, CTM £6.05, Pullao Rice £1.20. Minimum charge £5. Hours: 6pm-2am, (3am on Fri. & Sat. for the night owls).

JALAL BALTI SPICE TAKEAWAY   ©

505 Chorley Old Road, Bolton   © 01204 843397

Taken over in 1989 by Budur Miah. Chef Mofir Miah cooks the formula. Delivery: £7 minimum, 4-mile radius. Hours: 5pm (Sun. 4pm)-12am (1am on Sat.). Mon. closed.

LEENA

131-133 Bradshawgate, Bolton   © 01204 383255

'Took nine friends 'cos the "BIBLE" recommended it. Not disappointed at all. Friendly service, they even gave me a tour of the kitchen. Nicely decorated, glass fronted kitchen, so you can watch. Very nice special Mixed Karahi. Curries tasted very tomatoey, too similar. Garlic Nan needs more garlic. Free Papadams, free liqueurs, oranges, mints etc.' DP.

THE SPICE ISLAND

87 Tonge Moor Road, Bolton   © 01204 361678

Manager Joynal and chef Mohammed Mehbub cook some intriguing unusuals. I've never seen Ekuri (£2.10) served anywhere else. It is spicy scrambled egg, served with Puri, and it's delicious. Palak Shira (£1.35) is a tasty spinach-based soup. Reporters tell of good Baltis, maybe because Mehbub professes to like them himself, especially the Garlic Special Balti, which he describes on the menu as 'recommended if you are going vampire-hunting' – presumably missable if you want to impress a new partner who's not shared your indulgence, but in all respects mind-blowing and breath-blowing! The Bangladeshi Dishes are also in demand, we hear. Shandus Baja (£4.25) is chicken or meat,

roasted, then stir-fried with bamboo shoots, fresh hot chillies and
other delights. Joynal is the manager. Price check: Papadam 35p, CTM
£4.30, Pullao Rice £1.20. Sunday Thali £4.60. Delivery: £6 order,
3-mile radius, 95p charge (!!!); £12 order, 4-mile radius, £1.95. Hours:
5 (Sun. 4)-11.30pm/4.30pm-12am.

SUNAR GAW BALTI CUISINE

310 Manchester Road, Bolton   ✆ 01204 364915

Sunar Gaw means 'golden village'. Opened in 1992 by Abdul Shahid
and Abdul Hannan, the former is the manager front of house, the latter the chef behind the scenes. Seats 44 diners. Price check: Papadam
35p, CTM £6.50, Pullao Rice £1.30. Set meal for two £25.95. Minimum
charge £15. Hours: 5.30pm-12am. Branch: Sunar Gaw, Haslingden.

Bury

TANDOORI NIGHTS

135 Rochdale Road, Bury   ✆ 0161 761 6224

'Brilliant. Watch them cooking the food. Very friendly and free chutney.' PJ. Hours: 5.30-11.20pm (12.30am on Fri. & Sat.), Sun. 4-11pm.

CHEADLE TANDOORI TAKEAWAY   NEW ENTRANT

228 Stockport Road, Cheadle   ✆ 0161 428 4668

Owned by M.D. Tasadduk Hussain, who is also head of the kitchen.
Opened in 1997. Formula curries on the menu. Price check: Papadam
30p, CTM £4.80, Pullao Rice £1, Chutney 20p each. Hours: 5pm- 12am
(12.30am on Fri. & Sat.).

Hyde

NAWABI BALTI   NEW ENTRANT

162-164 Market Street, Hyde   ✆ 0161 368 9917

'For my best friend and me, Friday is Curry Night and has been for
many years. Our favourite favourite, for value for money. There is an
excellent choice of dishes and the quantities are good. Restaurant is
beautifully decorated and comfortable. Seats about 40 and the staff are

very friendly, polite and obliging. Fully licensed, there is an in-house taxi service. Free home delivery.' GW. Price check: Papadam: 30p, Balti CTM £5.25, Pullao Rice £1.15.

MANCHESTER CITY

The postcodes of Manchester and its surrounding suburbs were recently changed. For the purpose of this Guide we have included M postcodes in all our Manchester City entries, and have divided the area into Central, East, South, West and North, using major roads as our arbitrary boundaries.

Manchester Central M1 to M4

ASHOKA

Portland Street, Manchester   © 0161 228 7550

'A few notches above the formula curry house.' RC.

GAYLORD TOP 100

Amethyst House, Spring Gardens
Manchester, M2   © 0161 832 6037

Owned by P.K. Chadha and R. Kapoor, since '93. Seats 92 diners, Northern Indian cuisine. 'Chicken Tikka and Chicken Tikka Garlic are the most succulent I've ever tasted and their Rogan Josh is my all time favourite dish – the lamb is always tender and the sauce has to be tasted to be believed. Vegetables fresh and nowhere does a better Nan.' RC. 'Reasonable menu selection, but what they offer is excellent. Good service in a very relaxing atmosphere.' AKD. Sunday lunch buffet £7.95. Service: 10%. 'Expensive and mediocre meal. Place was virtually empty and did not fill up on Saturday night. Service was very slow, they were more interested in talking amongst themselves than taking orders. Curry sauce was thin and watery.' DR PAW. Price check: Papadam 60p, CTM £7.95, Pullao Rice £2.50, Peshwari Nan £2.25. House wine £8.95, mineral water £2.50. Takeaway 10% discount. Hours: 12-2.30pm/ 6-11.30pm (11pm on Sun.). Stocks Cobra.

KAILASH ©

34 Charlotte Street, Manchester, M1   ✆ 0161 236 6624

N.P. Bhattara's 75-seater basement restaurant is described as Nepalese and serves Northern Indian curries, but where are the Nepalese delicacies? 'Service very helpful and friendly, particularly as there was a large party already in the restaurant. Possibly needs some redecoration, carpets a little shabby, although tables spotless. Free Papadams and pickles. Lamb Rogan Josh had cashew nuts. Portions a little on the small side.' TOC. 'Food I would rate as very average, although I rate the Nan bread as one of the best I have had. Comfortable surroundings and decor.' AKD. Price check: Papadam 40p, CTM £5.20, Pullao Rice £1.40, Peshwari Nan £1.70. House wine £7.30, mineral water £4.50. Hours: 12-2.30pm/6.30-11.30pm. Closed Sat. and Sun. lunch. Stocks Cobra.

NAWAAB

47 Rochdale Road, Manchester, M4   ✆ 0161 839 0601

Restaurant divided into two dining rooms. Serves Kashmiri and Pakistani styled curries. 'Have yet to find fault with either the service or the quality of the food. My visits are always mid-week, the restaurant is always quarter full. Friendly and helpful waiters. Check out the Karahi Murgh!' GF. Takeaway 10% off. Price check: Papadam 35p, CTM £6.50, Bombay Potato £2.95, Pullao Rice £2.20. Hours: 6-11pm. Sat. 5.30pm-12.30am. Branches: Bradford, Huddersfield, Majorca.

RAJDOOT

**Carlton House, 18 Albert Square,
Manchester, M2**   ✆ 0161 834 2176

The Rajdoot is the 1966 creation of architect Des Sarda who also owns the Rajdoot in Bristol, Birmingham, Dublin and of all places, Fuengirola, Spain. 'They are all highly decorated and up market restaurants. I love the bar area, where little leather stools are arranged round a large beaten brass tables, it feels so exotic. I am always surprised when somebody writes in and says they had an awful meal, I have been to all the Rajdoots more than once (except the Spanish one and I am working on that!) and I have always had good meals in all the branches.' DBAC. Sadly we have received a number of truly awful reports about this branch in particular. Also see Rajdoot, Bristol. It has cost it its TOP 100 rating, and if this goes on, its appearance in this Guide.

Manchester East   Including M11, M18, M34, M35, M40, M43

LA MIRAGE TANDOORI

67-69 Kenyon Lane, Moston, M40   © 0161 681 9373

'After being a regular customer here for many years and never been disappointed, I feel La Mirage should be given recognition for its excellent curries and tandoori dishes. The decor is not brilliant, but the meals, service and prices are. The best Madras in Manchester.' BT.

Manchester South   Including M12, M17, M19 – M21, M32, M33

BALTI BRASSERIE   NEW ENTRANT

212 Mauldeth Road, Burnage,
Manchester, M19   © 0161 443 1966

'Adam Khan's restaurant is small, seating 40. The Chicken Madras and Pilau rice were perfect, large portions at a very good price. The Garlic Nan was fantastic (best ever).' SM.

GREAT KATHMANDU

140 Burton Road, West Didsbury, M20   © 0161 434 6413

Nepalese restaurant, also serving traditional curry house food. Taken over '96 by Chandra Kumar, who also manages his 55-seater establishment. Decorated with flowers, in red and brown, religious photos on the walls, giving a warm atmosphere. Specials include: Bhutan Chara, chicken cooked with fresh mushrooms and tomatoes £4.65, Bary Masala – mince balls with fresh onion, tomatoes and yoghurt £4.65, Lobster Masala £14.95 and Murghi Masala £15.50 and 24-hours notice. Price check: Papadam spicy 35p, CTM £4.95, Pullao Rice £1.40,

Peshwari Nan £1.90. House wine £6.75, mineral water £2.50. Hours: 12-2.30pm/6pm-12am. Stocks Cobra.

TONDORI ROYALE   ©

682 Burnage Lane, Burnage, M19   ✆ **0161 432 0930**

Bob Hoque's 110-seater is very well-established (1980) and very well spoken of by the locals. 'It was packed! It is not difficult to work out why when you taste the cuisine. Atmosphere is electric and food well worth the 40-mile trip.' MB. It has distinguished itself with a full house of familiar dishes plus some great Bangladeshi specials. Fish dishes include Boal and Ayre. NW's favourite is Zhal Golda Chingri, king prawn cooked with chilli and ginger. 'A good restaurant, which boasts about its entry in the Good Restaurant Guide. I bet that's a scam.' PW. [So do I. Ask him to show you one, Philip, or where to buy it!!!. -Ed] Price check: Papadam 45p, CTM £6.75, Pullao Rice £1.25. Minimum charge £6. Delivery: £15 minimum, 3-mile radius. Hours: 6pm-1am, Sat. and Sun. 5pm-2.30am.

Wilmslow Road, Rusholme – M14

Wilmslow Road extends for nearly 6 miles south from Manchester Centre. It passes through Rusholme, Manchester's main Asian area. To get there from the city centre it's best to walk — parking is normally a joke. Face south on the Oxford Road, with the BBC on your left, and go for about 800 metres, passing the Uni and then the Royal Infirmary. At the Moss Lane East junction, Rusholme and Little India starts. In the last five years the expansion has been amazing and is continuing unabated. Now, in the 600 metres from Moss Lane to Claremont Road, there are no less than 35 curry eateries — Indian snack and sweet shops, cafés and restaurants. As if that's not enough, there are numerous pubs, offies, chippies, Chinese, pizza joints, kebab houses and burger bars, Asian grocers and halal butchers. Some of the cheap and cheerful all-day cafés allow BYO (but always ask — it can offend some Muslims). Some are quite expensive licensed restaurants, the largest of which seats 350 and is planning an expansion to 400! A conservative estimate on curry consumption is 50,000 curries a week here. We believe this to be the curry record for a district. Any challenges? Go a further 900 metres along Wilmslow Road and there are some 30 more curry eateries, making this a genuine Golden Mile. With such rapid growth, we'd love full details on this phenomenon from all our scribes. Maybe it will merit a special extended feature in the next Guide. Meanwhile, here are some of your favourites:

CHUNI'S   NEW ENTRANT

1 Claremont Road, Rusholme M14   © 0161 224 0376

'The main course was a delectable vegetable curry, a dhal curry and a
lamb curry. The sweet and coffee that followed ensured it was the best
all-round meal we have had in an Asian restaurant.' SM&GB. 'Enter the
doors and upstairs to an enormous, tastefully decorated restaurant.
You are met by one of the lively Chuni brothers. All the old favourites
on the menu. A weight watchers platter exists. Warm and crisp Papadams await you served with a selection of home-made chutneys and
pickles. My favourite starter is Hasina Kebab, spicy chunks of succulent lamb straight from the tandoor. Main course, Chicken Chilli with
Lamb Handi, quality meat delicately infused with spices, a luscious
alternative to the Karahi! Perfectly cooked Pullao Rice and large Nan,
only Paneer Kulcha will suffice. A perfect night.' SW.

EASTERN TOUCH   BYO ©

76 Wilmslow Road, Rusholme, M14   © 0161 224 5665

Mohammad Akhtar took over this 72-seater restaurant in 1989.
Pakistani curries, specialising in Balti. 'My favourite. Lino floor and
glass-topped tables — a café, really. Warm Papadams, chutney and
sauces are brought to the table immediately — free to all diners. Kebabs
cooked freshly over charcoal in the corner, piping hot, highly spiced
and juicy, served with a large plate of salad. Chicken Madras, prime
quality, tender and succulent, very hot, sauce is rich and fiery, perfect
for mopping up with a meaty Keema Nan. PW. Price check: Papadam
25p, CTM £5.20, Pullao Rice £1, Peshwari Nan £2. Takeaway 10% discount. Sunday lunch £6.50. Pista (pistachio?) Nan £2. Lager £1.50 pint,
house wine £5, mineral water £2. BYO allowed, no corkage. Delivery:
£5 minimum. Hours: 3pm-3am (3.30am on Sat.), Sun. 12-12.

LAL HAWELI   NEW ENTRANT

68-72 Wilmslow Road, Rusholme, M14   © 0161 248 9700

M. Nawaz took over this 150-seater in '97. Head chef Hamid Abdul
and Jawad cooks Pakistani-style curries. Specials include: Balti Lahori
and Khasi Ko Bhutwa. Sunday lunch £4.95. Price check: Papadam complimentary, CTM £4.95, Pullao Rice £1.10. House wine £7.50, mineral
water £2.50. Hours: 12pm-1am. Stocks Cobra.

NEW TABAK   ©

199-201 Wilmslow Road, Rusholme, M14   ✆ 0161 257 3890

Now with 'New' in the name, Mohammad Nawab's simply decorated
restaurant seats a MASSIVE 350 diners, on two floors. Pakistani curries and acompaniments on the menu cooked by chefs Raj Kumar and
Abrahim Ali. Balti is very popular with diners. 'Another little gem.
Karahi Nawabi Bataire, quails. Afghani Bashyan, tender juicy lamb
chop marinated in cream, spices and barbecued – not to be missed.' MB.
£7.50 wine. Sunday lunch buffet £4.95. Price check: Papadam complimentary, CTM £4.95, Pullao Rice £1.10. Hours: 12pm-1am. Branch: Lal
Haweli, 70 Wilmslow Road, Manchester. Nasib, 90 Wilmslow Road,
Manchester. Stocks Cobra.

SANAM SWEET HOUSE   ©

145-151 Wilmslow Road, Rusholme, M14   ✆ 0161 224 8824

Despite AQ Akhtar's restaurant being huge (seating 160, plus a further
200-seat function room), it is so popular locally that it's often full,
with queues waiting to be seated. 'The standard fare was very, very
good . . . the Aloo Tikka was very tasty. A good first time visit.' TOC.
Hours: 12pm-12am. Branches: Abdul's, 121 & 318 Wilmslow Road, and
298 Oxford Road.

SANAM TAKEAWAY

167 Wilmslow Road, Rusholme, M14   ✆ 0161 257 3557

'More of a kebab-style takeaway than a restaurant, serving only
starters. Easily missed, as the frontage covers no more than about 10
feet. Dingy decor and formica tables belie the standard of the food.
Samosas, both meat and vegetable, are the best I've ever eaten. Shikh
Kebabs (three to a portion) are superb. All served on a metal dish with
no cutlery but a warm, large and deliciously moist Nan. Not the place
to impress a new girlfriend, maybe, but a must for those late nights out
with the boys.' DB.

©	Curry Club discount (see page 6)		Unlicensed
√	Vegetarian		
BYO	Bring your own alcohol	⊞	Delivery/takeaway

SANGAM

9-159 Wilmslow Road, Rusholme, M14   © 0161 257 3922

M. Salim's establishment has grown to a vast 340 seats. There are four
dining rooms on two floors and decorated in a pink and blue combination. Being so large this restaurant may be unique in having two
managers, Faisal and Tanveer. Bangladeshi and Pakistani formula curries are on the menu, cooked by head chef Shahid. 'Up-market, bright
and clean. Lamb Chop Tikka, one of the best and most filling starters
I have had. Will visit again.' RC. Hours: 12pm-12am.

SHERE KHAN

52 Wilmslow Road, Rusholme, M14   © 0161 256 2624

This is the MCR version of Khan's W2. It is popular beyond belief
and does a massive 'love-it or leave-it' trade. The decision is yours.
Here's an example of both. 'One of the busiest restaurants on the
Curry Golden Mile. Clean, a/c (sometimes) and so busy that people
stand around waiting for tables, wishing you to hurry up. Tasteless and
watery onion and yoghurt raita are placed on the tables for your
Papadams and charged for if you want it or not. Food quality can vary
widely on different days of the week, portions not generous and it is
not cheap. Uniformly surly staff, probably a result of their contant
harassment by management. Look after your valuables, had two purses
and a handbag stolen. No help and sympathy from the management –
only the bill. £131 for nine, no service, definitely no tip.' NSC. 'I've been
there 100 times and it's great, but still they don't recognise me!' GR.
Hours 12pm-12am.

SPICY HUT   NEW ENTRANT   ©

35 Wilmslow Road, Rusholme. M14   0161 248 6200

M.S. Mughal's simply decorated, 60-seater serves traditional Pakistani
curries and side dishes. Traditional Karahi Ghosht (sic.), lamb on the
bone, garlic, ginger, tomatoes, coriander, herbs and spices £5.90. Garlic
and Cheese Nan £1.90. Price check: Papadam 60p (2 in portion),
CTM £5.50, Pullao Rice £1.30, Peshwari Nan £1.50. House wine £5.90,
mineral water 90p. Delivery: £10 minimum, 3-mile radius. Hours: 5pm-
2am, Sun. 3pm-1am. Stocks Cobra.

TANDOORI KITCHEN
BYO

131-133 Wilmslow Road, Rusholme, M14   ℭ 0161 224 2329

Mrs Masooma Hussain opened her 130-seater Persian restaurant in 1970. Has been refurbished this year. Chef Majid Abdul cooks traditional Persian and curry dishes. Specialities include: Khoresteh Lapeh, spinach and lentil in a rich tomato curry sauce £4.40. Mirza Ghasemi – aubergine cooked with plenty of garlic, tomato and egg £4.80. Unlicensed, BYO, no corkage. Price check: Papadam 40p, CTM £5.70, Pullao Rice £1.10. Takeaway 20% discount. Hours: 12-2.30pm/5pm-12am. Sat. 12pm-12am. Sun. 1-11pm.

Manchester West Including M5, M7, Salford, M27, M31, M38, M41, M44, M46

Cadishead, M44

SUNDORBON

40 Liverpool Road, Cadishead, M44   ℭ 0161 775 2812/5

Iqbal and Raquib Uddin, owners, and manager Mofique Uddin cook the formula. Price check: Papadam 50p, CTM £6.95, Pullao Rice £1.20, Peshwari Nan £1.40. House wine £6.50, mineral water £1.50. Delivery: £10 minimum. Hours: 6pm-12.30am (2am on Sat., 1am on Sun.). Stocks Cobra.

Eccles, M30

PASSAGE TO INDIA
©

168 Monton Road, Monton, Eccles, M30   ℭ 0161 787 7546

M. Hassan Choudhury and H. Uddin's serves 90 diners all the formula curries. Open 12pm-11.30pm Branch: Gate of India, Swinton.

Urmston, M41

STANDARD

2-4 Victoria Parade, Higher Road,
Urmston, M41   *C* 0161 748 2806

Taken over in '97 by Mohammed Karim. 'Pleasant decor. Fairly priced. Name describes restaurant well – a good standard Indian meal.' IEF-E. Takeaway 20% off. Price check: Papadam 50p, CTM £6.95, Pullao Rice £1.50. Hours: 5pm (3pm on Sun.)-12am (1am on Sat.). Stocks Cobra.

Manchester North   Including M8, M9, M24 (Middleton), M25 & M45 (Whitefield), and M26 (Radcliffe)

Prestwich, M25

GARDEN OF INDIA   ©

411 Bury Old Road, Prestwich, M25   *C* 0161 773 7784

An 88-seat restaurant, opened in 1984 by Hafizur Rahman and managed by A. Quyum. 'Chicken Samber, very reminiscent of a Dhansak, hot, but not as sweet, which was a very pleasant change and one which I shall look out for again. Chicken Paneer met with total approval.' SN. and RA. 'Have visited several times and have always found it quite acceptable.' MB. TT likes the Fish Kufta Masala – fish balls in a creamy sauce. Hafizur Rahman has plans for refurbishing his 68-seater. Curries, cooked by head chef Ataur Rahman. Thalis from £10.50 to £11.90 per person, recommended. Service 10%. Cover charge £1.25. Price check: Papadam 40p, CTM £6.20, Pullao Rice £1.70, Peshwari Nan £1.60. Takeaway 20% off. Hours: 5pm-12am. Stocks Cobra.

©	Curry Club discount (see page 6)		Unlicensed
√	Vegetarian		
BYO	Bring your own alcohol		Delivery/takeaway

Radcliffe, M26

ALISHAN

21-23 Church Street, Radcliffe, M26   ✆ 0161 725 9910

Abdul Mumin's 60-seater serves formula curries cooked by Aziz Rahman. Sunday lunch buffet £7. Takeaway 20% off. Price check: Papadam 40p, CTM £6, Pullao Rice £1.20. House wine £6.95. Delivery: £8 minimum, 3-mile radius. Orders over £20 — free bottle of wine. Hours: 4.30pm-12am, (1am on Fri. & Sat.), Sun. 1pm-12am.

RADCLIFFE CHARCOAL TANDOORI   ©

123 Blackburn Street, Radcliffe, M26   ✆ 0161 723 4870

At MLA Khan's very smart, up-market 100-seater, chef S.N. Ali's interesting starters include: Balti Chana Masala and Puri £2.45. Lamb Chop Tikka £3.25. Takeaway 30% discount. Sunday lunch £6.50. Price check: Papadam 45p, CTM £6.50, Pullao Rice £1.35, Peshwari Nan £1.60. Delivery: 3-mile radius. Hours: 6pm-12.30am (1.30am on Fri. & Sat.). Sun. 12pm-12.30am. Branch: India Brasserie, 105, Stockport Road, Marple, Stockport. Stocks Cobra.

SHAHBAAZ

Old Barn, Radcliffe Moor Road,
Radcliffe, M26   ✆ 0161 724 0000

F.A. Syed and Capt. N.I. Moshin opened this restaurant in 1989 (as the Curry Cottage) with its easy-to-remember phone number and address. Even the postcode is apt — OWL. In fact, Mr Syed should have renamed it the Owl Tandoori at the Old Barn! But we've not heard a thing from any one about that idea or indeed anything else.

Whitefield, M25 & M45

AKRAM'S   NEW ENTRANT

Sefton Street, Whitefield, M25   ✆ 0161 796 0412

The decor is really striking. It is set in a spacious former Methodist hall, now decorated in a minimalist way. Our scribes tell of good à la carte food and set meal bargains, especially the set lunch at £4.95 and the enormous Sunday buffet at £6.95. Open 12-2pm/6-11.30pm, Sun. 12-11.30pm

DAWAT TAKEAWAY

184 Bury New Road, Whitefield, M25   © 0161 796 5976

MB's favourite. Price check: Papadam 25p, CTM £4.40, Pullao Rice £1.10.

LA IMRANS NEW ENTRANT   ©

Top of Elms Centre, Whitefield M45   © 0161 796 0557

Popular Balti Night – Tuesday and Thursday – seven dishes £7.50. Sunday Buffet between 1pm and 6pm e-a-m-a-y-l £7.95 adult, £4.95 children. Takeaway 30% discount. Free parking at rear. BYO wine only, but please ask. Price check: Papadam 40p, CTM £6.95 (incl. rice), Pullao Rice £1.50 (with meal 75p). Lager £2.60 pint, house wine £6.50. Hours: 5 (Sun. 1)-11pm, (1am on Fri. & Sat.).

Oldham

BRITISH RAJ NEW ENTRANT   ©

185-187 Lees Road, Oldham   © 0161 624 8696

Oldham's oldest, Atik Miah and Aysha Khanom's place is 'tasteful, right down to the Union Jacks embroidered into the chairbacks. The food is really good. The Shan Special Chicken and Bombay Chicken were both like a dream – hot and spicy and unlike the normal formula stuff. Pullao Rice exceptionally light and perfumed. The meal was finished off with hot towels and orange segments. The manager then brought us two free tall cocktails to finish off with. They do special evenings with home-cooking, food as eaten by Bangladeshi families. One to return to.' RK. Most popular dish – Balti Shan, chicken or lamb, cooked with spices, onions, tomatoes, green peppers and green chillies £4.95. Takeaway 10% off. Sunday lunch £7.50. Good value Pickle Tray 65p. Price check: Papadam 30p, CTM £4.95, Pullao Rice £1.30, Peshwari Nan £1.85. Delivery: £10 minimum, 4-mile radius. Hours: 5.30pm-12.30am (2am on Sat., 1am on Sun.). Stocks Cobra.

LIGHT OF BENGAL

114 Union Street, Oldham   © 0161 624 4600

Established in '80 by Abdul Hannan, who also manages front of house. Seats 86 diners between two rooms. Takeaway 10% discount. Minimum charge £5.50. Price check: Papadam 35p, CTM £7.15, Pullao Rice £1.75, Peshwari Nan £1.75. Hours: 5.30pm-12.30am.

MILLON RESTAURANT   NEW ENTRANT   ©

Westwood Business Centre,
Featherstall Road South, Oldham   © 0161 620 6445

Abdul Momin and Ashik Ullah opened their Millon, meaning meeting place, in 1993 in a purpose-built, elegant building. The inside is as smart as the outside. There is a pub-ish, comfortable bar and a 96-seat dining room, with alcoves and pillars and smart upholstery. Since the chef is Mr Momin, the food is of a high standard. 'Plush surroundings. Papadams and a lovely, very tangy chutney, Amishi Chicken, very creamy and fruity and Chicken Jhali Bhuna, spicier and better. Totally approved of the Sag Paneer.' RK. Price check: Papadam 45p, CTM £6.75 (incl. Rice), Pullao Rice £1.60, Peshwari Nan £1.60. House wine £6.45. Takeaway 5% off. Hours: 5-11.30pm (12.30am on Sat.), Sun. 4-11pm.

Ramsbottom

Known to residents as 'Rammy'.

EASTERN EYE

38 Bolton Street, Ramsbottom   © 01706 823268

Tomal Datta's restaurant seats 48 diners. Specials include Balti dishes from £6.50.'Though licensed, when busy, you may be asked to visit the pub over the road whilst your table is prepared. Chicken Tikka absolutely perfect.' MB. Sunday buffet – 12 dishes, £8.95 (£4.50 child). Takeaway 15-20% off [which ??? -Ed]. Price check: Papadam 50p, CTM £6.50, Pullao Rice £1.60, Peshwari Nan £1.80. Hours: 5pm-12.30am. Stocks Cobra.

Rochdale

DERAJ BALTI CROWN

244 Yorkshire Street, Rochdale   © **01706 358649**

At Abdul Bhuiyan's smart, 45-seater, well-appointed in dusky pink, Balti dishes are a speciality, CT Balti being the most popular dish. Takeaway 20% off. Sunday lunch buffet £6.95. Price check: Papadam 35p, CTM £5.95, Pullao Rice £1.20, Peshwari Nan £1.60. Delivery: £10 minimum, 3-mile radius. Hours: 5pm-2am, Sat. 5pm-3am, Sun. 3pm-1am. Stocks Cobra.

LA TANDOOR   NEW ENTRANT   ©

Unit A7, Bamford Precinct, Rochdale   © **01706 642037**

Mrs S. Habeeb's 68-seater is decorated with a paint effect of waves in the ocean and trees on banks. Eight spice boats have been fixed to the walls with sacks of spices in them. Fishing hammocks are tied to the ceiling. 'A superb restaurant, and be warned – book a table, as it gets very busy. We had Nargis Kebab and Vegetable Chaat for starters – a dream – and we followed with a main-course choice of Chicken Tikka Biriani and Chilli Chicken Balti, with a side dish of Malayee Kufta (vegetable balls in a coconut sauce with pineapple and peaches), Pullao Rice and Chupattis. It was all excellent, followed by ice cream, face towels, a free drink and after-meal sweets. All this cost us just £26.45. We'd eat there every day if we were locals!' RK. Price check: Papadam 40p, CTM £6.35, Pullao Rice £1.25. Takeaway 20% off. Hours: 12.30pm-12.30am (1am on Sat.). Family Banquets Sunday £8.50 – 12.30-6pm. Stocks Cobra.

Standish

AMIN'S   NEW ENTRANT

487 Preston Road, Standish   © **01257 426661**

Restaurant seats 110 diners in two rooms. Party room seats 40. Decorated in pastel shades. Balti Exotica, combination of meat, chicken, lamb, king prawns, cooked in Balti sauce £8.50, most popular dish. Sunday lunch £5.95. Takeaway 20% off. Price check: Papadam 60p, CTM £6.50, Pullao Rice £1.50, Peshwari Nan £1.50. Hours: 12-2pm/5.30-11.30pm. Stocks Cobra.

TASTE OF BENGAL

11 High Street, Standish   📞 01257 473119

One correspondent raves on about owner-manager G. Uddin's Korai
Coriander and Chilli Fish (£4.90 incl. rice). 'Fish is so good for you.
We have it with Balti Dopiaza Sag (£4 incl. Nan) – spinach and lashings of onion, served in the iron pot – a double dose of iron, and our
meal for two is barely a tenner.' NM. 'Was not disappointed. Chicken
Akbari – a mix of fruit, nuts and Chicken Tikka – superb. Fit for the
Emperor himself.' TJ. Established in '92 by G. Uddin, who is also manager. Bangladeshi curries cooked by head chef M. Miah. Chicken
Pasanda is the most popular dish. Ask for the Weightwatchers special
£7.30 – 650 calories. £2 pint lager, £6.90 wine. Price check: Papadam
40p, CTM £6.60 incl. rice or Nan, Pullao Rice £1.45. Peshwari Nan
£1.65. Takeaway 30% discount. Open daily, 5pm-12am. Branch: Wigan
Tandoori Takeaway, 50 Frog Lane, Wigan. Stocks Cobra.

Stockport

HEATONS TANDOORI   NEW ENTRANT   ©

33a, Shaw Road, Heaton Moor, Stockport   📞 0161 442 9766

Abdul Aziz's 48-seater serves Kulchi Lamb, a whole leg slow cooked
with freshly ground spices, enough for four, £66.90. Price check:
Papadam 50p for two, complimentary chutney, CTM £6.25, Pullao
Rice £1.50, Peshwari Nan £1.75. Hours: 5.30pm-1.30am. Stocks Cobra.

INDIA BRASSERIE   NAME CHANGE   ©

105 Stockport Road, Marple, Stockport   📞 0161 427 2558

M.L.A. Khan, who took over the former Marple Masala in 1996. Seats
75 diners. Price check: Papadam 40p, CTM £5.45, Pullao Rice £1.50,
Peshwari Nan £1.50. Delivery: 3-mile radius. Hours: 5pm-12am. Branch:
Radcliffe Charcoal Tandoori, Radcliffe. Stocks Cobra.

©	Curry Club discount (see page 6)	☕	Unlicensed
√	Vegetarian		
BYO	Bring your own alcohol	🍴	Delivery/takeaway

KUSHOOM KOLY   ©

6 Shaw Road, Heaton Moor, Stockport   ℰ 0161 432 9841

Meaning 'flowerbud', Mrs Kulsum Uddin's 80-seater with bow window
and an open kitchen has been in the same family since it opened in
1971, with Fakuk front of house. The 8 rooms are decorated in pastel
shades of peach and blue with carved teak screens on the walls. Sami
and Kashim in the kitchens will cook Bengali fish dishes to order. 'The
food is plentiful and if you like garlic then this is the place to go.' GC.
'The menu features the usual range of favourites. Jalfrezi cooked the
way I prefer it, very spicy and liberal use of green chillies.' PH. Price
check: Papadam 60p for two, CTM £5.20, Pullao Rice £1.80. Takeaway
15% off. Delivery. Hours: 5pm-1am (2.30am on Sat.). Branch: Kaya Koly
Takeaway, Heaton Road, Heaton Moor, Stockport. Stocks Cobra.

ROMILEY TANDOORI

6-7 The Precinct, Romiley, Stockport   ℰ 0161 430 3774

'A very plush establishment, clean and serves excellent food.' MB.

TANDOORI PARLOUR   NEW ENTRANT

115 Buxton Road, Stockport   ℰ 0161 483 9112

'My family have enjoyed a lovely meal in pleasant surroundings. Plentiful good food. Service good.' CFW. 'Mr Maleque (the owner), takes
great pride in the ambience and decor. His food is superb, with all the
usual favourites (each with vegetable, free-range egg, fish and Quorn
options as well as meats). Cookery demonstrations, freezer packs,
party menus etc. are all available on request.' JG. Price check: Papadam
30p, CTM £4.25, Pilau Rice £1.25.

Wigan

AJMEER MANZIL

76 Market Street, Wigan   ℰ 01942 235910

Established in 1976 by Islam (manager) and Miah (head chef). Their
curry house seats 50 diners and serves formula curries. Specials include:
Chicken Makonwala £5.55, chicken tikka in a mild creamy sauce with
cheese. Price check: Papadam 40p, CTM £5.85, Pullao Rice £1.40,

Peshwari Nan £1.40. Minimum charge: £5. Hours: 11-2pm/5pm-1am (3am on Fri. & Sat.). Sun. 1pm-1am. Branches: Bombay Duck Takeaway, 50 Frog Lane, Wigan; Taste of Bengal, 11 High Street, Standish, Wigan. Stocks Cobra.

MERSEYSIDE

Area: North West
Population: 1,444,000
Number of restaurants in county: 90
Number of restaurants in Guide: 12

Formby

HILAL BALTI HOUSE   NEW ENTRANT

6 School Lane, Formby   ✆ **01704 874444**

'Formerly Bhalo. Nice warm Papadams with an excellent chutney. Shami Kebab and Boti Kebab came with a rather good mustardy yoghurt. Chicken Mint Massala and Chicken Narangi were new to us and a dream. Superb Pullao Rice and large Chapati.' RK.

JEWEL IN THE CROWN

126-128 Church Road, Formby   ✆ **01704 873198**

'We feel privileged to have such a fine curry house so close. We have never been disappointed.' DG. Reports please. Stocks Cobra.

©	Curry Club discount (see page 6)	☕	Unlicensed
√	Vegetarian		
BYO	Bring your own alcohol	🔳	Delivery/takeaway

Liverpool

BALTI HOUSE   NEW ENTRANT

18 Stanley Street, Liverpool   © 0151 236 3456

'Unusual decor, through the door walk over a bridge over an indoor pool, fountain to the bar area, down steps to dining area. Chingy Achari £9.95, marinated king prawns, strong spicy, sour – superb.' PS. Business lunch £3.50. Hours: 12-2pm (Mon. to Fri.), 5pm-12am (1am on Fri. & Sat.).

GULSHAN   TOP 100   BEST IN THE NORTH

544-546 Aigburth Road, Liverpool, L19   © 0151 427 2273

One look at M. and S. Rahman's venue tells you that it is likely to be good. Along its three-shop frontage is a white facia, supported by twelve pillars, above each of which resides an attractive uplighter resembling an ice cream cone. Between each light is a small canopy that crowns each of the tinted, partially-curtained windows below, beyond which one can see an inviting restaurant scene. There's a smart lounge complete with leather Chesterfields, and the 76-seater restaurant, in 3 rooms, with equally impressive leather-backed chairs. The toilets are very expensively fitted out and they're spotless. The 'ladies' powder room' contains hairspray, perfumes, deodorants, hand-creams, cotton-buds and, its very own resident resplendent black elephant. Sorry, chaps, no can see, not even if you're Lily Savage in full drag. DR says 'you could eat your dinner in there' – you're welcome, Denise, and we get your drift, but the Toilet Tikka has limited appeal, no matter how long the queue. The waiters wear striped waistcoats, and the tables are all well-dressed too, with crisp linen and decent cutlery. 'Even before we started to study the menu, complimentary Papadoms and chutneys were discreetly served ... why doesn't every Indian restaurant do that?' asks GB. This is clearly a caring restaurant. They give a nuts-warning where relevant and are great with kids. Several regulars have remarked that the prices, though a little high, have hardly varied in several years. Starters include Chicken Tikka £4.30, Samosa and Onion Bhajia both £3.75. Gulshan Special, £5.75 contains king prawn, Chicken Tikka, Lamb Tikka, tomatoes, coconut and mushrooms in a cream and wine sauce, topped with egg soufflé and cheese. Chicken Zeera, £4.95 is chicken chunks cooked with cummin. 'Definitely a TOP 100. Took the

Guide's advice and had a Mustard Balti Chicken, £4.95 cooked with mustard and wine, and Green Balti Masala, £4.95 containing puréed coriander, tamarind, green chilli and green herbs. Great when places experiment, thoroughly satisfied and went to the good pub opposite, then braved Liverpool's occasional public transport.' RDL. 'Recommended. Delighted to go.' RC. The imaginative use of wine is rare in Indian restaurants and, done well as it is here by owner-chef M. Rahman, it gives traditional dishes an unexpected and subtle lift. Price check: Papadam 60p, CTM £6.95, Pullao Rice £1.95, Peshwari Nan £1.95. House wine £8.95. Takeaway: 30% discount. Hours: 5-11pm. Stocks Cobra.

TAJ MAHAL

57 South Road, Waterloo, Liverpool, L1   ✆ 0151 928 7050

'Superb restaurant – noted as being one of the best in north Liverpool. Pleasant decor and surroundings though the background music can be rather intrusive at times. Service rather slow but the food makes up for it.' PS. 'Papadoms were very light and crispy. Vegetarian Thali very good.' GF. Open 12-2.30pm/5.30pm-12am (2am on Fri. & Sat.), Sun. 2pm-1am Stocks Cobra.

Newton-le-Willows

TASTE OF INDIA   ©

56 Market Street, Newton-le-Willows   ✆ 01925 228458

Akhlaqul Ambia's 80-seat Taste's house specials include: Balti Exotica – meat, chicken, lamb and king prawn, medium spiced £6.50. Balti Ruhabja – tikka cooked in mincemeat, highly spiced £6.25. Balti Garlic Chicken – tikka with fresh garlic and green peppers £5.95. Takeaway: 15% discount. Sunday buffet £7.95 between 3pm and 10pm. Price check: Papadam 35p, CTM £5.95, Pullao Rice £1.50. House wine £8.95, mineral water £3.50. Hours: 5pm-12am. Branch: Haydock Tandoori, Kenton Lane, Haydock. Stocks Cobra

©	Curry Club discount (see page 6)		Unlicensed
√	Vegetarian		
BYO	Bring your own alcohol		Delivery/takeaway

Southport

LAL QILA NEW ENTRANT

---

35 Bath Road, Southport   ✆ 01704 544991

At B. Miah's recently refurbished 60-seater the three courses plus coffee for two banquets are value, from £17.95 to £25.90. Price check:
Papadam 40p, CTM £6.75, Pullao Rice £1.40. Set lunch under £5.
Delivery: £10 minimum, town area only, Fri., Sat. & Sun. Hours: 12-
2pm (2.30pm on Sun.) and 5.30-11.45pm. Stocks Cobra.

Wirral

*The Wirral is neither a town nor a county and, until 1965, was part of Cheshire.
Since then the northern part – a small, digit-like, curry-rich peninsula between the
rivers Mersey and Dee – has been part of Merseyside. Ellesmere Port (q.v.) remains
in south Wirral but is in Cheshire. Here are the Merseyside Wirral towns in alphabetical order:*

Moreton

SURMA TANDOORI NEW ENTRANT   ©

271-273 Hoylake Road, Moreton, Wirral   ✆ 0151 677 1331

Jamshed Ullah's first-floor restaurant seats 52 diners. 'Good food,
tasteful decor and friendly service. Side dish of Matter Paneer and the
Chappati were excellent.' RK. Takeaway 20% discount. Price check:
Papadam 45p, CTM £5.95, Pullao Rice £1.50. House wine £6.25.
Hours: 5.30pm-12am (12.30am on Sat.).

New Brighton

MAGIC SPICES

---

225 Seabank Road, New Brighton, Wirral   ✆ 0151 691 1919

'Nothing too much trouble. Meat Samosa light and flavourful.
Chicken Jalfrezi probably the best I've ever tasted' RK. 'Asked the waiter to choose the starters, we couldn't make up our mind and were going
to share anyway. Eight of us consumed a mountain of fresh Papadams
and chutneys while we waited. Impressive Onion Bhaji – good and

spicy, Prawn Puri – excellent, Shish Kebab and Samosa – good, but the star was Stuffed Pepper – magnificent. Chicken Tikka Rogan Josh – superb, Chicken Tikka Bhuna a little too hot. Portions were a bit on the small side.' DB. 'Recommended.' RC. Stocks Cobra.

Upton

SHAH JALAL TAKEAWAY   NEW ENTRANT   ▦

9 Arrowe Park Road, Upton, Wirral   ✆ 0151 606 1134

'We've especially enjoyed their specialties – Chicken Jhal is hot but very tasty with a citrus tang, Nadroo Kiyakni equally flavoursome but milder.' RC. Hours: 12-2pm/5-11.30pm. Fri. & Sat. 5-11.30pm.

UPTON HALAL BALTI HOUSE   BYO ©

167 Ford Road, Upton Village, Wirral   ✆ 0151 604 0166

Shofiul Miah's venture opened in 1996 and is not licensed, so BYO is a big attraction. Price check: Papadam 35p, CTM £6.80, Pullao Rice £1.60. Minimum charge £5. Set meal £9.50. Open every day except Tues., 5-11.30pm. Branch: Manzil, 73 Grange Road East, Birkenhead.

Wallasey

SURUCHI TAKEAWAY

105 Wallasey Road, Wallasey, Wirral   ✆ 0151 639 9404

We notice that the menu offers small and large portions and prices for all main dishes. What a great idea! DB may have the local attendance record here. Can anyone beat it (and prove it)? He has come here for a takeaway every Thursday evening, most Fridays and occasionally Saturdays since it opened. That's around 100 times a year, he tells us! And his girlfriend likes it too (just as well!) And he still visits other restaurants, and finds time to send us plentiful reports on them. We need more like you, Dave. 'Chicken Biryani (£3.70 small, £4.75 large) is excellent – ask for the omelette. Chicken Dhansak Madras-strength (£2.60 small, £3.60 large) is absolutely superb. CTM is thick and creamy, and when done to Madras-strength is exquisite. It's frequented by the cricket club. Owner Raj bends over backwards to ensure your meal is exactly what you require. Can't recommend highly enough.' DB.

Razu Miah's interesting starters include: Ranga Kebab, hot minced lamb and potato, seasoned with onion, herbs and spices £2.20. All main curry dishes can be ordered in small or large portions, good idea for those with a smaller appetite. Specials include: Khasia Lamb, fairly hot dish of sliced lamb tikka, simmered gently with garlic, herbs and spices £3.50 small, £4.50 large. Jhinga Saag, combination of Bengal prawns, spinach and garlic £5.20 small, £6.20 large. 'Samosas far too doughy, Nan too.' RC. Price check: Papadam 35p, CTM £3.50 small, £4.50 large, Pullao Rice £1.30, Peshwari Nan £1.50. Hours: 4pm-12am, (12.30am on Sat.). Closed Mon. except for bank holidays.

MIDDLESEX
Greater London

Area: All part of GL (west of London)
Population: 1,000,000
Number of restaurants in county: 284
Number of restaurants in Guide: 44

The county of Middlesex is very ancient. It once contained most of London, though this distinction became diminished when central London became autonomous during Victorian times. What was left of the county (located west and north of London) was completely 'abolished' when Greater London was formed in 1965, a move unpopular with Middlesex residents. Confusion exists because the Post Office still use Middlesex as a postal county. Postcodes add to the confusion. Enfield, for example, is EN1, 2, 3 in postal Middlesex but is in (Hertfordshire) GL county. Potters Bar EN6 is the same. Barnet is in postal Hertfordshire with EN4 and 5 codes. It used to be in geographical Middlesex but is now a GL borough! There is talk of reviving the county of Middlesex. It would certainly help beleaguered guide editors!

©	Curry Club discount (see page 6)	☕	Unlicensed
√	Vegetarian		
BYO	Bring your own alcohol	⊞	Delivery/takeaway

Bedfont

INDIAN PALACE NEW ENTRANT   ©

414 Staines Road, Bedfont   **℡ 0181 751 5822**

Managed by Mr Miah. Head Chef Somir Ahmed. A Bangladeshi formula curry house, seating 54 diners and as you would guess, CTM is
the most popular ordered dish. Specials include: Lamb Chilli Masala
£6.95. Butter Chicken £6.95. Sunday lunch buffet £5.95. Set dinner
£19.50. Minimum charge: £8.95. Price check: Papadam 50p, CTM £6.55,
Pullao Rice £1.65, Peshwari Nan £1.95. Lager £2.60 pint, house wine
£5.95, mineral water £2.10. Delivery: £20 minimum, 3-mile radius.
Hours: 12-2.30pm/6-11.30pm.

Edgware

SHREE GANESHA VEGETARIAN   √

4 The Promenade, Edgwarebury Lane,
Edgware   **℡ 0181 958 2778**

This superb vegetarian restaurant was opened in 1990 by Pamchandra
Tiwari, with his wife Hemantika supervising the kitchen staff, making
sure only the best was served from it. Bombay street food, such as Bhel
Poori with tamarind chutney, features on the menu along with south
Indian delights, Masala Dosa (wafer-thin pancake wrapped around
potato curry made from lightly spiced curry leaves, sautéed onions,
mustard seeds and turmeric) served with home-made coconut chutney,
delicious. Unusual and tasty curries such as pumpkin are also a delight.
Hours: 6-10.30pm. Open for Sunday lunch.

Enfield

ALBANY TANDOORI NEW ENTRANT

569 Hertford Road, Enfield   **℡ 0181 805 3027**

M.A. Awal and Masood Qureshi's 36-seater is decorated in dark pink,
with light green walls, with Mugul pictures, plants and brass fittings.
'Food excellent, service brilliant and staff are friendly, helpful and
cheerful and always polite. On my mother's 65th birthday a card and
cake were brought, a complete surprise!' AJF&JKH. Specials include:

Sizzling Nawabi – diced chicken barbecued on charcoal with green peppers and ginger £9.95. Sunday buffet 12.30pm to 4.30pm. Minimum charge: £7.50. Cover charge £1. Takeaway: over £10 – 15% discount. Price check: Papadam 50p, CTM £6.50, Pullao Rice £1.50, Peshwari Nan £1.95. House wine £6.95, mineral water £2.50. Delivery: £8 minimum, 3-mile radius. Hours: 5.30pm-12am. Sun. 12.30pm-12am. Stocks Cobra.

Greenford

SUNDARBAN NEW ENTRANT

3 Odeon Parade, Sudbury Heights Avenue, Greenford   ℂ 0181 900 0988

Opened in 1984 by Mr Abdul. Bangladeshi curries on the menu. Hours: 12pm-2.30pm/6-11.30pm. Branch: Pinner Tandoori, Pinner. Stocks Cobra.

Harrow

JHUPDI NEW ENTRANT   √

235 Station Road, Harrow   ℂ 0181 427 1335

Licensed, vegetarian restaurant. 'Friendly, with no frills. Plenty of assistance with menu, varied choice, 18 starters, Kachoris, Mogo Chips and Bombay Tiffin. Masala Dosa, huge portion, best I've tasted.' DD. Stocks Cobra.

Hayes

THAMOULINEE

128a Uxbridge Road, Hayes   ℂ 0181 561 3723

Sri Lankan restaurant owned and run by husband and wife Anthony and Jasmine Hyacinth's (cook). We parked at the bus stop, everyone else does! at around 8pm. The brickwork is down-at-heel, the awning torn, the plate window, dirty. The place was empty, but we were warmly welcomed by Mr H. Through a hatch, I saw Mrs H., waiting for her first order. It has been inexpertly painted pale pink, the bar decorated with coloured Xmas tree lights. The tables are covered with Xmas paper (it was July), the chair next to me was unstable, the carpet filthy. Mr H. handed us two curry stained menus. After choosing a bottle of red Merlot £5.95, we nibbled the lightest Papadam we've ever tasted, wiith mango chutney, mint raita and a red-tinged coconut chutney. Starters: Mixed Special, Vadai, Mutton Roll, Crab Claw and Prawn Kebab £2.50, with a green-tinged coconut chutney and tomato sambol all fresh, and enjoyed. Main courses were sweetly served by a young Sri Lankan, who could have flown in yesterday, his English not fluent. With every delivery, he piped up, 'cheers'. Kothu Rotti, chopped rotti prepared with mutton, egg, onions and spices £4.10, huge portion, dry, spicy and a lovely change to wet curries. Pat devoured a Thamoulinee Special Crab Curry, two crab shells, legs and claws, packed with meat, smothered in rich hot gravy, at just £3.90. Special Fried Rice £2.80, was huge with more coconut, tomato sambols and Achcharu (mixed pickle). I decided to check out the services. Under no circumstances was the door going to shut, the wood had warped too badly. It was reasonably clean with soap, pink toilet roll, paper towels and even a bottle of bleach; unfortunately, the toilet resolutely refused to flush. Of the three other tables occupied all night, one was by three Sun readers (regulars, it seemed) who chose to ignore the Sri Lankan dishes and ordered Chicken and Mushroom Curry, 'very light, medium, medium know-wot-I-mean'. How sad! Normally a restaurant in this state, would not get in the guide, but there's no doubt Mrs H can cook, and there are precious few Sri Lankan eateries. Price check: Papadam 35p, Pullao Rice £1.25. Takeaway: 10% off. Hours: 12-2.30pm/6pm-12am. Tues. closed. Cash and cheques only. Stocks Cobra.

Heathrow Airport

NOON TASTE OF INDIA

Mezzanine, Terminal 1, Departures Area, Heathrow Airport

'No phone – no booking at airports, just turn up. It's a 90-seater, on the mezzanine.' GK. Noon owns a vast Greenford state-of-the-art factory which churns out tens of thousands of curry ready-meals every week for the likes of Sainsbury's and Waitrose, as well as under the Noon name. All day you can have beverages, snacks and meals, Indian and western. We finally got to try it with hopeful expectations, particularly following its nomination by Egon himself as the best UK airport caterer. We ordered papadams which came with three chutneys

(Royal's range – another Mr Noon brand). We followed with Masala Dosa with Sambar £3.45. It lacked south Indian tastes and textures. The dosa was greasy, as though it has been reheated, the potato was hard, and though curry leaves were in evidence, the sambar a near miss of tastes. Raan Sandwich £4.95, thin slices of roast lamb, spread with curry paste sit on two small nans (no tandoori oven cooked these breads) also spread with paste (coriander?). No traditional spiced-to-die-for, fall-off-the-bone Raan this! The Goan Prawn, £7.50, came in a thick, almost gluey sauce which tasted of little more than creamed coconut and tomato, with, doubtless starch and factory 'stabilisers', accompanied by turmeric-dyed, over-salted, not-basmati, slightly-starchy rice. Cobra lager 330ml £2.25, and £3.50 for a very good glass of Shiraz were expensive, but it is Heathrow! Naively we expected a great Indian meal, after all Mr Noon is Indian. The food was none other than Noon ready-meals. We detest such products, and unless you happen to like supermarket curries, be warned! Pity – with so much expertise available in nearby Southall, this could be showcase Indian food. The whole bill was £23.90 and I did leave a tip. As for the Ronay nomination, it says more about the state of the other airport caterers, and possibly the limit of Egon's currinary knowledge, than the excellence of Noon's, which is only here (in the Guide) because it's there (at the airport). If one must eat there, I suppose Noon's is it. Hours: 7am-11pm. Serves Cobra.

Hounslow

ASHNA   √

368 Staines Road, Hounslow   ℂ **0181 577 5988**

A pure vegetarian restaurant. Try the specials, they are truly pleasurable. Masala Dosa and Bhel Poori are also on the menu.

HOUNSLOW BRASSERIE   ©

47-49 Spring Grove Road, Hounslow   ℂ **0181 570 5535**

Open-plan restaurant owned and managed by Naveed Sheikh. Chef Ali cooks Pakistani curries and side dishes. Specials: Zeera Chicken, cooked with ground cummin, fairly dry £6.25. Karahi Lobia, black-eye beans, herbs, spices, onions, capsicum and tomatoes £4.25. 'Meat Samosas, £1.50 are absolutely outstanding, the holy grail of samosas!

TE. Takeaway: 5% off. Price check: Papadam 60p, CTM £6.25, Pullao Rice £1.85, Peshwari Nan £2.25. Hours: 12-3pm/6pm-12am. Fri. closed lunch (off to the Mosque). Stocks Cobra.

KARAHI MASTER LAHORE TANDOORI ©

795 London Road, Hounslow   © 0181 572 2205

Pakistani (Halal) 40-seater opposite Hounslow Bus Garage. Taken over this year by Mohammad Akmal. Specials include: Roast Lamb Leg £17.50, or, if celebrating with friends, Stuffed Whole Lamb £100 sounds great. Lunch-time specials for £5.95, please ask. BYO is allowed, 1 bottle per person. Price check: Papadam 10p, CTM £4.50, Pullao Rice £1.50, Peshwari Nan £1.25. A free drink to Curry Club members from Mr Akmal – cheers! Delivery: £15 minimum (6 free Papadams), 4-mile radius. Hours: 12pm-12am. Stocks Cobra.

Northolt

EMPRESS OF INDIA

40-42 Church Road, Northolt   © 0181 845 4361

Est. 1974, Ali, Zaman and E.H. Khan's a/c 50-seater serves popular curries. Butter Chicken Masala and Murghi Masala are specials. Sunday lunch buffet – 12-6pm £5.95. Price check: Papadam 45p, CTM £5.45, Pullao Rice £1.65, Delivery: £12.50 minimum, 3-mile radius. Hours: 12-2.30pm/6pm-12am. Stocks Cobra.

Northwood

SHANTI NAME CHANGE

48 High Street, Northwood   © 01923 827856

Formerly the Viceroy, Mofiz Miah's restaurant seats 60 and serves Bangladeshi-Pakistani curries. Specials include: Elecha (cardamon) Kofta Jhoal. Bhuna Gost (on the bone). Lamb Shahjanee – lamb tikka cooked with spicy kebab mince and sautéed onions served with rice or nan £9.95. Sunday lunch £7.25. Minimum charge £5. Price check: Papadam 60p, CTM £5.95, Pullao Rice £1.80, Peshwari Nan £1.90. Hours: 12-2.30pm (Sunday Buffet to 3pm) and 6-11.30pm. Stocks Cobra.

Pinner

PINNER TANDOORI

141 Marsh Road, Pinner   © 0181 866 5474

Abdul Rafique's restaurant seats 50. Good formula curries on the
menu. Price check: Papadam 35p, CTM £5.95, Pullao Rice £1.60,
Peshwari Nan £1.75. Hours: 12-2.30pm/6-11.30pm. Stocks Cobra.

MALA NAME CHANGE

426b Rayners Lane, Pinner   © 0181 866 7363

Agreeable food and prices at Lipu Miah's former Village. Hours: 6pm-
12am (12.30am at weekends). Stocks Cobra

Ruislip

RICE N SPICE TAKEAWAY NEW ENTRANT   ⊞ ©

73 Station Approach, South Ruislip   0181 841 5498

Kaizer Ahmed Chowdhury has agreed a drink for CC members at his
(unlicensed) takeaway. Chef Cherag Ali's specials include: Chicken
Tikka Mushroom Korai £4.30 and Peshwari Chicken or Lamb £4.30.
Price check: Papadam 35p, CTM £4.30, Pullao Rice £1.50. Delivery: £12
minimum, 3-mile radius. Hours: 12-2pm/5-11.30pm.

RUISLIP TANDOORI   ©

115 High Street, Ruislip   © 01895 632859

A/c 52-seat Nepalese restaurant, recently refurbished in black and
white, flowering trees, Nepalese handicraft, pictures and a beautiful
golden Buddha, which is, we're told, 'the main attraction apart from
the Nepalese food'. Owner K.B. Raichhetri enjoys explaining about his
Nepalese house specials on the menu. Takeaway: 10% off. Minimum
charge: £8. Sunday buffet £6.95. Price check: Papadam 55p free chutney,
CTM £5.90, Pullao Rice £1.70. Delivery: £15 minimum, 2-mile radius.
Hours: 12-2.30pm/6pm-12am. Stocks Cobra.

Southall

From a single acorn (see Maharaja), there is an ever-growing number of sweet/snack centres, cafés and restaurants to be found, mostly on the the Broadway, the main artery through Southall. The current vogue is expansion westwards. Others are on South Road and the Green. These places cater primarily for their indigenous Asian population, a generally peaceful mix of Indian and Pakistani Sikh and Punjabi carnivores, enhanced by East African Asians. If you are none of these, do not feel inhibited from entering. Everyone is treated equally and all are welcome. However, if you are looking for lush decor, candlelight, carnations for the lady, etc., etc., you will not find them in most Southall venues. You'll find 'halal' not 'haute cuisine', nor curryhouse, nor alcohol in most. But you will find good, authentic cuisine in straightforward, functional eating houses, at realistic prices. The food is served fast, whether in self-service cafés or in sit-down restaurants. Below we examine our (and our correspondents') favourite eating holes.

BABU TANDOORI

156 The Broadway, Southall	© 0181 574 1049

Reasonable prices with friendly staff.

BRILLIANT TOP 100   ©

72-74 Western Road, Southall	© 0181 574 1928

Owned by Kewel and Davinder (Gulu) Anand since 1975, who settled in the UK, having been forced to flee from troubled Kenya. An expansion plan has added the next-door venue onto the main room and increased the seating to 200. There is a 1st floor party room, with its own bar and music equipment (for discos etc) which seats 80. And still the place is full to bursting, being especially popular with Asian families. The tables are large, and groups of 10 to 20 are the norm. Half of these will be kids, and Asian kids are always well-behaved at the restaurant, loving the experience as much as their parents. The restaurant has many large tables, laid out banquet style, white linen cloths and burgundy paper napkins. Small matching chandeliers and wall light fittings, padded velvet chairs. On busy nights you may find yourself sitting next to an unknown dinner companion, but conversation soon flows, as does the Punjabi cuisine, which is more spicy but not necessarily hot. 'Carrot and mint home-made pickles are on the table, Masala (only) Papadams, which can be either fried or roasted, will be served while you peruse the not overly large menu. Menu specials

include: Karahi Chicken £6, Palak (spinach) Lamb £6 and Masala Fish
£6. These are served in decorative copper beaten pots with serving
spoons to match, balanced on individual heaters. 'Most popular dishes
ordered and I always have these as a starter, are fabulous, and are Butter
Chicken and Jeera Chicken £12 whole bird or £6 half.' Parking and even
driving in Southall is chaotic, but you will find the odd spot on side
streets. Price check: Papadam 50p, CTM £5.50, Pullao Rice £2. House
wine £7.50, mineral water £2. Takeaway 10% off. Service: 10%. Hours: 12-
3pm (Tues.-Fri.)/6-11.30pm (12am on Fri. & Sat.). Mon. closed. Stocks
Cobra.

KARAHI TANDOORI KABAB CENTRE

161 The Broadway, Southall   © 0181 574 3571

A.F. Choudhury's café-style restaurant, with formica tables, seating 66.
Walking past you are immediately attracted to the display cabinets
containing all sorts of tempting snacks such as Pakora, Bhel Poori, Gol
Goppas, Jeera Pani (cumin water), Tikki, Samosa, Indian sweets, etc.
Inside is clean and waiter-served. Fabulous Tandooris, Kebabs and
breads, cooked by the chefs on show. Punjabi and curries are also
cooked in front of you in karahis, and are quite delicious. Great prices.
Gets very busy since it is immensely popular with the young trendy
Asians at weekends. Hours: 9am-12am.

LAHORE KARAHI AND TANDOORI   BYO

162-164 The Broadway, Southall   © 0181 813 8669

A huge plate-glass window with sliding doors dominates the front of
Asif Rahman's 100-seater . The open stainless steel kitchen runs down
one side, the tandoor oven being in view from the street. Sit at simple
tables at the front, or at the back in more 'glamorous' ones with high-
backed padded seats. Watch the chefs prepare Pakistani curries and
accompaniments. Kebabs are most popular. Specials: Niharhi – spicy
leg piece with spicy gravy £5.20, Paya – lamb trotters with thick gravy
£5.20, Haleem – crushed lentils and lamb £5.20. There is also another
counter with cold savoury items, Paan and sweets. 'My favourites
include: Dhai Vada, Alu Tikki and Chana Masala £1.80, Bhel Puri
£1.90, Papri Chat £1.70 – Yum Yum! Waiters have a leisurely approach
to service but are happy about it.' DBAC. BYO. Price check: Papadam:
complimentary. Delivery is free locally. Hours: 12pm-12am.

MADHU'S BRILLIANT TOP 100 ©

39 South Road, Southall   © 0181 574 1897

Opened in 1980 by J.K., K.K., Sanjay and Sanjeev Anand, nephews of
the great Mr Anand of the Brilliant (*see* entry). The restaurant seats 104
on two floors, the upper floor, toilets and second bar being reached by
a large spiral staircase at the front of the restaurant. You will often find
Sanjay in the restaurant, welcoming diners as old friends – you will
know which one he is, because of his very distinctive laugh. Our Guide
was the first to recognize this restaurant, back in 1984, when the clientele was mostly Asian. Today, and dozens of awards later, there are as
many non-Asians as Asians enjoying the food and ambience here. The
latter is rather basic, though the company is always animated, the Asians
sitting on large tables in family groups, kids and all, the Brits in twos
and fours and more reticent, but enjoying it nonetheless. Cooking is led
by brother Sanjeev (affectionately called Mint). The food is typical
Punjabi and far removed from the Bangladeshi curry house formula.
'Never been so disappointed in an Indian meal! Booked table for 7pm
on Saturday evening. Nothing was as I expected, the place was empty
so the ambience was poor. [Asians, like Spanish, emerge and dine late.
I bet it was full by 10pm. -Ed] You can only get spicy Papadam, with
thousands of little bubbles all over them, [Grilled -Ed] which I don't
like 'cos they stick in my teeth! I asked for help with the menu and got
a very condescending lecture from the waiter. I'm obviously out of line
with other reviewers.' AF. Yes, you must be. 'I ate here and can confirm
its status in the Guide. Food a little pricy, but probably reflects London effect and reputation. Wonderful atmosphere as it was crowded
with the local Asian community. Only 30 minutes from Heathrow, so
good place to eat between flights. Parking can be difficult.' DR PAW.
The Anand signature dishes, Butter Methis and Jeera Chicken, all £6.60
for half a chicken on the bone, are an absolute must when dining here.
House specials: Mniahma Chommah – spring lamb ribs seasoned and
marinated and cooked in tandoor. Machuzi Kuku – spring roaster –
on the bone, in a thin curry, medium-spiced, a Kenyan speciality –
three-person portion £16. Boozi Bafu – spring lamb chops from
Kenyan Boozi, cooked authentically in a spicy medium sauce, highly
recommended – three person portion £18. Price check: Papadam 50p,
CTM £6.50, Pullao Rice £2, Peshwari Nan £2. House wine £8, mineral water £3. Hours: 12.30-3pm (Sat. and Sun. closed) and 6-11.30pm.
Closed Tues. Stocks Cobra.

MAHARAJA   ©

171-173 The Broadway, Southall   © 0181 574 4564

Southall's very first Indian restaurant opened in 1955. Owned by A.A.
Sandhu, since 1972. Managed by H.S. Sandhu. 'I like this restaurant,
nicely decorated, seats 90 and is an oasis for those who like a pint of
beer or a glass of wine with their meal, as I do. It is surrounded by fabulous Pakistani eateries, which are an alcohol desert. Northern Indian
food is on the menu, all your regular favourites are there and cooked
well.' DD. 'What an excellent choice, Mixed Grill, (about £9), easily
enough for two. Jalfrezi, in my top ten. Chana Masala, possibly a little
heavy on the ginger. Two young waiters, very pleasant.' sw. 'Even my
carnivorous, fussy sister R actually likes it. In two phrases, I'd describe
the Maharaja as the formula done better, and an ideal starting place for
those unsure about the delights of Southall. Our meal for three with
drinks cost £42.' DBAC. Takeaway: 10% discount. Price check: CTM
£6.95, Pullao Rice £2.10, Peshwari Nan £2.25. House wine £7.95, mineral water £2.80. Hours: 12-3pm/6-11.30pm. Stocks Cobra.

OMI'S TOP 100

1 Beaconsfield Road, Southall   © 0181 571 4831

Owner-chef Mykesh Kharbanda cooks north Indian and Kenyan curries at Omi's off South Road on a side street, and with just 42 seats,
it gets harder to find a space, especially in the evenings. The shop front
stands slightly back from the pavement, making room for parking for
4 vehicles. A short menu above the counter describes what is on offer,
along with the Specials of the Day. The most popular dishes are
Ginger Chicken and Palak Chana. Since we were taken here years ago
by Indian journalist KN Malik ('I want to show you Indian food at its
best'), we can safely say this is the Indians' Indian restaurant. We love
his food and adore Mykesh's idiosyncrasies. The place doubles for van-
hire. So one phone call can order you lovely, soft, delicious Garlic Nan
and noisy diesel-fumey Transit Van! It has the usual plastic tables and
chairs, making for a clean and tidy restaurant, but it's the freshly-
cooked food you go for. Price check: Papadam 50p, CTM £4, Pullao
Rice £1.75, Peshwari Nan £1.20. Set lunch £3.75. House wine £1.50
glass. Delivery: small charge. Hours: 10.30am-9pm, Fri. & Sat. 11am-
9.30pm. Closed Sun. Remains in our TOP 100. Stocks Cobra.

PUNJABI KARAHI   ₽ ©

175 The Broadway, Southall   0181 574 1112

Chef Khurrum Choudhry's restaurant seats 150 and hewarns that parking after 6.30pm is 'thin on the ground'. Pakistani and Balti dishes are
his speciality, including Mixed Grill £10, Kebabs 60p, Chicken legs
£2.60 and Tandoori Batera (quail), £2.90 for starters and Methi
Chicken £5.40, Paya – lamb trotters in a spicy sauce £5. Price check:
Papadam 15p, CTM £5.40, Pullao Rice £1.80, Peshwari Nan £1.50.
Hours: 11.30am-11.30pm (12am on Sat.).

SAGOO AND THAKHAR ASIAN
TANDOORI CENTRES TOP 100   BYO

The Roxy, 114 The Green, Southall   © 0181 574 2579
157 The Broadway, Southall   © 0181 574 3476

Owners Mr Sagoo and Mr Thakhar's long-standing restaurants serve
the local community morning, noon and night. Strategically located at
either end of Southall. The Roxy is the larger, but they both serve identical food (almost). When you enter, there may be a queue, even outside
the door, but it won't take long before it's your turn. Long glass coun-
ters display tempting Indian sweets and savoury snacks (Bhajias, Kebabs,
Samosas, Aloo Tikki, Dahi Vasa, etc.), curries (Murgh Masala, on the
bone, Bombay Potato, Sag Paneer, Sag Gosht and more, all cold but will
be reheated in the microwave on request), Channa Dal, Rice (Plain,
Pullao and Biryani) and breads. 'Pick up a tray and tell the chap behind
the counter what you want and whether you are eating in or taking out.
Portions are generous and I have to restrain myself from over-ordering.
When you have paid (cash or cheques only), take your tray to the other
room and seat yourself.' DBAC. 'The absolute curry experience, should be
compulsory for all members to visit! Sample the vast range of dishes on
offer, all authentic and served up in a no-nonsense style. We ate vast
quantities of food, including Pakoras, Dall (black bean), Chicken and
Meat Curries, Rotis and rice. Service with a smile, staff friendly. Highly
recommended, must be very high in the TOP 100.' DB. They also serve
a wonderful chutney, sticks of carrot, slices of onion, embalmed in a
tamarind and yoghurt sauce, delicious, I can't get enough of it. You can
BYO as far as we know, which all makes for a great meal out. Fresh fruit
juice and Lassi are available. The Roxy is licensed for lager. Hours:
10am-10.30pm (11pm on Fri., Sat. and Sun.). It is high in our TOP 100.

SHAHANSHAH VEGETARIAN   🍴 √ ©

60 North Road, Southall   © 0181 574 1493

Gill Baljinder (manager) and Johl Sarbjit, have since 1984 specialized
in cooking from north and south India at their vegetarian restaurant,
which seats 30 diners. Samosas and other snacks are the most popular
items ordered. Indian sweets are made on the premises, so you can be
sure they are fresh. Set dinner £5. Sunday lunch £4. Price check:
Papadam 30p, Pullao Rice £1.50. No credit cards. Hours: 10am-8pm.
Branch: Shahanshah Vegetarian, 17 South Road, Southall.

TANDOORI EXPRESS ON JALEBI JUNCTION   ©

93 The Broadway, Southall   © 0181 571 6782

Owner Abdul Chaudhury, manager Mr Shauket, and head chef
Rassaq's bright and colourful venue appeals to the local young and
trendy population. It is often full of chattering, bright young Asians
babbling on in animated Southall cockney accents. A richly painted
and decorated rickshaw can be seen outside on the wide pavement
which enhances the environment. Also a cook makes Jalebis, those
crispy, deep-fried squiggles, immersed in syrup, right there on the
pavement. So if you've not seen it done, here's the only place in Britain
we know of that does it on view. Great Pakistani curries and fresh
breads are a big pull, along with snacks such as Samosas, Pakoras, etc.
There is also a vast sweet counter to pile on the pounds (weight that
is, not the bill). Starters include: Club Sandwich, finest chicken and
lamb BBQ fillings £3. Shami Kebab, mince meat and lentil burger 50p.
Dehi Bhalla, lentil flour doughnuts soaked in yoghurt £1.50. House
specials: Masaladaar Raan, whole leg of lamb roasted in the tandoor
with all the natural juices and flavours sealed within, a Moghul dish
from Lakhshmi Chauk, Lahore, £15. Alcohol is strictly prohibited.
Price check: Papadam 50p, CTM £4.50, Pullao Rice £2, Peshwari Nan
£80p. Hours: 9am-11pm.

TANDOORI KABAB CENTRE   ©

163 The Broadway, Southall   © 0181 571 5738

Known locally as TKC. Established in 1965 by A.M. Choudhry. Manager Dalawar, head chef Farooq. The menu quotes 'please specify your
taste of chillies when ordering.' Appetisers include: Reshmi Spring

Lamb Boti, tender succulent pieces of lamb marinated in double cream roasted in the tandoor £3.50. Paneer Tikka, chunks of vegetarian cheese marinated with spices and baked in tandoor £3. Main courses: Nehari, shank of lamb served in a spicy sauce £4. Zeera Chicken, made with butter and cummin seeds £5. Sarson Ka Saag, mustard and spinach leaf £3.50. House Specialities: Chargha, fully roasted and tenderly spiced, free-range chicken, a recipe from the inner Punjab £6.50. Chappal Kebab, beaten mince steaks cooked and served on a sizzler, a speciality from the North-West Frontier Province £4. Try the Kulfi Faluda, a Pakistani version of the Knickerbocker Glory £1.80. Pinad Da Buffet £6.99. All food is prepared with Halal meat. Alcohol is strictly prohibited. Price check: Papadam complimentary, CTM £4.50, Pullao Rice £2, Peshwari Nan 60p. Hours: 10am-11pm. Also, on the premises is the first (they claim) Halal Chinese restaurant, called Shan Wah. Reports needed on that one please. Branch: Tandoori Express on Jalebi Junction, 93, The Broadway, Southall.

Stanmore

PASSAGE TO INDIA   ©

905 Honeypot Lane, Stanmore   © 0181 952 9151

Owned by S. Miah and managed by S. Rahman. Price check: Papadam 45p, CTM £5.35, Pullao Rice £1.50. Set menu £4.95. Hours: 12-2.30pm/5.30pm-12am. Reports please. Stocks Cobra.

Sudbury

GANGES   ©

769 Harrow Road, Sudbury   © 0181 904 0011

Fully air-conditioned and licensed restaurant seating 45. Opened by Mr Haque in 1985 with Naz running front of house. A Bangladeshi-style curry house with all the usual curries and accompaniments, from Korma to Madras. Nepalese dishes also feature. Price check: Papadam 40p, CTM £5.95, Pullao Rice £1.60. Set menu £5.95. Delivery on orders over £12. Hours: 12-2.30pm/6pm-12am. Stocks Cobra.

Teddington

BENGAL BRASSERIE   ▦ ©

162 Stanley Road, Teddington   © 0181 977 7332

Managed by Ali Kausar, head chef Sufian Khan. Air conditioned, seats
44, decorated with Indian and Bangladeshi art on the walls and fresh
carnations on the tables. House specials include: Chicken or Lamb
Balaka, marinated, cooked with potato, egg, green chilli, red wine,
spicy hot £6.95. Jeera Chicken, marinated, cooked in cummin £6.50.
Collected takeaway: 10% discount. Minimum charge £8.50. Price check:
Papadam 60p, CTM £6.50, Pullao Rice £1.95. Delivery: £20 minimum,
2-mile radius. Hours: 12pm-2.30am/6pm-12am. Stocks Cobra.

Twickenham

SHEESH MAHAL   NEW ENTRANT

21 London Road, Twickenham   © 0181 892 3303

White and blue frontage this 66-seater (upstairs too) has been owned
and managed by A. Monaf, since '82. It describes itself as, 'nice and
simple, for us and the customers'. Yes, you've guessed it, Chicken Tikka
Masala is the most ordered dish. Takeaway 10% discount. Sunday lunch
buffet £6.95. Price check: Papadam 50p, CTM £6.25, Pullao Rice £1.95.
Delivery: £10 minimum, 3-mile radius. Hours: 12-2.30pm/ 5.30pm-
12am. Branch: Monaf's, 119 Station Road, Hampton.

Wembley

*Rapidly gaining ground as the second Southall. Unlike Southall, its large
Gujarati/East African population gives Wembley food a different (predominantly vegetarian) taste from Southall. As with Southall, there are many good sweet/snack
shops/cafés and restaurants crammed with Indian goodies. Here are your favourites:*

CHETNA'S BHEL PURI   TOP 100   √

420 High Road, Wembley   © 0181 903 5989

A vegetarian restaurant with vegan dishes. 'You often have to queue
here. We waited on the pavement until they called out our number, but

it is well worth it. They do deluxe Masal Dosas, and a great Vegetarian Thali main course. Their Bhel Puri is gorgeous, with its crispy, crunchy textures, and its tart, hot and savoury tastes, and there is a variant called Alloo Papdi Chaat'. JM. They serve pizzas alongside curries from south India,' reflecting the craze, not only amongst Wembley Asians, but sweeping Delhi and Bombay! Open 12-3pm/6-10.30pm.

CURRY CRAZE TOP 100   ©

8-9 The Triangle, Wembley Hill Road,
Wembley   ✆ 0181 902 9720

Owned by Mr and Mrs S..K. Malhorta, she is also the head chef, specializing in East African/Punjabi food. *See* the Brilliant (Southall) for more information. Opened in 1980 and proving to be a reliable restaurant. 'Excellent, each year there is a conference for diving instructors in London; for the past two years it has been in Wembley and both times our party has gone to the Curry Craze – we have not been disappointed yet. After eating our fill of Papadoms, we started the proceedings with Jeera Chicken. Good value in terms of standard of cooking.' SN. When there is a concert or football match at the Stadium, a set dinner buffet is provided. 'Dishes were full of spices and excellent. Service was very friendly. Certainly worth its place in the TOP 100.' MF. Recommendations: Butter Chicken, Jeera Chicken – half £6.50, whole £13 and Chilli Chicken – whole £15, Methi Chicken – whole £14. 'Worthy of TOP 100.' RL, Service 10%. Price check: Papadam 50p, CTM £6.25, Pullao Rice £1.95. House wine £7.55. Hours: 6-11pm, Tues. closed.

GEETANJAI

16 Court Parade, Watford Road, Wembley ✆ 0181 904 5353

From the outside, it looks nothing more than a typical curry house, but you would be wrong to pass it by. A well-decorated, stylish restaurant, linen tablecloths, copper serving bowls, high-backed padded chairs and plants a-plenty. If you usually order an Onion Bhaji, go for the Corn version instead, served with chutney for £2.90; it makes a refreshing change. Hours: 12-3pm/6pm-12am. Stocks Cobra.

KARAHI KING   BYO

213 East Lane, Wembley   © 0181 904 2760

Fabulous food, fabulous tandoori (including the breads), curries for
meat-eaters and vegetarians. Served up by the same staff. Open 12pm-
12am. No credit cards. No corkage, so BYO.

KARAHI RAJA   BYO

195 East Lane, Wembley   © 0181 904 5553

Established in 1993 by Mushtaq Ahmed. Restaurant seats 150 diners
between two rooms. Pakistani-styled curries cooked by B. Hussain.
House specials include: Haandi Chicken – chicken on the bone cooked
with herbs, tomatoes and spicy thick sauce £4.95. Paya – lamb trotters
Lahori style £4.95. Vegetarian dishes: Karahi Egg, scrambled egg, tomatoes, coriander and green chillies £4. BYO allowed, no corkage. Price
check: Papadam 30p, CTM £4.95, Pullao Rice £1.70, Peshwari Nan £2.
Sunday lunch buffet £10. Delivery: £15 minimum, 3-mile radius. Hours:
12pm-12am.

MARU'S BHAJIA HOUSE   NO ALCOHOL √

230 Ealing Road, Alperton, Wembley   © 0181 903 6771

This restaurant, opened by Maru over 20 years ago, provides superior
family unique style of vegetarian curries and accompaniments from
East Africa. Their Bhajias are the real thing, and they are even spelt
correctly, rather than the formula Bhaji. Try their Potato Bhajias,
besan-batter-coated, deep-fried and served with tamarind (imli) chutney as a real treat to die for. Hours: 12-8.45pm (9.45pm on Fri. & Sat.),
closed Mon. Alcohol not permitted.

MARUTI BHEL PURI   √

238a Ealing Road, Wembley   © 0181 903 6743

A vegetarian restaurant serving inexpensive melt-in-the-mouth
delights, such as Dosas with Sambar and, of course, the namesake Bhel
Puri. Try their Karahi Corn-on-the-Cob. 'All fantastic stuff for the
lucky residents of Wembley. I wish I lived nearer.' DBAC. Open daily
except Tues. 12-10pm.

PALM BEACH

17 Ealing Road, Wembley   ℂ 0181 900 8664

A Sri Lankan and south Indian restaurant, but this doesn't mean there is no meat on the menu. Alongside the Dosas, Vadias and Hoppers, you will find Mutton Ceylon Curry, tender lamb, steeped in a richly spiced, meaty, juicy gravy. Decorations are relaxed, with batiks and wood carvings. Open daily except Tuesday 12pm-3pm/6-11.30pm Branch: Palm Beach, 18 The Avenue, Ealing, London w13. Stocks Cobra.

RAJBHOG   BYO

140 Ealing Road, Alperton, Wembley   ℂ 0181 903 9395

A similar establishment to Sakoni (*see* entry below), selling Bombay street food and other snacks such as Bhajias. South Indian dishes, Idli (white, sponge-like UFO), Dosa (wafer-thin lentil pancake stuffed with potato curry lightly spiced with mustard seeds and curry leaves) and Sambar (a watery, yellow-coloured curry, thickened with lentils, medallions of carrot and potato with fingerlike pieces of drumstick) are must-haves, because they are quite delicious. Hours: 11am-10pm (10.30pm on Fri., Sat. and Sun.).

SAKONI

119-121 Ealing Road, Alperton,
Wembley   ℂ 0181 903 9601

Alcohol is not allowed at Sakoni, but there's no problem getting authentic Indian vegetarian snacks in a pleasant and informal atmosphere. Service good and quick. Run by Gujaratis who know about the food and tradition. Generous portions. Chutneys freshly prepared and are not removed from the tables every few minutes, which makes a change from most other Indian restaurants. 'Recommended.' RM. Hours: 11am-11.30pm Branch: Sakoni, 129 Ealing Road, Wembley.

TASTIEY LAND

537 High Road, Wembley   ℂ 0181 900 9919

Sri Lankan and south Indian curries feature highly on the menu in this restaurant. The set meals are good value, offering good and varied food. Egg Godhamba Rotti, Veechu Rotti, Katta Sambol, Mutton Curry all for £3.95 including a free Papadam. Hours: 6-11pm.

WEMBLEY COTTAGE NEW ENTRANT   ©

305 Harrow Road, Wembley Triangle   ℂ 0181 902 4039

Established in '85 by T. Moniz, this 45-seater is one of the few Nepalese restaurants. Baban in the kitchen cooks up unusual delights which include Mariz (pepper) Chicken £5.95, Nepalese Chicken Bhutuwa – highly spiced £6.25. Chicken Chowla – cooked in tandoor, mixed with ginger and garlic £5.95. 'Not terribly impressed with the food.' RM. 'Recommended to me by so many of my colleagues.' CT. Price check: Papadam 40p, CTM £5.95, Pullao Rice £1.90. Hours: 12-2.30pm and 6-11.30pm. Stocks Cobra.

Whitton

JOLLY'S TANDOORI NEW ENTRANT

2 Hounslow Road, Whitton   ℂ 0181 894 3122

Established in 1975, taken over in '78 by Shahid Ali and Ataur Rahman. Bangladeshi formula curry house, seating 58 diners. Dhansak, Masala and Balti dishes are most popular. Minimum charge £8.50. House specials include: Golden Curry Special – half chicken, tandoori cooked with minced meat, egg and lychees £7.50. Chicken Sharaf Khan – spring chicken on the bone cooked and marinated in thick almond and cream sauce £7.50. Price check: Papadam 50p, CTM £7.50 incl. rice, Pullao Rice £1.65, Peshwari Nan £1.60. Lager £2.30 pint, house wine £5.95, mineral water £2.25. Hours: 12-3pm and 6pm-12am.

©	Curry Club discount (see page 6)		Unlicensed
√	Vegetarian		
BYO	Bring your own alcohol		Delivery/takeaway

NORFOLK

Area: East
Population: 751,000
Number of restaurants in county: 41
Number of restaurants in Guide: 11

Aylsham

GATE OF INDIA NEW ENTRANT

14 Market Place, Aylsham	✆ 01263 734742

Owned by Messrs Abu Miah and Kelu Miah, who tell us their 54-seater, managed by Mr Kalam is 'very spacious, the walls are light pink with stripy, shiny wallpaper.' Chef F. Miah does Baltis, though CTM is the most popular dish ordered. Specials: Baharai, fairly hot, cooked with green chillies and ground pepper £5.35. 'Quite outstanding, food, service and friendliness are quite remarkable.' S&BF. Takeaway: 10% discount. Price check: Papadam 40p, CTM £5.35, Pullao Rice £1.50, Peshwari Nan £1.70. House wine £6.95 wine. Hours: 12-2.30pm and 6-11pm

Great Yarmouth

BOMBAY NITE ©

25a King Street, Great Yarmouth	✆ 01493 331383

Raza is the owner and Louise Hughes is manager. We hear well of the Roast Chicken Massala and the Sylhet Supreme. Price check: Papadam 40p, CTM £5.95, Pullao Rice £1.50. Minimum charge £12.50. Service 10%. Open daily 6pm-12am. Reports please.

King's Lynn

BOMBAY BRASSERIE

24 Railway Road, King's Lynn	✆ 01553 767666

'A smart medium-sized restaurant. I dined alone and could only sample a few dishes but all the smells coming from the surrounding tables were right. Papadams were fine with good chutneys and Sheek Kebab was very good. Chicken Tikka Jalfrezi used quality chicken with plenty of onions and fresh chilli but tasted somewhat metallic. Peshwari Nan sugary. Although there were no fights it is best to avoid Friday and Saturday nights perhaps! Some colleagues went for lunch the next day and reported good Vegetable Biriani.' CT.

INDIA GATE ©

41 St James Street, King's Lynn ℂ 01553 776489

Air conditioned. Taken over in August '97 by A. Miah (manager) and S. Ahmed (head chef). Bangladeshi curries and Balti. Tikkah Jafrezi, with fresh green chillies £6.45 is the most ordered dish. Minimum £5.95. Price check: Papadam 40p, CTM £6.05, Pullao Rice £1.50, Peshwari Nan £1.65. Lager £1.90 pint, house wine £6.95, mineral water 95p. Hours: 12-2pm/6pm-12am.

ISHALIMAR BALTI CUISINE

61 Railway Road, King's Lynn

'Papadams and Chutneys were fine and Peshwari Nan much better than the previous night at the Bombay Brasserie. Shahi Chicken was really superb, cooked in yoghurt, garlic, onions, tomatoes and green pepper, fantastic, thick, home-cooked tasting sauce with large pieces of chicken. Simply superb!' CT.

North Walsham

PRINCE OF BENGAL

13a Mundesley Road, North Walsham ℂ 01692 500119

Owner, Mr Folik Miah Choudhury, can be found in this 54-seater welcoming guests in for their meal, and always finds time for a chat with his guests, including Eastender Ross 'Grant' Kemp, who eats here (I have photo to prove it). Despite that, other luminaries dine here. R&MA with their colleagues, say 'the consensus of opinion is that the menu is varied and interesting, vegetable dishes are very good, pleasing vegetarians, and top marks for the clean toilets.' Sunday buffet £7.50. Takeaway: 10% discount. Cheques under £10 and credit cards under £15 will not be accepted — we think that's a bit off! Price check: Papadam

55p, CTM £6.50, Pullao Rice £1.75, Peshwari Nan £1.75. Lager £3 pint, house wine £7.95, mineral water £2.95. Hours: 12-2.30pm/6-11.30pm. Branch: 40, Cromer Road, Sheringham, Norfolk.

Norwich

Norwich has a number of attractions, including DBAC's sister. For the curryholic, there's the dubious distinction of the curry price-wars that have been plaguing Norwich for years. Thirteen curry houses and a population of 127,000 is not a remarkably high ratio of restaurants to people (see Bradford, West Yorkshire) but, by virtually halving prices, many seem to have achieved full houses, unlike Bristol, whose price-war result-ed in numerous bankruptcies. I said last time that price-wars are best left to giant corporations, such as supermarkets. And then as I write this (July '98) Bengal Spice opens at St Benedicts Street, Norwich. We wonder if it will cut away from the rest or join in with the price wars. I say again make Methi while the restaurants last, and tell us about it!

ALI NAME CHANGE   ©

12-14 Magdalen Street, Norwich   © 01603 666874

'Originally called the Bombay. Ali is a superb host and manager, his brother is an excellent cook. Crowds are flocking, have to book for a table virtually every day of the week. King Prawn Korai, superb. Chicken Dupiaza delicious and Chicken Makhani to be tried again. Overall exceptional. Well-drilled waiters.' DR GTC.

NAZMA NEW ENTRANT   ©

15 Prince of Wales Road, Norwich   © 01603 616101

In 1996 Mohabbat Ali was brave enough to open his Nazma venture on a site long-established with Indian restaurants (a Bombay, and more recently the short-lived Lal Toofan were there). But his branch seems to thrive, as does this one so, like his locals, we wish Mr Ali well. Price check: Papadam 35p, CTM £3.05, Pullao Rice £1.40. Minimum charge £5. Open daily for lunch and dinner. Branch: Nazma Brasserie, 15 Magdalen Street, Norwich.

NORWICH TANDOORI   ©

98 Magdalen Street, Norwich   © 01603 621436

Kuti Meah is the managing owner. His 50-seater restaurant has: 'A
straightforward comfortable interior. Lamb Pasanda best tried so far in
the city. Chicken Tikka Pasanda, mildly creamy, cooked with butter,
almonds and sultanas, exceeded expectations.' TW. Hours: 12-3pm/
6pm-12am.

PASSAGE TO INDIA   NEW ENTRANT

45 Magdalen Street, Norwich   © 01603 762836

A. Ali's 75-seater curry house serves formula dishes, CTM being the
most popular dish ordered. House specials include: Buhari, fairly hot
with fresh green chillies, Chicken £3.25, Lamb £3.30, Prawn £3.45.
There is parking at the back of the restaurant for ten cars. Takeaway:
half price. Price check: Papadam 35p, CTM £3.50, Pullao Rice £1.20,
Peshwari Nan £1.10. Lager £2.10 pint, house wine £7.95, mineral water
£2.50. Delivery: £25 minimum. Hours: 12-30pm/6pm-12am. Branch:
Prince of India, 19 Prince of Wales Road, Norwich.

PRINCE OF INDIA

19 Prince of Wales Road, Norwich   © 01603 616937

Owned by A. Rahman, since 1983. His 66-seater restaurant has, 'a spacious lounge for customers to enjoy'. Chef A. Bashir cooks formula
dishes. This is undoubtedly one of the city's most popular restaurants,
judging by the correspondence we receive: 'Beamed ceilings and divided alcoves give cosy atmosphere. Food quite good.' MB. 'Food tasty and
competently spiced and presented. Service was good considering the
restaurant was packed to capacity. Noticed at least 15 people in the
"Bombay Mix Zone" waiting to be seated.' GR. 'Food was very good
and my colleague enjoyed his CTM although it was vibrant with food
colouring. Rice good, Nan excellent.' CT. 'Typical curry house fare,
Patia can be variable, Korma always nice.' R&MA. Price check: Papadam
40p, CTM £3.80, Pullao Rice £1.30, house wine £7.95. Hours: 12-
2.30pm/6pm-12am. Branch: Passage to India, Norwich.

Thetford

NEMI INDIAN CUISINE ©

17 White Hart Street, Thetford   ✆ 01842 761260

A snug restaurant seating 48 diners, established by Abdur Rour in 1992. Restaurant seats 50 diners and head chef Alamgir Kabir cooks Bangladeshi formula curries, CTM being the most ordered dish. His specials include: Batak (tandooried duck) Masala £6.95, Horen (venison cooked in tandoor) Masala £7.95, Buaal Masala (Bangladeshi Fish) £5.75. Takeaway: 10% discount. Price check: Papadam 30p, CTM £5.75, Peshwari Nan £1.60. Lager £2 pint, house wine £6.30, mineral water £2. Delivery: £12 minimum, 5-mile radius. Hours: 12-2pm/6pm-12am.

Wroxham

STAR OF INDIA NEW ENTRANT

The Bridge, Norwich Road, Wroxham   ✆ 01603 784243

Unusual to find a pork dish on the menu, Special Pork £7.50 – pork steamed in tandoori sauce with cream and other trimmings. 'Small entrance, easily missable. Greeting most friendly and cheerful. Can recommend the Prawn Garlic Special, King Prawn Ceylon and Chicken Tikka Biriani. Truly delicious Kulcha Nan.' BT. Price check: Papadam 40p, CTM £5.25, Bombay Potato £1.60, Pullao Rice £1.30, Chutney 40p per person. Hours: 12-2.30pm/6pm-12am.

NORTHAMPTONSHIRE

Area: Central
Population: 580,000
Number of restaurants in county: 57
Number of restaurants in Guide: 12

Corby

BOMBAY DYNASTY

76 George Street, Corby   © 01536 400660

Akbor Ali's restaurant seats 46. Chef Abdul Quayum's Baltis are popular. Takeaway and delivery – please ask for special offers, free wine. Manager Golam Sarwar's menu lists all the curry house favourites with a few additions. Our attention is drawn to Kalmi (chicken) Kebab (£2.20), Murgh Bemisall (£5.60) – Chicken Tikka with onion, ginger, garlic, tomato and coriander – and Murgh La Jawab (£5.60) – tandoori chicken chunks in a thick gravy. Price check: Papadam 40p, CTM £5.35, Pullao Rice £1.45. Minimum charge £7.95. Set meal £7.95. Sunday eat-your-fill buffet £5.95, under 10's half-price. Delivery: £10 minimum, 7-mile radius. Hours: 12-2.30pm/6-11.30pm. Branch: Spice of Life, 169, Wellingborough Road, Rushden, Northamptonshire.

Kettering

THE RAJ   ©

50 Rockingham Road, Kettering   © 01536 513606

Owned by Goyas Miah since 1991. Formula Bangladeshi restaurant, decorated in 'subtle green, light, clean atmosphere.' Seats 74. House specials include: Raj E Jinga, whole king prawns marinated and cooked in thick rich garlic spicy sauce and served in cast iron karahi £8.95. Sunday buffet £5.50. Takeaway: 10% discount. Price check: Papadam 50p, CTM £6.95, Pullao Rice £1.60, Peshwari Nan £1.75. Delivery: £7.50 minimum, 5-mile radius. Hours: 12-2.30pm/5.30-12am (12.30am on Fri. & Sat.), Sun. 12pm-12am. Branch: Ancient Raj, 12, High Street, Long Buckby, Northampton.

RED ROSE

1 George Street, Kettering   ✆ 01536 510120

70-seater managed by Mr Rashid with Abu Bakorhelal as head chef cooking formula curries and side dishes. Sunday lunch £5.50. Price check: Papadam 40p, CTM £6.35, Pullao Rice £1.50, Peshwari Nan £1.50. Delivery: £6.50 minimum, 3-mile radius. Hours: 12-2pm/5.30pm-12am.

Long Buckby

THE ANCIENT RAJ   ©

12 High Street, Long Buckby   ✆ 01327 842193

Established in '93 by G. Miah (manager) and Raj Miah. Their restaurant seats 60 and chef B. Miah's specials include Ostrich Balti!!! For rugby fans, Ian McGeechan, British Lions rugby coach, eats here. Sunday buffet £6.95. Price check: Papadam 50p, CTM £5.95, Pullao Rice £1.60. Lager £2 pint, house wine £6.95, mineral water £2.95. Delivery: 10-mile radius. Hours: 12-2pm/5-11pm, Sun. 12-10.30pm. Open for Christmas Day lunch.

Northampton

BOMBAY PALACE   NEW ENTRANT

9-11 Welford Road, Kingsthorpe   ✆ 01604 713899

Abdul Ahad's reataurant seats 40 diners. Of chef Abdul Husian's curries, CTM is the most ordered. 'Arrived without booking, offered a choice of smoking or non smoking area (excellent). Girlfriend says this is the best Chicken Malaya in Northants! Jayne (girlfriend), given rose as we left! (Nice touch). Well worth trying – don't be put off by the location.' DL. Price check: Papadam 40p, CTM £6.75, Pullao Rice £1.75. Delivery: ring for details. Hours: 12-2pm/ 5.30pm-12am.

FAR COTTON TANDOORI   ©

111 St Leonards Road, Far Cotton, Northampton   ✆ 01604 706282

'Far out' wrote a local scribe (IM) of the three Alis: chef Haruni, Ansar and Soub's above-average takeaway in the southern outskirts of town.

Specials include: Mint Lamb, tikka meat, mint and almond £5.20. Chicken Dhakna, medium spiced, tomatoes, capsicums, fried garlic and mushrooms £3.85. Price check: Papadam 40p, CTM £5.20, Pullao Rice £1.35. Hours: 12-2pm/5-10.30pm (11pm on Sat., 10pm on Sun.).

IMRAN BALTI HUT   BYO

285 Wellingborough Road, Northampton   ℂ 01604 622730

'If you can get inside the door of this extremely popular restaurant and push through the crowds of people to try and get a seat you are guaranteed an excellent meal. Always best to book. At the weekend people queue out of the door! Simply decorated, pleasant waiters. A large vegetarian choice. After papadoms and chutneys, don't order starters unless you have a particularly huge appetite, though a must is the family Naan – 2 feet long by 18 inches wide – a highlight. Can BYO for a small corkage charge.' ss. Reports, please. Stocks Cobra.

RAJPUT BALTI   NEW ENTRANT   ©

224a Wellingborough Road, Northampton ℂ 01604 637336

Taken over in 1996 by Shahab Uddin. Seats 50, serves Bangladeshi formula curries, cooked by chef Shofor Ali. Set dinner £8.95. Free bottle of wine with orders over £20. Price check: Papadam 30p, CTM £4.95, Pullao Rice £1.50. Lager £3.50 pint, house wine £5.95, mineral water £2.50. Delivery: £8 minimum. Hours: 12-2.30pm/6pm-12am.

STAR OF INDIA

5 Abington Avenue, Northampton   ℂ 01604 630664

'Having dined at Abdul Noor and manager Bodrul Islam's exceptional 40-seater many times, we decided to try their 24-hr notice. Murgh Mossala, a complete meal for 4 including a bottle of Indian red wine. After crisp Popadoms, with the usual accompaniments, were starters, including Onion Bhajees, Samosas and Tandoori Shah Jahni. Main course, two whole chickens marinated and stuffed with spices and two whole boiled eggs! and Special Fried Rice – did not disappoint!' DL. Tandoori dishes and Vegetarian dishes can be ordered in half portions – what a great idea. Price check: Papadam 30p, CTM £5.65, Pullao Rice £1.40. Delivery: £9.50 minimum. Hours: 12-2.15pm/5.30pm-12am (1am on Fri. & Sat.). Sunday 12-3pm/5.30pm-12am.

TAJ MAHAL

7 Marefair, Northampton   © 01604 631132

Apart from its hours, this is a typical curry house, nothing more or less. It is Northampton's oldest, having opened in 1952, ranking it in the country's first ten Indian restaurants. With 47 years in the business, you'd expect them to be good at the job. I can't imagine why they find it necessary to stay open till 3am. But for those who pound up and down the M1 (yes, there are some of us who do it in the wee hours) anything is better than motorway food. Hours: 6pm-12pm (3am on Fri. & Sat.).

Rushden

CURRY GARDEN

24 Church Street, Rushden   © 01933 314121

Komor Uddin continues with a good local trade. Price check: Papadom 45p, CTM £5.35, Pullao Rice £1.40. Kurzi Lamb meal £26.50 for two. Open daily for lunch and from 6pm-12am. Stocks Cobra.

Wellingborough

AKASH TANDOORI

36 Cambridge Street, Wellingborough   © 01933 227193

Est. 1979 by Mr Choudhury, who says: 'Dining without wine is like a day without sunshine.' And so say all of us! Specials: Makhon Chicken. Sunday lunch £5.95. Price check: Papadam 30p, CTM £6.75 incl. rice. Delivery. Hours: 12-2.30pm/6-11.30pm. Stocks Cobra.

©	Curry Club discount (see page 6)		Unlicensed
√	Vegetarian		
BYO	Bring your own alcohol		Delivery/takeaway

NORTHUMBERLAND

Area: North East
Population: 305,000
Number of restaurants in county: 18
Number of restaurants in Guide: 8

Alnwick

ALNWICK TANDOORI ©

17 Clayport Street, Alnwick   ✆ **01665 510772**

Owned by Abdul Khalique and Abdul Tahid. Mr Khalique can be found in the restaurant welcoming guests and Mr Tahid can be found in the kitchen cooking up all our favourite curries and accompaniments. Hours: 5.30-11.30pm.

Berwick-upon-Tweed

MAGNA ©

39 Bridge Street, Berwick-upon-Tweed   ✆ **01289 302736**

Jahangir Khan 100-seater family business – a pretty restaurant with green and cream wallpaper, hanging plants and smart, black-tie waiters, has been in our Guide since we started it in 1984. 'And no wonder.' says CC member Michael Fabricant, MP. The food, which is the standard formula stuff beloved by all curryholics, is as well described on the menu as it is cooked. It's a port in a storm right there on the A1-Scottish border, with the ghosts of Lindisfarne not far behind. 'Most pleasing and memorable way to spend an evening with friends.' GFB. Pickles 80p per person. Breast of chicken 50p extra. Takeaway: 10% discount. Chandee Dishes, very mild with fresh cream and mango from £6.95. Shim Dishes, cooked with green beans from £6.95. Hours: 12-2.30pm/6pm-12am. Sunday 6pm-12am.

Corbridge

CORBRIDGE TANDOORI   ©

8 Market Square, Corbridge   *✆* **01434 633676**

SM Shahjahan's small restaurant hidden above a shop est. in '89. Specials: Murghi Masala, succulent cubes of chicken tikka, cooked with mincemeat £6.95. Takeaway: 15% discount. Lamb Karaya, marinated diced tender lamb, barbecued over charcoal then cooked in a slow process in a pot called karaya with garlic £6.70. DT MH continues to dine here regularly (though he lives in Wales) 'It is as good or better than the Valley.' [*see* entry] 'and I go to both. If you want excellent decor and different dishes, go to the Valley. If you want excellent "standard" dishes, come here. It has only two drawbacks: it is small and can get stuffy and hot when busy, and it does get busy, especially at weekends. I cannot recommend it highly enough.' Price check: Papadam 50p, CTM £6.95, Pullao Rice £1.95. Hours: 12-2.30pm/6-11.30pm. Stocks Cobra.

THE VALLEY   TOP 100   ©

The Old Station House, Corbridge   *✆* **01434 633434**

Corbridge station building in the beautiful Tyne valley, was built in 1835 for Stephenson's railway. It is no longer used as a station although it is on the important Newcastle-to-Carlisle railway line. Indeed, trains stop at Corbridge station throughout each day but passengers do not use the old building any more. That is until Daraz (Syed Nadir Aziz) turned it into a stylish, up-market Indian restaurant, offering a unique service, for parties of 10 to 80 at £20 a head, including return travel. Uniformed restaurant staff welcome you at Newcastle Central Station and escort you by train to The Valley. En route, choose four courses from the à la carte menu. The order is rung through on a mobile. Your starter is awaiting your arrival. 'It beats ordering a taxi.' GM. Of course, individuals can make their own way here and back by scheduled train – but beware a fairly early last train. Or, there is parking for 12 cars. Why not book your takeaway by phone en-route, collect, pay and eat it, without leaving the train? As for the restaurant, there is a reception room and 80 seats in four connecting rooms (one of which opens onto the eastbound platform). Decor is lush and Indian, though a total interior refurbishment is 'expected'. And the food? Chef Abdul Khalick's menu contains all the CC (currinary correct) favourites plus some good specials. Chingri Moslai, prawns with garlic and mustard, £3.50. Macher Bora, tuna fish kebab, £3.50. Luari Mangsho, medium hot lamb dish, cooked with tomatoes, green pepper and fresh coriander £7.25. Rajha Chingri Sagwala, king prawns cooked with fresh spinach, coriander and green chilli £9.95. Dhai Baigon, large grilled aubergine stuffed with spicy mixed vegetables, topped with yoghurt £5.95. 'I decided to visit having read the Guide write-up and was not disappointed. Food superb, one page devoted to house specialities, none of which I had ever come across before. An absolute must.' TOC. Price check: Papadam 50p, CTM £6.95, Pullao Rice £2.50. House wine £7.95, mineral water £2.95. Takeaway 20% off. Hours: 6-11pm. Sun. closed. Branch: Valley Junction 397, The Old Station, Archbold Terrace, Jesmond, Newcastle. Remains high in our TOP 100. Stocks Cobra.

Cramlington

LAL QILA   ©

Dudley Lane, Cramlington   © **01670 734268**

Established '86 by Sabu Miah. Seats 54, serves formula curries. Red brick building, with private parking for 20 cars. Framed Indian art hangs, padded yellow and blue chairs, yellow table cloth, red patterned carpet, flowery wallpaper and curtains, makes for quite an eyefull. Baingan Pakora, deliciously spiced, deep-fried aubergine served with minted sauce £1.95. Samba Gosht, lamb fairly hot, spiced cooked with lentils and fresh coriander £5.50. Business lunch Monday to Fri. £2.25 and £5.50. Price check: Papadam 50p, CTM £5.50, Pullao Rice £1.60, Peshwari Nan £1.25. Lager £1.65 pint, house wine £7.50. Hours: 12-2.30 and 6-11.30pm.

Hexham

ABBEY TANDOORI   ©

28 Priestpopple, Hexham   © **01434 603509**

Miah Sahid's 44-seat Abbey restaurant is plainly decorated but neat and tidy. A good selection of tandoori dishes on the menu with, as they call them, 'supporting dishes' and four different Nans. 'We found ourselves snowbound in Hexham en route to Essex from Scotland. Naturally we had our trusted *Good Curry Guide* in the car, and found the Abbey Tandoori. Meal was superb. King Prawn Vindaloo and Chicken Pathia. Naan bread one of the best I've tasted, crispy on the outside but beautifully light and fluffy on the inside. Too few king prawns in my Vindaloo. I'd have happily paid more for a few extra prawns.' S&KT. Hours: 12-2pm/6-11.30pm, Sun. 6-11pm only. Stocks Cobra.

Morpeth

MORPETH TAKEAWAY NEW ENTRANT

10 Chantry Place, Morpeth ✆ 01670 516144

Abdul Muhit and Awlad Miah's takeaway, serving Northern Indian food. Price check: Papadam 35p, CTM £4.30, Bombay Potato £1.50, Pullao Rice £1.30, Pickles 40p. Hours: 12-2pm/6pm-12am. Sun. 6-11.30pm.

TANDOORI MAHAL ©

17 Bridge Street, Morpeth ✆ 01670 512420

60-seater, owned by chef Afrus Miah whose menu gives very good descriptions of every dish. Specials include Murgh Masala, spring chicken off the bone, soaked in spiced cream, roasted and served with Basmati Rice £8.50. Sabzi Ka Khazana contains Bhindi Bhaji, Milijuli Sabz, Dal Masala, Palak Bhaji, Chwal and two chapatis £7.25. 'An absolutely first-class establishment. Prices fair, service good, decor of a very high standard, parking no problem.' MB. Manager Surot Miah has promised to give a discount to Curry Club members at lunchtimes. Price check: Papadam 50p, CTM £6.05, Pullao Rice £1.40. Takeaway: 10% discount. Hours: 12-2.30pm/6pm-12am. Stocks Cobra.

NOTTINGHAMSHIRE

Area: East Midlands
Population: 1,017,000
Number of restaurants in county: 87
Number of restaurants in Guide: 18

Mansfield

MODHU MITHA

11-15 Ratcliffe Gate, Mansfield   ✆ 01623 651203

Extensive menu with standard curry house stuff. 'Food quite delicious and always plenty of it. Fresh Bhindi in the Bhajee.' MB.

Newark

ASHA

2 Stodman Street, Newark   ✆ 01636 702870

'Decor, very wine-bar. Chicken Tikka Masala pleasant but lacked the creaminess that I am used to, though still well recommended.' DH.

Nottingham

BEESTON TANDOORI   ©

150-152 High Road, Beeston, Nottingham   ✆ 0115 922 3330

S. Choudhury's cosy 40-seater. Chef recommends Uri and Muki Specials, described as fairly dry but well-spiced. Hours: 12-2.30pm and 6pm-12am.

BOMBAY BICYCLE SHOP
TAKEAWAY   NEW ENTRANT   ▦ ©

511 Alfreton Road, Nottingham   ✆ 0115 978 6309

Takeaway only, interior in shades of grey, exterior red and yellow. Specials include: Chicken de Goa, fresh cream, flaked coconut, mango sauce £4.95. Sag Alloo Paneer £2.50. Garlic Chappati £1.20. 6 parking spaces behind takeaway. Credit cards not accepted. Price check: Papadam 45p, CTM £4.95, Pullao Rice 70p, Peshwari Nan £1.35. Delivery: £8 minimum. Hours: 5.30pm-12am.

CHAND TOP 100 ©

31 Mansfield Road, Nottingham ✆ 0115 947 4103

38-seat, jointly owned by Mohammed Shanaz, front of house, and chef Mohammed Riaz. The menu contains a very good selection of vegetarian dishes. Dhava Thaum £2.20 – garlic mushrooms served on a thin bread, and Mixed Vegetable Karahi £5.15. There are plenty of meat, fish and fowl dishes, too. Balti dishes are also on the menu. 'Comfortable and clean. Owner and staff always friendly. Good sized portions.' sw. 'As regular customers of the Chand, we were very pleased, but not surprised, to see it placed in your TOP 100 curry houses last year. We have spent many a pleasant evening enjoying generous helpings ... from a wide menu while solving innumerable Times crosswords.' sm&gs. 'The food is always of the same quality and the service is always very friendly.' sw. 'There are four reasons for visiting the Chand. Firstly, the friendly service; secondly, the excellent quality of the food; thirdly, the wide variety of dishes; and fourthly, the fact that I have never had a bad meal there.' pg. 'Chand deserves to be in the TOP 100 curry houses! The staff are great, the food excellent.' pb. Takeaway 15% discount. Pickle Tray £1.20 – too expensive! Paradise Balti, chicken, lamb, prawn and vegetables, all in one medium-spiced sauce with a mesh of omelette £7.50. Price check: Papadam 50p, CTM £7, Pullao Rice £1.50. Hours: 12-2pm (Sun. closed) and 5.30pm-12.30am (1am on Sat.). Stocks Cobra.

THE INDIAN ©

7 Bentinck Road, Nottingham ✆ 0115 942 4922

Pretty black beams, white frontage and inviting curtained windows at Naj Aziz's 40-seater in 2 areas (smoking and non-smoking). Very stylish restaurant, un-Indian, unfussy, light and bright, Wedgwood blue ceiling and magnolia walls. Walls are decorated with hanging carpets and back-lit fretwork, tiled floor, large palms in white pots. We hear that the food is family-style. 'Aubergine Paneer and Garlic and Mushroom Baji for starters, served with crisp salad. Murgh Makhani, Chicken Tikka cooked with garlic, coriander and brandy, and I can honestly say it was among the best curries I have ever eaten. Rice portions were large. Staff extremely friendly and food is outstanding.' CY. 10% service charge for parties of 6 or more. Takeaway 10% off. Price check: Papadam 75p, CTM £7.20, Pullao Rice £1.90, Peshwari Nan £2.20. House wine £9.50. Sunday lunch £16. Hours: 6-10.30pm Tues.-Sat. Closed 16th-30th August, a week at Christmas and two weeks in the summer. Stocks Cobra.

JEWEL IN THE CROWN NEW ENTRANT

25 Bridgford Road, Bridgford, Nottingham © 0115 981 1645

Owned by M. Ibrahim, since 1995. Tells us that his air-conditioned restaurant is, 'nicely decorated, top class outside sign'; that his 'customers enjoy the meals' and that he is 'a very busy restaurant.' Agreed? Specials: Jinga Sharab, king prawns are taken out of their shells, dipped in a tandoori sauce made from fresh cream, yoghurt, mint and tandoori spices, roasted in the Tandoor, blended in a sauce prepared with white wine £7.45, delicious! Price check: Papadam 40p, CTM £6.95, Pullao Rice £1.80, Peshwari Nan £2. Lager £2.30 pint. Delivery: £10 minimum, 3-mile radius. Pay by credit card over the phone. Hours: 12-2pm/5.30pm-12.30am. Branch: Pavilion, 1a, Radcliffe Road, West Bridgford.

KASHMIR   ©

60 Maid Marian Way, Nottingham   © 0115 947 6542

A.D. Satti's 90- and 100-seater in traditional Indian restaurant decor. 'Started with Mixed Kebab, Onion Bhajia, Seekh Kebab, Shami Kebab £2.50, no sauce was served, so too dry. I had literally put down my knife and fork and the plate with cutlery was snatched from me, no interest was shown in me, as a customer, so no tip. Can't recommend.' GGP&MP. Most-ordered dish: Kaghani, cooked in cream, fresh mint, dhania and mushrooms from £4.30. BYO allowed, no corkage. Price check: Papadam free, CTM £6.50, Pullao Rice £1.40, Peshwari Nan £1.30. House wine £6.50. Hours: 6pm-1am (Sat. from 2pm, Sunday from 1pm). Stocks Cobra.

©	Curry Club discount (see page 6)		Unlicensed
√	Vegetarian		
BYO	Bring your own alcohol		Delivery/takeaway

LAGUNA   ©

43 Mount Street, Nottingham   ✆ 0115 941 1632

Taken over in '85 by manager Tony Ranjit Verma. Seats 62, serves
Northern Indian curries, cooked by Bharat Desai. 'Very efficient, food
well above average. Laguna Special, a sort of Tandoori Masala sauce is
good, its vegetarian counterpart is potatoes in the same sauce, but is
curiously called Bombay Aloo. Many vegetarian dishes and beautifully
cooked.' PT. Service 10%. Takeaway: 10% discount. Price check: Papadam
80p, CTM £7.40, Pullao Rice £2.60, Peshwari Nan £2.20. House wine
£8.40. Hours: 12.30-2pm/6.30-11pm. Stocks Cobra.

MEHRAN   ©

948-950 Woodborough Road, Mapperley,
Nottingham   ✆ 0115 955 1005

Taken over in '98 by Mr and Mrs Mohamad Akram Khan. Balti –
chicken balti most popular – restaurant seats 80. Price check: Papadam
65p, CTM £8.50, Pullao Rice £2.30. House wine £7.50. Delivery:
2-mile radius. Reports please. Hours: 6pm-12am (2am on Fri. & Sat.).
Stocks Cobra.

MILAAP TANDOORI   ©

67 Chilwell Road, Beeston, Nottingham   ✆ 0115 925 4597

Owner chef Pervaz Iqbal seats a snug 28 diners and cooks Pakistani
curries. All prices include Papadom, rice and chutney. 'A welcoming
smile and friendly banter from manager Yousef (or "Chippy" as he is
better known) makes the journey seem worthwhile. The Makhani
Chicken Tikka is the mouth-watering combination of boulders of
fresh moist chicken served in an indescribable tandoori sauce . . . truly
magnificent!!!!!' PB. 'The clientele are welcomed as part of a family, and
many people who have met over a meal have become good friends.
Whatever I choose, I am never disappointed. The quality of the ingredients, and the care taken in the kitchen never vary.' CF. 'Whilst the
food is excellent, the service is second to none.' PB. ' Pervez is an excellent cook, who manages to combine just the right amount of spiciness
with the subtle flavours of Indian cuisine.' JB. 'Visited frequently over
last 10 years. Staff always friendly and welcoming, take a pride in the
food that they serve. Good value for money.' S&BA. Minimum charge

£8.50. Price check: Papadam 60p, CTM £6.90, Pullao Rice £1.90. Lager £1.95 pint, house wine £9.90. Hours: 5.30pm-12am (12.30am on Sat).

MOGAL E AZAM   ©

7-9 Goldsmith Street, Nottingham   ✆ 0115 947 3826

The Mogal was opened in 1977 by Mr SN Miah, and seats a huge 300 diners on ground and 1st floors, and serves very good, very popular formula curries, CTM the most popular dish ordered. 'Like the Taj Mahal inside, with arches and minarates built into walls and hallway, marble-effect look, creamy white in colour, with large brass bric-a-brac as decor.' SNM. Specials include: Bengal ka Boul, Bangladesh fish £11.95. Hours: 12-2.30pm/5.30pm-1am. Stocks Cobra.

MOUSHUMI   ©

124 Derby Road, Stapleford, Nottingham   ✆ 0115 939 4929

A tastefully decorated 70-seater decked out in sea greens and stained wood. Large and expensive engraved glass panels divide the restaurant. Proprietor Sanawor Ali is a romantic soul. His Valentine's Night at £25 per couple, with free cocktails for her and champagne for him, sounds good. No reports on proposals. Ataur Rahman. Specials: Dakeshwari Murgh, chicken in cream and yoghurt £4.95. £6.95 wine. Price check: Papadam 50p, CTM £6.95, Pullao Rice £1.70. 10% service. Delivery: £10 minimum, 3 miles radius. Hours: 12-2.30pm/6-11.30pm. Branch: Amrit Takeaway, Mapperley Top, Nottingham. Stocks Cobra.

MUGHAL TAKEAWAY   NEW ENTRANT   ⊞

222 Derby Road, Stapleford, Nottingham   ✆ 0115 939 9379

Opened in 1984 by Latib Ali. House Specials include: Macon Chicken £4.50, tandoori chicken off the bone, cooked with spices and fresh cream and Tandoori Special Cocktail £5.50. Great Indian breads include: Garlic and Tomato Nan, Chilli and Onion Nan, Coriander and Onion Nan, all at £1.30. Price check: Papadam 30p, CTM £4.10, Bombay Potato £1.85, Pullao Rice £1.20, Pickles and Chutneys 35p. Delivery: 3-mile radius. Hours: 5pm-12am.

RAJPOOT BALTI HOUSE NEW ENTRANT

8 Station Road, Sandiacre, Nottingham   ✆ 0115 949 1608

Formerly All India. Taken over in '98 by Mohammed Riaz and Omar Butt. A bright and modern 46-seater. Set dinner £7.95. Baltis feature big on the menu. Coriander Nan £1.25 – sounds lovely. Price check: Papadam 30p, CTM £6.45, Pullao Rice £1.30, Peshwari Nan £1.65. House wine £6.90. Delivery: £10 minimum, 5-mile radius. Reports please. Hours: 6pm-12am (1am on Fri. & Sat.). Stocks Cobra.

SAAGAR TOP 100   ©

473 Mansfield Road, Sherwood,
Nottingham   ✆ 0115 962 2014

Mohammed Khizer opened his Victorian-styled 98-seater in 1984. Front of house is managed by Imtiaz Ahmed, leaving Mr Khizer to do his thing in the kitchen, assisted by Amjaid Parvaiz. From the abundant correspondence we receive, the Saagar does its thing really well. Its 90 seats are split between two floors, and it is smart. 'Everything it is cracked up to be, expensive but worth it. Vegetarian Thali for two is not just a tray but a seemingly endless train of small bowls provided as fast as you can eat.' PT. 'The pops and picks were gorgeous. My Mixed Kebabs £4.90 were tasty. Chicken Kaallan £9.10 was very sweet, yet very sour too, with tender chicken cooked in a south Indian style, with mango, coconut and yoghurt. My girlfriend was brave enough to tackle Chilli Chicken Tikka Masala £9.50 incl. rice, and our Garlic and Tomato Naan £1.95 was excellent, covered in fresh tomato chunks. Everyone felt the food had been made freshly, and it was cooked to perfection. It makes a nice change to come to a decent restaurant which has the edge over others because of little things that just make a difference, like fresh flowers at every table, proper lemon-squeezers, spotless toilets, etc.' NH. Discounts for CC members at lunchtimes. £5.50 half carafe. Price check: Papadam 45p, CTM £9.50 (incl. rice), Pullao Rice £2.30. Hours: 12-2.15pm (Sun. closed)/5.30-12.30. Remains in our TOP 100. Stocks Cobra.

SHABAZ

142 Alfreton Road, Nottingham   ✆ 0115 979 0061

'Service polite and prompt. Decor mediocre and clinical, comfort acceptable. Free Pops, all credit to them. Chicken Rezala with Nan

£5.50, very hot, spicy and very tasty. Chicken Rai with Nan £5.50, good. Well worthy place.' GGP&MP. Hours: 6pm-3am, Fri.-Sat. 6pm-4am. Insomniacs, take note.

Southwell

SANAM BALTI HOUSE NEW ENTRANT   ©

15-17 King Street, Southwell   ✆ **01636 813618**

Early Victorian listed building, boasting a spendid spiral staircase with original stain. All rooms are open plan with ornate Moghul style arches to doorways. Beautiful jade colour, lighting subdued crystal reflecting the traditional Indian art. All tables are covered in fine contrasting linen, sparkling silverware and fresh flowers. Centre of attention has to be a 26-cubic-feet fish tank, which is set within an existing chimney and can be viewed from both rooms. Chef-owner, Khalid Mahmood or 'Chef Saab' as he is known to staff and customers, originates from Pakistan's Kashmir. 'Tastefully decorated. All food was hot, excellent Pullao Rice and Peshwari Nan.' LW. All main curry dishes include rice, pops and picks. Price check: Papadam 50p, CTM £7.10, Pullao Rice £1.30, Peshwari Nan £1.60. Lager £2.25 pint, house wine £10.95. Hours: 6-11.30pm.

OXFORDSHIRE

Area: Central
Population: 587,000
Number of restaurants in county: 78
Number of restaurants in Guide: 22

Abingdon

PRINCE OF INDIA

10 Ock Street, Abingdon   ✆ **01235 523033**

Established in '83 by manager Abdul Ahad, 'will be fully refurbished in '98', he tells us. Well, has it? – answers please in a report!! Chef

Mokddus Ali cooks formula curries, Tandoori Beef — slices of steak coked in a tandoori sauce with cream, ginger and garlic £9.95, Lamb Rajitha, medium curry, tender pieces of lamb cooked in tomato and fried raisins £7.50 — being specialities. Takeaway: 20% discount. Sunday buffet lunch £6.95. Price check: Papadam 60p, CTM £6.50, Pullao Rice £1.60, Peshwari Nan £1.65. Lager £2.50 pint, house wine £6.50. Delivery: £10 minimum. Hours: 12-2.30pm/6-11.30pm.

Banbury

MOGHUL

58 Parsons Street, Banbury   © 01295 264177

'I have used this place for years when in town, lovely inside, good food, first-class service.' J. 'Located in one of the more pleasant areas of Banbury. Exquisitely tender Chicken Korai, full of flavour. The chef-owner was concerned for our enjoyment. Heartily recommended.' JCC.

SHEESH MAHAL   ©

45 Bridge Street, Banbury   © 01295 266489

M. Khalid is the owner-chef here, and has been since 1986. It's a 70-seater, managed by M. Manwar, and it serves standard formula curries. 'Decided to visit on a friend's recommendation. Tandoori Fish for starters, very good. Chicken Moghlai, excellent, Naan breads were massive. Coffee pot and cream were left on our table so we could help ourselves.' JSK. Price check: Papadam 40p, CTM £6.75, Pullao Rice £1.55. Minimum charge £4.55. Hours: 5pm-12am.

Bicester

BICESTER TANDOORI   NAME CHANGE   ©

15 Market Square, Bicester   © 01869 245170

The Sahana was taken over in 1994 by Mrs Dilwara Begum, and renamed. Decorated in pink with a blue marble bar, seats 40. Formula curry house, CTM is most popular. Price check: Papadam 40p, CTM £5.50, Pullao Rice £1.60, Peshwari Nan £1.60. Delivery: £15.95 minimum, 3-mile radius. Reports please. Hours: 5.30-11.30pm (12am on Sat.). Stocks Cobra.

Chinnor

CHINNOR INDIAN NEW ENTRANT   ©

59-61 Lower Road, Chinnor   ℭ 01844 354843

'This restaurant has changed ownership recently (to Saidur Rahman since '97) and for the better. Cooking shows new influences. The food is superb. A great evening and I can't fault them. Highly recommended.' MS. Seats 60, decorated in green with artifical plants, to look like a garden, bamboo chairs, apricot table linen. Parking for 30 cars – side entrance. 'I recommend it to all my friends.' DGG. Price check: Papadam 50p, CTM £6.50, Pullao Rice £1.70, Peshwari Nan £1.80. House wine £6.90. Hours: 12-2.30pm/ 6-11.30pm. Stocks Cobra.

Chipping Norton

ANARKALI   ©

6 West Street, Chipping Norton   ℭ 01608 642785

'Good selection on menu, good-sized portions. Best-ever Naans, light and fluffy. Onion Bhajees out of this world. Bank Holiday weekend was busy but manager still had time to talk to us.' PA. Proprietor is A. Uddin. Hours 12-2.30pm/6-11.30pm.

Faringdon

AZAD TANDOORI AND BALTI NEW ENTRANT ©

14 Coxwell Street, Faringdon   ℭ 01367 244977

30-seater owned by Rabia Khanom Ali, since '95. 'Nicely decorated since he took it over.' RK. Serves Bangladeshi formula curries, Tandoori dishes are very popular. Takeaway: 15% discount. Price check: Papadam 50p, CTM £6.25, Pullao Rice £1.70, Peshwari Nan £1.75. House wine £6.95. Delivery: £10 minimum, 4-mile radius. Hours: 5-11.30pm. Sun. 12-11.30pm. Stocks Cobra.

©	Curry Club discount (see page 6)		Unlicensed
√	Vegetarian		
BYO	Bring your own alcohol		Delivery/takeaway

Henley-on-Thames

GAZAL ©

53-55 Reading Road, Henley-on-Thames　　© 01491 574659

Anwer Naseem named his restaurant after gentle Indian love songs, for that's what Gazal means. It has nothing to do with guzzling. ('I hope that puts one reporter right, who told me that's why he came here in the first place – to get big portions!' PJ.) He loves the place, though, visiting whenever he's in town. Reports please. Hours: 12-2pm/6-11pm.

VICEROY

40 Hart Street, Henley-on-Thames　　© 01491 577097

A large restaurant seating 100. A good and reliable establishment serving all the usual curries and accompaniments with a few specials thrown in, such as Chingri Jhol (king prawns served in a skillet) and Karahi Kebab Khyberi from the Khyber Pass. Reports please.

Kidlington

OVISHER TANDOORI

11- 13 Oxford Road, Kidlington　　© 01865 372827

M. Bari's smart 80-seater. 'One of my favourite restaurants.' JCC. 'The food was delicious and far too much. I can't think of a better place to do business.' MS. Price check: Papadam 50p, CTM £6.25, Pullao Rice £1.90. Reports please. Stocks Cobra.

Oxford

ALCAZAR

1 The Parade, Windmill Road, Headington, Oxford　　© 01865 760309

'A smallish restaurant serving Balti food. My wife and I had Balti Mughlai, an elegant, subtly-flavoured dish, as good as anything we've ever had. Pullao Arasta Deluxi, very finely-flavoured rice. Service was efficient, courteous and good-humoured. Impressed.' GG. 'One can enjoy a relaxed, unique feast.' DH. Reports please. Stocks Cobra.

AZIZ TOP 100   ©

230 Cowley Road, Oxford   ✆ 01865 794945

Smart 90-seater, white with gold lettering exterior. Inside, very well decorated, cane chairs, plants, subdued lighting, upmarket, sophisticated. Named after its owner, Azizur (Aziz) Rahman, this restaurant is 'one of Oxford's best.' MS. And we know that to be true. Mr Aziz is one of the spearhead founder members promoting Bangladeshi cuisine. There is no reason I can think of why, with 85% of our curry restaurants Bangladeshi, so few specialize in authentic cuisine. That country's capital, Dacca, has a few superb restaurants, most acclaimed of which is the Kastoori. Perhaps the location must be London, but sooner or later it must happen. And there are few better qualified restaurateurs than Mr Aziz and his ambitious colleagues. Meanwhile the Aziz is one place where you will find the Bangladeshi curry house formula done as well as it can be. 'My no 1 favourite.' DR JCC. 'Excellent quality, charming service. Very comfortable and relaxing atmosphere.' RT. 'Decoration immediately impressed. Tables simply but elegantly set with crisp white linen. Good vegetarian selection on menu. Generous quantities and delicately flavoured. Emphasis on subtlety. A splendid meal.' WC. 'Impressive reports confirmed. Mid-week the place was packed. Decor is upmarket and smart, the food well prepared and served in generous quantities. This is where the middle class, the academics and well-off students of Oxford eat and entertain. Service was slow but the place was very busy. Parking can be a problem.' DR PAW. Arramba – to begin, Maach Bora, fish cake with potato, eggs and green chillies £3.50. Chott Pottie, chickpeas, egg and potatoes spiced with coriander £2.75. House Specialities: Murgh Jal Frajee, stir-fried chicken in batter, with fresh chillies – hot £6.15, Jerre Koligi, lamb livers with cummin £6.15. Chitol Bhuna, Bangladeshi fish rolled into Kofta £6.65, Galda Chineri Kodu, king prawns with red pumpkin and green chillies £7.50. Dimm Dall, eggs and red lentils with coconut milk £4.50. Takeaway: 15% discount. Sunday buffet 12-5.30pm, £7.50 per person, children £3.75. Price check: Papadam 45p, CTM £6.25, Pullao Rice £1.85, Misti Nan £2.15. Hours: 12-2pm/6-11.30pm. Sunday 12-11.30pm. New Year's Day closed. High in our TOP 100. Stocks Cobra.

DHAKA BRASSERIE   ©

186 Cowley Road, Oxford   ✆ 01865 200203

Taken over in 1997 by Shams Uddin, seats 40. CC members will get a
percentage off the bill. Takeaway: 20% off. Sunday buffet £6.95.
Minimum charge £8. Price check: Papadam 45p, CTM £6.20, Pullao
Rice £1.85, Peshwari Nan £1.80. Lager £2.40 pint, house wine £6.95.
Delivery: £8 minimum, £6-mile radius. Hours: 12-2.30pm/6pm-12am.

KASHMIR HALAL   ▟ ©

64 Cowley Road, Oxford   ✆ 01865 250165

Opened in 1970 by Said Meah and seats 50 diners. A comprehensive
menu listing all your favourite curries and accompaniments. Halal
meat. Tandoori dishes a speciality of the house. Price check: Papadam
50p, CTM £5.60, Pullao Rice £1.80, Peshwari Nan £1.60. Delivery.
Hours: 12-2.30pm (Fri. closed)/6pm-12am.

Headington

MIRABAI   NEW ENTRANT

70 London Road, Headington   ✆ 01865 762255

Shabbir Ahmed Choudhury 44-seater has 6 cabins for 4 diners and
serves formula curries, CTM, Korma and Balti are most popular.
There is parking for 10 cars at the side and in front of the restaurant.
Price check: Papadam 50p, CTM £5.95, Pullao Rice £1.75, Peshwari
Nan £1.75. Lager £2.20 pint, house wine £6.95, mineral water £2.50.
Delivery: £8.50 minimum, 5-mile radius. Hours: 12-2.15pm/6pm-12am.

MOONLIGHT

58 Cowley Road, Oxford   ✆ 01865 240275

Established in 1974, one of the early ones, by A.L. Haj Wasid Ali. The
function rooms are really stylishly decorated in Wedgwood blue, crystal chandeliers, ornate plasterwork on the ceiling and walls, arches,
hand-painted murals on the walls depicting Royal court life, mounted
elephants hunting tigers and ladies dancing, petrol blue and gold velvet padded seats, blue and white table linen, they seat 75 and 25. The
main restaurant seats 100 and has pink and white table linen, pink pat-

terned velvet chairs. Serves Kashmiri-style curries. Specials include: Fried Fish, spicy chunks of Bangladeshi fish grilled with onions £3.40, Sag Puri, a fried chapati topped with spinach cooked in garlic and butter £2.30. Achari Gosht, sliced pieces of lamb spiced and pickled £5.80, Kashmiri vegetable Biriani, a mixture of vegetables and pulses £4.95. DR JCC.'s no. 2 favourite, and popular with students, too. Price check: Papadam 45p, CTM £5.80, Pullao Rice £1.80. House wine £6.90. Minimum charge £7.50. Hours: 12-2.30pm/6pm-12am. Stocks Cobra.

POLASH TANDOORI TOP 100   ©

25 Park End Street, Oxford   © 01865 250244

Owned by Tina Begum, Samad Ali, Ali Amzed (chef) and S. Islam since '95, seats 60, and has had a new frontage and carpet. The cooking by Mohana Pilliai is well above average and some of the specials are unusual, featuring duck, venison, pheasant and chitol and buaal – Bangladeshi fish, e.g. Buaal Mossala Maachli Samosa, filled with fish £2.75. Aloo Borah, mixture of potato, egg, green chilli £2.50. Brinjal Borah, aubergine mixed with potato, egg and green chilli £2.55. DR JCC. rates it his no. 3. JC (not the same person) says: 'This is quite the best in Oxford. Dishes are light and intriguing with distinctive spicings. Best vegetarian menu for miles. We have yet to tire of it. Starters vary slightly in taste depending on chef, which makes it rather pleasing.' 'We were impressed by the very polite waiters and speed of service.' MS. "I had a Murgh Jalfrezi which was ridiculously hot with green chillies in abundance – to be fair the manager did warn me. Staff were very courteous and apologetic when we were stranded with Papadoms but no pickle tray.' ND. 'Above average but portions small for price. Sheek Kebab £2.90, one kebab cut into five pieces with sprigs of salad. Chicken Jalfrezi with Chapattis and rice, very tasty, portions acceptable, but not generous. Not a TOP 100.' DR PAW. Despite this one voice, we are happy to retain the Polash in our TOP 100. Are we right? Manager Gous Uddin will give a discount to Curry Club members. Open 12-2.30pm/6-11.30pm. Price check: Papadam 45p, CTM £5.95, Pullao Rice £1.75. House wine £7. Hours: 12-2.30pm/6-11pm. Stocks Cobra.

©	Curry Club discount (see page 6)	☕	Unlicensed
√	Vegetarian		
BYO	Bring your own alcohol	⊞	Delivery/takeaway

SHEMON'S INDIAN CUISINE ©

135 High Street, Carfax, Oxford   ✆ 01865 242062

Aabul Kashem's 52-seater has red velvet chairs and sofas, red and white table linen, uplighting and ceiling fans. Special: Biriani, basmati rice, chicken, lamb tikka, mushrooms, prawns and omelette. Takeaway: 10% off. Minimum charge: £5. Price check: Papadam 50p, CTM £6.60, Pullao Rice £1.90, Peshwari Nan £1.90. Hours: 12-2.30pm/6-11.30pm. Stocks Cobra.

TAJ MAHAL

16 Turl Street, Oxford   ✆ 01865 243783

'For location and low price, you can't beat the Taj. But it is very standard high street curry style. It's really nothing special.' DRC JC. Yes, I know, I know, Doc, but it has been on the first floor above Whites since 1937. I simply can't omit it! It was only the third curry restaurant in England at the time and the first outside London, and has always attracted the *cognoscenti* from don to student. 'Varied menu, we chose from the specials. Massive quantities of quality food.' JF. 'Smart comfortable restaurant with splendid views. Karahi Chicken – exceptional, Methi Gosht and Vegetable Curry – very good. We rate them pretty highly.' DR GG. 'Birianis remain outstanding. Huge portions.' DR AGJ.

Thame

DE WANI SHAH'S ©

8 Swan Walk, Thame   ✆ 01844 260066

Daytime this 28-seater is a coffee shop, found behind the Swan Hotel. At night it becomes De Wani (hall of assembly), a licensed Indian restaurant. Nural Isam is owner and chef. DK liked the 'leave-it-to-us' set meal at £9.99. Takeaway: 10% off. Price check: Papadam 40p, CTM £5.50, Pullao Rice £1.65, Peshwari Nan £1.50. Delivery: £10 minimum, 5-mile radius. Hours: 5.30-11.30pm, Tues. closed.

Wallingford

PRINCE OF INDIA

31 High Street, Wallingford   ✆ 01491 837017

Mrs Shelina Begum's formula (CTM is most popular) restaurant seats
40. She tells us she plans a '98 full refurbishment'. Buffet lunch £5.99.
House specials: Murg or Lamb Acher, succulent chicken or lamb in
hot mango pickle £6.25. King Prawn Delight, cooked with Tia Maria
£11.95. Takeaway: 20% off. Price check: Papadam 6op, CTM £6.25,
Pullao Rice £1.60. Delivery: £15 minimum, Wallingford area only.
Hours: 12-2.30pm/6-11.30pm. Stocks Cobra.

Witney

CURRY PARADISE

39 High Street, Witney   ✆ 01993 702187

'Visited on the strength of the review in the Guide which states that
the chef is eager for you to try his curries. Well the rest of the staff
aren't! Not that is if you are a lone diner at 8pm on a Friday night.
Upon entering the restaurant and requesting a table for one, I was met
with a blank no, not at this time! No apology, or explanation. The
restaurant was not full and empty tables did not have reserved signs.
But it was "no" despite protest. I drove eight miles to Woodstock and
ate at the Palace Tandoori, who presented me with a very reasonable
meal.' JMFP. I've kept this restaurant in because it highlights a problem
we hear of often. The singles thing. It's quite outrageous. Who do such
restaraunts think they are? It would really have been no skin off their
noses to serve you. Singles always eat quickly, often in and out within
the hour, leaving the table for a second sitting – their loss! Curry
Paradise failed to return its questionnaire, but is welcome to reply and
will be published next time if it does. Pat and I were turned away from
an Austrian restaurant in Farnham, several years ago. They gave a lame
excuse that they were fully booked, but the restaurant was almost
empty with no signs of reserved tables. We got the definite impression
that we were dressed inappropriately, in jeans and trainers. We have
driven past the often empty restaurant several times, but have never
been back.

RUTLAND

Area: East Midlands
Population: 50,000
Number of restaurants in county: 3
Number of restaurants in Guide: 2

Leicestershire's bureaucratic loss is Rutland's gain. Back again after decades of non-existence, it is once again Britain's smallest county — it is geographically smaller than the city of Birmingham. Our plea last time has yielded the following response. Now DMC knows what they eat with their pints of Ruddles!

Oakham

EVEREST   NEW ENTRANT

28 Gold Overton Road, Oakham   ✆ 01572 724800

Price check: Papadam 35p (plain) 45p (spicy), CTM £5.50, Pullao Rice £1.40, Pickles and Chutneys £1.20 – OUTRAGEOUS. Delivery: £10 minimum, 3-mile radius. Hours: 6-11pm (11.30pm on Fri. & Sat.), closed Tues.

RUTLAND BALTI HOUSE   NEW ENTRANT   ©

18 Mill Street, Oakham   ✆ 01572 757323

Owned/managed by Abdul Khalique, since '95. Formerly Oakham Tandoori, plain white artex walls and ceiling, seats a cosy 32 diners, serves Bangladeshi formula curries. Sunday lunch £5. Takeaway 15% discount if order over £15. Price check: Papadam 40p, CTM £5.60, Pullao Rice £1.60, Peshwari Nan £1.50. Lager £1.90 pint, house wine £7. Hours: 5.30pm-12am (12.30am on Sat.). Sun. 12-3pm/5.30pm-12am.

©	Curry Club discount (see page 6)		Unlicensed
√	Vegetarian		
BYO	Bring your own alcohol	⊞	Delivery/takeaway

SHROPSHIRE

Area: Welsh Border
Population: 405,000
Number of restaurants in county: 43
Number of restaurants in Guide: 10

Bridgnorth

EURASIA

21 West Castle Street, Bridgnorth   ℰ **01746 764895**

The Eurasia is well-established, having opened in 1975. It changed
hands in 1987 to Azadur Rahman and I. Miah. Makni Chicken, Jalfrezi
and Tikka most popular. Price check: Papadam 50p, CTM £7.80 (incl.
Rice), Pullao Rice £1.75. Sunday lunch £5.75. House wine £6.50.
Hours: 12-2pm/6pm-12am. Sunday 1pm-12am. Stocks Cobra.

PUNJAB TERRACE BALTI   NEW ENTRANT

3-5 Mill Street, Bridgenorth.   ℰ **01746 768707**

'The Balti dishes are excellent, the Nan bread enormous and their
special Pullao Rice worth tasting. The restaurant is beamed and has a
lot of character. Well worth a visit.' CB&PD. Price check: CTM £4.85,
Balti Chicken £3.95, Nan £1.10.

Ludlow

SHAPLA BALTI   BYO ©

58 Broad Street, Ludlow   ℰ **01584 875153**

Owner chef Muzibur Rahman and manager Shalim Miah of this 44-
seater are 'enthusiastic and keen to help. Balti Sag, delicious – you wanted
it to go on and on. Naans, massive. Price, very reasonable. The restaurant
also does kebabs and cheeseburgers for philistines!' SR. And Donner
Kebabs, including a Donner Chicken Tikka Kebab (£3.25). BYO is
allowed, no corkage. Price check: Papadam 55p, TM £5.45, Pullao Rice
£1.60, Peshwari Nan £1.55. House wine £8.50. Hours: 12pm-12am. Branch:
Spice Empire, 17, High Street, Cleobury, Mortumere. Stocks Cobra.

Newport

SHIMLA ©

22 St Mary's Street, Newport   © 01952 825322

Set takeaway meals are excellent value at Nurul Islam's restaurant. Balti (£8.95) includes Papadam with mint sauce and onion salad, Tandoori Mix Kebab, Chicken (or Lamb) Tikka Balti, Sag Aloo, Pullao Rice (half-portion) or Nan, and sweet or coffee. Price check: Papadam 30p, CTM £5.95, Pullao Rice £1.50. Minimum charge £10. Open 6pm-12am.

Oswestry

SIMLA ©

42 Beatrice Street, Oswestry   © 01691 659880

Sufu Miah's Simla has been trading since 1976, and seats 100. We'd like more satisfied reports about the food, prices and service. Open daily 12pm-12am. Branch: Simla, 5 Grapes Hill, Llangollen, Clwyd.

Shrewsbury

COPTHORNE BRASSERIE TAKEAWAY

39, Mytton Oak Rd, Shrewsbury   © 01743 270336

'Picture window into Martin Kabir's kitchen. A joy to watch experts at work. Popadoms, onion and lettuce salad and a pot of creamy dip were part of the package and the smell was mouth-watering. I hastened to the car and headed for home. I have to admit that the food was gorgeous. The pieces of chicken in the Vindaloo were huge and succulent and there was a liberal sprinkling of fresh coriander in the sauce, which was aromatic, creamy, thick and wonderfully hot. Salads were crisp with none of the limpness so often associated with takeaway establishments. A delicious meal.' sc. Hours: 4.30pm until 'late.'

SHERAZ

79 Wyle Cop, Shrewsbury   © 01743 351744

Started in 1960, at a time when there were only a few hundred curry houses in the whole UK. Boktiar Uddin took over in 1982, and a best

seller is Balti Rowgoonjus, £4.10. Price check: Papadam 55p, CTM
£6.50, Pullao Rice £1.60. Set meal £12.50. Open daily 6pm-1 am.

Telford

MISTER DAVE'S   🍺 BYO ©

15 Burton Street, Dawley, Telford   ℰ 01952 503955

The very popular Mister Dave's is in fact owned by Mr Mel (Kirton)
who bought the 72-seater in 1988. Decorated with pale green walls,
with dark green paintwork. Authentic Baltis from £3.20 for chicken
and £2.95 for vegetables. Most popular dish Mr Dave's Balti Special,
meat, chicken, prawns, mince and vegetables £4.20. BYO, no corkage.
Papadam 25p, CTM £4.50, Pullao Rice £1, Peshwari Nan £1.50. Hours:
6pm-12am. Sunday closed.

Wem

SHABAB   ©

62b High Street, Wem   ℰ 01939 234333

Say 'Wem' to confirmed curryholic Mick Jagger, and he'll fondly remember Charlie Watkins, the father of rock and roll big sound systems,
whose Watkins Electronic Music amps and speakers achieved the first
ever 1000-watt outdoor system in Hyde Park in 1969. Now you can have
that level of sound in your car if you want to go prematurely deaf! This
has nought to do with ought, except to say that since 1993, when M. Lal
opened his Shabab, with Jay Bhatti as manager, Wem has been known,
locally at any rate, for its good Pakistani curries cooked by Shabir. Price
check: Papadam 40p, CTM £6.75 incl. rice or Naan, Pullao Rice £1.30.
Minimum charge £6.50. Open daily 5.30pm-12am.

Whitchurch

NICE'N'SPICY TAKEAWAY   ⊞ ©

20 Mill Street, Whitchurch   ℰ 01948 662282

Takeaway established in 1996 by manager Abdul Mozid: 'we like to
think that all our dishes are special and reasonably priced.' Decorated
in green and gold, plants, comfortable sofa with patterned curtains

and carpet. Chef's Special: Bombay Chicken, cooked with whole boiled egg and potato £4.30. Price check: Papadam 40p, CTM £4.55, Pullao Rice £1.40 large container only. Hours: 5pm-12am.

SOMERSET

Area: West Country
Population: 465,000
Number of restaurants in county: 43
Number of restaurants in Guide: 19

Bath

THE EASTERN EYE ADDRESS CHANGE ©

8a Quiet Street, Bath ℂ 01225 422323

120-seater, pink and blue with most impressive Georgian interior, owned by Suhan Choudhury. Specials: Mon Pasand – slightly hot, enlivened with herbs and yoghurt £7.50, Shah Jahani – chicken breast, slightly spiced, shallow fried in ghee, blended with homemade cheese and cream £7.50, Sultan Puri Pilau – from Uttar Pradesh, spiced rice with lamb and cashew nuts, served with a gravy £8.95. Price check: Papadam 50p, CTM £6.90, Pullao Rice £1.80. House wine £7.95. Service 10%. Minimum charge: £9. Hours: 12-2.30pm/6-11pm. Stocks Cobra.

JAMUNA ©

9-10 High Street, Bath ℂ 01225 464631

Beautiful upstairs views over an orange grove and Bath Abbey. Authentic Indian decor, carpet and furniture changed mid '97. Seats 64, serves Bangladeshi formula curries. Specials: Akbari Masala, half chicken and minced meat in cream sauce £9.95. Ba-Dhania, cooked with butter beans, fresh coriander and cream £4.95. Service 10%. Takeaway: 10% discount. CC members: 10% discount. Price check: Papadam 40p, CTM £7.15, Pullao Rice £1.80, Peshwari Nan £1.70. Hours: 12-2.30pm/6pm-12am. Stocks Cobra.

RAJPOOT   ©

4 Argyle Street, Bath   ✆ 01225 466833

At Ahmed and Mahmud Chowdhury's 92-seater, they tell us the decor
is 'unique, giving the feeling that you are in India.' Serves Bangladeshi
formula curries. Specials: Chasni Masala, sweet and sour with lime
£6.95. We still get mixed reports. 'They can do a good job, so we're
told, but maybe the clue is on JKG's comments: 'the Choudhurys own
nearly all the Indian restaurants in Bath – Pria, Desh, Spice Avenue,
Ruposhi, Jamuna and Bengal Brasserie, and in Bristol – Ganges and
Ruposhi. Quite a cartel!' JKG. As every year, one blaster, which mono-
poly or not, the Choudhury's must take note of: 'I was staying in Bath
and was interested in an entry in your book over the Rajpoot. You had
expressed doubts over the quality of the restaurant: this is the first time
I have ever made a written complaint about anything, but the food,
quality and service leave much to be desired. Remove the entry from
your book.' NLD. We'll give it one more chance. Takeaway: 10% discount.
CC Members: 10% discount except Set Lunch. Minimum charge £15
per person. Service 10%. Price check: Papadam 50p, CTM £7.95, Pullao
Rice £1.95, Peshwari Nan £1.95. House wine £8.95. Hours: 12-2.30pm
(Sun.-Thurs.)/6-11pm. Stocks Cobra.

RUPOSHI TAKEAWAY   ©

3 Sussex Place, Widcombe Parade, Bath   ✆ 01225 337294

A safe bet, reasonably priced lunch and dinner takeaway-only, managed
by Gous Ali. Price check: Papadam 30p, CTM £4.90, Pullao Rice
£1.20. Branch: Ruposhi, 110 Mount Road, Bath.

Bridgewater

TASTE OF INDIA   NAME CHANGE

31-33 Penel Orlieu, Bridgewater   ✆ 01278 446660

At the former Simla, Biriani is apparently the most popular dish. £6.95
wine. Takeaway: 20% discount. Price check: Papadam 50p, CTM £5.45,
Pullao Rice £1.75. Parking for 20 cars at back of restaurant. Hours: 12-
2pm/5.30pm-12am. Stocks Cobra.

Clevedon

MOGHULS TANDOORI   ©

33 Old Church Road, Clevedon   ✆ 01275 873695

'The place is not much to look at but comfortable enough with booth seating. Started with Chicken Tikka, big, succulent. Followed by Tandoori King Prawn Masala, lovely sauce with cream. Excellent Pullao Rice with chopped almonds and fried onions. Delicious Mixed Vegetable Curry, green peppers, cauli, beans, onion and mange-tout.' MS. Price check: Papadam 35p, CTM £6.75, Bombay Potato £2.25, Pullao Rice £1.75, Chutney/Pickles 30p. Hours: 12-2pm/6pm-12am.

Glastonbury

NEEL AKASH   NAME CHANGE   ©

62 High Street, Glastonbury   ✆ 01458 834104

Formerly Indian Ocean, taken over in March '98. Bangladesh curry house, 36 seats. Specials: Advocaat lamb, lamb cooked with fresh mint, very lightly spiced, flavoured with Advocaat liqueur £5.95. Is that as good as it sounds? MS will have to find out what that's like. and whether 'Glastonbury being a centre for strange religious practices, the menu now has such offerings as Druid Dopiaza or Chicken Solstice.' MS. How about a Sacrificial Shashlik? Reports please! Price check: Papadam 40p, CTM £6.15, Pullao Rice £1.70. Takeaway: 20% discount. Hours: 12-2.30pm/6-11pm.

Midsomer Norton

SHAPLA

43 High Street, Midsomer Norton   ✆ 01761 410479

Tiny, seats 24 diners, serves formula curries, CTM is most popular. LT especially liked their Dandag (sic.) and had not previously heard of their Chicken, Lamb or Prawn Dim (sic.) – 'cooked with egg in a sauce'. Neither have we! Price check: Papadam 35p, CTM £4.95, Pullao Rice £1.60. Takeaway 15% off. Delivery. Hours: 12-2pm/5.30pm-11.30pm. Branch: Tandoori Mahal, 13 Sadler Street, Wells. Next door is Shapla Indian Takeaway (tel. 01761 411887).

Nailsea

TIKKA FLAME

5-6 Ivy Court, High Street, Nailsea ℭ 01275 855700

Sohail J. Elahi's 44-seater is 'decorated in cream with dusky pink comfortable chairs and sofas, white table linen, lanterns hang from the ceiling, golden framed pictures and a pretty English girl in a salwar kameez serving behind the bar.' DD. Moghlai Murgh, chicken cooked in a creamy sauce with almonds, cashews and lychees £5.60. Tikka Biriani, chicken, lamb, prawn, garnished with omelette, tomato and onions £9.95. Takeaway: 10% off. Price check: Papadam 30p, CTM £6.85, Pullao Rice £1.70. Hours: 5.30-12am. Closed Sun.

Portishead

SPICY AROMA TANDOORI ©

Clarence House, High Street, Portishead ℭ 01275 845413

Another Chowdhury family restaurant which has, we hear, settled in well under the management of Samad who, like me, has by now heard all the gags about pongs! So save them for later, and enjoy the good things on offer here, which include in their not over-long menu a number of unusual specialities, such as Cobra Salon. No, it's not a beer cellar – it's chicken, lamb, egg, tomatoes and mushroom and X'cutti (pronounced dja-cewt-ee) – chicken cooked in a coconut, chilli and vinegar-tamarind purée – from Goa. More reports, please.

Taunton

SPICE NIGHTS NAME CHANGE

93-95 Station Road, Taunton ℭ 01823 334361

Formerly Ganges, taken over in February '98 by (manager) A. Muhit. Decorated in greens, padded chairs, green and white tableclothes, fretwork and Indian pictures. Price check: Papadam 50p, CTM £6.50, Pullao Rice £1.80. House wine £6.90. Takeaway: 10% discount. Sunday Buffet £7.95, 6-10. Delivery: £10 minimum, Taunton area only. Hours: 6pm-12.30am. Closed Mon. Stocks Cobra.

UDDINS NEW ENTRANT

23 East Reach, Taunton   ✆ 01823 351555

'Restaurant was clean, attractively decorated and inviting. Food was very good; Nan breads served extra large. A big thumbs up to Uddins – wish we lived nearer, rather than being refugees from hotel food!' SM.

Wellington

TASTE OF INDIA   ©

21 North Street, Wellington   ✆ 01823 667051

Naz Choudhury's Taste is a cosy little a/c 30-seater, which serves , for example, 'home Style: Fish Kurma, Murgee Razzla, Vegetable Kebaba, Achar Gust, Pilaw, chutney and pickle for four £55'. Buffet £9.95. £7.20 wine, also have off-license for takeaway trade. Price check: Papadam 50p, CTM £7.15, Pullao Rice £2.10. Hours: 12-2pm/6pm-12am. Tues. closed. Branch: Tandoori Spice, 12, Higher Street, Cullompton, Devon. Stocks Cobra.

Wells

TANDOORI MAHAL NEW ENTRANT

13 Sadler Street, Wells   ✆ 01749 670240

'Former shop has been converted to a 50-seater formula curry restaurant with standard menu. Shish Kebab pleasant, CTM served onto a cold plate, poor. Pullao Rice small portion, Sag Aloo excellent.' AG.

Weston-super-Mare

AVON TANDOORI   ©

16 Waterloo Street, Weston-super-Mare   ✆ 01934 622622

Opened in May '88, seats 49 diners, managed by A. Hoque, formula and Balti dishes. Specials: Tandoori King Prawn Zalfarazai, lemon juice, capsicum, onion, hot green chillies £10.95. Minimum charge: £7 per person. Takeaway: 10% discount. Price check: Papadam 40p, CTM £7 inc Rice, Pullao Rice £1.60, Peshwari Nan £1.65. House wine £5.50. Hours: 12-2pm/6pm-12am, Sat. 6pm-12.30am, Sun. 6-11.30pm. Stocks Cobra.

CURRY GARDEN   ©

69 Orchard Street, Weston-super-Mare   ✆ 01934 624660

Seats 65, in two dining rooms, Bangladeshi curry house. Owned by
Miah and Ali. Price check: Papadam 40p, CTM £7.15, Pullao Rice
£1.70. Lager £1.90 pint, house wine £5.50. Takeaway: 10% discount.
Minimum charge: £5. Hours: 12-2pm/6pm-12am.

VICEROY

57 Whitecross Road, Weston-super-Mare   ✆ 01934 628235

We hope it continues doing excellent food, service, decor, remember-
ing names, the pond with Koi carp and fountain, etc. If it's so good.
let's hear from it and from you please. Mind you if I delist it, out goes
their main claim to fame – its visit by *Silence of the Lambs'* Anthony
Hopkins (bringing a whole new meaning to Chef's Special!)

Wincanton

MIAH'S   ©

4 Church Street, Wincanton   ✆ 01963 34452

Akthar Hussain's place, serving good curry house food at good prices.

Yeovil

AKASH BALTI   NEW ENTRANT

101 Middle Street, Yeovil   ✆ 01935 472352

'Has become the best for miles around. Situated in one of the less
endearing parts of central Yeovil the premises has a modest 45 covers.
Staff are polite and helpful and service prompt. Cuisine is of the highest standard. Particularly good are the Chicken Dhansak, Patia and
Ceylon dishes, all of which seem to offer a perfect balance between
sweet, sour and spice. Garlic Nan is quite outstanding.' TWB. Hours: 12-
2pm/5.30pm-12am.

STAFFORDSHIRE

Area: North Midlands
Population: 1,041,000
Number of restaurants in county: 79
Number of restaurants in Guide: 21

Cannock

DILSHAD   NEW ENTRANT

1 Cannock Road, Chadsmoor, Cannock   ✆ 01543 570264

Faruk Uddin's a/c, recently decorated 60-seater serves formula curries. Special Combinations, served in a divided dish. Sample two curries in smaller portions. Good idea, eg: CT Patia and Lamb and Mushroom Delight, £6.95. Price check: Papadam 45p, CTM £7.40, Pullao Rice £1.45. Lager £1.95 pint, house wine £7.20. Takeaway: 10% discount. Delivery: £10 minimum, 6-mile radius. Hours: 5.30pm-1am (2am on Sat.).

JASMINE   NEW ENTRANT   BYO ©

**125 Hednesford Road, Heath Hayes,
Cannock   ✆ 01543 279620**

N. Islam's 50-seat Jasmine Balti Special: Prawn, King Prawn and Lobster is £9.75. BYO, no corkage. Minimum charge: £5. Takeaway: 15% discount. Price check: Papadam 40p, CTM £7.25, Pullao Rice £1.40. House wine £6.95. Delivery: £10 minimum, 3-mile radius. Hours: 5-12.30pm, Sat. 5.30pm-1am. Branch: Jasmine, 2nd, Bird Street, Lichfield, Staffordshire. Stocks Cobra.

SANAM BALTI HOUSE   NEW ENTRANT   BYO

193 Cannock Road, Chadsmoor, Cannock   ✆ 01543 573565

'Excellent food and very friendly service. Book or be prepared for a long wait at weekends. It allows you to BYO. Our bill for ten was £64!' Price check: Papadam 35p, Balti CTM £4.95, Pullao Rice £1.10. Open daily 5.30pm-1am (2am on Fri. & Sat.).

Codsall

RAJPUT

The Square, Codsall   © 01902 844642

Its Tudor building could fool you into thinking it's a pub. But it is a
smart place, with an upstairs 'rather cramped restaurant, though the
food is very good, and the service polite and friendly.' DG.

Hednesford

BENGAL BRASSERIE   NEW ENTRANT   ©

44 Market Street, Hednesford   © 01543 424769

Owner Kuti Miah's formula curry house seats 60. Specials: Chicken
Keema Matter — succulent pieces of marinated chicken cooked in a
spicy minced lamb sauce with chickpeas £5.25. Price check: Papadam
40p, CTM £5.75, Pullao Rice £1.50. House wine £6.95. Delivery: £15
minimum, 3-mile radius. Hours: 6pm-12am. Branches: Royal Indian
Brasserie, Albion House, New Quay, Dyfed. Bay of Bengal, Crackwell
Street, Tenby. Dilshad Brasserie, Whitford Street, Holywell, Clwyd.

Kingsley Holt

THORNBURY HALL RASOI   NEW TO OUR TOP 100

Lockwood Road, Kingsley Holt   © 01538 750831

This unusual restaurant is approximately 10 miles east of Hanley (off
the A52) in a renovated Grade II listed building, once a manor house.
Since 1994 it has been owned and managed by Mr and Mrs Siddique,
who have brought style and Pakistani food to this beautiful area. It has
three public areas, including a conference room. The main restaurant
leads from the bar and is decorated in gold and terracotta, ceramic
floor, open fire for winter evenings. The Shalimar room, named after
gardens in Pakistan, is decorated in green and gold, large windows and
doors leading to garden. Dance floor, sparkling globe and sound system. Lahore dining room, large, elegant, richly decorated Georgian
plaster ceiling, swagged curtains and a brass teapot, it nearly reached
the ceiling! Pakistani delicacies are on the menu at the pretty place.
'Could be tricky to find, but my in-laws live close by. The main hall is

very grand, but not always open. Other areas are elegant and comfortable. Service good, including some staff from the village in Pakistani dress. Excellent flavours and quality. Sensible portions.' DR HM. 'Fantastic restaurant. Magnificent settings in a listed building. Kumbi Pullao Arasta Rice cooked with mushrooms was out of this world. Karahi Mogulai, pieces of lamb cooked with cream, egg, ground nuts, garnished with almonds, superb. Karahi Murgh Jalfrezi, cooked in green chilli, ginger, garlic, yoghurt and spices, the best my husband has ever tasted.' MR & MRS C. We're pleased to promote it to our TOP 100. Price check: Papadam 50p, CTM £6.50, Aloo Jeera £3.50, Plain Rice £1.50. Hours: 12-2.30pm/6-11pm (11.30pm on Fri. & Sat.).

Kinver

SHANAJ TANDOORI NEW ENTRANT ©

122 High Street, Kinver ✆ 01384 877744

Three Alis run this 56-seat restaurant. Makmad Ali owns it, Mohammad manages it and Tabaruz cooks. Price check: Papadam 45p, CTM £5.80, Pullao Rice £1.45. Set meal £14.50, veg £10.50. Kurzi Murch £21.50 for two. Open daily 5.30pm-12am.

Leek

PABNA NEW ENTRANT ©

16-18 Ashbourne Road, Leek ✆ 01538 381156

Formerly India garden, Fazz Meah took over in March '98 and completely refurbished. Formula curry house, Rogan Josh most popular, seats 80. Price check: Papadam 45p, CTM £6.25, Pullao Rice £1.45. Lager £2.25 pint, house wine £7.25. Minimum charge: £7.50. Takeaway: 15% discount. Hours: 5.30-12. Reports please.

©	Curry Club discount (see page 6)		Unlicensed
√	Vegetarian		
BYO	Bring your own alcohol	⊞	Delivery/takeaway

Lichfield

EASTERN EYE   TOP 100   ©

19b Bird Street, Lichfield   ✆ 01543 254399

Abdul Salam's redec has achieve plenty of comment. Local artist Jenny Hobbs recreated Swat valley house, right up in Pakistan's northern mountain ranges (just a nan nudge from Baltistan). It is famous for its forests and ornate wooden carved furniture, showing Buddhist influences going back 2,000 years and predating Islam. In the restaurant, the beams, pillars and window are from Swat. The bar front is from neighbouring Afghanistan, the chairs are Rajasthani and the table tops are from 150-year-old elm. 'Count the rings,' enthuses Mr Salam. Internal decorating is by Jane Smith, with her 10-year-old daughter painting the radiators. Tracy Potts did the outside sign, and apparently she decorated the toilets, too. These are a 'must-see' on your list. The theme is Agra's Red Fort – probably India's best example of a Moghul residence. The food is formula done well. Specials include Murgh with Apricot, marinated chicken with apricot yoghurt sauce, cream and fresh coriander £7.45. Rajasthani Paro Breast – pigeon £6.95. Michael Fabricant, MP, MCC (member of the Curry Club) continues regularly to take his seat at the Eye as a loyal local, rating it highly, as do so many other reports we get, e.g.: 'Remains my favourite. Abdul Saleem is a fine host, producing outstanding dishes. Party of eight, a banquet of whole marinated leg of lamb, a huge steamed fish and eight other main dishes, all extremely impressed. Casual atmosphere. Wine list still consists of an armful of bottles placed on your table to take your pick from – a tradition I hope will remain.' PJ. 'Wonderful decor – beautiful old wood tables and hand painted radiators! The food was unusual and beautifully presented on huge oval china plates. Will definitely try it again if we're ever in the area.' K&ST. As with every TOP 100, we get a dissent now and again. The Eye is no exception, and I know Mr Salam takes complaints seriously: 'We were rushed, our food was chosen for us, and, when served, was ordinary and slapped on a plate. There was an air of turnover. The bill of £20 plus per head was a disgrace.' DR MPH. [Was it a Saturday night? Even if yes, it is still not TOP 100 behaviour. -Ed] Reports please. Discounts for CC Members on Sundays. Price check: Papadam 40p, CTM £6.95, Pullao Rice £1.70. House wine £6.95. Hours: 12-2.30pm (Sat. only) 5pm-12am. Stocks Cobra.

LAL BAGU ©

9 Bird Street, Lichfield   ✆ **01543 262967**

Formula curry house, seats 70, proprietor Masum Ahmed Chowdhury. Special: Shorti – chicken, lamb or prawn – cooked with chat masala, slight hot and sour, finely chopped green chillies and fenugreek £4.25. £6.25 wine. Price check: Papadam 40p, CTM £5.95, Pullao Rice £1.60. Delivery: £10 minimum, Lichfield area. Sunday lunch £6.95. Takeaway: orders over £20, free wine, papadam, onion salad and mint sauce. Hours: 12.30-2.30pm Sun. only/5.30pm-12am. Stocks Cobra.

Newcastle-under-Lyme

BILASH ©

22 Keele Road, Newcastle-under-Lyme   ✆ **01782 614549**

Mrs D. Choudhury's curry house, seats 92 in three dining rooms. Special: Akni Chicken – boneless chicken, egg, pineapple, sultanas, almonds, cherries and cashews served with vegetable curry sauce. 'It's by far the plushest restaurant in town, with wood-panel decor, nice cutlery and comfortable seating.' DE. Price check: Papadam 30p, CTM £5.99, Pullao Rice £1.40. House wine £6. Takeaway: 10% off. Hours: 5pm-12.30am. Branch: Monzil, Broad Street, Hanley. Stocks Cobra.

OSSIES NEW ENTRANT   BYO ©

39 Ironmarket, Newcastle-under-Lyme   ✆ **01782 662207**

Formula (CTM is most popular) curry house seats 86 in two dining rooms. Formerly Ali Baba, taken over in late '96 by M. Arshad. BYO no corkage. Minimum charge: £6.95. Price check: Papadam 50p, CTM £5.25, Pullao Rice £1.80. Lager £2 pint, house wine £5.95, Hours: 6pm-1am (3am on Fri. & Sat.).

Perton

FLAMINGO EXQUISITE BANGLADESHI CUISINE

7 Anders Square, Perton   ✆ **01902 745200**

Perton, a village just 3 miles west of Wolverhampton, is the location for Modhu Miah's 50-seater, managed by Rikki Haque. It must get points for the name, says one of our wags, though he speaks more of typical formula curries than exquisiteness. Parking for 10 cars at the rear. Price check: Papadam 50p, CTM £6.15, Pullao Rice £1.55. Delivery: £10 minimum, 7-mile radius. Buffet night on Sunday £5.95. Minimum charge £10. Hours: 5.30-11.30pm. Stocks Cobra.

Rugeley

BILASH   ©

7 Horsefair, Rugeley   ℭ 01889 584234

At Chowdhury, Rofique and Uddin's 90-seater: 'our favourite.' N&GD (party room 48). The specials include Chilli Chicken Tikka, with red and green chillies, served with salad £5.75. Price check: Papadam 45p, CTM £5.95, Pullao Rice £1.60. House wine £7.95. Takeaway: 10% off. Hours: 12-2.30pm/5.30-11.30pm.

GANGES

5 Horsefair, Rugeley   ℭ 01889 582594

Mahub Ahmed Choudhury runs Rugeley's longest-established restaurant. Special: Tandoori Golden Chicken — cooked in a creamy minced-meat sauce, served with salad £7.10. Price check: Papadam 40p, CTM £6.70 (incl. Rice), Pullao Rice £1.50. Delivery: £10 minimum, 5-mile radius, over £20 – 10% discount. Hours: 5.30pm-1am.

Shenstone Woodend

THE LODGE   NEW ENTRANT   BYO ©

The Lodge Cottage, 24 Birmingham Road,
Shenstone Woodend   ℭ 01543 483334

Shenstone Woodend is a small green-belt village on the W Mids border, 4 miles north of Sutton Coldfield. Jamal and Imam Uddin's Lodge is beautifully appointed, with carpet and pine floors, simple chandeliers, white ceiling-roses, arches and cornices, and magnolia walls. 'My family eats as often as possible in this luxurious restaurant with excellent parking facilities. Smart, efficient waiters remember customer names and preferences, and they adore children. Chef Motin Miah excels with a wide variety of Indian cuisine.' RLP. Hours: 5.30pm-12am.

Stafford

SPICE DELIGHT   NEW ENTRANT   ⊞

5a Lichfield Road, Stafford   ✆ 01785 245554

'One of, if not *the* best take-away we have ever tried. The menu boasts
'we only use fresh herbs and best quality spices' and 'the ultimate in
quality' – comments which we wholly endorse!!' MJB.

Stoke-on-Trent

GULSHAN

6-8 Swan Bank, Burslem, Stoke on Trent.   ✆ 01782 833157

'We regularly dine here and have never had reason to complain, the
food being of the highest quality. Extremely friendly welcome.' HLH
'Always receive a warm welcome. Have never been disappointed.
Chicken Tikka £2.50 is most tasty, tender and succulent.' L&BF. Price
check: Papadam 40p, CTM £5.60, Vegetable curries all £1.90, Mixed
Chutney Tray 95p. Delivery. Hours: 5.30pm-1am (2am on Fri. & Sat.).

MONZIL   ©

44 Broad Street, Hanley, Stoke-on-Trent   ✆ 01782 280150

A. Matin's Monzil's 1977, formula curry house, seats 120 in two dining
rooms. Chef's Special: chicken, meat, prawn, mushroom and tomato
with spices and boiled egg. Takeaway: 10% off. Price check: Papadam
25p, CTM £5.99, Pullao Rice £1.40. House wine £5.99. Hours: 7pm-
3am (2am on Sun.). Branch: Bilash, 22 Newcastle-under-Lyme, Staffs.
Stocks Cobra.

Tamworth

FOSTERS YARD HOTEL   NEW ENTRANT

12 Market Street, Polesworth, Tamworth   ✆ 01827 899313

'Party of 5 adults and 2 children under 4 years. Very courteous service,
children especially welcomed.' HS. Price check: CTM £7.45, Pullao
Rice £1.60, Nan £1.15.

Uttoxeter

KOHI NOOR   BYO ©

11 Queen Street, Uttoxeter   © 01889 562153

At S. Miah's 70-seater, specials include Chicken Sath, lemon flavoured vegetables (Shatkora), coriander, garlic herbs and spices, £5.95. 'Interesting decor, early curry house style, red velvet chairs and '70's carpet. Food good. Mixed Kebab starter average but Chicken Jalfrezi was hot and spicy, downed with three Chapattis. Good value.' PAW. CC members in parties of 10 or more will get a percentage off the bill, so gather up friends and family! Allows BYO, no corkage. Price check: Papadam 50p, CTM £4.95, Bombay Potato £1.95, Pullao Rice £1.50. Lager £2 pint, house wine £7. Delivery: £20 minimum, 3-mile radius. Hours: 5.30pm-12am (1am on Fri. & Sat.). Stocks Cobra.

SUFFOLK

Area: East
Population: 644,000
Number of restaurants in county: 53
Number of restaurants in Guide: 14

Brandon

BRANDON TANDOORI   ©

17-19 London Road, Brandon   © 01842 815874

Arjad Ali's 70-seater opened here in 1991, just a runway length from USAF Lakenheath. But the roar of the FIII's is drowned out here by the roar of the tandoor, and the roar of approval from the locals. Our aero-med colonel pilot has retired back to the Midwest corn-bowl of America but still writes that he and his Suffolk wife miss their curries: 'I got my wings on Phantom jets, and again on the Brandon's Chicken Garlic Chilli, £6.10. It's hotter than my bird's jet pipe!' (We don't think he's referring to his wife!) 'The food is always of a wonderful quality, quickly and cheerfully served, and you can always rely on it when taking friends from India. My mouth waters at the memory of the last Murghi Massala, marinated spring chicken, cooked with mincemeat, peas, potato and tomato, £6.10. Book well in advance especially on Saturdays!' RE. Price check: Papadam 40p, CTM £6.20, Pullao Rice £1.70. House wine £6.90. Takeaway: 10% off. Minimum charge: £10. Hours: 12-2pm/6-11pm.

Bury St Edmunds

MUMTAZ INDIAN   ©

9 Risbygate Street, Bury St Edmunds   ℰ **01284 752988**

Formula curry house, seating 44, opened in 1974 by Syed Nurul Haque, who tells us that during the Falklands War, he was asked to cook curries for the soldiers. His food was flown out by military aircraft and he believes that because the troops ate his food they won the war! Who am I to argue? Special Set Thai dinner: Onion Bhajai, Vegetable Curry, Chana Masala, Tarka Dal, Pullao Rice, Puri and curry sauce £6.50. Takeaway: 10% off. Minimum charge: £6.50. Price check: Papadam 50p, CTM £5.90, Pullao Rice £1.75. Delivery: £10 minimum, 12-mile radius. Hours: 12-2.30pm/6-12am (12.30am on Sat.). Stocks Cobra.

Felixstowe

BOMBAY NITE   ©

285 High Street, Walton, Felixstowe   ℰ **01394 272131**

Standard curry house, serving the formula. Owned and managed by Mahbub Alam. Seats 60 in three rooms, seating divided into booths. Decorated in cream and green. Price check: Papadam 30p, CTM £5.75, Pullao Rice £1.30. Lager £1.90 pint, house wine £7.50. Takeaway: 15% discount. Hours: 12-2.30pm/6-11.30pm.

©	Curry Club discount (see page 6)		Unlicensed
√	Vegetarian		
BYO	Bring your own alcohol		Delivery/takeaway

Hadleigh

ROYAL BENGAL

51 High Street, Hadleigh   ✆ **01473 823744**

'Small restaurant, well-lit, warm and comfortable. Chicken Tandoori
Biryani, £8.50, good quality and flavour; Chicken Tikka Madras, £6.75
approx, was too mild, unmemorable; Nan very good, Onion Bhaji
£1.80 very good.' NS. [Better order Phal next time, Nigel!]

Halesworth

RUCHITA   ©

26 Market Place, Halesworth   ✆ **01986 874524**

E. Miah and Z. Allam run this 60-seater, with able assistance from
John Gomez in the kitchen, whose handiwork is highly regarded. Try
the King Prawn Re Jala, in cream with dry fruits, very mild spices £6.95
or the Chicken Patiwala, £6.95, diced chicken cooked with cheese, yoghurt, garlic, garnished with stuffed tomato and capsicum. Price check:
Papadam 40p, CTM £5.20, Pullao Rice £1.30. House wine £5.85.
Hours: 12-2.30pm/6-11.30pm.

Ipswich

JORNA TAKEAWAY   NEW ENTRANT

29-33 Wherstead Road, Ipswich   ✆ **01473 680635**

Enjoy coffee and Bombay mix while waiting for your order at Idris
Ali's takeaway. Chef's Special, tandoori chicken cooked with minced
meat in a rich sauce, served with Special Fried Rice and green salad
£6.50. Price check: Papadam 50p, CTM £4.20, Pullao Rice £1.40.
Delivery: £12 minimum, 3-mile radius. Hours: 5-11.30pm.

TAJ MAHAL   ©

40-42 Norwich Road, Ipswich   ✆ **01473 257712**

Kamal Uddin's Taj Mahal opened its doors in 1964. ['It's older than
me.' DBAC] It seats 60, serves formula curries, but 'anything can be
arranged.' Special: Achar Chicken Masala, with pickled spices £4.95.

CC members will get 10% off the bill. Takeaway: 20% off. Price check: Papadam 50p, CTM £5.25, Pullao Rice £1.40. Lager £2.50 pint, house wine £5.95. Takeaway: 20% discount. Hours: 12-2pm/6pm-12am.

Lowestoft

AHMED   ©

150 Bridge Road, Oulton Broad, Lowestoft ✆ 01502 501725

Boshor Ali's cute little restaurant has just 28 seats. 'Brilliant.' says PJ. Open 12-2.30pm/6-11.30pm. Branch: Jorna Indian Takeaway, 29-33 Wherstead Road, Ipswich.

SEETA   ©

176 High Street, Lowestoft   ✆ 01502 574132

Is a 28-seater the norm round here? It's not why M. and M.M. Uddin chose that name. (Groan! esp. since it's last time's gag!) Sita is the Indian goddess of beauty and love. Alternatively, the Sitar is the melodic Indian stringed instrument. Now you'll remember the name! Either way, you like the Seeta. It's a pretty restaurant, with dusky pink walls, white ceiling, ornate plaster cornice and ceiling rose. Ceiling fan and brass light fittings, green velvet chairs, napkins, white table linen. It has the usual curries and accompaniments on the menu including, we're told, fresh scampi on request in the curries. But we think this is unique . . . You may order the 'Staff Curry' but please order the day before, so head chef Motin Uddin, can make extra portions. Price check: Papadam 45p, CTM £6.55, Pullao Rice £1.75. Takeaway: 10% discount. Hours: 12-1.30pm/6-11pm. Closed Tues. Stocks Cobra.

Newmarket

ARIF INDIAN RESTAURANT

30-32 Old Station Road, Newmarket   ✆ 01638 665888

Messrs Ahmed and Ahadi opened the Arif in 1995, and already we hear that you have to jockey for a seat on race days, in this now very popular, attractive restaurant. 'Our friends took the trouble to think ahead, and book ahead, for the Khurzi Lamb (£58 for four). It's a whole leg of lamb, apparently marinated for ever, and slowly cooked for ever in the oven, until it is too tender to believe. They do something with red wine in the cooking, but we can't fathom what. Anyway, who cares? It's a great way to be entertained by our friends. For over three hours we were stuffed full of papadoms, chutneys, starters, the magical lamb, curry side dishes, special fried rice, house wine, coffee, fabulous service and good will, at the end of which we simply rolled home in a taxi, and our friends have no washing up to do!.' JMCA. Price check: Papadam 50p, CTM £5.95, Pullao Rice £1.60. Hours 12-2.30pm/6pm-12am. Stocks Cobra.

NEWMARKET INDIAN CUISINE   NEW ENTRANT

150 High Street, Newmarket   ✆ 01638 660973

N. Ali (manager) and A.Uddin's (chef) formula restaurant seats 50 and specialises in Tandoori dishes. Price check: Papadam 60p, CTM £6.70, Pullao Rice £1.90. House wine £8.90. Takeaway: 10% off. Hours: 12-2.30pm/6-11.30pm (12am on Fri. & Sat.). Stocks Cobra.

Stowmarket

ROYAL TANDOORI   ©

16-18 Tavern Street, Stowmarket   ✆ 01449 674392

M. Ahmed and S. Miah's 60-seater is situated in a white Georgian building, in two blue and pink rooms with matching curtains and carpet. Formula curry house, seats 60. 'Food is gorgeous.' PJ. 'Once I got used to the idea of curry gravy with Chicken Jalfrezi, it was decidedly delicious.' LG. Price check: Papadam 60p, CTM £6.95, Pullao Rice £1.60. Lager £2.50 pint. Hours: 12-2.30pm/6-11.30pm.

Wickham Market

BENGAL

70 High Street, Wickham Market   ✆ 01728 747767

Opened '95 by Motin Khan, seats 42, serves formula curries, all favourites are there. Situated in a 16th-century beamed property. Takeaway: over £10 – 10% discount. Hours: 12-2pm/6-11pm. Closed Monday.

Woodbridge

ROYAL BENGAL TOP 100   ©

6 Quay Street, Woodbridge   © 01394 387983

We never seem to have much to say about Mr Malik's 52-seater. Yet it remains in our TOP 100, simply because it is CC (currinarily correct) in all departments. Amazingly, in all these years we have never had a complaint (we tempted fate with this comment last time). It must be the only TOP 100 not to have had one. The venue is spotlessly clean, including the toilets. The welcome is warm. The service is efficient, friendly, accurate, and positive. The untoward is handled with experience and tact, such as late arrivals, customer ordering error, spillages and small things that can become big things, such as a corked bottle of wine, spotted by the waiter and removed before comment was needed by the clients. There is nothing over-remarkable about the items on the attractive menu. But everything is here, and everything is cooked well, and everything is above average. Even the departure is handled well. Customer care is uppermost. A curryhouse should be as the pub is in the local area. It should be a place where locals can be comfortable, unwind, enjoy and not feel overcharged. This restaurant is all of these things. And if other restaurants modelled themselves on these simple rules everyone would be a TOP 100 restaurant, but then I suppose there would be no need for our Guide at all. Congratulations to you, Mr Malik and your staff. Price check: Papadam 45p, CTM £6.95, Pullao Rice £1.50. Lager £2.70 pint. Hours: 12-2pm/6-11pm.

SURREY

Area: Home counties (south of London)
Population: 1,033,000
Number of restaurants in county: 353
Number of restaurants in Guide: 63

Parts of Surrey were absorbed by Greater London in 1965. We note affected boroughs with the letters GL.

Addington, GL

SURUCHI ©

120 Headley Drive, New Addington ✆ **01689 841998**

50-seater formula curry house, run by Aklis Miah, with manager Junel Ali. Set Dinner: £9. Sunday lunch £6.95. Price check: Papadam 40p, CTM £6, Pullao Rice £1.50. Delivery: £9 minimum, 3-mile radius. Hours: 5.30-11.30pm. Sun. 12-3pm/5.30-11pm. Stocks Cobra.

Ashford

SHAPPI OF ASHFORD

7 Church Parade, Church Road, Ashford ✆ **01784 423266**

'Reasonably impressed with the quality and price. Onion Bhaji £1.55, Prawn Dhansak £3.65, Chicken Biryani £4.95, Pullao Rice £1.45 and Peshwari/Keema Nan £1.35. A decent local.' SR. Stocks Cobra.

Ashtead

BALTI HOUSE NEW ENTRANT

1-5 Rectory Lane, Ashtead ✆ **01372 277245**

Formerly Ashtead Tandoori. Seats 60, formula curry house. Gourmet night, Tuesday and Sunday buffet £6.95. Six parking spaces at the side of the restaurant. Price check: Papadam 50p, CTM £5.95, Pullao Rice £1.75. House wine £7.75. Takeaway: 10% off. Delivery: £12 minimum, 3-mile radius. Hours: 12-2.30pm/6pm-12am.

MOGHUL DYNASTY   ©

1 Craddock Parade, Ashtead   ✆ 01372 274810

Established in '86 managed by Adbul Mannan. Nicely decorated in
cream with white pillars, table linen, green plants, wooden chairs with
blue velvet seating, colonial fans. Formula curry house, CTM being
most popular. Price check: Papadam 70p, CTM £6, Pullao Rice £1.90.
Lager £2.90 pint, house wine £7. Takeaway: orders over £12, 10% off.
Minimum charge: £8.50. Hours: 12-2.30pm/5.30-11pm.

Banstead

BANSTEAD TANDOORI   ©

6 High Street, Banstead   ✆ 01737 362757

A/c curry house owned by Mr Ali. Balti dishes available. Minimum
charge: £8.50. Price check: Papadam 5p, CTM £5.95, Pullao Rice £1.75.
Lager £2.10 pint, house wine £8.20. Takeaway: 10% discount. Hours: 12-
2.30pm/6-11.30pm.

Bramley

CHAMPAN TANDOORI

High Street, Bramley, Nr Guildford   ✆ 01483 893684

'A delightful little restaurant. Seating split between two beamed rooms,
the smaller one is almost like a private dining room and would be great
for an exclusive party, seating about ten. I always order CTM as my
benchmark and can tell you that it is superb, the chef adds puréed
mango chutney which gives it a slightly sweet but tangy flavour.' DBAC.
'Small but cosy. Best Chicken Murgh I've ever had – so garlicky !' SV.

Byfleet

RED ROSE OF BYFLEET   ©

148-150 High Road, Byfleet   ✆ 01932 355559

An attractively decorated restaurant, with plaster cornices and dado
rails. Ivies and palms divide tables and chandeliers hang from the ceilings. King Prawn dishes are house specialities. Average prices.

Managing partner, Shuel Miah, enjoys giving a red rose to the lady on departure. Hours: 12-2.30pm/6-11.30pm. Branches: Gaylord, Weybridge; Red Rose, of Surbiton, Red Rose of Chessington.

Camberley

FRIMLEY TANDOORI TAKEAWAY   ▦ ©

47 High Street, Frimley, Camberley   © **01276 685537**

Established '85 by Hassan Ahmed (manager) and Hussain Ahmed (chef). 'In an effort to salvage an evening wrecked by a [now delisted] Camberley curry house, we decided to collect a takeaway and go home. As a recent convert to vegetarianism, I have not long left behind the delight of their Chicken Vindaloo. The staff were quite happy to cater for my new taste. Complimentary Popadoms and Onion Salad, service indeed!' ws. Popular lunch specials: Chicken Tikka Roll or Kebab Roll £2.95. Price check: Papadam 35p, CTM £6.10, Pullao Rice £1.55. Luncheon Vouchers accepted. Hours: 12-2pm/6-11.30pm.

POLASH TAKEAWAY   NEW ENTRANT

224 Frimley Green Road, Frimley Green,
Camberley   © **01252 834500**

Formula curries from chef/owner G. Khan. Special: Tropical Nawabi Balti, combination of chicken and lamb tikka, tandoori chicken and sheek kebab, served with Rice or Nan £7.25. 20 parking spaces in front. Price check: Papadam 40p, CTM £5.85, Pullao Rice £1.65. Delivery: £12 minimum, 3-mile radius. Hours: 5.30-11.30pm.

RAJPUR   ©

57d Mytchett Road, Mytchett, Camberley   © **01252 542063**

Manager Abdul Motin tells us his 46-seater is 'plush with Bengali paintings, comfortable cushioned seating, and a bright interior.' You tell us 'The food is outstanding. I commend the chef, Mr Khan, who I have followed to this restaurant. He can prepare a meal to your specifications, especially in terms of hotness. The sauces are very good, they use freshly ground spices and herbs.' DM. Special: Bangladesh Style Tandoori Masala, tandoori chicken, boneless, thick mild spicy sauce £5.95. Banquets Weds. evenings £9.95. CC members 10% discount.

Price check: Papadam 40p, CTM £6.20, Pullao Rice £1.70. Lager £2.95 pint, house wine £6.95. Takeaway: 10% off. Sunday buffet lunch £6.50, £3.95 kids. Hours: 12-3.30pm/6-11pm.

TARIQ'S INDIAN BRASSERIE

369 London Road, Camberley   🕐 01276 66441

Opened in 1995. 'Built up an excellent reputation in my eyes! Restaurant beautifully decorated with tasteful background music to add to the ambience. Staff are first-class, polite, helpful and attentive when required. Ample portions. Chicken Vindaloo (£4.20) could have been slightly more spicy for my own taste, I'll ask for that next time. Home-delivery service available.' WPS. Price check: Papadam 35p, CTM £6.20, Pullao Rice £1.60. Hours: Mon.-Sat. lunch & dinner, Sun. dinner only. Stocks Cobra.

Carshalton, GL

ASIA STANDARD   ©

140-142 High Street, Carshalton   🕐 0181 647 0286

Reliable, good curry house of managing owner, Abdul Hannan. Open 12-2.30pm/6-11.30pm. Stocks Cobra.

CLAY OVEN TAKEAWAY   ⊞ ©

15a Gordon Road, Carshalton Beeches   🕐 0181 647 9190

A takeaway-only establishment, opened in 1992 by Hermon Miah. Hours: 5.30-11.30pm. Branch: Gaylord, 141 Manchester Road, Isle of Dogs, London E14.

ROSE HILL TANDOORI   ©

320 Wrythe Lane, Rose Hill, Carshalton   🕐 0181 644 9793

A wee 30-seater, est. 1982, owned by Salequr Rahman, manager Mr E. Rahman, and unusually at a formula curry house, a lady chef, Mrs Rahman — a family business. And I bet if you ask she'll cook really authentic Bangladeshi food. I see Confederates' Coffee, made with Southern Comfort — nice one! Price check: Papadam 30p, CTM £3.50, Pullao Rice £1.40. House wine £5. Delivery: £12 minimum, 1½-mile radius. Minimum charge: £7 per head. Hours: 12-2pm/5.30pm-12am. Stocks Cobra.

Chipstead

CHIPSTEAD TANDOORI

32 Station Approach, Chipstead   © 01737 556401

Established in 1988, Abdul Munaim's 50-seater has a loyal following and a good London pedigree (*see* branches) seats 50. Recommendation: Balti dishes. Takeaway: 10% off. Price check: Papadam 35p, CTM £5.50, Pullao Rice £1.50. Lager £2.70 pint, house wine £6.50. Hours: 6-11pm (11.30pm on Sat.). Branches: Delhi Brasserie, Cromwell Road, Kensington; and Frith Street, WC2.

Cobham

COPPER CHIMNEY   ©

40 Portsmouth Road, Cobham   © 01932 863666

Abdul Alam and P.H. Choudhry's 72-seater is in two rooms of a quaint old building with lots of little alcoves, wooden beams decorated in peach and dusky apricot with rich damask tablecloths with matching napkins, and a fresh flower on each table. Chef Shaid Miah's 'menu is marvellous. Popadoms and relishes very good, one Popadom provided with the compliments of the waiter. King Prawn Suka, a large prawn pan-fried with a lovely thick, rich, slightly sweet and very oniony sauce £4.95. Onion Bhajias, four smallish spheres, very well spiced and not too stodgy. Butter Chicken £7.95, excellent. Pullao Rice, lovely texture. Nan, circular, quite light and deep. Salmon Kedgeree, unusual and good, very large plateful, spoiled by a large pile of inappropriate salad, served with thick lentil dhal. Brinjal Stuffed £2.95, two small aubergines, split, spread with spices and served in a rich creamy sauce, very good, not seen before. Service was absolutely first class, a very personable young waiter with a large smile, a full knowledge of the menu and competence added a great deal to the evening.' HC. Sunday lunch £7.95. £8.95 wine. Price check: Papadam 50p, CTM £6.95, Pullao Rice £1.75. Delivery: £15 minimum order, 3-mile radius. Hours: 12-2.30pm/6-11.30pm. Stocks Cobra.

Cranleigh

CURRY INN   NEW ENTRANT ©

214 High Street, Cranleigh © 01483 273992

Bangladeshi formula curry restaurant, smart, bamboo chairs, palm
trees, sugar pink table linen. Seats 93 diners, Bhel Puri dishes are most
popular, well spiced with lemon, mint , bay leaves, methi (fenugreek)
and dallcani (cinnamon), from £5.95. 16 car parking spaces at back of
restaurant. Curry Club members: 10% discount. Sunday lunch £6.95.
Price check: Papadam 50p, CTM £6.10, Pullao Rice £1.60. Lager £2.35
pint, house wine £7.95. Hours: 12-3pm/6-11.30pm. Stocks Cobra.

Croydon, GL

AKASH   NEW ENTRANT BYO ©

79 London Road, West Croydon © 0181 686 4464

Abdul Muktadir and Abdul Hussain look after the kitchen and the
front respectively. Croydon's price-war makes it one of the cheapest
around, made even more economical by BYO and the Curry Club discount. Price check: Papadam 30p, CTM £3.20, Balti Special £3.50,
Pullao Rice £1. Set meal from £5.50. Minimum charge £5. Hours: 12.30-
2.30pm/6pm-12am. Stocks Cobra.

BANANA LEAF ©

27 Lower Addiscombe Road, Croydon © 0181 688 0297

Taken over in '97 by Mr D. Sitha Raman. Masala Dosa is the most
ordered dish. 'Not very familiar with South Indian food, decided to
experiment. A small restaurant, tidy, clean and fresh. Friendly waiters.
Pappadams (65p), huge, crisp and fresh served with a variety of dips
(£1.30) and onion salad. Bonda (£1.95), hot, crisp, sensitively spiced
with a small bowl of curry sauce. Onion Dosai (£2.80), freshly cooked
with golden onions and fresh coconut chutney. King Prawn Fried
(£8.45), certainly had a good kick. I paid by credit card and when the
slip was presented to me the bottom line had been filled in, pleased me
tremendously!' LH. Price check: Papadam 35p, CTM £5.50, Pullao Rice
£1.85, Lager £2.30 pint, house wine £7.50. Hours: 12-2.30pm/6-11pm.
Stocks Cobra.

THE DEANS   BYO ALLOWED

241 London Road, Croydon   © 0181 665 9192

The Deans opened in 1993 and is named after its chef-owner Salam Ud Din and manager Zaka Ud Din. It is a massive, fully-licensed restaurant seating over 150 diners in two dining rooms, decorated in white with 'sparkly' mosaic mirror Indian arches to be found in the Moghul palaces. It has a small but typically authentic Pakistani Punjabi menu, serving tandoori items and well-spiced curries. Specials: Handi dishes, chicken £4.90, Methi Gosht £5. Handi Aloo Chana £3.50, Dhal-stuffed Karela (bitter gourd) £5. 'Always use their home delivery service.' sw. 'My favourites include the Karahi Fish and the Handi Palak Chicken. Bearing in mind the range of satisfying vegetarian dishes, it is possible to eat well for £6 or £7.' JDL. 'Rows and rows of fairly plain tables, often packed full. What we like about it is the number of Asians in the place, probably something like 80%, which is generally a good sign of the standards and quality offered. The food comes predominantly in iron karahis or earthenware pots (handis), which makes the whole meal look that much more interesting besides helping to retain heat in the food.' CD. BYO no corkage. Price check: Papadam 30p, CTM £5.50, Pullao Rice £1.50. House wine £7.50. Delivery: £10 minimum, 3-mile radius. Hours: 12-2.30pm/6-11.30pm (10.30pm on Sun.). Stocks Cobra.

INDIA PALACE   NEW ENTRANT

79 High Street, Croydon   © 0181 686 6730

'Decor is all pastel pinks and blues and there are fountains, hanging plants and so on. An Indian suite is available for private parties – seats 50. Unusual starters include Crab Claws £2.50 – rolled in breadcrumbs and deep-fried, side dishes Paneer Tikka Masala £3.95 – homemade cheese marinated, half done in the tandoor and cooked in a spicy sauce. Chicken Malai Kebab for me – I don't know what a "white tandoori sauce" is, but it was beautiful. Karahi Gosht for Salma, which was also wonderful. We were completely stuffed at the end of it!' SM. Price check: Papadam 30p, CTM £5.50, Bombay Potato £3.25, Pullao Rice £1.95. Hours: 12-3pm/6-11pm (12am on Fri. & Sat., 10pm on Sun.).

ROYAL TANDOORI 2

226 Addington Road, Selsdon, Croydon   © 0181 651 3500

M.B. Quadir's attractive 72-seater is decorated in green, with engraved glass panels separating diners. Restaurant is partitioned by plants, which splits up the large and long room. A few interesting dishes on the menu include Veal Karahi, Quail Karahi and Tandoori Trout. Kurma Tikka Masala most popular. Minimum charge: £7.20. Price check: Papadam 70p, CTM £7.10, Pullao Rice £1.65. House wine £8.95. Delivery: £15 minimum. Hours: 12-3pm/6-11.30pm. Sat. 6pm-12am. Branch: Royal Tandoori (1), 209, Godstone Road, Whyteleafe, Surrey. Stocks Cobra.

RUPALI TAKEAWAY   NEW ENTRANT   ⊞ ©

337 Brighton Road, South Croydon   © 0181 686 8460

M.A. Miah's popular takeaways include Chicken Jhalfrezi and King Prawn Ghalfry. Price check: Papadam 40p, CTM £3.75, Pullao Rice £1.25. Delivery: £10 minimum, 3-mile radius. Hours: 5pm-12am.

RUPEES TAKEAWAY   ©

184 Wickham Road, Shirley, Croydon   © 0181 655 1866

Enamul Karim Khan and chef Chand Miah's takeaway offers a view of the clean, tidy, well organised open kitchen. Specials: Lamb Chop Bhuna £5.95. Chilli Nan £1.40. Price check: Papadam 35p, CTM £4.95, Pullao Rice £1.40. Delivery: £8 minimum, 4-mile radius. Hours: 5-11pm.

SOUTH INDIA

16 London Road, Croydon   © 0181 688 6216

G. Dinamani and S. Vaman's licensed south Indian restaurant serves lovely vegetarian dishes; the former (ex-Sree Krishna, SW17) heads the kitchen and the latter is manager. There are also south Indian carnivorous dishes (though no tandoor, no CTM, and no formula items!) Try the Meat Fry (£4.90) – made dry with coconut and spicy with red chilli. And in-betweenies will love the Fish Curries £4.50 and Kerala Prawn Curry, tamarind and tomatoes £6.90. Oothappam (£2.50 – spicy pizza, Masala Dosai £2.50 – stuffed pancake, with potato curry,

Kalan (£2) – yoghurt curry with mangoes and Coconut Chutney (50p). Specials: Idli Sambar, steamed rice and lentil cakes served with sambar and coconut chutney £3.50. Thoran, green beans, green banana or cabbage, stir-fried lightly with curry leaves and coconut £2.20. 'Renowned for vegetarian creations. Marvellous food. Love the Do Piaza, the second batch of onions are actually fried and sprinkled on top, which you don't always see. Roast Masala, turned out to be one of those pancake things rolled up and stuffed with potato curry – about 3-feet long – delicious, very light, crispy and came with Sambar and Coconut Chutney. Cheap prices.' sw. Masala Dosa and Sambar most popular dishes. Price check: Papadam 60p, Pullao Rice £2.20. Lager £2.20 pint, house wine £7.90. Hours: 12-2.30pm/6-11pm. Monday evening closed.

Dorking

ASSAM NEW ENTRANT   ⊞

Unit 6, Old Char Wharf, Station Road, Dorking   ✆ 01306 886660

'A delivery service only. As many will realise, when one has a young child it severely restricts the ability to visit restaurants. The Assam is the ideal solution. The food that is prepared is of a very good standard and although they sometimes seem to have a lot of problems keeping to their 45-minute delivery time, the food is also cheap and extremely plentiful.' GF. Price check: Papadam 35p (plain), 40p (spicy), CTM £5.30, Pullao Rice £1.65. Delivery: £10 minimum, 3-mile radius. Hours: 5.30pm-12am.

MOGHUL

187 High Street, Dorking   ✆ 01306 876296

The best in town, says pw: 'Wide choice of meals consumed, all up to usual high standards.' Stocks Cobra.

©	Curry Club discount (see page 6)	☕	Unlicensed
√	Vegetarian		
BYO	Bring your own alcohol	⊞	Delivery/takeaway

East Molesey

GOLDEN CURRY ©

19 Hampton Court Parade, East Molesey   ✆ 0181 979 4358

A. Aziz's traditionally decorated 52-seater has been going since 1967. Three generations of regulars go for a stable, quality operation and friendly service, led by head waiter Abdul Karim. Sunday lunch £4.95. Minimum charge: £6. Takeaway: 10% off. Price check: Papadam 45p, CTM £5.50, Pullao Rice £1.70. House wine £6.25. Hours: 12-2.30pm/6pm-12am. Stocks Cobra.

PALACE INDIAN CUISINE NEW ENTRANT ©

20 Bridge Road, East Molesey   ✆ 0181 979 1531

E. Eshad's 60-seater is yards from Hampton Court palace. 'It's a wonderful place for a leisurely meal in a conservatory, perfect for warm summer evenings.' DD. Chef's special: Murag Tikka Rajella, yoghurt based, spicy cooked with massala sauce and fresh garden mint £6.10. Price Check: CTM £6.10, Pullao Rice £1.75. House wine £7. Minimum charge: £8. Takeaway: 10% discount. Delivery: £12 minimum, 2-mile radius. Hours: 12-2.30pm/6-11.30pm. Stocks Cobra.

Epsom

INDIA GARDEN NEW ENTRANT

132 High Street, Epsom.   ✆ 01372 722617

'All the food was well prepared, looked appetising on arrival and was in well sized portions. Definitely deserves to be in the guide.' HJC.

LE RAJ TOP 100

211 Firtree Road, Epsom Downs   ✆ 01737 371371

I said last time that owner-chef Enam Ali's cooking is light and innovative, and includes some Bangladeshi specials. There is no doubt that Enam, leader of the Bangladeshi Caterers' Association (BCA), is very capable, his brother, Tipu a good lieutenant and manager. But 'I sincerely worry that his outside interests are affecting things at the restaurant. A good tweak on the tiller is needed now.' Enam will agree I am a great supporter of him and his BCA. My Bangladeshi Cookbook was inspired by him, and no one wishes the trade to serve authentic Bangladeshi curries alongside the formula more than I do. So the criticism was intended to inspire Enam back into the kitchen. When I recently met him face to face, he quizzed me on my comments. I repeated that since he was not attempting to do formula curries, regular appearances are essential in the kitchen to maintain the standards he himself had set. I think this is vital for all restaurants. Names like Nick Nairn, Gary Rhodes, Worrall-Thompson, Brian Turner, Rick Stein and Cyrus Todiwalla soon find their signature quickly fades if they fail to make regular, preferably hands-on kitchen forays. Enam agreed and told me that in 1998 he has spent more time at the restaurant, including overseeing a much-needed expansion to 110 seats, now in two rooms. Much-needed because it is not from Enam's devoted locals who fill the place that I get the 'disappointed' comments. It is from those who, having read this Guide, treck to outer Epsom (it's on the A240/A2022). I have to say that I have had far fewer reports either praising or not this year, but maybe that's because we demoted it from the Top 100. I'm returning it now, because I believe Eman meant what he said. We'll see if you report, please! Incidentally, ask for it spicy if that's how you like things. Specials: Bahar E Sammunder, Bangladeshi fresh water fish cooked with fresh herbs £11.50. Murgh E Shandan, delicate strips of supreme chicken in a hot fragrant sauce £10.95. Sabzi Halim, mixed vegetable cooked in lentils, lime juice and chilli £5.95. Minimum charge: £15. Price check: Papadam 65p, CTM £7.50, Pullao Rice £2.50. Lager £2.95 pint. Hours: 12-2.30pm/5.30-11pm.

SAVAR BALTI HOUSE   ©

21 Waterloo Road, Epsom   ℭ 01372 724167

The menu has many old favourites and some nice changes, such as Salmon Samosa, Duck Muglai, Bangladeshi Fish, Shatkora Chicken or Lamb cooked with Bangladeshi citrus fruit or Savar Special, spring chicken hot with green chillies. Despite this, owner Moin Uddin tells us Tikka and Korma are the most popular dishes. As I always say, if we wish to see the call for authenticity maintained, we must encourage, order and enjoy these more authentic dishes. Price check: Papadam 40p, CTM £5.10, Pullao Rice £1.50. House wine £5.50. Delivery: £10 minimum, 5-mile radius. Hours: 12-2.30pm/6-11.30pm (12am on Sat.). Branch: Savar Tandoori, Cheam Road, Sutton.

Ewell

BOMBAY

332 Kingston Road, Ewell   © 0181 393 0445

Suruk Miah's curry house seats 60 on wooden chairs, upholstered in
blue and gold, matching carpet, white linen, glass engraved dividing
screens, plenty of plants and white stone elephants. Six parking spaces
at back of restaurant. Sunday buffet £5.95. Price check: Papadam 40p,
CTM £5.80, Pullao Rice £1.50. House wine £6.45. Delivery: £10 minimum order, 3-mile radius. Hours: 12-2.30pm/ 6pm-12am. Stocks
Cobra.

CURRY HOUSE

1 Cheam Road, Ewell   © 0181 393 0734

'Gosht Methi was particularly delicious and had a crunchy texture from
fresh onion. Tarka Dhal also deserves a mention, perfect for dipping
Naans into. Food piping hot, portions adequate.' JP. Stocks Cobra.

Farnham

BANARAS NEW ENTRANT

40 Downing Street, Farnham   © 01252 734081

MA Rahman's smart curry house is decorated in pink and white. 'All
the food we had was more than acceptable, but the decor was the best
thing about the restaurant and the service was a particular let-down.'
HJC. Special: Karahi Duck Tikka, marinated in a thick sauce, cooked
and served in a cast iron dish £9.95. Minimum charge: £10.50. Sunday
lunch £8.95. Price check: CTM £7.95, Pullao Rice £1.95. House wine
£7.50. Hours: 12-2pm/6-11.30pm. Branches: Darjeeling, Farnham.
Viceroy, High Street, Hartley Witney, Hants.

DARJEELING   ©

25 South Street, Farnham   © 01252 714322

M.A. Rahman and S. Islam's 46-seater is stylishly decorated, with
mahogany wood panelling everywhere, brass plates decorate the walls
and there is a large brass peacock in the window. 'Everything about this

restaurant is good. The decor is subtle, low light, tropical fish. Good carpeting and sumptuous table linen and crockery. The menu is extensive. Service is very good. Waiters are friendly but unobtrusive. Food is excellent, subtly spiced, generous portions, excellent quality. Continues to be our favourite restaurant.' JW. Special: Garlic Chilli Chicken £8.95. Takeaway: over £15, 10% off. Set dinner £26 for two. Price check: Papadam 45p, CTM £7.95, Pullao Rice £1.95. Lager £2.95 pint, house wine £7.50. Minimum charge: £15. Hours: 12-2pm/6-11.30pm. Branches: Banaras, Farnham. Viceroy, Hartley Witney, Hants.

Guildford

KOHINOOR

24 Woodbridge Road, Guildford   © 01483 306051

Chef Azizur Rahman's Kohinoor is a bit tricky to find, being adjacent to, but not directly accessible from, the bypass, but this does not deter the locals. 'Service and food are excellent and this is rapidly becoming my favourite in Guildford.' CD. 'Very reasonable prices considering the location.' EJR. 'Well done. A light, bright atmosphere. Had a special resembling a Madras crossed with a Jalfrezi – rich sauce and an abundance of green chillies – superb! Happy to return anytime.' RV. Price check: Papadam 50p, CTM £6.75. Pullao Rice £1.75. Lager £2.80 pint, house wine £6.95. Minimum charge: £8.50. Sunday buffet £6.95. Hours: 12-2.30pm/6-11.30pm.

RAJDOOT

220 London Road, Burpham, Guildford   © 01483 451278

S. and M. Miah opened here in 1992, with an air-conditioned restaurant. 'Taken with their Bengal Fish Massalam (£7.50) – a freshwater boal with onion, chilli, garlic and cumin.' DC. 'Attractive fairly sophisticated decor. Marvellous staff, friendly, helpful and efficient. Fairly extensive menu with a few more unusual dishes. Prices are very good for the quality and portions were average to generous. Tandoori Fish, a whole trout beautifully cooked. Lamb Jalfrezi, marvellous. Butter Chicken exceptionally good, very rich but with more bite. Absolutely sensational Brinjal Bhajis. Superb Mattar Panir. Deep and moist Plain and Peshwari Nan. Wonderful large Onion Bhajia, spicy and crisp onion. Cooking and spicing excellent. A candidate for the next TOP

100 list.' HC. Price check: Papadam 50p, CTM £6.50, Pullao Rice £1.80. Sunday buffet £6.50. Minimum charge £8.50. Open daily 12-2.30pm/5.30-11pm. Stocks Cobra.

Haslemere

SHAHANAZ ADDRESS CHANGE

Weyhill, Haslemere   © **01428 651380**

This, as avid Guide readers know, is the Editor's delivery local. It does perfectly average formula Bangladeshi curry house food, typical of so many such places up and down the land. As we write this they have just traded up to a new address providing a larger sit-down, and we wish them well. Like most places, we prefer the food on weekdays, the Friday-Saturday pressure meaning they lack the edge. But another factor, which affects most restaurants is quite evident here too. Food quality, though always acceptable, can be a little up and down depending which chef has what day off. Service is mild mannered, gentle and experienced. The Shahanaz is definitive when it comes to delivery. Some years ago, chef-owner M. Ullah pioneered home-delivery in this area. Indeed he was amongst the nation's 3% who did it at that time. It transformed the restaurant's fortunes. The sight of the little red Shahanaz van whizzing around Haslemere has been a familiar, reassuring sight to curryholics for years. Their free delivery radius is enormous, and we have heard of up to four cars doing this at the weekend. Mr Ullah has never completed his questionaire (which disqualifies most restaurants automatically from this Guide), and though he displays his window sticker proudly, I doubt that he reads his entry. But I do hear from a real regular that the previous 10% off for home delivery has been withdrawn without warning since the move. That regular DL says he used the service 40 times a year at £20 a go. He was so cross about the lack of warning re his discount that he vows not to use the Shahanaz ever again. That's £800 a year lost from a single customer. An object lesson for an otherwise astute operator. Price check: Papadam 55p, CTM £5.50, Pullao Rice £1.70, Chutneys and Pickles 60p. Hours: 6-11.30pm. Stocks Cobra.

Horley

FORT RAJ BALTI RESTAURANT

74 Victoria Road, Horley   ✆ 01293 822909

At Shah Ali Athar and Abdul Khan's 74-seater (party room 32) our attention is drawn to chef Ali Mokoddus's Balti Chicken or Lamb Tikka Shankapuri (£6.95), whose sauce contains coconut and red wine. 'Portions large and well-presented. Service very friendly. Decor is tasteful.' MR & MRS DNL. Minimum charge: £6.50. Price check: Papadam 50p, CTM £7.95, Pullao Rice £1.75. Takeaway: 20% off. Delivery: £12 minimum, 3-mile radius. Hours: 12-2.30pm/6pm-12am. Stocks Cobra.

Kingston upon Thames, GL

GOLDEN CURRY   ©

36-38 High Street, Hampton Wick,
Kingston upon Thames   ✆ 0181 977 1422

Mabashar Ali's menu lists all our favourite curries and accompaniments, with a few specials as well, such as Chicken Rejala – fairly hot with yoghurt and black pepper. Free delivery available. Hours: 12-2.30pm/6pm-12am. Stocks Cobra.

MONTY'S TANDOORI   ©

53 Fife Road, Kingston upon Thames   ✆ 0181 546 1724

70-seater Nepalese restaurant, owned by Kishor Shrestha. South Indian face-masks decorate the white walls and hang from cream drapes. Hand-painted silk pictures of Indian scenes cover the walls, the floor is tiled. Specials: Nepalese Murgh Masala, chicken on the bone £6.95. 'Service is excellent, unobtrusive, polite and no mistakes. Food is plentiful and piping hot.' ST. Price check: Papadam 50p, CTM £7.10, Pullao Rice £2.10. Lager £2.60 pint, house wine £7.50. Takeaway: 10% off. Hours: 12-2.30pm/6pm-12am.

©	Curry Club discount (see page 6)	☕	Unlicensed
√	Vegetarian		
BYO	Bring your own alcohol	▦	Delivery/takeaway

Leatherhead

CURRY QUEEN

41 Church Street, Bookham, Leatherhead   © 01372 457241

'Have always been impressed with the constant high standard of cooking. A true feast at a reasonable price.' EJR.

SAFFRON GARDEN

Guildford Road, Bookham, Leatherhead   © 01372 457241

'Building was originally a red brick house and later adapted, can hardly been seen from the road and is pretty unprepossessing, car parking is limited, can only be entered by the service road running parallel to the main Leatherhead/Guildford road (A246). Ordered a takeaway, the one waiter I saw was very helpful and friendly. Butter Chicken absolutely wonderful, and made spicier on request. Brinjal Bhajee, large chunks of meltingly fabulous aubergine, well spiced. Portions just right, excellent value.' DC.

Lingfield

LINGFIELD TANDOORI   NEW ENTRANT

9 High Street, Lingfield   © 01342 835101

Olde worlde theme with exposed beams, taken over in '96 by Muhib Miah (manager) and Abdus Salam (chef), seats 56. Formerly Curry Inn. Takeaway: 10% off. Price check: Papadam 50p, CTM £6.95, Pullao Rice £1.75. House wine £7.25. Sunday lunch £8.95. Hours: 12-2.30pm/ 6pm-12am. Stocks Cobra.

Oxted

GURKHA KITCHEN   NEW TO OUR TOP 100   BEST NEPALESE

111 Station Road, Oxted   © 01883 722621

Monday night, didn't book. Oxted town is divided by the railway, like Woking, which is very irritating, we drove up and down Station Road West twice before we realised about the 'other side'. We arrived at 8pm and our coats were taken immediately by the waiter, who sat us in the

reception/waiting area. The bench-style sofa was made very comfortable by large Nepalese patchwork and embroidered cushions; we
ordered aperitifs. The floor is boarded, which makes it slightly noisy,
but the whole look is very elegant. Beautiful hand-forged black steel
chairs, the seat and back were wickered, the seat then covered in a small
patterned carpet with a fringe on two sides. White linen table clothes
and napkins, large, fragile wine glasses, drinking receptacles for the
connoisseur, their slender stems making a lovely bottle of Argentinian
Norton red wine the more enjoyable. I asked our waiter if a lot get
broken. 'Yes,' he said proudly, 'and I break the most.' At the back of the
restaurant an area is decorated with a small roof as in a Nepalese village, fishing net and basket hanging from the wall. Restaurant busy,
table of eight ladies possibly an office party? Another table was laid up
and reserved for 16, which soon arrived as a birthday party of very
sophisticated young people. A few of the men drank lager, but most
of them drank red or white wine — cosmopolitan tastes indeed. Their
expertise with the menu was demonstrated by them all knowing exactly what they wanted to eat. Who says spicy restaurants are in decline?
[Wish I'd been so confident at eighteen. -Ed]

The food is first class Nepalese fare. But it isn't earthy village food.
It's slightly evolved and modern, yet indisputably Nepalese. Two spicy
Papadams, folded into quarters and three home-made chutneys:
tamarind, mango chutney, lime pickle, arrived as soon as we sat down.
Aperitifs were delivered promptly to the table. We ordered Vegetable
Khaja, crisp vegetable filling pastry with mint and mustard dressing
£2.30, filo pastry wrapped up like spring roll, but not so thick. They
were cut in half, diagonally, a small green salad with the dressing decor-
ating the centre of the plate, the Khaja in four corners. Extremely mild,
but tasty. Bhutuwa, stir-fried chicken liver, prepared in traditional
Nepali spices £2.45. The liver was coated in a light, spicy curry sauce
and came in a basket, encircled by slices of tomato and cucumber.
Presentation of both these starters, excellent. For our main course we
chose Pokhareli Lamb, a classic rich spiced lamb dish from western
Nepal £5; it was indeed rich, the lamb very lean and tender. Hariyo
Machha, steamed fish wrapped in spinach prepared in a mild, dry fruit
sauce £7, large portion of white fish in a creamy sauce. Palungo Sag,
steamed spinach sautéed with fenugreek seeds £2.60; the spinach was
fresh. Gurkha Aloo, diced delicately, prepared in turmeric and cummin
seeds £2.60, mild potato cubes fried a little brown on the sides.
Rashilo Bhat, rice cooked with bay leaf, cardamom, garnished with

brown onion £1.95, light, fluffy and flavoursome. Joano Patre, bread with carom seed £2, just like a Nan really, quartered, very good. Golbeda Ko Achar, fresh tomato pickle £1.25, spicy, a good accompaniment to all dishes. Everything was delivered in seperate white china dishes, the plates hot. All the waiters are smartly dressed and polite. For the surroundings, food, aperitifs I was expecting a bill of something around £60, but I was pleasantly surprised at a total of £43.45, service not included. A TOP 100 restaurant. Sunday Buffet 1-10pm. Hours: 12-2.30pm/6-11pm (11.30pm on Fri. and Sat.).

Purley, GL

INDIA PALACE

11 Russell Parade, Russell Hill Road,
Purley   © 0181 660 6411

Z. Haq's traditional curry house seats 48. Special: Chicken, marinated, cooked in butter, cultured yoghurt and ground nuts £5.31. 'Mother-in-law's favourite. Superb Tandoori Chicken OFF the bone, i.e., it was whole but boned.' TN. Price check: Papadam 50p, CTM £5.40, Pullao Rice £1.70. Takeaway: 10% discount. Hours: 12-2.30pm/6-11.30pm (12am on Fri. & Sat.). Stocks Cobra.

Redhill

EXOTICA TANDOORI   ©

18 Cromwell Road, Redhill   © 01737 778624

Chef/owner Ali Shazid's 30-seater is decorated in dark cherry, matching carpet, green plants. Specials: Chicken Chat, small juicy pieces of chicken, cooked in a hot and spicy sauce £2.10. Passanda, sliced meat cooked in fresh cream, cultivated yoghurt and ground nuts £5.25. Price check: Papadam 40p, CTM £5.25, Pullao Rice £1.20. House wine £6.95. Minimum charge: £10. Delivery: 4-mile radius. Stocks Cobra. Hours: 12-2.30pm/5.30-11.30pm (12am on Fri. & Sat.).

©	Curry Club discount (see page 6)		Unlicensed
√	Vegetarian		
BYO	Bring your own alcohol		Delivery/takeaway

Reigate

VILLAGE BRASSERIE   ©

10 West Street, Reigate   ℭ 01737 245695

40-seater curry house with some South Indian specials, Mossala Dosi (*sic.*), pancake filled with delicious spicy vegetables, served with salad £2.10, owned by MD A. Rashid. I like the sound of Green Kebab, spinach, cottage cheese, garlic and ginger cakes £2.50 and Choti Poti, chickpeas, potato, egg, garnished with Bombay Mix £2.50. Price check: Papadam 50p, CTM £4.95, Pullao Rice £1.50. House wine £6.80. Takeaway: 10% discount. Sunday lunch £7.25. Delivery: £10 minimum order. Hours: 5.30-11.30. Stocks Cobra.

Richmond upon Thames, GL

RANI   √

3 Hill Street, Richmond upon Thames   ℭ 0181 332 2322

Like Sheila and Jyoti Pattni's N3 Rani, this one does Gujarati and south Indian vegetarian cooking. I was critical last time and asked to be swamped with reports about both venues. I said if the Pattnis write to me, be sure I'll publish their comments here. You didn't and they didn't. Hours 4.30-11.30pm. Branch: Rani, London N3. Stocks Cobra.

Staines

ANCIENT RAJ   ©

157 High Street, Staines   ℭ 01784 457099

Owner-chef Syed Joynul's restaurant is 'appropriate for all occasions, from takeaways to family celebrations. A stylish setting. Moghul swordsmen decorate the walls. We are impressed with the consistently high standard of well-presented and hot food. Reasonably priced.' SR. Hours 12-2.30pm/6-11.30pm. Stocks Cobra.

Surbiton, GL

AGRA TANDOORI   ©

142 Ewell Road, Surbiton   © 0181 399 8854

Owner-manager HK Paul runs a good and reliable curry house, serving competent curries and their accompaniments. Hours: 12-2.30pm/6pm-12am. Stocks Cobra.

AJANTA   ©

114 Ewell Road, Surbiton   © 0181 399 1262

Rubel Ahmad will help you to find all your favourites. 'Set meal for four, looked good value and so it proved. Huge quantities, good selection of starters, sensitively spiced Lamb Dupioza.' cjc. Hours: 12-2.30pm/6pm-12am. Branches: Shapla, Bristol Road, Selly Oak, and Stratford Road, Shirley, Birmingham. Stocks Cobra.

RAJ   ©

163 Ewell Road, Surbiton   © 0181 390 0251

Aziz Miah's curry house seats 58 and 'offers the best value for money, excellent food, good-sized portions, attentive yet not overbearing waiter service and tasteful decor in clean and comfortable surroundings.' sh. Chef's Choice: Special Garlic Chicken, tikka cooked with garlic, onions, green peppers, in garlic sauce £5.85. Sunday buffet 12-6. Price check: Papadam 45p, CTM £5.85, Pullao Rice £1.60. House wine £6.95. Takeaway: 10% discount. Hours: 6-11.30pm. Stocks Cobra.

Sutton, GL

SAVAR TANDOORI

7 Cheam Road, Sutton   © 0181 661 93955

'Very friendly, but tables too close together. CTM £5.50, excellent chicken, smooth sauce, good flavour. Chicken Madras £3.80, good use of spices. Chicken Jalfrezi £5.50, good flavour and hot, big portion and great value. Mushroom Bhajee £2.10, just right, plentiful mushrooms. Absolutely superb, light and fluffy Special Rice £2.20.' an.

Thornton Heath, GL

BEULAH ROAD TANDOORI   NEW ENTRANT   ©

77 Beulah Road, Thornton Heath   ☏ **0181 771 7783**

M.R.A. Khan's 40-seater serves formula curries. Special: Tandoori
Karahi Mixed Grill, cooked with wine £9.25. Takeaway 10% discount.
Price check: Papadam 30p, CTM £4.75, Pullao Rice £1.30. House wine
£6.25. Hours: 6pm-12am. Stocks Cobra.

Tolworth, GL

JAIPUR   TOP 100   ©

90 The Broadway, Tolworth   ☏ **0181 399 3619**

The external decor makes this venue unmissable. Its huge pink stone
pillars make it stand out, a fact not unnoticed by the local council, who
in the early days spent a considerable amount of time, and presumably
money, trying to force owner S.U. Ali to remove them. Fortunately
bureaucracy lost, and the pillars remain; indeed, they continue inside,
giving a very Indian feel to the interior. India's Jaipur is the pink city,
where every building is made from pink sandstone. Naturally the
Jaipur's theme is pink too, with 'an amazing sugar-pink decor, with
friezes of dancing ladies seemingly sculpted out of the wall.' DD. 'A
thoroughly enjoyable restaurant.' DRC. 'One of my regular haunts.' PD.
In our TOP 100. We describe the food in the entry for the branch:
Jaipur, Woking. Stocks Cobra.

Virginia Water

VICEROY OF INDIA   ©

4 Station Approach, Virginia Water   ☏ **01344 843157**

M.S. Ali's Viceroy remains very popular. Stocks Cobra.

©	Curry Club discount (see page 6)	☕	Unlicensed
√	Vegetarian		
BYO	Bring your own alcohol	⊞	Delivery/takeaway

Weybridge

GOLDEN CURRY   ©

132 Oatlands Drive, Weybridge   ℂ 01932 846931

Good reports still received about owner Enayeth Khan's golden curries.
Stocks Cobra.

THE HUSSAIN   ©

47 Church Street, Weybridge   ℂ 01932 844720

All reports speak well of the food and the service at M. Suleman's
Hussain. 'Garlic chicken was memorable, even next day, according to
one wag.' HC. Branch: The Curry Corner Tandoori, Hersham, Surrey.

Whyteleafe

CURRY GARDEN   ©

242 Godstone Road, Whyteleafe   ℂ 01883 627237

An effort is made at Akhlaqur Rahman and Moynoor Rashid 54-
seater air-conditioned restaurant. On the ground and first floor, it's
decorated in 'light blue wallpaper, silk plants, with a superb bar.'
Special: Vegetable Malai Kofta, minced vegetables made into balls and
cooked in cream £4.50. Sunday buffet 12-3pm, £5.95 adult, £3.95 children. Minimum charge: £6. Service: £10. Takeaway: 10% discount. Price
check: Papadam 50p, CTM £5.75, Pullao Rice £1.50. House wine £5.50.
Delivery: £13 minimum order, 3-mile radius. Hours: 12-3pm/6pm-
12am. Stock Cobra.

Woking

JAIPUR TOP 100

49 Chertsey Road, Woking   ℂ 01483 772626

This elegant 60-seater is owned by Nizam Ali and his two delightful
sisters, Reggi and Sophi, all of whom I met in their gorgeous Sylheti
home, during a monsoon storm a few years ago. 'The ambience (of the
restaurant) is smooth and peaceful. The bar on the right invites you to
enjoy a relaxing drink, while the huge pillars in their subdued tones of

pink make you feel you are in India. The food is always an adventure, spiced with care and forethought by chef Rupa Kumar. The whole meal was outstanding.' DBAC. 'Basically traditional menu with a few interesting items. Food served with a smile. Chicken Dupiaza very light on onions. Could not fault the food but ordinary.' MP. 'We started with King Prawn Butterfly and Meat Samosa (both excellent). We followed with Sali Boti (sliced lamb with apricots) which was mild and beautifully cooked. The Nan bread (slightly crispy and buttery on top) was sensational. Service was perfect and this is definitely a worthy Top 100.' AF. Minimum charge: £6.95. Business weekday self-serve buffet lunches £5.95, Sunday e-a-m-y-l buffet: £6.95 adult, £3.95 kids. Price check: Papadam 50p, CTM £5.95, Pullao Rice £1.95. House wine £6.95. Delivery (tel. 770083): £12 minimum, 4-mile radius. Hours: 12-2.30pm/6-11.30pm. Branch: Jaipur, Tolworth, Surrey.

KHYBER PASS   ©

18 The Broadway, Woking   ✆ 01483 764710

It's a standard curry house, green decor and Hindi arches. 'Food is always good. Of particular interest to us is the lime pickle on the chutney tray.' DRC. Manager Jafar Abdul Wahab promises to give a generous discount to Curry Club members. Branches: Khyber Pass, 12 Lower Guildford Road, Knaphill and 54 Terrace Road, Walton-on-Thames. Stocks Cobra.

SUSSEX

Area: South
Population: 1,417,000
Number of restaurants in county: 239
Number of restaurants in Guide: 43

For the purposes of this Guide we combine East and West Sussex.

Bexhill-on-Sea

ANWAR

2 Sackville Road, Bexhill-on-Sea   ✆ 01424 210205

Owned by Jamir Uddin (manager) and Mrs Nurun Bibi (chef).
Northern Indian curries, 50 seats, parking for 8 cars. Price check:
Papadam 40p, CTM £5.50, Pullao Rice £1.30. Lager £2 pint, house
wine £7.95. Delivery: £15 minimum order, 3-mile radius. Hours: 12-
2.30pm/6pm-12am.

KASHMIR NEW ENTRANT

14 Village Mews, Little Common,
Bexhill On Sea   ✆ 01424 848082

Owner, Islam Uddin, seats 63. Formula curries. Specials: Tandoori
Lobster from £12.50. Takeaway: 10% less. Price check: Papadam 50p,
CTM £6.50, Pullao Rice £1.75. Sunday lunch: £6.95. Minimum charge:
£10. Hours: 6-11pm. Sun. 12.30-2.30pm/6-11pm.

SHIPLU   ©

109 London Road, Bexhill-on-Sea   ✆ 01424 219159

At Abdul Kalam Azad's Shiplu 'service couldn't be bettered, all dishes
were well cooked and presented in adequate quantities.' DJB. Open
12pm-2.30pm/6pm-12am. Stocks Cobra.

Bognor Regis

ELMER TANDOORI

76 Elmer Road, Middleton-on-Sea,
Bognor Regis   ✆ 01243 582641

Samim Ahmed Chowdhury tells us his 60-seater 'looks very nice, clean
and tidy.' Price check: Papadam 25p, CTM £3.45, Pullao Rice 85p.
House wine £6.95. Service: 10%. Hours: 12-2.30pm/6-11pm.

MAGNA

3 Argyle Street, Bognor Regis   © 01243 828322

Arrived at 6.30ish. Restaurant deceptively large, smart though typically colours clashed. Clean and well maintained. We were the first
customers, but others soon appeared and takeaways doing a good trade
for a Wednesday. Smart and polite waiters. As we sat a small plate of
Bombay Mix was delivered, very fresh and crunchy, certainly no other
hands had been rummaging in it. We virtually demolished this while
we looked at the menus. Started with two very crispy pops and picks
CT, at least eight generous pieces, fresh and succulent on a bed of
sautéed onions £1.95. Onion Bhajia – two flattish discs, spicy and
moist £1.60. Taste of Sylhet Sat Kora Chicken – a type of lime, with
potato and plenty of freshly sliced green chillies £4.65, made a good
change. CT Dansak served with Pullao Rice £6.90. Side orders of
Tarka Dal – topped with fried garlic £1.95. Specials include:
Bangladeshi fish – Rui Mas and Boal Mas both £8.95. With a bottle of
French red wine and an extra portion of rice the bill was a very reasonable £32.70 plus tip. I visited the toilets and can report that they
score 9 out of 10. Hours: 12-2.30pm/5.30-11.30pm.

PASSAGE TO INDIA

15 The Square, Barnham, Bognor Regis   © 01243 555064

Mr Rahman's 58-seater. Special: Butter Chicken £5.70. Price check:
Papadam 40p, CTM £5.90, Pullao Rice £1.60. House wine £6.50.
Hours: 12-2.30pm/6-11.30pm (12am on Fri. and Sat.). Stocks Cobra.

Brighton

ANCIENT CURRY DOME TAKEAWAY   ©

6 George Street, Brighton   © 01273 670521

Opened in 1990 by Ali Hussan. All meals are served with Rice,
Papadam and Onion Salad; if you don't want the Rice or Papadam you
will be charged £1 less. Price check: Papadam 40p, CTM £5.60, Pullao
Rice £1.20. Delivery: free over £6.50. Hours: 5.30pm-12am.

BALTI HUT NEW ENTRANT

2 Coombe Terrace, Brighton   © 01273 681280

30-seater, est. '97 by Dost Mohammed, serving formula curries and Balti specials from £4.80. Price check: Papadam 50p, CTM £6.80, Pullao Rice £1.45. House wine £7. Service: 10%. Takeaway: 10% off. Delivery: £8 minimum, 3-mile radius. Hours: 6-11.30pm (12am on Sat.).

BOMBAY ALOO NEW ENTRANT   √

39 Ship Street, Brighton.   © 01273 776038

'We loved it, wanted to share it, and hope that many more (vegetarian) curry lovers can satisfy their craving without too many shekels leaving their pockets. Vegetarian Buffet meal (14 dishes) £4.50 eat 'til you burst. Buy 11 buffet meals and have the 12th on us.' sk&ld.

POLASH   BYO ALLOWED ©

19 York Place, Brighton   © 01273 626221

Formula 60-seater, owned and managed by Nosir Ullah. BYO, no corkage. Takeaway: 10% off. Price check: Papadam 40p, CTM: £6.95, Pullao Rice £1.55. House wine £6.25. Delivery: £10 minimum. Hours: 12-2pm/6pm-12am. Stocks Cobra.

SHIMLA TANDOORI TAKEAWAY

92 Preston Drove, Brighton   © 01273 542626

'The best takeaway in Brighton. The Garlic Chilli King Prawn is amazing – whole cloves of garlic and whole (red hot) chillies. CT is also one of the best we've come across.' rs. Hours 5-10.30pm.

VICEROY OF INDIA

13 Preston Street, Brighton   © 01273 324733

Traditionally decorated, formula curry 48-seater, est. '85 by Mohammed Wasid Ali. Specials: Butter and Jeera Chicken £5, Jeera King Prawn, thick sauce with cummin seeds £6.75. Price check: Papadam 55p, CTM £4.85, Pullao Rice £1.65. Lager £3.10 pint, house wine £6.95. Service 10%. Hours: 12-2.30pm/5pm-12am.

Chichester

MEMORIES OF INDIA

Main Road (A259), Bosham Roundabout,
Chichester   ✆ 01243 572234

Abdul Jalil's formula curryhouse is nicely decorated, peach walls, tablecloths and napkins, and blue carpet. Separate bar, highly polished
floor, cane chairs and tables, green plants. 'Had a takeaway and despite
the decor which made us think it would be expensive we found it to be
very reasonable. My only complaint, Sag Paneer was made with ched-
dar. Helpful staff, despite being busy.' sw. Specials: Lamb Podina, thin
lamb with garlic, fresh mint and coriander £6.95. Ayre Jalfrey, Bengali
fish cooked with chillies, garlic, peppers in a hot spicy sauce £7.95.
£6.95 wine. Takeaway: 15% off. Minimum charge: £13.50. Price check:
Papadam 40p, CTM £6.25, Pullao Rice £1.95. Hours: 12-2.30pm/6pm-
12am. Stocks Cobra.

Crawley

BENGAL SPICES

71 Gales Drive, Three Bridges, Crawley   ✆ 01293 571007

An attractive restaurant in gold and green with engraved screens to
divide diners. 'The food was again exceptionally good and we were
more than satisfied. CTM absolutely wonderful, superb flavour. Balti
Mushroom Fry absolutely great, very deep tomato and green pepper
sauce with large moist whole mushrooms, perfectly cooked. Sag Panir,
marvellous, dry, very cheesy flavour. Has the cleanest and prettiest
Ladies' I know. Two young men from Wales sat at the next table and
both ordered Phalls. I have never seen anybody eat this incendiary dish
before, but they ate every morsel with no sign of anything out of the
ordinary – could have been totally bland from the reaction. Must have
been very hardened Phall eaters.' HC. Open 12pm-2.30pm/6-11pm.

RAJ TAKEAWAY   ⊞ ©

8 Broadfield Barton, Broadfield, Crawley   ✆ 01293 515425

S.U. Ahmed has a loyalty discount scheme: collect stars for a free
meal. As well as the goodies, chef A. Ali does curry sauce and chips,

kids' favourite. Price check: CTM £5.25, Pullao Rice £1.40.
Hours: 5.30-11pm.

RUBY MURRAY TAKEAWAY

4 Orchard Street, Crawley	© 01293 417417

Takeaway and delivery service. The menu covers a wide range of curries
with other foods (Donner £2.20 medium), Burgers (Chilli £1.70 single)
and Pizzas (Bombay Mix – curry sauce, Meat Tikka, Chicken Tikka,
cheese, tomato, onion, mushroom, sweetcorn, green peppers) £9.20
large. 'Meat Vindaloo, as always hot, with a wonderful sauce, £3.60.
Quick to arrive – free delivery in half an hour. Staff helpful and food
inexpensive.' GT. Price check: Papadam 50p, CTM £6.50 incl. rice, Pullao
Rice £1.30. Hours: 4pm-1am. The Ruby Murray stocks a selection of
canned and bottled lagers, but their licence says these are strictly delivered with food to customers over the age of 18 and before 11pm.

SULTAN'S BRASSERIE   NEW ENTRANT   ©

6-7 Orchard Street, Crawley	© 01293 427940

We'd arrived back at Gatwick at midnight from lands afar, with a huge
withdrawal symptom. The best bet at that hour was either the Ruby (*see*
above) or, in the same ownership, B. Khan's next-door 100-seater Sultan.
Sure enough it was doing a good sit-down trade. Standard fare, but
wonderful under the circumstances. Special: Lamb Sheryan – mince,
lamb, coconut, raisins, cashew nuts and cream, served with special fried
rice £11.95. Minimum charge: £10. Price check: Papadam 50p, CTM
£6.95, Pullao Rice £1.95. House wine £7.45. Corporate functions welcome. Multi storey parking opposite. Hours: 12-2.30pm/5pm-1am.

Crowborough

HENNA   NAME CHANGE

24 Crowborough Hill, Jarvis Brook, Crowborough	© 01892 661881

Reports please since it changed name from Akash. Stocks Cobra.

ROSE OF BENGAL   ©

3 Crowborough Hill, Crowborough   ✆ 01892 662252

We hear again about Esab and Moshud Ali's Hyrali (green) Chicken or Lamb Masalla, cooked with sag, mint, coriander, butter and cream. Hours: 12pm-2.30pm/6-11pm. Stocks Cobra.

East Preston

BENGAL TANDOORI

116 Downs Way, East Preston   ✆ 01903 777365

'All your favourites including wicked Phalls for the loonies. [Excuse me, that's one of my favourites!!! -Ed]. Quantities a bit small, although I am a big eater. Polite and friendly service.' RT. 'We've enjoyed Indian meals in many venues but none compare with the Bengal. Food excellent, generous portions. The surroundings are very comfortable and tastefully decorated. Parking is easy – right at the door. Never empty, weekend customers prepared to wait an hour for takeaways. Favourite dish is the Kurzi Lamb, ordered with two days' notice, serving four to five with the full meal costing around £60 – superb!' J&KT.

Eastbourne

INDIAN PARADISE   ©

166 Seaside, Eastbourne   ✆ 01323 735408

A. Khalique's bright restaurant has been serving competent curries and accompaniments to a local following for the last 15 years. Delivery. Hours: 12pm-2.30pm/6pm-12am.

Hailsham

RAJ DHUTT

48 High Street, Hailsham   ✆ 01323 842847

A.S. Ali's 36-seater's specialities include Chicken Silsila – Tikka chicken breast cooked in sauce of bay leaves, cardamom, cinnamon, ginger and garlic. Price check: Papadam 45p, CTM £5.55, Pullao Rice £1.50. House wine £5.95. Takeaway: 10% off. Hours: 12-2pm/6-11pm (11.30 on Sat.).

Hastings

SHIPLU ©

177a Queens Road, Hastings   © 01424 439493

Mr Hoque's Shiplu is 'tastefully decorated and clean. Service on the slow side but friendly. Pops warm and crisp, Onion B large, could not be beaten. Phall not on the menu but asked for it. Very hot as it should be.' BP-D. Hours: 12-2.30pm/6pm-12am. Stocks Cobra.

Haywards Heath

BENGAL LANCER   NEW ENTRANT

111 South Road, Haywards Heath   © 01444 454661

'Superb food, service and cleanliness.' M&BS. 'A very varied menu, spoilt for choice, but staff really helpful in explaining different foods. The quality of food is exactly what you would expect.' MSS.

CURRY INN ©

58 Commercial Square, Haywards Heath   © 01444 415414

At Abru Miah's 60-seater with blue and green marble effect bar, pillars, plants and chandelier lighting, Korma is the most popular dish. Price check: Papadam 50p, CTM £5.80, Pullao Rice £1.70. House wine £8.50. Hours: 12-2.30pm/6-11.30pm (12am Sat.).

NIZAM

139 South Road, Haywards Heath   © 01444 457527

Anwar H. Chowdhury's 83-seater serves formula curries. Specials include: Badmi Kurma Chicken – Chicken Tikka in a yoghurt, pepper and onion sauce and Methi Kalia Chicken – Chicken Tikka with spinach and lentils, both £6.50. Minimum charge: £10. Price check: Papadam 60p, CTM £6.50, Pullao Rice £1.95. House wine £8.25. Takeaway: 15% off. Hours: 12-2.30pm/6-11.30pm. Stocks Cobra.

Horsham

CURRY CENTRE

43 London Road, Horsham   ✆ 01403 254811

'Our regular haunt for over 20 years. Thoroughly recommended for consistent food. Excellent Niramish.' DRM.

Hove

AL RIAZ   ©

244 Portland Road, Hove   ✆ 01273 722332

Mrs Kosser Riaz's is noted for fabulous comfy chairs to sit in at the bar, the sort you could quite happily go to sleep in. Smartly laid tables, blue candles and crystal glasses. A very grand conservatory. Price check: Papadam 45p, CTM £6.95 incl. Pullao Rice; Pullao Rice £1.55. Service 10%. Delivery which can be paid for on the phone with your credit card – great! Hours: 5pm-12am.

ASHOKA   ©

95-97 Church Road, Hove   ✆ 01273 734193

100-seater owned by Bashir Meah and Rafique Miah. 'Nice roomy restaurant, clean and comfortable. Onion Bhaji, small but good and tasty. Chicken Ceylon with Pilau Rice and Nan, hot, as it should be, nicely served and plenty of it! Bill allowed for 10% discount to Curry Club member, but offset by service charge.' BP.-D. Madras most popular. Price check: Papadam 50p, CTM £7.25, Pullao Rice £1.75. House wine £6.95. Service: 10%. Sunday lunch: £6.95. Hours: 12-3pm/6pm-12am. Branch: Bombay, Preston Street, Brighton. Stocks Cobra.

GANGES

93 Church Road, Hove   ✆ 01273 728292

Abdul (front) and Karim (kitchen) run an attractive restaurant decorated in white and green. Poneer Shashlik £2.95 and Brandy King Prawn £13.95 sound interesting. Price check: Papadam 55p, CTM £7.25 incl. Pullao Rice; Pullao Rice £1.75. Minimum charge £6.95. Hours: 12pm-2.30pm/6pm-12am. Stocks Cobra.

HOVE TANDOORI   ©

175 Church Road, Hove   ✆ 01273 737188

Shofir and Shahed Ahmad's 42-seater. Hove Special: chicken, meat,
prawn cooked with garlic, ginger, tomato, mushroom, onion, green
pepper, coriander, green chilli in a thick sauce, served in a Korai with
Rice £7.95. Takeaway: 10% off. Price check: Papadam 40p, CTM £4.75,
Pullao Rice £1.30. House wine £4. Delivery: £8 minimum, 3-mile
radius. Hours: 12-2.30pm/5.30pm-12am. Stocks Cobra.

KARIM'S TANDOORI   ©

15 Blatchington Road, Hove   ✆ 01273 739780

Formula curry house, traditionally decorated, seats 38. Balti dishes
available. Price check: Papadam 50p, CTM £7.50, Pullao Rice £1.70.
Lager £2.60 pint, house wine £6.95. Minimum charge: £7.95. Service:
10%. Delivery: £8 minimum order. Hours: 6-11.30pm (12am on Sat.).
Branch: Balti House, Coombe Terrace, Brighton.

KASHMIR

71 Old Shoreham Road, Hove   ✆ 01273 739677

Owner chef Subab Miah celebrates 20 years of reliable business. 'The
food is always delicious, the service courteous and friendly.' HF. 'A consistently high standard of cooking and preparation.' JHW. 'Mr Miah
and family provide excellence at all expectations.' CRC. 'I've been coming since it opened. The seating and bar are very pleasant. The curries
are delicately spiced and individual.' LH. Established way back in '78, by
Subab Miah, who is a busy chap, being manager and head chef. Traditional decor, formula curries, specials include Balti dishes, seats 45.
Price check: Papadam 45p, CTM £5, Pullao Rice £1.80. House wine
£7. Delivery: Hove area. Hours: 12-3pm/6pm-12am.

Lewes

SHANAZ   ©

83 High Street, Lewes   ✆ 01273 488038

Taken over in '97 by Mrs L.B. Salim, her 98-seater (party room 44) is
decorated cottage-style with varnished wood panelling, Special: Jeera

Chicken, cooked with cummin seeds, onion, green pepper and herbs, chillies on request £5.95. Price check: Papadam 50p, CTM £5.95, Pullao Rice £1.65. House wine £6.95. Minimum charge: £6.95. Hours: 12-2.30pm/6pm-12am. Stocks Cobra.

Newhaven

LAST VICEROY   ©

4 Bridge Street, Newhaven   ℂ 01273 513308

AS Ahmed's 40-seater is divided into smoking and non-smoking zones and has a separate entrance for t/a customers and an off-licence – cigarettes can be delivered to your table! Specials: Garlic Duck Masala £8.95. King Prawn Zafrani £11.95. 'Our favourite, always offering good food and friendly service. Ample portions, very enjoyable.' BJMcK. Kid's half-price menu. Price check: Papadam 45p, CTM £5.75, Pullao Rice £1.75. House wine £7.25. Sunday, free starters with main meal, eat-in only. Minimum charge: £10. Takeaway: 30% off. Delivery: £10 minimum. Hours: 12-2.30pm/6-11.30pm. Stocks Cobra.

Nutley

GANGES

High Street, Nutley   ℂ 01825 713287

Mr and Mrs M.U. Haque own this 70-seater where Korma and Dansak are the most popular dishes. Price check: Papadam 60p, CTM £6.50, Pullao Rice £1.60. House wine £6.95. Hours: 12-2pm/6-11.30pm. Stocks Cobra.

Petworth

VICEREGAL LODGE

East Street, Petworth   ℂ 01798 343217

Here's last year's entry verbatim: 'Owned by Joe Choudhury who tells us that, to his regular customers (who are all, it seems, pilots and yachtsmen), his restaurant is their 19th hole, and that it is more like a private club than an Indian restaurant. Since Petworth is near neither the sea nor an airstrip, we are as bemused as you are, but Joe will give you a really warm welcome whatever!' I really thought this was fair comment, but it so upset Mr Choudhury, that he wrote to me saying the entry was 'borderline cheap humour, done without ever trying to get to know who we are. I am game for a laugh', he continues, ' but *you* have to be doubly careful when earning your bread and butter, dancing between two cultures. The people you profess to represent may grin from ear to ear when used as material for your jokes, but me and my family have heard them all.' Ouch!!! No offence intended, Joe, not to you or to anyone in the business, never, as *everyone* knows. I can only presume you misunderstood the meaning of the word 'bemused'. Seats 36 in two rooms. 'Excellent! Service friendly and competent. Popadoms warm and crisp and onion relish nicely chilled. Chicken Rezala consisted of pieces of breast fillet in a spicy plum-tomato sauce with garlic and coriander. Prawn Jalfry equally good, a spicy lesson in oral aerobics. Very good Tarka Dal, Madras Sambar and Sag Aloo. Fresh and fragrant Pullao Rice, Nan and Chapatis.' CT. Price check: Papadam 50p, CTM £6, Pullao Rice £1.80. Hours: 6pm-12am (Pre-ordered party bookings only at lunch). Stocks Cobra.

Ringmer

RINGMER TANDOORI   ©

72 Springett Avenue, Ringmer   ℂ 01273 812855

Balti dishes feature on owner, M.A. Uddin's, menu along with the favourites. Open 12pm-2.30pm/6pm-12am. Stocks Cobra.

Seaford East

BENGAL PALACE   NEW ENTRANT   ©

30 Church Street, Seaford East   ℂ 01323 899077

Air conditioned, traditional decor, saris hang on walls, engraved glass screens divide tables. Managed by Eleas Hussain, formula curries, seats 48. Sunday lunch £7.95. Price check: Papadam 50, CTM £6.45, Pullao Rice £1.65. House wine £7.15. Delivery: £10 minimum. Hours: 12-2.30pm/6pm-12pam. Stocks Cobra.

SUSSEX

Steyning

MAHARAJA

The Street, Bramber, Steyning   © 01903 812123

Our window cleaner, David Lambert and his wife Sheila love curry, in fact they have a Saturday night ritual of ordering a home delivery from the same restaurant, spending, they think, over £1,000 p.a. at it. On a caravan break, they stopped at this little hamlet and decided to try the only Indian. Despite being absolutely packed, as was the car park, they were immediately squeezed in and papadams and chutney tray was placed in front of them. (Not ordered so would they be on the bill?) Starters, Reshmi Kebab with omelette and a Puri dish, main courses and rice, two pints of lager and two glasses of white wine later, the bill arrived. The pops were not listed, but the total was a hefty £47. Good portions and lovely surroundings, they say, made it well worth while. Hours: 12pm-2.30pm/6-11.30pm. Stocks Cobra.

Worthing

MA'HANN   NEW TO OUR TOP 100

179-181 Montague Street, Worthing   © 01903 205449

1998 expansion has increased A. Monnan's Ma'haan to 140 seats (party room 30). Monnan is a qualified chef, and though he is to be found out front these days, he's very much respected in his kitchen. He and his energetic manager Abul Kabir are: 'most polite and friendly, greeting regular customers like old friends. An outstanding feature is the generosity of the portions, piping hot and very nicely presented.' GV. Specials: Chicken or Lamb Rezala, slightly hot and sweet, cooked in a tangy sauce £8.95; as Beef Jagannath (£8.25) – well-spiced fillets cooked with capsicum, green chillies and coriander, incl. rice. 'One of the best I have visited. Large restaurant, divided into smoking and non-smoking, decor good with background music. Lamb Jalfrezi, Madras hot, well spiced, tender meat and rich tasty sauce. Chicken Pasanda, mild, thoroughly enjoyable. Tasty Mixed Vegetable Curry, Garlic Nan, you could taste the garlic.' MPB. We have many satisfied reports from locals and others from far and wide. Welcome to our Top 100 and a formula curry house doing the job as well as it can be done. Price check: Papadam 45p (plain) 75p (spicy), Chutney or Pickle 45p each, CTM

£8.95 (incl. Pullao Rice), Bombay Potato £2.95, Pullao Rice £1.95. Wine £7.95. Takeaway: 10% off. Hours: 12-2.30pm/5.30-11.30pm. Stocks Cobra.

SHAFIQUE'S   ©

42 Goring Road, Worthing   © 01903 504035

Shafique Uddin decribes his 48-seater as '30s colonial.' Special: Bangladeshi Mass, fish curry, hot £9.95, Sunday lunch buffet £7.45 adult, £5.45 children. Price check: Papadam 50p, CTM £7.95, Pullao Rice £1.75. House wine £7.95. Takeaway: 10% discount. Delivery: £1, 3-mile radius. Hours: 12-2.30pm/5.30-11.30pm. Stocks Cobra.

TASTE OF BENGAL TAKEAWAY   ©

203 Heene Road, Worthing   © 01903 238400

Owned by Faruk Kalam (chef) and Salik Miah since '84. Formula takeaway. Special: Murgi Mossallam, spring chicken cooked in mild spices, almonds, minced meat, fruit and eggs, served with saffron rice £5.95. Price check: Papadam 40p, CTM £4.60, Pullao Rice £1.50. Delivery: £7 minimum order, 5-mile radius, charged at 95p! Hours: 12-2pm/5.30pm-12am. Branch: Golden Bengal, Lyndhurst Road, Worthing.

TYNE AND WEAR

Area: North East
Population: 1,127,000
Number of restaurants in county: 137
Number of restaurants in Guide: 32

Gateshead

BILLQUAY TAKEAWAY   NEW ENTRANT   ©

78 Station Road, Bill Quay, Gateshead   © 0191 495 0270

Est. '87 by Syed Amir Ali. Bangladeshi curry takeaway, CTM most popular. Price check: Papadam 35p, CTM £3.95, Pullao Rice £1.10. No Credit cards. Hours: 6pm-12am.

CURRY GARDEN TAKEAWAY NEW ENTRANT   ⊞ ©

53 Coatsworth Road, Bensham, Gateshead © 0191 478 3614

Owned by Abdul Malik Choudhury since 1996, 'splendid from decor
to menu,' serves formula curries. Special: Tandoori Bhuna Masala with
Pullao Rice £6.45. Price check: Papadam 40p, CTM £5.80, Pullao Rice
£1.60. Delivery: £5 minimum order, 3-mile radius, £1 charge. Hours: 12-
2pm (Sun. closed)/6pm-12am.

THE LAST DAYS OF THE RAJ   ©

218 Durham Road, Shipcote, Gateshead   © 0191 477 2888

A takeaway-only establishment serving Bangladeshi curry house food.
Price check: Papadam 55p, CTM £5.95, Pullao Rice £1.75. Hours 12-
2.30pm/6pm-12am.

LAST DAYS OF THE MOGUL RAJ   ⊞

565 Durham Road, Low Fell, Gateshead   © 0191 487 6282

Run by Ali and Ali. Formula curry house. Special: Raj Lamb and
Cabbage £4.95. Price check: Papadam 55p, CTM £5.95, Pullao Rice
£1.75. Hours: 12-2pm (Sun. closed)/6pm-12am.

THE LAST DAYS OF THE RAJ TOP 100   ©

168 Kells Lane, Low Fell, Gateshead   © 0191 482 6494

Athair Khan's up-market 100-seater has stylish decor – pure 30's Art
Deco, complete with grand piano. Live music Thursdays. Crisp linen
tablecloths laid on beautifully presented tables, brass light-fittings,
ceiling-fans, trellis-climbing plants, and fresh flowers. Luxurious surroundings, with friendly and efficient waiters. The bar is spacious and
well stocked. This restaurant must have one of the biggest and most
comprehensive menus in the country; it is quite a delight. You will find
all the regular formula curries with some regional and authentic dishes
including recipes from the British Raj – Country Captain £7.25, a dry
dish cooked with chicken breast, onion, ghee, chillies, ginger, garlic,
turmeric and salt. Raj Lamb and Cabbage (£7.25) is cooked with
yoghurt, poppy seeds, lemon juice, green coriander, garlic, onion, fresh
coconut, green chillies, ground coriander, ginger, cinnamon and cumin
with ghee and chilli. You will also find on the menu a few dishes with

an oriental flavour, such as Dim Sum £3.25, Oriental King Prawn Rolls £3.75 and Butterfly Breaded Prawn £3.75, and there is a Pizza or two – quite fabulous, definitely a TOP 100 restaurant. Handi Murgh £7.15, King Prawn Garlic Chili £10.55. Price check: Papadam 75p, CTM £7.85, Pullao Rice £2.55. Sunday buffet £10.95. Hours: 12-2.30pm (closed Sunday)/6-11.30pm. Branch: The Last Days of the Raj, 565 Durham Road, Low Fell, Gateshead. Stocks Cobra.

Houghton-le-Spring

PENSHAW TANDOORI

13 Chester Road, Penshaw,
Houghton-le-Spring   ℭ 0191 512 0015

'This is my local and I visit it frequently. It is a small, licensed establishment in a village location which does considerable takeaway trade. Excellent food and prices are reasonable. The Baltis are served in an enormous karahi, if you are a man; the fairer sex always gets a smaller version, much to the indignation of my girlfriend.' NW. Stocks Cobra.

TANDOORI NIGHT TAKEAWAY

98 Newcastle Street, Houghton-le-Spring   ℭ 0191 584 5037

A. Ahmed's specials include fish dishes, from £3.90. Madras Chicken most popular. Price check: Papadam 50p, CTM £4.30, Pullao Rice £1.15. Delivery: £5 minimum, 5-mile radius. Hours: 6pm-12am.

Newcastle upon Tyne

INDIANNA TAKEAWAY

6 West View, Forest Hall, Newcastle   ℭ 0191 270 0423

Luson Miah (chef), serves formula curries at his takeaway establishment. But how about this special: Naga Tikka Masala, exceedingly hot, made with naga chillies (a type of Habañero scotch bonnet) £4.70.[Beam me up Scotty, or is that Scotchy? -Ed]. 'My wife and I have a takeaway once a week. Friendly efficient service.' DH. Price check: Papadam 40p, CTM £4.80, Pullao Rice £1.60. Soft drinks also available. Delivery: £8 minimum, 6-mile radius. Hours: 5.30pm-12am.

LAHORE TAKEAWAY NEW ENTRANT

32 Vauxhall Road, Walkergate, Newcastle ℰ 0191 295 3818

'I have tried several of the curries and they are quite exquisite, oodles
of spices and fresh ingredients but nothing overdone. They are so delicious I find myself running my fingers around the empty cartons, a
thing I've never done before in 15 years.' LS. Price check : CTM £4.40,
Keema Pillau Rice £1.90, Papadam 45p.

LEELA'S NEW ENTRANT   ©

20 Deans Street, Newcastle   ℰ 0191 230 1261

Established in 1990, owned by Paul and Leela. Seats 60, serves South
Indian food. 'Best treat in Newcastle. Welcomes you, takes your order,
even makes your order for you if you'll give them a free hand. She suggested a vegetarian feast that was flawless. Food preparation is
supervised by her husband Paul, and is the best. Deserves to be
extremely popular!' WH. Special: Paper Dosa, lentil and rice pancake
with savoury sauce £3.95. Chemmen, marinated prawns stir-fried with
cashew nuts £5.50. Irachi Thoran, strips of lean lamb, soaked in
almond sauce and stir-fried £4.95. All sounds great! Price check:
Papadam 50p, Pullao Rice £2.50. House wine £10.95. Hours: 12.30-
2.30pm/6-11.30pm. Sunday closed. Stocks Cobra.

RAJ

Bigg Market, Newcastle upon Tyne   ℰ 0191 232 1450

'Got a great Garlic Chicken Tikka and Egg Pilau takeaway.' RDL. Stocks
Cobra.

RUPALI

6 Bigg Market, Newcastle upon Tyne   ℰ 0191 232 8629

'Being a CC member I booked a table and had a very nice meal. When
I was at University in Newcastle I regularly went to the Rupali.
However, when the bill came there was no discount. I asked Mr Latif,
who despite seeing my membership card tried to catch me out by asking how often the magazine came out. Eventually got a 10% discount,
which according to the guide should have been 20%. Who is right?' GL.
Naughty old Abdul. It was him, not us, who wanted to offer 20%. But

worse, we've heard of others refused the discount altogether. So we ask too, why say one thing and do another? True, it is up to Mr Latif to do the deal as stated on the last pages of this Guide. But rest assured he has heard of The Curry Club and the Guide. It's not up to him to ask you such questions. For that Latif, you are now delisted as a top 100. Indeed, you came near to a total delisting from the Guide, saved only by comments like these: 'Lovely Punjabi Thali at one of the town's finest, though service a little slow.' RDL. 'Even though Paul Gascoigne was a regular at the Rupali during his Newcastle days, the food's always been good.' AN. Price check: Papadam 50p, CTM £6.50, Pullao Rice £1.70. House wine £6.95. Takeaway: 20% discount. Hours: 12-2pm (Fri. closed)/5.30pm-12am. Sun. 7-11.30pm. Reports please. Stocks Cobra.

SACHINS TOP 100

Old Hawthorn Inn, Forth Banks,
Newcastle upon Tyne   © 0191 261 9035

We always seem to have so little to say about Sachins. Actually, contented reports rain in, and so be it, Sachins stays comfortably on our TOP 100, really for being spot on, unpretentious, non-exhibitionist, and well above average. Among the popular starter and main course favourites is Paneer Pakora, curd cheese deep-fried in a gram flour batter, Murgh Pakora, chicken pieces deep-fried in a gram flour batter, Murgh Marchi Masala, like a Chicken Tikka Masala but with fresh green chillies to give it a bite. 'Thoroughly enjoyed my Muglai Akbari.' FD. Scottish owner Liam Cunningham adds to the flair. Reports please. Stocks Cobra.

SHIKARA   ©

52 St Andrew's Street, Newcastle   © 0191 233 0005

Bodrul Haque's massive 150-seater is on two floors. Chef Tipu Sultan's specials include: Murg Tandoori Masala Panjabi Style £8.75. 'Great value for money.' MS. 'Impressive menu.' DC. Price check: Papadam 40p, CTM £6.25, Pullao Rice £1.75. House wine £8.50. Takeaway: 15% off. Hours: 12-2pm (Sunday closed)/6-11.30pm (12am on Thurs., Fri. and Sat.). Stocks Cobra.

SOLOMON'S NEW ENTRANT

Thorntree farm, West Road, Denton Burn,
Newcastle   © 0191 274 2323

Converted farmhouse. 'First problem, the menu, I have read shorter
novels. Chose Punjabi Murgh Tikka, very spicy. On clearing the table,
the waiter jokingly commented that I would have stomach problems in
2 hours!! – I didn't. Three main courses, superb. Angoori Chicken had
grapes in the sauce. Paratha appeared to be a fried Nan. No dessert,
by this stage the (no problem) stomach is sufficently full.' TOC. 'The
menu warned me that my starter was spicy, and it was. My Singapore
Curry was a little bit different. Why didn't this place exist when I lived
at home?' TOC.

VALLEY JUNCTION 397 NEW TO OUR TOP 100

397 The Old Station, Jesmond, Newcastle © 0191 281 6397

Daraz and his brother Locku have a penchant for purchasing old railway stations and making money from them. First they spend a great
deal to get the decor right. This one was formerly the Carriage Pub.
The carriage in question was built for the Great Northern Railway at
Doncaster in 1912. Numbered 397, it was a saloon for 'wealthy families
to hire for their journeys'. Now incorporated into the restaurant, it is
decked out in greens and golds, and still earns its keep for the well-
heeled. Like it's sister restaurant, it has quickly earned a reputation for
good food, indeed the menus are identical. Chingri Varkee, grilled
green pepper stuffed with spicy prawns £3.50. Tandoori Dhakna, chick-
en wings marinated in fresh herbs and spices, served with minty
yoghurt sauce £2.95. Murgh e Khazana, breast of chicken cooked
mainly with mild spices and honey, in a creamy sauce £7.50. Mangsho
Pesta Ke Shadi, top side of beef cooked with a blend of mild spices
and pistachio nuts. £7.95. Reports Please. Branch: The Valley, The Old
Station House, Station Road, Corbridge, Northumberland. Safe bet
new TOP 100.

VUJON TOP 100   ©

29 Queen Street, Newcastle upon Tyne   © 0191 221 0601

'Established in 1990 by Matab Miah (manager). Stylish restaurant, up-
market surroundings, seats 90 on two floors, party room 40.

Comfortable, well-lit and very clean. No standard curries, but starter and main courses proved interesting and a good choice.' KDF. Remains in our TOP 100, and gives discounts. Price check: Papadam 60p, CTM £8.90, Pullao Rice £1.90. House wine £8.90. Hours: 11.30-2.30pm/6.30-11.30pm. Stocks Cobra.

South Shields

INDIAN BRASSERIE

146 Ocean Road, South Shields   ✆ 0191 456 8800

Cheap and cheerful formula curries and accompaniments. Price check: Papadam 30p, CTM £4.45, Pullao Rice £1.30. Hours: 12-2.30pm/5.30pm-12am (2am on Fri. and Sat.). Stocks Cobra.

KHANA PINA

150 Ocean Road, South Shields   ✆ 0191 454 4407

At Syed Faruk and Feruz Hussain's Khana, 'menu well presented and informative. Quantities were more than ample and the quality first class. Second to none service. Pleasant seating and decor.' KR. 'Good variety on the menu, generous quantities. Excellent quality and flavours. Restful and comfortable and clean. Value for money.' JC. Price check: Papadam 40p, CTM £4.95, Pullao Rice £1.45. Minimum charge £5. Hours: 5.30pm-12am. Closed on Monday.

NASEEB

90 Ocean Road, South Shields   ✆ 0191 456 4294

'Impressed with the layout and decor. A bright and airy restaurant. The meals arrived hot, looking great and smelling wonderful. Very good portions were all eagerly consumed. No hesitation in recommending the Naseeb.' TH.

SAFFRON BALTI HOUSE   ©

86 Ocean Road, South Shields   ✆ 0191 456 6098

Abdul Kadir's 56-seater has 'light modern decor with traditional pictures on the walls, comfortable seating with tables for 2 to 8 people.' Sunday lunch £3.95. Takeaway: 15% off. Price check: Papadam 45p,

CTM £5.50, Pullao Rice £1.65. House wine £3.95. Hours: 12-2.30pm (Friday closed)/6pm-12.30am (2am on Fri. and Sat., 12am on Sun.). Stocks Cobra.

STAR OF INDIA ©

194 Ocean Road, South Shields   ℂ 0191 456 2210

The first curry house in South Shields, it opened in 1960, and was taken over by M. Faruque in 1972. Seats 60, light gold and white wall coverings, burgundy seats, alcove seating on both sides of restaurant. Specials: Chicken Tikka Jalfrezi £5.60. Chilli Pilau (£1.95) Takeaway: 15% off. Price check: Papadam 40p, CTM £5.60, Pullao Rice £1.85. Hours: 12-2.30pm/5.30pm-12am. Branch: Royal Bengal, Prince Regent Street, Stockton. Shapla, 192, Northgate, Darlington. Stocks Cobra.

TANDOORI INTERNATIONALE

97 Ocean Road, South Shields   ℂ 0191 456 2000

J. and N. Islam's 60-seater is situated in a converted boarding house. The restaurant is the former dining room. Special: Nargisi Kofta, boiled egg coated with pounded lamb, fried and soaked in a curry sauce £4.50. 'Good ambience with tasty food, reasonably priced. I ordered Nargisi Kofta with sauce, both were good, but no trace of a boiled egg.' DM. Special 3-Course Menu, Sunday to Friday until 11pm, only £5.40, including glass of wine. Takeaway: 10% off. Price check: Papadam 50p, CTM £5.50, Pullao Rice £1.50. Lager £2 pint. Hours: 12-2.30pm/6pm-12am.

Sunderland

CHESTER HALAL TAKEAWAY   NEW ENTRANT

169 Chester Road, Sunderland   ℂ 0191 510 8835

Owned and managed by Monwar Ahmed since 1978. Special: Brahmen's Thali £5.25. Sunday and Thursday special menu – 5-course £4.95, 7-course £7.75. Price check: Papadam 25p, CTM £4.50, Pullao Rice £1.15. Hours: 5.20pm-12.30am.

GRANGETOWN TANDOORI KITCHEN ©

1 Stockton Terrace, Grangetown,
Sunderland   ✆ 0191 565 5984

A takeaway-only establishment, managed by Shofozul Islam. Special:
Lamb Pudina, mint and imli £3.55. Price check: Papadam 25p, CTM
£4.45, Pullao Rice £1.25. Delivery: £5 minimum, 3-mile radius, £1
charge. Hours: 12-2pm/5.30pm-12am. Sun. 6pm-12am.

Wallsend

LIGHT OF INDIA

120 High Street East, Wallsend   ✆ 0191 234 5556

'Manager Mr Salik is always very helpful. Food more than enough,
does an excellent Chicken Tikka Chilli Mosala.' MS. Hours: 12-2.30pm/
6pm-12.30am, closed Sunday lunch.

Whickham

JAMDANI ©

3 The Square, Front Street, Whickham   ✆ 0191 496 0820

Opened in 1988 by Mr A. Miah. Try the Chicken Saffron £6.95 or King
Prawns £7.50 – delicious. Price check: Papadam 40p, CTM £5.95,
Pullao Rice £1.75. Open 12-2pm/6-11.30pm. Stocks Cobra

Whitley Bay

HIMALAYA ©

33 Esplanade, Whitley Bay   ✆ 0191 251 3629

Reliable curry house. Owner is Abdul Goffar. Hours: 12-2.30pm/
5.30pm-12am. Stocks Cobra.

KISMET ©

177 Whitley Road, Whitley Bay   ✆ 0191 297 2028

Originally opened in 1968, but taken over by Maklisur Rahman in
1996. Pakistani Punjabi cooking and Bangladeshi formula curries on

TYNE AND WEAR

the menu. Friday night is Balti night – six courses for £7.95 – great value. Price check: Papadam 35p, CTM £5.35, Pullao Rice £1.45. Open 12-2.30pm/6pm-12am, closed Tues. lunchtime. Branch: Jesmond Takeaway, Jesmond Road, Newcastle. Stocks Cobra.

SHAHENSHAH ©

187-189 Whitley Road, Whitley Bay ℂ 0191 297 0503

Established 1988 by Abu Taher, 'good-looking' decor. Bangladeshi formula curries cooked by A. Hannan.'Food first-class. Chicken Tikka terrific, full of flavour.' MB. 'My local for a year.' SN. 'We found the restaurant busy in a quiet and efficient way. Cobra the perfect accompaniment.' PP. Hours: 12-2.30pm/6pm-12am. Stocks Cobra.

TAKDIR ©

11 East Parade, Whitley Bay ℂ 0191 253 0236

Majibur Rahman's reliable 70-seater. Price check: Papadam 30p, CTM £5.10, Pullao Rice £1.50. Minimum charge £10. Hours: 5.30pm-12am. Branches: Akash, 3 Tangier Street, Whitehaven, Cumbria; Al Mamun Takeaway, 5 John Street, Cullercoats. Stocks Cobra.

Winlaton

BALTI HOUSE ©

18a The Garth, Front Street, Winlaton ℂ 0191 414 2223

A 34-seater. Owner F.I. Khan promises to increase his takeaway discount from 15% to 20% for CC members. You can't get fairer than that! Hours: 6pm-12am. Branch: Balti House, Newcastle. Stocks Cobra.

©	Curry Club discount (see page 6)	☕	Unlicensed
√	Vegetarian		
BYO	Bring your own alcohol	⊞	Delivery/takeaway

WARWICKSHIRE

Area: Midlands
Population: 483,000
Number of restaurants in county: 64
Number of restaurants in Guide: 16

Alcester

CELLAR

7 Market Place, High Street, Alcester   ✆ **01789 764635**

Formerly Balti Cellar. M. Hussain's 60-seater, traditional vaulted historical cellar. Specials: Crab and Duck dishes. Price check: Papadam 60p, CTM £6.95, Pullao Rice £1.95. Lager £2.25 pint, house wine £8.95. Hours: 6pm-12am.

Coles Hill

POLASH BALTI CUISINE   NEW ENTRANT

85 High Street, Coles Hill, B46   ✆ **01675 462868**

Opened in the new year by Enam Uddin and Adbul Mannan. Chef Taj Ullah cooks up the curries. Special: Bengal Fish Masala, Bangladeshi fish on the bone, cooked with herbs, coriander, served with rice £8.95. Cosy curry house, seats 32 diners, decorated in cream, blue velvet chairs and carpet, engraved glass screens divide seating. House wine £6.95. Takeaway: 10% off. Price check: Papadam 40p, CTM £5.50, Pullao Rice £1.70. Delivery: £15. Hours: 5.30-12. Stocks Cobra.

Henley-in-Arden

ARDEN TANDOORI   NEW ENTRANT

137 High Street, Henley-in-Arden   ✆ **01564 792503**

Owned by Nanu and Angor Miah, since 1984. Bangladeshi curry house, 'expensively fitted out in a nice light green and pink marble effect.' Specials: Nan Rathan Bhuna — succulent pieces of chicken, lamb and king prawn, medium-spiced. Price check: Papadam 45p,

CTM £6.25, Pullao Rice £1.65. Lager £1.90 pint, house wine £6.95. Takeaway: 20% less. Special: Lobster and Spinach Balti £8.25. Channa (chickpeas) Balti £4.75. Hours: 12-2.30pm/5.30pm-12am. Branches: Saleem Bagh, 476 Station Road, Dorridge, Solihull. Saleem Bagh, Queen Square, Cannock, Staffs. Plaza Balti, 4 Mill Street, Cannock, Staffs. Reports please.

Kenilworth

BALTI TOWERS

Kenilworth Lodge Hotel, 149 Warwick Road,
Kenilworth   © 01926 851156

60-seater managed by John Perrins. Specials: Tandoori Trout £5.50, Quorn Tikka Masala £5.95. Price check: Papadam 40p, CTM £5.95, Pullao Rice £1.30. Minimum charge: £5. Hours: 6pm-12am.

RAFFLES   NEW ENTRANT

57 Warwick Road, Kenilworth   © 01926 864300

'Ultra expensive, top-quality, extremely upmarket restaurant. Choice of Malaysian Malay, Malaysian Chinese or Malaysian Indian. Curry Puff, triangular samosa shaped pastry but very different inside, exquisite taste. Ikin Kelaph, plaice in a crumb coating, which included coconut, deep-fried and very crispy, served with stir-fried asparagus, carrots, sweet potatoes and a spicy dip, most enjoyable. Sambal Ikan, magnificently spicy fish in a beautiful sauce, quite superb! Ais Kacing, shaved ice, condensed milk, rose water, bits of jelly, assorted colours. Very cold; as it melted, I fished around and got bits such as red kidney beans, very unusual. Superb service.' GGP&MP.

SUNAM BALTI HOUSE   BYO ALLOWED

57 Abbey End, Abbey Court, Kenilworth   © 01926 863070

Amin Uddin's 62-seater. Northern Indian food on the menu. Licensed, but you are welcome to bring your own wines, strictly before 9.30pm, a small charge will be added to your table. House special is Garlic King Prawns £6.50. BYO, 25p corkage per person. Price check: Papadam 40p, CTM £4.95, Pullao Rice £1.50. Lager £1.90 pint, house wine £6.50. Takeaway: 10% off. Hours: 5-11.30pm.

Leamington Spa

ASHOKA TOP 100

22 Regent Street, Leamington Spa   © 01926 428272

'Consistently the best. Variety and quality of food speaks for itself.
Free popadoms when collecting a takeaway.' SN&RA. Hours: 6pm-2am,
opens 6.30pm Sun., closes 3am Fri. & Sat. We've not heard from them
or from you. Delist next time? Till then remains in our TOP 100.
Stocks Cobra.

BOMBAY TANDOORI   ©

38-40 Regent Street, Leamington Spa   © 01926 420521

Opened in 1990 by chef Anar Ahmed. Serves Bangladeshi and north
Indian curries. House specials Khata Masli, ayre Bangladeshi fish
steaks in tangy spicy sauce £6.75. Kooris Lamb – whole leg of spring
lamb spiced, marinated for at least eight hours, roasted tandoori-style,
garnished with mincemeat and served with Vegetable Bartha and Pillao
Rice – £58.50 for four. Minimum order £5.50. Special: Takeaway: 20%
off. Price check: Papadam 50p, CTM £5.95, Pullao Rice £1.50. House
wine £6.25. Delivery: £12 minimum, 3-mile radius. Hours: 6pm-1am
(3am on Fri. & Sat.). Stocks Cobra.

Nuneaton

RAJDHANI   ©

1 Cambourne Drive, Horeston Grange,
Nuneaton   © 01203 352254

Surat Miah's 56-seater. Opened in 1985. Unusual specials: Tikka Paneer
Jalfrezi, cooked with tomatoes, onion and green chillies, £6.95. and
Tandoori Quail £8.95 or Trout £6.50. Minimum charge £12. Price
check: Papadam 40p, CTM £6.95, Pullao Rice £1.75. Lager £1.90 pint,
house wine £6.45. Takeaway: 20% off. Hours: 5.30-11pm.

SUNDARBON   ⊞

39 Attleborough Road, Nuneaton   © 01203 344243

Owned by K. and S. Miah. 'Very, very good.' PJ. Price check: Papadam 20p, CTM £5.50, Pullao Rice £1.40. Hours: 5pm-12am (1am on Sat.).

Rugby

DILRUBA

155-157 Railway Terrace, Rugby   © 01788 542262

Owner Liaquat Ali's popular 54-seater. Special: Fish Rogon £5.50. Price check: Papadam 60p, CTM £6.50, Pullao Rice £1.60. Takeaway: 10% off. Delivery: £10 minimum. Hours: 6pm-1am (2am on Sat.). Stocks Cobra.

Stratford-upon-Avon

HUSSAIN'S

6a Chapel Street, Stratford-upon-Avon   © 01789 205804

Omor Khalid's 60-seater (party room 26) is close to all theatres, and popular with actors, apparently. 'Delicious curries, Chicken Biriani and Chicken Tikka Masala came with veritable slabs of succulent chicken breast. Superb featherweight Pillau Rice, best we've tasted! Cosy atmosphere. Good Nan.' HS. Special: Rup Chanda, skate-like fish from the Bay of Bengal, fried and cooked with onions, fresh tomatoes, herbs and green chillies £7.25. Price check: Papadam 40p, CTM £7.25, Pullao Rice £1.90. Delivery: £15 minimum order. House wine £7.50. Takeaway: 15% discount. Hours: 12-2pm/5pm-12am. Stocks Cobra.

LALBAGH BALTI   ©

3 Greenhill Street, Stratford-upon-Avon   © 01789 293563

Opened in 1989 by Abdul Aziz, who is also to be found in the kitchen as head chef. Decorated in maroon with patterned wallpaper, green carpet and Bangladeshi pictures on the wall. Specials: Mushroom on Puri £2.30, Fish Kebab £2.95. 'Conventional menu. Excellent comfort. Polite and reserved service. Papadoms served with delicious sauce and onion relish, very good. Lalbagh Special Chicken £5.95, large quantity, wholesome chicken, quality ingredients.' G&MP. Price check: Papadam 50p, CTM £6.25, Pullao Rice £1.80. Lager £2.30 pint, house wine £9.95. Takeaway: 20% off. Hours: 6pm-12.30am.

RAJ   NEW ENTRANT ©

7 Greenhill Street, Stratford Upon Avon   © 01789 267067

Formerly Baltiwalla. Owner/manager Nurul Zaman Khan. Decoration: mixture of burgundy and cream colours. Special: Chicken Sath Lemon Sylheti, diced chicken cooked in medium spiced sauce with sath lemon (shakora) £6.30. Price check: Papadam 35p, CTM £6.30, Pullao Rice £1.80. Delivery: £15 minimum, 4-mile radius. Hours: 12.30pm-12.30am. Sunday lunch closed. Stocks Cobra.

THESPIAN'S INDIAN CUISINE ©

26 Sheep Street, Stratford-upon-Avon   © 01789 267187

Opened in 1996 by chef-proprietor Habibur Rahman. Air-conditioned. Bangladeshi food features on his menu. For an interesting change, try Boal Biriani for a starter £3.25 – fillets of Bengal boal, lightly spiced. House specials include Lobster Beruda, aubergine-flavoured sauce, served with Pilau Rice £9.75. 'Very wide menu, unusual choices. Predominantly pink lounge with mock tudor bar. Very comfortable with pleasant surroundings. Variable quality and quantity.' GGP&MP. Price check: Papadam 35p, CTM £6.50, Pullao Rice £1.70. Minimum charge £10.95. Delivery: minimum £10, 3-mile radius. Hours 5.30pm-12am. Branches: Knowle Indian Brasserie, High Street, Knowle; Stockland Balti Takeaway, Marsh Lane, Erdington, Birmingham.

Warwick

CASTLE BALTI BYO

11 St John's, Warwick   © 01926 493007

'Asked three separate locals for their recommendation and it was recommended by all three. FAN-BALTI-TASTIC. Quality of food, service and value for money outstanding. Shami Kebab followed by Chicken Mushroom Balti with Nan – absolutely the best – superb.' CP.

WEST MIDLANDS

Birmingham

Area: Midlands
Population: 2,615,000
Birmingham — Britain's Second City,
    1,018,000
Number of restaurants in county: 469
Number of restaurants in Guide: 93

At the hub of the county of West Midlands is Birmingham city. Unquestionably Britain's number two city, Brum has come vibrantly alive with investment in its centre. The new convention-centre-concert hall-hotel complex has breathed excitement into the city, not least by placing the buildings, and a number of new pubs and restaurants, alongside the confluence of four canals. For those unaware of what flows beneath and between Brum's busy roads, there is no better place to view this astonishing network. There are even a couple of Birmingham's other assets nearby: Balti houses. It was here that the G8 heads of state met this year. Pictures of Clinton, Chirac, Kohl, et al being fussed over by new-boy Blair, were flashed round the world. It is even said they all ate a Balti! For the purposes of this Guide, we divide the city into geographical areas, in which are grouped postcode zones B1 to B48 although, as ever, there is no sequential logic to postcode numbering. We start with Birmingham Central, then go to the adjacent Balti Zone, next North, East, South East, South West, and West. Further B postcodes, B62 (Halesowen) to B93 (Solihull) follow, listed alphabetically by their suburb name.

Birmingham Central Postcodes B1 to B5 (restaurants listed in alphabetical order)

AGRA FORT ©

**14-16 Suffolk Street Queensway,
Birmingham, B1**   ℂ **0121 643 2230**

Situated next to the Alexandra Theatre, Jamal Chaudhuri's 150-seater is very smart. Its large plate-glass windows allow you a peep inside. If you come by car, it's valet parking. The decor is not typically Indian.

Polished wooden floor, creamy-gold walls with faint murals of zebras and peacocks. Comfortable, armchair seating makes this the sort of restaurant where you can relax and spend the evening. Specials include South Indian Garlic Chilli Chicken, North Indian Murgh-e-Shanazi, Bengali Lobster Masala, and the Thalis. Price check: Papadam complimentary, CTM £7.25, Pullao Rice £1.80. Open 12-2.30pm/6pm-12am (2am on Sat.). Closed Sun. Branch: Yew Tree Cottage, Birmingham, B25.

ALOKA

6-8 Bristol Street, Birmingham, B5   © 0121 622 2011

By 1960, Birminham centre had just one curryhouse. It was at the above address. I know because I always came here from as far afield as Coventry, where I lived and worked, which had none. I really don't remember if it was called the Aloka then, but it is now. During the 1960s, the spread of the curry house was as prolific as the city's building. Now it's Birmingham 280, Coventry 40. So here's to the Aloka, a pioneer indeed. Reports, please.

FESTIVAL BALTI   ©

204 Arcadian Centre, Birmingham, B5   © 0121 622 6289

Mojibul Haque's 48-seater is chic and modern and packed with smart young people on the night we looked in. Chef Abdul Ali's specials include Chicken or Lamb Shatkora, made tangy with the Sylhetti lemon (£5.95) and Seafood Delight (£4.95), medium-spiced with fish, prawns and scampi. Pops and free chutney. 'Lamb Tikka £2.60 sparse, Fish Pakora £3.50 good size. Very nice Chicken Rogan Josh £4.80. Presentation of food excellent. Restaurant clean and tidy.' GG&MP. Price check: Papadam 40p, CTM £4.80, Pullao Rice £1.80. Minimum charge £5. Hours: 5-11.30pm, Fri. & Sat. lunch 12-2pm.

MAHARAJAH   BEST IN THE MIDLANDS   TOP 100

23 Hurst Street, Birmingham, B5   © 0121 622 2641

I recall this restaurant serving Biriani topped with edible silver leaf (vark) when it first opened in the 1970s. It was the first time I'd seen it used in Britain, though traditionalists in India would not contemplate the dish without it. It was a Moghul fetish, of course, the emperor permitting a gold leaf garnish only on the food for himself and the chosen member of the harem (the dish of the day!), while his wives had to make do with silver leaf. They believed it to be an aphrodisiac. It is not for me to comment on the validity of this claim and, with the EU ban on vark, neither can anyone else in Britain. (The CC still sells by post pure silver vark purchased from Hyderabad.) So the Maharajah is no longer allowed to serve it, sadly. The menu looks a little ordinary, but the food is still outstanding. I came here unbooked alone one dinner time. Despite a full to bursting room, I was seated at once and served with every care and attention. There were the usual contented groups of Asians, always a good sign of authenticity, and I was not the only loner. A young Asian woman was uncomfortably alone, peering frequently out of the window, and explaining that her friends would soon arrive. Owner N. Bhatt did his utmost to relax her with nibbles and a drink, and smiling chat, *en passant*, and eventually her uncles and father arrived, with profuse apologies. Meanwhile the waiting bookers were deftly dispatched to the downstairs bar. Such competence is rare and welcome. On two floors, it's a small place, and booking is recommended. The food is Indian, cooked by Gurmaj Kumar and Jaskarn Dhillon, and it is always spot on. Ask about the Special Dish of the Day. We continue to receive plentiful reports on the Maharajah. Stays in our TOP 100, indeed, I'm happy to give it our BEST IN THE MIDLANDS Award. Price check: Papadam 65p, CTM £6.35, Pullao Rice £1.90. Set Dinner: £12.15. Hours: 12-2pm/6-11pm, Fri. & Sat. lunch 12-2pm. Closed Sun. and bank holidays.

MILAN INDIAN CUISINE   ©

93 Newhall Street, Birmingham, B3   ℂ 0121 236 0671

Dhirendra Patel's 120-seater is decorated in pastel shades, giving it a light and airy feel. The bar area is typically Indian with beaten copper drinks tables and large coffee pots. Chef Balbir Malhi's menu features all the usual curry house favourites from Korma to Jalfrezi but there is also an extensive vegetarian section. Paneer Tikka £2.25, spicy paneer cooked in the tandoor. Stuffed peppers filled with coconut, potatoes and coriander £1.95. Reshmi Mattar Paneer £4.50, homemade cheese with herbs, spices, peas, cashews and corn. Price check: Papadam 60p, CTM £6.25, Pullao Rice £1.75. Minimum charge £8.50. Open 12-2pm/6pm-12am. Branches: (t/a only Stoney Lane, B'hm and 296 S. Abel Street, Milpitas, nr San José, California, US. Stocks Cobra.

MOKHAM'S OF DIGBETH   🍵 ©

140 Digbeth High Street, Birmingham, B5   © 0121 643 7375

Of Naz Khan's venue AM says 'Mokham's pride themselves on their cooking so you may have to wait as all the food is freshly prepared. Tandoori Sheeksh Kebab is certainly one of the best I have ever tasted. Balti Exotica is meat, chicken, prawns, mushroom and pasta, without doubt unique in my experience. A very substantial dish, served up in the traditional black bowl, it was beautifully spiced and the pasta blended superbly but when combined with my Nan bread it left me feeling like Pavarotti.' Hours: 12-2.30pm/6pm till late.

RAJDOOT   ©

12 Albert Street, Birmingham, B4   © 0121 643 8749

MS Gill manages this 84-seat branch of Des Sarda's Rajdoot (the others are in Bristol, Manchester, Dublin and Fuengirola, Spain). He opened this one in 1972. As are all the Rajdoots, it is fully air-conditioned and tastefully and authentically decorated. Des is an architect and knows a thing or two about style. The chefs here are Nepalese (head chef Basu Mali) and their cooking is as delicate as you'll find. 'Absolutely superb, we find this establishment to be extremely reliable. Fish Tikka starter exquisite as usual as was the Chilli Chicken Tikka, generous portions. King Prawn Chilli Garlic was a favourite amongst our group again but I decided to try the Lamb Punjabi Massalla this time and what a good choice!! Meat extremely lean and well spiced, served in a dark onion and tomato gravy finished with balsamic vinegar and red wine. We ordered the usual side dishes, dal of the day, Bombay Allo Jeera and Sag Paneer as well as Pillau Rice and Peshwari Nan, all of which were fresh and cooked to perfection.' CT. I regret to say that like the other Rajdoots, (*see* entries) we do get complaints. Price check: Papadam free, CTM £7.60, Pullao Rice £1.80. Service charge 10%. Hours: 12-2.30pm (not Sun.)/6.30-11.30pm.

©	Curry Club discount (see page 6)		Unlicensed
√	Vegetarian		
BYO	Bring your own alcohol	⊞	Delivery/takeaway

Birmingham – Balti Zone
B10 to B13 postcodes
(restaurants in alphabetical order)

The Balti Zone starts about 2 miles south east of the city (follow the A34), and is thickly spread around the suburbs of Small Heath, Sparkhill, Sparkbrook and Moseley (B10 to B13). The population is largely north Pakistani, mostly from Kashmir's Mirpur, adjacent to which is the district of Baltistan, high up in the Pakistani mountains. You'll find recipes and more about this subject in my newly published 'Balti Bible' (see page 2). Those who doubt the existence of Baltistan should visit 2 baltihouse, upon whose walls is the biggest map of the region that I've seen, and it is from there that Balti originated. But for those who prefer to say it did so in a bucket in Birmingham, you are certain to get the nation's best Baltis here. Here are your favourites, and watch for comments from 'AM' the Balti King himself, Andy Munroe.

ADIL 1 BEST UK BALTI TOP 100   ☕ BYO ©

148-150 Stoney Lane, Sparkbrook, B11   ✆ 0121 449 0335

Mohammed Arif, Rashid and Abid Mahood opened here in 1975. Although they are not the first balti (it was a café called the Paris opened in 1973 by a Mr Ramzan, the former long-closed, the latter had retired back to native Baltistan before discovering that he had started an international cult). Arif is happy to claim first, and he is indisputably the longer at it. 'My grandafather' he says, 'ran a restaurant in Kashmir decades ago, called Adil meaning *Justice*. Customers chose their own fresh raw ingredients, and watched the entire cooking process. Apart from that, our Sparkbrook restaurant is identical.' Well, it was. There's been a sparkling modernisation recently, enlarging the place to 100 seats with 56 upstairs. It's a step upmarket (but not too far we hope) since I came here to do an evening chat show for BBC Radio W Midlands with Steve Nallon, Keith Vaz MP and Mr Ron (Aston Villa) Atkinson. Mrs A. nearly fainted when she observed the toilets as she delicately placed her high heels between the oil drums on her way upstairs! I'm pleased to see that the menu hasn't changed. Even the prices are much the same. It still offers 72 different Baltis, including their much-copied signature dish, meat 'chicken' mince with veg-dall-spi-chana. 'My birthday and what better, after a 7.30am champagne and Guinness breakfast in London's Smithfield Market, than to travel to Birmingham for a Balti at Adil's. After the initiation course of Green Chilli Bhajis 70p, we settled down to enjoy Balti Chicken Tikka Veg-Dall-Spi-Chana £5.20, two massive Table Nans £2.90 and two portions of rice £1. My colleague Ian (two puddings) Hunter could not contain himself, unable to decide between Rasmali 90p, Barfi 60p and Kulfi £1.40, and ate all three. Simple as ABC – Adil's for Balti Curry.' DB. 'If I'm anywhere near Birmingham I pilgrimage to Adil's. Oh! the Baltis! and so low a price. Avoid the starters, they are ordinary and the small portions make them poor value for money. Not licensed, but there is an off-licence next door run by his cousin. If you order a cab, the driver is another cousin! Family enterprise!' CD. Adil's own car park opposite. Often pioneers are best, and although Adil's took a dive in popularity and quality recently, I am happy to see it begin to thrive again in its second-generation-same-family management. Accordingly I am not only restoring Adils to our TOP 100, I am giving it our 1999 Best UK Balti Award. Price check: Papadam 35p, Pullao Rice: £1. CTM £4.50. Delivery: minimum £10. 3-mile radius. Hours: 12am-12am (1am Thurs.-Sat.).

ADIL 2   ©

130 Stoney Lane, Balsall Heath, B12   ✆ 0121 449 9296

Adil's other branch is really the overflow for Adil 1. Manager is M. Ashraf. Open 12pm-12am. Branch: Waterfront Balti, 127-129 Dudley Road, Brierley Hill.

ALAMGEER   BYO ©

811 Stratford Road, Sparkhill, B11   ✆ 0121 778 2388

G. Arif's unlicensed BYO 30-seater is always extremely welcoming. 'Onion Bhajias too salty, but the rest absolutely brilliant. Superb service, ample food, filthy, scruffy carpet.' GG&MP. Hours: 6pm-2.30am.

AL-FRASH   🍽 BYO ©

186 Ladypool Road, Sparkbrook, B12   ✆ 0121 753 3120

Mukhtar Ahmed's 85-seater is a smart and pleasantly decorated restaurant in pinks and blues with a spiral staircase. Quality high-backed chairs make for a comfortable evening. Starters include Onion Rings 65p, one of DBAC's favourites. It's one of Andy Munroe's top 10:

'Starters to die for – the mushroom and aubergine Pakoras come highly recommended. For main course try the "white rose" house speciality which is not a steal from a Bradford curry house but a popular Lahore dish comprising chunks of chicken breast languishing in a cardamom flavoured sauce with cashew and cream. Alternatively try Meetha Gosht which is tender lamb in fried onions, sultanas, coconut and almonds, a great balance of a spicy back taste off-setting the sweetness. Mop it all up with voluptuous garlic Nan, although the coriander version takes some beating.' AM. Price check: Balti Chicken and Mushroom £4.35, Nan 70p (small), £1.95 (medium) or £3 (large). Papadam 35p, CTM £4.80, Pullao Rice £1.30. Hours: 5pm-1am.

ALI BABA   🍺 BYO ©

250 Ladypool Road, Sparkbrook, B12   ✆ **0121 449 4929**

We like Mr Aslam's logo of a chap holding a sizzling Balti, sitting on a flying carpet (beats cars for home delivery?) 'Clean comfortable. BYO. Very good Sheek Kebab 70p, freshly cooked and spicy. Nice Roti, 60p. Lamb Bhuna, prepared with extra chilli, very accommodating £3.90.' RE. Price check: Papadam 30p, CTM £5, Pullao Rice 95p. Hours: 12-2.30pm/4pm till late. Branch: Nirala, Moseley Road.

DESI KHANA

706 Stratford Road, Sparkhill, B11   ✆ **0121 778 4450**

'This is my favourite. Decidedly Asian – European customers are rare – strict Muslim – a sign says "No Alcohol" so no BYO. Glass top tables and a shortish menu, but the food is good.' Seekh Kebabs £1.60 – freshly made in the front of the shop over coals – come in a sizzling platter with onions and are absolutely superb. Tarka Dhal £3.75 – excellent, but too much for one.' RE.

I AM THE KING OF BALTI   🍺 BYO ©

230-232 Ladypool Road, Sparkbrook, B12   ✆ **0121 449 1170**

Khalid Hussain's 44-seater is unlicensed, but if you bring your own wine they are very happy to chill it for you. King Kebab, £1.50 is the favourite starter with main course Kashmiri Chicken and Balti Chicken and Mushroom both £5. Beware the 5% charge on any payments made by credit or debit cards, though you're not likely to spend over £10. 'A regular eating place when we visit family. Never had a poor meal after half a dozen visits. Chicken Keema Balti is excellent for beginners. Nans as big as tennis rackets. Parking can be difficult.' PAW. Price check: Papadam 40p, CTM £6, Pullao Rice £1.60, Nan £1, Extra Large Nan £3.50. Delivery: £10 minimum, 3-mile radius. Hours: 3pm-12am, Fri. & Sat. 2pm-1am, Sun. 1pm-12am.

IB NE GHANI   ☕ ©

264-266 Green Lane, Small Heath, B9   ✆ 0121 772 8138

Competent curries and Baltis at Dawood Hussain's establishment. Hours: 5pm-1am, Fri. & Sat. 4pm-2am.

IMRAN'S BALTI HUT   ☕ BYO

264 Ladypool Road, Sparkbrook, B12   ✆ 0121 449 1370

'Baltis, superb. Family Nan, unbelievable – 3 feet by 2 feet. BYO from "offy" next door. Excellent value for money.' RS. 'Claims to have been around at the time of the first-ever splitting of Balti bread in Brum. Spacious and includes in-view cooking for those who like to see a Sheeksh Kebab being cooked live. My main course Balti Chicken and Mushroom had an impressively spicy kick. Unusually you can also get a family Chapatti also Quail Balti (a dish which has now achieved almost protected status).' AM. 'Lamb Jalfrezi, meat tough and lacked depth of flavour. Chicken Korma – too hot for a Korma and for my wife.' RE. Hours: 12pm-12am.

K2   ©

107 Alcester Road, Moseley, B13   ✆ 0121 449 3883

N. Pasha and M. Niam's 58-seater is named after the highest mountain in Pakistan, shown on the biggest map of Baltistan (to prove it exists to the doubters) on one wall. Peppered Chicken £3.10, is Chino-Tibetan (a Baltistan influence) with its sweet and sour chicken prepared with a mixture of black and green pepper, ginger, soya sauce, sugar and lime. Balti Chicken and Mushroom £5.50, Nan £1.20. Price check: Papadam served with mint sauce, 30p, CTM £6, Pullao Rice £1.30. Access and Visa accepted. Hours: 6-11.30pm.

KABABISH

29 Woodbridge Road, Moseley, B13   © 0121 449 5556

Khawaja Yaqub owns this 65-seater Pakistani restaurant. 'Very good service. Balti dishes were big and good value. Shame – out of okra. Aloo Mushrooms particularly good.' ST. Price check: Papadam 50p, CTM £5.95, Pullao Rice £1.50. Balti Chicken and Mushroom £5.55, Nan 95p. Minimum charge £5.50. Hours: 12-2.30pm/6-1130pm (12.30am on Fri. & Sat.), Sun. 6-11.30pm.

KASHMIR LODGE

132 Stratford Road, Sparkbrook, B12   © 0121 773 1632

'Housed in a former bank – the sort of grandiose building used before such establishments became virtually an excuse for a hole in the wall. Prices remain at a credible street level. There is a good range of Baltis including Balti Tinda (sweet potato) and Balti Karele (bitter gourd).' AM. Hours: 12-2.30pm/6-12pm.

KHYBER

365 Ladypool Road, Sparkbrook, B12   © 0121 449 5139

'Cosy family restaurant where the sign should read "enjoy as much as you like". Tasty Tikkas and no-nonsense Balti just like mom used to cook 'em. Lovingly prepared so expect to wait a little for a true taste of Birmingham's unique Balti experience'. AM.

KING'S PARADISE   ©

321 Stratford Road, Sparkhill, B12   © 0121 753 2212

Owned by Mahboob Hussain. 'Balti Tandoori Butter Chicken, very smooth-tasting, in bright red sauce with some onion in there. Peshwari Naan, large, tasty with just a hint of syrup.' G&MP. Mushroom Nan (£1.30) sounds great! Price check: BCTM £4.50, Pullao Rice £1.30. Open 12pm-2.30pm/5.30pm-12am. Private car parking.

©	Curry Club discount (see page 6)		Unlicensed
√	Vegetarian		
BYO	Bring your own alcohol		Delivery/takeaway

KUSHI   🍵 BYO ©

58 Moseley Road, Birmingham, B12   © 0121 449 7678

Messrs Mohammeda and Haydur's 62-seat 'Kushi appears to have picked up just about every cup apart from the Jules Rimet. However, never mind the awards, try the food. Kushi's Kebab is one of the best of its kind as are the sizzling Shashliks. Wide choice of main courses including Kushi's new and highly valued range of "saffron" dishes. Good selection of Nans from Keema to Kulcha'. AM. 'All nine of us agreed that this was a magnificent Balti house.' G&MP. Delivery: £10 minimum. Hours: 5.30pm-1am (2am on Sat.), Sun. 6pm-12am.

LAHORE KARAHI   NEW ENTRANT

357-363 Ladypool Road, Sparkbrook,B12   © 0121 447 9007

'Brash buffet-style where you can eat-as-much-as-you-like at a price.' AM. 'Albeit a buffet the quality of the food was excellent, with everything qualifying for the top "melt in the mouth" standard and for only £5.95 per person. The Lahore Karahi is highly recommended. Booking is advisable at weekends.' MJB.

PAKISTAN   NAME CHANGE   🍵 ©

127-129 Ladypool Road, Sparkbrook, B12   © 0121 440 1238

Formerly Kashmir Lake Balti, 'Seekh Kebabs 50p each – freshly made, good and spicy. Tasty and excellent value. One to go back to.' RE.

PLAZA TANDOORI   🍵 BYO ©

278 Ladypool Road, Balsall Heath, B12   © 0121 449 4249

The food at this unlicensed (BYO welcome) 80-seater is more Southall than Sparkbrook or Balti Heath, since owners R. Singh and G.S. Pank and chef Gurmit (1997 Birmingham Council Chef of the Year) are Sikhs who specialise in Northern Indian Punjabi food. This adds a different flavour to the cooking. 'Service attentive and friendly. Food good. Definitely one to return to.' RE. Price check (down on last year): Papadam 30p, CTM £4.60, Pullao Rice £1. Hours: 5pm-12am.

POPULAR BALTI   NEW ENTRANT   BYO

139 Ladypool Road, Sparkbrook, B12   © 0121 440 0014

'Cheap and cheerful Balti House. Food very good, complimentary Popadoms, freshly cooked Sheek Kebabs at 55p each. Nice and crisp Roti 40p. Reasonable toilets with soap and hot water. BYO.' RE.

POLASH   BYO

11 Hobmoor Road, Birmingham, B10   © 0121 766 8824

Yearning for the Bangladeshi curry house formula? BYO to Rafiqur Rahman's unlicensed 30-seater. Price check: Papadam 25p, CTM £3.50, Chicken Chilli Masala £3.25, Pullao Rice £1. Hours: 5.30pm-1am.

PUNJABI PARADISE   BYO

377 Ladypool Road, Sparkbrook, B12   © 0121 449 4110

'Mohammed Shabaz's popular place. One of the Balti glitterati featured on more TV programmes than Ulrika Jonsson. However, the food backs up the image – fresh coriander laden Baltis, yeasty Nan breads with a frantic but friendly atmosphere. Their special chicken Kebabs are worth a stab. Even has its own garage for all its valued (and that's everybody) customers.' AM. Price check: Papadam 25p, CTM £5.50, Pullao Rice £1.20. Minimum charge £6. Hours: 5pm-1am.

ROYAL AL FAISAL   BYO

136-140 Stoney Lane, Balsall Heath, B12   © 0121 449 5695

Spelt Faisal, or Faisel, the other venerable Balti, contemporary with Adil's from whom it is a few doors away, is Mohammed Ajaib's smartly decorated restaurant in shades of green. Seats 150 diners, tables of four and the usual banquet-style seating. Kashmiri Baltis on the menu. This is the place to get your Kharak Nan £3.30, absolutely huge. 'Very good Baltis.' CD. For the adventurous try their Balti Lotus Roots £3.50 or Balti Mustard Leaf (sarson) £3.50. Balti Chicken and Mushroom £4.30. Price check: Papadam 30p, CTM £4.60, Pullao Rice 90p. Minimum charge £6.50. Hours: 11.30am-12am.

ROYAL NAIM   TOP 100   🍴 BYO ©

417-419 Stratford Road, Sparkhill, B11   © 0121 766 7849

The Nazir brothers make Balti into an art form. Their restaurant is huge – 175 seats on two floors, yet it does not feel oversized. The decor is neither too much nor too little. It's open all hours, of course it's BYO, and the prices are very reasonable. You can fill yourself for £5, and blow up for £10. You are made welcome and are served with prompt efficiency throughout. Chef Shaffique and his crew are masters. The Royal Naim is a classic illustration of "Biggest is Best." Great food, big portions in voluminous sizzling black bowls, glass-topped tables and warm hospitality. Balti chicken with fresh fenugreek or mint is uniquely tasty. Like most royalty, the Naim had one weakness, in their case, precooked starters. Their Pakora has now been sent packing for a freshly prepared version which could batter any opposition. The Naim also produce deep frozen Baltis for retail outlets and local schools – no wonder Birmingham's education standards are starting to rise!' AM. 'When we had to go to Birmingham we took the opportunity to try the restaurant voted the Best Balti. The atmosphere was building before we found the actual restaurant because of the community in which it is situated and the numerous other Balti restaurants surrounding it. The basic nature emphasized the excellent food. Owner very attentive and helpful. Returned a month later. Once you get the Balti in front of you and taste it you don't want it to end.' SR. 'Visited on a busy Saturday night. Standard of service, choice, quality of food and value for money is very high. Party of eight, four adults, four children, plenty of choice for all. Our large Naan £3 covered the table. Washed down with a jug of Lassi. Ras Malai for pudding is hard to beat. Takeaway counter serves Samosas, Onion Bhajis just the thing for the journey home – if you live as far away as I do! My children insisted I make a detour two days later on our return from Kendal to Suffolk to revisit the Royal Naim.' DB. We were most disappointed to find the sweet cabinet crammed only with colas. Price check: Papadam 40p, BCTM £5.50, Pilau Rice £1.50. Delivery: 5-mile radius. Hours: 12-1am (3am on Fri. & Sat.). A Balti house not bettered by Adils, and very high in our TOP 100. Branch: Royal Stirchley Tandoori and Balti House, 1526-1528 Pershore Road, Stirchley, B30.

ROYAL KASHMIR LODGE   NEW ENTRANT

132 Stratford Road, Sparkhill, B11   © 0121 773 1632

'Very impressive decor, high ceilings, drape curtains, chandelier. Mixed Grill, Lamb Tikka, Chicken Tikka, Tandoori Fish, Sheesh Kebab at £3.50, wonderful mixture of flavours. Very large quantities, top-quality ingredients. Service slow with water and starters but these were obviously freshly cooked, so understandable.' GG&MP.

ROYAL NAWEED   BYO ©

44 Woodbridge Road, Moseley, B13   © 0121 449 2156

Mr Ali and Chef Shan's 'Free Popadoms with dips. Baltis very good. Huge Naan, eventually defeated us. No frills, clean, excellent value.' MJG. Price check: Papadam 30p, CTM £4.90, Pilau Rice 95p. Delivery: £6 minimum £1 charge! 4-mile radius. Hours: 12-2.30pm/6pm-12am.

SHAHI NAN KABAB

353 Stratford Road, Sparkhill, B11   © 0121 772 2787

'Long known for its vast range of barbecued starters including that protected species the liver tikka and combos of Bunter-like proportions (e.g. Rolly Polly – three Kebabs in a Shahi snacks including a large Paratha with salad and chutney) but make sure that you have got some room left for the spicy and tasty main course Baltis. Balti chicken and mushroom is a classic dish of its class but good selection of both meat and vegetarian dishes all at excellent prices!' AM Hours: 12pm-12am.

SHANDOR   NEW ENTRANT

353 Ladypool Road, Sparkbrook, B12   © 0121 449 5139

'Starters not to be trifled with including a Green Chilli Bhajia. Chicken Pakora £1 is excellent value. Tasty vegetarian dishes include Vegetable Black-eye bean and Mushroom Balti and the non vegetarians are recommended to try the Balti Chicken Jalfrezies. Shandar offer their Baltis cooked in low fat style but the secret behind this culinary breakthrough remains hidden. Incidentally it is licensed and £4.50 for a bottle of Sparkbrook's finest Liebfraumilch must make every hour a happy one.' AM.

SHEREEN KADAH

543 Moseley Road, Balsall Heath, B12   © 0121 440 4641

'One of the veteran Balti houses but a veteran with full honours. Over half the starters are below £1 but that doesn't affect the taste and authenticity as they are cooked in the open behind the counter. In the display cabinet is a selection of Kebabs on an array of sharp skewers which look like a Zulu armoury after an attack on Rourke's Drift. Fairly limited vegetarian choice but the menu does include some un-usual nuggets for meat-eaters including Balti Shahi Murgh, Tandoori Marinated Spring Lamb, charcoal cooked then served up in bay leaf juices with tomatoes onions, garlic and ginger. Giant family Nans are a snip at £2.50 with some nice rice including a lemon variety.' AM. Hours: 11am-12am.

SPICE AVENUE

526 Moseley Road, Birmingham, B13   © 0121 442 4936

Licensed corner-site with rear parking. 'Smart as any Avenue with a tempting selection of dishes. Starters include a challenging Lassan Shashlik which is pieces of chicken marinated in garlic and chilli sauce. Vegetarians aren't neglected with a vegetable Kebab which has at least nine(!) different vegetables fried in golden bread crumbs. For a main event the Balti ginger chicken is a straightforward but excellent com-bination. However, the lamb Shahan is an excellent exotic alternative with tender lamb cutlets stuffed with garlic mushrooms. Accompanying onion kulcha will make your eyes and mouth water.' AM.

Birmingham North
B6, B7, B19 to B24, B42 to B44 postcodes
(restaurants in alphabetical order)

BALTI SPICE TAKEAWAY   NEW ENTRANT   ©

1240 Aldridge Road, Great Barr, B44   © 0121 366 6548

Taken over in January '98 by Bilal Miah (manager) and Abdul Ahad (chef). Open kitchen, customers can see their formula curries cooking. Coke, Fanta and mineral water available. Price check: Papadam 30p,

CTM £4.95, Pullao Rice £1.20. Takeaway: 10% discount. Delivery: £8, 4-mile radius. Hours: 4.30-11.30pm (12.20pm on Sat.).

INDIA GARDEN

992 Tyburn Road, Erdington, B24   © 0121 373 9363

Gian Uddin's 80-seater 'venue is clean, modern and roomy. Staff friendly and efficient. 1st class menu, good choice of drinks. A BIG PLUS – security camera parking for the car.' GG&MP. Delivery: 5-mile radius. Price check: Papadam 50p, CTM £7.85, Pullao Rice £1.65. Buffet £8.50. Lager £2.15 pint, house wine £7.95. Delivery: £7, 4-mile radius. Hours: 5am-12.30am, Sat. 12am-2am. Sun. 1pm-1am.

RAJ INDIAN CUISINE

30 Birmingham Road, Great Barr, B43   © 0121 357 8368

50-seater, fully air-conditioned restaurant. Opened in 1990 (but originally in 1976) by M.A. Latif. Special: Lamb Tikka Green Masala, cooked with green masala hot and spicy £6.50. Price check: Papadam 40p, CTM £6.50, Pullao Rice £1.70. Sunday buffet £6.95. Takeaway: 20% less. Lager £2.10 pint, house wine £1.85 glass. Delivery: £12 minimum, 4-mile radius. Hours: 5.30-12.30. Branch: Arden Tandoori, Henley-in-Arden, Warks.

SAMRAT TANDOORI   ©

710 Chester Road, Erdington, B23   © 0121 384 5900

Samrat means Emperor, established in '83, managed by Mr Dey, chef Mr Choudhury. Air-conditioned, seats 50, party room 30. Special: Spicy Fish £3.30. Kurzi lamb, served with Basmati rice £21 for two. Price check: Papadam 45p, CTM £5.75, Pullao Rice £1.65. Lager £1.90 pint, house wine £1.35 glass. Delivery: £6, 5-mile radius. Hours: 5pm-1am (2am on Fri. & Sat.).

STOCKLAND BALTI   🍵 ©

221 Marsh Lane, Erdington, B23   © 0121 377 8789

A takeaway establishment, managed by Noor Ali, serving competent curries to a regular crowd. Open 5pm-12.30am (1am on Fri. & Sat.). Owned and managed by Mrs Amina Begum since '93. Price check:

Papadam 30p, CTM £4.10, Pullao Rice £1.05. Delivery: £10. Hours: 5pm-12am (1pm on Sat.).

Birmingham East
B8, B9, B25, B26, B33, B34, B36, B37 and B40 (NEC) postcodes (restaurants in alphabetical order)

SHABAR TANDOORI   ©

4 Arden Oak Road, Sheldon, B26   ✆ 0121 742 0636

Angur Miah Qureshi and Mozamil Ali's Balti restaurant, seats 62. Special: Chicken or Lamb Zarzara £5.95. Table Nan £2.40. Spiced Banana in ghee £1.95. Price check: Papadam 40p, CTM £6.65, Pullao Rice £1.25. Lager £2.90 pint, house wine £6.50. Sunday lunch: £5.95. Takeaway: 10% discount. Hours: 5.30pm-12am.

YEW TREE COTTAGE   ©

43 Stoney Lane, Yardley, B25   ✆ 0121 784 0707

Opened in 1979 by Jamal Chaudhuri, this 40-seater curry house is in old cottage-style with oak beams. Takeaway services on the ground floor, restaurant on 1st floor. Gourmet Nights, four courses £9.95. Special starters: Tikka Sandwich, chicken tikka with nan, salad and dressing £3. Mixgrill Sandwich, chicken and lamb tikka, sheek kebab and Nan £4.25. Banana Chicken, medium spiced £3.95. Madras sauce £1.50. Vindaloo Sauce £1.90. Price check: Papadam complimentary, CTM £5.75, Pullao Rice £1.70. Lager £1.90 pint, house wine £6.95. Minimum charge: £15. Sunday buffet £9.95. Delivery: under £40, £2.50 charge, over £40, free, 3-mile radius. Hours: 5pm (Sun. 6pm)-1 (Sat. 2am).

©	Curry Club discount (see page 6)	🍺	Unlicensed
√	Vegetarian		
BYO	Bring your own alcohol	▦	Delivery/takeaway

Birmingham South East
B27 and B28 Beyond this is Solihull
and Knowle (*see* entries)

MIZAN NAME CHANGE ©

1347 Stratford Road, Hall Green, B28 ✆ 0121 777 3185

Formerly J. Jays, K.A. Rahman's curry house, seats 66. Takeaway: 10%
off. Minimum charge: £5. Special: Saag Kamal Kakri, spinach and lotus
roots £2.70. Price check: Papadam 55p, CTM £5.80, Pullao Rice £1.60.
Lager £2.45 pint, house wine £6.95. Hours: 12-2pm/5.30pm-12am (12.30
on Fri. & Sat.).

MOGHUL ©

1184 Warwick Road, Acocks Green, B27 ✆ 0121 707 6777

At Mr Hassan's mahogany and pink venue. Special starters: Tandoori
Fish and Mushroom Garlic Fry £1.95. Price check: Papadam 50p, CTM
£6.95, Pullao Rice £1.60. Lager £2.10 pint, house wine £6.75. Takeaway:
20% discount. Minimum charge: £5. Hours: 5.30pm-12.30pm (1am on
Sat.). Branch: Diwan Balti, Alcester Road, Moseley, Birmingham.

PURPLE ROOMS

1076 Stratford Road, Hall Green, B28 ✆ 0121 702 2193

Established in 1988 by Faizur Rahman Choudhury, formula curry
house, seats 60, two dining rooms. 'Stuffed Peppers, excellent. Pakeeza
Chicken, could taste no coconut, chicken superb. Service was prompt,
but dimly lit for my liking.' GP. Sunday lunch buffet, 1-4, £5.95. Monday
and Thursday Gourmet Night, 5-course dinner £6.95. House wine
£7.95. Delivery: large parties only. Price check: Papadam 50p, CTM
£5.80, Pullao Rice £1.80. Hours: 12-2.30pm (Fri. & Sat.) and 6pm-
12am. Sun. all day. Stocks Cobra.

SPICE VILLAGE NAME CHANGE BYO ALLOWED ©

2 Robin Hood Lane, Hall Green, B28 ✆ 0121 745 5445

Formerly Kebabish, taken over by Rais Alam in January 1998, seats 60.
Special: Tandoori Fish £2. Balti Lamb kebab Masala with egg £5.90.

Balti Spice Aphrodisiac £7.90. BYO. Price check: Papadam compli-mentary, CTM £5.90, Pullao Rice £1.70. House wine £7.80. Hours: 12-2.30pm/6pm-1am. Sun. 6pm-1am. Reports please. Stocks Cobra.

Birmingham South West
B14, B29 to B32, B38, B45, B47, B48, B60 postcodes

BALTI BAZAAR

1267-69 Pershore Road, Stirchley, B30   © 0121 459 4517

'Bazaar in name and bizarre in menu – Bazaar Nan actually contains fresh fruit. Moreish aptly describes the food as well as the style of decor.' AM. '38 of us, split over two tables, they coped very well with such a large party, everything went very smoothly. Service was obvi-ously slower that normal, but never so slow that people were becoming irritated. Pops 35p with free brightly coloured dips. Paks 80p, fresh and very spicy. Tandoori Chicken £1.95, well marinated and very tasty. Prawn Puri, minute prawns, bread was beautifully done. Peshwari Nan £1.50, excellent.' GG& MP. Hours: 5pm-12am.

HIMALAYA   BYO

1716 Bristol Road South, Longbridge, B45 © 0121 453 4336

Miss Nazma Khanom and Mr A. Ali's curry house seats 55. Special: Dilruba Curry, chicken tikka and tandoori King prawn in masala sauce, served with rice £9.10. 'Nothing a disappointment.' MR. 'Price check: Papadam 25p, CTM £5.40, Pullao Rice £1.60. Takeaway: 10% off. BYO. Minimum charge: £7. Hours: 5.30pm-12.30am (1am on Sat.).

INDIANAS

68-9 The Green, Kings Norton, B38   © 0121 451 2907

At Shezad Inayat and Razwan Inayat's smart pastel 75-seater, you can watch your meal being cooked through the glass-fronted kitchen. Special: Chicken Pakora £1.95. Mushroom and Sweetcorn Masala Puri £1.95. Mixed Grill Balti Masala, shashlik, chicken, seek kebab, lamb and chicken tikka, rich mild masala sauce £4.75. 'Food above-average, portions generous. Word of warning: they charge an extra 50p should you decide to have your starter served in a sizzler!' CM. Another for the 'silly rules' book. Takeaway: 20% off. Price check: Papadam 40p, CTM £4.90, Pullao Rice £1.55. Lager £1.90 pint, house wine £6.95. Hours: 5.30pm-12.30pm (1am on Sat.).

KASHMIR GARDEN NEW ENTRANT

855 Bristol Road South, Northfields, B31   © 0121 475 1714

'Service prompt, attentive and polite, superb. Extremely impressed. Vegetable Samosa 90p, Tandoori Chicken £1.90, Chicken Pakora £1.90, Onion Bhajia 80p.' GG&MP.

KINGS BALTI NEW ENTRANT

13 York Rd, King's Heath B14   © 0121 443 1114

Owned and managed by Salim Miah. Special: Panir Tikka, cubes of curd cheese dipped in marinated gram flour and fried £2.05. Balti Chicken Tikka Naryl, delicate coconut sauce £4.95. Balti Chicken Dan Gali, cashew, sultanas, almonds, pistachio, fresh banana £4.95. Price check: Papadam 30p, CTM £4.95, Pullao Rice £1.20. Delivery: £8, 2-mile radius. Takeaway: 10% off. Hours: 5.30-11.30pm.

RAJPOOT   ©

1831-1833 Pershore Road, Cotteridge, B30 © 0121 458 5604

Watir Ali's 94-seater does all your favourite curries and Balthis (*sic.*). 'A glitzy little place with friendly service. All the family use it regularly.' JAD. Hours: 6pm-2am.

SPICE EXCHANGE NEW ENTRANT

1845-1847 Pershore Road, Cotteridge. B30 ©0121 451 1007

Tandoori Fish, served with salad £3.25. Gusthaba, speciality from Kashmir, minced lamb, turmeric, black pepper, garam masala formed into meat balls, pan fried in sweet and hot tomato sauce £5.75. Cocktail Balti's – have your favourite balti cooked with French wine and brandy for £1.50 extra. Please exchange your reports here!

YASSER TANDOORI
<svg>🍵</svg> BYO ©

| 1268 Pershore Road, Stirchley, B30 | © 0121 433 3023 |

A. Hussain and Sarwar Khan's (seats 80, parking for 12 cars) specializes in Pakistani and Kashmiri cooking. Special: Tandoori Fish £1.70. Balti Chef Special Tropical, prawn, chicken, meat, mushroom £5.20. Garlic Family Nan £4.90. BYO. Price check: Papadam 40p, CTM £4.80, Pullao Rice £1.30. Minimum charge: £4.50. Hours: 4pm-1am.

Birmingham West
B15 to B18 and B32 (alphabetical order). Beyond this is Halesowen, Warley, West Bromwich (*see* entries)

BANU
BYO ALLOWED

| 353 Hagley Road, Edgbaston, B17 | © 0121 434 3416 |

Formerly the 1969 Gaylord. Taken over in '92 by Mohammed Mostafa. Chef M.M. Helal. Bangladeshi formula restaurant, seating 50. BYO. Price check: Papadam 50p, CTM £4.75, Pullao Rice £1.60. House wine £6.50. Takeaway: 10% discount. Delivery. Hours: 6pm-1am (2am on Sat.). Stocks Cobra.

SHIMLA PINKS

| 214 Broad Street, Birmingham, B15 | © 0121 633 0366 |

Just north of Central TV. Fully licensed, upmarket pricy home-base for a long-proposed national chain of franchises. 'Nans the best I've had. Bhuna Chicken particularly good. Service courteous. Plenty of space. Strange decor.' MJG. 'Minimalist decor. Food out of this world.' SR&LG. Branches: East Indian Company and Varsity Blues, Stirling, Central; Killermont Polo Club, Glasgow, Strathclyde; Shimla Pinks, Johnstone, Strathclyde.

©	Curry Club discount (see page 6)	<svg>🍵</svg>	Unlicensed
√	Vegetarian		
BYO	Bring your own alcohol	⊞	Delivery/takeaway

SOHO INDIA   NEW ENTRANT   ©

417 Hagley Road West, Quinton, B32   ✆ 0121 421 3242

Bangladeshi formula curry house, seats 50, established in 1985 by
Mohammed Abdul Muquit. CC members will get 10% off their bill.
Special: Village Special Soup £1.75, I wonder what that tastes like?
Lager £1.85 pint, one of the lowest prices in the guide. Price check:
Papadam 35p, CTM £5.85, Pullao Rice £1.75. House wine £5.95. No
takeaway. Minimum charge: £6.50. Hours: 5pm-12am. Stocks Cobra.

Elsewhere in the West Midlands
Brierley Hill

WATERFRONT BALTI HOUSE   BYO ©

127-129, Dudley Road, Brierley Hill.   ✆ 01384 476929

Mohammed Ashraf's 80-seater serves Kashmiri-style curries and Balti
BYO. 10% off for students and nurses. Tuesday Balti night, 3-course
meal £4.30. Price check: Papadam 30p, BCTM £4.50, Pullao Rice £1.30.
Delivery: £12 minimum, 3-mile radius. Minimum charge: £6.50.
Delivery: £7. Hours: 5.30pm-12pm.

Coventry

BALTI ROYAL TAKEAWAY   NEW ENTRANT

142 Jardine Crescent, Tile Hill, Coventry   01203 460237

Formerly Al Madina taken over by Bosir Miah in '98. Special: garlic
Chilli Bahar, diced tandoori roasted chicken cooked with garlic, green
chilli, yoghurt and fenugreek £4.95. Price check: Papadam 30p, CTM
£4.95, Pullao Rice £1.20. Delivery: £6.95 minimum, 4-mile radius.
Credit cards not accepted. Hours: 5pm-12am (12.30am on Fri. & Sat.).

BENGAL DELIGHT

166-168 Holbrook Lane, Coventry   ✆ 01203 686789

S.M. Hussain's 66-seater is in pretty shades of peach with mint green
table linen, and a fountain. Special: Asar Ghosht lamb meat in dry

slightly hot flavour sauce with a sour taste £8.95, Jeera Murgh chicken in medium sauce, cooked with tomato, cummin and peppers £8.95. Price check: Papadam 70p, CTM £5.45, Pullao Rice £1.60, Sunday lunch £9.95. Minimum charge: £15. Hours: 5.30-1130pm. Stocks Cobra.

CAFE SPICE NEW ENTRANT

244 Hipswell Highway, Coventry   ℰ 01203 659800

As far was we know, not related to the London Cafe Spices. 'Very luxurious, obviously a lot of money has been spent. Popadoms 60p and chutney. Starters, Tandoori Chicken, beautifully presented and well marinated £1.95, Kebab Roll with salad, absolutely superb £2.20, huge. First class service.' GG&MP.

DHAKA DYNASTY

292-294 Walsgrave Road, Coventry   ℰ 01203 636615

'Predominantly beige and green decor, in good state of repair. Popadoms 65p, Balti Chicken with Vegetables £4.50, Chicken Tikka Biriani £6.90, Pullao Rice £1.50. Menu extensive in every respect although nothing really unusual. Reasonable quantities. Excellent service, but two items of crockery were chipped.' GG&MP. Stocks Cobra.

KING WILLIAM IV PUB TOP 100   ©

1059 Foleshill Road, Coventry   ℰ 01203 686394

Some 6,500 British pubs serve curry. Not long ago, you were lucky if you could get a decent sausage at the pub, and then only at set times. But along in 1986 came Pele and Jatinder Bains, whose origins are north India. They were already experienced publicans, but this was a new idea. They put only authentic curries on the menu at their 160-seater pub. And guess what? From day one, it's been a resounding success. All the regular curries are there, with the cooking by Pele. 'Very wide menu, quality apart from greasy popadoms, generally excellent, although some of the potato in Balti Mince £4.50 was burnt. Tandoori Chicken, very good £1.85. Service very prompt.' GG&MP. Specials include Murg Angar, half spring chicken marinated in yoghurt and delicate herbs, served with salad £4.10, Gosht Fukht Biriyani, saffron-flavoured rice, with lamb £4.50. [What the fukht is this – a viagra substitute??? Do they mean Dum Pukt or this is a mean printer's misprint?

– Reports please! Ed]. Good ale with good curry. Roll on, I wish there were more like this. Strings of good reports keep it in our TOP 100. Price check: Papadam 30p, CTM £4.70. Lager £1.70 pint, house wine £6. Hours: 12-2pm/6pm (Sun. 7pm) -10.30pm (Sun. 10pm).

MONSOON   ©

20-21 Far Gosford Street, Coventry   ℭ 01203 229651

Owned by J. Raj and G. Judge, since 1996. 'Modern, zazzy music.' Pakistani curries, 'Superb quality, enormous quantities. Excellent Popadom 45p crispy with spicy chutney dip, Balti Chilli Chicken Masala £3.95 was a feast, wonderfully spicy with sumptuous chicken, Balti Mince £3.95 with vegetables including okra, pepper, chana, tomatoes, potatoes and courgettes was mouthwateringly good. Peshwari Nan £2.10. The bees' knees for Balti houses.' GG&MP. Karahi Monsoon Special, chicken, meat and prawns, cooked in a balti with green peppers and onions £6.25, Balti Chicken Tikka Keema £5.95, Coriander Nan £1.90. Price check: Papadam 45p, CTM £5.55, Pullao Rice £1.50. Lager £2 pint, house wine £6.99. Takeaway 10% off. Delivery: £10 minimum, 4-mile radius. Hours: 6pm-12am (1am on Sat.).

QUICK STOP BALTI   🍺 BYO

80 Far Gosford Street, Coventry   ℭ 01203 632578

'Unlicensed and unpretentious restaurant. Fairly basic menu, service very good. Balti Chicken Jalfrezi, well marinated.' GG&MP.

RED ROSE BALTI   ©

31 Silver Street, Coventry   ℭ 01203 222702

Last time, I asked which was the first curry restaurant to open in Coventry. The year was 1960. I dined at it then, but can't remember its name or address. Mr Mukaddas Ali bought this place in 1993, and says this was it. Well according to Anthony Mead it was the Modern on Primrose Hill next to the Leopard Pub, now both demolished. Any advances on that? Anyway, the Red Rose Indian has good curries on the menu, plus a good selection of Baltis. Balti Chicken and Mushroom £3.75, Nan £1. Price check: Papadam 45p incl. chutney, CTM £4.95, Pullao Rice £1.10. Minimum charge £4.

RUPALI TOP 100   ©

337 The Hill Lane, Coventry   ✆ 01203 422500

Ashik Ali's very attractively decorated huge 200-seater, serving the formula. Chef Rois Ali has attracted some notoriety since winning a Chef
of the Year award. He can cook, but, like others before him, must
beware of letting apparent 'fame' take him from the kitchen. We do
continue to get one in five poor reports. Portion size is one gripe,
something easily and, frankly, cheaply remedied. 'Decor and service
certainly exceptional but having both gone for the Chicken Jalfrezi we
were disappointed at the quality and the quantity. Both dishes were
'nice' but did not justify a price of £9.95. Naan were excellent as were
the Popadoms and pickle tray. Two lagers and two soda waters came to
£7 – scandalous!' DH. 'Quantities very substantial, outstanding quality,
service very prompt and courteous, decor simply wonderful. Top notch
food in every respect, maintaining its reputation and providing a wonderful variety of dishes within the Thali format.' GG& MP. CC members
10% off, so plenty more reports please; meanwhile we will retain the
Rupali in our TOP 100. Price check: Papadam 60p, CTM £8.95,
Pullao Rice £1.95. Lager £2.50 pint, house wine £8.95. Takeaway: 25 %
off. Sunday lunch: £7.95. Minimum charge: £9.95. Hours:5.30-11pm.

SHAHI PALACE   ©

367 Foleshill Road, Coventry   ✆ 01203 688719

It had a record four names in 10 years (Palace, Kashmir, Balti). Since
1995 it's been Iqbal Hussain's Shahi Palace, a licensed 90-seater, nicely
decorated in greens. Special: slices of Bangladeshi boal fish in hot and
tangy taste with green chilli and shatkora £7.95. Nawabi Murgh, pieces
of chicken marinated cooked in mince lamb sauce and freshly garnished with chilli, coriander and egg £8.50. Daily banquets £5.95. Price
check: Papadam 40p, CTM £5.50, Pullao Rice £1.50. Minimum charge
£10. Service 10%. Delivery: £10 minimum, 4-mile radius. Hours:
5.30pm-12.30am. Stocks Cobra.

©	Curry Club discount (see page 6)		Unlicensed
√	Vegetarian		
BYO	Bring your own alcohol		Delivery/takeaway

THAI DUSIT   NEW ENTRANT

39 London Road, Coventry   © 01203 227788

'A Thai restaurant, and a must. Totally entranced. Spicy Fish Cakes
£3.95. Golden bags, thin pastry ships filled with minced pork and
prawn, deep-fried with sweet chilli sauce £3.95. Excellent, beautifully
presented starters, served with dip, carrot, parsley and cabbage. Spicy
hot Jungle Curry with Thai herbs £6.95. Friendly service, calm music
helped to create pleasant ambience.' GG&MP.

Dudley

CHEF DEE BALTI   NAME CHANGE   ©

44-45 High Street, Quarry Bank, Dudley   © 01384 412757

'Raffat and Majid Hussain's 70-seater does Pakistani curries and Baltis.
BYO, no corkage. The chef is Chef Shoukat Hussain. This was the
Tim Tandoori, so who is chef D? Special: Tropical Multi Masala Balti,
chicken, lamb and prawns in a medium hot masala £7.50. Price check:
CTM £5.50, Pullao Rice £1.45. Lager £2 pint, house wine £7.95,
Hours: 5pm-2am.

CLASSICAL BALTI HOUSE   🍺 BYO ©

63 Halesowen Road, Netherton, Dudley   © 01384 240230

At R. Khan's small restaurant we continue to hear of the Happy Hour
special menu from 6-9pm Hours: 6pm-2am (3am at weekends).

Halesowen

AMEENA   ©

192 Hagley Road, Hasbury,
Halesowen, B63   © 0121 550 4317

Hiron Miah's 78-seater (est. 1974) is nicely decorated in shades of
blue, Special: Shahi Tandoori Masala served with Pullao Rice £7.50,
Bangladesh Special King Prawns £7.15. Chicken Tikka Sagwala Balti
£6.35. Price check: Papadam 35p, CTM £5.95, Pullao Rice £1.60.
Minimum charge: £6.50. Takeaway: 10% off. House wine 5.95. Hours:
5.30pm-12.30am. Stocks Cobra.

BALTI TOWERS   ©

85 Long Lane, Halesowen, B65   © **0121 559 5118**

No news from Mohammed Sadique nor from Basil. Reports please.
Hours: 6-11.30pm daily. Lunch Sun. only 12-2.30pm.

Kingswinford

BALTI NAME CHANGE   🍽 BYO

847 High Street, Kingswinford   © **01384 294861**

Formerly Mr Daves. 'BYO, quite cheap, excellent standard of Balti.
Chicken Pakora is the greatest we've ever had.' SR&LG.

RANI BALTI NEW ENTRANT

49-51 Market Street, Kingswinford   © **01384 294861**

Ikbal Hussain and Mohammed Miah's 60-seater (party room 32).
Special: Lamb Passanda, sliced lamb cooked in fresh cream, cultured
yoghurt and mixed ground nuts, served with Pullao Rice £5.95. Price
check: Papadam 35p, CTM £5.40, Pullao Rice £1.45. Minimum charge:
£7.50. Delivery: £8 minimum, 3-mile radius. Hours: 6pm-12am (1am on
Sat.)

Knowle

BILASH   ©

1608 High Street, Knowle   © **01564 773030**

Mashud Uddin and Nowab Ali's Bangladeshi curry house seats 64,
party room 40. Set in black and white surroundings, dating back to the
16th century. Special: Jeera Chicken Dilkush, spring chicken, coconut,
jeera, tomato and mixed spices £5.55. 'Very good quality.' J &. MCL. Lager
£1.95 pint, house wine £7.25. Takeaway: 10% off. Hours: 5.30pm-12am.
Branches: Bilash, 82-90 Priory Road, Kenilworth. Bejoy Takeaway, 763
Old Lode Lane, Solihull, West Midlands.

KNOWLE INDIAN BRASSERIE ©

1690 High Street, Knowle, B93   © 01564 776453

Hossain Miah's air-conditioned Bangladeshi curry house seats 40.
Nicely decorated in cream and pale pink, plaster cornices and velvet
upholstered chairs. Special: Fish Bhuna Bengal Style, chunks Bangladeshi fish, cooked in medium sauce with spices, herbs and green
chillies £6.35. 'Malai Kebab, chicken marinated in cream with herbs and
spices and baked in a clay oven – very tasty. Chicken Tikka Sylhet,
boneless chicken with minced lamb and egg cooked with spices and
herbs – unusual mixture of mince and chicken, very spicy with good
texture and flavours. Bombay Aloo, well-marinated potato although
not as spicy as they promised in the menu. Quantities – enormous.
Not as expensive as one might expect. A top-quality restaurant.' G & MP.
Price check: Papadam 40p, CTM £5.25, Pullao Rice £1.50. Minimum
charge: £6. Lager £1.90 pint, house wine £7.25. Takeaway: 10%. Hours:
5.30-11.30pm (10.30pm on Sun.). Branches: Stockland Balti Takeaway,
332 Marsh Lane, Erdington, Birmingham; Thespian's Indian Cuisine,
Stratford upon Avon, Warwickshire.

SEVEN SPICES   NEW ENTRANT

1594-1596 High Street, Knowle   © 01564 771595

Taken over in Feb '98 by Mohammed Shabaz, seats 75, serves Pakistani
– Punjabi style curries. Says AM: 'Shabaz made his name in Birmingham, and having won the battle of the Balti decided to move to finer
surroundings. Smart minimalist nouveau decor with polished wooden
floorboards, mini spotlights, terracotta walls with black chairs and
marbled tables. Chicken Pakora is unbeatable with tender goujons of
chicken breast in a light spicy batter. Mind you it's a photo finish with
the tandooried lamb chops. For main course the Punjabi Korma amply
lives up to its description of a mild creamy sauce with lashings of fresh
cream, grated coconut, sultanas, cashew nuts, saffron and selected
Punjabi spices. Notwithstanding, Shabaz does not forget his roots
with Balti Chicken, the trademark dish of sizzling chicken languishing
in a sea of clean fresh spices.' AM. Sunday and Monday buffet £8.95.
Courtesy bus for large parties, from Sunday to Thursday. Price check:
Papadam 50p (incl. dips), CTM £7.50, Pullao Rice £2. Lager £2.30
pint, house wine £8.25. Takeaway: 10% off. Hours: 5.30pm-12am
(12.30am on Sat.).

Solihull

JAIPUR

79 Hobs Moat Road, Solihull, B92   © 0121 722 2982

Owned by J. Ali, since '93. Bangladeshi curry house, with Balti dishes
on the menu, from £3.95 to £6.75, decorated in light green, seats 70.
Price check: Papadam 40p, CTM £5.85, Pullao Rice £1.60. Minimum
charge: £7. Hhouse wine £6.50. Hours: 5.30pm-12am. Stocks Cobra.

OASIS TANDOORI   NEW ENTRANT

130 Stratford Road, Shirley, Solihul B90   © 0121 733 6079

'Being addressed as "mate" is not acceptable! Reasonably wide menu,
good comfort. Balti Chicken £4.80, Peshwari Nan £1.55, Nan £1.20.'
GG&MP. 'Portions quite large, the food excellent. Chicken Chilli
Massala very good. The waiters were very jolly and friendly. Well worth
a visit and we'll be going again.' JSC. Price check: Papadam 35p, Chicken
Garlic Masala £4.64, Bombay Potato £2.50 Pilau Rice £1.50.

Stourbridge

BALTI BAZAAR   🍴 BYO

1a Pedmore Road, Lye, Stourbridge   © 01384 353800

Opened in 1997 by R. Miah, with Ali Akbor managing front of house
and Noor Miah is head chef. 'The service was prompt and pleasant,
with a reassuring "quality check" by the staff midway through the
meal. The food was above average.' LW. Price check: Papadam 35p,
CTM £4.30, Pullao Rice £1.20. Hours: 5pm-12am.

INDIA HOUSE TANDOORI AND BALTI

22 Lower High Street, Stourbridge   © 01384 393301

Opened 1969, so one of the originals. Since 1980 it has been under the
ownership of Abdul Ahad. Seats 85. Bangladesh and Pakistani curries
on the menu cooked by Ashique Ahmed. They tell us they were once
warned by Dudley Heath Authority, so reports please. Price check:
Papadam 45p, CTM £5.35, Pullao Rice £1.55. Hours: Mon.-Thurs.
5.30pm-12am. Fri.-Sun. 5pm-1am.

KAMRAN BALTIS   BYO

34 High Street, Lye, Stourbridge   © 01384 893030

Ansar and Asdaq Farakh's Pakistani curry house seats a considerable
105. BYO, waiters will chill and serve. What service! Price check:
Papadam free, CTM £4.50, Pullao Rice £1.30. Delivery: £8 min., 3-mile
radius. No credit cards. Hours: 5.30pm-12am (1am on Fri. & Sat.).

NASEEB OF LYE   BYO

15 High Street, Lye, Stourbridge   © 01384 891353

Taken over in 1996 by M. Ahmed, manager of the former Mr Daves
Balti House. Nicely decorated in light blue with matching blue chairs
and carpet, seats 55. Special: Lye Multi Balti, all meats and vegetables
served in a Balti pan £4.95. Buffet nights Monday and Wednesday
£5.95. Price check: Papadam 35p, CTM £4.85, Pullao Rice £1.20.
Takeaway 10% off. Delivery: £8 minimum, 3-mile radius, free
papadams. Daily buffet £5.95. Credit cards not accepted. BYO. Hours:
5.30-11.30pm (12.30am on Sat.).

NEEL AKASH BALTI AND TANDOORI   ©

2F High Street, Wollaston, Stourbridge   © 01384 375919

Chef Mujibur Rahman's 60-seater. Bangladeshi formula curries including Bengal Masala £5.75 and Bhoona Shashlik £5.75. Balti Chicken and
Mushroom £4.75, Nan £1.20. Price check: Papadam 50p incl. chutney,
CTM £5.75, Pullao Rice £1.50. Minimum charge: £5. House wine
£6.95. Special: Acher Special, chicken, meat or prawn with pickles
£4.95. Takeaway: 10% off. Delivery: £8 minimum, 3-mile radius. Hours:
5pm-12am. Stocks Cobra.

PEPPER AND SPICE   BYO ALLOWED ©

4 High Street, Lye, Stourbridge   © 01384 893933

At Sabber Iqbal's 40-seater you can get these intriguing specials:
Pepper Chicken, capsicum stuffed with tandoori chicken £2.25. Fish
chat, fish in a sweet and sour sauce £2. Balti Chicken and Mushroom
£3.30, Nan 75p. BYO. Price check: Papadam 45p, CTM £4.50, Pullao
Rice £1.50. Lager £1.50 pint, house wine £6. Credit cards not accepted.
Delivery: £7 minimum. Hours: 6pm-12am.

REDFORTE ASIAN CUISINE TAKEAWAY

70 Bridgnorth Road, Wollaston,
Stourbridge   © 01384 835555

Takeaway only, situated next door to the village bakery. Owned by
Shaun Hussain Shah (manager). Price check: Papadam 35p, CTM
£4.80, Pullao Rice £1.30. Hours: 5.30pm-12am (12.30on Fri. & Sat.).

Sutton Coldfield

ASIAN GRILL

91 Park Road, Sutton Coldfield, B73   © 0121 354 7491

Opened way back in 1968. If you, or any other business for that matter, have survived that long, you must be good. Bangladeshi curries on
the menu including Balti Chicken Tikka £5.90, Nan £1.30. Seats 76
diners. Price check: Papadam 40p, CTM £7.25, Pullao Rice £1.60.
Minimum charge £8. Open 5.30pm-12am (1am on Fri. & Sat.).
Stocks Cobra.

BASHUNDORA

Lichfield Road, Sutton Coldfield, B74   © 0121 354 8397

'Behind Guildhall and opposite the nick. 'Excellent value and safe
parking.' GG&MP. 'Excellent meal. A real find.' JAG. On the takeaway
menu, I see something for the 'silly rules' book — I quote: 'One meal
cannot be shared between two persons.' [!!!] Price check: Papadam 55p,
CTM £7.60, Pullao Rice £1.55. Hours: 12-2pm/6pm-12am.

STREETLY BALTI   BYO

188 Chester Road, Streetly,
Sutton Coldfield, B73   © 0121 353 2224

'Excellent food, generous portions. One interesting feature, the
availability of divided serving dishes allowing one to order smaller
portions of two different dishes. No licence, but the offie is almost
next door. Not open on Sundays.' BP. 'Not only is the food excellent
but the staff are most pleasant and helpful at all times.' VY. 'Enjoyed
one of their combination meals, Balti Methi Gosht and Balti Chicken
Rogan.' DC

Walsall

EAST END   ©

9 Hawes Close, Broadway, Walsall   ✆ 01922 614800

Muhibur Rahman is proud of his veteran 1967 curry house. Special is
Green Chilli Chicken Tikka Masala (£4.95). Balti Chicken and Mush-
room £3.50, Nan 90p. Price check: Papadam 35p, CTM £5.25, Pullao
Rice £1.35. Open 5.30pm-12am.

KING BALTI   🍴 BYO ©

89 Ablewell Street, Walsall   ✆ 01922 620376

48-seater owned by Dudu Miah. Chicken Tikka Jalfrezi most popular.
Price check: Papadam 30p, CTM £4.95, Pullao Rice £1.40. Takeaway:
10% off. Delivery: £12 minimum, 3-mile radius. Hours: 6pm-1am.
Branch: Malabar, 7, Anchor Road, Aldridge, Walsall.

SAFFRON   ©

42-43 Bradford Street, Walsall   ✆ 01922 627899

130-seater, smart restaurant opened in 1963. Taken over in 1997 by
Monjur Choudhury, now a Southern Indian restaurant, South Garlic
Chicken most popular. Price check: Papadam 35p, CTM £5.25, Pullao
Rice £1.55. Lager £1.85 pint, house wine £6.95. Delivery: £8 minimum.
Hours: 12pm-12am.

SALMA BALTI KINGDOM   BYO ©

41 Caldmore Green, Caldmore, Walsall   ✆ 01922 635162

Established in 1995 by Shah Motashirau, seats 60, serves Bangladeshi
formula curries. Mosaic wall decoration. Special: Sylheti Shatkora,
chicken or lamb marinated, cooked with tangy citrus fruit, slightly hot
£5.50. Price check: Papadam 30p, CTM £4.95, Pullao Rice £1.30.
Delivery: 6 minimum, 4-mile radius. Hours: 5pm-12.30am (1.30am on
Fri. & Sat.).

Warley

AL MOUGHAL   ☕ ©

622 Bearwood Road, Smethwick,
Warley, B66   ✆ 0121 420 3987

100-seater managed by Mumtaz. Pakistani-style curries on the menu.
'Reasonably clean, down-market but cheap and cheerful. Chicken
Karahi Tikka Massala Special and three Chapatis, waiter advised only
two – spot on. Food competent and tasty. Tremendous value. If this
place was a wine it would be a Blue Nun.' PAW. [Yuk! Let's settle for a
'Brown Nan' -Ed] Price check: Papadam 30p, CTM £5.50, Pullao Rice
£1.15. BYO. Special: Balti Chicken Tikka Aloo Jalfrezi £5.25. Onion
Nan 95p. Delivery: £10 minimum, 3-mile radius. Hours: 6pm-12am.

RAJ   NEW ENTRANT   ©

7 Halesowen Street, Rowley Regis,
Warley B65   ✆ 0121 559 5537

Formula curry house, nicely decorated in shades of blue, wooden fretwork partitions, hanging plants, seating 54, Chicken Balti £3.95 and
CTM most popular. Sunday buffet £5.95. BYO. Price check: Papadam
40p, CTM £4.50, Pullao Rice £1.40. Lager £1.40 pint, house wine
£5.95.Takeaway: 10% less. Hours: 5.30pm-1am (2am on Fri. & Sat.).

ROWLEY VILLAGE   TOP 100

10 Portway Road, Rowley Regis,
Warley, B65   ✆ 0121 561 4463

Not a peep from the ebullient Mr Moin Udin, nor indeed anyone else
in the whole wide world. So we make do with last time's quotes: 'It is
without doubt the best tandoori restaurant in the Midlands if not the
whole of the UK.' DH. 'Starters are like main courses and the main
meals are, well, enormous! Everything tried on the menu, so far, has
been of a very high standard. Watch out for their special mixed dishes,
which represent extremely good value for money. Highly recommended.' CM. Reports please to remain a TOP 100. Open 5.15pm-12am.

STANDARD   ©

2 High Street, Blackheath,
Rowley Regis, Warley, B65   ℂ 0121 561 2048

Kazi Ashafuz and Kazi Wahiduz Zaman's tiny 30-seater (pretty, green
wallpaper and wood-panelling) serves formula curries. Special:
Chicken Jaipur, creamy, egg and nuts £5.05. BYO. Price check:
Papadam 50p, CTM £5.50, Pullao Rice £1.50. House wine £6.
Takeaway: 10% off. Delivery: £10 minimum. Hours: 6pm-1am (2am on
Sat.). Stocks Cobra.

West Bromwich

CLOCK TOWER BALTI   ©

33 Carters Green, West Bromwich, B70   ℂ 0121 553 4167

H. and Joginder Singh's Punjabi/northern establishment. 'Extremely
tasty, good sized portions, polite staff, clean and friendly atmosphere'
NB. 'Super Balti Dupiaza, Nan bread exceptional. Free Popadom and
Pickle!!!' AL. 'An excellent meal at a fair price. TRY IT!' TE. 'Meal was
great, plenty of it!' BH. 'Friendly service. Actually managed to recognise
us from our previous visit 12 months earlier.' PK. 'Menu 10/10. Excellent
Vegi variety.' SF. Price check: Papadam 35p, CTM £5.95, Pullao Rice
£1.30. Delivery free on orders over £8. Stocks Cobra.

Willenhall

WILLENHALL COTTAGE   NEW ENTRANT   BYO ALLOWED

High Road, Lane Head, Willenhall

'Takeaway Only. Hit consistently high standard of formula curry.
Chilli Chicken and Chicken Tikka Madras are wonderful. One Sunday
they delivered within 25 minutes, before we had laid the table!' SR&LG.

©	Curry Club discount (see page 6)		Unlicensed
√	Vegetarian		
BYO	Bring your own alcohol		Delivery/takeaway

Wolverhampton

BILASH

2 Cheapside, Wolverhampton   © 01902 427762

'Sampled the midweek lunch buffet – excellent.' MB. 'Kitchens visible behind a fully glazed wall and the food was superb.' IB. Stocks Cobra.

REAL INDIAN BISTRO NEW ENTRANT   BYO ALLOWED

28 Cleveland Street, Wolverhampton   © 01902 425101

Manjit Dabb's 60-seater serves Balti dishes and formula curries. Special: Samosa Chat, samosa covered with chickpeas in sauce £1.80. Chappel Kebab, mince meat shaped like a foot, tawa-cooked, served sizzling £2.25. BYO. Price check: Papadam 30p, CTM £4.95, Pullao Rice £1.35. House wine £6.95. Takeaway: 10% off. Delivery: £10 minimum, 3-mile radius. Hours: 6pm-12am. Stocks Cobra.

WILTSHIRE

Area: Mid West
Population: 562,000
Number of restaurants in county: 50
Number of restaurants in Guide: 18

Chippenham

AKASH TANDOORI AND BALTI   ©

19 The Bridge, Chippenham   © 01249 653358

Established in '79 by Nurul Islam, an old friend of this Guide, having been in our first edition. Decorated in 'red dado and curtains with green plants and doors, incorporates framed pictures and tropical fish tank'. Special: Passanda, creamy fragrantly spiced dish £6.70. House wine £8.50. Price check: Papadam 50p, CTM £6.70, Pullao Rice £2.20. Takeaway: 10% off. Hours: 12-2pm/6pm-12am (12.30am on Fri. & Sat.).

TAJ MAHAL NEW ENTRANT   ©

51 The Causeway, Chippenham   ℂ **01249 653243**

Arju Miah says 'it always takes time to prepare good food, why not try
a few of our starters while you wait?' While you do, admire the 50-
seater's red flock wallpaper. Lobster Butter Fried £4.75 and Tandoori
Lobster £5.50 sound delicious, though CTM is most popular. Minimum charge: £12. Takeaway: 10% off. Price check: Papadam 50p, CTM
£6.50, Pullao Rice £1.75. Delivery: £10 minimum, 8-mile radius. Hours:
12-2pm/6pm-12am.

Cricklade

GOLDEN DELIGHT NEW ENTRANT   ©

47, High Street, Cricklade.   **01793 752242**

Two-roomed 44-seater owned by M.M. Ali. Specials: Ginger Chicken
£6.25, Mushroom Biriani £5.25. Price check: Papadam 60p, CTM
£6.25, Pullao Rice £1.75. Lager £2.50 pint, house wine £6.75. Takeaway:
10% off. Hours: 12-2.30 (Sun.-Fri.) and 6-11.30pm (12am on Sat.).

Devizes

DEEDAR

2 Sidmouth Street, Devizes   ℂ **01380 720009**

Joshim Ahmed's 24-seater's kitchen is in full view. Chutney Deedar,
chicken, lamb or prawn cooked with mango chutney and lime pickle
£4.50. 'Appearance of this restaurant is basic and very simple, no frills
with formica tables. A very welcoming atmosphere and the food is
cooked in full view. Madras and Dhansak curries are full of flavour
and the Peshwari Nan was plump and puffed up, dripping with melted butter – delicious.' PGN. Price check: Papadam 30p, CTM £4.80,
Pullao Rice £1.30, Pickles 20p. House wine £7.50. Takeaway: 10% less.
Hours 12-2pm/5.30-11.30. Stocks Cobra.

©	Curry Club discount (see page 6)	☕	Unlicensed
√	Vegetarian		
BYO	Bring your own alcohol	▦	Delivery/takeaway

Everleigh

GOA BALTI HOUSE

Filling Station, Everleigh, Nr Tidworth ✆ 01264 850850

'As its adddress tells, it was a filling station – the pumps actually remain in the forecourt. A fine small bar, comfortable restaurant. A good sign is the genuine linen napkins. While visiting my son near Andover, had a friend staying from Canada who claimed he had curried moose. He apparently marinated it for a couple of days and then curried the lot – some sixty pounds of delicious meat! At the Goa, we indulged in a dazzling variety of dishes – a stupendous Chicken Madras, rich, hot, spicy. Garlic Chilli Chicken, tamarind sauce, marinated spicy chicken, full rounded edge on it. Lamb Vindaloo, a rich sauce, kick like a mule. Chicken Rhogan Josh, full and mature. A felicitous Karahi Murgh (Tandoori chicken cooked in a brilliant curry gravy served sizzling hot), Murag Rossa (Tandoori chicken, cinnamon sauce, served in a sizzling dish), all supported with a splendid series of vegetable curries, including fresh Bhindi Bhajee. Charming service, nothing spared to ensure we had truly splendid evening. Other temptations include Goa Special (Tandoori baked chicken cooked with almonds, coconut, sultanas and cashew nuts in a heavenly yoghurt based sauce and a definitive Lamb Jalfrezi. Sadly, there's no Moose Curry, but it's still a filling station indeed.' RG. 15% discount for collected takeaways. Price check: Papadam 40p, CTM £5.75, Pullao Rice £1.85, Pickles 40p per portion. Hours: 12-2.30pm/6pm-12am. Stocks Cobra

Ludgershall

MUGHAL NEW ENTRANT ©

33 Andover Road, Ludgershall 01264 790463

Of Mrs Bushra Rahman's 44-seater's curries, Tikka and Balti are the most popular. Special: Jhingi Kodv £5.50. Price check: Papadam 45p, CTM £5.95, Pullao Rice £1.50. House wine £6.95. Delivery: £15 minimum, 3-mile radius. Hours: 12-2.30pm/6pm-12am. Stocks Cobra.

Marlborough

ASIAN GRILL

8 London Road, Marlborough   © 01672 512877

'Place was busy, staff courteous and pleasant. Sag Bhajee should be renamed Sag and garlic, it was excellent – definitely no vampires visiting that night!' CL. Hours: 12pm-2.30pm/6pm-12am.

Melksham

MELKSHAM TANDOORI   ©

26 Church Street, Melksham   © 01225 705242

Mr Mahammed Mayna's attractive Cotswold stone building is adjacent to a car park. Its bar/reception are in a long narrow room with 50 seats beyond. 'Asked for a Papadom and got three (not charged). Chicken Tikka, great lumps, very well cooked, nice and succulent. Lovely mint sauce. Lamb Jalfrezi rich and loads of green chillies lurking in there for the unwary – I love 'em. Portions huge, cooking great and amazing value. Recommended.' MS. Price check: Papadam 30p, CTM £5.50, Pullao Rice £1.50. Hours: 6pm-12am. Branch: Saadi Takeaway, Silver Street, Bradford on Avon.

Salisbury

ASIA

90 Fisherton Street, Salisbury   © 01722 327628

When the Asia opened in 1963, there were barely any curryhouses outside London. Experience shows and we have constantly heard, since our first Guide, that it is above average. 'A thriving business, always packed. Service extremely fast, very efficient and absolutely charming. Kashmiri Chicken, beautifully done. Sag Bhaji was the best I have had – very spicy with guts and edge.' RG.

©	Curry Club discount (see page 6)	☕	Unlicensed
√	Vegetarian		
BYO	Bring your own alcohol	⊞	Delivery/takeaway

Swindon

BHAJI'S TAKEAWAY   ©

76 Thames Avenue, Swindon   © 01793 533799

Owned by Iqbal Shishir. Special: Tandoori Garlic Chilli Chicken or
Lamb £5.45, most popular. Price check: Papadam 50p, CTM £5.15,
Pullao Rice £1.50. Delivery: £10 minimum order, Swindon area. Hours:
5pm-12am.

BIPLOB   ©

12-14 Wood Street, Swindon   © 01793 490265

Rokib Alo and Fozlur Rahman's 60-seater has a separate lounge/bar
area seating 20. House specials include Begun Bahar £5.95. Price check:
Papadam 45p, Masala 50p, CTM £5.95, Pullao Rice £1.50. Minimum
charge £10. Hours: 12-2.30pm/6pm-12am. Branch: Raja Takeaway,
Cheltenham, Rajdoot, Cirencester, Glos. Stocks Cobra.

CURRY GARDEN   ©

90 Victoria Road, Swindon   © 01793 521114

R. Khan's large restaurant seating 80 diners remains popular. Chef
specials include: Tandoori King Prawn Jalfrezi, with green chillies
£9.95. CC Members will get a 10% discount. Takeaway: 15% less. Price
check: Papadam 50p, CTM £5.95, Pullao Rice £1.70. Minimum charge:
£6. Hours: 12-2pm/5.30pm-12am.

GULSHAN   ©

122 Victoria Road, Old Town, Swindon   © 01793 522558

Owned and managed by Abdul Kahhar. Seats 80 on two floors
connected by a spiral staircase. 'Very smart decor, pleasant attentive
waiters. Extensive menu, mainly Bangladeshi. Muglai Paneer, cheese,
mixed fruit, almond, sultanas, fresh cream in mild sauce served
with Onion Bhajias and beer, cost £9.40. A nice idea was the revolving
sweet tray with the bill.' DS. Sunday all-day buffet £7.50. Takeaway: 15%
discount. Hours: 12-2.30pm/6pm-12am. Sat. 6pm-1am. Stocks Cobra.

MAHARAJAH   NEW ENTRANT   ©

6 High Street, Purton, Swindon   © 01793 770253

At Abdul Khalique Ali's 48-seat (party room 24) curry house, CTM
is most popular. Special: Peshwari Mushroom £6.50, Lobster Chilli
Masala £11.95. Price check: Papadam 50p, CTM £6.75, Pullao Rice
£1.95. Lager £2 pint, house wine £7.95. Takeaway: 10% off. Hours: 1-
3.30pm (Sun. only buffet) 5.30pm-12am (12.30am on Sat.).

RAFU'S TANDOORI

29-30 High Street, Highworth, Swindon   © 01793 765320

Opened in 1982 by Mr Rafu as the Biplob; renamed to prevent confusion. It remains popular. 'Menu large and varied choice. Quantity –
very filling. Quality good. Service good.' JWH. 'I find Rafu's a very nice
place.' RF. 'The wine list is very good for an Indian restaurant.
Whenever we go to Rafu's we know we are going to have a top class
meal, with friendly people, in pleasant surroundings.' JS. Price check:
Chicken Tikka £6.50, Mixed Veg. £2.30, Papadam 45p, CTM £6.95,
Pullao Rice £1.60. Set menu £6.95. Hours: 12-3pm/6pm-12am.

SPICY AROMA   NEW ENTRANT   ©

144 Cricklade Road, Gorse Hill, Swindon   © 01793 488700

Abdul Rouf Ali's Aroma seats 46 in two dining rooms decorated with
'mahogany effect with cream background, with a classic wooden effect
bar'. Mr Ali is a Spice Girls fan. 'Ginger: she appears fresh in most of
our exciting dishes; Sporty: see our waiters race around you, yet remain
polite and courteous at all times; Posh: as you would expect because
we're brand new; Baby: she's a sweetheart – why not bring yours to
Spicy Aroma? Scarey: after paying us a visit you'll be scared to go anywhere else, in case it doesn't meet with our standards.' Price check:
Papadam 45p, CTM £5.50, Pullao Rice £1.70. Delivery: £10 minimum
order. Minimum charge: £6.95. Sunday lunch buffet: £7.95. Hours:
lunch by appointment only, 5pm-1am. Stocks Cobra.

Warminster

AGRA NEW ENTRANT

---

32 East Street, Warminster   © 01985 212713

Mr M. Rahman's 1984 ownership of this 50-seater coincided with the publication of our first Guide, in which it appeared. We've always regarded it as a useful currying hole in an otherwise devoid area. Special: Duck Jhalferezi, with fresh green chillies, £7.95. Price check: Papadam 30p, CTM £7.95 (incl. rice), Pullao Rice £1.95. Lager £1.90 pint, house wine £6.95. Minimum charge: £9. Takeaway: 10% off. Hours: 12-2.30pm/6-11.30pm. Branch: Assam Takeaway, East Street, Warminster.

Wootton Bassett

SALIK'S NEW ENTRANT

---

21 High Street, Wootton Bassett   © 01793 852365

Situated opposite the Curriers' Arms! 'Bhajia £1.95 and Samosa £1.95, freshly made, nicely presented and delicious! Fragrant, fluffy Pullao Rice. Lots of meat in Keema Nan £1.65. Massive portion of Chicken Biryani £4.95. Chicken Tikka Bhuna £4.65, lots of well-marinated breast meat.' TE. 'This little gem deserves a mention. Extraordinary food, quality and service at a low price.' AE. Price check: Papadam 40p, CTM £5.25, Pullao Rice £1.55. Delivery: free on orders over £10. Hours: 12-2.30pm/6pm-12am (1am on Fri. & Sat.). Stocks Cobra.

©	Curry Club discount (see page 6)		Unlicensed
√	Vegetarian		
BYO	Bring your own alcohol		Delivery/takeaway

WORCESTERSHIRE

Area: Midlands
Population: 476,000
Number of restaurants in county: 37
Number of restaurants in Guide: 16

Bewdley

THE RAJAH OF BEWDLEY ©

8 Load Street, Bewdley   ✆ 01299 400368

Anwar Uddin's 34-seater is in a grade 2 listed cottage with soft light-ing and exposed beams. 'Food excellent, the people extremely friendly, offering a high standard of customer service.' SH. Special: Tandoori Lobster. Price check: CTM £5.95, Pullao Rice £1.50. House wine £6.95. Takeaway: 10% off. Minimum charge: £4.95. Hours: 5-11.30.

Kidderminster

EURASIA TAKEAWAY ▦ ©

Unit 1, Stourbridge Road, Kidderminster   ✆ 01562 825861

Syed Mumshad Ahmed's takeaway is reportedly popular. Special: Rung Pur, marinated chicken, onions and capsicum and Chicken Gulshan, barbecued chicken with minced lamb, garnished with salad £4.50. Price check: Papadam 30p, CTM £4.50, Pullao Rice £1.20. Delivery: £7 min-imum, 5-mile radius. Hours: 5pm-12am.

NEW SHER E PUNJAB ©

48 George Street, Kidderminster   ✆ 01562 740061

Evenings only at Puran Singh's restaurant which has been open a long time (since 1971). Stocks Cobra.

Malvern

ANUPAN

85 Church Street, Malvern   ✆ 01684 573814

'Friendly efficient service, decor pleasant and comfortable. Chicken Tikka Masala, excellent flavour, not too hot, good-sized portion. Chicken Patia, not on menu, was also excellent.' DR. Stocks Cobra.

Malvern Link

AJANTA

243 Worcester Road, Malvern Link   ✆ 01684 569820

'Chicken Tikka Masala and Chicken Jalfrezi both excellent, especially the Jalfrezi with the use of lemon, gave an exquisite dimension, eaten with Naan. Finished off with Kulfi and washed down with the best chai I've ever had.' JFM. Stocks Cobra.

Pershore

SHUNARGA   ©

44 High Street, Pershore   ✆ 01386 555357

Mosnul Haq says of his 50-seater there's a 'cosy atmosphere, with bamboo chairs, screens. Korma the most popular dish. Special: Sylheti Chicken, tender pieces of chicken, in a mild, thick sauce, with Basmati Pullao Rice £6.95. 'Warm welcome and Bombay Mix on arrival. Starter, Chicken Bhuna on Puree £2.20, very good and spicy. Chicken Vindaloo £4.25, good, nice and hot, not overpowered, with plenty of taste. Pullao Rice watery. Nan bread £1.10, very good and piping hot.' MG. Credit cards are not accepted on meals under £10! Price check: 35p, CTM £4.95, Pullao Rice £1.45. House wine £6.95. Takeaway 10% off. Hours: 1-2pm/6pm-12.30am. Stocks Cobra.

©	Curry Club discount (see page 6)		Unlicensed
√	Vegetarian		
BYO	Bring your own alcohol		Delivery/takeaway

Redditch

AKASH   ©

31-33 Unicorn Hill, Redditch   © 01527 62301

Opened in 1979 by Akil Choudhury. A reliable and well-established 65-seater in two rooms, tastefully decorated in pale pink, with Moghul arches around pictures of India. Special: Balti Kebab, £2.60. Kashmiri Lamb chop, with chickpeas in a rich sauce, served with Rice £5.50. Minimum charge: £5.50. Price check: Papadam 50p, CTM £7.25 incl. rice, Pullao Rice £1.50. House wine £6.50. Delivery. Hours: 5pm-12am. Branch: Balti Desh Takeaway, Alvechurches; Balti Raj Takeaway, Unicorn Hill; Tilla Balti Takeaway, 1242 Evesham Road, Astwood Bank, both Redditch. Stocks Cobra.

BALTI RAJ TAKEAWAY   NEW ENTRANT   ▦

41 Unicorn Hill, Redditch   ©01527 60292

Miah (chef) and Ahmed (manager) do the takeaways. Special: Chicken Jointha, very hot, cooked with plentiful green chillies £3.95. Price check: Papadam 30p, CTM £4.85, Pullao Rice £1.25. Delivery: £10 minimum. Hours: 5pm-12.30am (1.30am on Sat.). Branches: *See above.*

NAWAB

17-21 Unicorn Hill, Redditch   © 01527 64594

Ajaib Hussain's 60-seater's special is noted: Lamb Tikka Jeera, marinated and roasted in the tandoor, with onions, fresh tomatoes, fenugreek, coriander, cummin and spring onions £5.50. Minimum charge: £4.95. Credit cards not accepted. Price check: Papadam 40p, CTM £5.50, Pullao Rice £1.35. House wine £5.75. Delivery: £12 minimum, 3-mile radius. Hours: 5.30pm-12am. Stocks Cobra.

Tenbury Wells

SHAMRAJ BALTI HOUSE   ©

28 Cross Street, Tenbury Wells   © 01584 819612

Owned by Mr Rahman, seats 60, party room 14, formula curries, 'marble-effect painted interior, light blue.' Special: Shamraj Shahi Special

£7.95. Price check: Papadam 55p, CTM £5.60, Pullao Rice £1.60. House wine £7.40. Takeaway: 15% off. Hours: 12-2.30pm (Sat. & Sun.)/5pm-12am. Stocks Cobra.

Worcester

AKAASH

63 Lowesmoor, Worcester   © **01905 611124**

'The Akaash was taken over by an "up market" restaurant in St Johns (the Pasha). Since then staff uniforms have arrived. Seekh Kebabs £1.95, Papadoms 35p.' RE. Reports please.

ASHLEY'S BALTI HOUSE   🍴 BYO ©

11 The Tything, Worcester   © **01905 611747**

Formula Pakistani curries at Mohammed Altaf's 65-seater in two rooms. 'There are 5 restaurants and 3 takeaways in a half mile stretch of this road out of Worcester. All of them, except Ashleys, serve unremarkable food. Busy, bustling, spit and sawdust. Shish Kebab 70p, reheated in microwave, bright red, tasted OK. Lamb Balti, tasty, good quality meat. Korma, a little on the hot side for my wife. Tandoori Roti 95p – very good indeed; Lamb Balti Madras with Dhal £4.05 – very tasty, a nice combination. Unlicensed, but there is an off-licence opposite. The best in Worcester so far.' RE. Baltis are 'the talk of the town', says EM. BYO, no corkage. Price check: Papadam 25p, CTM £4.30, Pullao Rice £1.10. Sunday lunch £3.95. Minimum charge: £4. Hours: 12-3pm (Sun.-Fri.)/5.30pm-12am (1am on Sat.).

BOMBAY PALACE   ©

38 The Tything, Worcester   © **01905 613969**

Abdul Rob tells us his 40-seater has 7 parking spaces at the back. Special: Lamb Pasanda Nawabi, tender sliced lamb, cream, yoghurt and ground nuts £5. Price check: Papadam 40p, CTM £5.20, Pullao Rice £1.35. Minimum charge: £6.55. Delivery: £10 minimum charge, 3-mile radius. Hours: 6pm-12am (1am on Sat.). Stocks Cobra.

PASHA

56 St Johns, Worcester   © 01905 426327

Abdul Haie does 'Bangladeshi cuisine of a high standard. Pleasant staff
and surroundings. Chana Puri was very tasty. Vegetable Dhansak Balti
was served in a shallow cast-iron pan and had a sharp and interesting
flavour.' DS. Price check: Papadam 45p, CTM £5.50, Bombay Potato
£2.25, Pullao Rice £1.50. Delivery. Hours: 12-2pm/5.30pm-12am.

PURBANI   ©

27 The Tything, Worcester   © 01905 423671

75-seater owned by Abdul Haie and T. Hussain. 'Indian Moghul styles,
with classical English' decor. Special: Chicken Tikka Bhoona £6.95.
Price check: Papadam 40p, CTM £5.75, Pullao Rice £1.50. House wine
£5.75. Delivery: 3-mile radius. Minimum charge: £3.75. Takeaway: 10%
off. Hours: 12-2pm (Sun.-Fri.)/6pm-12am. Stocks Cobra.

SPICES TAKEAWAY NEW ENTRANT   ©

9 Barbourne Road, Worcester   ·   © 01905 729101

Open kitchen, owned and managed by M.A. Hoque. Special: Kabeb
Ka Karishma, mixtures of Tandoori items £2.40, Lamb Shahjahan,
with garlic and mushrooms £5.75. Credit cards not accepted. Hours:
5.30pm-12am (1am on Sat.). Branch: Shunarga, 44, High Street,
Pershore.

©	Curry Club discount (see page 6)		Unlicensed
√	Vegetarian		
BYO	Bring your own alcohol	⊞	Delivery/takeaway

YORKSHIRE

1997 county changes created a 'new' Yorkshire county — East Yorks, and gave back Cleveland south of the Tees to North Yorks, restoring Britain's biggest county. Because the area is so large, we deal with these four counties in compass order, N, E, S, W or, as DBAC remembers it, Nice Eating Shredded Wheat!

North Yorkshire

Area: North
Population: 726,000
Number of restaurants in county: 54
Number of restaurants in Guide: 17

Harrogate

GANJA NEW ENTRANT

34 Oxford Street, Harrogate   ✆ 01423

'Interior not what one has come to expect, very modern furnishings and quality high. Rather tatty loo door leads to a very clean and well appointed toilet. Subtlety of spicing was excellent with new flavours percolating the taste buds throughout the meal, rather than the instant "wham bam" experience of many meals which so quickly fades. Prices a little higher but acceptable.' JL. Price check: Papadam 40p, CTM £6.95, Pullao Rice £1.80, Pickles 30p per person.

RAJPUT NEW ENTRANT

Cheltenham Parade, Harrogate   ✆ 01423 562113

Opened in 1992 by Mrs Perveen Khan — head chef. 'No complaint about the food — it concerns the pickle tray. Myself and two friends went for a meal, only one of us had the pickle tray, but we were charged for three. I queried the amount, and was met with a very curt response from the owner's husband, "Well, I can't be responsible for seeing who has and hasn't had pickles." I said that I didn't see why we should pay for something we hadn't eaten. He then replied, "Are you going to pay or not?", and rather than cause a scene, I paid the full bill. On leaving I said I wouldn't be back. He commented, "Good, we don't want your sort here anyway." The pickles are a small matter, but I know a lot of people don't check their bills. This restaurant has been prosecuted by North Yorkshire trading standards for blatantly overcharging customers.' JMFP. We don't want this sort of restaurant in the guide, but it's here to warn everyone else.

RAJ RANI TAKEAWAY   ▦ ©

235 Skipton Road, Harrogate   © 01423 529295

Ahad Miah, the proprietor of this takeaway only, is offering Monday and Tuesday CC customers 15% discount on collected takeaways over £15. Special: Special Lamb Tikka, sliced lamb tikka, mince lamb, green peppers, onions, herbs and coriander £4.95. Price check: Papadam 40p, CTM £4.95, Pullao Rice £1.25. Delivery: £8.50, 4-mile radius. Hours: 5.30-11.30pm (11pm on Sat., 10.30pm on Sun.).

Malton

RAJ TANDOORI   ©

21 Church Street, Norton, Malton   © 01653 697337

S. Islam's friendly 34-seater has dusky pink and petrol blue walls, white cornices, Indian art, pink and white linen and spot lights. Special: Akhini Chicken, pineapple, almond, sultanas, peas and rice, served with vegetable curry £6. 'Has been a satisfying experience following their progress, to what is now a very good restaurant. My seven-year-old daughter's favourite eating establishment.' AT. Price check: Papadam 40p, CTM £5.95, Pullao Rice £1.50. Lager £1.80 pint, house wine £6.95. Takeaway: 20% off. Delivery: £1.50 minumum, Malton area. Hours: 5.30pm-12am, Mon. closed except for Bank Holidays.

Middlesbrough

CLEVELAND TANDOORI   ©

289 Linthorpe Road, Middlesbrough   © 01642 242777

Owner-chef Abid Hussain's 32-seater serves formula curry, but there are some Pakistani gems: Shalgum Gosht is meat with turnip and

Lahori Gosht both £4 is meat with okra. For the yet-to-be-converted-to curry, try the Anglo Indian Coronation Chicken, created in 1953 by the London's Cordon Bleu school in honour of QE II's Coronation: diced chicken cooked with apricots in a creamy sauce £5.80. Price check: Papadam 30p, CTM £5.60, Pullao Rice £1.80. Buffet, Sunday, Monday, Tuesday £8.50, incl. glass of wine. Delivery: £6 minimum, 3-mile radius. Hours: 6pm-12am (2.30am on Fri./Sat.). Stocks Cobra.

KHAN'S BALTI HOUSE   ©

349 Linthorpe Road, Middlesbrough   ℂ 01642 817457

Seats 65, formula Pakistani curry. Authentic Karai (aka Balti) dishes, cooked with tomatoes, capsicums, garnished with fried onions (tarka), served sizzling £5.95. Takeaway 20% off. Sunday lunch £12.50. Minimum charge £5. Price check: Papadam 30p, CTM £6.50, Pullao Rice £1. House wine £2.20 – glass! Delivery: £5 minimum. Hours: 6pm-1am (1.30am on Sat. & Sun.). Branch: Khan, 417, Linthorpe Road, Stocks Cobra.

Ripon

MOTI RAJ   ©

18 High Skellgate, Ripon   ℂ 01765 690348

Abdul Malik's philosophy is: 'the only path to good food, like good wine, is time.' Special: Sliced Chicken Tikka with Keema, £5.95. 'For main course I had Chicken Karahi, served in a proper cast iron karahi and piping hot. One of my friends had Prawn Bhuna, not on the menu, but not the slightest trouble for them to provide. Total bill (for 3) came to £24. I thoroughly enjoyed the meal.' JMFP. Price check: Papadam 40p, CTM £5.25, Pullao Rice £1.35. Takeaway 10% off. Delivery (tel. 602030): 3-mile radius. Hours: 5.30pm-12am.

©	Curry Club discount (see page 6)		Unlicensed
√	Vegetarian		
BYO	Bring your own alcohol	🎴	Delivery/takeaway

Settle

GOLDEN GATE TANDOORI

Fern Cottage, Market Square, Settle   © 01729 822901

40-seater taken over in 1997 by N. Uddin Ali. Decorated in green and white contrasting the wooden beams. Thursday and Friday set meal £14.99 for two. Balti dishes are new on the menu, from £5.50 for Chicken Balti. Special: Chicken Tikka Chom Chom, green chillies £6.95. Takeaway 10% off over £6. Price check: Papadam 40p, CTM £6.30, Pullao Rice £1.50. House wine £7.95 litre. Minimum charge: £6. Hours: 5pm-12am. Stocks Cobra.

Skipton

AAGRAH   BEST RESTAURANT CHAIN TOP 100   ©

Devonshire Place, Keighley Road, Skipton   © 01756 790807

Managed by Mostafizur Rahman, this 52-seater is the third of seven very popular Aagrahs (so booking advisable) and good enough to be awarded a collective TOP 100 cachet. (*See* Shipley, W Yorks for detailed comment.) Hours: 6pm-12am (11pm on Sun.). Stocks Cobra.

NAAZ   NAME CHANGE   ©

21 Keighley Road, Skipton   © 01756 792473

40-seater, changed name from Royal Bengal when taken over in '97 by N. Uddin. Price check: Papadam 40p, CTM £6.10, Pullao Rice £1.60. House wine £6.95. Takeaway 20% off. Delivery: £10 minimum. Reports please. Hours: 12-2pm (Sat. closed) and 6pm-12am (12.30am Sat.). Stocks Cobra.

RAJ BALTI HOUSE

11 Keighley Road, Skipton   © 01756 795697

Owner-manager Mastab Ali's restaurant seats 42. Special: Balti Tikka £7.95, Chicken Passanda £7.95. Takeaway 15% off. Price check: Papadam 40p, CTM £6.10, Pullao Rice £1.60. Hours: 6pm (Sat. & Sun. 5.30pm)-12am (1am on Sat., 11.30pm on Sun.). Stocks Cobra.

Tadcaster

AAGRAH BEST RESTAURANT CHAIN TOP 100   ©

York Road, Steeton, Tadcaster   ✆ 01937 530888

Managed by Aagrah boss, Mohammed Aslam, this 100-seater, which opened in 1996, is the sixth of seven very popular Aagrahs. It's on the A64 near York, with easy parking. All the Aagrahs are rated with a collective TOP 100 cachet. (*See* Shipley, W Yorks for fuller comment.) Hours: 6-11.30pm (11pm on Sun.). Stocks Cobra.

Yarm

BALTI HOUSE

49 High Street, Yarm   ✆ 01642 788998

In the mid-1960s I used to fly over tiny Yarm, landing RAF jets at Middleton St George, now Teesside Airport, but there wasn't a curry house there then, nor indeed anywhere within a 50-mile radius. Now there are over 100 in that area, and even this one at Yarm. We hear that Johir Uddin's 80-seater is a curry house with a difference, decorated rather like a pub, great idea, seats 80. Special: Beef Munro, mild dish cooked with garlic sauce, ground almonds, served with Pullao Rice £8.95. Price check: Papadam 40p, CTM £6.95, Pullao Rice £1.50. House wine £8.95. Takeaway 10% off. Minimum charge £6.95. Hours: 12-11pm (2am on Fri. & Sat.). Stocks Cobra.

York

AKASH

10 North Street, York   ✆ 01904 633550

Chef/owner J.U. Ahmed's 38-seater does a set dinner for £9.50. Special: Kabuli Chicken or Lamb, chickpeas, tomato and fresh coriander £6.20. Price check: Papadam 50p, CTM £6.20, Pullao Rice £1.50. Takeaway 20% off. Hours: 12-2pm/6pm-12am. Stocks Cobra.

JINNAH BALTI   ©

105-107 Micklegate, York   ℭ **01904 659999**

Saleem Akhtar's 135-seater can be full at a weekend, we hear. 'I started
with the Seekh Kebabs and thought I was going to be disappointed
with the place as the Kebabs were of the red-colouring variety and possibly microwaved (the best I've tasted were at Bharat in Bradford).
However, the main course, Jinnah Special Balti which was chicken,
lamb, prawn and mushrooms was excellent.' RC. Price check: Papadam
45p, CTM £6.95, Pullao Rice £1.95. Hours: 12-2.30pm/6pm-12am.
Branch: Jinnah, 845 York Road, Leeds; Jinnah Takeaway, 18 The Village,
Haxby; Taj Mahal and Viceroy of India, York. Stocks Cobra.

LAL QUILA   NEW ENTRANT

17-19 Bishopthorpe Road, York   ℭ **01904 670684**

'Extremely impressed by the service, atmosphere, surroundings and
food quality and variety. Reasonable prices. Definitely for those who
like their food spicy, hot and rich. Mixed Kebab, Prawn Puri, Meat
Tejab (hot!) and Chicken Madras, to cool off with!' AE. Delivery: £15
minimum, 3-mile radius. Price check: Papadam 40p (plain), 45p
(spicy), CTM £6.95 (incl. Pullao Rice), Pullao Rice 1.40. Hours: 12-
2.30pm (Sun. closed)/6pm-12am. Takeaway: 20% off.

TAJ MAHAL

4 Kings Staith, York   ℭ **01904 653944**

'Food and prices excellent.' AA. Hours: 12-2.30pm/6pm-12am.

©	Curry Club discount (see page 6)	🍺	Unlicensed
√	Vegetarian		
BYO	Bring your own alcohol	🏠	Delivery/takeaway

East Yorkshire

Area: North
Population: 800,000
Number of restaurants in county: 23
Number of restaurants in Guide: 7

1997 transferred the territory and towns from North Humbs into East Yorkshire. Prior to 1965 it was, in any case, part of Yorkshire.

Beverley

NASEEB   NEW ENTRANT   ©

9-10 Wednesday Market, Beverley   ✆ **01482 861110**

Established in 1988 by Abdul Muzir, seats 44 diners, Bangladeshi formula curries. Very pretty restaurant, Indian painting, white walls, arches, ceiling fans, blue tablecloths and napkins, velvet chairs and curtains. Roshoon Mirch Murgh, hot, thick sauce, fresh garlic, green chillies, green pepper, chopped tomatoes and fresh coriander leaves £6.10. Price check: Papadam 40p, CTM £7, Pullao Rice £1.60. House wine £6.95. Delivery only available to club members, ask for details. Takeaway: 10% discount. Hours: 6-11.30pm. Stocks Cobra.

Bridlington

BRIDLINGTON TANDOORI

124 St John Street, Bridlington   ✆ **01262 400014**

At S. Miah's 48-seater MB had the 'BEST Chicken Madras that I've EVER tasted, expertly spiced with a most delightful lemony flavour.' Special: Chef's Special, chicken, meat, prawn and mushroom £5.90. Price check: Papadam 55p, CTM £5.50, Pullao Rice £1.55. Hours: 12-2.30pm/6pm-12am (12.30am on Fri. & Sat.).

Hessle

LIGHT OF INDIA   ©

27 The Weir, Hessle   ✆ 01482 649521

Saiful Islam Tarafdar's Light is under the shadow of the fabulous
bridge, and does 'fabulous takeaways only' KY. Special: Indian Burger,
pitta bread with spicy kebab and salad £1.90. Curry Sauce and Chips
£1.90! Price check: Papadam 30p, CTM £4.60, Pullao Rice 90p. Set
dinner £16.95. Delivery: £7 minimum, Hessle area and £10 minimum
local area, possibly small charge! Hours: 5pm-12am (12.30am on Sat.).

Hull

JEWEL OF ASIA   ©

328 Beverley Road, Hull   ✆ 01482 445469

Syed Amir Ali and manager Asrob Ali always 'make you welcome.' BD
at their 'blossom-pink-walled curry house.' SAA. Price check: Papadam
30p, CTM £6.50, Tandoori Salmon £10.95, Balti Garlic Chilli Chicken
£6.50, Pullao Rice £1.20. Set dinner £22.95 for two. Delivery: £1, 2-mile
radius, £2 over. Hours: 5.30-12am (1am on Sat.). Stocks Cobra.

MAHARAJAH

245 Holderness Road, Hull   ✆ 01482 224647

Abdul Hamid's 46-seater is well-spoken of by RK. Balti specialities.
Price check: Papadam 35p, CTM £3.90, Pullao Rice £1.05. House wine
£6.75. Hours: 12-2pm/6pm-1am. Stocks Cobra.

TANDOORI MAHAL   ©

589 Anlaby Road, Hull

Abu Maksud and Mizanur Tarafder's 64-seat restaurant is one of RK's
favourites. 'Have been regular customers for over three years. We have
always received first class service and excellent food.' PT. Price check:
Papadam 40p, CTM £4.60, Garlic Chilli Chicken Tikka £7.85 incl.
rice, Pullao Rice £1.10. Kurzi Lamb £45. Set dinner £16.95. Hours:
6pm-12am.

Pocklington

TANDOORI MAHAL   NAME CHANGE

13-15 Railway Street, Pocklington   ✆ 01759 305027

Shelim Ahmed's curry house has changed name from Tandoori Mahal. Special: Jalfreji, tikka, tomatoes, capsicum, green chilli, coriander £5.20. 'One of our two favourites.' BT. Price check: Papadam 40p, CTM £5.10, Pullao Rice £1.35. House wine £7.20. Takeaway: 10% off. Hours: 12-2pm (weekdays)/6-11.30pm (12am on Sat. & Sun.).

South Yorkshire

Area: North
Population: 1,296,000
Number of restaurants in county: 98
Number of restaurants in Guide: 11

Barnsley

INDIAN GARDENS

---

16 Peel Square, Barnsley   ✆ 01226 282612

At R.A. Rahman's 66-seat curry house, the 'staff are very friendly and attentive. Specials marginally more expensive than standards, but are superior. Naans wonderfully light, but on the small side. Personal favourite Chicken Karahi comes to the table sizzling in a blackened cast-iron karahi on a wooden base.' NW. Other specials include: Begon Took, fried aubergine bathed in tangy sauce of yoghurt and gram flour paste £1.60. Palong Sag, spinach, lentils and fresh coriander £3.70. Even hotter than a Vindaloo, comes the Sindalo, cooked with Chinese dry chillies, from £3.50. Price check: Papadam 40p, CTM £4.90, Pullao Rice £1.50. Hours: 6pm-12.30am (1am on Sat.). Stocks Cobra.

JALSA   ©

7 Pitt Street, Barnsley   © 01226 779114

'Comfortable, smart, 50-seater with a delightful reception area and bar.' so proprietor Emdadur Rahman tells us. And we know it's popular. Takeaway 15% off. Price check: Papadam 40p, CTM £6.95, Pullao Rice £1.70. House wine £6.95. Hours: 6-11.45pm (12am on Sat., 11.30pm on Sun.). Stocks Cobra.

K2

5 Royal Street, Barnsley   © 01226 299230

Kashmiri Balti takeaway-only establishment. 'Excellent.' TH. Price check: Papadam 20p (one of the cheapest in the guide), CTM £4.70, Pullao Rice £1.20. They don't do lunch and we're not surprised, owner/manager/chef Ditta must be exhausted with these hours! 10% off for students before 10.30pm. Hours: 6pm-3am (4am on Sat., 12.30am on Sun.).

Doncaster

AAGRAH BEST RESTAURANT CHAIN TOP 100   ©

Great North Road, Woodlands, Doncaster © 01302 728888

Opened in 1995, the fifth of seven very popular (so booking advisable) Aagrahs. This 70-seater is a franchise run by cousin Liaquat Ali. Like its sisters, it is awarded a collective TOP 100 cachet. 'I would put it at no. 1 in Doncaster, and there's a lot of competition.' JF. (*See* Shipley, W Yorks for detailed comment.) Hours: 6-11.30pm (12am on Fri. & Sat., 11am on Sun.). Stocks Cobra.

INDUS   ©

24-26 Silver Street, Doncaster   © 01302 810800

Long-established (1968) 185-seater, owned by Karim Din, with manager M. Ilyas. Special: King Prawn Tandoori, served with rice and sauce £10.90. 'A sophisticated restaurant.' DC. Price check: Papadam 70p, CTM £8.40, Pullao Rice £1.90. Takeaway: 5% off. Delivery: £20. Sun. buffet £12. Hours: 12-2pm/7pm-12.30am. Stocks Cobra.

Sheffield

AMBAR NEW ENTRANT

740 Ecclesall Road, Sheffield   © **0114 268 0886**

N.K. Dasgupta's 36-seater does blackboard specials (why don't they all
do this?) Chef's banquet: Lamb Massalam (4 diners) whole leg of
roasted lamb is carved at your table. Chicken Massallam (for 2 diners)
£26. Price check: Papadam 40pCTM £5.95, Pullao Rice £1.40. Hours:
12-2pm/6pm-12am. Fri. & Sat. 6pm-1am.

ASHOKA NEW ENTRANT

307 Ecclesall Road, Sheffield   © **0114 268 3029**

Established in 1967 by Mrs M. Ahmed, this 38-seater is managed by
Mr Ahmed. Most ordered dish Bhel Puri – £2.95, Liver Puri – chick-
en livers, stir-fried in masala, served on bread £2.95. Price check:
Papadam 70p, CTM £7.25, Pullao Rice £1.75. Lager £2.60 pint, house
wine £8.90. Takeaway: 10% off. Hours: 6 (Sun. 7)-11.30pm.

BALTI KING   ©

216 Fulwood Road, Broomhill, Sheffield   © **0114 266 6655**

110-seater on two floors, owned by Hanif Hussain (known as Tony to
his regulars) serving Pakistani food. Decorated in cream and red, traditional statue reliefs on walls, plaster dome with chandelier and long
bar for you to 'prop' up, while waiting for a table. If it is your birthday Hanif presents his guest with a bottle of Bucks Fizz and a
birthday card. House special Tropical Balti £7.90 consists of chicken,
lamb, prawn, mushroom, potatoes, channa, pineapple and fruit cocktail, tomatoes and onion, garnished with fresh coriander leaves. Sounds
like starter, main course and pudding mixed into one! New fish dishes
on menu, e.g.: Kashmiri style curry. Fish Masala and Chips(!) served
with Rice £7.50. Price check: Papadam 35p, CTM £5.70, Pullao Rice
£1.30. House wine £7.90. Delivery: £10, 3-mile radius. Hours: 12-3pm
(1am on Sun.). Stocks Cobra.

BILASH TAKEAWAY   ⊞ ☕

347 Sharrow Vale Road, Sheffield   © 0114 266 1746

Established by chef Abdul Jahir in 1986. Price check: Papadam 30p,
CTM £3.95, Pullao Rice £1. Hours: 5.30pm-12am.

JAFLONG NEW ENTRANT   ©

182 Northfield Road, Crookes, Sheffield   © 0114 266 1802

A cosy Bangladeshi formula curry house, seating just 36 diners. Balti
dishes on the menu, from £3.50. Special: Jahangir Bhuna Prawn, medium, onions, tomatoes and mushrooms £4.20. Price check: Papadam
40p, CTM £5.50, Pullao Rice £1.50. Lager £2 pint, house wine £7.
Hours: 6pm-12am (1am on Fri. & Sat.).

NIRMAL'S TOP 100   ©

189-193 Glossop Road, Sheffield   © 0114 272 4054

Nirmal's was in our 1984 Guide, and was in our TOP 100 in the 1992
edition. Erroneously I dropped her in the 1995 edition, and this carried
through into 1998. Mercifully she has politely reminded me of her
existence, and I take great pleasure in restoring her to her rightful position in the Guide, TOP 100 *et al.* Mind you, her many regulars needed
no such reminding. I say 'her' and 'she', because Mrs Nirmal Gupta is
the owner chef, with the front going to Mr P.L. Gupta. But Nirmal is
no retiring backstage person. She makes appearances on the restaurant
floor and 'enjoys talking about food'. PM. She is a huge personality and
has no hesitation in telling customers like William Hague and Jamie
Lee Curtis such snippets as 'curry is an aphrodisiac'. But not all her
clients are stars. She opened in 1981 near the University 'to feed hungry students', indeed many of her regulars work and study there. Mrs
Nirmal's has virtually doubled in size since we first reported on it, and
now has a reception area, cocktail bar and 80 seats on two floors. Its
famous Special Board, upon which are chalked the dishes of the day,
fortunately remains. The technique would hardly merit a mention in
1001 bistros up and down the land, but it is rare in the world of curry.
I mentioned this back in 1984, and I'm still waiting for the formula
wallahs to cotton on! The menu is northern Indian with, on the face
of it, just standard Tandoori, Tikkas, Kormas, Bhunas, Madrases,
Vindaloos and the rest. 'But do not expect one-sauce cooking here.' RS

'All is cooked superbly, as at an Indian home.' GA. Of those specials: 'Nirmal's Potato Chops £2.25, are amazing mashed potato rissoles with a central stuffing of spicy lentils topped with almond tikka. The vegetable dishes prove the point that this is exceptional cooking. The paneer is always light and fresh, and stuffed Bhindi (okra) is always the test of a good chef — they can so easily go sappy! I've not seen that happen here.' BR. 'She is a magician with lentils.' SG. Price check: Papadam 45p, CTM £6.95, Pullao Rice £1.95. Tomato Paneer, £4.95. Parsnips with peppers and tomatoes £4.50. Aubergine Green Pepper £4.95. Gourmet Buffet night on Tuesday, £9.95 from 7.30-11pm. Sun. buffet £9.95. Service charge: 10%. Hours: 12-2.30pm/6pm-12am. We welcome Nirmal's back to our TOP 100. Stocks Cobra.

West Yorkshire

Area: North
Population: 2,070,000
Number of restaurants in county: 293
Number of restaurants in Guide: 53

Batley

BOMBAY PALACE 　　　　　🍵 BYO ©

3 St James Street, Batley 　　　　© 01924 444440

Balti 60-seater in an old converted bakery, with many features still apparent, such as the dough mixers, opened in 1992 by G. Maniyar and Shahid Akudi. Brick walls display Moghal paintings, open fire. 'My wife and I have been regulars since it opened. Our current favourites are Seekh Kebabs — beautifully spicy, not too hot, fresh and tasty. Nargis Kebabs — full of flavour with a velvety texture. For special occasions there are banquet menus, which again represent excellent value for money.' TN. Special: Palace Raan, whole leg of lamb, marinated for 24 hours in herbs, yoghurt, almonds and cashews, cut into slices, plenty for 4, £60. Delivery £10, 3-mile radius. Price check: Papadam 20p, CTM £7.50, Pullao Rice £1.50. Hours: 6pm-12am.

SPICE GARDEN   🍺 BYO ©

2 Market Place, Birstall, Batley   © 01924 471690

Specials at Abrar Hussain's Pakistani 74-seater include the Grand-Slam – it's four different meats, vegetables, prawns, massive portion – so now you know! Price check: Papadam 40p, CTM £4.95, Pullao Rice £1.50. Takeaway: 10% off. Delivery: £7, 3-mile radius. BYO. Hours: 5pm-12am.

Bradford

Bradford has a high pedigree curry background, with its very well-established largely Pakistani population. This means Halal meat and few veg at the many unlicensed cheap n' cheerful spit n' sawdust caffs. Since many are strict Moslems, not all welcome BYO. Where we know they do, we say so. Even so, please check with the staff then always drink discreetly and in moderation in such places. The restaurants, sweet shops and cafés are much more widely spread around than, say, in Southall. Curryholics must locate them, for their excellent, uncompromising ethnic food at real value-for-money prices. With more curry establishments (160) per head of the population (475,000) than in any other city in Britain (the ratio is 1:2968), Bradford remains Curry City UK (see Leicester and Glasgow). Here are your favourites:

AMEER   ©

415 Thornton Road, Thornton, Bradford   © 01274 833673

P. Quresh's licensed 60-seater serves good, standard curries. Hours: 5.30am-1am. Stocks Cobra.

ASHA   ©

31 Cheapside, Bradford   © 01274 729358

Special Feast Night on Sundays and Thursdays at owner Abdul Anwar's Asha. Hours: 6pm-12am. Stocks Cobra.

BENGAL BRASSERIE   ©

198-200 Keighley Road, Frizinghall,
Bradford   © 01274 543350

55-seater taken over in '97 by manager, Ali Ahmed. Decorated in blues. Has a spiral staircase, colonial fans, shamiania (Indian tent) and two

massive brass coffee pots. Specials: Murgh Sagarana, serves two £29.95.
Throughout the centuries the traditional Kashmiri wedding feast.
Consumed only by the bride and groom, it was always thought to have
had special romantic, potent powers. [Comments in a brown envelope
please! -Ed]. The dish consists of a whole spring chicken, barbecued
and stuffed with eggs and mincemeat. Served on a platter of Akhni
Pilou, which is tender chunks of lamb and fine grains of basmati rice.
Mas Masala, diced fish, medium sauce, peppers, onions, tomatoes,
fresh coriander leaves, served with boiled rice £5.95. Price check:
Papadam 25p, CTM £6.95, Pullao Rice £1.45. House wine £7.50.
Takeaway: 10% off. Hours: 12-2.30pm/6pm-12am. Stocks Cobra.

BOMBAY BRASSERIE

1 Simes Street, off Westgate, Bradford   © 01274 737564

Taken over in 1998 by Ali Shan. The building was a place of worship
and makes a fantastic venue, seating 120.'Most enjoyable.' DC. Price
check: Papadam 30p, CTM £6.50, Pullao Rice £1.20. Hours: 12-2pm
Mon.-Fri./6pm-12am (1am on Sat.). Stocks Cobra.

HANSA'S GUJARATI VEGETARIAN   √

44 Great Horton Road, Bradford   © 01274 730433

A Gujarati vegetarian restaurant in Pakistani-meat-eating Bradford is
unique. In fact Mr and Mrs Dabhi have been unassumingly doing their
thing here for years. All Gujarati items mentioned on page 38 will be
found here, plus many delightful vegetable curries. 'Drumsticks were
new to me and enjoyable.' GR. 'Spinach and Potato Curry was first-
class.' GH. Reports please. Branch: Hansa's, Leeds. Stocks Cobra.

KARACHI

15-17 Neal Street, Bradford   © 01274 732015

'. . . the food has never varied, and is always excellent. For years the
menu has displayed "new" dishes – which have remained unchanged.
[as it seems does this entry! -Ed]. The waiter, Ali, knows exactly what
we are going to order. My favourite, Chicken Karahi, is the best I've
ever tasted, brought sizzling to the table. The kitchens are open and
you can observe your meal being cooked and sometimes be entertained
when the staff have a minor dispute. Finally the toilets – definitely a

black mark – they have to be seen to be believed. The Gents smells like a horse box – enough said. [is that also unchanged?] However, all this is an eating experience, cheap, good-quality food, but absolutely no frills – a real curryholic's delight.' JP. Reports please.

KASHMIR

27 Morley Street, Bradford　　　© 01274 726513

'It holds about 200 on two floors. It is clean, floors are tiled and partially, the walls. The toilets were not a big hit with the ladies. The gents were passable. We sat at a clean table and were then asked to move, being told, "Reserved". So we moved to another clean table except no clean ashtray. Waiters not friendly, in fact quite surly. Started with cold Popadoms, excellent Sheek Kebabs and Chicken Tikka, Pakora – nice and spicy. We were not given any napkins to wipe our now greasy hands, and had to go and ask for a supply. We got, without prompting, a generous supply of water. Main course Korma, bit too sweet, CTM, more sauce needed, Karahi, about right and Madras, hot!. Garlic Nan was perfect. Staggering value at £21.60.' JMFP. 'Very good food, very very cheap, free Chapattis with every main course (takeaway).' KH. It's all quite tatty looking from the outside. However, downstairs the food was very good indeed. My main course Chicken Jalfrezi was extremely tasty. The decor is "Curry Caff" with plain cheap tables and chairs etc.' CT. Price check: Papadam 20p, CTM £3.80, Pullao Rice £1, Chutneys or Pickles 90p each. Hours: 11am-3am.

KHYBER　　　　　　　　　　　　　　　

6 The Green, Idle, Bradford　　　© 01274 613518

Light, airy Kashmiri-style curry restaurant, seats 52, owned and managed by Mohammed Ammer. Minimum charge: £5. Price check: Papadam 20p, CTM £5.10, Pullao Rice £1.10. Hours: 4-11.30pm.

NAWAAB　TOP 100

32 Manor Row, Bradford　　　© 01274 720371

We went to Messrs Mahboob Hussains' 80-seater after doing a cooking demo at Waterstones, unannounced (as normal) and without booking, at about 1030pm and it was packed. But the welcome was good and they squeezed us in. The decor is very notable. The service was willing, but quite disorganised, with no concept of stations, so we had a series of waiters asking the same questions, then long gaps when we needed them, like buses. Adjacent was a group of 20 experiencing much the same, though they, like all those present, were evidently enjoying their local. Eventually the food came. We felt it was below average, the portions tiny. For example Bombay Potato consisted of four small (canned?) potatoes covered in tasteless red dye. The Sag Keema lacked definitive tastes, the rice was unmemorable. We wondered why we get such good reports about the place, good enough for us to have awarded it a TOP 100 slot. 'I've enjoyed great meals here.' DC. 'Impeccable service. Large pickle tray waiting on each table, Popadoms crisp. So many excellent main dishes to choose from, we have been through most of them, every one being of a very high standard. It isn't the cheapest but for the quality who can complain.' NDM. Not the Nawab's adoring locals, obviously. We don't mind £40 with wine, if the experience deserves it. Reports please, to keep it in the TOP 100. Price check: Papadam 35p, CTM £6.50, Pullao Rice £2.20. House wine £7.90. Takeaway: 10% off. Hours: 12-2pm (Fri. & Sat. only)/6-11.30pm (12.30am on Fri. & Sat.), Sun. 1-11pm. Branches: Nawaab, Huddersfield, Manchester and Palma Mallorca.

PAZEEKAH NEW ENTRANT   BYO

1362 Leeds Road, Thornbury, Bradford   © 01274 664943

Ex bus driver Mazhar-ul-Haq's tells us he likes to change the decor and the menu regularly, 'because that's what customers want to see.' Successful Pakistani restaurant, seats a considerable 130 diners. Chef/ manager is son Mohammed Jamil. Price check: Papadam 25p, CTM £5.95, Pullao Rice £1.40. Also own an 18,000sq ft Superstore, selling Halal Meat and Poultry, Groceries, Spices, Hardware, Fresh Fruit and veg, and utensils at 91 Edderthorpe Street, off Leeds Road, Bradford. Reports please. Hours: 4pm-12.30am (1.30am on Sat.).

RAWAL   BYO 🍺 ©10%

3 Wilton Street, off Morley St Bradford   © 01274 720030

Owner Chef Abdul P. Butt cooks Pakistani curries in his open kitchen, Mobin Iqbal manages the 50-seater and promised a 10% discount to CC members. Special: Grand Slam, mixture of meat, chicken, keema and fresh vegetables, served with Pullao Rice £5.70. Zam-Zam Special,

meat, chicken, king prawns, and chick peas, served with Pullao Rice
£5.70. Price check: CTM £5.30, Pullao Rice £1.20. Takeaway: 10% off
for students, 3 chappatis or boiled rice with each order. Hours: 5pm-
2am (3am on Fri. & Sat.). Mon. closed.

SABRAAJ

20 Little Horton Lane, Bradford   ✆ 01274 724316

'Relaxed, friendly, speedy service. Excellent quality, food prepared with
fresh herbs and spices.' N&MI. 'Enjoyable.' DC. Reports please.

SHAH JEHAN   ©

30 Little Horton Lane, Bradford   ✆ 01274 390777
6 North Gate, Baildon,Bradford   ✆ 01274 582500

Aka. Omar's, owner/chef Omar Gulzar Khan's two branches have
identical menus. The Horton Lane branch seats 150 and is spread over
three rooms. It is stylish and luxuriously decorated, with lovely leather
sofas to relax on, while waiting for a takeaway, and pretty red chairs for
your table. 'An extremely smart and well laid out restaurant with
friendly service throughout. We had the whole leg of lamb ordered 24
hours in advance. Superb. Highly recommended.' CT. The menu is the
same at both branches. Paneer and Chick Pea Roll, in crispy pastry £2.
Good selection of Balti dishes, eg: Balti Milli Juli Sabzi, fresh mixed
vegetables, herbs, spices, tomatoes, ginger, garlic, yoghurt and methi
leaf £5. Price check: Papadam 30p, CTM £6.50, Pullao Rice £1. Daily
Buffet £5.95. House wine £3.70. Hours: 12-2.30pm/5.30pm-12am.
Stocks Cobra.

SHIRAZ   🍺 BYO ©

133 Oak Lane, Bradford   ✆ 01274 490176

Owned by Mohammed Gulbahar, with Mohammed Aslam managing
and Mohammed Afzal cooking competent Kashmiri curries and Baltis.
Price check: Papadam 30p, CTM £4.60, Pullao Rice £1.50. Hours:
4pm-2am. Closed Christmas Day and for Muslim festivals.

SHISH MAHAL BYO ©

6 St Thomas Road, Bradford © 01274 723999

Mohammed Taj's 54-seater 'is next door to one of the best pubs in Britain, The New Beehive, tremendous real ale with genuine character. The food at this BYO restaurant is nothing short of marvellous. Flavour literally explodes in the mouth. Sensational garlic chicken. Friendly and informal service.' SL. Hours: 4pm-3am.

SWEET CENTRE

Lumb Lane, Bradford

Welcome back to our Guide. At the counter you order savouries and sweets by the pound. I know because way back, I purchased 120 samosas here for a CC function, and we all found the measuring process a wee bit complex. Eventually they settled for 15p each and the sams were worth the sum! The sit down's fun too: 'Unlicensed all-hours cafe, cutlery on request. Asian clientele. Food cheap.' DC. 'Excellent. The service is good and the food very tasty.' SL.

TANDOORI NIGHTS BYO ALLOWED ©

53 North Parade, Bradford © 01274 305670

At owner Abdul Ghafoor Malik's 52-seater, Mir Hamid cooks fine Kashmiri curries, eg Goshtabay £6.95, a Kashmiri wedding dish, thinly-sliced lamb fillets soaked overnight in yoghurt, then ground into meat balls, cooked in yoghurt sauce with Kashmiri Mirch (chilli) and lychees, then garnished with fresh coriander, pistachios and almonds. Handy Gosht, meat is cooked (and served) in the clay pot – with herbs and spices, £5.95. 'Excellent, the prices reasonable, well worth a visit.' NH. Price check: Papadam 30p, CTM £4.80, Pullao Rice 90p. House wine £5.95. BYO £1 corkage. Minimum charge £8. Takeaway: 15% off. Hours: 12-2pm/6pm-12am (1am on Sat.). Sun. closed. Stocks Cobra.

TASTE OF BENGAL ©

79 Bradford Road, Idle, Bradford © 01274 618308

Abdus Subhan's cosy restaurant, decorated in, 'simple, plain wallpaper, minty colour, Axminster carpet' has just 28 covers, so book at weekends, or be disappointed or have a takeaway. Abdul Qayum runs the front with

Uddin Khan in the kitchen. Balti and Bengal Specialities feature on the menu with a Dine Bangladeshi-Sylhet Special £4.95 – cooked in a thick blend of spicy sauce with king prawns, mixed vegetables and (more) prawns. Price check: Papadam 25p, CTM £4.95, Pullao Rice £1.10. Lager £1.80 pint, house wine £5.45. Minimum charge £5.50. Takeaway: 10% off. Hours: 6pm-12am. Branches: Moghul, Horsforth, Leeds and Ilkley.

Brighouse

BENGAL BRASSERIE   NAME CHANGE

6 Huddersfield Road, Brighouse   ✆ **01484 719818**

Formerly the Thipti. 'The food looked and tasted wonderful, portions were right for both of us and the Nans were fresh and light' – MR&SM.

Dewsbury

GULSHAN   ☕ ©

Northgate House, Northgate, Dewsbury   ✆ **01924 456289**

Rahim Bostan's Gulshan seats a cute 22 covers, 'possibly the smallest restaurant in GB, and ab-fab.' DBAC. 'An incredible eating experience. Basic service is via a counter, where the kitchen can be seen. Cooking is by Asian women who are veiled, led by chef Saddique. Baltis, Masala dishes and Korma very popular. 'Food is great. Chicken Dhansak, especially. The facilities – upstairs through a room of sleeping people (Asians). We won't tell the Health Dept because we want the Gulshan to stay as it is.' ID. Delivery. Price check: Papadam 20p, CTM £5.50, Pullao Rice £1. Delivery: £5, 3-mile radius. Hours: 5pm-2am.

MOONLIGHT   NEW ENTRANT   BYO

**Springwell House, 14, Halifax Road,
Dewsbury**   ✆ **01924 462222**

'Owner Raf Hussain, very friendly, nothing is too much trouble for the staff. Nicely decorated and has a good atmosphere. Curries cooked to your personal taste, the portions generous and prices reasonable.' L&CH. Delivery. Price check: Papadam 30p, Balti CTM £4.70, Bombay Potato £2.30, Pullao Rice £1.10. Mango Chutney £1.10 and Pickle 80p! Hours: 5pm-1am (2.30am on Thurs., 3am on Fri. & Sat., 2am on Sun.).

Garforth

AAGRAH BEST RESTAURANT CHAIN TOP 100   ©

Aberford Road, Garforth   © 0113 287 6606

Nephew Wasim Aslam manages this 110-seater, opened in 1993, and the fourth of the very popular Aagrahs. (*See* Shipley entry.) Hours: 6 (5.30 on Fri. & Sat.)-11.30pm. Stocks Cobra.

Halifax

SHABAB   ©

---

25 Union Street, Halifax   © 01422 345655

Taken over in 1997 by Omer Farooq Ayub. The lounge area is richly decorated with wooden screens, gold embroidered cushions, silk painting and huge brass trays as drinks tables. The 62-seat restaurant is adorned with Moghul arches, brass lanterns with stained glass and those fabulous hand-made chairs with the bells. Price check: Papadam complimentary, CTM £4.95, Pullao Rice £1.30. House wine £7 litre. Hours: 12-2pm/5.30pm-1am. Reports please. Stocks Cobra.

Huddersfield

KABANA TAKEAWAY NEW ENTRANT   🍵

---

43 Trinity Street, Huddersfield   © 01484 422940

Pakistani cooking at this takeaway. Opposite the Tech. Watch MTV with the students while you wait! Special: Nan Kebab, minced lamb, 2 pieces of chicken, Seikh (*sic.*) kebab served with salad and sauce in a Tandoori Nan £3.50. Vegetarian Kebab, all salad in hot pitta bread £2. Price check: Papadam 15p (congratulations, you do this Guide's 2nd cheapest Pop!), CTM £3.50, Pullao Rice 90p. Set lunch: £5.50. Delivery. Hours: 5pm-1pm.

©	Curry Club discount (see page 6)	🍵	Unlicensed
√	Vegetarian		
BYO	Bring your own alcohol	▦	Delivery/takeaway

NAWAAB   TOP 100

35 Westgate, Huddersfield   🕾 01484 422775

Last time CT said: 'In short, the restaurant was superb and deserves to be placed well towards the top of your 100. However, we think it has become a victim of its own success and needs a damn good kick up the Aloo Chaat!' CT. We asked for more reports, please. You said: 'Food and service are usually very impressive. Balti dishes are my favourites. Tandoori dishes are also good, if a bit overdone at times.' RC. We believe our remarks on the equally popular Bradford branch also apply here, and we urge Messrs M. Hussain to do some staff re-training. We'll leave it for now shakily in our TOP 100, and await your reports. Price check: Papadam 35p, CTM £6.50, Pullao Rice £2.20. E-a-m-a-y-l £8.99. Daily buffet £7.99. Takeaway: 10% off. Lager £2.10 pint, house wine £7.90. Hours: 5.30-11pm (12.30am on Sat.). Sun. 12.30-4.30pm/ 6-11pm. Branches: Manchester, Bradford and Palma, Majorca.

SERENA   NEW ENTRANT   ©

12 St Peters Street, Huddersfield   🕾 01484 451991

Ihsan Elahi's 'modern and chic' Pakistani formula curry house seats 62, the party room, 40. Chef Khalid Hussain's special: Hawahan Muragh, chicken with pineapple, cream, £5.50. 'Good quality, well prepared dishes. It is not cheap but it is value for money and service excellent.' JT. Price check: Papadam 40p, CTM £5.75, Bombay Potato £3, Pullao Rice £1.50, Pickle Tray £1.20! You're right, it is not cheap. Bombay Potato is very expensive for a side dish, the menu says that vegetarians can have it as a main course for £5.50!!! Service: 10%. Lager £2 pint, house wine £7.95 litre. Takeaway: 15% off. Hours: 6-11.30pm.

SHABAB

37-39 New Street, Huddersfield   🕾 01484 549514

M. Nazir's 120-seater is decorated with hand-made chairs from Lahore. Chef Saddique's specials include Jhinga Biryani, basmati rice, herbs, spices, prawns, saffron, garnished with egg, served with vegetable curry £7.10. 'Everything very enjoyable and nicely presented. Service excellent.' AH. Price check: Papadam free, CTM £6.20, Pullao Rice £1.80. Sunday lunch £6.95. Wine £8.70. Hours: 11.30am-2.30pm (4pm on Sun.)/6-11.45pm. Branch: Seraj Takeaway, Bull Close Lane, Halifax. Stocks Cobra.

Ilkley

ILKLEY TANDOORI   ©

10 Church Street, Ilkley   ✆ **01943 607241**

Shah Marshal Alom's traditionally decorated 50-seater has golden arches and hanging plants. Special: Boul Mas, Bangladeshi fish £7. Price check: Papadam 30p, CTM £5.95, Pullao Rice £1.40. House wine £3.95 half-litre. Takeaway: 10% off. Hours: 5.30pm-12am. Stocks Cobra.

SABERA

9 Wells Road, Ilkley   ✆ **01943 607104**

Mrs Bilquis Jamal Choudhury's 1973 clean restaurant with pine panelling and 44 seats is an old friend of the Guide. 'I enjoyed my Kalajee Gurda Dil and will return to try some of their other dishes.' DM. Price check: Papadam 45p, CTM £7.50, Pullao Rice £1.40. Takeaway: 10% off. Minimum charge: £5. Hours: 12-2pm (Sat. only)/5.30-11.30pm.

Keighley

BALTI HOUSE NEW ENTRANT   BYO

1 Russell Street, Keighley   ✆ **01535 611600**

Managed by Mr Akhtar. Secluded cabins, pleasant atmosphere. Special: Jalfrezi, chillies, capsicum, tomato and herbs £5.50. Price check: Papadam 30p, CTM £6.25, Pullao Rice £1.45. Delivery: £8, 5-miles. No credit cards. Hours: 6pm-12.30am (1.30am on Fri. & Sat.).

SHIMLA SPICE NEW ENTRANT   BYO ©

14 South Street, Keighley   ✆ **01535 602040**

A newly established Pakistani restaurant, opened in 1998 by Mohammed Ayub and his two brothers, who had their 70-seater built from scratch on a useful corner site. Interior is decorated beautifully, ornate plasterwork on ceiling and walls, colonial fans, large chandelier, 'Tiffany' lamps and cane furniture. Takeaway: 15% off. Delivery: £8. Special: Murgh Makhani £5.75, Achari Murgh £5.75, Shima Fish Masala £5.95. Price check: Papadam 30p, CTM £6.25, Pullao Rice £1.45. Hours: 6pm-12.15pm (1.15pm on Sat.). Reports please.

Knottingley

JEWEL IN THE CROWN   ©

110 Weeland Road, Knottingley   ✆ 01977 607233

Pakistani curries at Manager Adnan Miraf's 40-seater. 'Excellent food
at reasonable prices. Service friendly and efficient. Recommend the
Punjabi (Tandoori) Mixed Grill £5.40.' IB. Price check: Papadam 25p,
CTM £5.50, Pullao Rice £1.40. £1.70 pint lager. E-a-m-a-y-l £8.
Takeaway: 20% off. Delivery: £8, 2-mile radius. Hours: 6pm-12am.

Leeds

CHIRAAG BALTI   NEW ENTRANT   ©

30-32 Chapel Hill, Morley, Leeds   ✆ 0113 253 5720

40-seater, taken over in February '97 by T. Hussain. Special: Fish
Pakora £2.50. Mushroom Pakora £1.95. Sweetcorn and Mushroom
Biryani £4.60. Price check: Papadam 30p, CTM £5.80, Pullao Rice
£1.50. Takeaway: 15% off. Delivery: £8, 3-mile radius. Hours: 6pm-12am
(12.30am on Sat.). Closed Tues. Stocks Cobra.

CORNER CAFE   NEW ENTRANT   🍴 BYO ©

104 Burley Road, Leeds   ✆ 0113 242 2026
83 Buslingthorpe Lane, Leeds   ✆ 0113 262 3958

Two good corner sites, as Parvez Al's name choice tells you, both with
the same menu. 'Unlicensed, and cutlery on request, it's opposite the
Queens Head pub. Waiter will come and collect you when your table
is ready. Have a significant Asian clientele and the food is excellent and
mind-blowingly cheap. Starters no more than £1.50 and main dishes,
served on soup plates, were typically around the £3 mark. Murgh Chan
stunning.' DC. Good selection of vegetarian curries: Spinach Nan £2.
Mince Rice £2.50. Expensive chutney tray £2.75. Price check: Papadam
35p, CTM £5.30, Pullao Rice £1.50. Delivery: £10, 3-mile radius. Credit
cards not accepted. Hours: 12-2.30pm (weekdays)/5.30pm-12am.

DARBAR TOP 100

16-17 Kirkgate, Leeds   ✆ 0113 246 0381

A turbaned doorman welcomes you at 'a very ordinary street-level door, but upstairs the decor is a revelation.' HJC. It's exotic, with traditional Moghul paintings and an antique Hawali (palace) door, specially brought from India. 'Has a very impressive interior. Room is large and the decor promotes the Indian Palace feeling — spacious yet warm and elegant'. AG 'Excellent restaurant, especially at lunchtime, self service buffet. Probably deserves TOP 100, although I am always slightly suspicious of Indians with grandiose decor.' RC [You'd be suspicious of India then, Robert! -Ed]. 'Very good service and cooking. And, the decor is marvellous.' SL. 'Overall this restaurant is superb and complements the Shabab very well. Indian food-lovers in Leeds are very fortunate to have two such restaurants'. HJC. Special: Murgh Lahori, bone-off spring chicken, tangy spices, green coriander, cream, yoghurt, tomatoes and ginger £7.25 (t/a). Daal Mash, white lentils cooked in butter with ginger, garlic and fried onions £2.50 (t/a). Strawberry Lassi (large jug) £3.75. Price check: CTM £8.50, Pullao Rice £1.50. House wine £11.95. Minimum charge: £16 eves. Lunch e-a-m-a-y-l £4.95. Hours: 11.30am-2.30pm (Mon.-Sat.)/6-11.30pm, Sun. closed. Stocks Cobra.

DAWAT

4-6 Leeds Road, Kippax, Leeds   ✆ 0113 287 2279

54-seater owned by Mr and Mrs Arora, with him front of house and her cooking north Indian specialities. Specials include Malli Kofta Curry £5.95. Price check: Papadam 20p, CTM £5.95, Pullao Rice £1.40. Service: 10%. Hours: 6.30-10.45pm, Sun. closed. Stocks Cobra.

HANSA'S GUJARATI VEGETARIAN   √ ©

72-74 North Street, Leeds   ✆ 0113 244 4408

Owned by Mr and Mrs Dabhi. 'I particularly enjoyed the crunchy, spicy flavour of the Shrikhand.' DM. 'As a non-veg I went with an open mind. Food was fine but portions small.' DB. 'Exquisite Lassi, portions small.' DO'R. Reports please. Hours: 12-2pm/6-11pm. Branch: Hansa's, Bradford. Stocks Cobra.

KASHMIR   🍷 BYO ©

162a Woodhouse Lane, Leeds   © 0113 245 3058

Unlicensed, 72-seater restaurant, managed by T. Mahmood. Price check: Papadam 20p, CTM £4.60, Pullao Rice 95p. Hours: 12pm-3am.

MOGHUL BALTI HOUSE

8-9 The Green, Town Street,
Horsforth, Leeds   © 0113 259 0530

Abdul Aziz's Bangladeshi curry house seats 40. Takeaway: 10% off. Price check: Papadam 30p, CTM £6.40, Pullao Rice £1.20. House wine £6.95 litre. Hours: 6-12. Stocks Cobra.

POLASH   ©

103 Town Street, Stanningley, Leeds   © 0113 256 0989

M. Arif's huge 150-seater is popular, it seems. 'Recently I had a family party at home and asked the Polash to cater for me. The resultant banquet was beyond praise.' EF. 'Our daughter, 14, says that the Polash Chicken Korma is her favourite, even though she has tried others in many other Indian restaurants.' BT. 'We were impressed. Food tasty. Service a little stretched at busy times.' IEF-E. 'How much we enjoy our visits. Excellent food, courteous staff.' MG. 'Always welcoming and courteous, high standard, always consistent, always start with Chicken Tikka follows by King Prawn Khass.' JS. 'Combination of service and freshly cooked food, makes the Polash our favourite.' MH-R. Price check: Papadam 30p, CTM £4.95, Pullao Rice £1.40. House wine £7.95. Hours:5.30-1130pm. Mon. closed. Stocks Cobra.

SHABAB   ©

2 Eastgate, Leeds   © 0113 246 8988

'Checked at lunch to see if opened at 6pm. Told them limited in time – told us OK. Arrived to find restaurant in darkness, one member of staff sitting alone. Sat in darkened bar. Few minutes later more staff arrived in street clothes. Minimal lighting switched on. Given menus. Told of 15-minute delay – not pleased. Staff reappeared in Indian dress, clearing debris from lunch, laying tables, vacuuming carpet. Again stressed shortage of time. Bowl of nibbles put on table. Couple arrived, treated to same darkness and delay. Within minutes three other tables were occupied. Decor very attractive, lots of carved wood, huge brass salvers on the walls, all furniture Indian style, generally very exotic. Modern, very repetitive Indian music, rather irritating. Grumbles somewhat erased when food arrived. Really completely different league – presentation, quality, spicing, whole competence – wonderful. Spiced Popadoms the best and lightest, relishes very good. Onion Bhajia, small flattish style, marvellous flavour. Chicken Podyarsi fabulous, very spicy, very rich, gorgeous. Excellent Pullao Rice. First class Machli Marsala, haddock dish, rich tomato sauce, lots of chunky onion, peppers. Enormous and light Nan. Portions were generous. Deserves TOP 100 for style and cooking, but everything else needs attention. Prices very good value.' HC. 'Had one of the worst meals ever.' SL. 'Overall this restaurant is superb and complements the Darbar very well. Indian food-lovers in Leeds are very fortunate to have two such restaurants'. HJC. TOP 100 removed until we get plentiful good reports. Stocks Cobra.

TARIQ'S NEW ENTRANT ©

12-16 St Michaels Road, Headingley, Leeds ✆ 0113 275 1881

Owned and managed by Bobby Sharma. Balti house seats 64. Special offer meal deal, Thursday and Sunday before 10pm. Dining in – free papadams and chutneys. Price check: Papadam 20p, CTM £4.90, Pullao Rice £1.20. Lager £2 bottle, house wine £6.50. Delivery: £6, 3-mile radius. Hours: 5.30pm-2.30am (3am on Sat., 12.30am on Sun.).

Otley

JEWEL OF INDIA NEW ENTRANT

1 Bridge Street, Otley ✆ 01943 467138

'Seats 35. Bright decor, ubiquitous murals of Indian gods. Excellent quality and generous portions of Chicken Madras (sauce a little too thick) and Keema Rogan Josh. Melt in the mouth Peshwari Nan. Pleasant waiting staff, well turned out in traditional dress.' JMFP. Price check: Papadam 40p, CTM £5.55, Bombay Potato £1.95, Pullao Rice £1.50, Pickle Tray £1.20. Hours: 6pm-12am (1am on Fri. & Sat.).

Pontefract

ROTI   ©

North Baileygate, Pontefract   © **01977 703915**

Arshad Mahmood's 110-seater (party room 40) is bright and airy with tented ceiling, beams, cream-with-green napkins, marble table tops, wicker furniture. Abdul Aziz's kitchen is in view behind glass. Pakistani food. 'Excellent quality, but bordering on the expensive.' KH. Price check: Papadam 50p, CTM (Kerhaay Choosa Makhan) £6.95, Pullao Rice £1.75. House wine £7.25. Hours: 5pm-12am. Stocks Cobra.

VICEROY   ©

6 Front Street, Pontefract   © **01977 700007**

Chef Akram Hussain Lohn cooks Pakistani food at his 60-seater, managed by Susan Ruckladge. Mushroom Pakora £1.30 a speciality. Price check: Papadam 30p (25p t/a), CTM £5.25, Pullao Rice £1.50 (£1.20 t/a). Delivery £6, 3-mile radius. Lager £1.80 pint. Hours: 5pm-12am.

Pudsey

AAGRAH   BEST RESTAURANT CHAIN TOP 100   ©

483 Bradford Road, Pudsey   © **01274 668818**

The second Aagrah is Head Office, as well as a 70-seater managed by Arshad Mahmood opened in 1986. Hours: 6-11.30pm (12am on Fri. & Sat.), Sun. 12.30-11.30pm. Full details next entry. Stocks Cobra.

Shipley

AAGRAH   BEST RESTAURANT CHAIN TOP 100   ©

27 Westgate, Shipley   © **01274 594660**

Today there are seven Aagrahs, all in Yorkshire, and all TOP 100s in this guide. It was here in 1977 that this 50-seater was opened by Mohammed Sabir. The notion to expand came from son Mohammed Aslam (then a London bus driver) assisted later by brother Zafar Iqbal, who now runs this one. It is notable for its Kashmiri-style decor with attractive block-print table linen and those fabulous hand-made, hand-painted colourful lacquered chairs with the cute tinkly bells, especially commissioned in Pakistan (£60 each). Gradually Aslam encouraged his extended family to join the enterprise as managers, staff and cooks. With increasing impetus the other branches have been brought on-stream, as stylish and up-market restaurants. We hear contentedly from many regulars who visit twice or more a week, and visitors from afar. Their average age is over 25 (no after-pub teenage louts here). Their average spend of £15 gives the chain a turnover of c.£2 million. The food is Pakistani, which self-taught cook Aslam has insisted that all family members also learn, training in both the kitchens and out front to NVQ level. This way the service and food in all the Aagrah restaurants is of equal standard. There is ample choice in the identical menus. Starters include Yahknee £1.80, spicy chicken soup, and Panir Pakora £2.20, Indian curd cheese fritter. Balti Liver £5.90, is a main-course dish, with garlic, ginger, chillies, tomatoes and coriander. There are many meat, chicken and fish dishes. Aslam's current pièces de résistance are Murgh Hydrabady, spring chicken, tangy spices, coriander, cream, yoghurt, tomatoes, ginger, £6.95. Balti Bhindi Aloo Paneer, curd cheese, bhindi and potato, onions, ginger, garlic, coriander, £5.90. Family Nan £2.80, Cheese and Onion Nan £1.80. Takeaway: rice and 3 chapattis free. Price check: Papadam 30p, CTM £6.50, Pullao Rice £1.50, Pickle Tray £1.20. Hours: 6pm-12am (11pm on Sun.). Branches: Garforth, Pudsey, Wakefield, W Yorks; Skipton Tadcaster, N Yorks; Doncaster, S Yorks. Stocks Cobra.

Wakefield

AAGRAH BEST RESTAURANT CHAIN TOP 100 ©

108 Barnsley Road, Sandal, Wakefield © 01974 242222

The seventh of seven Aagrahs, a 100-seater, opened in 1986. Parking for 40 cars. Like its sisters, it is justifiably very popular and good enough to be awarded a collective TOP 100 cachet. (*See* above entry for detailed comment.) Hours: 6-11.30pm (11pm on Sun.).

©	Curry Club discount (see page 6)		Unlicensed
√	Vegetarian		
BYO	Bring your own alcohol		Delivery/takeaway

AL AKBAR NEW ENTRANT ⊞ ☕

57 Bank Street, Ossett, Wakefield © 01924 263387

Taken over in 1988 by Mohammed Rahoof, parking in back yard for 12 cars. Chef Ajmal's Kashmiri curries for takeaway. Soft drinks available. Delivery: £5, 3-mile radius. Price check: Papadam 20p, CTM £4.20, Pullao Rice £1. Credit cards not accepted. Hours: 6pm-1am.

RAJ POOT

134 Kirkgate, Wakefield © 01924 371215

Ashik Miah's 52-seater, with Mashuk Miah in the kitchens has a 'friendly atmosphere.' 'I ate the Gurda Kaleja, which does not feature on the takeaway menu. I was brought up to appreciate offal and I am pleased to see it is included in Indian cuisine. Worthy of its entry.' DM. 'I have had the pleasure of eating here on several occasions and have never been disappointed. Chicken Chaat a delight.' AKD. Special: Chicken Tikka Biryani £5.95. Takeaway: 10% off. Monday and Tuesday – 3-course meal £5.95. Price check: Papadam 35p, CTM £5.95, Pullao Rice £1.30. House wine £7.50. Delivery: £12, 3-mile radius. Takeaway: 10% off. Hours: 5.30pm-12am (1am on Fri. & Sat.). Sun. 2pm-12am. Branch: India Palace, 36 Smyth Street, Wakefield. Stocks Cobra.

Wetherby

JAFLONG TANDOORI

31 High Street, Wetherby © 01937 587011

Bangladeshi curries at Mashook's 40-seater. Chef Ali's Murg Jalfry most popular. 'A small restaurant. Food very good indeed, service first-class.' DCO'D. Takeaway: 10% off – cash only. Hours: 5pm-12am. Branch: Kushi Takeaway, Kings Road, Harrogate. Stocks Cobra.

©	Curry Club discount (see page 6)		Unlicensed
√	Vegetarian		
BYO	Bring your own alcohol	⊞	Delivery/takeaway

THE ISLES AND ISLANDS

Population: 250,000
Number of restaurants in the isles: 52
Number of restaurants in Guide: 21

When he failed to capture the British Isles, Napoleon dismissed us as a nation of shop-keepers. Were he around today, he might observe that we are now a nation of curry house keepers. Some isles, including Lundy, the Isles of Scilly, Uist, Mull, etc., have no curry houses but for neatness, we group those that do together. For those who delight in collecting useless information, Lerwick, capital of the Shetland Isles, contains the nation's most northerly curry house (and probably that of the whole globe). It is 600 miles from London and 800 miles from our most southerly curry house in St Helier, capital of Jersey.

Channel Islands

Alderney

NELLIE GRAYS INDIAN CUISINE NEW ENTRANT ©

Victoria Street, Alderney ✆ 01481 823333

Established 1996, owned by Matin Miah (formerly the head chef of Jersey's Bombay Brasserie), and managed by Ashraf Makadur. Seats 50 in two dining rooms. Two parking spaces at rear of building. Jalfrezi most popular, chef's special Tarkari £6.95. Price check: Papadam 50p, CTM £7.75, Pullao Rice £1.75. House wine £6.95. Set dinner: £14.95.

Sunday lunch buffet: £9.95. Service: 10%. Hours: 6-11pm. Sun. 12-2pm. Stocks Cobra.

Guernsey

L'Eree

TASTE OF INDIA   ©
Sunset Cottage, L'Eree   ✆ 01481 64516

Owned and managed by the Fernandes family. 'Two Popadoms waited at the table which was neatly laid out. Fish Tikka, marinated in a sauce, very succulent. First-rate Methi Gosht with highly-flavoured sauce.' JT. Hours: 12-2pm/6-11pm. Branch: Taste of India, St Peter Port.

St Peter Port

TAJ MAHAL   ©
North Esplanade, St Peter Port   ✆ 01481 724008

Mujibul Hussain's 60-seater is located in the heart of St Peter Port opposite the main public car park. 'Popadoms, onion salad and mint sauce waiting on the table. Sampled Sardines on Puree, rich. A clean, cosy, and well-decorated place in jade, royal blue, gold and plum. Service good.' JT. Special: Bengal Chicken £7.95. Price check: Papadam 40p, CTM £7.95, Pullao Rice £1.90. Set menu £8.95. Minimum charge £8.95. House wine £7.95. Delivery: £15 Hours: 12-2pm/6-11.30pm (12am on Sat.). Stocks Cobra.

TASTE OF INDIA   ©
2 Mill Street, St Peter Port   ✆ 01481 723730

Owned and managed by the Fernandes family, with Batu front of house. Chef Ahmed's house special is Garlic Chilli Chicken (£8.95). Price check: Papadam 35p, CTM £8.75, Pullao Rice £2.15. Set menus £14.95 and £17.95. Minimum charge £15. Hours: 12-2pm/6-11pm. Branch: Taste of India, L'Eree.

Jersey
St Aubin

SHAPLA

Victoria Road, St Aubin   ℂ 01534 46495

'Decor very high standard with rich reds, golds and blues. Hasna Kebabs, lamb pieces marinated in yoghurt, then tandooried with onions, peppers and tomatoes, really very tasty indeed. Chicken Jalfrezi, aroma terrific. Simply perfect Lamb Rogan Gosht.' MB.

St Helier

THE NEW RAJ

8 St Saviours Road, St Helier   ℂ 01534 874131

Owned and managed by the Malik family since 1984. Decorated in green and coral with tented dining and bar areas. Seats 60 in two dining rooms. Special: Thali Dinners. Price check: Papadam 40p, CTM £5.25, Pullao Rice £1.75. Set menu £5.95. Service 10%. House wine £6.25. Takeaway: 5% off. Hours: 12-2pm/6pm-12am. Stocks Cobra.

SHEZAN

53 Kensington Place, St Helier   ℂ 01534 22960

A small restaurant seating 40. 'Meal very good. A bit expensive, but worth it.' SC. 'Owner, Shani Gill, is always the gentleman. His endeavours to satisfy all his customers has made him many friends.' GDM.

TAJ MAHAL CENTRAL

La Motte Street, St Helier   ℂ 01534 20147

'Classy and luxurious restaurant. You are surrounded by running water and tropical fish. Had best ever Tarka Dal.' TM.

Isle of Man

Douglas

SAAGAR ©

1 South View, Queens Promenade,
Douglas   © 01624 674939

Mr and Mrs Chowdhury and Mr Jaigirdar's 60-seater is 'the best I've
been to.' RR. 'One time we tried the special Kachee Biriani – 12 hours'
notice is required to prepare it. It's partially cooked Basmati rice layered over meat marinated in spices, yoghurt and herbs then cooked in
the oven – perfumed with saffron.' £25 for two. Delicious. Next time
we brought friends and tried Kurzi Lamb – 24 hours' notice is required
for this extravaganza (£48 for four). We've yet to try £70 whole leg of
lamb marinated in fresh ground spices with lamb mince meat cooked
in the oven. Mixed starters, side dishes, rice and breads for four are also
included.' AN. They allegedly sold a takeaway which was flown, with
two chefs, to Spain for a party of four, costing a staggering £2,995!
Makes the Kurzi Lamb look a snip. Price check: Papadam 70p, CTM
£6.55, Pullao Rice £1.95. Hours: 12-2pm/6pm-12am.

TAJ MAHAL

3 Esplanade Lane, Douglas   © 01624 674741

'"Welcome" the sign said. What it didn't say was, "Britain's most
expensive restaurant" – Chutney Mary was cheaper. It is the IOM and
it was worth it. All very tasty and well presented. Friendly staff.' MB.

Ramsey

SPICE OF LIFE

8 Peel Street, Ramsey   © 01624 816534

'We enjoyed the food, and would have done had it been in Manchester'
GB. 'Bizarre note on the door, "We do not serve drunks".' D.McC.

Scottish Isles
Isle of Bute
Rothesay

INDIAN PAVILION

---

7 Argyle Street, Rothesay, Isle of Bute   ℭ **01700 504988**

Est. 1993 by Bobby Mahey, 30-seater. Dave Mahey cooks north and south Indian and Goan food. Price check: Papadam 50p, CTM £7.50, Pullao Rice £1.30. Lager £1.95 pint, house wine £7.95. Delivery charge 95p. Hours: 5pm-12.30am.

Isle of Lewis
Stornoway

ALI'S

---

24 South Beach, Stornoway   ℭ **01851 706116**

We've not heard from them, so reports please.

Isle of Skye
Portree

GANDHI

Bayfield Road, Portree   ℭ **01478 612681**

'Don't be put off by the horrendous tartan carpet that awaits your entrance. Food took a long time to come. When it did come, however, it was excellent.' SN. 'Pleasant surprise. Bank Holiday and was packed, we were seated promptly, a bit of a delay but service friendly. Delicious food. Gobi Panir – spicy cauli-cheese – unusual.' EO'D. 'I've eaten better food on the mainland, but inclusion in the Guide is an absolute must to make visitors aware of the opportunity. On a rough count I would say that diners were 50% local and 50% visitors.' DM.

Orkney Islands

Birsay

HEIMDALL

Earls Palace, Birsay

'Operates from a farmhouse kitchen, with an adjoining three-table café area. Humble menu. Portions are handsomely ample and reveal a scintillating flavouring only arrived at by using fresh spices and herbs.' ES. Open Fri., Sat. & Sun. 5-10pm.

Kirkwall

MUMTAZ

---

7 Bridge Street, Kirkwall   © 01856 873537

'Comfortable and modern restaurant. All food very tasty. Service good and efficient.' PAWW. Hours: 12pm-12am.

Shetland Islands

Lerwick

RABA INDIAN

---

26 Commercial Road, Lerwick   © 01595 695554

'Warm decor. Well-cooked Indian cuisine at reasonable prices. Samosas, Bhajia and Chicken Tikka Masala were all delicious.' AIE.

Isle of Wight

It's a ferry-ride from the mainland so we put it in this section. There are 10 curry houses dotted around the island. However, MM has been telling us for years that she and her husband do a three-hour round trip to Portsmouth for a 'serious curry'! For those with less stamina, or who need a quick fix, these are the three you've talked about.

Cowes

BOMBAY PALACE

10a Shooters Hill, Cowes   © 01983 280942

'Ordered Achari Gosht Ka Salon, very very tasty and very very hot!! I'd definitely return.' DP.

COWES TANDOORI   ©

40 High Street, Cowes   © 01983 296710

At Ashid Ali's 64-seater. DB loves the Podina Gusht and Garlic Chicken. Hours: 12-2pm/6-12.

Newport

NABAB PALACE   ©

84 Upper Street, James Street, Newport   © 01983 523276

Jila Miah's 54-seater serves good, competent curries and accompaniments at reasonable island prices, eased by his will give a 10% discount to CC members. Hours: 12-2pm/6pm-12am.

NORTHERN IRELAND

Population: 1,600,000
Number of restaurants: 11
Number of restaurants in Guide: 6

Belfast

ARCHANA

13 Amelia Street, Belfast   © 01232 323713

'Menu very comfortable. Vindaloo very hot, excellent. Balti Chicken Chilli, also excellent. Decor and comfort good. Value for money.' JP.

ASHOKA   ©

363-367 Lisburn Road   ✆ 01232 660362

Back in the Guide is Ravi and Ms Sonal Chawda's 130-seater with its
elegant, pillared dining room (apparently the only Indian restaurant in
Northern Ireland with an Indian chef – Ishtiaque Khan). Frequented
by politicians and celebrities, including Ian Paisley, David Trimble,
members of U2 and Liam Neeson. Specials: Lobster dishes (prices
vary), Baltis £10-15.95. Price check: Papadam 30p, CTM £8.95, Pullao
Rice £1.75. Takeaway: 20% off. Hours: 5.30-11.30pm. Stocks Cobra.

BITHIKA TAKEAWAY

135 Lisburn Road, Belfast   ✆ 01232 381009

Price check: Papadam 50p, CTM £5, Pillau Rice £1.25. Hours: 5pm-
2am (12am on Sun.). Delivery service. Branches: Jharna, Belfast;
Tamarind, Carrickfergus.

JHARNA

133 Lisburn Road, Belfast   ✆ 01232 381299

Large a/c 110-seater. 'We found the Tandoori Crayfish superb
and different £11.95.' CD. Price check: Papadam free, CTM £8.95 incl.
Pullao Rice, £1.50. Set menu £4.95 (3 courses). Hours: 12-2pm/ 5.30-
11.30pm. Branch: Tamarind, Carrickfergus; Bithika Takeaway, Belfast.

Carrickfergus

TAMARIND

32-36 West Street, Carrickfergus   ✆ 01960 355579

Popular with its locals, we hear. Price check: CTM £5.95, Pillau Rice
£1.20. Hours: 12-2pm/5.30-11.30pm. Sun. -11p. Delivery service.

©	Curry Club discount (see page 6)	🍺	Unlicensed
√	Vegetarian		
BYO	Bring your own alcohol	⊞	Delivery/takeaway

Lisburn

HIMALAYA ©

---

13 Bachelors Walk, Lisburn   ℂ **01846 660044**

Feroz Talukder's 48-seater has 10 parking spaces out front. 'The Jalfrezi £6.95 is outstanding.' GR. Price check: Papadam: 40p, CTM £6.50, Pullao Rice £1.40. House wine £1.60 glass. Delivery: Free over £40, £1 within 3-mile radius. Hours: 12-2pm/5-11.30pm. Sun. 5-11. Branch: Gandhi, Belfast. Stocks Cobra.

SCOTLAND
BORDERS

As with England, the Guide goes alphabetically in county order, using the former regions for a convenient division of the Scottish mainland.

Area: South-east Scotland
Population: 104,000
Number of restaurants in county: 6
Number of restaurants in Guide: 2

Hawick

SHUGONDA BALTI HOUSE NEW ENTRANT

---

4 Station Building, Dove Mount Place   ℂ **01450 373313**

B.M. Talukder's 50-seater Bangladeshi curry house has 10 car parking spaces. Specials: Harsa Mossalla Chi, Masooru Dall Chi, Bengal Begun Mushroom Jal Hours: 12-2pm/6-11.30pm. Reports please.

Kelso

SWAGAT

Inch Road, Kelso   © 01573 225159

'This tiny restaurant is difficult to find. Mr Kumar, the proprietor, has
converted his garage into a restaurant. Sounds awful, doesn't it? Well,
it isn't. The food, service, prices are all excellent, I cannot commend
this little place enough.' JR.

CENTRAL

Area: Mid Scotland
Population: 272,000
Number of restaurants in county: 21
Number of restaurants in Guide: 7

Bridge of Allan

ASHOKA

23 Henderson Street, Bridge of Allan   © 01786 833710

'Food good in all aspects, especially the Garlic Nan and side dishes.
Service is friendly, attentive and quick. Seating is uncomfortable.' AGJ.

Denny

OMAR KHAYYAM   NEW ENTRANT

1 Church Walk, Denny   © 01324 825898

Est. 1980, M. Ahmed's Pakistani and Balti curry house seats 70 with
free car parking behind the restaurant. Price check: Papadam 80p,
CTM £9, Pullao Rice £1.90. Lager £2 pint, house wine £8. Set Dinner:
£10. Takeaway: 15% off. Hours: 12-2pm/4.30pm-12am (1am on Sat.).

©	Curry Club discount (see page 6)		Unlicensed
√	Vegetarian		
BYO	Bring your own alcohol		Delivery/takeaway

Dunblane

INDIA GATE

Fourways, Perth Road, Dunblane   © 01786 825394

'Wednesday night 9pm, went for the Buffet (£9.95) which looked appetizing, but turned out to be lukewarm, but apart from that quality was OK.' KH. 'Lots to eat, lots of taste, but not lots of price.' SH.

Falkirk

MEHRAN   ©

4 Weir Street, Falkirk   © 01324 622010

Shahid Shakir's Pakistani 48-seater has ample car parking. Baltis from £6.50. 'Haleem, lamb, mince and wheat was great' PC. Price check: Papadam 50p, CTM £7.95, Pullao Rice: £1.40. Lager £1.95 pint. Delivery: 2 miles. Takeaway: 10% off. Hours: 12-2pm/5pm-12am (1am on Sat.).

Larbert

GULNAR TANDOORI

50-64 Main Street, Larbert   © 01324 562189

Mr Singh's dishes include Parsee Fish £7.75, Achari Gosht, meat cooked in pickle £7.35. Price check: Papadam 45p, CTM £7.25 incl. rice, Pullao Rice £1.15. Delivery £10. Hours: 5pm-12am (1am on Fri. & Sat.).

Stirling

EAST INDIA COMPANY & VARSITY BLUES

7 Viewfield Place, Stirling   © 01786 471330

'Down a flight of stairs to a dark oak-panelled room, a fire burning brightly, walls huge with pseudo paintings. Sat at a highly-polished mahogany repro table. We found no argument with "The key to our success is a delicacy of flavour".' PW. 'Really bouncing on Thursday.

Got the last table at 9pm. Buffet £9.95, available every night except Friday and Saturday. Food excellent and piping hot.' KH. Delivery service. Branches: Killermont Polo Club, Glasgow, Strathclyde; Shimla Pinks, Birmingham North and Johnstone, Strathclyde.

TAJ MAHAL   ©

39 King Street, Stirling   © 01786 470728

Run by the Singhs. Raj manages the 100-seater and Jasminder cooks 'Naan bread to demand in front of you.' DL. Price check: Papadam 50p, CTM £7.75, Pullao Rice £1.45. Set lunch: £4.75. Lager £2.20 pint, house wine £4.95. Takeaway: 10% discount. Delivery: £1 local area. Hours: 12-2pm/6-11.30pm. Sat. 2pm-12am. Sun. 1-11.30pm. Branch: Curry Canon's Dorchester Avenue, Kelvindale, Glasgow.

DUMFRIES & GALLOWAY

Area: South west Scotland
Population: 148,000
Number of restaurants in county: 7
Number of restaurants in Guide: 1

Dumfries

JEWEL IN THE CROWN   ©

48-50 St Michael Street, Dumfries   © 01387 264183

Manager A. Muhit. 'Attentive staff. Bombay Mix on the table as we perused menu. Pops & pics immediately ready. Good starters – Vegetable Pakora and Mix Kebab. Chicken Dhansak and Chicken Methi reasonable. Good value.' AY. Hours: 12-2.30pm/6-11pm.

©	Curry Club discount (see page 6)		Unlicensed
√	Vegetarian		
BYO	Bring your own alcohol		Delivery/takeaway

FIFE

Area: East Scotland
Population: 346,000
Number of restaurants in county: 23
Number of restaurants in Guide: 4

Dunfermline

KHAN'S ©

33 Carnegie Drive, Dunfermline   ℭ 01383 739478

Ismail Khan's venue seats a massive 160 diners. 'Good value for money. Portions large and they make a mean Phal! Balti is included on the menu along with delights such as Bombay Tiffin, served with tamarind chutney.' LR. Hours: 12-2pm/5.30-11.30.

Glenrothes

NURJAHAN ©

Coslane, Woodside Road, Glenrothes   ℭ 01592 630649

Manirul Islam's 110-seater. Decorated in pinks to a very high standard. Roomy carver-chairs at all the tables. Striking menu with photographs of spices, dishes of curry and breads. 'A truly magnificent meal. Decor tastefully outstanding and spotless. More than generous quantities. The best quality we have ever tasted. Delighted to hear we were Curry Club members and gave us an unsolicited discount of 10%. A superior restaurant in every aspect.' MAJF. Hours: 12-2pm/5-11pm.

Rosyth

TASTE OF INDIA

130 Admiralty Road, Rosyth   ℭ 01383 413844

'Starters set a high standard of promises to come – the main courses let down. Raita that accompanies the Pakoras was made with yoghurt, mint and mango, very tasty.' NS. Reports please.

St Andrews

NEW BALAKA
BANGLADESHI TOP 100 BEST BANGLADESHI

3 Alexandra Place, St Andrews   © 01334 474825

Even before you enter Abdur Rouf's up-market and sophisticated 52-seater, note the frontage floral display. He has won awards for it. The unique feature is the huge kitchen garden at the rear, in which Mr Rouf grows all his own herbs and many vegetables. He says everyone is welcome to p-y-o. More foliage inside with palms dividing tables and Indian tapestries on the walls. Unusual dishes on the menu include Mas Bangla – salmon marinated in lime, turmeric and chilli, fried in mustard oil, garlic, onion, tomato and aubergine. I had the privilege of being trained to cook this dish by chef Abdul Monem which I reproduced at a lecture at St Andrews University for the Chemical Soc and all of Mr Rouf's friends. I hope they enjoyed it as much as I did. We then moved on to the restaurant for a fabulous meal. Amazingly the restaurant has no tandoor, which is detectable in the flavours of the breads and tikkas. But that aside, Mr Rouf's team continues to provide outstanding food in superb surroundings. We have lots of contented customer reports. All show a friendly, caring patron, and here's proof: We said last time: 'My husband remembered this restaurant as Kate's Bar while at the uni in the 1950s. Menu extensive and comprehensive. Quantity sufficient. Quality very good. Lacked the little touches that complement a meal, only plain Popadoms and no spoon in the Raita.' MAJF. Mr Rouf was so concerned that he made a point of assuring me that such things will not occur again!!! If only all restaurateurs took note of our comments we'd have a perfect curry-house world. It seems to me it's always busy, so please book. Meanwhile Price check: Papadam 60p, CTM £7.85, Pullao Rice £2.75. Delivery: Local only, £1.75. Hours: Sun.-Thurs., 5-1. Fri. & Sat. 12am-1am. Open Christmas Day. Comfortably in our TOP 100.

©	Curry Club discount (see page 6)		Unlicensed
√	Vegetarian		
BYO	Bring your own alcohol		Delivery/takeaway

GRAMPIAN

Area: North Scotland
Population: 506,000
Number of restaurants in county: 35
Number of restaurants in Guide: 9

We have received a letter from NC *saying that the first
Indo-Pak restaurant to open in Aberdeen, in 1963, was called Asia Kathon,
Holburn Junction. Does anyone else remember it? Reports, please.*

Aberdeen

KHAN'S NEW ENTRANT ©

22 King Street, Aberdeen ✆ **01224 646434**

Aman Khan's 175-seater has a helpful menu describing his Pakistani
food. Price check: Papadam 50p, CTM £6.75, Pullao Rice £1.90. House
wine £8.95 litre. Delivery: town centre, minimum two meals. Takeaway:
10% off. Hours: 5pm-12.30am. Stocks Cobra.

SERENA INDIAN BRASSERIE NEW ENTRANT ©

75 Holburn Street, Aberdeen ✆ **01224 213355**

Zafar Iqbal's 120-seater has 18 parking spaces, and specialises in
Pakistani curries. Nightly e-a-m-a-y-l, £10.95, 6-10pm. Price check:
Papadam 50p, CTM £7.95, Pullao Rice £1.90. Lager £1.95 pint, house
wine £5.50. Delivery: Minimum order £15, free within 4-mile radius,
otherwise £1.50. Takeaway: 10% off. Hours: 5pm-12am

Buckie

NEMAT TANDOOR NEW ENTRANT ©

52 West Church Street, Buckie ✆ **01542 832653**

Nemat Ali's 80-seater specialises in Balti, Pakistani and Southern
Indian cuisine. Price check: 50p, CTM £7.95, Pullao Rice £1.70. Lager
£2 pint, house wine £1.40 glass. Takeaway: 10% discount. Hours: 5pm-
12am (1.30am on Sat.). Closed Weds.

Elgin

QISMAT

202-204 High Street, Elgin   © 01343 541461

Liaquat Ali's 100-seater does a Monday night e-a-m-a-y-l £10.50. 'Good
food in good surroundings.' AM. Price check: Papadam 50p, CTM
£8.70, Pullao Rice £1.70. House wine £7.95. Delivery: within Elgin,
£10. Takeaway: 10% off. Hours: 12-2pm/5pm-12am (11.30am on Sun.).

Ellon

NOSHEEN   ©

5 Bridge Street, Ellon   © 01358 724309

Jointly owned by Tariq Mahmood and Joe Raj Ghaly. Major refurbishment planned for 1998, currently seats 88, with provision for 10 car
parking spaces behind restaurant. Banquets and buffets available. Price
check: Papadam 40p, CTM £7.95, Pullao Rice £1.95. Minimum charge
£5. Delivery: £12 in Ellon, £18 outside. They also have an off-licence
and can deliver wine, beer and cider. Lager £1.80 pint, house wine
£5.50. Takeaway: 10% off. Hours: 5-11.30pm (12am on Fri. & Sat.).
Branch: Shish Mahal, Union Street, Aberdeen.

Inverurie

ALO CHAYA   ©

56 Market Place, Inverurie   © 01467 624860

A well-established restaurant, owned since it was opened in 1987 by
Syed Mujibul Hoque. 'Waiters efficient and friendly. Buffet night is
worth a visit.' AMCW. Open 12-2.30pm/5.30-11.30pm.

©	Curry Club discount (see page 6)	🍵	Unlicensed
√	Vegetarian		
BYO	Bring your own alcohol	🔡	Delivery/takeaway

NAZMA TAKEAWAY ⊞

42 West High Street, Inverurie   © 01467 629100

A takeaway-only establishment. 'Has a large TV as you enter, so you can see what's going on in the kitchen. Spotless.' RK. See next entry.

Peterhead

NAZMA TANDOORI

22a Queen Street, Peterhead   © 01779 478898

One of a chain of four restaurants in the area run by the four Ullah brothers. Established in 1989, seats 60. Balti buffets every Mon. night, e-a-m-a-y-l Wed./Sun. £9.95. Special: Murgh Massala, chicken on-the-bone cooked in medium spicy sauce with mince and fresh coriander, garlic and ginger £9.95. 'Our local favourite for years. Service courteous and efficient. Food of consistently high standard.' DL. Price check: Papadam 70p, CTM £7.50, Pullao Rice £1.75. Lager £1.90 pint, house wine £7.90. Hours: 12-2pm/5-11pm. Branches: Nazma, Aberdeen; Banff, Nazma Takeaway, Inverurie.

Stonehaven

TANDOORI HAVEN ©

54 Allardice Street, Stonehaven   © 01569 762793

Shofiqul Hoque's 68-seater has a special menu for children which includes Herby Fish-Fry, Indian-style fish and chips. Price check: Papadam 50p, CTM £7.20, Pullao Rice £1.90. Sunday lunch buffet: £9.95. Takeaway: 10% off. House wine £7.90. Hours: 12-2pm/5-11pm. Branches: Currymount Takeaway, Rosemount Place, Aberdeen; Tandoori Port, The Green, Portlethen. Stocks Cobra.

HIGHLAND

Area: North Scotland
Population: 204,000
Number of restaurants in county: 18
Number of restaurants in Guide: 6

Aviemore

ASHA

43 Grampian Road, Aviemore   **& 01479 811118**

'Our first impression of the menu was that it seemed expensive, but most main courses included rice. Katta Murgh Masala was very tasty with a tang of lime.' EO'D. Hours: 12-2pm/5.30-11.30pm.

Fort William

INDIAN GARDEN

88 High Street, Fort William   **✆ 01397 705011**

'Service slow but the food's good.' GM. This restaurant has been under the present ownership for 12 years and seats 60 diners.

Inverness

RAJAH INTERNATIONAL

2 Post Office Avenue, Inverness   **✆ 01463 237190**

A spacious restaurant seating 60 diners. HB. says: 'The best curry experience in over 10 years.' Hours: 12-2pm.

ROYAL TANDOORI

99 Castle Street, Inverness   **✆ 01463 712224**

All the favourites at Moosa Kutty's. Price check: Papadam 40p, CTM £6.50, Pullao Rice £1.60. Delivery: £10. Hours: 12-2.30pm/5pm-12am.

Nairn

AL RAJ ©

25 Harbour Street, Nairn   © 01667 455370

Mobarok Ali's 70-seater has built up a good reputation. Even Nick Nairn himself has been seen here. Hours: 12-2pm/5-11pm.

Tain

THE FAR PAVILIONS NEW ENTRANT ©

11 St Duthus Street, Tain   © 01826 893003

Frank Ward and Iris Dow's tiny 26-seat up-market restaurant is the most northerly on the British mainland. Chef Hornal trained at Glasgow's Cafe India, Creme de la Creme and Ashoka. Most ordered dish: South Indian Garlic Chilli Chicken. Balti nights on Tuesdays. Children welcome (£2.50 menu). Price check: Free Papadams, CTM £6.80, Pullao Rice £1.60. Lager £1.90 pint, house wine £7. Takeaway: 15% off. Delivery: Local charge £1. Hours: 12.30-2.30pm/5pm-12am. Sat. 4pm-12am, Sun. 5-11pm.

LOTHIAN

Area: Mid Scotland
Population: 750,000
Number of restaurants in county: 87
Number of restaurants in Guide: 21

Edinburgh

CHILLI CONNECTION ⊞ ©

47 South Clerk Street, Edinburgh   © 0131 668 1171

P. Anwar took over this open-plan kitchen takeaway in 1998. 'Smart gear, smart place, smart food' AN. Price check: Papadam 45p, CTM £4.95, Pullao Rice £1.45. Delivery: Local, £10. Hours: 5pm-12am.

THE FAR PAVILIONS NEW ENTRANT TOP 100   ©

1-12 Craigleith Road, Edinburgh   © 0131 332 3362

Est. 1987, this 85-seater in two rooms is 'no ordinary curry house. It's
high time it was in the Guide. It's sumptuous outside and in.' GR. *The
Scotsman*'s Gillian Glover says 'the walls bore dimpled panels of but-
toned velvet. Even the staff were upholstered.' Owners Wasim and
Aasim Chaudhry say 'the aim of true Indian cooking is never simply
to bring a flush to the face and take a layer of skin from the tongue.
We prefer to call each dish a presentation'. Chef Abdul Aziz's 'chilli-
rated' menu is a well-worded presentation in its own right. Eye-
catching specials range from Kashmir to Goa. 'I had my favourite Pala
Gosht from Punjab, £8.25, and it had the correct Pakistani flavour, and
the suggested Tarka Dhal was gorgeous in authenticity – wafts of garlic, loads of flavour.' PL. Expect to spend £20 a head plus drinks, and
watch those extras. The Pickles Tray is £2.50, for example! But that
said, this restaurant is a welcome new addition to our TOP 100. The
CC discount eases the bill as does the e-a-m-a-y-l Tuesday 6.30-10pm,
£11.95. Price check: Papadam 55p, CTM £8.95, Pullao Rice £2.25.
House wine £10. Takeaway: 10% off. Hours: 12-2pm (weekdays)/5.30pm-12am. Closed Sun. except December. Stocks Cobra.

GULNAR'S PASSAGE
TO INDIA TOP 100 BEST IN SCOTLAND   ©

46 Queen Charlotte Street, Leith,
Edinburgh   © 0131 554 7520

'Over the last ten years Leith has evolved from a derelict dock area into
a tasteful commercial area surrounded by designer flats and yacht
marina, and now the Royal Yacht Britannia. Another attraction is
Mohammad Ridha Saleh's 82-seater Passage, not only for north Indian
and Kashmiri food, but for more: I cannot resist it! Every time I visit
Edinburgh, I am drawn to the consistently high quality, most unusual
cuisine at very nominal cost. Invariably superb, with exciting, fresh
spices. Lunch menu is outstanding value at £4.75 for a choice of
starters, main course curry, ice-cream and coffee. If you are feeling
global, try the Arabic specials. Starter of Dolma, vine leaves stuffed
with mince and rice and marinated in Arabic spices £2.10. Ordered
Lamb Samosas, amazed by generous size and excellent quality of
spiced lamb – absolutely delicious, a meal in themselves. Followed by

Kabolie Red Fort – a chef's special, spicy chicken, cashews, medium hot, spicy sauce and superb Paratha. A new initiative is the "belly dancing" nights, if you can stomach it!' TE. 'The proponent I saw was more skinny Scot or lanky Leithian than ample Arabian, but it's a fun night out, enhanced by Mohamed and the staff in red Moroccan fez, embroidered waistcoats and long white gowns.' AMCG Other specials include Aloobora – spicy potato balls filled with minced lamb £2.10. Potahari Sangam – minced lamb fried with fresh herbs and spices, garnished with coconut, wrapped in a puri £2.50. Rooflifter £6.75, lamb and chicken marinated, tandoor-cooked and prepared with mint, nuts and spices. Such delights promote Gulnar's to our TOP 100. Price check: Free Papadams, CTM £6.25, Pullao Rice £1.80. Delivery: Leith area. Hours: 12-2pm/5.30pm-12am (1am on Sat.). Stocks Cobra.

GURU BALTI   BYO ALLOWED ©

Dundee Terrace, Edinburgh   ℂ 0131 221 9779

Every dish is Balti at owner chef M. Afzal's and manager Mustafa Iqbal's 45-seater. Specials: Balti Chicken Jaipuri– with mushrooms and Punjabi spicing, Balti Chicken Jhalfrezie, fresh tangy tastes, Balti Kash-Afghan Palok Gosht, lamb with spinach, all £5.95. 'Very, very good. Good menu, food, comfort, decor and service. Very friendly. My family are all very experienced in spotting a good Indo-Pak restaurant.' NC. Price check: Papadam 60p, CTM £7.95, Pullao Rice £2.25. Set Dinner: £10.95. Sunday night special, kids eat free. House wine £8.95. Delivery: charge £1.50. Hours: 5pm-12am. Stocks Cobra.

INDIAN CAVALRY CLUB

3 Atholl Place, Edinburgh   ℂ 0131 228 3282

'Smart up-market restaurant on two floors. Officers' Mess on the ground floor, and the tent-canopied Club, downstairs. Service quick. Food excellent. The hottest Jalfrezi I have tasted. Prices high but on the whole worth it.' EM. For vegetarians and other diners try the Pineapple Samber, pineapple in a lentil and tamarind sauce. 'Ate an excellent Bharatiya buffet. This establishment thoroughly justifies its place in the Guide.' DM. Hours: 12-2pm/6-11pm.

KALPNA √

2-3 St Patrick's Square, Edinburgh   © 0131 667 9890

This vegetarian restaurant, established in 1983, remains very popular,
under the auspices of owner-chef Ajay Bhartdwaj. It serves a mix of
Gujarati, Bombay and south Indian items, such as Bhel Puri and Dosas
(*see* glossary), with some distinctive Moghul non-meat items too, such
as Aloo Dom – Kashmiri stuffed potatoes. Wednesday evening buffet.
Hours: 12-2pm/5.30-10.30pm (from 6pm on Sun.).

KHUSHI'S   BYO

16 Drummond Street, Edinburgh   © 0131 556 8996

'Nice short menu, good helpings, very good meat, perfectly marinated.
Fair service, nice Italian waiter. Clean, light-painted decor, very clean
toilets. Good comfort on padded benches and formica tables. Excellent big starters. No alcohol, but most people brought big jugs (2-3
pints) of beer from the pub next door. Madras was now a Vindaloo;
Bhuna and Korma could have been Madras.' NC. Branch: Khushi's of
West Lothian, Mid Calder.

KINGS BALTI

79 Buccleuch Street, Edinburgh   © 0131 662 9212

100-seater, managed by Nunir Abu with chef Ibrahim Ali. 'This is the
one the Uni students use. Unlicensed (the waiters nip round to the
off-licence next door for you!) GREAT!!!. Their low, low prices make
for a really inexpensive but high-quality meal. Crisp, warm Pops, generous pickles, light Paratha, high quality meat, fragrant sauces and
amazingly swift service from friendly waiters, all combine to enthuse
the customer.' TE. Delivery service. Price check: Papadams 45p (plain &
spicy), BCTM £5.10, Balti Bombay Potato £1.90, Pullao Rice £1.80.
Hours: 12-2pm/5pm-12am. Fri. & Sat. 12pm-12am.

©	Curry Club discount (see page 6)		Unlicensed
√	Vegetarian		
BYO	Bring your own alcohol		Delivery/takeaway

LANCERS BRASSERIE TOP 100

5 Hamilton Place, Edinburgh   ✆ 0131 332 3444

70-seater opened in 1985 by Wali Udin JP, managed by Alok Saha, head chef Badrul Hussain. Beautifully decorated, stylish restaurant has pink suede on the walls, tiled floor, highly polished tables. A smart eating atmosphere for business lunches and special occasion dinners. Downstairs is a private dining room for 12 diners. Chippendale-style furniture, banquet-style. Raj prints decorate the walls. A small but selective menu. Price check: Papadam 60p, CTM £6.95, Pullao Rice £2.25. Set Lunch: £9.95. Set Dinner: £15.95. Takeaway: 20% off. Delivery: £15, 4 miles. Hours: 12-2.30pm/5-11.30pm. Stocks Cobra.

MAHARAJAH'S

17-19 Forrest Road, Edinburgh   ✆ 0131 220 2273

'Magnificently designed, with hand-painted murals, to resemble a tented pavilion set within a beautiful palace garden', and set in the heart of the university area (10% discount for students and nurses). Buffet on Monday and Tuesday. Price check: Papadam 50p, CTM £6.75, Pullao Rice £1.95. Hours: 12-2pm/5.30pm-12am. Stocks Cobra.

RAJ

91 Henderson Street, Leith, Edinburgh   ✆ 0131 553 3980

Benefiting from Leith's reincarnation, Tommy Miah's restaurant retains its Victorian architecture. Most tables are on a large raised floor section. Good food, portions and knock-down prices. His own mango chutney is served with Papadams and starters and can be bought at the restaurant along with other own-labelled products.

SHAMIANA TOP 100

14 Brougham Street, Edinburgh   ✆ 0131 228 2265

Brothers Nadim (manager) and Mohammed (head chef) Butt co-own this award-winning 38-seater in two rooms, specialising in Pakistani Kashmiri cuisine. Mohammed was awarded the Best Chef Award in *The 1998 Good Curry Guide*. One of his specialities is Shahi Murgh £30, spiced whole roast chicken with salad, rice, nan and side dishes. It is good to see Kulfi Pista, Gulab Jaman and Garjar Halwa on the dessert menu. Last year I had the privilege of judging Mohammed at a London Indian chef competition cutely named 'Spindian' because it was promoted by a spinach grower (W. Emmett) and Tesco. Mohammed's Kashmiri Chaman Gosht (lamb and spinach with peppers – a Sag Gosht variant) was undoubtedly the best dish there. Price check: Papadam 40p, CTM £6.85, Pullao Rice £1.95. House wine £7.95. Service 12½%. Hours: 6-10pm. Sun. 6-8pm. Stocks Cobra.

SINGAPORA   ©

69 North Castle Street, Edinburgh   © 0131 538 7878

Malaysian-Singaporean 65-seater owned and managed by chef C. Pang. Decor is 'dominant decorative wood and high ceiling reminiscent of colonial-style romance, the waitresses in national dress.' AG. Most popular dish Satay: Chicken, Beef, King Prawn or Tofu, marinated, skewered and chargrilled, served with a delicious peanut sauce (five sticks), £5.90. The Malay Kari, £6.30 – chicken, beef, or vegetables in a coconut base, and Redang Beef, the national dish curry. Set Lunch: £6.90. Set Dinner: £18.90. Takeaway: 10% off. Delivery service. Hours: 12-2.30pm/6-10.30pm. Sun. closed in Winter.

SURUCHI   ©

14a Nicolson Street, Edinburgh   © 0131 556 6583

Unique at Herman Rodrigues' 70-seater is his careful selection of his own beautiful photographs of India which hang on the walls. Suruchi means, in most Indian languages, good taste, an apt name when considering the decor has been imported from India, and is clean and smart. Jaipur blue/turquoise tiles adorn the walls. Table linen is vegetable-dyed pink and tableware is beaten coppered brass. It serves real home-style Indian food. Well-situated for a pre-theatre (which is opposite) curry dinner. Regional Indian food festivals held monthly. Specials: Shakuti, from Goa with coconut and black pepper, £7.95 and Upperi, shredded cabbage with coconut and mustard seeds, £3.95. Most ordered dish: Kumbhi Narial, mushroom with coconut. Price check: Papadam 50p, CTM £7.95, Pullao Rice £2.50. House wine £7.95. Takeaway: 33% discount. Hours: 12-2pm/5.30-11.30pm. Stocks Cobra.

TANDOORI LAND   ©

63 Clerk Street, Edinburgh   © 0131 667 1035

What a title! S. Chowdhury's 32-seater, serving – yes, you guessed it ...!
Hours: 5pm-12am. Branch: Morningside Road, Edinburgh.

TIPPOO SAHIB   ©

129a Rose Street, Edinburgh   © 0131 226 2862

A Pakistani restaurant opened in 1982 as the Shanaz by the Parvez family. In 1996 Anjam Parvez renamed the 60-seater. Tippoo Sultan ruled
south India in the late 17th century. His battle collaborations with the
French caused the British severe problems, but left Tippoo's name in
legend. Tippoo's Tiger, his famous favourite mechanical 'toy', is now
housed in the British Museum, his portrait by Sir David Wilkie is in
the Scottish National Gallery. It was Edinburgh's 'Wild Macrea's regiment who defeated Tippoo. The colourful murals at the restaurant
depict the story. Chicken Mancharry, tandoor-cooked, with freshly
grated chilli, garlic and ginger, Chicken Nentara, cooked with onions
and methi, and Massalidar Gosht, meat cooked with pickles, all £7.95,
and Karella Gosht meat with bitter gourd, £6.95. 'First class quality
food, staff and atmosphere. Reasonable prices.' RC. Price check: Papadam 60p, CTM £6.95, Pullao Rice £1.95. Lager £2.10 pint, house wine
£8.95. Takeaway: c.25% off. Hours: 12-2pm/5pm-12am. Sat. 12-11.30pm,
Sun. 5-11.30pm. Branches: Ballis, Hanover Street; West End Balti
House, West Maitland Street, both Edinburgh.

VERANDAH   TOP 100   ©

17 Dalry Road, Edinburgh   © 0131 337 5828

44-seater opened in 1981 by Wali Tasar Uddin, MBE, JP, and his nephew,
Foysol Choudhury, who describe it as 'reassuringly low-key' serving
northern Indian and Bangladeshi cuisine. A pretty, relaxing restaurant
with cane chairs and bamboo-slatted wall blinds, a clever and effective
illusion. A very popular and well-established restaurant. House specials
include Amer Murghi, mild chicken cooked with mango pulp and cream
£6.95 and Chilli Garlic Chicken £6.95. Price check: Papadam 60p, CTM
£7.25, Pullao Rice £2.25. Set menus £5.95 and £6.95 for lunch and £16.95
for dinner. The wine list is very much above average, and includes a
drink-what-with-which-curry-guide. Delivery: £15. Hours: 12-2pm/

5pm-12am including Christmas Day. Stays in our TOP 100. Stocks Cobra.

Linlithgow

KISMET   ©

88 High Street, Linlithgow   ℭ 01506 671812

At Mahbub Hussain Khan's 38-seater specials include Chahat King Prawns (£8.50). Price check: Papadam 40p, CTM £5.75, Pullao Rice £1.45. Set menu £4.95. Hours: 12-2.30pm/5pm-12am.

Mid Calder

KHUSHI'S OF WEST LOTHIAN   🍵 BYO ©

11 Bank Street, Mid Calder   ℭ 01506 884559

Mr Islam Mohammed has plans to increase his 30-seater to 50. Banquet nights. Price check: Papadam 20p, CTM £5.95, Pullao Rice £1.50. Sun. e-a-m-a-y-l: £9.95. Delivery: £15 local area. Hours: 5-11pm.

Musselburgh

SHISH MAHAL   ©

63a High Street, Musselburgh   ℭ 0131 665 3121

46-seater, opened in 1979 by Idris Khan, manager Shezad. Chef Tariq's specials include Shajaman Murgh, half barbecued chicken, on or off bone, in medium curry sauce, £8.50, Shish Garlic and Chilli, £6.95, Nawabi Bhindi Gosht, okra with lamb £7.50, and Sabzi Pasanda, all vegetables £6.50. Buffet Tuesday 'As usual, outstanding. My favourite.' LW. Price check: Papadam 65p, CTM £6.95, Pullao Rice £1.75. Minimum charge £10. Delivery: £10. Hours: 5pm-12am. Stocks Cobra.

©	Curry Club discount (see page 6)		Unlicensed
√	Vegetarian		
BYO	Bring your own alcohol	▦	Delivery/takeaway

North Berwick

JOYPUR ©

114 High Street, North Berwick © **01620 895649**

Manager A. Hye and chef D. Rahman's 100-seater has clean, fresh-looking decor with cane furniture. 'Truly excellent. Prices are very reasonable and decor is great, friendly staff.' IP. Price check: Papadam 45p, CTM £5.95, Pullao Rice £1.85. Set lunch £4.95. Minimum charge £8. Takeaway 10% off. Hours: 12-2pm/5.30-11.30pm Stocks Cobra.

STRATHCLYDE

Area: West Scotland
Population: 2,306,000
Number of restaurants in county: 245
Number of restaurants in Guide: 25

Coatbridge

PUNJAB EXPRESS NEW ENTRANT ©

22 West Canal Street, Coatbridge © **01236 422522**

Opened in 1993 by the Dhanda brothers, Kally and Tari. The Punjab Express is part of the former Coatbridge Central Station House. Built in 1899, the building still has many of the period features. The station was closed by Lord Beeching in 1963 and the restaurant is situated in what used to be the station master's accommodation. Downstairs, in the former ticket office, is the Pullman Lounge. Reports please.

Glasgow

Glaswegians are at pains to tell us that Glasgow curries are 'the real thing, the best anywhere' . . . 'everywhere else is a pale imitation, especially the pakoras', writes one person frequently. The other thing they lay claim to is that Glasgow is the curry city of the world! As to the first claim, what they've got, lucky people, is a largely Pakistani population, and this means gutsy, spicy Punjab-style curries, as are found in Southall and Bradford, which are quite removed from the Bangladeshi curry house formula. Put another way, Glasgow's curries are the authentic thing, once tasted, never forgotten. As to 'curry city' sorry lads and wee lassies, you are still number three, measured by the number of curry restaurants to the number of citizens. At 132 to 700,000 (1:4375), this puts you behind Bradford, and Leicester.

ALISHAN TANDOORI

250 Battlefield Road, Battlefield   © 0141 632 5294

M.A. Qureshi's 44-seater has an extensive range of specials. Basanti, tandoori items in a creamy sauce with a tangy touch of pickle; Nashilee, ditto with wine, Nashidar, with brandy, all £9.50 Price check: Papadam 60p, CTM £6.90, Pullao Rice £1.30. House wine £8.50. Takeaway: 10% discount. Delivery: £10. Hours: 12-2pm/5pm-12am, Sat. 12pm-12am, Sun. 5pm-12am. Stocks Cobra.

AMBALA SWEET CENTRE

178 Maxwell Road, Glasgow   © 0141 429 5620

'Lamb Bhoona is amazing!' DF. This is a franchise operated by Mrs S. Ahmad. (*See* Ambala Drummond St, London, NW1.) As well as the counter takeaway sweets and snacks, chef Akmal cooks a small range of curries for the 26-seat restaurant. BYO not allowed. No credit cards. Price check: Papadam 40p, CTM £4, Pullao Rice £1.90. Hours: 10am-10pm.

THE ASHOKA TOP 100

108 Elderslie Street, Glasgow   © 0141 221 1761

Originally opened 1968, it was taken over in 1995. Owned by brothers Bhpoinder and Parminder Purewal, who assure you it now has no connection with the many other Ashokas in the area. Ashoke, incidentally, was an Indian emperor from centuries ago. Recently 110 seats in two dining rooms. Had a £250,000 facelift by restaurant designer Harris Khan. Critics have described it as 'Baroque into fantasyland' and 'rich opulence'. What do you say about that and chef Alexandré Paaeschi's cooking? The new menu has plenty of play on the words 'spark' and 'flame' (Old Flame for example are the old favourites like CTM). 'We hadn't booked, it was midweek, it was packed, we got the penultimate table. Popadoms crispy, good chutney tray, but naughty, naughty — don't put tomato ketchup in the cachumber ever again! Samosa, was shaped like a spring roll, but tasted very good. Main course portions good. Pat ordered his beloved Methi Chaman Gosht, with spinach, fenugreek, fresh oriental herbs and hot spices – £4.95, and pronounced it authentic and delicious. I had the Pakistani equivalent of CTM – Kashmiri Chasni Tikka, spicy, and equally good. Rice and breads enormous.' DBAC. Price check: Papadam 80p, CTM 7.95, Pullau Rice £1.95. Lager £1.95 pint, house wine £9.95. Takeaway: 10% off. Hours: 12-11.30pm, Sun. 5pm-11pm.

CAFE INDIA NEW TO OUR TOP 100 ©

171 North Street, Charing Cross, Glasgow © 0141 248 4074

Described (by its owner Abdul Sattar) as 'Britain's first-ever designer buffet restaurant'. It certainly has changed since it opened in 1979, its seating having reached a monumental 500. The 'first-ever' claim will have older-hand restaurateurs reaching for their pens, though designer it certainly is. The exterior tells you that. The ground floor is open-plan and bright. The seats are expensive high-backed pale wood with pink or blue upholstery, depending which zone you are in, and there are some alcove tables. The area called the galleries in the lower floor is moody, with darker reds and wrought iron. There is provision for self-service via a smart counter. Both floors have eye-catching artwork and light fittings. Sattar again: 'it's arty decor, attracting young clientele.' Of course, nice though it is, you can't eat the decor. Set menus are a speciality, and the Friday/Saturday e-a-m-a-y-ls (at £12.50) are popular. Specials: South Indian Garlic Chilli Chicken (£8.90), Lobster £18.90, Lamb Redfort £8.90. Price check: Papadam 70p, CTM £8.95, Pullao Rice £1.60. Lager £1.90 pint, house wine £1.90 (glass). Takeaway: 10% off. Hours: 12pm-12am. Sun. 3pm-12am.

CHANDIGARH

28 Vinicombe Street, Glasgow © 0141 400 0483

45-seat Tandoori restaurant owned by S. Singh since 1985. Funny piece from 'me-and-the-Moll' by 'Diner Tec' on the back of the takeaway menu. Specials: Chef's Special Masala (with medium-spiced wine creamy sauce), Chicken Halim (green capsicum sauce). Price check: Papadam 65p, CTM £7.30, Pullao Rice £1.95. Lager £1.95 pint, house wine £8.50. Takeaway: 25% off. Delivery: £6 minimum, 3-mile radius. Hours: 5pm-12am.

CHAPATI 1   ⊞ ©

2017 Dumbarton Road, Glasgow   ℂ **0141 576 0118**

Chain of 11 takeaways, est. 1983 by Iqbal S. Gill each of which has its own personnel, but are overseen by Deepa Gill (service) and Harnak Singh (chef). Curries, Kebabs and Pizza. Prices are not cheap for take-away: Onion Bhajia £2.25, Mango Chutney 70p, Potato and Cauiflower Curry £3.50. Most ordered dishes: Karahi Chicken and Chicken Jullander. Hours: Sun.-Thurs. 4pm-12.30am, Fri. & Sat. 4pm-1.30am. Branches: (All Glasgow area) Chapati 2, 1576 Dumbarton Rd, 0141 954 3154; Chapati 3, 339 Dumbarton Rd, Partick, 0141 337 1059; Chapati 4, 20 Byres Rd, 0141 334 4089; Chapati 5, 354 Paisley Rd W, 0141 427 6925; Chapati 6, 468 Dumbarton Rd, Dalmuir, 0141 952 9210; Chapati 7, 182 Paisley Rd W, Renfrew, 0141 885 2313; Chapati 8, 5 Lennox Dr, Faifley, 01389 879914; Chapati 9, 3 Greenock Rd, Bishopton, 01505 862 222; Chapati 10 39 Main St, Busby, 0141 644 1971; Sajjan, 2372 Dumbarton Rd, Yoker, 0141 951 1839. Neelim, 1590 Dumbarton Road, Glasgow, 0141 959 6265.

LA CREME DE LA CREME

1071 Argyle Street, Finnieston, Glasgow   ℂ **0141 221 3222**

400-seater in a former cinema aiming up-market, former stalls and dress circle in use. No expense has been spared, creating a style reminiscent, in parts, of London's Bombay Brasserie. Its claim to be Europe's largest Indian has never held water, especially now, with Café India's 500-seater. 'Food good, service poor.' BG. 'Service superb. Prices dear, but portions large.' DMCK. 'Tried the buffet, my first experience of this type of spice inhalation. All reasonable.' CW. Weekday lunch prices 20% off until 3pm. Balcony evening e-a-m-a-y-l buffet served 6-10pm, £8.95 weekdays, £11.95 weekends. Hours: 12pm-12am.

KILLERMONT POLO CLUB

**2022 Maryhill Road, Maryhill Park,
Bearsden, Glasgow**   ℂ **0141 946 5412**

The young go-ahead brothers Kal and Parmjit Dhaliwal opened this ultra-smart place in 1991, revealing considerable style. Firstly, it really is a polo club, and if you fancy a pukka chukka your mount awaits outside. Inside are two dining areas. One is oak-panelled with

Georgian-style chairs, polished tables and polo items decorating the walls. The other is more traditional with high-backed chairs and flowing table linen. The third partner, Jas Sagoo, runs the kitchen with Balbir Farwaha, from whence comes 'good food.' LM. Hours: 12-1.45pm, except Sun./5-10pm. Branches: East Indian Company and Varsity Blues, Stirling, Central; Shimla Pinks, Birmingham, and Johnstone.

KOH I NOOR

235 North Street, Charing Cross, Glasgow   ✆ 0141 204 1444

Glasgow's earliest Indo-Pak opened in 1961, and boasts to be the originator of the famous buffet nights (Mon.-Fri. 7-9pm). The staff and management pride themselves on having the largest and most authentic Indian Buffet in Glasgow, seating over 150 people at any one time. Northern Indian formula curries. Authentic Asian decor, with hanging rugs, arches etc. 'Excellent. Samosas so filling, had to leave most of my main course!' SF. 'Starters very impressive, quantities large. Garlic Nan not for the faint-hearted: beautiful. Chicken Tikka Chasini and Chicken Nentara memorable.' HB. 'Absolutely superb. In a class of its own.' BS. Price check: Papadam 80p, CTM £8.95, Pullao Rice £1.80. House wine £1.40 (glass). Hours: 12-3pm/12pm-12am. Sat. 12pm-1am. Stocks Cobra.

MR SINGH'S INDIA   ©

149 Elderslie Street, Glasgow   ✆ 0141 204 0186

Satty Singh, manager Mano Khan, and the waiters wear kilts at this 80-seater, whose new decor combines ethnic and traditional Scottish. Younis Ahraf (who wears chef's whites, by the way) does curried Haggis! 'Without question the best I have visited! Vast menu. Fantastic food, good portions. Booking essential, even mid-week. Brandy-drinkers beware. They have a 200-year-bottle of Napoleon's brandy at £35 a shot!' GD. Price check: Papadam 60p, CTM £8.95, Pullao Rice £1.85. Takeaway: 10% off. Hours: 12-3pm/5-11.30pm. Sun. 2.30-11.30pm.

MURPHY'S PAKORA BAR   ©

1287 Argyle Street, Glasgow   ✆ 0141 334 1550

Murphy's owner Teresa Doherty says 'We Scots are a fiery race!' [We Scots? Doherty? Murphy? Sounds like a bit of the blarney to me!] 'It was love at first bite! As we sank our baby teeth into our first chunk of pakora, there were loud karahis of more mum!' [groan] 'The word Pakora, to a Scot, slips off the tongue as easily as haggis, neeps and tatties. It's one of those snacks that can be eaten at any time of day or night . . . one bite is never enough.' At Murphy's the chef's a Scot (R. McGregor) which is why there's Haggis Pakora. 'Beam me up, Scotty.' cw. And there are 30 others including Chilli. 'Handkerchiefs supplied, but be warned, you'll be dumb struck . . . or is that struck dumb?' [Oh ha!ha! But what happened to the fiery race ?] Or there are Pizzas — traditional or with an Indian twist. Of course, it is a licensed bar, selling, well Murphy's of course! Price check Pakoras from £3.15. Takeway: 10% off. Hours: 12pm-12am. (1am on Fri.& Sat.).

NEELIM   ©

1590 Dumbarton Road, Scotstoun,
Glasgow   ✆ 0141 959 6265

Iqbal Gill is a well-known Glaswegian curry restaurateur. Well, to be exact, he also owns, with partners, ten 'Chapati' takeaways (*see above*) plus one called Sajjan and one restaurant. Harachan Singh manages this 60-seater and of chef Deepa Gill's north Indian curries, the most ordered dish is Chicken Jullander, the staff's favourite, with Punjabi spices, £7.50. Price check 60p, CTM £6.95. Pullao Rice: £1.45. Service 5%. Takeaway: 10% off. Free delivery. Hours: 5pm-12am.

SHALIMAR   NEW ENTRANT   ©

23/25 Gibson Street   ✆ 0141 339 6453

Rahmat Ali's 96-seater, opened in 1971. ('Time it was in the Guide.' AN). Specialises in Pakistani dishes. Nightly buffet. Price check: Papadam 50p, CTM £7.25, Pullao Rice £1.80. Takeaway: 20% off. Delivery: £1. Hours: 12-2pm/5pm-12am. Sat. 12pm-12am, Sun. 5pm-12am.

SHISH MAHAL   BYO ALLOWED ©

66-68 Park Road, Glasgow   ✆ 0141 334 7899

Glasgow's second oldest opened in 1964 in Gibson Street as a family business with five tables. Today it is a 100-seater in two dining rooms currently under the direction of brothers Ali Aslam and Nasim Ahmed. The real Shish Mahal is Lahore's 300-year-old palace of mirrors, built to enthral the Mohul emperors. It was once Glasgow's finest, but took a dive when all the smart young places started opening. But, following its move, it has regained its reputation for very good Pakistani/Punjabi food served well. Should we reinstate it to our TOP 100? Only you can decide. Price check: Papadam 60p, CTM £6.75, Pullao Rice £1.40. House wine £5. Takeaway: 10% off under £20, 20% over £20. You may BYO, corkage £2. Hours: 12-2pm/5-11.30pm. Fri. & Sat. 12-11.30pm (Sun. from 3pm). Stocks Cobra.

TURBAN TANDOORI

2 Station Road, Giffnock, Glasgow   ✆ 0141 638 0069

70-seater owned by Kulbir Purewal since 1982, and managed by Bobby Purewal. Northern Indian curries. Price check: Papadam 70p, CTM £8.95, Pullao Rice £1.70. House wine £11.95 litre. 'Great name, great people, great food.' A.MCV. Takeaway: 20% off. Delivery: £10. Hours: 5pm-12am.

Hamilton

CAFÊ MANZIL   NEW ENTRANT

23 Gateside Street, Hamilton.   ✆ 01698 285823

Tandoori restaurant. Seats 90 in four dining rooms. Special: Chicken Tikka Jammur (fruity, medium to mild, £7.50). Price check: Papadam 50p, CTM £7.50, Pullao Rice £1.95. Lager £1.95 pint, house wine £7.50. Takeaway: 15% discount. Delivery: Free, £10 minimum. Hours: 11.30-5.30pm/5.30pm-12.30am. Sun. 2-5pm/5pm-12am.

TAJ MAHAL   NEW ENTRANT   ©

154 Almada Street, Hamilton   ✆ 01698 420076

Pakistani and Balti cuisine. Seats 40. Price check: Papadam 60p, CTM £6.95, Pullao Rice £1.40. Lager £1.85 pint, house wine £1.95 (glass). Hours: 12-2.15pm/5-12. Sun. 3pm-12am.

©	Curry Club discount (see page 6)		Unlicensed
√	Vegetarian		
BYO	Bring your own alcohol	⊞	Delivery/takeaway

Irvine

GULAB   ©

2 Stanecastle Road   ℭ 01294 279141

Tandoori restaurant. Seats 100 with 30 car parking spaces. Price check: Papadam 50p, CTM £5.60, Pullao Rice £1.10. Most popular dish: Chicken Korma. Loyalty takeaway: 10% discount, minimum order £10. Hours: Mon.-Thurs. 12pm-1.30pm/4.30pm-12.30am. Fri. 4.30pm-12.30am, Sat. 12pm-1.30am, Sun. 4.30pm-1am.

Johnstone

ASHOKA

3 Rankine Street, Johnstone   ℭ 01505 322430

Same menu as at the Glasgow branches. Set meals are good value for money. Branches: Ashoka Ashton Lane, Glasgow; Ashoka West End, Glasgow.

SHIMLA PINKS

4 William Street, off Houston Square,
Johnstone   ℭ 01505 322697

Modern restaurant. Polished floors, tubular stainless steel chairs arranged round black tables. Branches: East Indian Company and Varsity Blues, Stirling, Central; Killermont Polo Club, Glasgow; Shimla Pinks, Birmingham, B15, West Midlands. Reports please.

Largs

KOH I NOOR

84 Gallowgate Street, Largs   ℭ 01475 686051

This restaurant is situated on the shorefront and has a good view. 'Varied menu, good-sized quantities, quality of meal very good.' ww.

Paisley

SHEZAN   NEW ENTRANT   ©

82 Glasgow Road, Paisley   ℰ **0141 887 2861**

Established by Manjit Singh in 1987. Open plan with 45 seats. Privilege card entitles customer to 25% discount. Price check: Papadam 65p, CTM £7.95, Pullao Rice £1.55. £9.50 wine. Takeaway: 20-30% off (depending on times). Delivery 90p charge. Hours: 12pm-12am, Sun. 5pm-12am. Stocks Cobra.

Prestwick

TAJ   ©

141 Main Street, Prestwick   ℰ **01292 477318**

Rabinder Singh's Taj seats 136 diners. Specials: Chicken Jira, Chicken Manana, Chicken Noorpuri. Price check: Papadam p50, CTM £5.60, Pullao Rice £1.20. Delivery: Free, £9 minimum. Hours: 12-2pm/5-12.15am. Fri. & Sat. 12pm-1.15am. Sun. 4.30pm-12.15am.

Renfrew

RAJPUT BALTI AND TANDOORI   ©

9 High Street, Renfrew   ℰ **0141 885 0026**

Opened in 1996 by Jameel Tahir Mohammed. He runs a VIP Privilege Card promotion, which entitles the cardholder and guests to 15% off the à la carte menu. Delivery. Hours: 12pm-12.30am. Branch: Asman, 22 Bath Street, City Centre, Glasgow. Reports please.

©	Curry Club discount (see page 6)	☕	Unlicensed
√	Vegetarian		
BYO	Bring your own alcohol	⊞	Delivery/takeaway

TAYSIDE

Area: East Scotland
Population: 394,000
Number of restaurants in county: 40
Number of restaurants in Guide: 7

Auchterarder

SHERAY PUNJAB ©

97 High Street, Auchterarder ℂ **01764 664277**

Proprietor, Paul Chima. Specialises in Balti. Seats 28. Price check: Papadam 95p, CTM £9.95, Pullao Rice £2.50. Lager £2.50 pint, house wine £8. Minimum charge £10. Takeaway: 10% off. Delivery: £25, and a £2 charge!!!. Hours: 5pm-12am.

Broughty Ferry

GULISTAN HOUSE ©

Queen Street Halls, Broughty Ferry ℂ **01382 738844**

'Impressive decor. Some meals excellent. Tandoori dishes are normally very good.' FC. Owner is M.A. Mohammed. Hours: 5pm-12am.

Dundee

CHAAND ©

104 Dura Street, Dundee ℂ **01384 456786**

Riaz Sheik and manager Naz's 80-seater serves Northern Indian and Balti formula curries. Price check: Papadam 60p, CTM £7.25, Pullao Rice £1.75. Lager £1.80 pint, house wine £7.25. Takeaway: 20% discount. Hours: 4-11pm, Sun. 5-11pm.

©	Curry Club discount (see page 6)	☕	Unlicensed
√	Vegetarian		
BYO	Bring your own alcohol	⊞	Delivery/takeaway

THE NAWAB   NEW ENTRANT

43 Gray Street, Dundee   © 01382 731800

Balti and tandoori restaurant established in 1994. Seats 88. Price check: Papadam 50p, CTM £6.95, Pullao Rice £1.50. Lager £1.90 pint, house wine £1.75. Hours: 5pm-12pm.

Kinross

RAJ MAHAL

132-4 High Street, Kinross   © 01577 864884

Owner-chef, Abdul Gafur, has a very unusual house special – Raj Mahal Rooflifter £9.95 – the hottest of the hot! Price check: Papadam 45p, CTM £6.85, Pullao Rice £1.75. Set menu £5.95. Seats 70. Price check: Papadam 65p, CTM £7.85, Pullao Rice £1.95. Takeaway: 10% discount. Hours: 12-2pm/5-11.30pm. Sun. 5-11.30pm.

Perth

MANZIL   NEW ENTRANT   ©

13 York Place, Perth   © 01738 446222

Rana Ali's 85-seat curry house. The most popular dish: South Indian Garlic Chilli. Price check: Papadam 50p, CTM £7, Pullao Rice £1.50. Lager £1.90 pint, house wine £6.95. Takeaway: 10% discount. Delivery: free local. Hours: 12-2pm/5-11.30pm. Branch: Tandoori Knights, Princess Street, Perth (takeaway only).

SHALIMAR

56 Atholl Street, Perth   © 01738 634204

The Shalimar first opened way back in 1983, but its current owner, Bal Krishan, took over the restaurant in 1996. 'The best I have found in years!' NC. Agreed? Reports please.

WALES

As with England, the Guide runs alphabetically in town and county order. We retain the former counties which provide a convenient geographical division of Wales.

CLWYD

Area: North Wales
Population: 412,000
Number of restaurants in county: 21
Number of restaurants in Guide: 6

Colwyn Bay

BENGAL PALACE   ©

The Clock House, 55-57 Abergele Road,
Colwyn Bay   ℰ 01492 531683

Manager A.M. Khan's large, air-conditioned restaurant is divided between two rooms, seating 85 in one and 40 in the other. Reliable curries we're informed. Hours: 12-2.30pm/6-11.15pm.

Deeside

BALTI NIGHTS   NEW ENTRANT

286a High Street, Connahs Quay, Deeside   ℰ 01244 830969

Used to be a Nat West bank. 'Nice food but not thrilling, after Popadoms and the Pickle tray, Onion Bhajia (four) and Meat Samosa covered in a yoghurt sauce. Service fine, had a soccer-mad waiter.' RK. 'Very polite staff. Very reasonable meal.' DV-W.

BENGAL DYNASTY   TOP 100   ©

106 Chester Road East, Shotton, Deeside   ℰ 01244 830455

Opened in 1991 by Mohammed Monchab Ali, with Rico managing, seats 92 with an additional lounge area for 40, in air-conditioned, purpose-built, airy and elegant, luxurious surroundings. Chef Foyzur Rahman's north Indian and Bangladeshi specials include Bengal Fish Curry, £6.95, Chicken Bonduk, £7.95. 'Immense size of the restaurant, huge. Politely greeted and guided to bar. Can see why this restaurant features so highly in the Guide.' MW. 'Outstanding.' WAJ. 'Slightly disappointed. Waiter swearing at his colleague – not a good start. Popadoms were not warm with standard chutneys. Reasonable Chicken Tikka Bhoona with Pullao Rice. Nearly died when I was charged £4 for a pint of Cobra.' RL. Price check: Papadam 60p, CTM £6.25, Pullao Rice £1.95. House wine £6.50. Takeaway: 10% discount. Hours: 12-2.30pm/5.30-11pm. Branch: Bengal Dynasty, Llandudno, Gwynedd. Stocks Cobra.

PLAZA AMANTOLA NAME CHANGE ©

Welsh Road, Sealand, Deeside ✆ **01244 811383**

Formerly Amantola International Foysol Miah's Plaza, managed by Habibur Rahman, seats a vast 205. Chef Gous Ali's specials include the cutely-named Indian Summer – hot chicken, Jewel in the Crown – variety of spices, Himalayan Delight – very mild, Asian Love, tender pieces of lamb, and Bollywood Chicken – creamy with Keema, all £7.95. 'Nothing impressive from outside. Huge inside, large lounge bar. Service was very helpful throughout. Huge menu, including Chinese selections. Excellent, enjoyable, good value.' JG. Price check: Papadam 60p, CTM £6.95, Pullao Rice £1.75. House wine £8.95. Takeaway: 25% off. Delivery: 5-mile radius, minimum charge £15. Hours: 12-2pm/5.30pm-12.30am. Stocks Cobra.

Holywell

DILSHAD   BYO

1 Whitford Street, Holywell ✆ **01352 712022**

'Situated over a takeaway. Pops and chuts fine. Onion Bhajia and Vegetable Samosa OK.' RK. 'Lots of choice. Twelve starters, seven breads, fourteen house specials. Balti, Tandoori and all the usual curries. Good quantities, never disappointed. Restaurant can be cold.' WJ. No credit cards. Hours: 5-11pm (1am on Fri., 2am on Sat.).

Llangollen

SIMLA

4-5 Victoria Square, Llangollen   © 01978 860610

Shofique Uddin owned this 50-seater since 1982. 'Staff were clean, smart, smiling and attentive. Tandoori Chicken Biryani, with egg white laced over the presentation, plus Vegetable Bhoona, Tarka Dal, Chicken Tikka, Nan bread and chilli chutney. Quantities were more than enough. A superb evening.' DMD. Price check: Papadam 40p, CTM £7.50, Pullao Rice £1.40. Lager £1.75 pint, house wine £7.95. Hours: 12-2pm/6pm-12am.

DYFED

Area: West Wales
Population: 354,000
Number of restaurants in county: 29
Number of restaurants in Guide: 6

Aberystwyth

ROYAL PIER TANDOORI

The Pier, Marine Terrace, Aberystwyth   © 01970 624888

'Something of a novelty, situated on the end of the pier. Served by a helpful waiter. Mixed Tikka prepared at my request without the usual salad, just tomatoes, cheerfully served.' JL. Reports please.

Cardigan

ABDUL'S TANDOORI CUISINE

2 Royal Oak, Quay Street, Cardigan   © 01239 621416

'This restaurant is small, best described as "cosy". The decor is clean and pleasant, the staff friendly and helpful. We have eaten here on a number of occasions and both the food and service have been consistently of a high standard. The quantities are not large but sufficient, we have never left still hungry.' TV. Hours: 5pm-12am.

Carmarthen

TAJ BALTI ©

119 Priory Street, Carmarthen © **01267 221995**

Opened in 1995 by Lias Miah. 'My husband and I always enjoy their fare. Elegant decor, service excellent and friendly, with superb food. Muted traditional music, intimacy of individual booths, a special atmosphere. Tandoori Mixed Grill declared the best ever.' JF. Price check: Papadam 40p, CTM £5.50, Pullao Rice £1.50. Set menu £7.95. Minimum charge £6. Sun. e-a-m-a-y-l buffet. Hours: 6pm-12am.

Llandeilo

THE REDFORT NEW ENTRANT ©

64 Rhosmaen Street, Llandeilo © **01558 824224**

Est. in 1998 by Bashir Miah. Newly furnished. Seats 38. Most popular dishes: Chicken Kurme, Bolti Tikka Mosolle, Murg Nobab. Price check: Papadam 40p, CTM £5.40, Pullao Rice £1.60. Lager £1.75 pint, house wine £5.95. Sun. buffet 20% for CC. Takeaway: 20% off. Hours: 5.30pm-12.30am. Sun. 3pm-12am.

Llanelli

BENGAL LANCER ©

43 Murray Street, Llanelli © **01554 749199**

78-seater opened by Ahmed Ali in 1986. Muzaffar cooks Bangladeshi curries. Refurbishment planned for 1999. Price check: Papadam 40p, CTM £5, Pullao Rice £1.40. Wine £6. Set menu £12. Minimum charge £12.50. Takeaway: 10% off. Hours: 12-2.30pm/6pm-12am. Stocks Cobra.

©	Curry Club discount (see page 6)		Unlicensed
√	Vegetarian		
BYO	Bring your own alcohol		Delivery/takeaway

SHEESH MAHAL

53 Stepney Street, Llanelli   © 01554 773773

'Food and service gets better every visit.' DV-W. Northern Indian formula curries at A. Ali's 85-seater. Price check: Papadam 50p, CTM £5.35, Pullao Rice £1.50. Lager £1.95 pint, house wine £6.50. Hours: 12am-2pm/6-11pm.

GLAMORGAN

Area: South Wales
Population: 1,310,000
Number of restaurants in county: 129
Number of restaurants in Guide: 17

Barry

BARRY BALTI   NEW ENTRANT   ▦ ©

10 Broad Street Parade, Barry   © 01446 7221717

Balti takeaway established in 1996 by Abdul Khan. Comments card for customer to complete in own time and return to restaurant. Price check: Papadam 30p, CTM £3.70, Pullao Rice £1.30. Delivery: Free. Hours: 5.30apm-1am, Sat. 5.30pm-2am.

MODERN TANDOORI TAKEAWAY   ▦ ©

290 Holton Road, Barry   © 01446 746787

Mr A. Akbar opened his takeaway in 1982. Try the Staff Special – three courses at £15.95 for two. Price check: Papadam 30p, CTM £3.95, Pullao Rice £1.10. Minimum charge £5. Hours: 5.30pm-12.30am. Sat. 5.30pm-1.30am. Branch: The Balti House Tandoori, 14 Crwys Road, Cathays, Cardiff. tel. 01222 482923.

©	Curry Club discount (see page 6)	☕	Unlicensed
√	Vegetarian		
BYO	Bring your own alcohol	▦	Delivery/takeaway

ROYAL BALTI TAKEAWAY   ▦ ©

44 Vere Street, Barry   © 01446 421366

Iqbal Miah's formula takeaway. Special: Chilli Balti. Price check: Papadam 30p, CTM £4.30, Pullao Rice £1.25. Delivery: Free, £15 minimum. Hours: 5pm-12am.

Bridgend

THE RAJ BALTI HOUSE   NEW ENTRANT   ©

59-61 Nolton Street   © 01656 647229

Northern Indian/Bangladeshi curries at S. Rahman's 48-seater. Price check: Papadam 40p, CTM £5.95, Pullao Rice £1.40. House wine £6.95. Takeaway: 10% discount. Delivery: 3-mile radius, £15 minimum. Hours: 6pm-1am. Branch: The Rose Balti House, 28 Station Road, Port Talbot, South Wales. Stocks Cobra.

Cardiff

BENGAL BALTI   NEW ENTRANT

156 Penarth Road, Grangetown, Cardiff   ©01222 396226

You've tried the rest – now try the best – or so their advert tells us. You tell us it's: 'an unimaginative restaurant, Aloo Chat – small with a bit of salad, Chicken Tikka Masala – small pieces of chicken in a highly coloured, bland sauce and OK Pullao Rice.' JB. Price check: Papadam 30p and 35p, CTM £4.05, Bombay Potato £1.50, Pullao Rice £1.10. Hours: 6pm-1.30am (3on Fri./Sat.). A restaurant for insomniacs.

INDO CYMRU   NEW ENTRANT

173 Cowbridge Road   © 01222 344770

'Not a vast menu, with an even smaller dessert menu. Chicken and Mushroom Balti, sauce very mild, with several large chunks of chicken. Service friendly but slow, had to ask twice for the dessert menu. A narrow restaurant but bright and clean. No attempt was made to take our coats, so we kept them on our chairs.' JB. Price check: Papadam 25p (plain), 30p (spicy), CTM £4.50, Bombay Potato £1.20, Pullao Rice £1.15, Chutney and Pickles 30p, per person.

JUBORAJ 2   TOP 100 BEST IN WALES

10 Mill Lane, The Hayes, Cardiff   ©️ 01222 377668

Return to the Guide following numerous good reports. 'Fairly large, comfortable restaurant, good reputation, very popular. Visited by Tom Jones [wow!] CTM fine and the Chicken Biriani tasty. Rice wasn't coloured – I like that.' HS. 'A very good extensive menu, large portions, very good service, luxury surroundings. A bit on the expensive side, but well worth it.' PAH. 'Probably the only Indian restaurant in Cardiff City Centre and in my opinion, one of Cardiff's best.' JB. Price check: Papadam 60p, CTM £7.35, Bombay Potato £2.95, Pullao Rice £1.95. Hours: 12-2pm/6pm-12am. Branch: Juboraj, 11 Heol-y-Deri, Rhiwbina, Cardiff. New to our TOP 100. More reports please.

STAR OF WALES   ©

438 Cowbridge Road East, Canton, Cardiff ©️ 01222 383222

This 60-seater first opened way back in the 1960s. Managed by Diloar, its present owner since 1987 is Kadir Miah, who is also the chef. His specials include Jaipuri Chi, Murgi Mossalla, Lamb Bahar, and Anarkali Bahar. 'Nice polite staff. Good average portions. Keema Nan especially delicious.' HS. Price check: Papadam 35p, CTM £5.75, Pullao Rice £1.45. Lager £1.75 pint, house wine £5.95. Takeaway: 15% off. Hours: 12-2.30pm/6pm-1am.

Hengoed

LIGHT OF ASIA   NEW ENTRANT

64 Main Road, Maesycwmmer, Hengoed   ©️ 01443 816968

Northern Indian formula curries. Owned and managed by Ansar Miah since 1988. Seats 36. Special: Tandoori Chicken £6.95. Price check: Papadam 35p, CTM £5.95, Pullao Rice £1.20. Lager £1.90 pint, house wine £4.95. Hours: 12-2pm/5.30-11pm.

©	Curry Club discount (see page 6)		Unlicensed
√	Vegetarian		
BYO	Bring your own alcohol	⊞	Delivery/takeaway

Merthyr Tydfil

NEW BALTI PALACE

1 Morlais Building, High Street,
Merthyr Tydfil   ✆ 01685 388344

Owned by Abdul Karim. House specials include Shahi Chicken Tikka Masala £4.75. Good prices all round. Free Papadams and Mint Sauce with takeaway orders over £7. Price check: Papadam 35p, CTM £4.45, Pullao Rice £1.50. Minimum charge £7. Delivery. Hours: 12-2.30pm/6pm-1am.

Penarth

TROPICAL TANDOORI TAKEAWAY

14 Glebe Street, Penarth   ✆ 01222 707555

'Two good Birianis with tasty cardamom flavours. Sometimes portions get a little smaller on a busy night. I think, Pat, that the Tropical deserves to stay in the guide, because tonight my meal was again delicious, and they are proving their consistency in quality and flavour.' HS.

Swansea

ANARKALI

80 St Helen's Road, Swansea   ✆ 01792 650549

Bangladeshi and Balti 60-seater est. by A. Rahman in 1978. Price check: Papadam 45p, CTM £5, Pullao Rice £1.50. Lager £2 pint. Hours: 12-2.30pm/6pm-12am. Branch: Bengal Lancer, Llanelli, Dyfed.

BONOPHOL TAKEAWAY   NAME CHANGE

93 Sterry Road, Gowerton, Swansea   ✆ 01792 875253

Owned by Mohammed Al Imran since 1990, name changed from Gowerton Tandoori in 1997. 'Exotic Bangladeshi cuisine'. Special: Lobster, prawns, crabs etc. Buna in Bangladeshi style; vegetable thali for two £13.90. Starter for CC discount. Price check: Papadam 30p, CTM £4.30, Pullao Rice £1.10. Delivery: £10 minimum, 3-mile radius. Hours: 5.30pm-12.30am.

INDIAN COTTAGE

69 Herbert Street, Pontardawe, Swansea   © 01792 830208

52-seater, opened in 1985 by Abdul Razzak who is also the head chef, managed by Shan Prescot. Serves northern Indian and Bangladeshi curries, with popular items like Karahi Kebab and Chicken Badam Passanda. Price check: Papadam 40p, CTM £5.45, Pullao Rice £1.50. Set Dinner: £23.75. House wine £4.40. Takeaway: 15% off. Hours: 12-2pm except Sun./5.30pm-12.30am. Sat.-1. Stocks Cobra.

MOGHUL BRASSERIE   NEW TO OUR TOP 100

81 St Helen's Road, Swansea   © 01792 475131

58-seater, opened in 1989 by Shazan Uddin, who is also the chef, managed by Ashik Rahman. Bangladeshi and Balti cuisine. Seats 58. Special: Lamb/Chicken Kochi £6. Sun. e-a-m-a-y-l buffet £7 for adults, £4 for children from the selection of lamb, chicken, prawn and tandoori delicacies and three different vegetable dishes plus bread and rice. 'Have been regulars for several years. Consistency is the key word for Mr Uddin. Efficient service in very pleasant surroundings. Excellent Chicken Tikka Karahi, Sali Boti and my favourite Pathia (prawn and chicken). Mr Uddin recently exhibited a wonderful Cockle Masala, at a Culinary Festival. Superb!' A&AP. 'We have never come across anywhere that comes even close to the wonderful cuisine served at the Moghul.' E&ME. Price check: Papadam 40p, CTM £5, Pillau Rice £1.30. House wine £6.50. Set menu – six choices from A to E, ranging in price from £14-22. Takeaway: 10% off. You want it in our TOP 100. Hours: 12-2.30pm/5pm-12am (2am on Fri. & Sat.). Stocks Cobra.

LAL QUILA

480 Mumbles Road, Mumbles, Swansea   © 01792 363520

Formerly Ocean View. 'Completely refurbished, now has very attractive decor, waiters wear smart uniforms. Probably Swansea's most up-market restaurant. Everything is spotless with quick and friendly service. I particularly like the Chicken Methi with lots of fresh fenugreek. Food generally good, only weakness heavy, greasy Nans.' JD. Reports please.

RAJPUTANA   ©

44 High Street, Gorseinon, Swansea   © **01792 895883**

Formula curry house seating 36 owned by Lal Miah since 1978. Fozlu
cooks the curries. Price check: Papadam 40p, CTM £5.90, Pullao Rice
£1.50. Set Dinner: £10.95. Buffet: £6.95. Takeaway: 10% discount.
Hours: 6pm-12.30am/Sun. 12pm-12am. Branch: Bilash, 19 Wind Street,
Ammanford; Curry Villa, Port Talbot.

GWENT

Area: South Wales
Population: 448,000
Number of restaurants in county: 53
Number of restaurants in Guide: 11

Abergavenny

THE RED ROSE

35 Frogmore Street, Abergavenny   © **01873 854790**

'Restaurant specialising in Handi and Bengali cuisine. New ownership,
newly decorated, clean and comfortable, exceptional service. Medium
strength Handi with good portions of chicken and vegetables in thick
sauce, pullao rice well cooked with topping of crisp onions. £28.90 for
2.' PH.

SUNDARBON   NEW ENTRANT

7 Monk Street, Abergavenny   © **01873 855785**

'By far and away the best. Serving formula curries, standard of presentation much higher than the others. Very crisp and clean table linen,
overall impression of a well-to-do establishment.' JL. Price check:
Papadam 30p (plain), 35p (spicy), CTM £4.50, Bombay Potato £1.75,
Pullao Rice £1.30, Chutney, Pickles and Mint Sauce 30p each.

Bedwas

INDIAN COTTAGE   ©

Bridge Cottage, The Square, Bedwas   ℭ 01222 860369

The foundations of Mohammed Riaz's cosy 28-seater were laid around the time that Queen Elizabeth I came to the throne. There is an interesting and detailed history of the building on the back of the menu. The cottage now dispenses 'very good, tasty.' GR. Pakistani food. Delivery charges: Bedwas and Trethomas 80p; Llanbradach, Caerphilly, Machen £1.20. Hours: 6-11p (12pm on Fri. & Sat.).

Cwmbran

KHAN TANDOORI TAKEAWAY

**6 Commercial Street, Pontnewydd,
Cwmbran   ℭ 01633 867141**

Siraj Khan started his takeaway in 1984. Eleven types of bread are listed under the heading of 'good companions'. Price check: Papadam 25p, CTM £4.90, Pullao Rice £1. Delivery: charge £1 Cwmbran/Newport. Hours: 5.30pm-12.30am (1am on Fri. & Sat.).

MAHRAJA BALTI

6 General Rees Square, Cwmbran   ℭ 01633 483627

76-seater owned by Mohammed Omar Sheik since 1992. Serves Pakistani and Balti curries. Price check: Papadam 40p, CTM £6.10, Pullao Rice £1.90. House wine £5.90. Minimum charge £7. Delivery: £8, 6-mile radius, ordered by 12am. Hours: 12-2.30pm/6pm-1.30am (2.30am on Fri. & Sat.). Stocks Cobra.

Monmouth

MISBAH TANDOORI

9 Priory Street, Monmouth   ℭ 01600 714940

D. Miah opened his 32-seater restaurant in 1990. Plans to expand. Chef A. Rahman does a good range of Baltis served with Nan bread ranging from King Prawn Balti at £9.95 to Vegetable Balti at £5.50. Special four-course Sun. lunch £6.95. Special: Bengal Fish Mossala (freshwater fish from Bangladesh cooked in tomato and onion, £7.95). Price check: Papadam 45p, CTM £6.75, Pullao Rice £1.75. Lager £1.95 pint, house wine £6.95. Takeaway: 10% off. Hours: 12-2pm/6-11pm.

Newport

DILSHAD INTERNATIONAL CUISINE NEW ENTRANT   ©

30/34 Clarence Place, Newport   ℂ 01633 254062

Mozadul Hussain and Moshaid Ali's 80-seater, est. 1989 has been recently refurbished, and has car parking for 20 cars. Chef Sirajul Islam cooks Bangladeshi and Balti curries, Rogon and Persian dishes such as Murug Zallander, Korahi. Price check: Papadam 40p, CTM £4.90, Pullao Rice £1.60. Lager £1.90 pint, house wine £7.50. Takeaway: 10% discount. Delivery: £10, 4-mile radius. Hours: 6pm-1.30am (11.30pm on Fri. 2.30pm on Sat.). Branch: The Prince of Caerleon Takeaway, Caerleon, Newport.

INDIAN COTTAGE TAKEAWAY

18 Malpas Road, Newport   ℂ 01633 821196

Del Ramzan assures us that his dishes are 'clearly distinguishable from the others because of their distinctive features'. House special: Chilli Garlic Chicken Massalah £7.20. Price check: Papadam 40p, CTM £5.30, Pullao Rice £1.70. Set menu £8.50. Delivery over £10, Newport and £12, Cwmbran. Hours: 5pm-12am (1am on Fri. & Sat.).

KING BALTI HOUSE NEW ENTRANT

248 Corporation Road, Newport   ℂ 01633 220662

Owner T. Torofdar specialises in Balti, Bangladeshi and Handhi dishes at his 56-seater. Price check: Papadam 45p, CTM £6.60, Pullao Rice £1.95. Hours: 12-2.30pm/6pm-12.30am (1am on Sat.). Stocks Cobra.

THE KOH I NOOR   ©

164 Chepstow Road, Maindee, Newport   ℂ 01633 258028

Mrs L. Khanan's venerable 60-seat Koh i Noor was established in 1978, and appeared in our first few guides, so welcome back. We've said before that nothing on the menu changes. Chef Tahir Ullah's curries are listed under such categories as mild, fruity, fairly hot, very hot, hottest and most favourite. In other words this is one of the early standard curry houses with its clutch of once-a-week regulars. Price check: Papadam 50p, CTM £5.40, Pullao Rice £1.90. (Well not quite everything on the menu is the same! The price check for 1984 was pops 15p, CTM £1.90, Rice 65p). Hours: 12-2.30pm/6pm-1am. Sun. 6pm-12am.

Risca

BOMBAY EXPRESS TAKEAWAY

14 Tredegar Street, Risca   ✆ **01633 601033**

Opened in 1996 by Mohammed Yamin, who also is the head chef. Price check: Papadam 30p, CTM £4.80, Pullao Rice £1.60. Delivery: £8, 4-mile radius. Hours 5.30-11.30pm, Fri. & Sat. 5pm-12am.

GWYNEDD

Area: North Wales
Population: 241,000
Number of restaurants in county: 26
Number of restaurants in Guide: 6

Bangor

MAHABHARAT   ©

5-7 High Street, Bangor   ✆ **01248 351337**

M. Sholayman took over this 1968 curry house in 1990. 'Spacious and comfortable. Service very efficient except for the late arrival of the mint sauce which was supposed to accompany the starter. Portions very generous and food of a high standard.' IM. Free Papadams and dips with every takeaway order. Price check: Papadam 40p, CTM £6.50, Pullao Rice £1.45. Minimum charge £9. Hours: 12-2pm/6pm-12am.

Caernarfon

GANDHI

11 Palace Street, Caernarfon   ℰ 01286 676797

'Standard menu with above-average food and service. King Prawn Butterfly followed by Lamb Tikka Masala, Pilau Rice and Keema Nan. Bombay Potato, particularly spicy – excellent. A very pleasing meal all round, good portions.' JL. Hours: 12-2pm, not Sun./5.30-11pm.

Llandudno

BENGAL DYNASTY   TOP 100   ©

1 North Parade, Llandudno   ℰ 01492 878445

Llandudno is a really fabulous seaside town with gorgeous Georgian buildings running in an arch along the waterfront. Lewis Carroll wrote *Alice in Wonderland* in this seaside resort. The 86-seat Bengal Dynasty is situated upstairs in one of these fine buildings. 'I was about to settle for fish & chips when I saw it, upstairs above a shoe shop. I had Lamb Tikka to start and then Chicken Bhuna, which was excellent.' AG 'King Prawn Butterfly followed by my usual main courses. A very accomplished meal. Keema Nan was the highlight together with a homemade Kulfi. Gets my vote.' JL. 'Service was welcoming, prompt and polite. Pops and chuts fresh and crisp. Main meals were large, everything was hot and well presented. An enjoyable experience, but not outstanding.' SR. 'Menu was wide and varied. Papadoms and chutneys excellent. Raita exceptional. All meals were served piping hot with hot plates and the portions were satisfying. Waiters were very accommodating in making changes to dishes for our individual tastes. Smart, clean and tasteful surroundings. Highly recommended.' NC. New Specials: Chicken Bondhuk £7.95, Lamb Satkora £8.95. Price check: Papadam 60p, CTM £6.25, Pullao Rice £1.95. Lager £2.20 pint, house wine £6.50. Takeaway: 10% off. Hours: 12-2.30pm (4.30pm on Sun.) and 6-11.30pm. Branch: Bengal Dynasty, Deeside, Clwyd.

©	Curry Club discount (see page 6)		Unlicensed
√	Vegetarian		
BYO	Bring your own alcohol		Delivery/takeaway

Llangefni

MOONLIGHT   ©

40 High Street, Llangefni   © 01248 722595

Emdadur Rahman, the owner-manager, is offering authentic Bangladeshi and northern Indian dishes using fresh ingredients and spices. Price check: Papadam 50p, CTM £5.95, Pullao Rice £1.60. Hours: 12-2pm/6-11.30pm. Takeaway available until midnight. Reports please.

Porthmadog

PASSAGE TO INDIA   NEW ENTRANT

26 Lombard Street, Porthmadog   © 01766 512144

'Tandoori Sheek Kebab was very spicy and dry and required nearly a pint of lager to get it down! The Chicken Shashlic was very good.' AG. Price check: CTM £6.35, Pulao Rice £1.75, Onion Bhaji £2.25.

POWYS

Area: Central Wales
Population: 117,000
Number of restaurants in county: 10
Number of restaurants in Guide: 2

Builth Wells

BALTI HOUSE

11 Market Street, Builth Wells   © 01982 551131

Owned by Rokib Ali since 1997. 'Pleasantly furnished and the staff most obliging and friendly. Chefs working can be viewed from the dining area. Ate there three times while on holiday and each meal was better than the last.' JP. Northern Indian formula curries. Price check: Papadam 45p, CTM £6.10, Pullao Rice £1.45. Hours: Mon.-Thurs. 5.30pm-12.30am. Fri. & Sat. 12-2pm/5.30pm-12.30am. Sun. 5.30-11.30pm.

Newtown

BALTI HOUSE

2 Wesley Street, Newtown   © 01686 622186

'Exterior of building does not encourage you to enter, though once inside all is of a high standard. Lamb Madras with Pilau Rice and Garlic Nan. Quantities were very good as was the presentation. My only gripe is that the pieces of meat are so large that you have to put your bread down while you cut the meat.' JB. Complaints like that we can handle! Reports please.

©	Curry Club discount (see page 6)	🍵	Unlicensed
√	Vegetarian		
BYO	Bring your own alcohol	🏠	Delivery/takeaway

List of Contributors

This Guide is possible thanks to the many Curry Club members, and others, who have sent in reports on restaurants. Especial thanks to the following regular, prolific and reliable reporters (apologies for any errors, duplications, omissions, and for the tiny print necessitated by space considerations).

A: Martin Abbott, Gloucs; Colin Adam, Kilwinning; Ray Adams, Kimberley; Meena Ahamed, London; Paul Allen, Chatham; Tony and Lesley Allen, Rugby; MF Alsan, Rugby; G Amos, Wirral; Capt R Ancliffe, BFPO 12; Apryl Anderson, Ponteland; Karen Andras, Nottingham; Lisa Appadurai, Benfleet; Robin Arnott, Stafford; Mrs M Asher, Woodford Green; Dave Ashton, Warrington; Jo Ashton, Elland; Allan Ashworth, York; Berry Ashworth, Compton Bassett; Michelle Aspinal, Chester; Darius Astell, Southampton; Rachael Atkinson, Cheshire; Simon Atkinson, N5; Y Atkinson, IOM; Claire Austin, Stoke; Arman Aziz, N4.

B: Tom Bailey, Alresford; John Baker, Loughton; Kim Baker, Hatfield; Mr & Mrs ML Banks, Enfield; Keith Bardwell, Hertford; Ian Barlex, Ilford; Trevor Barnard, Gravesend; Christopher Barnes, Ashton; Derek Barnett, Colchester; Tony Barrel, Hounslow; Joanne Bastock, Saltash; Mike Bates, Radcliffe; Shirley Bayley, Worthing; Karin and Angela, Rugby; Mr MJ Beard, Stafford; Joyce Bearpark, Murcia Spain; Dave Beazer, Cornwall; DJ Beer, Ross-on-Wye; Derick Behrens, Bucks; Matt Bell, Derbys; P Bell, Carlisle; Sam Bell, Coventry; TW Bennett, Sherborne; Becky Benson, Worcs; John Bentley, Northampton; Ron Bergin, Gerrards Cross; Ian Berry, Goole; Martyn Berry, SE3; Kenneth Beswick, Lincoln; DJ Betts, Bexhill; Jonathan Bick, Cardiff; Brian and Anne Biffin, Fleet; Colin Bird, Welwyn Garden City; BH Birch, Hyde; Jim Birkumshaw, Derbys; James Birtles, Manchester; Chris Blackmore, Bristol; David Bolton, Lichfield; Mrs C Bone, Norfolk; A Boughton, SE27; L Le Bouochon, Jersey; Mrs I Bowman, Rochester; Robert Box, Knottingley; Alan Boxall, Burwash; Sean Boxall, Andover; F Boyd, Stranraer; Iain Boyd, Wealdstone; Roderick Braggins, Peebles; Amanda Bramwell, Sheffield; Dave Bridge, Wallasey; Michael E Bridgstock, Northants; Sandra Brighton, Nelson; Steve Broadfoot, Anfield; John and Susan Brockington, Sutton Coldfield; Paul Bromley, SE13; Robert Brook, London; Nigel John Brooks, Stoke on Trent; David Brown, Leeds; IA Brown, Fernhurst; Mark Brown, Scunthorpe; Steve Brown, Twickenham; DA Bryan, York; RC Bryant, Witney; Robert Bruce, Thornaby; Heather Buchanan, Inverness; Dr TM Buckenham, SW11; Mrs J Buffey, Sutton Coldfield; LG Burgess, Berkhamsted; A Burton, Weston-super-Mare.

C: D Cadby, Swindon; Barry Caldwell, Chesterfield; David Caldwell, Brownhills; Stan Calland, Kingsley; Hugh Callaway, Cleethorpes; Duncan Cameron, Fordoun; Frank Cameron, Dundee; HS Cameron, Wirral; Alex Campbell,

Ramsey Campbell, Wallasey; Hartley Wintney; Mrs E Campbell, Harrogate; N Campbell, Edinburgh; Josephine Capps, Romford; L Carroll, Huddersfield; James Casey, Wiltshire; Peter Cash, Liverpool; Mark Caunter, Guildford; TM Chandler, Farnborough; Desmond Carr, N8; J Carr, Birkenhead; TO Carr, Warrington; BR Carrick, Wakefield; DL Carter, Huntingdon; Mrs M Carter, Colchester; Madeline Castro, Bury St Edmunds; Dr WF Cavenagh, Norfolk; Neil Chantrell, Warrington; Hilary J Chapchal, Leatherhead; Mr & Mrs DR Chapchal, Leatherhead; John Chapman, Leics; Paul Chapman, Leighton Buzzard; Mr & Mrs Chatfield, Wimborne; Rajender Chatwal, Bicester; Dr GT Cheney, Salhouse; Paul Chester, Cuffley; Sqn Ldr PF Christopher, Ferndown; Alexis Ciusczak, Capistrano Beach, CA; Peter Clyne, SW11; VA Coak, Penzance; Louise Coben-Sutherland, Enfield; CH Coleman, Sussex; Robin Collier, Mid Calder; Billy Collins, Wirral; Mrs J Collins, Portsmouth; CJ Comer, Basingstoke; Rhys Compton, Cheltenham; A Conroy, Durham; Joseph Coohil, Oxford; Neil Cook, Royston; Mr LW Coombes, Devon; Alan & Margaret Cooper, Llansteffan; Kim Cooper, Basildon; DW Cope, Whitchurch; Dr JC Coppola, Woodstock; Will Coppola, Oxford; Nigel Cornwell, Orpington; John Costa, Tunbridge Wells; MJ Cotterill, Bristol; Stephen Cowie, SW16; Steve Cowling, Shropshire; Julie Cozens, Oxon; Dr AM Croft, Cornwall; Roderick Cromar, Buckie; C Cross, Poole; Yasmin Cross, Huddersfield; Major & Mrs FJB Crosse, Salisbury; Robert Crossley, Huddersfield; Frank and Elizabeth Crozier, Redruth; R Cuthbertson, Southampton.

D: S Daglish, Scarborough; P Dalton, Wirral; Jan Daniel, Felpham; Mr & Mrs PE Dannat, Eastleigh; Martin Daubney, Hitchin; Gary Davey, W4; Alasdair Davidson, Heswall; Adrian Davies, NW3; Gwyn Davies, Wirral; Mrs JC Davies, Leeds; Josephine Davies, Swansea; Lucy Davies, Essex; Paul Davies, Chiddingfold; Mrs G Davies-Goff, Marlow; Colin Davis, Tatsfield; Ian Dawson, Mirfield; DM Day, Preston; Michael Day, West Bromwich; Peter Deane, Bath; Gary & Katy Debono, High Wycombe; David Dee, Ruislip; Elizabeth Defty, Co. Durham; Neil Denham, The Netherlands; R Dent, Bishop Auckland; Les Denton, Barnsley; Richard Develyn, St Leonards; Nigel Deville, Uttoxeter; Ken Dewsbury, Somerset; Richard Diamond, Romsey; RC Dilnot, Broadstairs; Graham Divers, Glasgow; James Dobson, Burscough; S Dolden, Rochester; R Dolley, W11; Clive Doody, Surrey; Keith Dorey, Barnet; Neil Downey, Worthing; Sarah Dowsett, Swindon; Anna Driscoll, Cape Province; Mrs J Driscoll, BFPO; Diane Duame, Wicklow; Eric Duhig, Hornchurch; Sheila Dunbar, Pinner; James Duncan, West Kilbride; Mark Dunn, E18; Robin Durant, Brighton; Martin Durrant, Chester; Mr & Mrs JA Dywer, Birmingham.

E: A Edden-Jones, Bristol; Bruce Edwards, Norwich; Dave Edwards, Rugeley; CM Eeley, Witney; Rod Eglin, Whitehaven; Wendy Elkington; Ray Elliott, Worcester; PT Ellis, W'rtn; Mrs G Elston, Woodley; Tony Emmerton, Chorley; Mark Evans, Caersws; Mr & Mrs A Evans, Manchester; Brian Exford, Derbys.

F: Gary Fairbrother, Crosby; Hazel Fairley, Guildford; Chris Farrington, Cherry Hinton; Graham Faulkner, Dorking; John Fearson, Bucks; Denis Feeney, Glasgow; Kevin Fenner, Rothley; Bill and Laraine Field, Newcastle-upon-Lyme; Stephen Field, Norton; Mick Fielden, Glossop; AJ Finch, Enfield Wash;

Duncan Finley, Glasgow; Maureen Fisher, Woodford Green; Bernard Fison, Holmrook; John Fitzgerald, Great Missenden; Merly Flashman, TN12; Colin & Toni Fleet, Dorset; Dr Cornel Fleming, N6; KD Flint, Kempsey; Fiona Floyd, Truro; Stephen & Elizabeth Foden, Lynton; Chris Fogarty, Enfield; Gareth Foley, Porthcawl; Neil Foley, Essex; IE Folkard-Evans, Manchester; SR Tracy Forster, Beds; Rod Fouracres, Glos.; Rosemary Fowler, Midhurst; John W Fox, Doncaster; Linda Foye, Barry; Theresa Frey, Fareham; Chris Frid, North Shields; Steve Frost, Kingston; Alan Furniss, Wraysbury; June Fyall, Bronwydd; Mrs MAJ Fyall, Dyfed.

G: Stephen Gaines, Middlesex; MJ Gainsford, Burbage; Leo Gajsler, Geneva; Mrs FE Gaunt, Stonehouse; Phillip Gentry, Bexleyheath; Brian George, Wolverton; CM Gerry, Cyprus; G Gibb, SE21; Robert Giddings, Poole; Michael Gill, Leeds; Andrew Gillies, Edinburgh; AV Glanville, Windsor; Ms D Glass, Liverpool; A Glenford, Lincoln; Nick Goddard, Stevenage; Andrew Godfrey, Seer Green; Matthew Goldsmith, Burgess Hill; Mr & Mrs A. Goldthorp, Halstead; John Goleczka, Pensford; Michael Goodband, Perhore; Bryn Gooding, Corfu; Dr G Gordon, Kidlington; Mrs J Gorman, Strood; Ian Gosden, Woking; Bill Gosland, Camberley; David Gramagan, Formby; DC Grant, Enfield; Kathryn Grass, Wigan; Alan Gray, Erskine; DR Gray, SW11; A Greaves, Chesterfield; Andrew Greaves, Derbyshire; Rachel Greaves, Tavistock; Denise Gregory, Nottinghamshire; Jonathan Green, Cathays, Michael Green, Leicester; Nigel Green, Orpington; Richard Green, Gerrards Cross; Sheila Green, Barrow; A Gregor, Boston; Frank Gregori, NW10; Andrew Grendale, Ingatestone; A Griffiths, Milton Keynes; JK Greye, Bath; M Griffiths, Northampton; Dave Groves, Walsall; Lynda Gudgeon, Willenhall;Louis Gunn, Chelmsford.

H: Karen Haley, Telford; John Hall, Cullercoats; Andrew Halling, Leigh; Stephen Hames, Bewdley; Alan Hamilton, Wakefield; Tina Hammond, Ipswich; Geoff & Janet Hampshire-Thomas, Kirkland; Neil Hancock, Derby; Ray Hancock, Chester; Dorothy Hankin, Fordingbridge; Sharon Hanson, Derby; Glynn Harby, Knaresborough; Martyn Harding, Powys; Roger Hargreaves, Stoke; J Harman, Brentwood; Gerald Harnden, Westcliff-on-Sea; Dawn Harris, Dubley; Paul Harris, BFPO; David Harrison, Dursley; Patrick Harrison, Cambridge; David Harvey, SE24; S Harwood, Lewes; John K Hattam, York; Sally Haseman, Surbiton; Christopher & Linda Haw, Dewsbury; Ann & David Haynes, Bournemouth; John Haynes, Saffron Walden; DI Hazelgrove, West Byfleet; M Hearle, Tunbridge Wells; Kevin Hearn, Newcastle; Bernice Heath, Nottingham; Andy Hemingway, Leeds; Terry Herbat, Barnsley; Georgina Herridge, W9; J & J Hetherington, Preston; Victoria Heywood, Burton; Roger Hickman, N1; Pat & Paul Hickson, Chorley; Janet Higgins, Blackburn; Mrs S Higgins, Blackburn; Mrs B Higgs, Cotty; Dave Hignett, Newcastle-upon-Tyne; Alec Hill, Wigan; Carolyn Hill, Nottingham; Stephen Hill, Chesterfield; Barry Hills, Surrey; David Hindle, W5; Bharti Hindocha, Richmond; Daniel Hinge, Bishop Auckland; Mrs MJ Hirst, Kent; SC Hodgon; Daniel Hodson, Abingdon; Peter Hoes, Bingley; P Hogkinson, Sheffield; Duncan Holloway, Windsor; Kevin Hooper, St Austell; Linda Horan, Wirral; Peter Hornfleck,

Farnborough; Jerry Horwood, Guildford; Dr MP Houghton, Rugby; Neil Houldsworth, Keighley; JK Howard, Enfield Wash; P Howard, Hornchurch; Mrs J Howarth, Oldham; Kathy Howe, Carlisle; Simon Howell, Gillingham; Bruce Howerd, Tongham; Lynn Howie, Sanderstead; Jan Hudson, Hemel Hempstead; Tom Hudson, Jarrow; Chris Hughes, Wraysbury; Paul Hulley, Stockport; SP Hulley, Reddish; HL & S Humphreys, Stoke-on-Trent; AG Hunt, Southend-on-Sea; John & Frances Hunt, Langport; Paul Hunt, Essex; Roger Hunt, Sidmouth; Vince Hunt, Manchester; Penny Hunter, Brighton; Sheila Hunter, Dundee; Dr M Hutchinson, Gwynedd; Mrs V Hyland, Manchester.

I: DM Ibbotson, Sheffield; Nick & Mandy Idle, Ossett; Ken Ingram, Leeds; G Innocent, Dawlish; Mrs G Irving, Redditch; Robert Izzo, Horsham.

J: Dr AG James, Wigan; O Jarrett, Norwich; Sue Jayasekara, Essex; Sally Jeffries, Heathfield; L Jiggins, Dagenham; G John, Wirral; Maxine & Andrew Johnson, Leiden; Colin Johnson, Southall; Peter Johnson, Droitwich; Paul Jolliffe, Exeter; CML Jones, St Albans; Gareth Jones, Tonypandy; Kate Jones, Leiden; RW Jones, N9; Shirley Jones, SE13; WA Jones, Flints; Wendy Jones, Clwyd; Michael Lloyd Jones, Cardiff; Esther Juby, Norwich.

K: Tessa Kamara, W13; AD Kantes, Northants; Chris Keardey, Southampton; Anthony Kearns, Stafford; Russ Kelly, Seaforth; Prof. and Mrs Kemp, Royston; Mr & Mrs MJB Kendall, Hook; David Kerray, Akrotiri; John Kettle, Dover; JS Kettle, Banbury; Saul Keyworth, Essex; Stephen Kiely, N16; David King, Biggleswade; John & Jane Kingdom, Plymouth; Alyson Kingham, Oldham; Frances Kitchen, Langport; Peter Kitney, Banbury; J & P Klusiatis, Reading; Drs Heather & Mark Knight, Oxford; Drs MJ & A Krimholtz, SW14.

L: Caz Lack, Kent; Martin Lally, Chester; Alan Lathan, Chorley; Cass Lawson, Swindon; Jonathan Lazenby, Mamhilad, Gwent; Gary Leatt, St. Brelade, Jersey; Andrew Lecomber, Durham; DH Lee, Waltham Abbey; Jackie Leek, Dartford; Simon Leng, Wakefield; David Leslie, Aberdeen; Russell D Lewin, NW2; A Lewis, Sherborne; Margaret Ann Lewis, Ashford; R Lewis, Rayleigh; Pat Lindsay, Hampshire; David Lloyd, Northampton; David Lloyd, Oswestry; Eleanor & Owen Lock, Geneva; Peter Long, Cheltenham; J Longman, Bodmin; John Loosemore, Orpington; DA Lord, Hove; Julia & Philip Lovell, Brighton; AP Lowe, Tolworth; Mr & Mrs DN Luckman, Horley; Jeremy Ludlow, Dorset; Mrs H Lundy, Wallasey; Graeme Lutman, Herts; Tim Lynch, Romford; Jamie Lyon, Burscough.

Mac/Mc: M Mcbryde, Watford; David Mackay, Twickenham; David Mackenzie, Darlington; Lin Macmillan, Lincoln; Deb McCarthy, E6; Patrick McCloy, N8; Vanessa McCrow, Teddington; David McCulloch, NW11; Michael McDonald, Ellesmere Port; David McDowell, Telford; BJ McKeown, Seaford; Ian McLean, Brighton; Dr and Mrs J McLelland, Mid Calder; Alan & Jean McLucas, Solihull; Dr FB McManus, Lincolnshire; Alan McWilliam, Inverurie.

M: Chris Mabey, Swindon; Rakesh Makhecha, Harrow; Richard Manley, Wirral; Cherry Manners, Hatfield; E Mansfield, Camberley; Clive Mantle; JF Marshall, Bedford; Geraldine Marson, Winsford; Colin Martin, Nuneaton; Derek Martin, Marlow; Jane Martin, SW19; PR Martin, Southend; DH

Marston, Southport; DJ Mason, Cleveland; LJ Mason, Leeds; John Maundrell, Tunbridge Wells; Gilian May, Hayes; Peter F May, St Albans; Simon Mayo, Farnborough; Simon Meaton, Andover; John Medd, Nottingham; Tim Mee, Harrow; Sue & Alf Melor, Hanworth; Nigel Meredith, Huddersfield; Sujata Mia, Middlesex; H Middleton, Coventry; Simon Mighall, St Neots; PJL Mighell, Canterbury; Robert Miles, Hertfordshire; Catherine Millar, BFPO; DR Millichap, Horsham; BW Milligan; AJ Millington, Woodford; Sally Millington, N10; Mr & Mrs P Mills, Mold; Mary Mirfin, Leeds; Al Mitchell, Belfast; Jonathon Mitchell, Alton; F Moan, Cuddington; Sarah Moles, Buxton; Jon Molyneaux, Peterborough; Mrs SE Monk, Gisburn; AV Moody, Portsmouth; Christy Moore, Dublin; Christy Moore, London; DM Moreland, Willington; S Morgan, Feltham; Ian Morris, Gwynedd; Peter Morwood, Wicklow; A Moss, Colchester; Caroline Moss, Solihull; Mrs L Muirhead, Glasgow; David Muncaster, Stoke; Andy Munro, Birmingham; Joan Munro, Leyburn; Annette Murray, Thornton Cleveleys; JL Murray, Enfield; RG Murray, Carlisle; Drs Heather & Harry Mycook.

N: Simon Nash, Cheshire; Mrs PG Naylor, Salisbury; Hugh Neal, Kent; Jeff Neal, Bolton; A Nelson-Smith, Swansea; Liam Nevens, Stockton; Tony Newman, Margate; Rebecca Newman, Hayes; Clive Newton, Northwich; P & D Nixon, Basildon; Mrs DA Nowakowa, Tiverton; Robert Nugent, SE31; Canon Peter Nunn, Gloucestershire; Jody Lynn Nye, Illinois.

O: Beverley Oakes, Essex; AM O'Brien, Worthing; Eamon O'Brien, Holland; Pauline O'Brien, London; DC O'Donnell, Wetherby; Elise O'Donnell, Wolverhampton; Mary O'Hanlon, N Oliver, London; Helensburgh; Sheila Openshaw, Hampshire; David O'Regan, Leeds; Jan Ostrom, Felpham; Judith Owen, SW6; William & Sue Oxley, Southampton.

P: Trevor Pack, Rushden; RH Paczec, Newcastle; M Padina, Mattingley; Mr & Mrs GG Paine, Coventry; Keith Paine, Tilbury; GJ Palmer, Gainsborough; RS Palmer, Norfolk; Mrs A Parker, Birmingham; Mr GM Parker, Birmingham; John MF Parker, North Yorks; Bill Parkes-Davies, Tunbridge Wells; Bill Parkes-Davis, Tunbridge Wells; Angela Parkinson, Clitheroe; M Parsons, Fareham; Roy Parsons, Richmond; Donald Paterson, East Grinstead; GM Patrick, London; Mrs PA Pearson, Bristol; Mrs G Pedlow, Hitchin; Mrs Barrie Penfold, Bourne End; J Penn, Southampton; AJW Perry, Bristol; Ian Perry, Essex; MJ Perry, E17; Ian Pettigrew, Edinburgh; Christopher Phelps, Gloucester; Adrian & Angela Phillips, Ammanford; Diane Phillips, Hyde; Jonathan Phillips, Saffron Walden; Steve Phillips, Wokingham; Colin Phipps, Scarborough; Sara Pickering, Northolt; Jack Pievsky, Pinner; Mike Plant, Essex; Susan Platt, Bury; D Pool, SE2; K Pool, Leyland; SR Poole, Runcorn; Tony Pope, Derbyshire; Steve Porter, Walsall; RL Power, Sutton Coldfield; Dave Prentice, Dartmouth; Steve Prentice, Devon; Tim Preston, Barrow; Alison Preuss, Glencarse; Jeff Price, Bristol; Mr J Priest, Sawbridgeworth; Dr John Priestman, Huddersfield; D Pulsford, Marford; Janet Purchon, Bradford; Steve Puttock, Chatham; Julie Pyne, County Down.

Q: Sheila Quince, E11.

R: Diane Radigan, Welling; Clive Ramsey, Edinburgh; Alison Ratcliff, Halstead; KJ Rayment, Hertford; RC Raynham, Chelmsford; CR Read, Epsom; Mark

Read, Romford; Kim Reeder, South Shields; Debbie Reddy, w12; Francis Redgate, Nottingham; Steven Redknap, Ashford; I Reid, Fife; Lorraine Reid, Edinburgh; Duncan Renn, Dursley; Derek Richards, Bewdley; Sean Richards, Dover; Simon Richardson, Gainsborough; Mike Ridgway, Buxton; Mathew Riley, se3; Lindsay Roberts, Lancaster; Margaret Roberts, Rubery; Peter Roberts, Shipston; Stewart & Anne Robertson, Leamington; Simon Roccason, Willenhall; Pat Roche, Chislehurst; J & P Rockery, Leicester; KG Rodwell, Harston; R Ronan, IOW; John Roscoe, Stalybridge; Brian Roston, Pontefract; John Rose, Hull; WJ Rowe; Steve Rowland, Matlock; Mrs EM Ruck, Darlington; DC Ruggins, Chalfont; JA Rumble, Rochford; Paul Rushton, Nottingham; K Ruth, w1; Bob Rutter, Blackpool; EJ Ryan, Effingham; N Ryer, Mansfield.

S: George and Mrs J Sadler, Thetford; MB Samson, Hertfordshire; Pauline Sapsford, Milton Keynes; MR Sargeant, Cornwall; Mark Sarjant, Guildford; GM Saville, Egremont; Mike Scotlock, Rayleigh; Mike Scott, Holmer Green; MJ Scott, se26; Nicky & Don Scowen, Romford; Tim Sebensfield, Beeston; M Seefeld, w5; Patrick Sellar, Maidstone; Philip Senior, Liverpool; N Sennett, Hull; David Sewell, Aldershot; Mrs DA Seymour, Burnham-on-Sea; Richard Shackleton, Wakefield; Brian Shallon, Camberley; Jeane Sharp, St Albans; Howard & Mary Sherman, Upton-by-Chester; Mark Shaw, Swindon; Michelle Shaw, Ilford; Deborah Shent, Nottingham; Barrie Shepherd, Bishopston; Howard Sherman, Chester; Theresa Shilcock, Derbyshire; Ewan Sim, Leeds; Carolyn Simpson, se13; Jennifer Singh, Enfield; Jeff Slater, e6; William P Sloan, Camberley; Else & Harald Smaage, Sauvegny; David Smith, Norwich; David Smith, Swindon; Denis Smith, Swindon; EK Smith, Edinburgh; Gillian Smith, St Andrews; Hazel Smith, Llandrinio; Howard Smith, Cardiff; Jim Smith, Cork; LP & A Smith, Gibraltar; Mark Smith, Lancashire; Nora Smith, Cardiff; RB Smith, BFPO; Sue Smith, Northampton; Susan Smith, Devon; Colin Snowball, Cheltenham; Tim Softly, Leigh; Robert Solbe, Surrey; Peter Soloman, Middlesbrough; M Somerton-Rayner, Cranwell; Maurice Southwell, Aylesbury; Gill Sparks, Halifax; Andrew Speller, Harlow; GD Spencer, Stonehaven; Mrs P Spencer, Norwich; Andy Spiers, Brighton; R Spiers, Wolverhampton; CP Spinks, Church Langley; Chris Spinks, Ilford; John Spinks, Hainault; Martin Spooner, Wallsend; DJ Stacey, Cambridge; Mrs WL Stanley-Smith, Belper; Mr & Mrs M Stanworth, Haywards Heath; John Starley, Birdingbury; Nigel Steel, Carlisle; Avril Steele, Crossgar; Bob Stencill, Sheffield; John Stent, Liss; Ian Stewart, Potters Bar; Tim Stewart, Norfolk; Tina Stone, Illford; Barry Strange, Kent; Rob Struthers, Brighton; Mrs MB Such; FD Sunderland, Plympton; FC Sutton, Poole; Andrew Swain, Sudbury; Carolyn Swain, Leeds; Gary Swain, Coventry; DL Swann, Parbold; Frank Sweeney, Middlesbrough; Gill & Graham Swift, Beeston; MS Sykes, Dorrington.

T: Nigel & Gill Tancock, Newbury; Steve Tandy, Cleveleys; Bernard Tarpey, Failsworth; Andrew Tattersall, North Yorks; CB Taylor, Wolverhampton; Colin Taylor, Preston; Kevin Taylor, Sevenoaks; Ken Taylor, Sevenoaks; Peter Taylor, Kingston-upon-Hull; Philip & Vivien Taylor, Cromer; Roger Taylor, Hamela; Len Teff, Whaddon; Mrs PF Terrazzano, Leigh-on-Sea; RL Terry, Kent;

Christopher & Niamh Thomas, Barnet; DG Thomas, Gloucestershire; DL
Thomas, Peterborough; Mrs J Thomas, Cumbria; Mark Thomas, Exeter; Nigel
Thomas, Lincoln; Dr DA & AHE Thombs, Slimbridge; Alan Thompson,
Clwyd; David & Lisa Thompson, SE10; Richard Thompson, Rainham; Bill
Thomson, Ramsgate; Paul Thomson, Salford; J Thorne, South Benfleet; Richard
Tilbe, Wokingham; Mrs BM Clifton Timms, Chorley; Joan & Ken Timms, West
Sussex; Mrs M Tindale, Beverley; Alan Tingle, Hayling Island; Graham Todd,
Crawley; Joan Tongue, Huddersfield; Alex & Sarah Torrence, Cleveland; SR
Tracey-Forster, Bronham; Bernard Train, Barton; Leigh Trevitt, Bishops
Stortford; R Trinkwon, Ferring; Kevin & Sarah Troubridge, Chelmsford; Dr JG
Tucker, SW17; Paul Tunnicliffe, Cleveland; Martin Turley, Belgium; Don
Turnball, Geneva; Mrs SM Turner, Stroud; R Twiddy, Boston; S Twiggs, Lower
Kingswood; Jeremey Twomey, Leamington; John Tyler, Romford.
V: David Valentine, Forfar; Alan & Lesley Vaughan, Paington; D Vaughan-
Williams, Penyffordd; Mrs B Venton, Chipstead; Richard Vinnicombe, Camber-
ley; Mr & Mrs T Vlismas, Crymyoh; Sarah Vokes, Dorking; Gordon Volke,
Worthing.
W: Phil Wain, Merseyside; PM Waine, Manchester; R Waldron, Oxon; Alison
Walker, Droitwich; Andrew Walker, Aklington; Dr JB Walker, Burnham; John
Walker, Chorley; Dr PAW Walker, Wirral; William Wallace, West Kilbride;
Alison Walton, North Shields; Mrs J Ward, Wakefield; Cathy Ward, Slough;
Pamela Ward, Birmingham; Simon Ward, Croydon; John Warren, Lancs; Mrs G.
Warrington, Hyde; Nicholas Watt, Houghton; RG Watt, Bromyard; Andy Webb,
Aberdeen; Peter Webb, West Byfleet; TG Webb, Peterborough; Nick Webley,
Llandeilo; Dave Webster, Gateshead; Harry and Marina Webster, Nottingham;
Andrew Wegg, SW16; Michael Welch, Reading; J Weld, Eastleigh; Dave Weldon,
Hale; John Wellings, Edinburgh; AD West, Leicestershire; Laurence West,
Torquay; Dr PJ West, Warrington; Joyce Westrip, Perth, Australia; Sarah
Wheatley, Leavesden; George Whilton, Huddersfield; Andy Whitehead,
Swindon; Mr & Mrs DW Whitehouse, Redditch; George Whitton,
Huddersfield; Peter Wickendon, East Tilbury; Jennette Wickes, Fleet; PM Wilce,
Abingdon; Malcolm Wilkins, Gravesend; Chris Wilkinson, Cumbria; Geoffrey
Wilkinson, Orpington; Babs Williams, Bristol; Mark P Williams, Bromley; P
Williams, St Austell; Raoul Williams, Cambridge; Ted Williams, Norwich;
David Williamson, NW3; David Williamson, Stamford; BP and J Willoughby,
Devizes; Bob & Eve Wilson, NW2; Dr Michael Wilson, Crewe; Major Mike
Wilson, BFPO 140; John Wirring, Swindon; Mrs AC Withrington, Hindhead;
David Wolfe, SW1, W Wood, Hornsea; John Woolsgrove, Enfield; Geof
Worthington, Handforth; Mrs C Wright, Glasgow; Mrs CF Wright, Stockport;
Clive Wright, Halesowen; D Wright, Rotherham; John D Wright, St Ives;
Georgina Wright, Nottingham; Lynn Wright, Newark.
Y: Stephen Yarrow, NW11; EJ Yea, Cambridgeshire; Rev. Can. David Yerburgh,
Stroud; Andrew Young, Cumbria; Andy Young, Penrith; Mrs B Young, Basildon;
Carl Young, Nottingham; Mrs E Young, Ilmington.

Index of Towns

What We Need to Know

We need to know everything there is to know about all curry restaurants in the UK. And there is no one better able to tell us than those who use them. We do not mind how many times we receive a report about a particular place, so please don't feel inhibited or that someone else would be better qualified. They aren't. Your opinion is every bit as important as the next person's.

Ideally, we'd like a report from you every time you dine out – even on a humble takeaway. We realize this is hard work so we don't mind if your report is very short, and you are welcome to send in more than one report on the same place telling of different occasions. You can even use the back of an envelope or a postcard, or we can supply you with special forms if you write in (with an S.A.E., please).

If you can get hold of a menu (they usually have takeaway menus to give away) or visiting cards, they are useful to us too, as are newspaper cuttings, good and bad, and advertisements.

So, please send anything along with your report. Most reports received will appear, in abbreviated form, in the *Curry Magazine* (the Curry Club members' regular publication). They are also used when preparing the next edition of this Guide.

We do not pay for reports but our ever-increasing corps of regular correspondents receive the occasional perk from us. Why not join them? Please send us your report after your next restaurant curry.

Thank you.

Pat Chapman
Founder, The Curry Club
PO Box 7
Haslemere
Surrey
GU27 1EP

Fax it to: 01428 645045

E-mail it to curryclub@costa.email.com

Internet Home Page: http://www.gcosta.co.uk/finefoods/

CURRY CLUB MEMBERS' DISCOUNT VOUCHER SCHEME SAVE POUNDS ON DINING!

To make big savings on your curry meals or takeaways, you must become a Curry Club member. It's easy: contact us at the address below. Members get our colourful *Curry Club Magazine* three times a year. In it are six vouchers, so you get eighteen vouchers a year.

Each voucher is valid at any one of the restaurants that have agreed to participate in this scheme. To identify them look for the © sign at the top right hand of the restaurant's entry.

The actual discount each restaurant is willing to give varies from restaurant to restaurant. Some will give a free bottle of wine, or free starters, others 5% off the bill, and some are offering as much as 10%, or even more.

We have agreed with the restaurant owners that these discounts are available at the discretion of the restaurant, at their quieter times, and that each Curry Club member will book in advance when using a DISCOUNT VOUCHER.

To find out how much discount you can get, and when they will give it to you, please PHONE THE MANAGER. (Where possible we have given the name of the individual owner or manager who has agreed to give the discount in the participating restaurant's entry.) Then please BOOK.

There is no limit to the number of people Curry Club members may take. One voucher is valid for a discount on one meal, and must be handed over when paying the bill.

REMEMBER, YOU MUST BE A MEMBER OF THE CURRY CLUB TO GET YOUR VOUCHERS. SO JOIN NOW TO SAVE POUNDS.

More information about the scheme and the Club from:

THE CURRY CLUB
PO BOX 7, HASLEMERE
SURREY GU27 1EP

Please send an S.A.E.